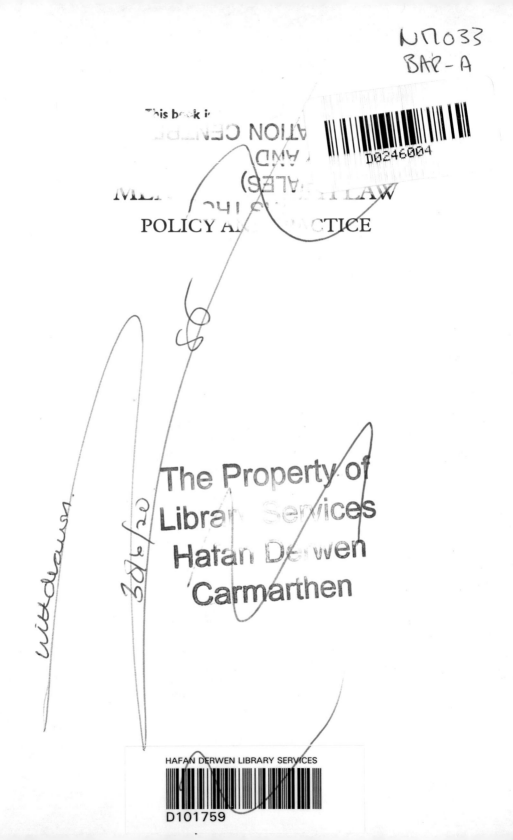

Mental Health Law
Policy and Practice

Peter Bartlett

and

Ralph Sandland

BLACKSTONE
PRESS LIMITED

First published in Great Britain 1999 by Blackstone Press Limited,
Aldine Place, London W12 8AA. Telephone (020) 8740 2277
www.blackstonepress.com

ISBN: 1 85431 941 8

British Library Cataloguing in Publication Data
A CIP catalogue record for this book is available from the British Library.

Typeset by Montage Studios Ltd, Horsmonden, Kent
Printed by Ashford Colour Press, Gosport, Hampshire

Contents

11 Mental Capacity (II: Specific Contexts)   376

12 Legal Responses and Advocacy for Clients   421

Preface

The prime reason for writing this book is that we needed it for our students. Since 1995, we have together taught a module in mental health law at the University of Nottingham. From the beginning, textbooks have been a problem. Certainly, there are books, often designed for the practitioner market, which cover the legal rules. Jones's *Mental Health Act Manual,* currently in its sixth edition, and Eldergill's *Mental Health Review Tribunals Law and Practice* are two particularly fine examples; but they are too detailed for general use by students and other newcomers to the field. Hoggett's *Mental Health Law* is more accessible in that regard, but at the expense of pragmatic issues. More important, all three of these works restrict themselves to legal analysis. They do not consider the legal rules in their social, political, or theoretical context.

In our view, it is almost immoral to divorce the study of mental health law from the social situation of the people directly involved. At its core, mental health law involves the coercive power of the state in one of its most raw forms: the confinement and forcible medication of individuals. The issue at the moment is not whether the use of such powers is justified, although that will of course be examined in the text which follows; it is merely that the realities of the power, and the problems implied, must be considered. The powers do not fall equally on everyone. Psychiatric powers are applied differentially by gender and race, and disproportionately on the poor. While cheap Marxist platitudes are unhelpful, the realities of psychiatric power in society equally cannot be ignored. A number of undergraduate sociology texts take account of these issues; but where the legal sources tend to ignore sociology, the sociologists tend not to provide an adequate account of the role of law in constructing and regulating these power relations.

Mental health law is also, by its very nature, interdisciplinary. It is not merely a site of legal regulation and control; it is also a system where a wide variety of professionals have jobs to do. That places its own set of pressures on the development of mental health law, and a purely internal legal analysis is misleading for failing to take those pressures into account. The tradition in some of the literature has been to see these professional approaches as conflicting with legalism. We would challenge the neat dichotomies that such arguments imply and, in the work which follows, will try to show why we take this position.

The intellectual appeal of mental health law thus lies not merely in the legal rules, but in the tensions between the rules, psychiatric practice, social administration, and the ways in which mental illness is characterised and understood by professionals and lay people alike. In our view, there was a need for a text which incorporated the substantive law, social policy and empirical work.

While primarily designed as a textbook for law students, we hope this book will equally be of interest and assistance to practitioners of law as well as the medical professions and social workers, and to the students of medical and social science disciplines. Appropriate materials on mental health law would equally appear to be lacking in these disciplines. It was, we admit, rather an eye-opener to realise how little medical professionals are taught about the assessment of mental capacity, for example, notwithstanding that it is the cornerstone of the law of medical treatment. We were able to find few introductory medical texts which dealt with that subject in the depth we have provided in Chapters ten and eleven, even though much of the theoretical framework upon which Chapters ten and eleven rely was developed by medical, rather than legal academics.

This book, therefore, endeavours to place the academic study of the law in the context of social issues and professional practice. That said, it is not a book which is designed to provide simple answers, for we think that such answers do not exist. That would also, in our view, mistake the purpose of an educational text. A text should inspire to further inquiry. It should reinforce the point that law is the place of investigation, dispute and argument, rather than of snappy answers to snappy questions. Throughout, we have tried to present varieties of countervailing arguments, to press the reader to interact with the subject and formulate increasingly sophisticated views. Occasionally, this has required the authors to develop arguments against their own works, published elsewhere. This has been a peculiarly liberating experience, both intellectually challenging and humbling at the same time. It also re-enforces our commitment to the view that this is an area where there are no easy answers. There are instead extraordinarily interesting problems and arguments regarding ways forward. We will have succeeded, not if our readers think they have the solution; but instead if we have inspired them to greater consideration of the problems.

This open-ended view of problems and solutions is not merely of academic relevance. Mental health law is currently in a state of flux. The current law, developed at a time when institutional confinement was increasingly the norm, cannot readily cope with the policy move in the last few decades towards care in the community. In addition, the development of anti-discrimination law relating to people with disabilities, including mental disabilities, has created tensions in the legal framework in which services are to be provided and standards set. How can one legally regulate mental health law in a way which does not discriminate on the basis of mental disability? As a result, much of the law is currently up for grabs. The Law Commission's work on mental incapacity was published following long gestation in 1995. Subsequent consultation by the Lord Chancellor's Department regarding implementation was completed in 1997. As we go to press, and after the final typesetting of chapter eleven, the government has issued a policy statement as to the future of the Law Commission proposals. Most of what we describe in chapter eleven is expected to be implemented, although the government is not planning to implement the proposals for public law protection of those at risk, nor do they plan to place advance statements about healthcare on a statutory footing. While this is the current plan, no doubt there will be much further discussion before legislation is passed into law. Further, in 1998, the Government established a 'scoping study review team' to consider a root and branch rewriting of mental health law. This panel reported to the government in July 1999. The Government's response was the Green Paper *Reform of the Mental Health Act 1983: Proposals for Reform*, cm 4480, London: Department of Health, published in November 1999. The Green Paper invites views (by 31 March 2000) on a large number of proposed major and minor reforms of the 1983 Act regime. Perhaps the most significant of these, hardly unexpected (see 9.5), is to extend powers of compulsory treatment and control of patients in the community, both as an alternative to hospitalisation and after discharge. If implemented this would constitute a major shift in the axis of mental health law. It is also proposed that significant changes be made to the civil admissions process, with only one route into compulsion available under civil law. The triggering medical condition for all powers of compulsion would be 'mental disorder' broadly defined, with the abolition of the more specific concepts currently to be found in s. 1(2) of the 1983 Act. Some form of safeguard for informal patients lacking capacity would be introduced, addressing problems highlighted in *Bournewood* (see 4.2). Further safeguards over the use of some controversial treatments are also put up for discussion. The Government disagrees with, but seeks views on, the suggestion of the Scoping Review Committee that capacity play a more prominent part in the powers to treat without consent. Review tribunals would be significantly altered, although the form and powers of these tribunals are not yet clear.

The Green Paper is bound to incite further controversy. Professional interest groups are put under threat; for example there is a suggestion that social workers need not continue to play a part in the compulsory admission process. Similar issues are at stake in the constitution of the proposed independent tribunals, and in the prospect of increased limitations being placed on clinical discretion. As is appropriate with a Green Paper, there is little detail or prescription in the proposals it puts out to consultation. As readers of this book will soon discover, however, the devil is often in the detail. Opponents of both 'legalism' and 'medicalisation' will find much in the Green Paper to dispute; and many of the criticisms of the present mental health system, rehearsed in this book, are not referred to in the Green Paper. For all concerned, there remains everything to play for.

These are merely the latest developments in a debate which has continued for much of the last two hundred years. While such specific reforms coming down the pipe suggest the particular relevance of this book now, mental health law is problematic by its very nature, and similar debates can be expected to continue well into the future.

In writing a book such as this, we of course become indebted to a considerable number of people. Mona Gupta has read some parts of the work, to ensure that we are not saying things that are too foolish from a medical perspective. Michael Gunn has kindly responded to a variety of queries. The staff at Blackstone Press have behaved with a refreshing blend of professionalism, flexibility and good humour. We ofer our thanks to them, and particularly to our editor, Heather Saward. Our thanks are also due to Julie and Rick, our domestic partners, for the considerable patience they have shown in the grind which writing a book inevitably creates. Perhaps our greatest debt, however, is owed to our students in the mental health module, since its commencement in 1995. Particular thanks are in order to those of them that shared their experiences of the mental health system with us and with their colleagues, either as patients or as staff. They have not merely provided invaluable insights into the law in practice; they have also served as a reminder that the dividing line between 'them' and 'us' is largely illusory.

19 November 1999

Table of Cases

Table of Statutes

Table of Secondary Legislation

ONE

Conceptualising mental health law

In the serene world of mental illness, modern man no longer communicates with the madman: on one hand, the man of reason delegates the physician to madness, thereby authorizing a relation only through the abstract universality of disease; on the other, the man of madness communicates with society only by the intermediary of an equally abstract reason which is order, physical and moral constraint, the anonymous pressure of the group, the requirements of conformity. As for a common language, there is no such thing; or rather, there is no such thing any longer; the constitution of madness as a mental illness, at the end of the eighteenth century, affords the evidence of a broken dialogue, posits the separation as already effected, and thrusts into oblivion all those stammered, imperfect words without fixed syntax in which the exchange between madness and reason was made. The language of psychiatry, which is a monologue of reason *about* madness, has been established only on the basis of such a silence.

Foucault, 1965, pp. x-xi

1.1 INTRODUCTION

In his usual rather dense style, Foucault encapsulates many of the paradoxes at the root of the study of mental health and illness, and sets the stage for many of the themes which will be of significance in this volume. The centrality of a medical model of insanity is asserted, imposing a scientific order onto the profoundly un-ordered world of the mad. While madness is displayed in the form of a disease, sanity is a constraint, both physical and moral, into which the insane person is confined through pressure of the group, the sane. All this is a construction of the reasoned, and reflects the world of the reasoned; to the insane person, it is an alien landscape.

The situation is yet more complex than Foucault posits here, however, for mental health law, like psychiatry, is also a language 'of reason about madness'. The two languages, law and psychiatry, speak sometimes symbiotically and sometimes in uneasy juxtaposition in the pages which follow. Each are paradigms of rationality in their way, and thus each is faced with the same problem: how to impose order onto madness, a realm which would seem *ex hypothesi* to be lacking order, to be irrational.

This may sound hopelessly abstract, but a few examples will clarify. How exactly, if at all, can mental health (or perhaps more importantly, mental illness) be defined; and are the existing legal and medical definitions clear, consistent, and appropriate? How can we impose reason, rationality, onto the irrational? Does the process of definition not imply a logical structure in madness, a structure which cannot exist in madness by its very nature? At what point do mad people acquire rights and corresponding responsibilities and authority over what happens to them? Are we content that these languages of mental health and illness remain exclusive of the voices of their client groups, and if not, how are those voices to be included in an understanding of law and policy in the mental health area? And if mental health law and psychiatry are both discourses of reason about madness, what do those discourses tell us about the reasoned people who create them? If, as Foucault claims, the languages of mental health law and psychiatry develop in the silence of those they affect, what do our views of how the insane are understood and when we should intervene in their care tell, us about us, the people who construct the languages about the insane?

These are some of the big issues at the heart of this book. There is no pretence that they will be solved; indeed, it is a fundamental belief of the authors that the purpose of a textbook such as this is not to present solutions, but instead to articulate problems for discussion and investigation. The first three chapters concern broad issues of interest, such as the general structure of mental health services, including (in Chapter two) the definitions of mental health. Chapters four and five concern civil confinement, and Chapter six criminal confinement. Chapter seven concerns treatment for mental disorder, Chapter eight the law and procedure surrounding mental health review tribunals, and Chapter nine community care. Chapters ten and eleven concern the law of civil capacity, and Chapter twelve contains an overall discussion of the efficacy of legal remedies for those with psychiatric difficulties, and an introduction to advocacy for this particular client group.

1.2   WHO ARE THE INSANE?

Issues of psychiatric and legal definition will be reserved for Chapter two, but it is appropriate at the outset at least to start the discussion of who the insane are. The newspapers would leave us in little doubt. In their eyes, the insane are a threat, a lurking menace in society, a hidden and violent element, which may erupt without notice. The Glasgow Media Group analysed news items about the mentally ill for the month of April 1993, mainly in the tabloid press and on television. It found 323 stories relating to dangerous or violent behaviour by people with mental illness — roughly twice as many as concerned their other categories (stories about harm to self, prescriptive or advice columns related to treatment or care, and stories critical of accepted definitions) combined (Glasgow Media Group, 1996, pp. 47-81). These may no doubt be in part a function of the economics of publishing — scaremongering sells newspapers — but the Glasgow group further makes a persuasive case that these representations have their effects on public perceptions. The image is profoundly misleading. The vast bulk of those with psychiatric difficulties are simply not dangerous (Bowden, 1996, pp. 17-22).

The images do not stop with violence, however. The mentally ill are perceived as homeless and poor, the deserted of society. There may well be some truth in these allegations in many cases, although much depends on how mental illness is defined, and in particular regarding homelessness, whether substance addiction is considered a mental illness. Certainly, many of those who have been involved with the psychiatric system are poor, although it is a fair question to ask the degree to which this is due to a prejudice of employers against hiring people who have been institutionalised. The image is nonetheless of people who have fallen through the net, tragic figures, lonely, to be pitied rather than valued.

These images cannot tell the whole story. There are countervailing images. When we think of the mentally ill, we might alternatively think of Virginia Woolf, Robert Schumann, Sylvia Plath, or Vincent Van Gogh. The image of the mad artistic genius is in its way a part of western cultural imagination. The connection between madness and genius excited considerable academic debate in the nineteenth century, and more recently, the American psychologist Kay Redfield Jamison has argued for a correlation between manic depression and artistic genius (Jamison, 1993). The image of the insane person as genius, warranting respect rather than pity or fear, is a refreshing counterweight to the images of the insane person as dangerous lunatic, or homeless vagrant. It becomes possible to ask whether madness is something to be valued rather than disparaged. Rather than silencing the mad, should we encourage them to speak?

In the end, all these images must be approached with considerable caution, since the mad artistic genius like the mad killer focuses on the statistically rare exception. The reality in the overwhelming number of cases is likely to be characterised by banality rather than extremes. Current estimates are that mental illness will affect roughly one in six adults in Britain per year, although psychotic illnesses are much less common, closer to one per cent of the population. Depression alone will affect roughly half of women and a quarter of men before the age of 70 (Department of Health, 1998a, p. 10). This would suggest that it is not appropriate to think in terms condescendingly of 'them', but rather, somewhat more humbly, of 'us'. The frequency suggested by the statistic would suggest that any generalisation may well mislead as much as it informs.

That is perhaps particularly important in so far as it challenges the popular sense that everyone with mental difficulties must somehow be the same. Different difficulties affect people differently. It is simply wrong for example to expect that people with mental illness will also have intellectual limitations. The fact that an individual is profoundly depressed or hearing voices, for example, does not mean they are unable to understand complicated information, and process it at a reasonably sophisticated level. Certainly some people with mental illness are not intellectually very bright; but others are very bright indeed, and most are somewhere in the middle. The experience of people affected would suggest that the stereotype associating mental illness with lack of mental ability remains widespread, a depressing comment on how far society has yet to come in understanding both mental illness and developmental disabilities.

A similar warning ought to be made regarding developmental disabilities. Frequently, one hears the phrase 'mental age' used regarding people in this group. It is at best a caricature. People develop in different ways, and at different rates, and the person 'with a mental age of six' may well have little in common with a six-year-old child. To refer to a twenty-five-year-old woman in this way is unhelpful: in a very real sense, she is still a twenty-five-year-old woman. Rather than to identify her with the child she manifestly is not, it is far more sensible to consider her actual situation, understanding and abilities, and proceed accordingly.

Romanticisation of mental illness, whatever image is adopted, is unlikely to be helpful. That said, it is surely appropriate to provide some sort of starting point to understanding what it feels like to be mentally ill. The writings of those who have experienced mental illness first hand provide invaluable reading to the student beginner in the area. A selection is provided in the bibliography (Mays, 1995; Hart, 1995; Dunn *et al*, 1996; Jamison, 1996; Read and Reynolds, 1996; Styron, 1990). These readings drive home the point that mental illness, particularly in its more extreme forms, can be a profoundly unsettling and unpleasant experience. Consider U. A. Fanthorpe's description (1996, pp. 52-4) of the experience of depression:

Again I find myself waking miserably early, even before the summer birds; again I find music unspeakably painful; again my speech becomes slow, and my arms seem grotesquely long; again I'm afraid to go out, because people will see at a glance that there's something wrong, and shun me; I can't face the garden because, although in one part of my brain I know the blackbirds are just making their usual evening calls, I'm convinced that the cats are after them and that it's my fault; above all, my vocabulary shrinks to such an extent that the only word I'm really at home with is 'sorry'.
...

When I'm badly depressed I long above all things to be a prisoner. I imagine this as a life where you don't make choices, where the pattern of life is plain and involuntary. Life in depression is like this anyway, but it retains the illusion of choice. If you had to do the sad things you are doing because someone had ordered that you should, indeed because you'd deserved it, the despair might (you think) go.

Linda Hart (1995, p. 19) described the sensations accompanying her schizophrenia as follows:

The top half of my head feels quite light but the thread that runs down from my head to my stomach is soaked in a deep despair. Maggots in my belly multiply. Rotting flesh. Want to drink bleach to cleanse them or a sharp knife to cut them out. They told me I needed a psychiatrist and not a medical surgeon back in September. They said Graham [the psychiatrist] would get rid of the maggots but he hasn't.

These are not pretty images, and one would be inhuman not to feel considerable sympathy for the individuals affected by these experiences. Yet sympathy is a double-edged sword, for it can easily lead to a paternalist impulse to intervene whether the individual likes it or not, 'for their own good'. The result is a risk of marginalising the person we intend to help, and the re-enforcement of the gulf of silence of which Foucault speaks.

This is not merely a civil rights point, nor an abstract issue of discourse construction. It is in part a practical point: if intervention is to be successful in the long term, its subject must in the end be supportive of the intervention. In the environment of intrusive surveillance in a psychiatric facility it is possible to force a patient to take drugs they do not wish to take. It is much more difficult outside that environment, and if the patient is not convinced at that time of the continuing benefits of medication, it seems unlikely that he or she will continue taking it.

Perhaps as significant is the fact that it is not obvious that the disorder is readily distinguishable from the person with the disorder. This ambiguity is apparent in Marie Cardinal's description (1996, p. 108):

But for my children, I might let myself go completely, stop fighting, perhaps, for the struggle against the Thing was exhausting. More and more, I was tempted by the medication that delivered me to a nothingness which was dull and sweet.

In this articulation, the alternative to the disorder is a void, a nullity. This image of mental illness as constructive of self is similarly evident in Sheila MacLeod's description (1996, p. 81) of her anorexia:

Two facts emerge immediately from this résumé. The first is that I felt my battle to be with authority, whether in the form of teachers, matrons, parents, or even nature itself. The second is that, up until this point, I was winning. It seems to me that anorexia nervosa acts as a metaphor for all the problems of adolescence. But instead of meeting each problem separately and assessing it for what it is, the anorexic thinks she has a master plan, designed to solve them all at one stroke. She is convinced that it works; it can't fail. It is like a dream come true. It is euphoria.

When I first came across Szasz's dictum, 'Mental illness is a self-enhancing deception, self-promoting strategy', I considered it to be a harsh judgement on a fellow creature. But when I substituted 'anorexia nervosa' for 'mental illness' I could see the truth in what Szasz was saying, and realize at the same time that his judgement was not so harsh. After all, if the self is felt to be nothing, any strategy adopted to enhance or promote it, desperate though it may be, is a step towards what most of us would consider to be health, and an action necessary for survival. The anorexic's skinny body proclaims, 'I have won; I am someone now.'

This view of mental illness as intrinsic to self receives judicial acknowledgement in the case of *B* v *Croydon District Health Authority* (1994) 22 BMLR 13 (HC). That case involved a patient suffering from a personality disorder, not anorexia, which nonetheless manifested itself in the refusal of food to the point of near self-starvation. The primary issue before the trial court was whether the patient had the capacity to consent to treatment, in this case feeding. Thorpe J cites (at p. 19) an expert witness, a forensic psychiatrist, as identifying the relation between the individual and the personality disorder as a factor for the court's consideration:

The third feature is the patient's necessity to control her own internal world and her relationship with others. In a pathological way, she uses maladapted methods to control distress in herself and to control others around her. Her need to use abnormal coping mechanisms stems from her abnormal development. In relation to this feature, Dr Eastman poses the question: Have we the right to remove the only mechanism that remains to her without the prospect of being able to help her to cope in other ways?

The court gives considerable credence to this concern (at p. 22):

Here the patient has developed in adolescence an individual personality which can be medically classified as disordered. But the disorder is the person and we must question the justification of depriving such a person of all that is available without the prospect of being able to help her to cope in other ways.

Various points may be made about this approach. First, the comments occur in an appraisal of capacity. While a similar logic may ethically apply to other branches of mental health law, capacity is a field with its own idiosyncrasies: see Chapters ten and eleven. Secondly, the decision of Thorpe J on capacity was expressly doubted by the Court of Appeal. The Court of Appeal's judgment was summary and obiter on this issue. It took a different view of the evidence, and did not refer to the autonomy point at all. That said, its reasons suggest that Thorpe J's approach would not be adopted, at least by that panel of the appellate court: see [1995] 1 All ER 689.

Finally, while the relation between the individual and the disorder was clearly a matter considered by Thorpe J, and a factor in his decision that B had the capacity to consent to treatment, it did not in the end preclude him from ordering the provision of tube-feeding as treatment, pursuant to s. 63 of the Mental Health Act (MHA) 1983. The intricacies of this part of the decision will be discussed in Chapter seven. The instant point is instead that the centrality of the disorder to the individual is a factor which raises ethical issues regarding intervention; it does not necessarily determine whether intervention is ethically justified. A number of positions may be potentially adopted here. At one extreme, it might be claimed that intervention, and particularly intervention over the patient's objection, is rarely if ever justified on the basis that it constitutes extraordinarily intrusive meddling with an individual's personality and psyche. At the other, it might be argued that intervention is frequently justified, on the basis that, after the intervention, many people are grateful. This 'thank-you theory' will be examined in more detail in Chapter four, in the context of civil confinement. Intermediate positions are also possible. Presumably, the wishes of the affected individual may be a significant factor; it would seem positively cruel not to support an individual who wishes to be free of the trait. Thorpe J distinguishes between alterations to an individual's normal personality, and a situation where the disorder is intrinsic to the personality. In *B v Croydon*, there was 'no overlay of illness upon the patient's norm' (p. 22). This might be distinguished from a situation where a medically defined variation appears in an already existing personality, where intervention might be justified to restore the pre-existing personality. The difficulty with this approach, of course, is to determine how long the disorder must exist before it becomes integral to personality. In addition, it does not solve the question of what to do when the cure will remove more than the disorder. Marie Cardinal's reference to a 'nothingness which was dull and sweet' suggests a cure removing not only the disorder, but also other parts of her nature as well.

Students of mental health law are often quick to adopt a medicalised model of mental illness, that it is appropriately the realm of a specialised, medical practitioner. Certainly, medicine will often have a role to play, and this is acknowledged by most but not all people affected by mental disorder. Those in the subject group, however, will often understand their experience in a multi-faceted way. William Styron, for example, writes (1996, p. 57):

I shall never learn what 'caused' my depression, as no one will ever learn about their own. To be able to do so will likely for ever prove to be an impossibility, so complex are the intermingled factors of abnormal chemistry, behaviour and genetics. Plainly, multiple components are involved — perhaps three or four, most probably more, in fathomless permutations.

Certainly, those with mental health problems often receive medical attention. Usually this is voluntary on their part, but at the same time, there may be an element of ambivalence to it, even when the treatments work relatively according to plan, and thus alleviate the condition. U. A. Fanthorpe describes (1996, p. 52) this ambivalence as follows:

When depression hits me, the last thing I want to do is see the doctor, because it seems hard to define anything 'wrong'. When I have finally made myself go, and the doctor has slotted me back into a medical definition again, the reactions are odd: relief at knowing where I am again and what I have to do, but at the same time resentment that this has happened again, the same symptoms, prescriptions, general fears, and dreariness.

John Bentley Mays describes (1995, pp. xiv, xv) the medicalisation of his condition, in his own eyes as much as those of the doctors, more expressly in terms of alienation, reflecting the Foucaultean vision with which this Chapter commenced:

> Yet the forensic language I invoke springs from nothing in my own heart or mind, is no more original than my routine complaining. Rather, it slides down on the page out of clinical case histories and medical records, a portrait of the *nobody*, nameless, extinguished, who is the topic of the technical literature on depression.
>
> I have read the literature now that provides me with terms of order, pretending to study the technical language of depression — but really studying the way of looking, of writing, embodied in such texts. It is a poetry of the scalpel's quick slash, the spurt and stanching of blood, clamping back successive layers of skin, fat, muscle, the probe with a point of gleaming metal of the nothingness at the centre. Writing myself up as a *case*, I experience myself, pleasurably, obscenely, as object. The former exacerbation of subjectivity is gone, now that the cyst known as *soul* is lanced, and all that remains is flesh, killed by the invasion of medical power, stiffening, cooling.

Both Fanthorpe and Mays describe continuing and successful relations with their respective medical advisors: there is no element of sour grapes here. At the same time, the sense of ambivalence to a medical model of their experience is real.

This is significant not merely as an insight into the way those in the affected group perceive their condition; it is also significant because of the way the world, or at least social policy, reacts to this uncertain relationship with the medical model. In a recent press release (22 September 1998), Minister of State for Health, Paul Boateng stated that 'with our safety-plus approach, the law must make it clear that non-compliance with agreed treatment programmes is not an option.'. This position is problematic in the context of the nature of relations articulated above. Is it reasonable or appropriate to expect unswerving adherence to treatment in a professional context perceived by the patient as alienating? Will this breakdown not be exacerbated if the doctor/patient relationship is not as successful as it appears to have been in the cases of Mays and Fanthorpe?

The view of the affected is given some support by some public perceptions of insanity. The British studies uniformly indicate that the public perceives behaviour typical of mental disorders as caused by a wide range of factors. Social and environmental factors are identified as causes more frequently than physiological or moral factors (see analysis contained in Glasgow Media Group, 1996, pp. 5-8). Nor is this multi-faceted view the preserve of the laity. While medical professionals hotly dispute the relative significance of various factors, few would now question the relevance of social and environmental factors to the occurrence of mental disorder. There is a risk that this view may fuel a different stereotype, that the mentally ill individual is really a malingerer, who should simply buck up and get on with their life. It is difficult to see this view accurately describing many of the people affected with mental illness. At the same time, the public perception of mental illness as more than just medical gives additional credence to the broader views of those affected. In short, everyone else agrees: mental disorder is not just a medical matter, suggesting that this view by people directly affected should not be dismissed lightly.

Students new to mental health law sometimes perceive mental illness as something which can be cured permanently, rather like measles, where with appropriate treatment the patient is free of the malady forever. This is often a misleading view particularly in the case of serious mental illness. The better image is of a chronic condition, at best controllable, which may affect the individual for much of their life. This again has social policy implications: if intervention is to be enforced on the individual, is it to be enforced in perpetuity? This seems extremely intrusive to the life of the individual affected, and must therefore be approached with considerable hesitancy.

Viewed in this light, mental health law and policy might be seen as disspiriting subjects. Those affected by mental illness often face a selection of possible courses of action, none of which on balance is particuarly appealing. Continuation with the experience of disorder is hardly an attractive option, medicine does not necessarily provide a complete answer. Alteration of the social, cultural and environmental factors which may contribute to the malady is extremely difficult to achieve in practice. Forced intervention, either through confinement in hospital, enforced medication or control of the individual in the community, seems both intrusive and not obviously effective except perhaps in the very short term. One of the difficult things for new students in this area to understand fully is that here, as with many areas of law, there will often be no good solution possible for a client. Instead, there will be a selection of problematic or downright bad possibilities from which a choice must be made.

At the same time, it would be wrong to assume that all persons with mental health difficulties live miserable lives. Again, generalisations are likely to be unhelpful here, but like most of the rest of us, it is reasonable to understand this client group as happy with some parts of their lives, unhappy with others, having some good times and some less good times. While it is inappropriate for the student of mental health law to ignore the realities of the life imposed by the reality of the mental condition, it would be equally inappropriate to romanticise the mental disorder in a way which obliterates the remainder of the life of the individual.

1.3   OTHER INTERESTS: MENTAL HEALTH CARE

People with mental disabilities or disorders are of course the client group who are the objects of the psychiatric system, and thus of mental health law, but they are not the only people with interests in the delivery of mental health care. Mental health care is delivered in a system, in part based in the National Health Service, in part elsewhere in the state social services network, and in part in the private sector. A detailed survey of the range of interests operating in this system, and the sociology of how those interests interact, is beyond the scope of this Chapter; but a brief survey of some of the players will provide an indication of the complexity of the influences on mental health policymaking.

The prime medical personnel involved in the care of the mentally ill are of course nurses and doctors, primarily general practitioners and psychiatrists. These people work in conjunction with social workers, psychologists, community mental health nurses, health visitors, social service agencies and, particularly in recent years, health administrators in the administration of the mental health system.

It is abundantly clear that the vast bulk of these people have a real and honest concern about the people in their care. The power-hungry doctor who has no interest in his patients but merely a desire to control may make good television drama, but it has little to do with the reality of the individuals involved in the mental health system. That said, the individuals listed above are all professionals, operating in an administrative system. Vast sociological literatures exist on the way people operate in such bureaucracies, and strive to enhance professional status. The tensions may be within individual professions: psychiatrists for example have tended historically to feel undervalued among medical specialisms. The tensions may run between groups: nurses have long been working to see their own profession recognised in the broader medical hierarchy, and social workers have similarly struggled for professional recognition. Such professional issues will be noted further in Chapters five and seven.

Such projects of status enhancement are clearly a part of the sociological and historical fabric of the administration of mental health. They are not generally crass attempts at power-grabbing, but manifest themselves instead primarily in articulation and formation of the values and expertise of the group in question. The group will no doubt sincerely believe, often entirely appropriately, in the value of the expertise it has to bring to a specific set of issues; but the result is nonetheless the privileging of a set of assumptions, or of a specific way of looking at things. It is this process which may result in the person with the mental health difficulty being unable to recognise himself or herself in clinical descriptions. Other ways of looking at things, whether those of the individual with the difficulty or of the other professions, are implicitly challenged in the process. Perhaps unintentionally, the knowledge or expertise of the profession becomes the exercise of power, in potential conflict with other professions or ways of looking at things.

On a more mundane note, the professionals noted above are also all human, with understandable concerns about job satisfaction and job conditions. The image of the doctor, willing to abandon all family or personal life and devote himself or herself entirely to the care of patients, has a romantic appeal, but does not represent reality in most cases. The professionals, entirely reasonably and like the rest of us, must balance priorities.

These day-to-day pragmatic issues have become increasingly important in recent years. The policy drive in the last twenty years has been towards economic efficiency in services provided by the state. The result has been a service stretched beyond reasonable limits. Deahl and Turner describe general psychiatric wards, particularly in London, where bed occupancy rates are routinely in excess of 120 per cent of capacity, where virtually all admissions are emergencies (Deahl and Turner, 1997, p.6). Government moves to introduce supervised discharge and supervision registers for those released from psychiatric facilities (see further 3.4 and 9.5), are a further pressure to hold hospital and other medical personnel responsible when things go wrong following discharge, with no extra resources. The results are perhaps predictable: there would appear to be a crisis of morale in much of the mental health services. Deahl and Turner claim that the burnout period for a psychiatric nurse on an adult general psychiatric ward is seven months, and cite a study that eighty-eight per cent of consultant psychiatrists wished to leave the profession (Deahl and Turner, 1997, p. 6). The picture is of a set of professionals, overworked and disillusioned, unable to provide the sort of service which they think it appropriate to give, and which would match their professional ideals and ideology.

How are we to approach this in a social policy or a legal context? Will the current government substantially alter this situation? If not, should we abandon our vision of a health service able to provide the continuing framework of care required by those suffering from chronic conditions, such as many mental illnesses? Should we design policy on the basis that service will be minimalist, able to intervene only in crisis situations, targeting care at those in most need while leaving those with less pressing problems to their own devices? How should law approach these situations? In the law of negligence, for example, should doctors be given an increased margin of appreciation for their errors, on the basis of working conditions which are far from ideal? Or should the courts continue to insist on standards of professional practice which the professionals themselves feel they are no longer able to provide?

Not all those with an interest in the care and treatment of the mentally ill are contained within the public sector. The health care reforms of the former Conservative government opened up care to the private sector. The effects in the mental health arena have been various. Overflows of patients from NHS psychiatric wards may be moved to private facilities, simply to alleviate space pressures. Further, many of the facilities such as group homes through which community care is offered are provided by the private sector. Sometimes these private sector providers are non-profit organisations, established through charities such as MIND; in other cases, they are standard businesses, run with a profit motive. Either way, the shift to the private sector means that maintenance of standards and control of staffing are out of direct government control. Regulation is theoretically possible, but complicated by the fact that if unattractive standards are set, the private operator can fold up shop, a possibility the government can little afford given the inability of the NHS to service the demand. This is not a desirable option from the private operator's viewpoint either, since considerable investment will have been made. In this balance policy must be made.

Care is not, of course, the exclusive preserve of the professionals. Families and friends also provide care. The specific role of these informal carers will depend on the circumstances. Sometimes, they provide housing, with or without a day centre providing a formalised programme during the day.

Sometimes, the person with mental illness will reside elsewhere, be it in hospital, at a group home, or alone in the community. Here, the role of family and friends may be to provide a sense of community and support, or it may also be to provide some sort of overview, to ensure that the appropriate services are being provided.

These services and the people who provide them have traditionally been largely taken for granted in the administrative structure of mental health. This is difficult to justify, for such carers provide important services, in conditions which may be very difficult. Some public support is available for these activities (see Carers (Recognition and Services) Act 1995) and there have been some recent moves to increase public funding to assist or relieve carers, as for example by allowing them to take the occasional weekend break from their caring duties (*The Guardian*, 9 February 1999, p. 9). Such programmes seem appropriate acknowledgements of services performed which, at their best, provide the person with the mental disorder an optimal home environment, at minimal cost to the state.

Other forms of acknowledgment of the family role can be much more problematic. Here, perhaps even more than with the professional actors, the interests of the service provider and those of the mentally ill person are difficult to disentangle, suggesting difficulties with formal control of these individuals over the decisions which are made about mentally ill family members. Like other service providers, but perhaps more than other service providers, the family and friends of the individual will have an emotional interest in the fate of the individual. It can be profoundly painful to witness the onset of mental illness in a loved one. The effect of the condition on relations within the family and, if the affected person is a breadwinner forced to cease employment, on the life of the family, can be profound. It is difficult to see how family members can be expected to divorce these feelings from their views of the person with the disorder, and what ought to happen to that person. The result is a paradox: it is their intimate knowledge and relationship with the affected person which creates the appeal of their greater involvement; but at the same time, this same factor creates the risk that decisions will be made on criteria other than the best interest of the affected person.

The private interests in the mental health field extend well beyond carers. Pharmaceutical manufacturers are a particularly clear example of these other interests. Pharmaceuticals are big business: roughly one quarter of the prescriptions dispensed by the NHS are to affect the central nervous system, to alter moods, states of mind or behaviour (Lacey, 1996, p. xiii). The pharmaceutical manufacturer SmithKline Beecham sells over £1 billion of anti-depressant medication every year. Clearly, medication for mental illness has brought considerable benefits in many cases. At the same time, the adverse effects of medication can be profoundly unpleasant. The precise nature of these adverse effects will, of course, depend on the patient and medication in question, but they can be significant enough to dissuade patients from continuing the treatment. Ron Lacey (1996, p. 118) makes the point this way, regarding depot anti-psychotic medications, long-lasting medications injected into patients at intervals of weeks or months.

Whilst they can relieve the torment of the symptoms of serious mental illness for many people, they can also reduce an individual to an unprotesting zombie-like state. For some patients the use of depot antipsychotics is little more than an exchange of one form of human misery for another. Drowsiness, lethargy, loss of motivation, impotence, stiffened muscles, shaking hands, physical restlessness, severe anxiety and persistent constipation may be more distressing to some people than a fixed belief that their thoughts are being controlled by the international brotherhood of Freemasons. For others these side effects are a small price to pay for the relief that the drugs give them from a much more distressing and terrifying psychotic inner reality.

The varieties of psychiatric medication and their adverse effects will be discussed in greater detail in Chapter seven; suffice it here to say that while their benefits should not be ignored or underestimated, they are not problem-free, miracle drugs.

Pharmaceutical manufacturers spend a considerable amount of money advertising their products, particularly in specialist medical journals such as the *British Journal of Psychiatry*. Unsurprisingly, the advertisements emphasise the potential benefits of the medications, and place the adverse effects in very small print, either at the bottom of the page or off to the side. More interesting are the images used to sell the drugs, often reflecting themes discussed elsewhere in this Chapter, although usually with a particularly sugary gloss. Thus images of a patient's return to true self-hood as a result of the drug, or scenes of restored domestic bliss, are common. Perhaps more worrying are advertisements which, often very subtly, suggest the use of medications as an efficient control of patients. These are presumably directed to the harassed doctor, presenting a fast and efficient way to restore order onto their ward or into the local psychogeriatric nursing home. Are the advertisements effective? The continued use of large advertising budgets by these firms would suggest that they think so. A field trip to the medical library for a critical viewing of these advertisements is instructive to the student who is new to mental health law.

These groups, patients, the varieties of medical personnel, social workers, hospitals and NHS health trusts, private caregivers, families, and pharmaceutical companies, make use of lobbyists and pressure groups to press their views. Sometimes these roles are performed by professional organisations, such as the Royal College of Psychiatrists, the College of Physicians, or the British Medical Association. Sometimes, they are performed by charities, such as MIND, Mencap, or the National Carers' Association. Sometimes, large organisations such as pharmaceutical companies will hire lobbyists directly. Once again, there is a considerable sociological literature on how these bodies work. If the group represents a variety of different persons or providers, decisions as to what position is to be lobbied for may become complex. This may be particularly complex in some of the groups in the charitable sector, for example, which do not 'represent groups' per se, but exist instead primarily to focus attention on sets of issues. While MIND, for example, endeavours to give particular consideration to the views of users, its mandate and membership is considerably broader than this.

Lobby or pressure groups may further have independent interests involving their reputations or financial integrity which may influence them in addition to, or, occasionally, at odds with the interests of the groups they represent. If a private firm of lobbyists is hired, for example, the firm will have a profit motivation. Even in the charitable sector, the financial integrity of the organisation must remain a factor in its priorities. Amendments to the way in which services are provided has complicated this, since in the last two decades, government has increasingly provided funding in the charitable sector. Nationally, the government provided £175 million of £3,000 million in charitable revenues in 1976, or roughly six per cent; by 1984 this had grown to £1 billion of charitable revenue of £10 billion, or ten per cent (Prochaska, 1988, p. 4). Currently, somewhere between thirty-five and forty per cent of charitable income is thought to come from government sources (Whelan, 1999, p. 3). While these figures reflect the entire charitable sector, mental health charities have garnered at least their share of this new money. Indeed, as the charities have found an increasing role for themselves in the provision of community mental health services, the financial relations with government have intensified. The effect on these organisations is ambiguous. On the one hand, government relies on these organisations more than ever before to fulfil government objectives; at the same time, the organisations rely on government increasingly, to provide the funding for their activities. It is difficult to see that this uneasy relationship would not have its effect on the role of these charitable organisations to comment upon and to influence government policy.

Lying across all these interests is of course the government. It would be an error to think of the government as a monolith; like the remainder of the system, it is composed of parts, which may be characterised as much by competition as cooperation. The clearest of these possibly divergent interests arises between central and local government. The tradition in this country has long been for local government to have a particularly central role in service provision. Thus the actual purchase, and some of the provision, of community care rests at the local authority level, where policy-making rests primarily with central government. The same is true of health care provision, which will be administered at the local level, consistent with policy set centrally. In each case, much of the core funding will originate with the central government. This suggests that local and central interests may well disagree on a wide variety of issues, from priorities in service provision, to, most pivotally, the appropriate level of funding for service provision.

Even central government must be understood as a complex entity. Mental health care will span a variety of offices and departments. Disability benefits for those living in the community are a social security issue. The Court of Protection, which handles the property and affairs of those found incapable of so doing themselves under part VII of the MHA 1983, is a part of the Lord Chancellor's Department. Psychiatric treatment in hospital is of course a matter for the Department of Health. Within government, status is measured largely in terms of staff allocations and budget. The way in which programmes are divided between departments is thus profoundly relevant to the status of the departments concerned, with corresponding impact on government policy.

The interests of a variety of departments in mental health services re-enforces that mental health policy may be as much a function of competitive negotation between government departments as it is of cooperation.

Throughout the system, lawyers can be expected to be active. They will be hired, either to lobby for specific interests or to represent clients in specific situations, by all the parties noted above. Here again, while the lawyer should of course defend the interests of those clients with all ferocity, limited only by professional standards such as the duty to uphold the dignity of the court, other factors can creep into the picture. Practising lawyers quickly learn that their individual reputations are profoundly significant to the attainment of their career aspirations and, sometimes, to the success of their causes. In practice, this may affect how the lawyer presents a case, and occasionally, what arguments will be made. Similarly, the realities of private legal practice require a cash flow. The lawyer representing clients in mental health as much as any other cannot in the end ignore that reality. This is seen with clarity in some of the debates surrounding legal aid. Certainly, availability of legal aid is likely to be vital to many poor psychiatric patients if their rights are to be protected. At the same time, the reason it is vital is because without an appropriate legal aid structure, lawyers simply cannot afford to accept many cases: the issue here is about the economics of running a law office as much as it is about abstract notions of rights.

The resulting picture is of a complex system of actors and interests in the provision of mental health care. It would be unduly cynical to take the view that the people with the mental health problems, the people whom the system ought most to support and assist, are ignored. It would be fair to say that the users of mental health services have not traditionally been as successful as the professional groups in having their voices heard directly. This problem is complicated by the fact that the users of mental health services do not speak with one voice. They range from enthusiastic proponents of medication to people denying the relevance of a medical model to insanity entirely. User views instead tend to be filtered through a professionalised view of best interests. While it would be inappropriate to deny the good faith of much of this professional concern, the other factors noted above may distort or influence the message. If it is inappropriate to say that the person with mental health difficulties is absent from policy formation, it is certainly inappropriate to deny the other factors which influence policy formation.

1.4 SOURCES OF LAW

1.4.1 The roots of the Mental Health Act

Mental health law is as old as law itself. The earliest codified reference in the English statute book is contained in a 1324 statute defining the Royal Prerogative, giving the king jurisdiction over the persons and property of 'idiots' and those who 'happen to fail of [their] Wit': *De Prerogativa Regis* c. ix, x. Nonetheless, much of the care of the insane in medieval and early modern England occurred outside the realm of statute, and it was not until the eighteenth and particularly nineteenth centuries that the insane became, increasingly, subject to statutory jurisdiction. These statutes may have been the precursors of the MHA 1983, but they were markedly different in form. Specifically, for much of the nineteenth century, mental health law was not contained in a single Act, but instead in a variety of streams of statutes, each quite distinct from the others. Four nineteenth-century streams, and one additional one from the early twentieth century, warrant particular note, as they combine in somewhat amended form to comprise the MHA 1983.

One set of legislation governed private madhouses. The Madhouses Act of 1774 required private madhouses to be licensed by the College of Physicians if in London, or otherwise by the local magistracy. In 1828, this legislation was replaced by a new Madhouses Act. While amended repeatedly over the course of the century, this Act set the structure for these establishments for much of the the the nineteenth century. The College of Physicians lost its formal role. Up to 1845, madhouses outside London were inspected and licensed by the justices of the peace. In London these inspection and licensing functions were conducted by a new body, the Metropolitan Commissioners in Lunacy. With an amending statute of 1845, the Metropolitan Commissioners were renamed the Commissioners in Lunacy, with jurisdiction to inspect madhouses through-out the country, although their licensing authority remained restricted to London. Admission to private madhouses was upon the application of a family member, supported by two certificates of insanity signed by medical practi-tioners not directly associated with the madhouse.

The Madhouse Acts covered private madhouses and charitable hospitals only. While these might occasionally be quite extensive in size, they were not the vast public asylums of popular memory, which were instead governed by a series of County Asylum Acts. The first of these was passed in 1808. This Act allowed asylums for the relief of the insane poor to be built on the county rates. The facilities were overseen by a committee of justices of the peace until 1888, when they were passed to local authority control: Local Government Act 1888, ss. 3(vi), 86, 111. Throughout the nineteenth century, these facilities were generally restricted to paupers, although in practice a somewhat wide definition of that term might sometimes be employed. Admission was by order of a justice of the peace, upon the application of a poor law relieving officer, supported by one medical certificate, almost invariably signed by the poor law medical officer. The frequent rewritings of and amendments to the County Asylum Acts in the nineteenth century did little to change this structure, although legislation in 1845 made county asylum provision mandatory for the first time.

The nineteenth century also saw a string of statutes relating to clarifying, modernising, and rationalising the procedures relating to the Royal Prerogative powers. These powers allowed control over the person or property and affairs of an individual to be taken over, once incapacity to make relevant decisions had been shown (see further Chapters ten and eleven). This power thus related to decision-making authority, not institutional confinement. Technically, the Royal Prerogative vested authority over lunatics and idiots in the monarch, who by tradition granted the power to make determinations of lunacy and idiocy to the Lord Chancellor at the beginning of each reign. By the beginning of the century, the Lord Chancellor in turn delegated the inquisition into the lunacy of an individual to three Commissioners. This panel of three was reduced to a panel of one in 1833. Where originally the Commissioners had been judges, they became in 1842 barristers of at least ten years' standing. In 1862, the Commissioners lost the authority to try lunacy and idiocy matters where a jury was requested. That was removed to the common law courts, where the Commissioners continued to try lunacy or idiocy when no jury was requested. This gives a flavour of the nineteenth-century statutes relating to Chancery jurisdiction.

Finally, the nineteenth century saw a stream of statutes devoted to the detention of criminal lunatics. The initial statute was forced by *Hadfield's Case* (1800) 27 Howell's St Tr 1281, where it was held (at p. 1854) that notwithstanding a successful plea of insanity in defence of an attempted murder, the prisoner 'for his own sake, and for the sake of society at large, must not be discharged'. Legislative authority was provided for such detentions later that year. For the next half-century, criminal lunatics were included in county asylum legislation, but the construction of Broadmoor Asylum, opened in 1863, was reflected legislatively by a new stream of statutes devoted to criminal lunacy specifically, commencing with the Criminal Lunatics Act 1860.

The Lunacy Act 1890, is sometimes perceived as a watershed statute. In a sense it is, in that for the first time it combines the four legislative streams relating to the laws of insanity into one statute. Further, it was in effect for much of the twentieth century, not being formally repealed until 1959, and the MHA 1983 still resembles it in general structure. In its historical context, however, it is something of an anticlimax, although it did make some changes. For the first time, for example, privately paying patients could not be admitted to psychiatric facilities without the order of a justice of the peace. If the 1890 Act consolidated the various strands into one statute, however, it did not consolidate the strands themselves; for example the paupers who had been under the jurisdiction of the County Asylum Acts continued to be subject to a set of rules quite different from private patients.

The first half of the twentieth century offered two significant developments. The first was to add yet another strand of legislation, the Mental Deficiency Acts, commencing in 1913. These seem to have been given short shrift by legislative historians of insanity. That is unfortunate. Not only did they provide the basis of the current guardianship provisions of the MHA; they also provided the legislative framework for some early care in the community, before the Second World War (Thomson, 1998; Walmsley et al, 1999). This provision was not negligible: by 1939, almost 90,000 people were controlled by these Acts in England and Wales, almost half of which were living in the community (Walmsley *et al*, 1999, p.186). Further, they provided a legislative framework for an increasingly ornate social discourse relating to developmental disabilities. While 'idiocy' was expressly covered under the nineteenth-century legislation, for much of that period little distinction was made beween this and 'lunacy'. The Idiots Act of 1886 began to acknowledge the distinctness of problems relating to developmental disability; the differential nature of the issues, and a different set of social responses, was given clearer articulation by the Mental Deficiency Act 1913.

The second development was that the Mental Treatment Act 1930 introduced informal admissions for the first time. In law, this is extremely significant. Up to this time, there was no distinction between admission to and confinement in a psychiatric facility. From 1930, it became possible for an individual to be admitted to a psychiatric facility without a formal and binding order of admission. For the first time, the patient might also be free to leave. While this admission route took some time to gain widespread popularity, it now accounts for around ninety per cent of psychiatric admissions.

It is in this legislative context that we must understand the Mental Health Act 1959. The creation of the National Health Service in 1948 had largely removed the distinction between public and private facilities, with the incorporation of charitable hospitals into the public sector. The old legislative distinctions appeared to make less and less sense. Where the 1890 Act had left the distinctions largely untouched, but included all legislative strands in one statute, the 1959 Act actually tried to consolidate the divergent strands into one. The solution of the 1959 Act was largely to ram the different processes together. For example, where compulsory admission before that time had been in the hands of poor law/social service officials if the patient was poor and the family if the patient was able to afford private care, under the new system both admission mechanisms were combined for all patients, so that all compulsory admissions required both family and social services involvement.

The 1959 Act did make a few significant changes. First, admissions were now removed from justices of the peace. The process allowed admission instead upon the agreement of a mental welfare officer and the nearest relative of the patient, accompanied by certification of two doctors of mental disorder. This may have reflected existing practice in any event, for there is evidence that in some areas at least, justices of the peace were signing multiple copies of blank orders of admission, in anticipation of applications from poor law relieving officers and medical officers (Forsythe, Melling and Adair, 1999, 83). Nonetheless, albeit perhaps unintentionally, the 1959 Act is said to have had the effect of moving power from hospital administration and judicial officers directly to treating physicians (Fennell, 1996, pp.168-9). Secondly, the Act introduced mental health review tribunals. For the first time, a dedicated mechanism was created by which patients could challenge their confinement. Finally, the 1959 Act moved the *parens patriae* power to an entirely statutory footing. Where the previous legislation of this power had functioned as amendments of the common law, the 1959 Act subjected guardianship and conservatorship to a purely statutory régime.

The MHA 1959 once again placed mental disorder and developmental disorder in the same statute, an approach continued under the MHA 1983, currently in force. The result has been a mixed blessing. On the one hand, legislation combining the responses to be available in appropriate circumstances irrespective of whether an individual suffers from mental illness or developmental disability increases the flexibility of responses in a way which must be to the benefit of both groups. At the same time, the combined statute means that the legislative space to consider problems specific to each of these groups has disappeared. This would seem to have worked to the disadvantage of those with developmental disabilities, which in discussions related to the current Act are overshadowed by issues of mental health and illness. This is reflected in the title of the Act: why should people with developmental disabilities be subject to a 'mental health' Act, when they are not, per se, mentally ill. Indeed, this book can be justly criticised for this bias. While purporting to discuss the ambit of the MHA 1983 as a whole, much of the discussion does show an inappropriate assumption that the prime users of the legislation are mentally ill, not developmentally disabled.

The MHA 1983, still currently in force, albeit as amended, kept the basic provisions of the 1959 Act. The new Act was passed in a climate where patient rights were treated more seriously than ever before in this century. There were some changes in nomenclature: 'mental welfare officers' became 'approved social workers', and 'mental subnormality' and 'severe mental subnormality' became 'mental impairment' and 'severe mental impairment' respectively, for example. Some more substantive changes were also made at this time, however. Treatment while in a psychiatric facility was for the first time brought into the legislative realm, albeit only for those confined in the facility. That inclusion nonetheless made it equally clear for the first time that those not covered by the provisions, that is, those informally admitted, had the same rights regarding treatment as the common law provides to people outside the facility. In addition, the powers of personal guardians were significantly reduced. This was later taken by the courts to require an expansion of common law to fill an apparent gap: see further, Chapters ten and eleven.

What are we to make of this long and somewhat tortuous history? Perhaps what is striking is less how much things have changed, as how much they have remained the same. While the distinctions between public and private admissions have disappeared under the current Act, the structure is otherwise reminiscent of the strands of nineteenth-century law identified above: parts II and VI on admission to facilities, including removal of patients to the various parts of the United Kingdom; part III on criminal confinement; part VII on management of property and affairs. On a more minute level, the continuities are similarly notable. The current role of the approved social worker (ASW) looks remarkably similar to that of the poor law relieving officer, 150 years ago.

At the same time, the context of the Act has changed markedly, making interpretation complex. When the Act contains the old nineteenth-century clauses, as it often does, their relevance or applicability is no longer clear. Take for example the provisions defining the right of the nearest relative to insist on the release of a patient, contained in s. 23(2). This originates in the nineteenth-century statutes. If the confinement was in the private sector, the relative was responsible for paying the patient's upkeep, and therefore was perceived to have the right to demand the release of the patient, to limit their financial exposure. If instead the patient was confined in a county asylum, the right to order release was conditional on an undertaking by the person ordering the release that the individual would no longer be chargeable on the poor law. The right to release was thus a way to enforce public economy in care provision, and to limit the shame of the family at receiving poor relief. Neither of these justifications continues to exist; yet the section remains in relatively unamended form. Justifications may continue to exist for the inclusion of the role; but they are *ex post facto*.

These nineteenth-century rights to order the release of the patient were circumscribed if the patient were 'dangerous to other persons or to himself', a restriction remaining in s. 25 of the Act; yet how are we to read that section given the standard of confinement introduced in 1959 and still in force, that the civil confinement is 'necessary for the health or safety of the patient or for the protection of other persons'? If it is the same standard, the right of the nearest relative is removed in all cases where the patient is rightly confined, rendering the power a nullity. If the standards are different, how are they different? The answer would have to be to introduce a relatively low standard for 'health' in the 1983 provision, since it is difficult to see how 'safety' of the patient or 'protection of other persons' provides the necessary flexibility to provide a standard different from 'dangerous'; but is that really consistent with the meaning of the 1959 standard as a whole? Does the phrase 'the health or safety of the patient or for the protection of other persons', when read as a whole, not instead imply a relatively high standard of risk to health? And should the determination of modern standards of confinement be based on arcane arguments about nineteenth-century legal history?

The MHA 1983 is full of this sort of difficulty. Its construction and interpretation can be fiendishly difficult. A Code of Practice, revised in 1999, has been issued to assist those charged with the Act's administration (Department of Health and Welsh Office, 1999). In a sense, this only complicates matters further, since the Code contains material supplementary to the legal standards of the Act. While the Code is not legally binding on practitioners, it is identified as something the Secretary of State is obliged to produce by s. 118 of the Act. The result can appear to establish ambiguities in the standards to be applied: one is reminded of the Japanese proverb that a person with a clock knows the time; a person with two clocks is never sure. Even without reference to issues of social policy in interpretation, the MHA therefore provides a veritable panoply of difficulties, testing the lawyer's skills in statutory interpretation to their limit.

1.4.2   Other law and mental disorder

The MHA 1983 may provide the core of the law for this textbook, but it will be clear from the preceding discussion that it cannot stand on its own. In the silence of the statute, common law will continue to apply. In addition, other legal subject areas may come into play in understanding the rights of those with mental health problems. The modern law curriculum, frequently modular, is appropriately criticised for treating legal subjects as self-contained packages, with little to do with each other. The study of mental health law allows the law student an ideal opportunity to think across legal subjects, analysing which approach will yield a desirable result. A brief survey will show how some of these related areas intersect with mental health law.

The MHA 1983 itself involves subjects such as confinement and enforced treatment, performed on statutory justification. These matters tend to be controlled by judicial review, and students should be aware of the relevance of their study of public law to mental health law.

The treatment of those informally admitted to psychiatric facilities is governed by common law, with the standard rules of consent and medical negligence applicable. In addition, personal guardianship has been severely curtailed by the MHA 1983. The common law is moving in to fill this void (see Chapters ten and eleven). The precise legal nature of the movements into this area are not yet entirely clear. Tort and contract seem to be involved, and fiduciary duties seem a possible candidate for a structure in the future.

Capacity is of course not merely about guardianship; it is a threshold whenever people enter into legal relations, and the law has developed not merely prospective rules to allow individuals to make decisions on the incapable person's behalf, but also rules to take effect when the incapable person has nonetheless entered into relations with others. Here, capacity law, a close cousin of mental health law, reaches into virtually the entire law school curriculum. As an illustrative list, there are rules regarding capacity to marry, to engage in sexual relations, to file for divorce, to sign contracts, to commit crimes, to serve as trustee or corporate director, to execute a will, to vote in elections, and of course to consent to medical treatment. Some of these will be discussed below, requiring some consideration of the broader laws in these areas.

Even regarding mental disorder distinct from incapacity, the Mental Health Act does not of course affect all of the individual's life. A variety of other statutory regimes may also be significant. People with mental disorders face with embarrassing frequency problems of maintaining jobs and finding places to live. The former of these will be subject to employment laws, which articulate the degree to which mental illness can be used to justify dismissal. Similarly, both employment and housing are covered by the Disability Discrimination Act 1995. This may be particularly helpful, as it can require the employer or landlord to make reasonable accommodation to take account of the needs of the disabled person. Disability rights are also noted in the Treaty of Amsterdam 1997, suggesting that a European dimension may become increasingly relevant as that treaty is implemented. Particularly if employment fails, the individual may be in need of social services, where a range of disability benefits may be available under social security legislation.

Finally, the Human Rights Act 1998 provides possibilities for future developments and litigation challenging provisions of the Mental Health Act and related law. The European Convention on Human Rights has tended to treat mental health issues in a relatively procedural way, insisting for example on the provision of due process safeguards. Thus *Hussain* v *United Kingdom* (1996) 22 EHRR 1 concerned the right to a court hearing for those detained at Her Majesty's pleasure, that is, the insane in the criminal system. Further, in *X* v *United Kingdom* (1981) 4 EHRR 188, the European Court of Human Rights was not prepared to restrict the wide powers of the Home Secretary to recall persons conditionally discharged from psychiatric facilities; but the court was prepared to insist on procedural requirements, specifically that judicial review of those decisions be available, and that reasons for the recall must be provided. The incorporation of the Convention into English domestic law with the 1998 Act, however, may have unforeseen consequences as lawyers cite North American jurisprudence, which has sometimes been more successful on similar language in challenging mental health law. Can it be argued, for example, that enforced treatment of a patient with capacity, particularly without a hearing allowing the patient's view to be considered, could constitute inhuman treatment under art. 3? Can enforced treatment in the community be subject to challenge as a violation of the right to private life under art. 8? Are disability in general, and mental disability in particular, contained by implication in the general non-discrimination provision of art. 14? Are there restrictions on the scope of art. 5(1)(e), which creates an exception to the right to liberty and security of the person in the case of persons of unsound mind; and if so, what precisely is the scope of that exception? It remains to be seen whether the English courts will adopt a robust approach to the 1998 Act. If they do, there may be interesting times ahead in mental health law.

Mental health law spans almost all legal disciplines. The student of mental health law should see this as an opportunity, not a threat, for it allows a reassessment of those disciplines from a new and different angle from that usually forming the base of law school curricula.

1.5   CONCLUDING COMMENTS

This book views mental health law both as a subject in its own right, and as a case study. In the former context, it provides an opportunity for law students to exercise their skills in statutory interpretation and case analysis, but it requires more. Mental health law and policy is by its very definition an interdisciplinary study. It is not an area where law should be considered independently, divorced from the realities of clinical practice or life for the client in the community. It requires the student to consider how various actors work together, and which interests take precedence over others. Thus empirical research and sociological approaches will often be as enlightening as pure legal analysis.

Mental health law as case study instead requires the student to consider the nature of law. As we have seen, mental health law spans the curriculum. In this, it is typical of other types of law — a secret often kept from students, who seem determined to view law in discrete and unrelated subject packages — and the skills acquired by the student in thinking across these legal areas should be expected to assist him or her in any sort of law they eventually practise. If critical theory and sociology may be required to make sense of what mental health law is about, so mental health law provides a way for the undergraduate student to approach these subjects, and once again, these approaches will prove valuable in other contexts. No law operates divorced from the real needs of clients and the pressures of social policy. Mental health law creates a suitable study of how these interact, and an understanding of this can certainly be applied by students to other areas of law.

In closing, this chapter returns to its beginning: silence. It will be clear that in our view, the silence must be broken. This is, in a sense, a lawyer's conceit, for law glorifies the representation of the individual client: in our professional ideology, based in rights theory and liberalism, the model of the lawyer defending the interests and acting on the instructions of the individual client is pivotal. Yet this is not merely conceit. The more offensive conceit would be to treat mental health law as a set of academic constructs, and ignore the people contained within the system. These are real people with real problems. This is true of everyone in the system, but is perhaps most true of the people with mental health difficulties or developmental disabilities; yet it is their voices that remain largely outside the hearing of policymakers.

If this book argues for the necessity to break down the silence described by Foucault, it should also challenge the reader to question the discourse which has resulted from that silence. If policy has developed through silencing the mad, if it is, as Foucault claims, a discourse of reason about unreason, it then tells us as much or more about the reasonable as the mad. For reason to articulate insanity, it must do it with reference to sanity, for that is the only way the border can be understood. In this way, mental health law and policy can be seen as a mirror, in which we see our own values reflected. For Foucault, this language of reason bears no particularly enhanced status. It is instead 'that other form of madness, by which men, in an act of sovereign reason, confine their neighbors, and communicate and recognize each other through the merciless language of non-madness' (Foucault, 1965, p. ix). Yet if reason is madness, it is nonetheless our madness, and thus something we should strive to acknowledge and understand.

In the first chapter of *Madness and Civilization*, Foucault uses the imagery of the ship of fools, the *stultifara navis*, as the paradigm of a Renaissance view of madness. Foucault seems to have believed that these ships actually existed, a view which has attracted criticisms from historians (e.g., Midelfort, 1980). He also draws a symbolic meaning from this image: 'It is possible that these ships of fools, which haunted the imagination of the entire early Renaissance, were pilgrimage boats, highly symbolic cargoes of madmen in search of their reason' (Foucault, 1965, p. 9). This is, in a sense, as appropriately a metaphor for Foucault's view of the result of the enlightenment: the journey of 'that other form of madness' in search of its reason. It is also the project of this book.

TWO

Problems of definition

When I assert that mental illness is a myth, I am not saying that personal unhappiness and socially deviant behavior do not exist; what I am saying is that we categorize them as diseases at our own peril.

The expression 'mental illness' is a metaphor that we have come to mistake for a fact. We call people physically ill when their body-functioning violates certain anatomical and physiological norms; similarly, we call people mentally ill when their personal conduct violates certain ethical, political, and social norms. This explains why many historical figures, from Jesus to Castro, and from Job to Hitler, have been diagnosed as suffering from this or that psychiatric malady.

Szasz, 1970, p. 23

Szsaz's arguments are not only wrongheaded, they are also inhumane, since they deny the possibility of help for a condition [schizophrenia] which claims the life of one in ten sufferers.

Leff, 1993, p. 78

2.1 INTRODUCTION

The problem posed by Szasz is real enough. A finding of mental disorder in law can have profound effects on an individual. It serves as a dividing line between the acknowledgement that individuals are responsible for their actions and have authority to make decisions as to what happens to them, and possible intervention depriving the individual of basic rights of citizenship. The MHA 1983 contains extreme powers. People may be confined against their will, or lose control of their property and affairs. They may be treated against their will with powerful chemicals. Some of these have adverse effects which may significantly curtail the individual's quality of life, or sense of well-being. Such powerful violations of civil rights require powerful justifications.

At the same time, as the quote from Leff illustrates, there is a sense in society that it is somehow wrong to leave without protection those who are vulnerable to abuse and unable to cope with day-to-day decisions. This too is occasionally expressed in terms of rights. Thus the United Nations Declaration on the Rights of Mentally Retarded Persons contains a specific right to a guardian able to protect the rights and interests of an incapacitated person: 1971 UN General Assembly, 26th sess., resolution 2856, para. 5. The failure to intervene in an appropriate situation here can leave the individual open to physical, mental or financial abuse, results which are remarkably similar to the risk of overintervention identified by Szasz.

Whichever way the argument is phrased, whether as the liberal right to be free from intervention, or the more paternalist question of who should or should not be protected, the issue involves the deployment of power over individuals. This is most easily seen in the overtly legal context: civil confinement under the MHA is obviously the deployment of power. The development of social policy is also the deployment of power, however, for it involves the structuring of society and the creation of social programmes into which the participants will be expected to fit. Even naming individuals as mentally disordered is an exercise of power, since it changes their perceptions of themselves, and the perception of them by other people.

If power is to be exercised, it is appropriate to insist that it be exercised properly, for cogent justifications, according to reasonably clear and defensible criteria. The gateway to the powers under the MHA is the concepts of 'mental disorder', and four of its subcategories. This chapter will challenge the stability and clarity of these concepts and the justifications for their use. The result is a quandary which is at the base of mental health law and policy: if we are to take Leff's view seriously, we are obliged to exercise power in aid of those who are most vulnerable; yet it is profoundly problematic to determine who those vulnerable people are, leaving open the possibility of significant civil rights abuses and criticisms.

2.2 THE STATUTORY STRUCTURE

The conditions to which the MHA 1983 is to apply are defined in s. 1(2) of that Act:

'mental disorder' means mental illness, arrested or incomplete development of mind, psychpathic disorder, and any other disorder or disability of mind and 'mentally disordered' shall be construed accordingly;

'severe mental impairment' means a state of arrested or incomplete development of mind which includes severe impairment of intelligence and social functioning and is associated with abnormally aggressive or seriously irresponsible conduct on the part of the person concerned and 'severely mentally impaired' shall be construed accordingly;

'mental impairment' means a state of arrested or incomplete development of mind (not amounting to severe mental impairment) which is associated with abnormally aggressive or seriously irresponsible conduct on the part of the person concerned and 'mentally impaired' shall be construed accordingly;

'psychopathic disorder' means a persistent disorder or disability of mind (whether or not including significant impairment of intelligence) which results in abnormally aggressive or seriously irresponsible conduct on the part of the person concerned.

All of these are subject to s. 1(3) of the 1983 Act:

Nothing in subsection (2) above shall be construed as implying that a person may be dealt with under this Act as suffering from mental disorder, or from any mental disorder described in this section, by reason only of promiscuity or other immoral conduct, sexual deviancy or dependence on alcohol or drugs.

2.2.1 'Mental disorder'

Section 1(2) defines 'mental disorder' broadly. While mental illness, severe mental impairment, mental impairment and psychopathic disorder will become significant in their own right for some purposes, it would be incorrect to view mental disorder as simply the sum of these categories, for the definition also includes 'any other disability or disorder of mind'. Thus any arrested or incomplete development of mind will suffice to render an individual 'mentally disordered', even if there is no resulting aggressive or irresponsible conduct which would bring the individual into the scope of one of the defined mental impairment categories. Similarly, the Court of Protection, which is in charge of assuming control and management of property and affairs of those lacking capacity, is able to take the view that persons with difficulties of short-term memory, spatial or temporal orientation, or reasoning difficulties may be placed under its remit in appropriate circumstances. While medical evidence is required prior to the Court assuming jurisdiction, a specifically psychiatric diagnosis is not necessary, and as long as a disorder or disability of mind is present, a specific medical diagnosis is not pivotal.

'Mental disorder' is the gateway definition for a number of provisions of the Act. It is the term used for example in s. 2, which allows an individual to be confined for up to twenty-eight days; in s. 5, which allows the formal detention of an individual already in hospital for up to six hours; in s. 6, which allows an individual to be confined for seventy-two hours on a more summary procedure than used for s. 2; in s. 94, which defines the jurisdiction of the Court of Protection; in s. 131, which allows an individual to be admitted on a voluntary or informal basis to a psychiatric hospital; in s. 135, which allows justices of the peace to issue warrants to search for and remove individuals believed to be ill-treated; and in s. 136, which allows detention by a police officer for up to seventy-two hours. Mental disorder is of course not the only requirement for the use of these powers; but it is the disorder required for the use of the sections.

Other sections of the Act do not require 'mental disorder', but instead a more specific mental condition. Longer term admissions under s. 3, guardianship under s. 8, criminal confinements under ss. 35 and 37, and transfers from prisons to mental hospitals under s. 47, for example, all require that the individual be suffering from one of four specific types of mental disorder: mental illness, severe mental impairment, mental impairment, or psychopathy. In addition, where two doctors are required to certify the disability in these sections, they must identify the same category of disorder: see s. 11(6).

Mental illness is not defined under the Act. Discussion of its nature and possible definition will be discussed in detail below. To understand the discussion of the other categories which follows, however, it is appropriate to say that the courts have held that the words of the statute are not specialist terms. Instead there is some authority that they are terms of ordinary English usage, to be understood as the reasonable person would understand them.

2.2.2 The mental impairments

'Mental impairment' and 'severe mental impairment' are defined in the statute. Both definitions require a 'state of arrested or incomplete development of mind'. The causation of these conditions seems irrelevant: they can be a function of genetic, constitutional, or environmental factors, or be caused by disease of the brain (Hoggett, 1996, p. 39). That said, the definitions would not be broad enough to include degeneration of or injury to a mind 'occurring after that point usually accepted as complete development'. (Department of Health and Welsh Office (1999, 3rd edition), Code of Practice, para. 30.5).

The definitions do not cover all such cases, however, but only those where the deficit entails impairment of intelligence and social functioning, and is associated with abnormally aggressive or seriously irresponsible conduct on the part of the individual. The Code of Practice emphasises the importance of direct observation of behaviour (para. 30.5) and the importance of a multi-disciplinary assessment prior to classification in either category of mental impairment (para. 30.4).

It is with these criteria associated with social functioning and behaviour that we begin to see the use of conduct to determine whether the Act should apply. Here, the use of these factors seems relatively benign from a civil rights perspective. The behaviour here does not define the impairment; it rather serves to restrict the cases of impaired intelligence where the Act may be invoked. Nonetheless, it does start to raise the question of what the priorities of the Act are, and to hint at its social control functions.

The statutory definitions of mental impairment and severe mental impairment are remarkably similar. The difference appears to be a matter of degree. In the former, the arrested or incomplete development of mind is specific:lly identified as 'not amounting to severe mental impairment'. The former must include 'significant', and the latter 'severe' impairment of intelligence and social functioning. It is not obvious that these adjectives actually add very much to the understanding of or differentiation between the two categories.

The case of *R* v *Hall* (1988) 86 Cr App R 159 discusses the scope of severe mental impairment, and of mental impairment by implication. This case involved a charge of intercourse with a 'defective' (to use the term of the statute), pursuant to s. 7 of the Sexual Offences Act 1956. The defendant Hall had been the principal of a special school, where Alison Hames had been a student for two years, when she had been aged sixteen to eighteen. At that time, Ms. Hames moved to a different institution for those with developmental disabilities. Some year-and-a-half later, Hall went to the new institution, collected Ms. Hames, and brought her to a hotel. There, he encouraged her and assisted her to masturbate. He admitted that they had engaged in similar conduct while she had been under his care, at the special school. The issue was whether Ms. Hames was capable of consenting to this behaviour.

The Sexual Offences Act 1956 as amended holds that consent may not be given by a 'defective', defined as 'a person suffering from a state of arrested or incomplete development of mind which includes severe impairment of intelligence and social functioning'. This is effectively the first half of the test for severe mental impairment. At issue was whether 'severe' in this context was to be gauged in comparison with the population as a whole, or instead with the population of people with impaired intelligence and social functioning. The court favoured the former (at p. 162):

> The words of the phrase 'severe impairment of intelligence and social functioning' are ordinary English words. They are not terms of art. The phrase appears in a section which deprives two classes of person of the capacity to consent, girls under 16 and women who are defectives. It is clearly designed to protect girls under 16 because, albeit normally developed mentally, they are clearly regarded by Parliament as not sufficiently mature to consent to what, consent apart, would be indecent assaults. It is also designed to protect women over 16, if defectives, from exploitation. We can see no reason to suppose that Parliament intended to protect only those who were severely impaired compared with other mentally defective persons, but not those who were severely impaired as compared with normally developed persons. The sections do not say so and, on a natural reading of the words, it is in our view clear that severe impairment is to be measured against the standard of normal persons.

While medical evidence would be admissible to determine an individual's level of intelligence, it had no weight on the question of whether the individual was 'severely' impaired; that was an issue for the jury (p. 162). Indeed, in *R v Robbins* [1988] Crim LR 744, which dealt with a similar issue, a finding of 'severe mental handicap' under s. 1(3), (3A) of the Sexual Offences Act 1967 was made without expert evidence being led at all.

The *Hall* case is taken by some commentators as a guide to the reading of the MHA 1983 definitions (see, for example Jones, 1999, p. 14–15). The similarity of wording is striking, but the respective contexts should equally be noted. While the MHA 1983 is certainly to ensure protection of people with mental impairments, it also provides them with civil rights, and in determination of those rights, the distinction between mental impairment and severe mental impairment can be significant. For example, those with non-serious mental impairment can only be civilly confined under s. 3 of the Act if treatment is available which 'is likely to alleviate or prevent a deterioration of his condition' (s. 3(2)(b)). This provision does not apply to people with severe mental impairment. The broad reading of 'severe mental impairment' which would follow from an uncritical application of the *Hall* decision would correspondingly limit membership in the class of 'mental impairment', limiting the application of s. 3(2)(b). It may be open for the court in *Hall* to find that Parliament intended to protect all mentally impaired people from indecent assaults; but it is difficult to make the parallel argument for the MHA 1983 classes, where Parliament has itself drawn distinctions in the Act. The criminal statutes do not contain a distinction between 'severe' and non-severe classes; the MHA 1983 does, and that perhaps makes a difference. It may still be open to be argued that in the context of the Mental Health Act 1983, the severity of mental impairment should be assessed in comparison with other people with mental disabilities, not with the public at large.

It is appropriate to note in passing the difference between *Hall* and the Code of Practice on the issue of medical expertise. *Hall* emphasises the lay determination of the 'severity' of mental impairment; the Code of Practice emphasises the professional role in determinations through multi-disciplinary assessments. Neither reading can be read as a definitive approach for the interpretation of the MHA 1983, *Hall* because it is about a criminal law defence, and the Code because it is only issued for guidance as to good practice. Nonetheless, it is another example of ambiguities and uncertainties as to the role of medical professionals in the interpretation and administration of the Act.

2.2.3 'Psychopathic disorder'

The mental impairments are perhaps the easiest starting points in the discussion of s. 1(2), MHA 1983, for at least everyone agrees that arrested or incomplete development of mind exist in an intellectually coherent fashion. The same cannot be said to be true about the other defined term in the subsection, i.e., psychopathic disorder. The difficulty with this disorder is that its criteria of definition are not distinct from its behavioural ramifications: abnormally aggressive or seriously irresponsible conduct do not merely characterise the malady; they are indistinguishable from it, at least in current medical understanding. Indeed, the term itself is viewed as out-dated by the medical profession, which prefers instead to speak of anti-social or dis-social personality disorder.

In the defining of psychopathy, the image of mental health law as a mechanism of social control is perhaps at its strongest. Some aspects of behaviour or personality are defined as illness, without any obvious mechanism to distinguish them from similar, non-ill traits. Do these individuals fail to conform to fundamental behavioural norms because they are unable, or unwilling to comply? Mental abnormality is inferred from anti-social behaviour, and anti-social behaviour is explained by mental abnormality, in an apparently sealed loop. An examination of the core criteria defining the condition do little to ease concern about this. Classic characteristics include egoism, immaturity, aggressiveness, low frustration tolerance, and the inability to learn from experience. More recently, Prins lists additional indicators: a 'lacuna of super-ego'; the greater-than-usual need for excitement; a capacity for the creation of chaos among family, friends and carers; thrill-seeking; pathological glibness; anti-social pursuit of power; and absence of guilt (Prins, 1995, p. 311). The result is hesitation even within the psychiatric community. Prins refers to it (1995, p. 309) as the 'Achilles heel' of psychiatry, citing Peter Tryer:

[T]he diagnosis of personality disorder is similar to an income tax form; it is unpleasant and unwanted, but cannot be avoided in psychiatric practice.

As noted above, psychopathy as defined in the 1983 Act requires a mental disorder which results in 'abnormally aggressive or seriously irresponsible conduct'. Consistent with, or perhaps compounding, the ambiguities in the categorisation, the courts are content to view a finding of psychopathy as a hybrid between medical professionals and lay opinion. In R v Trent MHRT, ex parte Ryan (1991) unreported CA, Nolan LJ said:

No doubt whether the conduct is the result of the disorder is again a medical question. Whether it amounts to seriously irresponsible or abnormally aggressive behaviour seems to me, as Dr Shubsachs himself said in his report, to raise questions other than of a purely clinical nature. ... The fact that medical evidence is involved in the definition is of course in itself no reason why it should not be decided by members of the tribunal in the light of their own expertise and examination of the patient.

At the very least, the approach of the court is expressly normative. As with the distinction between mental impairment and severe mental impairment, the pivotal issue is not a matter of medical expertise.

Psychopathy is handled differently in the different mental health legislation in the United Kingdom. It does not exist as a separate category either in Northern Ireland or Scotland. The Northern Ireland Order appears to exclude it entirely, and the best view appears to be that those with the disorder cannot, for example, be civilly confined under that ordinance (see Northern Ireland Order, SI 1986 No. 595 (NI 4); Reed, 1996, p. 5). Until recently, the Scots legislation, by comparison, included it by implication in the broader category of mental illness. Section 17(1) of the Mental Health (Scotland) Act 1984 referred specifically to individuals suffering from a mental disorder which 'is a persistent one manifested only by abnormally aggressive or seriously irresponsible conduct'. The implied status is now express. The first statute passed by the new Scottish parliament altered the 1984 definition so that it now explicitly includes personality disorder: Mental Health (Public Safety and Appeals) (Scotland) Act 1999, asp 1, s. 3.

There would appear to be no consensus even in the psychiatric community as to how these cases ought to be dealt with, and what reform if any is appropriate to the English legislation. A survey by Rosemarie Cope of psychiatrists working in regional secure units and special hospitals showed a near-even split as to whether psychopathy should remain within the MHA 1983: 53 per cent in favour and 47 per cent against. Of those proposing removal from the Act, roughly 60 per cent favoured the Scots system, where psychopathic disorder would be contained within the broader concept of mental illness (Cope, 1993, p. 217). Nonetheless, roughly 10 per cent of Cope's sample appear to have favoured removal of psychopaths from the current Act entirely, presumably resulting in something analogous to the Northern Irish model (Cope, 1993, p. 226).

Cope's survey was restricted to forensic psychiatrists, however, and may therefore be more supportive of a continued use of the concept in the Act. Unlike the pattern in forensic services, diagnoses of personality disorders in general psychiatric settings have been falling off considerably in recent years (Pilgrim and Rogers, 1993, p. 142). This may be a complex statistic to read, however. Unlike criminal confinements, civil confinement of psychopaths under s. 3 of the Act is possible only if treatment is available which will 'alleviate or prevent a deterioration' of the individual's condition (s. 3(2)(b)). The fall in numbers does not necessarily mean a challenge to a medical paradigm of psychopathy or personality disorder, therefore; it may instead reflect a scepticism as to whether people with these disorders are amenable to treatment. This would appear to be a serious question: while some of these people do, apparently, respond to different treatments, there does not seem to be any mechanism to determine what treatment, if any, will be effective on a specific individual (Reed, 1996, pp. 6-7).

In 1992, a joint working group was established by the Department of Health and the Home Office to examine the treatment of persons with personality or psychopathic disorders. This group recommended that the term 'psychopathy' ought to be replaced in the Act, on the basis that it was no longer in clinical usage. It recommended that 'personality disorder' ought to be included in the statute in its stead, on the express condition that 'personality disorder' would not be further defined (Reed, 1996, p. 6). It is difficult to see that this solves the problems of circularity identified above, where conduct was identified as illness, which in turn explained the conduct. And how would a court interpret this new term? The tendency of the courts not to read the statute in a technical, medical fashion will be clear from the preceding discussion. Would 'personality disorder', not further defined, be read as words commonly in English usage, as other controversial terms of the statute have been? In that event, would the new term create an exceptionally broad point of entry into the provisions of the Act? Alternatively, would the court recognise the new phrase as a medical term of art? If so, the decision-making role would presumably be removed entirely to the medical professional, and the normative aspects of the current definition, which are the province of the non-medical view, would be removed. Are we content, particularly in matters where the definition of the disorder dissolves into behaviour failing to match a social norm, to entrust this entry criterion entirely to doctors?

2.2.4 Section 1(3): promiscuity, immoral conduct, sexual deviancy and drug dependency

Section 1(3) provides that no person may be dealt with as mentally disordered under the 1983 Act, 'by reason only of promiscuity or other immoral conduct, sexual deviancy or dependence on alcohol or drugs'. This restriction applies both to 'mental disorder' and also to the four specifically enumerated types of mental disorder. The word 'only' is significant: the subsection does not, of course, preclude the operation of the Act in cases where the impugned conduct is but one manifestation of a more complex disorder.

This section, as so much of the MHA 1983, must be understood in its historical context. Victorian and Edwardian social policy had to a considerable degree been intended to enforce morality, particularly onto the poor and marginal. The public, county lunatic asylums were but one mechanism to this end. In addition, the Inebriates Act 1898, ss. 1, 2 allowed detention in reformatories for up to three years of habitual drunkards and those committing serious crimes while drunk. While originally conceptualised in terms of moral control, the first decade of implementation saw the role of inebriate regulation increasingly in psychiatric terms (Zedner, 1991, pp. 259-63). A similar ambiguity between socially inappropriate behaviour and institutional control may be seen in the subsequent Mental Deficiency Act 1913, where 'feeble-mindedness' was not clearly distinguished from immoral behaviour. Thus an unmarried woman giving birth while on poor relief was deemed by the Act to be feeble-minded and was to be subjected to confinement in an asylum; no further proof of mental state was necessary (Zedner, 1991, p. 275).

The MHA 1959 can be seen as introducing a sea change in this regard, by introducing an earlier version of the current s. 1(3). In part, this can be understood as the continuation of a reconceptualisation of the role of regulation and institutions for the insane, away from overt control and towards a more medicalised vision of treatment. The fact that the impugned behaviour is not of itself to be sufficient evidence of mental disorder does not make the behaviour acceptable. If the behaviour in question constitutes a crime, as much of the behaviour in the scope of s. 1(3) may, it will instead be categorised as criminal. The express addition in 1983 of drug dependency to the conduct which does not, of itself, indicate mental disorder provides a good example of this new ambiguity. The express removal of drug dependency from the definition of mental disorder does not normalise the behaviour in question, for people are still convicted of drug-related crimes in considerable numbers. In understanding the effect of the section, and the scope of the definitions in s. 1 as a whole, the issue may well not be simply the distinction between mentally disordered as opposed to non-disordered behaviour; it may be the choice of category of deviance, between mad or bad.

The leading case on this subsection is *R v MHRT, ex parte Clatworthy* [1985] 3 All ER 699. That case involved a man convicted in 1967 of two counts of indecent assault involving inappropriate touching of young girls. On the basis of this conduct, which represented part of a pattern of similar behaviour, he was diagnosed as having a psychopathic disorder. He remained in a secure hospital for eighteen years, whereupon his doctors concluded that he could no longer be detained, on the basis that the sole justification for his confinement was his sexually deviant behaviour towards young girls. As it was a confinement under the criminal jurisdiction of the mental health legislation, however, they could only recommend his release, and the review tribunal with the actual decision-making authority did not follow their advice, providing only the barest of reasons for its decision. Clatworthy sought judicial review.

The facts of the case provide a hint of some of the other dynamics of decision-making in this sort of situation. Clatworthy had been confined under the MHA 1959, which contained a provision substantively similar to s. 1(3) of the 1983 Act (MHA 1959, s. 4(5)). While that section refered only to 'promiscuity or other immoral conduct', rather than sexual deviance specifically, it is nonetheless difficult to see that the 1959 phrase is not wide enough to encompass the inappropriate touching. If the doctors in 1985 were serious in their view that this conduct had been the only justification for confinement, it is open to be asked why this objection had not occurred to them eighteen years previously.

The issues before the court were not limited to the scope of s. 1(3), but also included an issue as to the adequacy of reasons provided by the tribunal: see Chapter 8. On this latter point, Clatworthy was successful and the case was remitted to the tribunal. Perhaps for this reason, the court is somewhat coy in its treatment of the former point, suggesting but not expressly making a finding based on a rather fine distinction (pp. 701-2):

It may at once be observed that the effect of sub-s. (3) is apparently to prevent there being a condition of psychopathic disorder when the abnormally aggressive or seriously irresponsible conduct consequent on the persistent disorder or disability of mind is conduct which is a manifestion of sexual deviancy. It may also be observed that it can be contended that sexual deviancy does not mean tendency to deviation but means indulgence in deviation. That contention would achieve support from its context, the context being promiscuity or other immoral conduct and dependence on alcohol or drugs.

The suggestion would seem to be that the tendency, a sexual attraction to children, may be outside the scope of s. 1(3), but the conduct, the inappropriate touching of little girls, is covered by the section. The suggestion seems to be that one may treat the sinner, but not the sin.

If tendency is theoretically distinct from behaviour and s. 1(3) were to apply only to the latter, however, it would presumably be the case that an individual could be brought within the scope of the Act if they have the tendency to behave in one of the ways enumerated by s. 1(3), even if they have never in fact acted on that tendency. Thus to have paedophiliac desires would justify the invocation of the Act, even if the desires had never been acted upon. Can it really have been the intent of the legislature that a desire to drink alcohol to excess could be taken into account in understanding an individual as mentally disordered, even if the individual were in fact teetotal? Or that a desire to behave promiscuously could be taken into account even if the individual remained chaste?

Such a reading would seem to fly in the face of the historical context of the provision, discussed above. There was no distinction in the framing or implementation of the earlier legislation between the behaviour and the tendency, and confinement in the facilities in question was to curb the tendency as much as the behaviour. Thus Zedner notes that nineteenth-century advocates justified detention of inebriates for up to three years reformatories 'in order to keep them away from drink long enough to fortify their will to abstain' (Zedner, 1991, p. 232). The objective was to create moral character, to remodel the individual, not merely to control behaviour (Zedner, 1991, pp. 237, 241-5). It was this sort of violation of liberty that s. 1(3) was to address; yet if the distinction between tendency and behaviour is adopted, it would seem instead to have paved the way for a more expansive violation of the individual's freedom. The earlier legislation at least required that the individual actually have engaged in the specified activity, thus to be a habitual drunkard or to engage in immoral sex, for example.

The distinction between tendency and behaviour is in any event problematic, since mental disorders do not comfortably divide from the behaviours which characterise them. Psychopathy is perhaps the paradigmatic example: the condition is defined by the behaviour. This difficulty is acknowledged by the court in *Clatworthy*, in its criticism of the reasons provided by the tribunal (at p. 703):

The grounds for the reasons invite immediately the question: what are the features of psychopathic disorder as defined by the 1983 Act apart from sexual deviancy? The evidence as I read it is that there is no other feature and sexual deviancy is to be discounted under the Act.

In so far as this is the case, the distinction between behaviour and tendency ceases to be meaningful, and in such cases, s. 1(3) should be read as precluding the application of the Act.

Is the distinction between tendency and behaviour defensible based on the statutory wording itself? Does the subsection really refer to behaviour as distinct from tendency? The wording as it relates to promiscuity, other immoral conduct, or sexual deviancy may be at least arguably consistent with the comment of the court; but the phrase 'dependence on alcohol or drugs' is more problematic. The conduct which attaches to this phrase is presumably drunkenness and the actual ingestion of drugs. *Dependence* on such substances would appear instead to refer not merely to the conduct, but also to the tendency to engage in the conduct in question. If that is the case, it would have to be asked whether it was really the intention of the legislature to refer to conduct in some of the subsection and conduct plus tendency elsewhere, without express indication of what is, in the end, a very fine distinction.

It may, nonetheless, be inappropriate to dismiss the distinction too quickly, for it is in a different sense consistent with a continuing reconceptualisation of the realm of mental health law away from simple control of behaviour, towards the cure of the individual. The problems to be faced no longer centre on physical control, but instead on remedying a condition. Institutions are to be about treatment, not about simple detention; and psychiatrists are to be understood as doctors, not as gaolers. It would be consistent with this approach to distinguish between tendency and conduct in the definition section of the Act.

The control of the tendency requires, of course, very different mechanisms from the control of conduct. The tradition has been to view this as a benevolent shift, with physical control associated with a particularly miserable existence for the insane person, and medicalisation with humanitarianism and liberation. Certainly, the intrusiveness of physical confinement ought not to be underappreciated. At the same time, the intrusiveness of the newer techniques has its critics. For Michel Foucault, for example, the move to new forms of control of madness is problematic. For Foucault, this theme of intrusive control of the mind of the individual is consistent from the beginning of nineteenth-century psychiatry. Traditional medical history had accorded the Tukes of York with accolades as great liberators of the insane, for their pioneering work in removing physical restraint from patients at the beginning of the nineteenth century. Foucault's view of this move is much more circumspect (1965, p. 247):

> In fact Tuke created an asylum where he substituted for the free terror of madness the stifling anguish of responsibility; fear no longer reigned on the other side of the prison gates, it now raged under the seals of conscience. Tuke now transferred the age-old terrors in which the insane had been trapped to the very heart of madness. The asylum no longer punished the madman's guilt, it is true; but it did more, it organized that guilt; it organized it for the madman as a consciousness of himself, and as a non-reciprocal relation to the keeper; it organized it for the man of reason as an awareness of the Other, a therapeutic intervention in the madman's existence.

In this vision, where the old ways controlled physically, the new control through imposing self-restraint on the individual, altering the way the insane perceive themselves. Where the old ways left the thoughts and feelings of the individual essentially private, the new used this altered self-perception as a method of control.

2.3 'MENTAL ILLNESS'

As we have seen, the MHA 1983 sometimes requires one of the four specific categories of mental disorder, i.e., mental illness, severe mental impairment, mental impairment or psychopathy, to be specified. Mental illness has a particular importance among the four, simply because of the frequency of its use. In 1996-7, roughly 97 per cent of the people detained for treatment under s. 3 of the Act were categorised as mentally ill (Department of Health, 1998d, p. 5).

The term is not further defined by the Act. Once again, the case law and official information are ambiguous and inconsistent as to how the term is to be read, and the degree of professional involvement in its interpretation. A memorandum provided by the Department of Health states that the term's 'operational definition and usage is a matter for clinical judgment in each case' (Department of Health and Welsh Office, 1998, para. 10). This would suggest that it is a medical matter, to be interpreted by doctors in a medical framework.

This is difficult to reconcile with the case law, such as it is. The leading case, *W* v *L* [1974] QB 711, involved a man who engaged in sadistic behaviour towards animals. There was clear evidence that the man suffered from a psychopathic disorder, but the MHA 1959 then in effect allowed only relatively young psychopaths to be confined. The man was over the relevant age, and was therefore unable to be confined on that basis. One of the issues, therefore was whether he could also be understood to suffer from 'mental illness'. The majority of the Court of Appeal found that evidence of unusual performance on an electroencephalogram (EEG) indicated that he was also suffering from mental illness. It is however the minority judgment of Lawton LJ which has attracted the bulk of the attention. His Lordship interprets the words 'mental illness' as plain English (at p. 719):

> The words are ordinary words of the English language. They have no particular medical significance. They have no particular legal significance. How should the court construe them? The answer in my judgment is to be found in the advice which Lord Reid recently gave in *Cozens* v *Brutus* [1973] AC 854, 861, namely, that ordinary words of the English language should be construed in the way that ordinary sensible people would construe them. That being, in my judgment, the right test, then I ask myself, what would the ordinary sensible person have said about the patient's condition in this case if he had been informed of his behaviour to the dogs, the cat and his wife? In my judgment such a person would have said: 'Well, the fellow is obviously mentally ill.' If that be right, then, although the case may fall within the definition of 'psychopathic disorder' . . . it also falls within the classification of 'mental illness'; and there is the added medical fact that when the E.E.G. was taken there were indications of a clinical character showing some abnormality of the brain. It is that application of the sensible person's assessment of the condition, plus the medical indication, which in my judgment brought the case within the classification of mental illness and justified the finding of the county court judge.

This passage has been read as emphasising a lay interpretation of mental illness. Brenda Hoggett, for example, rather pointedly refers to it as the 'man-must-be-mad' test (1996, p. 32). Michael Cavadino (1991, pp. 299-300) has criticised the test on the basis that it assumes a known and consistent view among lay people as to what mental illness is. He argues that it in fact has a medical usage, drawing into question Lawton LJ's statement that it has 'no particular medical significance', and that it is based on an assessment of behaviour rather than on mental condition. He also stresses that Lawton LJ was a minority decision, and therefore the legal status of the test is suspect.

Some criticisms of the test are undoubtedly justified. Would the reasonable person on the street view an individual engaged in abnormally aggressive or seriously irresponsible conduct as mentally ill? If so, and the point seems at least arguable, psychopathy becomes its own category of mental illness; all people with 'psychopathic disorder' are also 'mentally ill'. This does not seem far-fetched, as it represents the situation under the Scots legislation, as we have seen. That cannot be the legislative intent in England, however, since the statute sometimes provides different conditions for the application of the Act to the two classes; the relevance of these different provisions to psychopaths would be nullified if they could simply and alternatively be categorised as mentally ill.

At the same time, the test is not entirely inconsistent with the approach of the courts to psychopathy and the mental impairments, discussed above. As in those cases, medical expertise is acknowledged, but the decision as to whether the medical facts are sufficient to satisfy the standard in the Act is a matter which is not restricted to clinical judgment. Such a hybrid approach admittedly fits more easily into the express definitions of those other disorders, where the issues of degree to which the lay view attaches are expressly spelled out in the statute; but a move from such a hybrid view for mental illness begs the question of why medical views should be definitive for that category, but not for the other categories of mental disorder. Consistency could alternatively be achieved if lay views were removed from the determination of all four subcategories of mental disorder; but in that event, the question arises as to whether we are content to place extraordinary powers over individual rights in the hands of one profession, no matter how well-intentioned.

The use of a purely medical approach to the administration of the disorder definitions in the Act is problematic for a variety of reasons. The first question is *which* medical approach? There are two primary medical nosologies of mental illness. The one in use primarily in North America is the Diagnostic and Statistical Manual of Disorders, currently in its fourth edition (DSM-IV), published by the American Psychiatric Association. Most of the rest of the world relies primarily on the World Health Organisation standard, the International Classification of Diseases and Related Health Problems, currently in its tenth edition (ICD-10), which contains a classification of mental disorders in Chapter five.

While converging in format, ICD-10 and DSM-IV are not yet identical, and their content is determined both by cultural specificities and by administrative momentum of the respective formulating organisations (Kendell, 1991). The content reflects political issues and approaches within these organisations. Thus the framers of DSM-IV were criticised by some feminists, within and without the medical professions, for advocating the inclusion of self-defeating personality disorder and premenstrual dysphoric disorder in the nosology, as the classifications were perceived to pathologise women. A rather pointed account of the internal political wrangles of the American Psychiatric Association in the formulation of DSM-IV, and in particular regarding the continued inclusion of these two categories, can be found in Caplan (1995). The internal administrative tensions she documents serves as a salient reminder that, as discussed in the previous Chapter, mental health law is never far from a collection of other complex interests.

Even viewed in its most sympathetic light, the use of these purely medical criteria in a legal context is problematic. Classification systems such as DSM-IV and ICD-10 can be seen as having a variety of objectives. They promote a unified nomenclature for professionals active in research or diagnosis, to ensure consistency in medical professional discourses and practice. They define the direction of those professional discourses, by determining the disorders to be studied (see Boyle, 1990, p. 4). Neither was designed as a mechanism to determine appropriateness of legal intervention.

The medical model of mental illness is developed by doctors and other medical professionals with the objective of providing cures, or, at the very least, alleviating undesirable effects of conditions. Severity of disorder, for example, is not necessarily a factor in development of that approach. Just as we would expect a doctor to treat minor as well as major physical ailments, so psychiatry is appropriately concerned with conditions of varying degrees of severity. This search for causes and cures is quite a different project from that of the Act, which may concern appropriateness of intervention, sanctioned by the state and over the objection of the subject. Certainly, the Act requires other legal requirements to be met before these powers can be invoked, but the question remains: is there any obvious reason to use a system developed to promote cure, in the rather different context of rights determination? Are these not simply two separate projects?

A variety of theoretical problems also lie at the root of the medical model of mental illness, which at least arguably suggests that we should embrace it in a legal context only with considerable hesitation. The medical paradigm comes wrapped in a scientific cloak, suggesting objectivity, reliability, and a confirmed basis in physical reality. There is an irony to this public perception, since few pure scientists would characterise their work in such pristine terms (see, e.g., Bird, 1990). For them, science is more likely to be understood as a collection of hypotheses which explain phenomena to a greater or lesser degree. This may well fit the medical model of mental illness, but its more modest claims equally serve to undermine the desirability of the model in a legal context: should we really be removing rights on the basis of hypotheses?

While a medical model of mental illness would generally suggest a physical cause of a disorder, such causes are generally at best disputed and often entirely unknown in practice. Often, there will be no test of a mental disorder, in the way in which an x-ray may reveal a broken bone. Instead, diagnosis will initially be through patient symptoms, that is, the history as reported by the individual. These will be supplemented by signs, indications actually witnessed by the doctor. In neither case is this likely to involve identifiable physical abnormalities, but instead behaviours or phenomena. For major disorders these may involve things such as hallucinations; or the belief in things which are profoundly unlikely, such as that the individual is being controlled telepathically; or that the individual is abnormally frightened or depressed without cause; or that they are behaving or threatening to behave in a way which self-damages, as in the case of a person with a personality disorder who wishes to self-mutilate, or an anorectic patient refusing food. The use of phenomena in this way is both theoretically and practically problematic. Why are they associated with a disease model at all, when the physical disorder which is central to that paradigm is often unknown?

The absence of objective tests further risks rendering the diagnoses self-fulfilling: individuals believed to have a specific form of disorder will have their behaviour used to confirm that diagnosis. Thus the hallucinations and delusions which are at the base of psychotic disorders such as schizophrenia may alternatively be caused by known physical factors such as toxic reactions. While good doctors may consider this possibility, the risk is that the doctor may diagnose schizophrenia and further inquiry not be conducted, because for schizophrenia, there is no further test.

Indeed, once an expectation of psychiatric disorder is raised, all sorts of behaviour may be viewed through a pathological lens further to justify that conclusion. In Rosenhan's study (Rosenhan, 1973), a variety of sane people gained admission to psychiatric facilities. Rosenhan's paper discusses the fate of these 'pseudo-patients'. To gain admission, they attended at the facility and complained (disingenuously) of hearing unfamiliar voices; the message of the voices was often unclear, but as far as could be understood, they said 'empty', 'hollow', and 'thud'. No further falsifications to the patient's personal history were made. Gaining admission was apparently not a problem, perhaps unsurprisingly as they were describing psychotic delusions, and in almost all cases, a diagnosis of schizophrenia was reached. The falsity of the presenting symptoms was not open to be discovered, of course, because there was no additional, objective test for schizophrenia: symptoms, as described by the patient are all the doctor has to go on.

What is perhaps more unnerving in the present context is the pathologisation of behaviour on the ward, and of the patient's history. Relationships with parents were reinterpreted and, in Rosenhan's view, distorted to match the existing psychodynamic theories. Aggression was understood as a sign of the continuance of the disorder, never as flowing from heavy-handed or marginalising behaviour by an attendant, nurse or doctor. Even arriving at the cafeteria early for lunch was reformulated by a psychiatrist in one case as indicating the 'oral-acquisitive nature' of the disorder (Rosenhan, 1973, p. 253). Such reinterpretation to justify existing conclusions is well-known in the sociological literature, both in medical contexts and beyond (see, e.g., Garfinkel and Bittner, 1967; Smith, 1990). The fact that this makes diagnoses difficult to falsify ought to give cause for pause, however, when legal controls result.

2.4   SCHIZOPHRENIA: A CASE STUDY

Schizophrenia provides a case study to examine these problems, although much of what will be discussed in this context will apply by analogy to other psychiatric disorders. It is selected here because its nature and the applicability of a medical model to understand it are matters of current debate, discussed in a variety of sources readily accessible to students (for example Thomas, 1997; Boyle, 1990; Wing, 1988; Bentall et al, 1988, 1988a). Its significance should further not be understated: it is one of the most frequent diagnoses under the Act, and serves as a paradigm in many people's minds for what mental illness is.

Contrary to popular usage, schizophrenia does not in the overwhelming number of cases have to do with a so-called 'split personality'. It is instead a psychotic disorder: fundamental to its nature is a fractured relationship to reality. This is typically manifest in hallucinations, particularly hearing voices. An interference in the thinking process is common (i.e., 'delusions'), where the individual believes that others are controlling their thoughts, or know what they are thinking. Similarly, a loss of autonomy may be experienced, where strange physical sensations may be felt, or movements occur without the patient's will. A lack of emotional engagement with surroundings, poverty of or minimal speech, lack of drive, lack of pleasure, and poor attention may also appear, generally gradually over a longer period than the earlier symptoms.

Schizophrenia is thus diagnosed solely according to symptoms as reported by the patient and observed behaviours. Two separate concepts should be identified in moving from these indicators to a diagnosis. The first is 'reliability': is the medical definition of the disorder clear enough that individuals will be categorised accurately, no matter who is doing the assessment? The second is 'validity', whether the definition actually relates to anything in reality. The difference can be illustrated by using David Pilgrim's example of Santa Claus (Pilgrim, 1995). We all know the characteristics of Santa Claus: delivers goodies on Christmas Eve from a sleigh drawn by reindeer, white beard, red coat, black boots, unrepentant pipe smoker, and so forth. We would all know him if we saw him; the definition is reliable. That does not mean Santa Claus exists; the definition is not in that sense valid.

The reliability of schizophrenia diagnosis has been problematic in the past (Bentall et al, 1988, pp. 305-6). Practice may be improving in this regard. Both the ICD and DSM criteria have become more specific in determining when a diagnosis of schizophrenia can be made. With the development of ICD-10 and DSM-IV, diagnostic criteria are converging, although there are still some differences (see Gelder et al, 1996, pp. 257-9). Increased reliability nonetheless does not settle the issue of whether the definition actually refers to anything or whether, like Santa Claus, it is a definition devoid of validity.

The causal theories relating to schizophrenia are various, and span genetic, biochemical and social factors. The genetic studies are summarised by Thomas (1997, pp. 31-6). If genetics were the cause of schizophrenia, one would expect the identical twin of a schizophrenic also to have the disorder, since identical twins have the same genetic code. Studies do indicate a much higher probability of this occurring. Thomas cites a study by McGue et al, for example, showing first cousins of people diagnosed as schizophrenic as having a 1.6 per cent chance of developing the disorder, where identical twins of schizophrenics have a 44.3 per cent chance (Thomas, 1997, p. 33, citing McGue et al, 1985). The difference is indeed suggestive, but hardly conclusive. Certainly, the probabilities of schizophrenia in the identical twin of a schizophrenic are impressively high; but as Thomas points out, one could equally argue the inverse: notwithstanding identical genetic codes, less than half of identical twins of schizophrenics go on to develop the disorder. While there would thus appear to be a genetic susceptibility, it is not clear whether the triggers in development of the actual disorder are genetic or environmental (Gelder et al, 1996, pp. 268-9). Further, the mode of inheritance is unknown (Gelder et al, 1996, p. 280). It is thus not obvious that genetics are the whole story.

Biochemical factors are similarly problematic. The most popular theory is that schizophrenia results from an oversupply of a chemical called dopamine in the brain. This view is not without support. Certainly, neuroleptic medication can assist in the control of symptoms in at least some patients, and this medication would appear to affect dopamine levels. The fact that chemical treatments can control the manifestations of a disorder does not necessarily mean that the disorder itself is biochemically caused. During the press attention and legal proceedings following the disclosure of her relationship with American President, Bill Clinton, Monica Lewinsky admitted to feeling depressed and taking medication to control that depression. The medication may well have helped her; but that is not a reason to adopt a biochemical model to understand the causes of her depression.

The first neuroleptics pre-date the dopamine theory: they were discovered to work before the dopamine theory was developed. At least arguably, the theory can be seen to account for the efficacy of the drug, rather than the drug being developed to match a separate theory (Thomas, 1997, p. 125). Drug efficacy is an awkward measure to use in any event. Not everyone receives the beneficial effects (see Pilgrim and Rogers, 1993). Further, the beneficial effects are not limited to schizophrenia, but also occur in mania. This suggests a more complex picture than simple causation based on dopamine imbalance.

Beyond the issue of drug efficacy, the theory has at best mixed empirical and experimental support (Thomas, 1997, p. 38). While post mortem studies of the brains of people who had schizophrenia show an increase in dopamine, this may be the result of antipsychotic medication (Gelder et al, 1996, p. 274). Thus Gelder et al state that while 'the evidence that dopamine is central to the action of antipsychotic drugs is strong, evidence for the corollary — that dopamine neurotransmission is abnormal in schizophrenia — is weak' (1996, p. 274).

Neurodevelopment models of schizophrenia also exist (Thomas, 1997, pp. 39-44). Here, the idea is that for any of a variety of reasons, be it maternal illness, birth injury, genetics or other factor, an abnormality in the brain occurs, and schizophrenia is the result. This, like the genetic factors discussed above, seems to apply for a subgroup of the schizophrenic population.

What we are left with are medical theories. Even those relatively devoted to a medical model of schizophrenia acknowledge that the cause is unknown (e.g., Frith, 1994). Validity cannot be shown. While that may give cause for pause, a lack of evidence does not necessarily bespeak a negative: the inability to demonstrate validity does not necessarily mean that the definition is invalid. Should we continue to rely on it, notwithstanding its questionable validity?

The continued utility of the concept in a research context has been disputed. Mary Boyle, for example, applies the work of Imre Lakatos on the philosophy of science to claim that schizophrenia has outlived its usefulness (Boyle, 1994). Her argument is considerably more sophisticated than a claim that a theory needs to explain all evidence. It is instead acknowledged that theories require adjustment in the face of new or inconsistent evidence. The theory is still helpful in a research context if these adjustments are 'content increasing'; if not, the theory itself is open to question. In other words, if adjusting the theory to cope with anomalies actually provides new information or insights, the theory remains useful; if it is merely making excuses for its anomalies, it is no longer helpful.

Boyle suggests that on such criteria, the concept of schizophrenia ought to be abandoned. In her view, the current research into the disorder is not producing new and helpful knowledge, but rather getting mired in its own contradictions. While she acknowledges increasing definitional rigour has increased reliability of diagnosis, she argues this does nothing to address whether the disorder as defined will be valid. She is critical of the research attempting to move towards validation, again on the basis that it is failing to produce new insights. Thus she criticises the theory that schizophrenia is a result of brain dysfunction on the basis that research has not been able to identify which part of the brain it is which is at issue, and the lack of evidence that any schizophrenic people suffered from brain dysfunction prior to treatment. The finding by proponents of schizophrenia that it may have multiple causes is criticised on the basis that these causes have not been identified, notwithstanding considerable empirical investigation. The suggestion that schizophrenia is actually a collection of many sub-types is similarly seen by Boyle as problematic: they have, in her view, never been convincingly identified (Boyle, 1994, p. 402).

Needless to say, such views are extremely controversial. They are nonetheless important for the student to consider, lest there be an unjustified sense that the medical conceptualisation of mental illness is somehow accepted or uncontroversial among the experts. Indeed, it is perhaps appropriate to note that some of the most radical critiques of concepts of mental illness have come from practitioners, or at least those with practice experience, themselves. Obvious examples include Thomas Szasz, R.D. Laing, and Michel Foucault.

The search for validation of the concept of schizophrenia can be understood in professional terms: geneticists, neurologists, and medical bio-chemists each attempting to find an explanation for the condition, based on the training they have received and the intellectual structures of their sub-disciplines. Social scientists have made similar enquiries, based on social science methodologies. Reflecting the history of social science research generally, social causes, social reactions, and social constructions of schizophrenia have all been identified. For reviews of the literature, see Thomas (1997, pp. 51-6), Pilgrim and Rogers (1993, pp. 13-21). Regarding social causes, sociologists have identified class, poverty, and social disintegration as correlatives of schizophrenia. As schizophrenia is geographically centred in inner cities, sociological debate developed around the question of whether it is caused by increased stress in such environments. The alternative explanation, of course, is that the onset of schizophrenia precipitated a fall in socio-economic status, resulting in a disproportionate move by people with the disorder to the inner cities.

Similarly, sociologists have looked at the ways in which people react to behaviour, labelling it as deviant. The issue here is how people become defined or understood as 'deviant', again a subject considered by sociologists regarding psychiatric patients at about the same time it was considered for prisoners and other 'deviant' classes. The study here was of patient 'careers', beginning with the way an individual became identified as insane. The argument was that this followed when they were identified by professionals as failing to conform appropriately to their appropriate social roles. Once they became so identified, the individuals then moved on to conform to the new role, the 'person with mental illness' role, to which the professional had now assigned them, adopting behaviours and attitudes which were expected of them in this new situation. The work of Erving Goffman, which will be considered more thoroughly in the next Chapter, provides a particularly good example of such an approach, carried from the stage of diagnosis or identification into the adoption of the role by the individual. The Rosenhan study, discussed above, is a further example of this: 'illness' was created in the interaction with the professionals. For a view which challenges Rosenhan on some of his conclusions, though, see Spitzer (1976).

2.5 CAUTIONARY TALES?

What are we to make of all this, for purposes of legal regulation? Scholars challenging schizophrenia as a concept do not necessarily argue that people diagnosed with schizophrenia are 'really' just like everyone else. As Boyle points out, challenging an existing paradigm is not to deny the existence of the phenomena which it is intended to explain (Boyle, 1990, p. 193):

It is not claimed that some people do not behave in strange and disturbing ways or have disturbing experiences. Nor is it claimed that these behaviours and experiences may not cause considerable distress, that they may not be preceded by changes in brain chemistry or that they may not be altered by certain drugs. What is challenged is the current interpretation of these phenomena; the usefulness of 'schizophrenia' or any of its sub-types as an inference from them.

This is all well and good; but it does not provide much assistance in a legal context. Boyle goes on to provide interesting suggestions on how research might be conducted in the future, but does not purport to analyse how legal intervention and regulation should proceed. In her view, the use of the concept as a basis for legal regulation is problematic not merely because of the claimed unscientific nature of schizophrenia, but also because science cannot be expected to perform what are essentially moral tasks relating to decisions as to when intervention is appropriate. She does argue that '[a]cceptance of its [schizophrenia's] non-scientific status, however, might at least help to make clear the need to articulate and radically rethink the assumptions and practices surrounding the law as it relates to bizarre behaviour' (Boyle, 1990, p. 194).

A radical rethink it would be, for law prides itself on its rationality, and its objectivity. The attachment of law to a medical approach can be seen in this light: with the use of a 'scientific' paradigm, the law can use standards which at least appear neutral. If intrusive intervention such as physical confinement and the removal of other civil rights is to be justified, it must be done according to clear and objective criteria. Scientific or medical frameworks are one, but not necessarily the only approach which yields such apparent objectivity. Thus the insanity defence, for example, will often in practice include expert medical testimony, but the test remains (in simple terms) whether the accused understood that the actions in question were wrong, a matter which is not essentially medical (see 6.4). Intervention in anticipation of future events is more difficult to structure without reference to some scientific characterisation of the individual, however. Thus we acknowledge suicide as within the rights of an individual, but would tend to hesitate before allowing a person with a mental illness to commit suicide, if the suicide was thought to be a manifestation of the disorder. Without some form of scientific base, how are we to distinguish these two cases?

At the same time, the problems remain. The apparent neutrality of the medical model may mask inequalities. As we shall see in Chapter four, people of Afro-Caribbean origin are markedly statistically over-represented in mental health admissions. There is hot dispute as to whether this represents a real, higher incidence of a medical disorder, or whether instead the apparent neutrality of the medical paradigm is masking discriminatory implementation. Black people are also over-represented throughout the criminal and policing system; does the supposed neutrality of the medical model protect such over-representation in the psychiatric system from appropriate scrutiny? Similarly, different diagnoses are reflected in differing proportions in people of different genders. Thus women are considerably more likely to be diagnosed with depressive disorders, senile and pre-senile dementia, and neurotic disorders than men; where men are somewhat more likely to attract diagnoses of schizophrenia, and alcoholism or alcohol psychosis (Pilgrim and Rogers, 1993, p. 23). Such statistics are not necessarily inconsistent with true neutrality of the model. Thus the increased incidence of senile and pre-senile dementia may in part be explained by the statistically shorter life span of men, which is likely to affect the incidence of a disorder which tends to occur late in life. At the same time, fierce debate continues to exist about how women are characterised by the mental health system (see 7.3.2).

The difficulty remains as to how a medical model can formulate what is, in the end, a social choice both as to what constitutes an illness or disorder, and as to when intervention or differential treatment is warranted. Homosexuality provides an instructive illustration. It is an interesting example, since this is a case where the psychiatric profession, along with society as a whole, simply decided that something which had been understood as an illness in the past, would no longer be considered in pathological terms.

In many ways, theories of homosexuality have mirrored and continue to mirror theories of mental illness. In both cases, there have been genetic, physical, and environmental explanations of behaviour which is statistically abnormal. Like mental disorders, homosexuality was for years treated with drugs, psychotherapy, or electrical aversion therapy, with ambiguous claims to success, in psychiatric environments. Notwithstanding its disease-like status in scientific terms and this history of treatment, it was decided that an illness model was no longer appropriate. A certain type of behaviour which had previously indicated a mental illness would no longer do so, emphasising the social nature of the whole project of mental illness. In the United States, the matter was decided by vote of the American Psychiatric Association, in 1974. It was not until the introduction of ICD-10 in 1993, nineteen years later, that it disappeared from the WHO classification.

It may well be that many psychiatrists in this country had not considered homosexuality a mental illness for years before that time. While that may be relevant for the human rights and dignity of gay people, it raises a different set of problems for mental health law, policy and regulation, for it suggests that professionals use criteria other than the medical standards to determine who is or is not mentally ill. If professionals are making such individualistic decisions, in what sense is the scientific or medical paradigm being relied on? Are we not left with doctors making individual choices as to what qualifies as an illness, and for intervention? If they are expanding beyond the standards provided, is there any reason that their views should be given particular credence?

Homosexuality also provides an important example as to how old ideas die hard. The topic is still frequently raised in Chapters relating to sexual disorders in psychiatric textbooks (see, e.g., Cohen and Hart, 1995, pp. 364-5; Goldberg et al, 1994, pp. 273-4). In the former text, it is expressly recognised that homosexuality is not a disorder under ICD-10. While the latter text, directed to general practitioners, makes no reference to treatment or cure, it equally does not specifically note that the condition is not a disorder, and its discussion is placed between transsexualism and sexual disorders of adult life, conditions which may call for medical intervention or assistance. In their discussion of the causes of homosexuality, Goldberg et al further do not merely cite genetic, biochemical and parental role models. In addition, they indicate that 'effeminate' boys are likely to become homosexual, and suggest that boys lacking confidence about their masculinity may be unattractive to the opposite sex, 'so that the adolescent enters the rather less competititive homosexual world' (Goldberg et al, 1994, p. 274). It is difficult to see that this description matches the experiences of gay men. Instead, it would appear to re-enforce imagery of gay men as morally weak and social failures — hardly the imagery of equality and respect which is reflected on the modern political agenda.

The older, pathological conceptions of homosexuality continue to influence current practice. Gay and lesbian psychiatric patients speak not merely of overt discriminatory behaviour in the mental health services, but also of how their sexuality is likely to be used to explain their mental health difficulties. In a survey by MIND in 1997, half of gay and lesbian users of mental health services surveyed were told they would have fewer problems if they tried to alter their sexuality. The continued view of sexuality as a mental health problem is perhaps unsurprising, as homosexual experiences may attract particular attention in the textbook instructions on good practice in taking patient histories. Thus while Cohen and Hart specifically disclaim homosexuality per se as a disorder under ICD-10 (Cohen and Hart, 1995, p. 364), they also specifically urge that information about 'any homosexual activity or other deviations' be specifically requested and noted in compiling the sexual history of a patient (p. 23).

The example of homosexuality can be seen in part as a cautionary tale. For years, intrusive and often unpleasant treatments were used in an attempt to alter a condition which is no longer viewed as pathological. One wonders if there are other disorders which, in time, will benefit from similar changes in social attitudes. In this context, it is an example of the normative side of diagnosis and mental health regulation, and raises the question whether mental illness or disorder, as defined by the medical profession, is an appropriate gateway to the MHA 1983 or whether a standard reflecting broader social interests should be introduced.

This example further emphasises the difficulties of moving between administrative contexts in the use of medical categories. To be realistic, people concerned about their sexual orientation will, at least sometimes, consult doctors. Unless doctors are to abandon those people, some form of medical understanding of homosexuality must be developed, and the role of the medical profession in this context must be articulated. That does not necessarily mean a 'cure' for homosexuality; it may well mean appropriate psychotherapy or peer counselling to come to terms with the individual's concerns. Nonetheless, it is not obvious that homosexuality can simply be removed from the medical universe. This raises from another angle the question of how medical nosology and models relate to legal regulation. Is the threshold of humane medical intervention necessarily the same as for legal or policy regulation? Certainly other requirements will be necessary to invoke the powers of the MHA, but is the same standard or definition of mental disorder appropriate for the individual who seeks medical involvement as for the imposition of state power, through civil confinement? Is the use of a system designed by doctors to provide a structure for care and cure really the appropriate one to use to determine administrative or legal interventions?

The problems of definition discussed in this Chapter lie at the heart of mental health law and policy. If a coherent understanding and articulation of the fundamental definitions of mental disorder which serve as the gateway to the 1983 Act is not attained, it is fair to ask how the Act is to be justified in a civil rights framework. Why is one set of behaviours treated one way, and another differently, if there is no coherent meaning to the terms which define the prerequisite conditions of the Act's application? Medical frameworks are problematic in this regard, and it is not obvious what other criteria could reasonably be used. On this basis, the justification for the Act is, arguably, dubious.

At the same time, reread some of the personal accounts of mental disorder cited in the last Chapter. Is it really justifiable that society does not develop social and legal support for these individuals? Can we really pass by? Is enforced intervention never appropriate? But why?

THREE

An overview of the contemporary mental health system

3.1 INTRODUCTION

The study of any area of law will be deficient unless the legal rules and procedures in question are studied in their operational context. This truism is, if anything, especially applicable to mental health law, the study of which can never pretend to be an end in itself. This is because law functions here, in the arena of mental health, not as an abstract discourse to be evaluated solely in terms of its internal coherence (although this is obviously an important question), but variously as the most formal and the most coercive expression of the policy of the state towards persons with mental disorder; as permission and limitation; as the authorisation of a hierarchy which licenses some to invade, even significantly curtail, the freedom of others. Mental health law is at once a mere tool, a function of policy in the same way that a decision to build a new hospital or fund an outreach programme is a function of policy; at the same time as it (as with these other things) is an expression of values, or of compromise between competing values or considerations, which can themselves be unpacked to reveal an untidy conglomeration of political, economic, moral, professional, systemic, as well as legal and other forces. Moreover, law must be seen as source of the mental health system in its own right (Fennell, 1986). Law, in terms of discourse, ideas, structures, and so on, has had a *constructive* influence on the contemporary system. Thus it can be said that a psychiatric facility is both a physical structure and a legal entity. There is little point in studying the operation of one without reference to the operation of the other. The same, it must follow, is true of those who enter the system. The patient, or client, is in some sense a *product* of the legal regime, just as he or she is a product also of social and medical policy and practice. The tradition in some of the literature has been to see these approaches as conflicting. This is not necessarily appropriate. As Roger Smith (1981) has shown, legal and medical discourses have had considerable similarity in the past. The mutual reliance of these discourses in both the past and present will be a theme of this Chapter, and indeed a recurring theme in this volume.

Crucial to understanding the contemporary system is an awareness of its history. The intimacy of the relationship between past, present and future in the delivery of mental health services cannot be overestimated. Mental health policy over the last two and a half centuries or so has tended to be reactive, and as a consequence has had continually to live with its ghosts, in terms of physical plant, professional discourse, vested interest and, to a greater or lesser extent, public perceptions. To provide an example, it has been, at least until recently, the policy of successive governments since at least 1960 that the preferred mode of delivery of mental health services, all things being equal, should be in the form of 'care in the community'. Yet throughout the entirety of that period mental health law, in the form of the Mental Health Acts of 1959 and the current Act of 1983, has been predicated on the view that 'confinement' is the norm; a view which is an inheritance from earlier legislation that gave expression to such policies. In consequence, the five per cent or so of patients who are detained in hospital are administered under a relatively developed (albeit controversial) legal regime; but for the majority of hospital inpatients, and the many more who are treated in the community, the relevant law is sketchy and must be pieced together from any number of sources, many of which give expression to a different order of policy imperatives — concerned for example with the housing, benefits and general health care systems — in addition to a hotchpotch of overlapping legislation, case law and other forms of guidance dealing specifically with community care for mental disorder. The result is both that the policy on care in the community is incoherent and that law and policy are out of kilter.

3.1.1   A sketch of the contemporary mental health system

Part of the explanation for such discrepancies is that immediately on attempting to define the contemporary mental health system, problems of delimitation present themselves. For example, from the perspective of one 'client group', namely patients judged dangerous enough by a court or the Secretary of State to require the making of a 'restriction order', what counts as 'the system' may be limited to the special hospitals and prisons, with transfer into medium and low security hospital facilities being little more than a postscript to many years spent in 'deep end' provision. Many of those who have been transferred to a special hospital from prison will be returned to prison, rather than be transferred into hospital conditions of lesser security, if treatment in hospital proves successful or is shown to be fruitless. Should prisons be considered as part of the mental health system? Arguably they should; as discussed in Chapter six, the population of our prisons includes a high number of mentally disordered persons. Such discussion, however, falls outside the scope of the present text. At the other 'end' of the system, there is a blurring between hospital and community care provision in terms of physical plant: while in terms of user experience, a patient whose condition involves episodic acute periods may well experience 'the system' as comprising a combination of inpatient and outpatient services, and might also want to include other departments of state — local authority housing departments or benefits agencies for example — as component parts of the same system. There are clearly significant quantitative and qualitative differences in how, from the point of view of those on the receiving end of the provision of mental health services, 'the system' is experienced.

From a more philosophical point of view, how one understands the concept of 'system' is far from clear. If one conceives of a system in terms of specific physical locations within society — hospitals, prisons, and so on — it can be described fairly easily. But of course the premise of community care is that, wherever possible, services should be delivered to persons in their own homes: are the homes of service users to be understood as part of the system? If so, a definition that moves beyond a description of physical plant is required. If the mental health system is seen instead in discursive terms — that is, as a set of doctrines and corresponding practices — the limitation of a 'physical' definition of the system seems to have been overcome. But where then is the line to be drawn?

One might attempt to define the system in terms of the professionals who administer it; but this too is problematic. Considerable numbers of people with conditions which the Mental Health Act 1983 would identify as 'mental disorders' are cared for primarily informally, by their families or private facilities. People with developmental disabilities and vulnerable elderly people are perhaps the obvious examples. The existence of family care for these people may mean that the state has little involvement other than the provision of a GP, or specialised teaching for a child with learning disabilities, or inspection and licensing of a residential facility for a senior citizen. This sort of private care provision is a part of state policy; but are these people in 'the system'? The answer to this question may depend on the reason the question is being asked. Thus if the issue is state encroachment on individual care, the answer may be doubtful, since control of care is largely private, although even here, the existence of some supervision over the nursing home, although not over the specific care of the individual, shows how grey the boundaries of the system can be. If the issue is instead the imposition of power relations onto people who may be vulnerable, these people must be considered a part of the subject class of this book, since such private arrangements for care can be as oppressive as the public and more visible psychiatric facilities. A part of the legal tradition involves assuming some responsibility for the protection of such persons; in that context, even purely private care cannot be perceived as outside the system.

Inevitably, there is a degree of intractability inherent in such questions. It can be said, however, that the contemporary mental health system is conceptualised by the state as a system of service provision, which is not limited, in theory at least, to specific physical locations. That said, institutional provision remains the dominant mechanism for service delivery. It is the duty of the Secretary of State for Health to promote a comprehensive health service: s. 1(1), National Health Service Act 1977; and s. 3(1) of the Act lists a number of forms in which that duty may be performed, comprising various inpatient and outpatient services. This duty is usually delegated to health authorities (which have responsibility for the provision of services at local level), who in turn delegate it to individual units of provision. Health authorities may provide services 'in house' but increasingly following the passage of the National Health Service and Community Care Act (NHSCCA) 1990, the typical unit of provision has been the National Health Service Trust (NHS Trust). An NHS Trust might have exclusive occupation of a hospital site or, more commonly these days, a number of separate NHS Trusts will provide accommodation and services on the same site. Alternatively, an NHS Trust might manage accommodation across a range of sites, perhaps in the form of a psychiatric inpatient facility and a 'satellite' hostel for patients who require some form of assisted accommodation before returning to the community, or perhaps in the form of a number of specialist units. In 1998 131 psychiatric NHS Trusts were in operation in England, providing 45,878 inpatient beds. Of these, slightly more than 3,000 were to be found in 30 facilities all with less than 201 beds. A similar number were available in provider units with accommodation of between 801 and 1,000 beds, and two hospitals each offer more than 1,000 beds. The bulk of provision is in middle sized units: 16,767 in the 201 to 400 bed range; 12,701 in the 410 to 600 bed range and 7,698 in the 601 to 800 range (Government Statistical Service, 1998, table B17). These statistics are misleading to the extent that an individual unit of provision may well be split across a number of smaller, relatively discrete, sites. But in global terms, around one in four of all beds within the NHS are provided for mentally disordered patients.

The Secretary of State has a specific duty, currently to be found in s. 4, NHSCCA 1990, to 'provide and maintain' so called 'special hospitals', defined as those for patients 'who in his opinion require treatment under special security on account of their dangerous, violent or criminal propensities'. There are three special hospitals that provide such services for England and Wales, namely Broadmoor hospital in Berkshire, Rampton in Nottinghamshire, and Ashworth in Lancashire. These institutions opened in 1863, 1912 and 1989 respectively, although Ashworth hospital is the combination (in 1989) of two earlier institutions, Moss Side Hospital, which opened in 1933 and Park Lane Hospital, the newest special hospital accommodation, built in the 1970s. The average population of each of these hospitals is around 500 patients, and all three accept patients with all types of mental disorder, although there are differences in emphasis. At Rampton, 80 per cent of the inmate population is female. Other facilities offer a range of accommodation in terms of security. There are around 25 Regional Secure Units (RSUs) within the psychiatric NHS Trust sector, offering an interim level of security, and the emergence of Medium Secure Units (MSUs), offering an intermediary level of security between that offered in general psychiatric facilities and that offered by RSUs, has been a feature of the 1990s. The initiative for the development of such accommodation has come from within the health service. Neither RSUs nor MSUs are statutory concepts.

The duty to secure the provision of services to patients in the community lies primarily with local authorities, which are required to make and revise regularly a care plan for the provision of community care services, although in consultation with health authorities, housing authorities, and service providers in the charitable, voluntary and independent sectors: s. 46, NHSCCA 1990, Department of Health (1993a). The 1990 Act is a coordinating piece of legislation and marks the point of entry into a web of services, and of legislation, delegated legislation and guidance. (The legal framework for the provision of community care services will be considered in detail in Chapter nine.) A significant proportion of the community care budget is consumed in the provision of residential accommodation of one sort or another. The two main types of unit are residential care homes and mental nursing care homes. In 1998, 7,700 residential care homes, of various sizes, provided accommodation for 40,500 adults with learning disabilities, and 3,200 such homes provided 34,250 beds for persons with mental illness (19,260 of which were earmarked for elderly patients) (Government Statistical Service, 1998, tables B23, B24). Nursing care homes, in which there is a greater emphasis on the provision of medical treatment, offered 3,360 places for persons with learning disabilities and 28,510 beds for mentally ill persons, three-quarters of which were designated geriatric beds (ibid.). These statistics overstate the number of beds actually available, as 2,100 nursing homes (one third of the total) are 'dual registered' to provide services to both health authorities (and so are likely to be counted as 'hospitals') and local authorities. Much of this provision is in the private sector (Department of Health, 1998c, paras. 48-51). Accommodation provided for mentally disordered persons in the form of residential care in the community is only a small part of the broader community care system. In 1998, there were a total of 347,400 beds in 24,500 locations, the majority of it provided in the form of residential care for the elderly. Thus although mental health services comprise a significant percentage of hospital provision, such services only occupy a moderate corner of the provision of care in the community. And in terms of occupied bed days, despite the fact that there are substantially more beds available in the community care sector, it is hospital provision that is the main contributor, at least as far as mentally ill patients are concerned. In 1997-98, there were 11.5 million occupied psychiatric bed days in the hospital sector, compared with 4.2 million in the community care sector (Government Statistical Service, 1998, table B22).

It has been policy since 1990 (DH, 1990a) that care should be provided wherever possible to people in their own homes rather than in residential accommodation. Accordingly, the community care system also comprises primary care provision, preventative care and after care. For most mentally disordered persons, their GP is the first point of contact with the mental health system. In addition, s. 46(3) of the NHSCCA 1990 requires local authorities to provide (with more or less room for discretion) a wide range of services, which are to be found in an equally diverse number of statutes, to mentally disordered persons in their own homes. These services will be delivered by social workers, in tandem with community psychiatric nurses, increasingly working out of Community Mental Health Centres (CHMCs), but may also be delivered in the form, for example, of domiciliary and other services geared to support independent living. CMHCs will also be amongst the forms in which day care provision is made. The role of social workers and community psychiatric nurses in the *mandatory* provision of treatment and other services, and in exercising powers of surveillance and control over mentally disordered persons in the community has increased markedly over the last decade, as successive governments have sought to respond to public concerns about the 'failure' of community care in this regard.

Completing the picture is the relatively 'invisible' but crucially important component, in the form of caring provided by the family and friends of learning disabled or mentally ill persons. Such provision is recognised in the Carers (Recognition and Services) Act 1995, which gives informal carers the right in certain circumstances to require that assistance be provided by a local authority. Conversely, local authorities may properly consider care that is being provided informally when assessing a person's need for services, and decide that it can in a given case play a residual role, offering respite care to both clients and their carers: *R* v *North Yorkshire County Council, ex parte Hargreaves* (1994) Medical Law Reports 121 (HC). This 'invisible' element in the system obviously distorts the pattern of community care expenditure. Even so, local authorities continue to spend greater amounts on residential care than on provision to persons in their own homes. In 1996-7 £185 million was spent on residential care for persons with mental health problems and £665 million on such care for persons with learning disabilities. This contrasts with the expenditure on 'at home' provision, of £153 million and £451 million respectively (Government Statistical Service, 1998, table E5).

This then, in bare outline, is the shape of the contemporary mental health system. But is it the system that we want? How, when and why did it come into being? What is its function or functions (intended or unintended)? To what extent has the 'shape' of the system changed, and with what implications? How well does the system actually work? More pertinently, what is the relevance of such questions for the student of mental health law? Although this book as a whole should be read as an attempt to begin to answer at least some of these questions, they will be particularly to the fore in this chapter.

3.2   THE RISE AND FALL OF ASYLUM-BASED PROVISION

To say that the interpretation of the historical genesis and development of the contemporary mental health system is a matter of controversy is a substantial understatement. And the more one learns of the history of madness and its responses, the better the reasons for this controversy are appreciated. It is both the most fascinating and the most frustrating aspect of this history that in its detail one finds the negation of easy generalisation, on more or less any aspect of it. Let us begin with what is uncontroversial: from a relatively small number of relatively small asylums at the end of the eighteenth century, specialised institutional provision for the insane grew over the course of the nineteenth and twentieth centuries, up to about the end of the Second World War. From that point, asylum provision has been in a fairly precipitous decline, as public policy has increasingly focused on community care as the primary mode of care provision for people with mental disabilities.

The change in provision can be seen with a few statistical indicators. In 1847 there were 21 county asylums in existence, by 1914 there were 97. The size of the average asylum also grew markedly after 1850. The average population was 1,000 by 1900, with a number of institutions at double that rate (Prior, 1993, p. 67). This growth is matched by the total number of people confined in these asylums. In 1850, total inpatients in county asylums numbered 7,140 (4.03 per 10,000 population). By 1930, they contained 119,659 people (30.14 per 10,000 population) and by 1954, 148,000 people (33.45 per 10,000 population). At this point, however, the decarceration movement was beginning to take effect, and the total inpatient population fell more rapidly than it rose: by 1981, the rate of confinement had more than halved to 15.5 per 10,000. This downward trend continued throughout the 1980s and 1990s. Between 1980 and 1990 there was a further 25 per cent reduction in the number of hospital beds available. Bed numbers fell below 100,000 by 1990, and by 1997-8 the total stock of available psychiatric hospital beds stood at 45,878 (see 3.1.1). By 1997-8 there remained only two hospitals with more than 1,000 beds (Government Statistical Service, 1998, table B17).

There are a variety of explanations for these trends. Regarding the growth of asylums, Jones (1972) emphasises the nineteenth-century social reform movements, and the great men who were their tireless advocates, Sir George Onesiphorus Paul, Charles Wynn, and, perhaps most significantly, Anthony Ashley Cooper, the seventh Earl of Shaftesbury, as promoting an increasingly civilised and humane response to the social problem of madness. The object of these figures was to bring decent and rational provision to some of the most pitiable people of society. Through tireless lobbying, they brought about the expansion of the county asylum movement to the point where it became a symbol of nineteenth-century philanthropy, and the provision of standards both in those asylums and in private facilities, through the introduction of legislative standards and an effective system of inspection.

This broadly progressive image of nineteenth-century social policy of asylums cannot entirely be dismissed. Certainly, there was an interest in the legislation of lunacy in the nineteenth century, such as had not occurred before; and the 1845 County Asylums Act, which made county asylum provision mandatory for pauper lunatics, no doubt was a significant boost to asylum construction. The progressive nature of the reforms is perhaps open to question, however. The nineteenth-century commentators were fond of citing the horrific care provided in environments where reform had not penetrated. A report from as late as 1845 tells of insane persons outside asylums kept by their families in that place 'commonly devoted to the reception of coals', this being a 'confined, dark and damp corner' between the stairs and the ground floor in which 'may be found at this very time no small number of our fellow-beings, huddled, crouching and gibbering, with less apparent intelligence and under worse treatment than the lower domestic animals' (in Jones, 1972, p. 12). Was previous provision really so bad? And did it really become so much better upon admission to asylums?

Certainly, some of the accounts are extremely unpleasant, but modern scholars are looking to these accounts with an increasingly critical eye. Patricia

Allderidge (1985) for example has challenged much of the disparaging imagery of Bethlem hospital in the eighteenth and early nineteenth centuries, and Roy Porter (1987a) and Rab Houston (1999) have both painted broadly positive pictures of the care of the insane in the private sector in the eighteenth century. For the poor, provision of care was surely more frugal; but research by Akihito Suzuki (1991, 1992) would suggest that it would be wrong to perceive even the poor insane as simply ignored by the system. Instead, they appear to have been treated within the poor law system, much as other paupers were.

The question therefore becomes not so much a matter of improvement in treatment on an objective scale, but rather how the Victorians understood the reforms as progressive. Certainly the perception of improved standards was a part of the concern; but equally important were the ideas that society could be regulated, and individuals controlled on a large scale. By 1845, the reforms in their legal form matched a fairly classic Benthamite paradigm. Central legislation was put in place, designed to ensure that poor 'lunatics and idiots' would come to the attention of justices of the peace, and would be confined in a new system of county asylums. Both these, and the private madhouses catering to the more monied classes, would be inspected regularly, by a specialised board of inspectors, the Commissioners in Lunacy. And consistent with such a Benthamite model, the asylum itself— both its architecture and the regime it would create — would be pivotal to the conception of the reform of the insane person. Surveillance both of the insane in the asylum and at least of the poorer classes of society became pivotal to the ideology of the statute.

The approach which became symbolic of nineteenth-century asylum care was moral treatment. This form of therapy had diverse origins. In England, it originated in a private facility run by Quakers, the York Retreat, in the years following its opening in 1796 (see Digby, 1985, 1985a). In France, it is attributed to Philippe Pinel, at roughly the same period. In contrast to the intrusive physical treatments of his day, Pinel claimed that 'experience affords ample and daily proofs of the happier effects of a mild, conciliating treatment', and 'giving my most decided suffrage in favour of the moral qualities of maniacs' who would exhibit 'indescribable tenderness' and 'estimable virtue' if treated 'morally'. Although not the first to use such techniques 'Pinel, however, explicitly completed the circle: that which is psychologically caused is most effectively psychologically treated' (Bynum, 1981, p. 42). A similar philosophy was to be found at the York Retreat: 'moral treatment as practised at the Retreat, and elsewhere, meant a concentration on the rational and emotional rather than the organic causes of insanity' (Digby, 1985, p. 53). This entailed a regime which although varying from exponent to exponent essentially comprised the provision of a protective, peaceful, civilised and contemplative environment in which 'to help the patient gain enough self-discipline to master his illness' (ibid.). As the nineteenth century progressed, and scandalous conditions were revealed to exist at asylums, hospitals and madhouses up and down the country, the York Retreat became a watchword for the humane treatment, and cure, of the insane. By shortly after the middle of the nineteenth century a somewhat mutated form of the Retreat's approach was broadly adopted throughout the country, under the name 'non-restraint'.

The system never worked the way its framers intended. The notion of a coordinated, centrally directed network of county asylums, and of surveillance throughout the country, whereby the poor insane would be routinely identified and removed to asylums, came up against well-established local interests, and management of and admission to asylums remained in local hands. Similarly, while it is certainly true that even in the largest of county asylums few people were subjected to physical restraint, moral treatment was not relied upon to the exclusion of chemical intervention, particularly later in the century when the use of opiates became relatively common.

As noted, the issues of surveillance, regulation, and control are central aspects of the system: surveillance of the community, to ensure the routine diversion of the insane to asylums; surveillance of the insane in the asylum, through appropriate architecture and staffing, to ensure that the insane are properly cared for and appropriately employed; surveillance of the asylum, to ensure that the officers and staff are doing their job properly; and surveillance of the insane by themselves, as a method of treatment. Certainly, this can be portrayed as progress. For the insane exposed to the worst of eighteenth-century conditions, there can be little doubt that the nineteenth-century asylum offered an improvement in standard of care: basic comforts, including adequate food, were provided. Work was offered to those who were able to do it — generally farm work for men and laundry and needlework for women — but only six hours per day. Perhaps unsurprisingly, there is evidence that some (although not all) individuals wanted admission to this environment (Bartlett, 1999, 1999a). At the same time, there is a sense in which the systemic approach glorified in the nineteenth century implied its own set of particularly intrusive controls and confinements. In theory, the poor were always under surveillance by local officials; there was to be no escape. Asylums were similarly open to the prying eyes of inspectors.

Similarly, the treatment at the centre of the new ideology has not always been portrayed in positive terms. For Castel (1985, p. 256) moral treatment is 'this authoritarian pedagogy'. For Foucault, moral treatment differed from what had gone before, the lunatic in chains, not so much because of its greater humanity but rather because of its greater, more penetrative control of the recipient. Now, the mad would police themselves. The moral treatment practised at York was important not so much for its religious element, but rather its more general strategy (Foucault, 1986, p. 145):

> to place the insane individual within a moral element where he will be in debate with himself and his surroundings: to constitute for him a milieu where, far from being protected, he will be kept in a perpetual anxiety, ceaselessly threatened by Law and Transgression 'the madman' must feel morally responsible for everything within him that may disturb morality and society, and must hold no one but himself responsible for the punishment he receives.

This may sound harsh, but such apparent harshness in part emphasises the success of the project upon which the new asylums were engaged, a project now completely assimilated into our modern understanding. Cure in the asylum is to be understood as a journey to normalcy. Where previous approaches to mental illness, based on somatic theories, may have implied such a base line in their diagnostic criteria, moral treatment places a concept of normality at the core of treatment: where previously, it might have been how the insane person was identified, now it becomes that which the insane person must want. This remains pivotal to our understanding of mental health: success is measured in terms of reintegration into society, and invisibility of the individual when returned to that society.

The nineteenth-century reforms further serve as a marker of a new attitude to people with mental health difficulties: they were a class to be treated differently. This is in fact merely a stage on a considerably longer progression, commencing with the 1714 Vagrancy Act, which allowed the confinement of the 'furiously mad' poor. A 1744 Vagrancy Act continued this trend, allowing such lunatics to be excused from corporal punishment for failing to work. In this context, the nineteenth-century statutes constitute a continuation of this strategy of classification and differential treatment. It represents a change from previous legal understanding, however, when the insane poor were dealt with as just another category of deviant. In the eighteenth and nineteenth centuries, they became a unique class, warranting special treatment or attention. It is a theme which permeates our modern view of the appropriate social approach to insanity. It is what makes it somehow socially acceptable to argue for the protective detention of the insane, or for their increased control in the community, in contexts which would be unthinkable in other elements of the population — again, a profoundly important epistemological shift at the root of our understanding of the insane.

While the social reform theory explains much of the theoretical context of asylum provision, both in the nineteenth century and today, it is problematic in that the legislation was not implemented in the way which would appear from the statute to be intended. And the emphasis on the Benthamite model obscures some fundamentally non-Benthamite influences on the shape of the legislation. The control of the new county asylums remained almost entirely outside the scope of the specialist inspectorate, the Commissioners in Lunacy. They were instead managed by the local justices of the peace until 1888, when they were transferred to local authorities. Similarly, as discussed in Chapter 1, justices of the peace controlled admission and discharge processes throughout the nineteenth century. The Commissioners in Lunacy could inspect the facilities. They could only protest, which they occasionally did in their annual reports, but they had minimal actual power to enforce change. Thus the City of London did not build a county asylum for its pauper lunatics until 1866, more than twenty years after such provision became mandatory, notwithstanding a continuing series of complaints by the Commissioners. Effectively, if local administrations did not wish to comply with the legislation, there was little to force them. Their situation was similar relating to private madhouses outside London, although inside the metropolis they did have licensing power for such private institutions. As a percentage of asylum provision, however, such private establishments were of minimal significance: the large growth in asylum provision in the nineteenth century was in the county asylum sector, where the Commissioners had no direct influence.

To understand the actual structure and growth of the nineteenth-century asylum system, therefore, it is necessary to understand the dynamic of the individuals who were actually doing the administration. Here, the presumptions of the previous discussion become almost universally problematic. Certainly, the nineteenth-century statutes appear to create the insane as a separate class of deviant, and in a sense they were; but in the county asylum system, they remained a separate class of deviant *poor*, and pauper status was required in order for admission. Arguably, the county asylum Acts of the nineteenth century are appropriately considered to be a branch of the poor law itself (Bartlett, 1999).

This makes sense chronologically. The County Asylums Act 1808 was of limited effect. The 1845 Act was of considerably greater effect, based not merely on the numbers of asylums built, but also on the numbers of people confined. Arguably, the significant change occurring between the two Acts is the replacement of the largely voluntary parish officers of the old poor law, with the professional workforce of the new. While the 1808 Act had given poor law officials the duty to enforce the Acts at the local level, it was only with the post-1834 staffing that the admission processes could be run on the scale the Acts intended.

If this approach is correct, the question arises as to when the provision of asylum and other services to people with mental disorders really separates from the provision of poor law, or social services as we would now call it. The question is perhaps whether they have ever become separate. A reasonable case can be made for the separation for asylum provision when the NHS was created, since it was at that time that the final vestiges of the poor law were laid to rest. For community care, however, the argument looks as strong as ever. Thus as will be seen below, it is only when community care services became claimable on social services budgets rather than health budgets that significant provision began to be made for care in the community.

The poor law connection is significant not merely for its administrative relationship to the asylum, but also because it was reformed at roughly the same time as the asylum law, and it too, at least on paper, introduced an institutional solution through the nineteenth-century workhouse. Prisons also grew apace in this period. Institutional solutions were popular throughout social policy at this time. Can these parallels be considered as flowing from the same causes? Can both reforms be related to the economic changes prompted by the industrial revolution?

Again, arguments are not straightforward. Certainly, population growth was rapid and unyielding, and there was a shift from rural to urban living for a significant proportion of the population. Traditional communities and social ties were broken. The result was the beginnings of the creation of a great swathe of urban poverty. However, as Scull has pointed out, the asylum had already been adopted as policy when the majority of the population still lived outside new cities, and before the Acts of 1845 the decision, at county level, to construct an asylum bore little relation to the extent of urbanisation and industrialisation. Scull offers instead an analysis that echoes that offered by Foucault in relation to the previous century. He suggests that explanation should focus on 'the effects of the ever more thoroughgoing commercialization of existence' (Scull, 1979, p. 29), resulting in 'the abandonment of long-established techniques for coping with the poor and the troublesome' (ibid., p. 30) without recourse to institutionalisation. For Scull, the new logic of commodification undermined informal methods of responding to insanity based on feudal relations of patronage, essentially converting them from social to economic relations based on waged labour. Madness in the era of capitalism is defined in terms of the requirements of that system, which is to say in terms of the ability to work. Incarceration of the insane freed former carers to work outside the home in the new factories, and in addition 'seemed ideally suited to the means of establishing "proper" work habits among those elements of the work force who were apparently more resistant to the monotony, routine, and regularity of industrialised labour' (ibid., p. 35).

Proof of such a theory is problematic. It would be naïve to ignore the social change which occurred in this period, and the consequent changes to the possibilities of domestic care of the insane. Certainly, the values cited by Scull were significant in the ideology of the new asylums. As we have seen, work was to be provided in the asylum for those able to pursue it. Similarly, an inability to work was one of the factors which might be considered in determining the appropriateness of an asylum admission. It was not, of course, the only one; but Scull's theory is not so crass. It acknowledges that confinement of an insane person may be necessary because of the absence of other care possibilities. It also acknowledges the possibility that those with insane relations might increasingly expect the state to provide care. While certainly an arguable view, such motives are difficult to substantiate. It does not inspire confidence, however, that patterns of institutionalisation of the insane in the period bear no obvious correlation to patterns of economic growth or recession and unemployment in the period, as one might expect if the growth of asylums is to be understood in economic terms.

In all this discussion of the nineteenth century, doctors in general and specialists in mental disorders in particular have been conspicuous by their absence. They have long been involved in the treatment of the insane, of course; and at some point in the last two hundred and fifty years, they became particularly central to the administration of insanity. Precisely how and when that colonisation occurred is controversial. Certainly, by the middle of the eighteenth century, the process had begun. Jones (1972, p. 35) argues that the madness of George III, cured by Dr. Willis, gave the image of the mad-doctor a considerable boost. That seems undisputed, though the rudiments of professional formation were falling into place before that time, with the opening of a variety of hospitals for the insane in the second half of the eighteenth century. First of these was St Luke's in London, opened in 1751. St Luke's was to be a teaching hospital and centre for medical research, and admitted medical students from the start. Other hospitals or asylums, funded like St Luke's by way of public subscription,opened in quick succession: Manchester Lunatic Hospital in 1766, others in Newcastle, Liverpool, York

and elsewhere soon followed. Certainly, the doctors running these establishments, and particularly those involved in private madhouses, would complain
of low professional status; but in time 'madhouse-keeping became an object
of pride not shame, helping, not hindering, a medical career' (Porter, 1987a,
p. 167), who points out that William Battie, the driving force behind St Luke's,
was to become President of the Royal College of Physicians.

The movement of medical specialists into the treatment of insanity continued with the development of the county asylums. Andrew Scull (1993), has
devoted considerable talent and insight into a claim that the nineteenth century
was the period when specialist doctors consolidated their professional status
over the insane. Much of his work is extremely perceptive in this regard,
examining how the new specialist class of mad-doctors form a profession,
complete with professional journals and a professional organisation, the
Association of Medical Officers of Asylums and Hospitals for the Insane. It is
indisputable that significant medical theory developed in the nineteenth
century. That said, for key developments, the medical profession can be seen
as followers rather than leaders. Thus notwithstanding the myth that the policy
of non-restraint was introduced by John Conolly at the Hanwell Asylum in
London, it would seem instead that it was introduced by the justices of the
peace in charge of the asylum (see Suzuki, 1995). This is significant of a
considerably wider phenomenon: while specialist doctors were appointed as
medical superintendents of county asylums for much of the nineteenth century,
they had remarkably little power. Specifically, they did not control who came
into the asylum; that was the role of justices of the peace, poor law relieving
officers, and poor law medical officers. They similarly did not control who left
the asylum: that, once again, was in the hands of the managing committee of
justices. In the private sector, things were different, since often the facility
would be owned by a doctor. If it was not, however, the relations between the
owner and the medical officer might presumably be complex. For both the
private and county facilities, medical certificates were of course required for
admission (two for the former, one for the latter); but individuals with an
interest in the facility to which admission was sought were specifically
precluded from signing the forms. As a result, they would frequently be signed
not by specialists, but by general doctors.

All of this did not, of course, stop the specialist doctors from developing a
professional expertise in the treatment of insanity, but it is difficult to see that
this specialist group enjoyed particularly administrative or political influence in
the nineteenth century. That would occur instead in the twentieth century.

So why did asylums grow? The centralised theory of Jones is problematic, in
that the growth required the acquiescence, if not the outright enthusiasm, of
the local officials, and the central authorities had no way of enforcing that.
Bartlett's theory may account for that more effectively, but it does not explain
why private provision also increased markedly in the nineteenth century
(although not as greatly as county asylum provision). The fact that such
provision increased outside the administrative framework Bartlett describes
suggests that internal administrative dynamics of the poor law cannot solely
account for the growth of the asylum system: this must, at least in part, reflect

a broader paradigm shift. The increased promise of cure is similarly problematic as an explanation. The use of data sets by modern historians would suggest that the asylums did have a curative role: roughly two-thirds of people admitted were released cured within two years of admission (Wright, 1997). Nineteenth century observers seemed to be unaware of this fact, however, and their reports tended to read from the earliest times as justifications for the failures of cure (see Scull, 1993). Certainly, the nineteenth century favoured institutional solutions more broadly, but it is difficult to see how that broad principle related to specific causal factors. It would seem that we are left with a selection of partial and not entirely convincing explanations; the issues will no doubt be debated by historians for a long time to come.

Accounts of the retreat from the asylum are no less problematic. Contemporary accounts tended to link the fall-off in hospital inpatient numbers with the emergence of a new generation of major tranquillising drugs in the 1950s. The first and most well-known of these was Chlorpromazine, which was first produced in France in 1950. The drug was first used in the UK in 1954 (where it is known as Largactil), and in the USA in 1955 (under the name Thorazine). There is no doubt that there was a 'drug revolution' in psychiatric practice at this time. As Scull (1977, p. 80) points out, in the USA in late 1953 Thorazine was only used (in trials) on 104 patients; by 1955 an estimated 2,000,000 prescriptions were written. Smith Kline French aggressively marketed the drug, and the company's turnover increased from $53m in 1953 to $347m by 1970.

This explanation seems to have a logical ring to it. If drug therapies can, at the very least, hold symptoms in abeyance, and possibly even 'cure' mental illness, the rationale for a general policy of inpatient treatment is undermined. Of course, huge benefits accrued to the status of the psychiatric profession within the medical, and broader, establishment with the advent of the new drug therapies. Here was confirmation of the organic, somatic model of mental illness, which allowed psychiatry to conform more explicitly to a medical model. The drug revolution also precipitated a change in government policy. The Mental Health Act 1959 recast the relation between 'legalism' and 'medicalism' in favour of the latter (although the process had already begun with the introduction of 'informal' admissions by the Mental Treatment Act 1930: see Chapter one), and also redrew the map of service provision. From now on there was to be a greater emphasis, at least at the level of policy, on outpatient and community-based service provision. Community care, which had in fact been a constant feature of the *social* response to mental disorder throughout the age of the asylum, now became government policy. In 1960 Enoch Powell, then Minister of Health, announced that the old Victorian asylums were 'doomed institutions'. According to his Hospital Plan of 1962, inpatient services were to be relocated to the greatest extent possible within general hospitals (and Departments of Psychiatry were indeed a feature of many general hospitals from the early 1960s) and, so the theory ran, investment was now to be channelled into community care schemes of one sort or another rather than into the maintenance of the Victorian asylum system (see 3.3). Moreover, this was seen to be *politically* feasible, as there was by this time a more tolerant attitude on the part of society in general towards mentally disordered persons.

However, there is good reason to think that this explanation is altogether too neat. For a start, inpatient numbers in some hospitals began to fall *before* the emergence of Chlorpromazine. Mapperly hospital in Nottingham, for example, had started to reduce inpatient numbers from 1948 (1948 1,310; 1956 1,060), and this pattern continued 'at an unchanged pace even after drugs arrived on the scene' (Scull, 1977, p. 82). This was a pattern that could also be seen in hospitals in the USA (ibid). In some European countries asylum numbers continued to rise after the introduction of the new drug treatments (Rogers and Pilgrim, 1996, p. 67). In the UK, there was little correlation between diagnosis, treatment and decarceration, so that, although the new treatments were not appropriate for the majority of hospital inpatients this did not prevent their de-institutionalisation (Butler, 1993, p. 37). In short, the preponderance of academic opinion today is to the effect that the link between decarceration and the drug revolution is little more than a modern myth (see e.g., Butler, 1993, p. 36; Rogers and Pilgrim, 1996, p. 67; Scull, 1977, p. 82).

So what does explain the undeniable fact of decarceration? Scull's argument, which is well known, is that, first, asylums did not cure people, but merely institutionalised them. However, those working in the system did not need radical sociologists to tell them this. Maudsley, for example, was making the point in the late nineteenth century. But the nineteenth century campaign for a policy of care in the community failed, or rather it lay dormant until its time came. That is, when its interests coincided with wider ideological and political agendas. Scull's second factor is the development of the welfare state after the Second World War. Scull locates the emergence of decarceration policies in the 1950s in the context of 'the internal dynamics of the development of capitalist societies' (1977, p. 134). As seen above, Scull has offered a similarly economically oriented explanation of the rise of the asylum a century earlier. In respect of decarceration he argues that with the emergence of the welfare state and an accompanying rise in state expenditure on the provision of welfare services, the asylum became too expensive to justify when 'outrelief' was as a general rule easier on the state's pocket. Scull points out that expenditure on social services as a percentage of GDP increased from 10.9 per cent in 1937 to 24.9 per cent in 1973, which has led to 'acute budgetary strains' (1977, p. 138). For Scull, the impact of the drug revolution should be seen as a subset of these broader economic considerations. The virtue of the new drug treatments, as such, is not so much that they 'work' but that they give credence to a strategy of service provision outside the asylum which is geared by considerations of cost rather than therapy.

Scull's analysis cannot easily be dismissed. It has been pointed out, however, that it is an analysis that is easier to apply to the 1960s, when financial problems, the 'sterling crisis' in particular, were a matter of acute concern for the government of the time. The 1950s, by contrast, were not a time of economic crisis, but rather of rapid economic growth (Rogers and Pilgrim, 1996, p. 67). Rogers and Pilgrim emphasise 'changes in ideological factors not economic factors' (1996, p. 68), in particular the link between Nazi concentration camps and other forms of incarceration that had been made, amongst others, by Deutsch (1973). However, Scull in turn has argued that such comparisons represent little more than 'the hyperbole of muck-raking journalism' (1996a, p. 385). Another undoubtedly important development was the spread of 'open door' policies from the mid-1950s, as psychiatric professionals developed a sensitivity to critical accounts of asylum life, and attempts were made to identify psychiatric facilities more closely with hospitals. The 'open door' policy was itself a function of broader changes within psychiatric practice. Prior (1993) has shown how the objects of psychiatric discourse have changed throughout the twentieth century, as research in the early decades of the century (Rosanoff, 1917; Lewis, 1929; cited in Prior, 1993) revealed both that psychiatric disorder was much more prevalent than had previously been appreciated and that many psychiatric disorders had to be evaluated — and treated — in terms of their social context. As Prior explains 'the discovery of the reservoir of mental illness in the community suggested that the presence of the asylum wall no longer acted as a natural boundary between the sane and the insane' (1993, p. 110). Many of the mental health problems identified tended to be minor in nature, and inappropriate for hospitalisation.

Although it may not be immediately apparent how the discovery of greater amounts of mental illness (and learning disability) in the community at large is linked to the policy of decarceration, the point is that there has been a shift in the focus of hospital-based services, from dealing with both acute and chronic cases, to a marked focus on the former. This is especially evident over the last few years. The total number of short-stay psychiatric hospital beds for elderly patients rose slightly from 5,770 in 1992-3 to 7,380 in 1997-8, and for other patients remained fairly constant at around 15,000. In the same period long-stay beds for elderly patients fell from 13,660 to 7,140 and for other patients from 11,000 to 4,190 (Government Statistical Service, 1998, table B24). Busfield (1986) has suggested that this shift in orientation can explain the apparent paradox in patterns of hospitalisation in the 1960s, when falling total inpatient numbers coexisted with significant increases in admission rates, from 78,500 in 1955 to 170,000 in 1968 (Scull, 1977, p. 67). Bott (1976) has argued that the beginnings of this trend are discernible in the 1930s, when first admissions, and numbers discharged, began to rise. It is likely that, as well as reflecting changes in the orientation of psychiatry, these features are a function of the availability after 1930 of admission to hospital, and discharge, on an informal basis. Scull is more cynical, arguing that the increase in admissions in this period should be seen in terms of a rearguard action on the part of asylum staff and managers to demonstrate that the asylum was not unable to cure people. A high turnover implies a high cure rate, although in reality this meant that patients were discharged whether 'cured' or not, and, in the case of long-stay patients, whether 'deinstitutionalised' or not. According to Bean and Mounser, (1993, p. 12) 'everyone gets out, and some, it appears, whether they are ready or not'.

Can the change at least in part be attributed to a broader policy shift away from institutional solutions? The beginning of decarceration at the end of the 1940s corresponds to the final end of the poor law and its workhouses, and a move in poor relief generally towards financial assistance to live in the community. If the rise of the asylum can be understood in terms of the favouring of institutional solutions in nineteenth-century social policy, can the twentieth-century move away from the asylum similarly be perceived as just another manifestation of a broader social policy?

In this context, it should be emphasised that notwithstanding the policy focus on asylums in the nineteenth and early twentieth centuries, care in other settings by no means ceased to exist. In part, this emphasises that local practice did not necessarily match official policy discourses. Thus a steady 25 per cent of those found to be insane in the nineteenth century were cared for in workhouses, and contrary to popular myth, these workhouse wards were not necessarily substandard in accommodation (Bartlett, 1999). Indeed, many became NHS hospitals after 1948. In addition, care outside institutions continued throughout the so-called heyday of the asylum. Systems of boarding out patients existed in both Scotland and Wales through the nineteenth century, whereby insane persons would be housed with family, friends, or paid carers in the community, or lodged on farms (Hirst and Michael, 1999; Sturdy and Parry-Jones, 1999). In England, arrangements tended to be less formal, but outdoor poor relief (doles) to people identified as insane continued throughout the nineteenth century, albeit on a diminishing scale. In the years between the two World Wars, there was increasing experimentation relating to care in the community, particularly of those identified as mentally defective (Thomson, 1996). Indeed, by the Second World War, almost 44,000 people in England were living outside the traditional asylum system under statutory guardianship under the Mental Deficiency Acts 1926 and 1939 (Walmsley et al, 1999, p. 186). On this basis, a move to increased community care can perhaps be seen as a policy reorientation waiting to happen.

3.3   COMMUNITY CARE

3.3.1   The development of community care and its impact on hospital-based services

The term 'community care' was first coined by the Royal Commission on Mental Illness and Mental Deficiency (the 'Percy Commission'), which sat from 1954 to 1957 (1957). The 1959 Act introduced the concept of guardianship from the Mental Deficiency Act 1913, giving a 'guardian' the powers 'of a parent over his or her 14 year old child' over a person subject to an order, the criteria for which were, and remain under the 1983 Act, broadly similar to those for confinement. Although nobody was quite sure what such powers entailed (and their detail was amended in 1983), the intention behind guardianship was to provide a community-based alternative to compulsory institutionalisation. Enoch Powell followed up his Hospital Plan of 1962 with *Health and Welfare: The Development of Community Care* (Ministry of Health, 1963) a year later. All of this seems to fit neatly with the view that the policy of decarceration did not exist in isolation, but rather was the mechanism through which a fundamental change was to be effected in the structure of the mental health system: a relocation of the client base of mental health services from institutions to 'the community'. However, as with decarceration, the actuality is somewhat more complex, indeed paradoxical. No more than a brief outline of some of the relevant factors at play will be considered here. The current legal framework for community care service provision and latest round of plans for reform will be considered in Chapter nine.

The first paradox is concerned with the very existence of community care. On the one hand, the policy document published in 1963 was to be the first of many such government documents with similar sounding names. Amongst the most important of these are: *Better Services for the Mentally Handicapped*, a White Paper published in 1971 (DHSS, 1971); its companion document *Better Services for the Mentally Ill*, published in 1975 (DHSS, 1975); the Audit Commission report *Making a Reality of Community Care* published in 1986 (Audit Commission, 1986); the Griffiths Report *Community Care: Agenda for Action* (Griffiths 1988). Each of these documents in its own way spoke to the failure to translate community care policy into community care practice. As Murphy (1991, p. 60) points out, by 1974 there were 60,000 fewer hospital inpatients than in 1954 'but very few services existed in the community . . . in most cases these people simply 'disappeared' from the official statistics since no one followed up their progress or knew anything about their fate'. In the cash-strapped 1960s, the attraction of care in the community as a *cheaper* option than institutionalisation, buttressed by *permissive* legislation regarding the provision of services, ensured that the policy was chronically under-funded. The White Paper of 1975 pointed out that in the year 1973-4 £300 million was spent on hospital services and only £15 million on community care provision, and by March 1974 31 local authorities had no residential accommodation for the mentally ill and a greater number, 63, did not even have day provision (Busfield, 1986, p. 348). Although the number of inpatients continued to fall, mental hospitals remained the key locus for the delivery of services. In the early 1980s, all of the hospitals marked for closure by the Hospital Plan of two decades earlier remained open. In part this is a 'chicken and egg' situation. Decarceration policies were delimited by the lack of residential provision 'in the community', but whilst funds remained tied up in hospital services, and hospitals remained willing to admit patients — indeed, as seen above, in ever greater numbers, and usually informally — and the public at large continued to construct the mentally ill as 'other', fuelled by a number of notorious cases, such as that of Graham Young (see 8.3.4), there was a lack of political will, both centrally and locally to make community care a 'reality'. In a very real sense, community care simply did not happen.

On the other hand, recent re-evaluations of the age of the asylum have shown that care in the community has been a constant feature of the *social* response to mental illness and learning disability: and that there have always been elements within psychiatry and its (particularly middle class) client base which have pursued and sought care outside the asylum (Bartlett and Wright, 1999a). In a sense, therefore, 'community care' is nothing new but rather is an approach that existed both before and during the period of the 'great confinement'.

The key to understanding this paradox, which throws much light also on the more recent developments, lies in unpacking the concept of 'community'. At a minimum, 'community' is a geographical location, but more importantly it is also a malleable discursive construct, and is capable of being put to use in a variety of different ways. Bartlett and Wright, for example, use the term as shorthand for care 'outside the asylum', and, in particular, in and by the family. The *policy* of community care after 1960 was also predicated to a large extent on the assumption that much care which had hitherto been provided in the form of inpatient treatment could be provided — at a fraction of the cost — by and in the family (Lewis, 1989). As women in fact provide the vast bulk of 'informal' care (although men may more recently have come to play a greater role in this regard, see Arber et al. 1988), whether in a family setting or by way of voluntary work for charitable organisations, the concept of 'community' used here, therefore, implicitly draws on an underpinning set of assumptions about the link between the concepts of care and femininity (Finch, 1984). Post-1960 community care policy, however, also drew on the notion of *social reintegration*. 'Community' here is used in a broader sense, to connote not simply the family of the person in need of 'care' but also the community at large. This much is evident from the social work theories that have developed around the concept. Normalisation theory, which emphasises the need for the community to value more highly the contribution which people with mental disorder problems, and learning disabilities in particular (Brown and Smith (eds), 1992), can be seen as 'treatment' not so much for the client as for the community. The Independent Living Movement argues that community care policy should be geared towards ensuring that persons who might otherwise be hospitalised are provided with the means to live independent, participatory lives as members of the broader community (Morris, 1993). Others (see Hume and Pullen (eds), 1994) advocate the 'rehabilitation model', the key elements of which involve helping individuals to (re)learn socially necessary skills, and which, like the Independent Living Movement, emphasises such things as the recognition of the rights of clients, their empowerment in decision-making, and the promotion of normal patterns of life. It is now government policy to acknowledge that 'community care has failed' (DH, 1998a, 1998b). One significant reason, although not the reason emphasised by the government, for this failure is that the 1950s view — that the broader community was prepared for the reintegration of its mentally disordered members — was mistaken. And this, in turn, is in significant measure explicable in terms of a failure adequately to understand the multifaceted nature of the concept of 'community' (and its ever-present companion, the 'other', that which is not 'community') before attempting to build a policy on that basis. As early as 1957 research suggested that 'on the whole 'people' do not wish to have very much contact with mental illness either on the personal or social level' (Cumming and Cumming, 1957, cited in Prior, 1993, p. 124).

However, to say that community care has failed should not be taken to imply that nothing has changed. By 1977 one third of admissions into psychiatric hospitals were to wards in general hospitals rather than mental hospitals (Barham, 1992, p. 20). Psychiatry became more fully medicalised, and from the start of the 1980s the old large-scale asylums have begun to close. Initially, this was a painfully slow, ward-by-ward, process, but in the last decade the rate of closure has speeded up. Accordingly, the 'shape' of the mental hospital system has changed, although the process is by no means complete. As seen above (see 3.1.1), there were just under 46,000 hospital beds available in England in 1998, across a range of facilities of various sizes. But the general trend in hospital provision is down. In 1991-2, for patients with mental illness or who have learning disabilities (together the 'mentally disordered' as per s. 1(2) of the MHA 1983) hospital occupied bed days totalled 14.6 million, falling to 11.5 million by 1997-8, constituting a 21 per cent reduction. Over the same period, community occupied bed days rose from 2.3 million to 4.2 million, a rise of 86 per cent (Government Statistical Service, 1998, table B22). Local authorities had long been reluctant fully to accept their responsibilities for the long-term mentally ill and (although to a lesser extent) learning disabled. Various policy initiatives attempted to galvanise local government into action, but it was not until the decision was taken (in 1980) that the cost of residential accommodation could be claimed by way of social security benefits that the residential community care sector finally began to expand as '[s]uddenly patients could be transferred into the community without burdening the budgets of health and local authorities' (Muijen, 1996, p. 145). Guaranteed payment by way of benefits provided the incentive required for the rapid development of privately run residential homes. The Department of Health's *Community Care Statistics 1998* (DH, 1998c) show that in 1998 there were 49,900 places for persons with learning disabilities and 38,400 places for mentally ill persons (21,500 of which are for elderly mentally infirm persons) in residential care homes, which constituted a virtual doubling of accommodation over 1994 (DH, 1998c, paras 20-22). Nursing care homes provided 3,500 beds for learning disabled clients and 25,500 beds for mentally ill persons (ibid., paras. 31, 32). These institutions vary in size from a few hundred to a handful of beds. The latter type of accommodation often takes the form of a so-called 'group home', in which residents live in a semi-communal, family-like arrangement. Perring (1992) identifies four types of group homes:

- independent flats for patients immediately leaving hospital
- homes with 24-hour staffing
- group homes with day-time staffing
- hostels on hospital sites.

The 1980s also saw an increase in the number of Community Mental Health Centres (CMHCs), from 1 in 1977 to 54 ten years later, and about 75 today, although their development nationally has been uneven. CMHCs are intended to provide services to clients in their own homes and to offer day care facilities. These tend to be staffed by a community mental health team comprising community psychiatric nurses, social workers, and psychiatrists, in some combination. Research by Barnes, Bowl and Fisher (1990) found that in areas where there are CMHCs there was a reduction in admissions to hospital.

There has, then, been a sizeable increase in the provision of mental health services in the form of 'community care'. Yet, as the above statistics also indicate, services remain hospital-based and community-based alternatives still suffer from a resources shortfall. Further initiatives were announced by the Department of Health early in 1996 (DH, 1996a), as the then Health Secretary, Stephen Dorrell unveiled plans to build a further 400 group homes with 24 hour nursing care. It was planned that these homes would facilitate the decarceration of patients on acute wards or in secure units, and provide an alternative to hospital admission for others. It was envisaged that 5,000 further community care beds would thereby be made available. Part of the strategy of the current Labour administration is to continue to increase the stock of beds in the community. The White Paper published at the end of 1998 (DH, 1998a) promised a further investment of £700 million over the following three years. As far as the future is concerned, although there are forces at work which, for some mentally disordered persons as defined by the MHA 1983, chiefly the 'psychopathically disordered', look likely to result in a renewed emphasis on compulsory hospitalisation, the overall trend towards the provision of care outside of hospital looks set to continue for a while yet.

3.3.2 Community care: divergence, convergence and colonisation

In order to understand the general social significance of the contemporary mental health system it is not sufficient simply to attempt to measure the degree to which there has been a shift from hospital-based to community-based sites of service delivery. An assessment of the degree to which there has been *qualitative* and/or *functional* change in the 'shape' of the system must also be made: and this requires that concepts like 'hospital-based' and 'community-based' must again be unpacked. It also requires that the provision of community care for those suffering from mental disorder be located in the wider context of the provision of welfare services in the era of decarceration. As noted above, social work theories have their place in the provision of care in the community. The services that are the particular concern of this book must be set in the broader context of the development of the welfare state in the period after the Second World War. The establishment of the National Health Service by the National Health Service Act 1946 drew on consensus-based theories of community and 'cradle to grave' protection for all citizens. Other key legislation, notably the National Assistance Act 1948, which finally abolished the workhouse and ushered in the modern social security benefits system, marks the end of incarceration as the policy response to poverty. Community care for mental disorder must be set against this broader context, not simply in terms of a renewed policy preference for 'outrelief', but also in terms of the material development of the welfare state, in particular, in the form of local authority social services departments.

The assumption built into the Powell scheme of the early 1960s was that in general terms the responsibility for the provision of social services in the community was to lie with local authorities, but the provision of services for the mentally ill was the province of health authorities. The consequence was inertia, as hospital-based spending dominated health budgets and local authorities tended to prioritise poverty and disability rather than mental health. The 1975 White Paper redrew the map to an extent, underlining the point that the appropriate response to chronic mental disorder was small scale residential units in the community, funded by local authorities, but it was not until the National Health Service and Community Care Act (NHSCCA) 1990 that the relationship between local and health authorities in the provision of community care services was drawn with anything approaching precision. This Act removed from the NHS the primary responsibility for the provision of non-hospital services for those requiring long-term care. Now the responsibility for overall planning of service provision was to lie primarily at the door of local authorities, in consultation with health authorities, independent sector providers and voluntary agencies: s. 46(1), (2), NHSCCA 1990. Although from one point of view this might be seen as something of a poisoned chalice, such an arrangement also has the potential to mark a qualitative shift in the shape of the mental health system to the extent that now mental disorder in 'the community' was as much a social work issue as it was a medical one.

This was certainly the intention of the social work profession, and well before 1990. The involvement of social workers in the delivery of mental health policy was slight in the early years of community care. The first psychiatric social worker had only been appointed in London in 1936, although social workers had a presence in American service delivery as early as 1905 (Prior, 1993, p. 88). But by the 1970s social work had become a recognised profession requiring training, and its knowledge base began to build up. The British Association of Social Workers campaigned for specialist mental health training for social workers to be built into the law by the reforms that took place in 1983, and s. 114, MHA 1983 now provides that 'Approved Social Workers' who have various statutory functions in relation to detained patients must be persons of 'appropriate competence in dealing with persons who are suffering from mental disorder'. It is not only involvement in hospital matters that social workers are concerned with. As discussed above, there now are various well-developed social work theories of community care. The post-1990 regime devolved power for the provision of services at ground level to social workers as 'care managers' in social services and 'key workers' in mental health services, and the role of social workers has recently been given sharper definition by legislation concerning the 'supervised discharge' of patients from hospital and their continued monitoring thereafter (see Chapter nine). Social workers may also take the role of advocate in respect of the entitlement to services of their clients. Yet to date, in so far as the social work profession has had aspirations to usurp the role of medical professionals in the delivery of community care services, the project must be counted as unsuccessful. The psychiatric profession still dominates. Further discussion of this point in relation to the admissions process into hospital can be found in Chapter five. As far as community-based services are concerned, it is clear here too that psychiatry remains the dominant profession (Prior, 1992). There was to be no central funding of specialist mental health training for social workers, and the numbers of such specialists has remained problematically low in the years after 1983 (see 5.2), This dominance by the psychiatric profession of services for mentally disordered persons outside of hospital will require further discussion shortly. Staying for the moment, though, with the NHSCCA 1990, it has to be said that this Act is more often discussed in terms of a definitive moment in the emergence of 'managerialism' rather than of medicalism in the delivery of health care services.

In the years following 1979, welfarism has been recast, as the concept of 'community' has been given a new inflection, emphasising the responsibility of service users and service providers to the broader community in terms of economic efficiency. State services have been increasingly infused with market principles and practices, and the mental health system is no exception. The 1990 Act was concerned not merely to systematise the provision of community care but to revolutionise the structure of the NHS. The immediate precursors of the 1990 Act were the White Papers of 1989. *Caring for People* (DH, 1989a) was concerned with community care, *Working for Patients* (DH, 1989b) with the National Health Service. The immediate concern of each was the same: the cost of community care and the health service respectively. For instance, in the case of the former, the availability of supplementary benefits (from an uncapped central government fund) for funding residential accommodation had played a large part in causing a rise in expenditure on supplementary benefit from £80 million in 1978 to £1.5 billion in 1989 (Muijen, 1996, p. 145). The Audit Commission Report of 1986 (Audit Commission, 1986) pointed out that not only was this a very expensive way of funding community care, but it also built in a tendency for preference to be given to residential accommodation, funded by supplementary benefit, rather than the provision of services to clients in their own homes, the bill for which had to be met from local authority funds.

The 1990 Act abolished this use of supplementary benefit and set in place a system under which the financing of 'residential care' was to be the responsibility of local authorities, 'nursing care' that of health authorities. However, this was only a small part of the picture. The fundamental change ushered in by the 1990 Act was the division of both hospital and community care systems along market lines, with players defined as either 'providers' or 'acquirers' (purchasers) of care: s. 4, NHSCCA 1990. Local social service authorities and health authorities (along with fund-holding general practitioners and private clients) were to be 'purchasers' of services. Hospitals and local authority social services departments were to be 'providers' of services, now in competition with private sector suppliers. Subsequently, the new system has become to a large degree entrenched. Hospitals have been broken up into individual units of provision known as NHS Trusts, often operating independently on the same site. The extent to which a 'free market' operates in the provision of mental health services is debatable, as there remains a significant degree of central government control, both in terms of the control of funds and in the way that they are spent (Hughes, 1991). And the 1990 Act did not come out of the blue, but was part of a process of change which had gathered momentum throughout the 1980s. Nevertheless, it is difficult not to read the 1990 Act, and the simplifying amendments to the NHS structure which took effect in April 1996 when the Health Authorities Act 1995 came into force, as a significant change to the structure of the system in that it is here, in the advent of managerialism, that the real challenge to the dominance of the clinical psychiatrist has been posed.

The third element of this shift, along with that from hospital-based to community-based service provision, and from demand-led to supply-led service provision and managerialism, has been a shift from public to private sector provision. Although the cost of residential care following the coming into force of the 1990 Act now had to be met by local authorities rather than the social security budget, the shift was sweetened by the availability of grant aid to be spent on acquiring services for persons in need by reason of mental illness. However, the availability of grant aid, which was time-limited to three years, depended on the abilities of local authorities to raise 30 per cent of the revenue, which in practice limited its availability to some local authorities, and could not be spent on capital projects (Butler, 1993, pp. 88-9). Moreover, it was stipulated that 85 per cent of grant provision must be spent on the acquisition of independent sector care. This not only limited the potential of local authorities to work in tandem with health authorities (Muijen, 1996, p. 147) but gave further momentum to the trend of the 'privatisation' of welfare services. By 1994, the independent sector provided 82 per cent of all residential home or nursing home places, rising to 88 per cent by 1998 (DH, 1998c). These statistics refer to the totality of community care services, and the pattern for provision for mentally ill and learning disabled persons is more marked: in both cases 93 per cent of provision of residential accommodation in 1998 was in the independent sector (DH, 1998c, table 4). The number of admissions into such accommodation is lower (at around 70 per cent), which is explicable on the basis that independent sector provision tends to be smaller in size than that provided by local authorities, although there are some homes which are 'dual registered' to offer both nursing and residential accommodation, which tend to have a larger capacity (DH, 1998c, para. 6, table 2).

On one view, which tends to be voiced by those who associate with the 'old' communitarian values of the post-war welfare state (Butler, 1993, Cowen, 1999), this process of reform of the mental health system is seen in terms of a betrayal of that ethos. From a different perspective, one that draws on the Foucaultian themes of service provision as 'discipline' and social control, there is an altogether more sinister aspect to these developments. The most influential and wide-ranging version of this thesis has been provided by Cohen in his book *Visions of Social Control* (Cohen, 1985). For Cohen, the development of community-based alternatives to institutionalisation in various contexts — poverty, criminality and mental disorder — should be read as the 'dispersal' of disciplinary strategies, from specialist institutions into society as a whole, involving a widening of the net of social control; a 'thinning of its mesh', which brings a greater percentage of the population under supervision; a 'blurring' of the distinction between formal and informal methods of control; and a greater 'penetration' of the state penal-therapeutic complex into the fabric of society. In its broadest version, this thesis has distinctly Orwellian connotations, of society at large continually under the disciplinary gaze of the state's organs of social control (Mathiesen, 1983). More nuanced versions, however, concede that the target population is limited to society's 'deviant' populations, including persons suffering from mental disorders, but nevertheless argue that the move out of the institution should be seen in terms of the greater 'psychiatrisation' of social problems. Applied to the context of mental health service provision, this is an attractive thesis. As detailed above, the early decades of the twentieth century saw an increase in the scope of psychiatry as new 'illnesses' were discovered in ever-wider sections of the general population (see 3.2). Rose explicitly couples this with the process of decarceration (Rose, 1986, pp. 83-4, in Rogers and Pilgrim, 1996, p. 82):

> Rather than seeking to explain a process of de-institutionalisation we need to account for the proliferation of sites for the practice of psychiatry. There has not been an extension of social control but rather the psychiatrisation of new problems.

In terms of the present discussion perhaps the most important point here is that to conceive of community care in terms of new sites for old practices raises the question of the qualitative differences between hospital and community care. It can be argued that, given the rapid growth of residential community-based accommodation, 'decarceration' has meant little more than patients being relocated from one institution to another. Perring (1992) found that, amongst former hospital inpatients discharged into group homes, although there was a preference for the latter, there were distinctly mixed views. It was widely remarked by residents that the new homes are too much like hospitals. Residents remain under supervision, visits by relatives are not encouraged, and there is a tendency amongst staff to 'infantise' residents: classic traits of hospital life (see further below). It has been an increasingly notable feature of the 1990s that patients who have been made subject to compulsory detention in a hospital under both civil and criminal powers of confinement, have been admitted into privately run nursing homes. For patients detained civilly, under part II, MHA 1983 the numbers so admitted rose from 281 in 1987-8 to 957 in 1997-8, and for patients sent to hospital by a criminal court under part III of the 1983 Act there were 92 such admissions in 1997-8 compared with 22 a decade earlier, although the numbers had been higher in the intervening years (DH, 1998d, table 9).

Although such admissions constitute only a tiny proportion of the whole (see Chapters 4 and 6), they nevertheless raise crucial questions about the qualitative difference between hospital accommodation and community care accommodation. For the purposes of the MHA 1983, 'hospital' is defined broadly in s. 145(1) to include any accommodation provided by a local authority for use as a hospital, and s. 34(5) explicitly provides that a mental nursing home which is registered to accept detained patients (under s. 23 Registered Homes Act 1984) is to be defined as a hospital for the purposes of part II of the 1983 Act. Other nursing homes or registered homes are not hospitals for these purposes, but to be registered as a nursing home the establishment in question must offer nursing or medical treatment (ss. 22, 23, Registered Homes Act 1984) and are *de facto* hospitals. As Eldergill (1997, p. 137) has pointed out, whether a 'detained' patient is 'discharged' into 'the community' can depend solely on whether local provision of hostel accommodation and the like has been made, or purchased, by the health authority or the local authority: if it is the former, it may be defined as a hospital, but not if it is the latter. It can be suggested, therefore, that what constitutes a 'hospital' is essentially an arbitrary question which, ironically, at least in the context of the compulsory admission of patients into 'hospital' is determined more by the custodial rather than therapeutic qualities of the institution in question. Moreover, the vast majority of residential community-based accommodation is outside the provisions of the MHA 1983, which apply only to 'sectioned' patients, and as such is a space of virtually unfettered medical discretion.

This thesis also garners plausibility from the proliferation of mechanisms for the control and monitoring of mentally disordered persons in their own homes. In the 1990s 'supervision registers' were introduced along with systems designed to provide continual monitoring in the form of the 'care plan approach' and 'after care under supervision', to sit alongside the already existent powers of guardianship (see Chapter nine). To date there are, as a matter of law, no general powers to allow the administration of treatment without consent 'in the community', but it is in any case possible to treat without consent in a community setting if that setting is in the form of accommodation provided by a health authority as it will count as a 'hospital' for these purposes. The strengthening of measures to control the behaviour of, in particular, mentally ill persons in their own homes has been carried forward on a wave of public concern about the threat to society that such persons constitute and has, in addition to the developments mentioned above, spawned such measures as the Sex Offenders Act 1997. In addition, there have been problems in attempting to provide group home accommodation because of opposition both from local residents and local authority planning authorities. In an illuminating but pessimistic piece of research, Jodelet (1991) found that the social stigma of insanity had not left mental disorder, but rather continued to prefigure the interactions of persons so labelled with their 'normal' counterparts, for whom mental disorder continues to function as a motif for 'otherness'. In short, there is plenty of evidence to suggest both that, although patients can be taken out of the asylum, it is not so easy to take the asylum (as the symbol for otherness) out of the patients, and that in a very real sense, the move to community care should therefore be seen as a spreading out of the hospital system into a broader and more diverse range of sites rather than constituting an alternative to hospitalisation. The provision of mental health services to persons in their own homes can in the same way be seen as the ever greater diffusion of that (medicalised) disciplinary strategy.

There is no doubt that the 'dispersal of discipline' thesis accurately captures one important element of mental health policy over the last few decades, and particularly in respect of the development of control-oriented powers over the last decade. But it also misses some important truths about both policy and, in particular, practice. As will be discussed in greater detail at 9.5, the powers of control in the community as framed by the Mental Health (Patients in the Community) Act 1995 represent a compromise between the interests of control and the civil liberties of the individuals concerned, and bear the influence of a consideration of the provisions of the European Convention of Human Rights. In other words, it is the case that, if by 'control' what is meant is the medicalisation of those pockets within the wider community which are inhabited by mentally disordered persons, then, to date at least, 'control' has been hemmed in by the presence of a legalistic discursive input at the level of policy formation.

At the level of practice, there is an obvious difficulty with theories of social control. This is that the failure of community care has been seen, most often, as a failure of control. Perhaps the dominant theme in public and political discourse concerning mental health over the last decade has concerned homicides and (but to a much lesser extent) suicides committed by mentally disordered persons. In part this is a failure of service providers to coordinate services effectively. A new blueprint for inter-agency working was published by the Department of Health in 1995 (*Building Bridges: a guide to arrangements for inter-agency working for the care and protection of severely mentally ill people* (DH, 1995a), but as the Labour government now accepts, the ability of local authorities and health authorities to act in tandem is also limited by various legal structural factors, and by continual under-funding. But it is the failure of community care as control that has dominated the political agenda. In the 1990s there has been a constant stream of independent inquiries, which have published reports, into homicides and suicides, following the killing of Jonathon Zito by Christopher Clunis in December 1992. It is true that these cases have been picked up and amplified by the media, and that the public and political reaction has often been out of all proportion to the scale of the problem: there is not an epidemic of murderous mental patients roaming at will throughout society, as some seem to believe (see 9.5.1). Nevertheless, read together, the independent reports — 34 as at February 1998 with a further 24 expected (Howlett, 1998, p. ix) — paint a depressing picture of over-stretched, under-resourced and under-staffed community mental health teams, unable to maintain contact with patients who have little wish to cooperate with their 'care plan'. As it is put in the White Paper (DH, 1998a) 'while [community care] improved the treatment of many people who were mentally ill, it left far too many walking the streets, often at risk to themselves and a nuisance to others'. Moreover, it is often not a matter of chance as to who 'falls through the net'. Community Mental Health Centres have been criticised (e.g. Bean and Mounser, 1993) on the grounds that they tend to concentrate on acute patients at the expense of chronic patients. According to Scull, in the USA, where the same centres can be found, 'very few members of the chronic patient population find themselves being treated [by CMHCs]'. In part this is because such centres verge on bankruptcy 'but more importantly, from the very outset, those running these facilities made it clear that the very last people they wished to treat were the psychotic' (Scull, 1996, p. 388). Howlett (1998, p. 3) found that there was 'no ownership of the chaotic and dangerous patients', and a key element in explaining this was that very often such patients were diagnosed as suffering from an untreatable 'personality disorder'. The debate over the non-treatment of Michael Stone, who was found guilty in 1998 of the murder of a mother and daughter in Kent, typifies the situation. Stone was previously known to the mental health services, but had not been offered treatment because his condition was deemed untreatable. The Home Secretary lambasted mental health professionals for their 'refusal' to 'treat' Stone, seeing it as an abdication of responsibility, but the response of professionals was that it was not appropriate to detain and/or treat a person deemed untreatable. The Home Secretary has recently announced that a form of preventive custody will be introduced for such persons; but the point here is that this is evidence, not of the spread of medicine-as-control into the community, but of a general reluctance on the part of both psychiatric and social work professionals to undertake the control of such individuals. And as far as the spread of residential accommodation is concerned, it is hard to see this as 'social control' in any conspiratorial sense, given that it tends to be those who are least in need of control and most in need of treatment who are provided with accommodation. This is not to dispute that civil liberties issues are absolutely pertinent to the treatment of those who occupy residential or nursing home beds. For Scull, the new system resonates with its history, comprising little more than neo-feudal styles of control (Scull, 1996). And although there is a system of registration and inspection in place (under the Registered Homes Act 1984) scandals, such as that concerning the sexual and physical abuse of residents over a period of many years in registered homes licensed and inspected by Buckinghamshire County Council (*The Independent*, 24 June 1998, p. 10), give rise to grave doubts about the ability of the system to detect and prevent this sort of abuse. This raises the issue of the experience of life as a hospital inpatient or client of community care residential accommodation. Before leaving our discussion of the mental health system, it is necessary to give this topic separate consideration.

3.4 INSIDE THE INSTITUTIONS

Within the sociology of medicine, the Weberian model, of modernist institutions as bureaucratic organisations characterised by the complexity of their social interaction, is a popular way of conceptualising the functioning of hospitals. Such models, although useful, can marginalise the experience of the client population. In this latter respect one author, whose work has provided the template for many people's understanding of life in a mental hospital, is Erving Goffman. His highly influential *Asylums* was first published in 1961. The book is the product of fieldwork carried out at St. Elizabeth's, a large asylum in Washington DC, in the mid-1950s, although it also draws widely on secondary material to support its general thesis. Goffman argued that mental asylums have less in common with general hospitals and more in common with other 'total institutions' such as monasteries or convents. Total institutions are those which erect 'a barrier to social intercourse with the outside and to departure that is often built into the physical plant such as locked doors, high walls, barbed wire, cliffs, water, forests, or moors' (1991, pp.15-16). These institutions are problematic for Goffman because '[a] basic social arrangement in modern society is that the individual tends to sleep, play, and work in different places, with different co-participants, under different authorities, and without an overall rational plan'. Hence the 'central feature of total institutions can be described as a breakdown of the barriers ordinarily separating these three spheres of life' (1991, p. 17). For Goffman, then, the inmates of total institutions have had their lives spatially collapsed and rationalised, and must adhere precisely to a timetable conceived by somebody else, and to a rational plan to the details of which they may not be privy. They must do this within a confined space and 'in the company of a large batch of others, all of whom are treated alike and required to do the same thing' (ibid.). Moreover, society within the institutions is split artificially into two groups; the inmates and the staff, and '[e]ach grouping tends to conceive of the others in terms of narrow hostile stereotypes' (ibid., p. 18). There is no public/private split here. The most personal or private aspects, not merely of inmates' lives, but of their minds, are public domain: a legitimate target for psychiatric intervention. This constitutes what Goffman describes as 'a violation of one's informational preserve regarding self' (1991, p. 32). The most profound or obvious effect of this is 'disculturation' or 'institutionalisation'; the inability of inmates to cope with the demands and strains of life outside, the fostering in inmates of absolute dependency on the system not only to satisfy but also to *define* their needs: the 'self is systematically, if often unintentionally, mortified' (1991, p. 24). Institutionalisation signifies a radical departure in the *moral career* of inmates. The sense of 'self' developed on the outside, in the context of family and other relationships, is left at the gates, along with the inmate's physical possessions and human dignities. Inmates are, quite literally, 'mortified'.

There is an obvious irony here, which Goffman is keen to bring out. If the purpose of mental hospitals is to cure or rehabilitate inmates for 'life outside', it seems a peculiar way of going about things to suspend 'life outside' as part of this process. This suspension of 'real life', however, is not 'simply' total, but instead plays on the very fact of that suspension (1991, p. 23-4):

> total institutions do not really look for cultural victory. They create and sustain a particular kind of tension between the home world and the institutional world and use this persistent tension as strategic leverage in the management of men.

Total institutions are coercive. Goffman talks for example about the 'obedience test' that new inmates have to go through (1991, pp.26-7). This, he argues, consists in the inmate accepting the total authority of the staff. The lesson to be leant here, however, is not merely obedience but *unquestioning obedience*. There can be no visible sign that the inmate questions or disagrees with or feels injustice at a staff decision. Inmates learn how to keep their facial expressions to themselves, to remain inscrutable, because attitude is as much a target for intervention as is action. The inmate must learn *subordination* as much as *obedience*. This is really the key distinction between institutions in general and total institutions: in the latter the new inmate must make a number of 'primary adjustments' to the self in order to 'fit' appropriately within the institutional world. However, there are degrees of totality, and this is because inmates also develop 'secondary adjustments': ways to 'buck the system', including for example the development of an inmate culture in opposition to that of the institution; the smuggling of contraband of various descriptions; the development of an economic system based on barter, the 'colonising' of vacant space within the institution, and so on. This is done partly to make life more bearable, but partly just for the sense of defiance that comes from 'breaking the rules' per se (1991, parts 2 and 3).

Goffman does not deny that patients do get out of mental institutions, but his point here is that on release much of what the inmate has learnt inside dissipates (1991, p. 70), and from his point of view this is not surprising because institutionalisation prepares inmates only for institutionalisation. What dischargees take with them back into the community is the stigma of their incarceration and an anxiety about being able to cope with the freedoms and responsibilities of life on the outside. Goffman says that in his experience it is these factors, rather than those relating to the patient's medical/mental condition, which occupy the thoughts of staff charged with the responsibility of deciding who gets out. The problems, in other words, which face dischargees and decision-makers, are caused by the fact of institutionalisation and not the reasons for institutionalisation in the first place (1991, pp. 70-1).

This, then, is the general thesis of *Asylums*. The rest of the book adds the detail, but we have already seen enough to realise that Goffman paints a dismal picture of the asylum, as a place where the logic of control has a far greater influence than medical discourse. There is certainly evidence to substantiate the claims that Goffman makes. The recent history of the three Special Hospitals — Broadmoor, Ashworth, and Rampton — is a case in point. Over the last two decades, Inquiries at each hospital (in 1980 at Rampton (Home Office, 1980); 1988 at Broadmoor (NHS Advisory Services/DHSS Social Services Inspectorate, 1988); and 1992 at Ashworth (Home Office, 1992)) found conditions not too dissimilar from those of the 'total institutions' described by Goffman: 'insular, closed institutions whose predominantly custodial and therapeutically pessimistic culture had isolated them from the mainstream of forensic psychiatry' (DH, 1999, para. 1.19.7), unable to attract and retain medical staff, with the Prison Officers' Association the dominant professional body. Such institutions cater mainly although not exclusively for persons sent to hospital by a criminal court, who can expect to spend a considerable period under detention. Although for the majority of special hospital patients there is a reasonable prospect of eventual transfer into conditions of increasingly lighter security followed by discharge into the community, the process is held up by the well-known problem of delay in securing transfer. One reason for this is the reluctance of those (psychiatrists) who control access to medium security accommodation to accept a Special Hospital patient (Dolan and Shetty, 1995). If a criminal court has ordered that a defendant be detained in a hospital, and has also made a 'restriction order' or a 'restriction direction' in respect of that defendant (see 6.5), significant powers are given to the Secretary of State for the Home Department by the 1983 Act, including the power of veto over any proposal that may be made by a Mental Health Review Tribunal or the patient's doctor, for the transfer of a 'restricted' patient out of a special hospital: s. 19, sch. 1, part II, para. 5. A patient may be given leave of absence under s. 17 by way of a 'trial transfer'. This too can only be done with the consent of the Secretary of State: sch. 1, part II, paras. 2, 3), who may properly consult others including the Aardvold Board on Restricted Patients (see further 8.3.4), before making any decision, and may take into account questions of public safety: *R v Secretary of State for the Home Department, ex parte Harry* [1998] 3 All ER 360 (HC). Not surprisingly, the Home Office adopts a cautious approach to the giving of consent to transfer proposals from a special hospital doctor or a tribunal. By a combination of these factors the consequence is that a significant number of patients remain inappropriately in special hospital accommodation (Gostin, 1986a; Hamilton, 1990). Of course, all of this tends to increase the likelihood that such institutions will fit the 'total institution' model.

The circumstances surrounding the Reports mentioned above were similar to those which were at force over the last century; with government action prompted by scandal, concern, and the lobbying activities of a concerned few. This was also the pattern of events preceding the most recent Inquiries, at Broadmoor in 1997 and Ashworth in 1997-9, but the nature of the complaint had now changed: now the special hospitals were not too austere, but instead too open. Both recent Inquiries were prompted by concerns that security was lax, and that drugs and pornography were widely available. The inquiry at Broadmoor was brief and showed that, on the whole, the regime had improved since the report of a decade earlier, although there were still significant concerns about security. In contrast, the *Report of the Committee of Inquiry into the Personality Disorder Unit, Ashworth Special Hospital* (DH, 1999) (the Fallon Report) presented to Parliament by the Secretary of State for Health in January 1999, showed that most of the allegations that had prompted the setting up of a Committee of Inquiry in 1997, were indeed true. The allegations in question had been made by a former patient of the personality disorder unit (PDU). The most serious concerned the availability of pornography including child pornography, and the presence in the PDU of the child of a former patient, brought in by him, so the Inquiry team found, as part of a plan to have her 'groomed for paedophile purposes'. There were many other lapses or plain absences of security and of management: patients ran businesses from the hospital and there was very little in the way of the barriers to communication with the outside world that were described by Goffman: internet access, for example, was freely available. At the same time, the institutions remained isolated in terms of their relation to the rest of the hospital system. The Fallon Inquiry concluded that the custodial, security-inclined regimes that had been detailed in the reports of the 1980s and early 1990s no longer existed, but now 'the pendulum may have swung too far away in the other direction', making a mockery of the notion of a 'high security' hospital. *The Independent* newspaper put the point more bluntly in the headline to its coverage of the publication of the Fallon Report: 'Ashworth run by inmates not staff' (*The Independent*, 6 January 1999, p. 6).

In Goffmanian terms, the Fallon Report details the extent to which 'secondary adjustments' can fashion an entirely different regime if 'policy' becomes a vacuum. However it would seem that since the latest round of scandals broke, policy is beginning to change again. The courts have recently been called upon to adjudicate on various questions relating to security measures in special hospitals. In *R v Broadmoor SHA, ex parte S and Others* (1998) *The Times*, 17 February, three patients at Broadmoor had sought judicial review of the decision of the hospital authority to introduce a policy of random and routine searching, replacing the 'for cause' policy that had hitherto been applied. Not surprisingly, the application was rejected in the High Court and that decision was upheld in the Court of Appeal. It was held that the power to detain for treatment implied a power to do that which was necessary for the success of that treatment, which included the right to search, as long as that was not exercised unreasonably in the circumstances. A similarly expansive reading of the 1983 Act was provided in *R v Mental Health Act Commission, ex parte Smith* (1998) *The Times*, 15 May) (HC), which relied on the above decision, and that in *Poutney v Griffiths* [1976] AC 314, to hold that the powers of admission, detention and treatment necessarily implied broader powers of management and control. In the present climate the courts are likely to give short shrift to attempts by special hospital patients to use litigation to protect the 'liberties' to which they have become accustomed in recent years, in at least some quarters. There has been one recent decision, in *Broadmoor Hospital Authority v Robinson* (1998) *The Times*, 15 October (HC), in which a more restrictive approach to the interpretation of the 1983 Act was taken. Special hospital managers have powers under s. 134(1)(b) of the 1983 Act to withhold outgoing mail from a special hospital patient to avoid 'likely' distress or danger to other persons, and under s. 134(2) in respect of incoming mail, which may be withheld in the interests of the safety of the patient or for the protection of others. Managers have corresponding powers to open and inspect any mail: s. 134(4). *Robinson* involved a patient who had written an account of his time in Broadmoor, which had been submitted to a publisher. An injunction had been obtained by the hospital managers on the grounds that the publication of the patient's memoirs would distress other patients and expose the defendant to risk of assault. The court held that s. 134 could have no effect when an item of post sent by a patient had reached its destination, and that the injunction should be discharged as it had the practical effects of undermining the limitations of managers' powers found in that section. However, even here, when the hospital managers were unsuccessful in their attempt to use law to enforce the inside/outside barrier, there is nevertheless evidence that the recent round of scandals has sent a shock wave through the management structure of special hospitals. It is therefore to be expected that the pendulum will continue to shift back in the direction of an emphasis on security and control.

It may of course be argued that special hospitals are atypical institutions. Indeed they are, yet there is evidence to support a Goffman-influenced understanding of the modern experience of hospitalisation from all sections of the hospital system. The Rosenham research, discussed in Chapter 2, provides one example. Research by Bott (1976, p. 133) discussed by Barham (1992, p. 8) found that the barrier between staff and inmates was rigidly enforced: '[t]alking to patients is dangerous because it threatens to puncture the barrier that keeps sanity and madness in their proper places', while Christine Perring (1992, p. 134), found that clinical staff take a fatherly role; nursing staff a motherly role, and that inmates are correspondingly infantised, irrespective of the actual gender of the participants. The strategic deployment of 'family' is a well-documented feature of the regime in women's prisons, particularly the New Holloway which after opening in 1976 used 'family' as a structuring dynamic within the regime (which was overtly therapeutic), for example, by dividing inmates into 'family units'. The enforcement of discipline and subordination through regulation of contact with family is also a well-documented research finding. Many more examples of institutions and regimes which exhibit this or that feature of Goffman's model could be drawn from the literature. There is also much autobiographical work which supports Goffman's contention that hospital inpatients must adhere to the regime or suffer the consequences; which places therapy of the mildest kind in a continuum with the use of shock treatment or drugs and, ultimately, when all else fails, straightforward violence and torture-like techniques based on deprivation or segregation, and which sees them as a function of the 'mortification' rather than 'treatment' of patients (Perrucci, 1974). The boredom of institutional life is well documented (see, for example, Anon, 1996). In short, there is little doubt that the characteristics and techniques described by Goffman have been widely deployed in both time and space, and although the view of many former inpatients who have been transferred into community-based residential accommodation is that the latter is less 'total' accommodation than that provided by mental hospitals, it is also well documented that many of the conditions of total institutions pertain in such accommodation (see Perring, 1992 and Barham, 1992, pp. 21-8). Within the general hospital sector, 'restraint' and 'seclusion' are still practised: moral treatment and medical treatment have still not totally ousted their historical predecessors, but have rather colonised their techniques. As will be discussed later (see 7.4.2), these practices today come under the definition, in s. 145(1), MHA 1983, of 'treatment'.

As the continued, even increased (Mental Health Act Commission, 1997, para. 10.2.3.) use of such practices indicates, mental hospitals continue to be institutions characterised by high levels of violence (Shah, 1993). It is difficult to give precise details of the incidence of patient attacks on staff which although clearly a problem (Royal College of Psychiatrists, 1998), is significantly under-reported by staff (Thakrey and Bobbitt, 1990), and much of the research tends to be retrospective, based on analysis of reported incidents (Cheung et al, 1997). In a prospective study, Cheung et al (1997) aimed to provide a more accurate picture of the situation. This study took place in an eleven ward facility comprising both locked and unlocked wards and housing both short-stay and long-stay patients. The study reports assaults by a patient population of 220 against a staff complement of 279 across an eight-week period. Four hundred and seventy-seven assaults were recorded. Of these, 296 or 62.1 per cent were verbal, 181 or 37.9 per cent physical, with or without accompanying verbal abuse. Although around a third of all assaults had no obvious precursor, the majority stemmed from interactions with staff, with the staff member either denying some request or 'assisting with patient's activities of daily living' (Cheung et al, 1997, p. 48) (whatever that means) or requesting the patient to take medication. Use of weapons was rare and physical injuries usually minor. Only two incidents required the attention of a doctor, with a further seven requiring some sort of first aid. However, around a third of those assaulted felt 'substantially shaken' by the incident. Of the 220 patients covered by the research, around half committed an assault (whether verbal or physical), although men were markedly more aggressive than women. In general patients on locked wards were involved in a greater mean number of incidents than other patients, and assaults on such wards tended to be less likely to arise out of interactions with staff and therefore less predictable. Schizophrenia and schizoaffective disorders accounted for 80 per cent of physical assaults, and only six patients were responsible for nearly two-thirds of all violent incidents. The authors found 'all of them to be suffering from treatment resistant schizophrenia' (Cheung et al, 1997, p. 51).

Although the frequency of assaults varies between hospitals (Davis, 1991), the findings of Cheung et al (1997, p. 49) confirm that assaults on staff are heavily under reported: only 9 verbal and 53 physical assaults were recorded, yet the data indicated that the facility in question could expect 3.89 physical attacks per member of staff annually. This research also confirmed the *patterns* of inmate violence against staff that have emerged from a large number of research projects. The findings that a high number of violent incidents are attributable to a few patients, and that men are more likely to be aggressive than women are typical. Violence against staff is not the only reason for some form of active intervention. The prevention of patient-on-patient violence and self-harm are also pressing concerns (Crichton, 1995). Nationally, there are more than 4000 deaths annually from suicide, and one-quarter of these are of people who were in contact with the mental health system in the year before their death (Department of Health, 1998a, paras. 1.7, 1.8). Suicide in hospital and prison facilities is a matter of particular concern. Around four in every 1000 persons admitted to a mental hospital will commit suicide (Ganesvaran and Shah, 1997), although the greatest risk is in the days immediately after discharge (Johnson et al, 1993). Suicides are statistically more probable for all categories of mental disorder (Ruschena et al, 1998), although those suffering from schizophrenia seem to be more at risk than others (Rossau and Mortensen, 1997). Patients at most risk tend to be young, male and with antisocial personality traits (Johnson et al, 1993), and there is evidence to suggest, although for reasons that are not clear, that, controlling for other variables, secure hospital accommodation carries a higher risk of suicide than either prison or general hospital facilities (Haycock, 1993). There is also evidence from Australia that suicide rates in hospitals can be affected by legal changes requiring staff to be more sensitive to the risk (Ganesvaran and Shah, 1997). In Goffman's terms, suicide is the ultimate 'secondary adjustment'; but the starkness of the statistics on suicide, and the complexity of the situation, makes one think long and hard about the role of theory. It must not be to offer glib or easy explanations for such problematic issues.

Goffman's thesis, as might be expected, has not gone unchallenged, on philosophical, methodological and empirical grounds. Sedgwick (1982), for example, has argued that Goffman's theory is too sweeping and so both underplays the extent to which mental hospitals resemble other hospitals, even from the point of view of the patient, most of whom are not detained; and is insensitive to the historical contingencies that must be taken into account when applying a theoretical model. For instance, Goffman draws, in quick succession, on T. E. Lawrence's description of barracks life in the airforce, practices in a nunnery, and the practice of flogging on ninetenth-century warships, to illustrate his thesis, all in the space of a few pages (Goffman, 1991, pp. 37-9), and gives the reader the impression that all are mere examples of a general phenomenon with no particularities or variation to speak of. There is no well-defined *qualitative* element in Goffman's understanding of a total institution.

There is, for example, as much autobiographical work that contradicts Goffman's views as supports them. Many patients experience their treatment as beneficial, even if their first impulse had been to resist. Moreover, a central tenet of Goffman's thesis has been undermined by the shift in focus of hospital services to acute care (Cavadino, 1989, Chapter 5). In the years of the great confinement a considerable number of patients spent years if not decades inside asylums. The average length of stay in the 1950s had fallen to approximately 10 years, compared with 20 to 40 years before the Second World War. Today, 60 per cent of hospital admissions spend less than a month as an inpatient (Ramon, 1992, p. xii). Rather than being 'total' institutions, contemporary mental hospitals are better characterised in terms of managed chaos. The biennial reports of the Mental Health Act Commission (MHAC, the latter-day version of the Lunacy Commissioners) leave the reader in no doubt. The relevant Chapter of the most recent report (MHAC, 1997) opens with an account of: '[t]he same heavy pressure on beds cited in the last two Biennial Reports', the consequences being that 'leave beds are occupied; patients are discharged early; patients may be kept in police cells for one or two days while a bed is found; patients are placed out of district' (MHAC, 1997, para. 4.1). At some hospitals bed occupancy stood at 150 per cent and patients who were in theory 'detained' under the MHA 1983, had to be sent home on leave to attend hospital on a day care basis. The problem is particularly acute in London (ibid.), and this goes some way towards explaining the greater involvement of London police with mentally disordered persons in public places, many of whom will be homeless (Abdul-Hamid and Cooney, 1997). The policy of bed closure has left the remaining system under-resourced for the numbers with whom it is required to deal. Moreover, in some facilities living conditions can be of questionable quality, with 'shabby, scruffy and poorly furnished' wards (MHAC, 1997, para. 4.2.1). There is little incentive to invest in ward comforts in hospitals scheduled for closure, but there is no doubt that general resource shortages often prevent substantial expenditure on items considered less than necessary. The extent to which such a picture corresponds to Goffman's model is open to question. There is limited interaction between patients and nursing staff, for example, although this seems to be more because of the pressure caused by staff shortages, which is particularly acute in regional secure units (MHAC, 1997, para. 4.4.2.), than because of an 'us and them' philosophy. This in turn affects the standards of care and the ability of institutions to provide individualised attention. Staff morale is often low, and some hospitals have been forced to close beds (ibid.). At registered mental nursing homes, which must be visited by the MHAC if accommodating 'detained' patients under the MHA 1983, concerns were with failure in record-keeping and adherence to procedures rather than with ward conditions. But as discussed above, the residential home sector is periodically rocked by scandal, which tends to encourage a certain degree of scepticism about the abilities of third party inspection always to detect even significant problems. Of course there are some parts of the system, the newly built medium secure units for example, that are said to provide high quality accommodation (MHAC, 1997, para. 4.4.1.).

3.5 CONCLUDING COMMENTS

It is not easy to digest of all this information, and it may be that this is because it sends out conflicting messages. In a very real sense, it is misleading to think of the state provision of mental health services as a singular system. Notwithstanding the move toward statutory integration of administrative structures and standards, the various 'streams' identified in Chapter one continue to coexist. The special hospitals should be thought of as a separate system, in which the emphasis is very much more on containment than cure, and in the wake of recent scandals is likely to stay that way. The Fallon Report recommended, in straightforward terms, that the special hospitals should be closed, and provision made for their patients in a range of smaller units. This plan was rejected by the Secretary of State for Health the very day that the Report was published. The matter had already been raised a year earlier in a confidential report made by the High Security Psychiatric Commissioning Board to the Secretary of State, which was leaked to the media (*The Independent*, 23 March 1998, p. 2). Resource limitations simply do not allow the abandonment of the three special hospitals, whatever their limitations; but the civil liberties implications are significant. The confidential report also expressed the view that between 850 and 1000 of the 1,520 persons detained in special hospitals do not need to be held in conditions of high security but cannot be transferred for want of alternative accommodation. Black people are significantly over-represented in special hospitals, and this in itself is a real cause for concern (Boast and Chesterman, 1995). But it seems highly likely that the special hospitals will continue to function in the foreseeable future as the nearest approximation to an ideal-type 'total institution' that is to be found in our mental health system.

General psychiatric hospital provision by contrast has moved significantly into the mainstream of health care provision and such facilities are very much more part of that general hospital system. As such, they share the problems of that system — limited funds, staff shortages, an emphasis on 'throughput' and the dominance of managerial rather than clinical (or social-control oriented) imperatives. If the problem for patients in the special hospitals is getting out, for those in need of acute care services the problem can be getting in — and staying in long enough. In some respects these facilities, when adequately funded, can conform most closely to the ideal of the asylum as 'refuge' or 'retreat' from the rigours of society that inspired the pioneers of moral treatment (Wallcraft, 1996). If a Goffman-type thesis can be made out in respect of this sector, it can only be through a detailed consideration of the treatments that it provides. This will be undertaken in Chapter seven.

Even so, generalisation remains a problem. For example, different wards in the same facility negotiate the balance between treatment and control differently. Wards ostensibly in 'the community' may in fact be more secure than those in hospitals. Detained patients may be held in conditions of lesser security than 'informal' patients. The recently-begun process of unearthing the hidden history of care in the community (Bartlett and Wright, eds, 1999) is a reminder that for much of what has passed as 'the' history of the treatment of mental disorder is only a part of that history, and that the role of institutional-isation has been routinely over-emphasised by 'traditionalists' and 'revisionists' alike. The second half of the twentieth century has witnessed the lingering, painful death of the asylum. Even now, at the end of the century, it is hanging on and, rather like the villain in a Victorian melodrama, may yet prove to have the strength for one more fight for survival. Although it seems highly improbable that inpatient treatment will become a rarity in the foreseeable future, the long-term shape of service provision can only be a matter of speculation. For some patients, those deemed suitable for special hospital provision, community care is not an alternative, but for the vast majority of patients prospects are not so clear-cut. Whatever the shape of future develop-ments, however — and the Review of Mental Health Law under the leadership of Professor Genevra Richardson has a brief, in the words of Health Minister Paul Boateng, to undertake 'a root and branch review of the law' (DH press release R1199-06, 17 September 1998) in order to implement what had been described in an earlier DH press release as a 'third way for mental health' (DH, 1998, 98/311) — one feature of the system does seem likely to remain fundamentally unchanged, and this is that our response to mental disorder will continue to be framed within the two polar points of the history considered in this Chapter. Our response to mental disorder is prompted both by concern about the plight of fellow human beings and by a desire to control behaviour judged to be dangerous or anti-social. Managerialism and the influence of market principles are vital questions when investigating how the system works. But in terms of function, the overarching perspectives, of benevolence and control, medicalism and custodialism *are* accurate: they reflect our motives, and their inherent ambiguity. In large part, the degree to which one or the other is emphasised is a matter of perspective, judgment and interpretation. But to understand the mental health system fully in terms of its broader social function and in its microscopic interactions with service users, it is perhaps necessary to learn to live with the paradox that it is both at once: and often the failure of both. Caught in the middle of this juxtaposition of the mundane, the bizarre and the poignant, as the intended beneficiaries of political and professional initiatives, and of social work and sociological theories, are the users of the service. And although the voices of service users risk being drowned out by those of the others, this must be resisted, lest we lose sight of the special contribution to our understanding of our mental health system that its users can make.

Joe's making a stool
I'm weaving a basket
someone's making coffee
Dee says I can sing
and she does.
Jane won't make an ashtray
Arthur's sulking because the priest wouldn't rechristen him *Jesus*.
Jane still won't make an ashtray. Instead she becomes a dog
grr Woof!
Dogs don't make ashtrays.
Dee's singing the national anthem
Arthur blesses me.
Sydney hasn't spoken all morning, or yesterday or the day before, gggrrrr
Woof!
Shit said Joe
I'm going to discharge myself from this place it's driving me mad
realising what he had said, he starts to laugh
I also start to laugh
the man on my left (who didn't hear Joe) starts to laugh as well. We all laugh,
except Sid who wants to die (and means it)
then we had coffee

(Lewis, 1996)

FOUR

Admission to hospital

I came out of my dream and back to stark reality when I opened my eyes that October morning. I looked around me: four grey walls reached to a high ceiling . . . There was a dirty blood-stained blue door with a small port-hole of reinforced glass in it but it was covered over the outside by a curtain: the door, too, was locked from the outside. There was no furniture in my tiny cell, nothing save a mattress, a pillow and a blanket. I had not even got my clothes, and there was no chamber pot. I huddled under my blanket for warmth . . .

(Zaki, 1995, p. 3)

On the whole, the picture given here is of a large degree of satisfaction on the part of patients and their relatives.

(Hoenig and Hamilton, 1969, p. 130, cited in Pilgrim and Rogers, 1993, p. 163)

4.1 INTRODUCTION

Roughly 250,000 persons per year are admitted to psychiatric facilities in England and Wales. They arrive through a variety of legal mechanisms. The overwhelming majority — about 90 per cent — are admitted 'informally' under s. 131, Mental Health Act 1983. People admitted under this section are not confined in any legal sense. While we will argue below that the practical situation of these people often makes it misleading to think of them as entering and remaining in the facility voluntarily, nonetheless in law, they are free to leave at will. The preponderance of these admissions must be emphasised, since the litigation and the literature are rather misleadingly skewed towards persons civilly or criminally confined. In fact, persons subject to detention are a relatively small minority of the hospital population. Of those formally confined ('sectioned'), most are admitted for assessment under s. 2. About two-thirds as many (3 per cent of admissions) are admitted for treatment under

s. 3. In addition, a much smaller number are admitted pursuant to the police powers contained in s. 136, or findings of mental disorder at various stages in the criminal process (see Chapter 6).

The mechanism of entry is important not merely because of the right to leave. Persons admitted informally keep the same rights to consent to treatment as anyone else in society. Persons confined have very different rights regarding treatment (see Chapter 7). The different categories of confinement further have some variations in length of confinement permitted and discharge procedure (see further below, and Chapters five and eight), so even between classes of confinement, the mechanism of admission is of considerable importance.

While the distinctions between the formal categories are thus definitive of legal rights, patients are often sufficiently uninvolved in the mechanics of the admission that they do not know what category they are under. This is further complicated by the movement of numerous patients between categories at various times in their hospital stay. Studies suggest that notwithstanding the duty in s. 132 that detained patients be informed of their status and of avenues of redress, 40 to 50 per cent of civilly confined patients did not know they had been confined (Toews et al, 1984; Bradford et al, 1986; Monahan et al, 1995; Goldrick, 1997). This emphasises the divergence of law on the books and law in practice, since large numbers of patients appear to lack basic information relevant to their situation.

4.2   INFORMAL ADMISSION

Section 131 of the MHA 1983 allows the admission of anyone who 'requires treatment for mental disorder'. 'Mental disorder' refers to the definition in s. 1 of the Act, discussed in Chapter two. The court in *R* v *Kirklees Metropolitan Borough Council, ex parte C* [1993] 2 FLR 187 (CA) held that s. 131 applied to treatment only, not assessment of a patient, creating a potential lacuna in the Act. The court dealt with the problem by holding that 'there has never been any doubt that an adult patient may be lawfully admitted to hospital for assessment, provided he or she consents, just as he or she may be admitted to hospital for an operation' (p. 191, per Lloyd LJ). The court thus established a second and independent basis for informal admission, founded in the common law.

As a matter of law, the existence of such an authority for informal admission outside the statute is not self-evident, for informal admission appears to be a concept unknown to the common law. In the eighteenth century, in law if not in practice, cases such as *R* v *Clarke* (1762) 3 Burr 1362 and *R* v *Coate* (1772) Lofft 73 would suggest that legal authority had to be sought to house a lunatic in a psychiatric facility. Certainly the care of the insane in this period was not understood on the model of an informal patient. This was clarified by nineteenth-century statutes which expressly precluded informal admission. This was built into the initial legislation establishing county asylums in 1808, where all admissions were by order of justices of the peace, and no inmate was permitted to be at large without order of the justices: see ss. 17, 23, County

Asylum Act 1808. For private sector institutions, the restrictions date from s. 29, Madhouse Act 1828. It is only with the statutory intervention of s. 1, Mental Treatment Act 1930, that informal admissions were generally permitted (see Chapter one). Prior to that, consent of the patient to admission does not appear to have been relevant to legal substance. It was instead relevant merely to the question of procedure: throughout the period, strangers acting without apparent encouragement of the patient were denied standing to press for a remedy (see *R* v *Clarke*, and *Ex parte Child* (1854) 15 CB 238).

If the finding in *Kirklees* is surprising in law, it is less so given modern attitudes sympathetic to voluntary admission, particularly in comparison with civil confinement. On the surface at least, the problems of coercion, of concern to the civil libertarian, disappear. In addition, the patient is likely to be more involved in the treatment programme, to be less alienated and dissatisfied with the experience of hospitalisation, and therefore more amenable to seeking assistance in hospital in the event that he or she encounters problems in the future. The balance of power between patient and psychiatrist is at least partly redressed, creating a closer approximation of a regular doctor-patient relationship. The increased trust between doctor and patient may improve treatment compliance after release, and create a better medical result.

These are laudable arguments indeed. The difficulty is that often, these admissions are not 'voluntary' in any conventional sense. Since the pioneering study by Gilboy and Schmidt in 1971, it has been recognised that coercion often operates in voluntary admissions. North American studies find that something like one-half of informally admitted patients feel coerced during their admission (Monahan et al, 1995). Pressure may be effected in a variety of ways. At its simplest, it may be purely situational. Psycho-geriatric patients, for example, may be unable due to physical weaknesses to exercise their right to leave. At a slightly more complex level, an individual living with a caring family may have no option but to follow the family's decision to admit the individual, since they have nowhere else to live and, often, few means of finding alternative accommodation and living support. As 'relief of carers' was the prime major reason for admissions to acute wards of the London hospitals studied by Flannigan et al (1994), this sort of coercion might be expected to be not uncommon.

Carers and others may not rely simply on the situational vulnerability of the client, but may use other tactics, from gentle encouragement or reasoning, through to threats or physical violence to encourage the individual to enter the facility. The motives are legion. A lawyer representing a client on a minor criminal charge may see 'willingness' to undergo psychiatric treatment as a useful bargaining chip in a sentencing hearing. Police officers or medical staff may wish to avoid the increased bureaucracy which flows from civil confinement. Medical staff may believe the therapeutic justifications for voluntary admissions noted above, and encourage patients to adopt that route rather than confinement for that reason. The medical staff also have an additional power, however, they can threaten confinement unless the patient consents to voluntary admission, and perpetuate that threat each time the patient expresses a wish to leave the facility (see Rogers, 1993). When such a direct manipulation is used, it is difficult to see the confinement as voluntary in any meaningful sense.

While the statistics would suggest that most people admitted to hospital found their stay beneficial overall (Monahan et al, 1995, and studies cited therein; Nicholson et al, 1996), there are obvious drawbacks to even informal hospital admission. Institutional rules limit freedom, and the individual is removed from society for a period. Hospitalisation is also expensive both to the taxpayer and, if private care is received, to the patient or the insurer. The practical situation of these informal patients can sometimes be worse than that of confined patients. As will be discussed in Chapter eight, at least a confined patient can challenge his or her committal. If the patient is competent to consent to medical treatment, his or her position is stronger as an informal patient, since he or she can refuse medication (although problems of coercion similar to those we have been discussing will arise in the case of such 'voluntary' treatment as well). If the patient lacks that capacity, however, he or she is in a considerably weaker position than confined patients, since the Act provides safeguards relating to second opinions and board hearings only for confined patients prior to medication. An informal patient lacking capacity, by comparison, may be treated by the doctor without any procedural safeguards, on the basis of the doctor's view of the patient's best interests (see further Chapters seven, ten and eleven).

Informal admission does not affect all groups equally. Statistically, women, and particularly white women, are admitted at a considerably higher rate than their proportion of the population as a whole (Pilgrim and Rogers, 1993, Bebbington et al, 1994, 746; Ineichen et al, 1984, 601). The indications are that this imbalance is particularly prevalent in the informal category, with women admitted informally at roughly one and one-half times the rate of men. If the system is working properly, this preponderance of informal admissions is a good thing, suggesting a relationship of trust between women and the psychiatric establishment; but it seems equally fair to question whether the statistics instead represent the disempowerment of women in current society. In this latter scenario, women's informal admission would result from acquiescence to the non-legal forms of authority discussed above, rather than an active choice of hospitalisation as the best available option.

The law has dealt with these non-voluntary informal admissions in a variety of ways. The first concerns the power of a guardian appointed under s. 7 of the 1983 Act. The details of these appointments will be discussed in Chapter nine. For here, suffice it to say that the Act allows guardians to be appointed for persons with mental disorders, where warranted by their welfare or the protection of others. The powers of these guardians are restricted by the Act, but s. 8(1) allows the guardian to require the patient to reside in a specific place. According to *R v Hallstrom (No. 2)* [1986] 2 All ER 306, p. 312, there is nothing in the Act to prevent this power being used to admit the patient into a hospital. The patient would not be detained under the confinement powers of the MHA 1983, and would therefore be an informal patient. Paragraph 13.10.a of the Code of Practice argues against the use of this power in this way for anything other than a short stay, but it is difficult to see statutory support for that limitation. In *Kirklees* (above), the Court of Appeal held that violation of the Code would not create a wrong which could be subjected to judicial scrutiny if the statute was complied with, even, as in that case, where the guardian was a public authority. The Code's prohibition may thus discourage guardians from admitting patients, but cannot prevent it should it occur. The result would be an informal patient without the legal authority to leave, and no obvious forum to require some form of assessment of his or her predicament. He or she could of course challenge the guardianship order before a review tribunal, but that would involve a set of criteria quite different from a challenge to a specific decision of a guardian to place the patient in the psychiatric hospital.

A similar difficulty concerns the admission of children as informal patients, on the authority of a parent. It is clear from *Kirklees* that a parent (or, more correctly, a person or body, such as a local authority with 'parental responsiblility') has the right to admit a child to a psychiatric hospital. Section 131 of the 1983 Act specifically allows children over the age of sixteen years capable of expressing wishes to be admitted informally on their own authority. If the child wishes not to be admitted, however, his or her competence seems not to be an issue here, since at common law, the wishes of a competent child under the age of eighteen years can be overriden by his or her parent: *Re R (A Minor) (Wardship: Consent to Treatment)* [1991] 4 All ER 177; *In Re W (A Minor) (Medical Treatment: Court's Jurisdiction)* [1992] 3 WLR 758. At the end of three months, the Health Authority is under a duty to notify the local authority of the residency, and the local authority must investigate to ensure that the welfare of the child does not require its intervention (s. 85, Children Act 1989), but such *post facto* investigation is not a substitute for admission standards (see Sandland, 1993).

The patients in these cases are effectively left without remedy. Other jurisdictions expressly allow review tribunal applications in such situations: see, e.g., Ontario Mental Health Act, RSO 1990, c. M.7, s. 13 regarding children over the age of 12. There has as yet been no significant pressure for such a reform in this country.

Both these situations concern the patient who has a guardian. What happens in the case of an adult patient without a legal guardian, and without the capacity to consent to admission? This was the situation in *R v Bournewood Community and Mental Health NHS Trust, ex parte L* [1998] 3 WLR 107 (HL). In that case, L, an adult with profound developmental disabilities, was admitted as an informal patient to a psychiatric facility. While agitated in the admission ward, he was generally compliant, and did not attempt to leave the acute ward following the admission. Had he made such a move, formal confinement proceedings would have been commenced, and L would not have been allowed off the premises; but such formal proceedings had not been necessary. At issue was whether individuals such as L, who acquiesced rather than assented to their admission, and who lacked the capacity to make a decision as to where they would reside in any event, could be admitted informally.

The Court of Appeal held that such persons could not be admitted informally. Lord Woolf MR, for a unanimous court, held that 'a person is detained in law if those who have control over the premises in which he is have the intention that he shall not be permitted to leave those premises and have the ability to prevent him from leaving': [1998] 2 WLR 765 at p. 769. On this definition, L was detained, since those in charge of the facility would not have permitted him to leave, had he wished to do so. In His Lordship's view (at pp. 775-6), detention was not permitted except in accordance with the statutory scheme: there was no additional common law detention power open to hospitals in England.

The House of Lords reversed this decision. On the question of detention, Lords Nolan and Steyn held that L had been detained. Lord Goff, speaking for himself and Lords Lloyd and Hope, held that detention arose only if L had attempted to leave the ward and been prevented from doing so. It does seem that this was the intent of the legislature when the 1959 Act, which introduced the current provision for informal patients, was passed. The Royal Commission which preceded the introduction of the 1959 legislation did advocate informal admission, not merely for assenting patients, but for 'all who need [treatment] and are not unwilling to receive it' (Royal Commission, 1957, para. 291). It is not obvious, however, that the wording of the statute clearly allows this reading.

In addition, the House of Lords held unanimously that whether or not L was detained, the detention could be justified according to the principle of necessity. This will be discussed in greater detail below: see Chapters seven, ten and eleven. The use of the principle in an incapacity context grows from the case of *F* v *West Berkshire Health Authority* [1989] 2 All ER 545. That case involved whether treatment could be provided to a person lacking authority to consent, since the existing law provides no provision to allow for appointment of someone to consent in the patient's stead. The House of Lords in that case held that the doctor could treat without consent in such a situation, in the best interests of the patient, and that treatment under such circumstances would be neither a battery nor a criminal assault. In a way, the situation in *ex parte L* provides a reasonable parallel: in both cases, a potential tortfeasor (for battery in F and wrongful confinement in *Bournewood*) seeks protection for actions benefiting an incapacitated person.

The parallel breaks down because of different guardianship rules, however: where the law does not allow a guardian to be appointed with authority to consent to treatment (see further below), s. 8, MHA 1983 does allow a guardian to be appointed to determine where an individual will live. Certainly, the authority of the guardian to determine residence does not provide authority to detain a person in that place; but *ex hypothesi* this is not the situation in *Bournewood*: if L had wished to leave, formal confinement processes would have been commenced, and nothing in that case would seem to provide any authority to confine individuals on the ward forcibly. Further, guardianship appointments carry with them legal remedies before the review board in the event of misuse; it is not obvious why persons in L's situation should not have access to those processes. One may have sympathy with the court's attempts to fashion a solution in *F*, where a lacuna in the law did exist; it is not obvious why the principle of necessity ought to be invoked in *Bournewood*, where the law already provides a solution.

None of this, of course, is an argument against the principle that truly voluntary admissions are a desirable admission mechanism. Instead, the caveat is merely raised that informal does not necessarily mean voluntary. The Dutch patient advocate Johan Legemaate has argued for increased regulation of informal admissions to take account of these pressures (Legemaate, 1988). In some cases, such as admissions on the authority of parents, greater process protections might indeed be effective. They will not present a panacea, however. For those whose coercion results from their vulnerability and dependency on others — those with nowhere else to go when their carers 'suggest' admission for example — the problem of coercion can only be addressed by the provision of options to hospitalisation. Procedural protections may be useful to ensure that existing options are considered. This may be a useful and important protection. A recent London study indicated that 41 per cent of persons admitted to the psychiatric hospitals studied, and 64 per cent of their carers, had no access to a key worker or to ways of seeking informed help (Flannigan et al, 1994) suggesting a problem of accessing such options as now exist. The process protections cannot of course provide those options where they do not exist.

4.3 CIVIL CONFINEMENT: STANDARDS AND JUSTIFICATIONS

In theory (but as we have seen, not necessarily in practice), informal admission does not involve intervention by the state to confine the individual in the psychiatric hospital. With civil confinement ('sectioning'), this is not the case. The sectioning of an individual is clearly an instance of the state coercive power intruding on the freedom of the individual. While the objective of civil confinement is not punitive, the intrusiveness of the violation must be understood as requiring clear justification.

Traditionally, the justifications have concerned the need to protect the individual or others in society (the 'dangerousness' criterion); or the more paternalist justification of acting for the benefit of the individual, with 'benefit' usually understood in medical terms. There has been an implication in some of the discourse regarding these criteria that the former is a creature of American constitutional law, while the latter is consistent with the English way of doing things. This is misleading on both counts. While the American Bill of Rights has certainly resulted in a more interventionist jurisprudence than has existed in England, it has always stopped short of finding dangerousness as an express requirement for confinement, and indeed when alternative options are considered at the end of this Chapter, a system of therapeutic criteria designed to meet the rights standards of the American constitution will be discussed.

Similarly, the dangerousness criterion is not an American invention. Prior to the statutory development of asylum law in the nineteenth century, the legal issue was a defence to an action for wrongful confinement. Confinement of a lunatic would be allowed 'to prevent apparent mischief, which might ensue: as, to restrain the plaintiff, non sane, from killing himself, or others, burning a house, or other mischief' (Comyn, 1822, vol. 6, p. 544, pl. 3.M.22.) While thus well-established by the beginning of the nineteenth century, the roots of the criterion are much older. Brook's abridgement from the sixteenth century contains another similar statement referring specifically, as in Comyn, to restraining the lunatic from killing, or doing mischief such as setting fire to a house (Brook, 1573, 'Faux Imprisonment', pl. 28, vol 1, p. 330).

In the nineteenth century, confinement criteria were codified by a series of statutes. With minor variations over the century, the standard required that a lunatic, idiot or person of unsound mind was 'a proper person to be taken charge of and detained under care and treatment': see Lunacy Act 1890, form 8. Notwithstanding this broad wording, out of a concern for civil rights of the insane, the courts imported the dangerousness language from the wrongful confinement context. The legislation was held to be justified by public order. Thus in *Re Fell* (1845 3 Dowl & L 373, 15 LJ (NS) MC 25 QB, Patteson J commented (at p. 29) that 'These statutes were passed for the protection of the public. . .'. That in turn led to a standard of dangerousness. In *Nottidge* v *Ripley*, *The Times* (London), 27 June 1849, p. 7, for example, Sir Frederick Pollock CB stated in his charge to the jury, 'it is my opinion that you ought to liberate every person who is not dangerous to himself or others . . . and I desire to impress that opinion with as much force as I can'. See also *R* v *Pinder, in re Greenwood* (1855) 24 LJ (NS) QB 148 at 151, per Coleridge J).

Far from being a foreign interloper, therefore, the dangerousness standard forms a part of English legal culture. In so far as it reflects an attempt to preserve public peace and safety, it represents an obviously legitimate public interest. The desire to protect individuals from harming themselves is less evidently a public interest, but if paternalist, it is at the less interventionist side of that spectrum. As a guiding justification for civil confinement, it also has the disadvantage that a person, even if not susceptible to treatment, could remain confined in perpetuity, due to mental illness and the mere risk of behaving in a fashion dangerous to self or others. This is particularly problematic since, as we shall see, dangerousness is notoriously difficult to predict. It also reinforces imagery of the asylum as a place of confinement and, by implication, not of treatment. Neither governments, nor the medical professionals working in the facilities, nor the public, find that imagery attractive.

Even in the nineteenth century, the dangerousness criterion was contested. In an open letter to the Lord Chancellor, responding to *Nottidge*, the Commissioners in Lunacy expressly denied a requirement of dangerousness prior to confinement, claiming instead that '[t]he object of these Acts is not, as your Lordship is aware, so much to confine lunatics, as to restore to a healthy state of mind such of them as are curable, and to afford comfort and protection to the rest' (Parliamentary Papers, 1849 (620) xlvi 381 at 4.) The twin justifications of the desirability of treatment and need for protective custody are essentially paternalist. The two strands are worth distinguishing, however. The former is an essentially medical paternalism, which continues to resonate in the mental health discourse and the MHA 1983. Its attractiveness lies in its promise, accurate or not, that things will be made better for the individual.

The attractiveness is nonetheless problematic in terms of legal logic. As several commentators have pointed out (Hoggett, 1996, Price 1994) it is a *non sequitur* to hold that because a patient's condition can be said to require hospitalisation, the patient should be *forced* to enter hospital. As a matter of law, what is the public interest which justifies such extreme intervention as the confinement of an individual to effect his or her treatment or cure? There may be an economic benefit, in that the individual may, if sufficiently improved in mental state, be much more employable; but if the claim is an economic one, the benefits presumably need to be balanced against probable costs of treatment, an exercise for which few would argue. The more appealing claim has to do with doing something good for somebody, a justification based on charity. This too is problematic, however. Intervention is justified only if there is likely to be real benefit to the proposed patient; but how likely and how much benefit?

A claim that intervention is permissible on behalf of those unable to help themselves is not justified, since the standard is based on treatability, not incapacity in decision-making. These two classes are considerably different in membership. It remains a distinct problem to locate a state interest in imposing confinement for purposes of cure or assistance on people who do not lack mental capacity, and do not want the help.

These difficulties are even clearer regarding the second justification of the Commissioners. The argument for protective custody is a different sort of paternalism, a claim that even if the patient's condition will not be improved, it is an act of kindness to confine the individual. This attitude is generally absent from the Mental Health Act 1983, although it does still exist for people with mental illness or severe mental impairment who are already detained under s. 3. Renewal of such detention can be justified in part when 'the patient, if discharged, is unlikely to be able to care for himself, to obtain the care which he needs or to guard himself from serious exploitation.' (s. 20(4)). The notion of protective custody is further much diminished in the professional discourses. It does still exist in the popular discourse regarding people on the streets rightly or wrongly understood to have psychiatric difficulties, particularly when those people are begging or sleeping rough. Arguments for confinement of this class must be approached with some care. Options, perhaps including hospitalisation should be offered to these people, but it is difficult to see the state interest in using a coercive power to confine them.

The current English legislation is a conjunction of a variety of approaches. For example, a prerequisite for most confinements refers to 'the health or safety of the patient or for the protection of other persons' (MHA 1983, s. 3(2)(c); see also ss. 2(2)(b), 5(4)(a)). Criteria relating to dangerousness and therapeutic benevolence are expressly included, even in the space of a single paragraph of the statute. Defenders of the 1983 Act would claim a triumph of English pragmatism and compromise. The rationales of the approaches are markedly different, however, and they do not necessarily sit easily together. Detractors would call the statute incoherent (Price, 1994). The tensions between the various approaches will be apparent throughout the discussion which follows.

The 1983 Act is somewhat complex, and an overview in advance may be of assistance in understanding the more detailed discussion which follows. The civil confinement structure is summarized graphically in *figure 4.1*. Essentially, civil admissions may be for assessment (s. 2) or for treatment (s. 3). An admission for treatment allows the detention of the individual for up to six months for initial admission and first renewal, and for up to a year for subsequent renewals. An admission for assessment allows detention of the individual for twenty-eight days. It is not renewable. At the end of that time, the individual must either be released, continued as an informal patient, or admitted for treatment under the usual procedures for a s. 3 admission.

For admission under either s. 2 or s. 3, an application must be made by the nearest relative of the individual or, in practice much more frequently, by an approved social worker ('ASW') (see further Chapter 5). The application must in general be accompanied by certificates from two medical practitioners. There are several ways in which short-term intervention may be instituted, to allow for the assessments of the medical practitioners or social worker to be completed. First, in an emergency (s. 4) one medical certificate will suffice for an admission for assessment, so long as the second is furnished within seventy-two hours. Secondly, an informal patient may be detained for up to seventy-two hours by a doctor, or, when immediacy is necessary, up to six hours by a nurse (s. 5). A justice of the peace, upon application by an approved social worker, may require detention in a place of safety for up to seventy-two hours of mentally disordered individuals who are being ill-treated, neglected, or not kept under proper control, or who are living alone and unable to care for themselves (s. 135(1)). Finally, mentally disordered individuals found by police officers in public places may also be removed to a place of safety for up to seventy-two hours (s. 136). Prescribed forms for most of these purposes are contained in the Mental Health (Hospital, Guardianship and Consent to Treatment) Regulations 1983 (SI 1983, No. 893).

The substantive criteria differ for each of these interventions. A brief outline of these criteria, along with the basic effects of confinement under the various categories, is in *figure 4.2*. There is a curious failure of the literature to analyse in detail the meaning of these criteria. As we will see, the courts have sometimes given relatively broad interpretations to the substantive criteria. Given the intrusion into the civil liberties of those confined, however, we would respectfully argue that the statutes ought instead to be strictly construed (see *In re Dulles' Settlement* [1950] 2 All ER 1013). Careful consideration of the standards is therefore appropriate.

Figure 4.1: An Overview of Civil Confinement

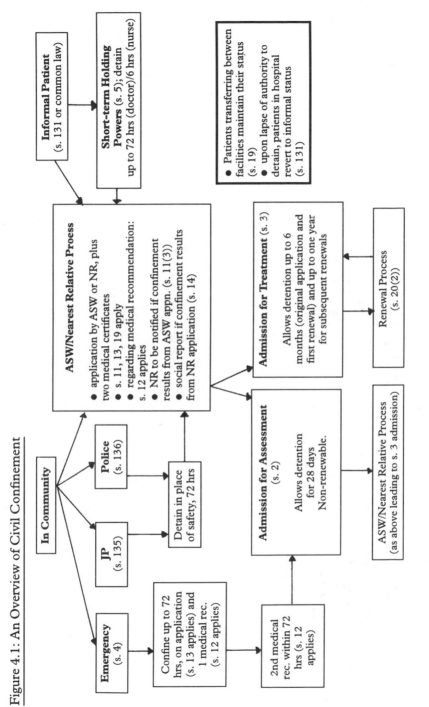

Figure 4.2: Confinement Criteria

	For Assessment	For Treatment	Emergency	Urgent In-patient	Justice of the Peace	Police
Section	2	3	4	5	135(1)	136
Mental Disorder Criteria	any mental disorder which warrants patient's detention in hospital for assessment for at least a limited period	must suffer from one of the specific categories of disorder defined in section 1, to a nature or degree which makes it appropriate to receive medical treatment in a hospital. If psychopathic disorder or mental impairment, treatment must be likely to alleviate or prevent deterioration of condition	as section 2 admission	If application by doctor, no separate criteria. If application by nurse, as s. 2 admission	any mental disorder	any mental disorder
Substantive Thresholds	Ought to be so detained in the interests of his own health or safety or with a view to the protection of other persons	Necessary for patient's health or safety, or for protection of other persons, that such treatment be provided, and it cannot be provided unless detained under this section	Compliance with section 2 would involve undesirable delay	If application by doctor, merely that application 'ought' to be made under part II regarding in-patient. If by nurse, in-patient receiving treatment for mental disorder, necessary for patients health or safety or for the protection of others that he or she be immediately restrained from leaving hospital, and not practical to refer to doctor	Has been, or is being, ill-treated, neglected or kept otherwise than under proper control; or living alone and unable to care for him/herself	In public place, and in need of immediate care and control, and necessary in the interests of the person or for the protection of other persons

	For Assessment	For Treatment	Emergency	Urgent In-patient	Justice of the Peace	Police
Section	2	3	4	5	135(1)	136
Maximum Detention Authorised	28 days, non-renewable	6 months (original certificate and first renewal); 1 year (subsequent renewal)	Absent second medical certificate, 72 hours. If second certificate, becomes s. 2 admission	By nurse: 6 hours. By doctor: 72 hours.	72 hours in place of safety	72 hours in place of safety
Treatment Rights	Treatment provisions of ss. 58 and 63 apply	Treatment provisions of ss. 58 and 63 apply	Treatment provisions of ss. 58 and 63 do not apply	Treatment provisions of ss. 58 and 63 do not apply	Treatment provisions of ss. 58 and 63 do not apply	Treatment provisions of ss. 58 and 63 do not apply
Other Notes	Discharge under s. 23 et seq. Review of detention available under ss. 66(1)(a) and 66(2)(a) within first 14 days of confinement.	Discharge under s. 23 et seq. Review of detention available under ss. 66(1)(b) and (f) and 66(2)(b) and (f), once prior to first renewal and once per renewal thereafter. Duty exists to provide aftercare under s. 117.	Discharge under s. 23 et seq.	Designed to allow assessments by ASW and doctor(s); discharge under s. 23 et seq.	Designed to allow assessment by ASW and doctor(s). No statutory provision re discharge.	Designed to allow assessment by ASW and doctor(s). No statutory provision re discharge.

4.4   DETENTION FOR ASSESSMENT OR TREATMENT: SUBSTANTIVE ISSUES

4.4.1   Admission for assessment under s. 2

The substantive criteria for admission for assessment are contained in s. 2(2) of the 1983 Act:

2(2) An application for admission for assessment may be made in respect of a patient on the grounds that—
(a)   he is suffering from mental disorder of a nature or degree which warrants the detention of the patient in a hospital for assessment (or for assessment followed by medical treatment) for at least a limited period; and
(b)   he ought to be so detained in the interests of his own health or safety or with a view to the protection of other persons.

To begin with, the patient must be suffering from 'mental disorder', in the sense of the *generic* definition in s. 1(2): see Chapter two. It is not necessary to specify the patient's condition with any greater clarity at this stage: this, after all, is the purpose of the intended assessment. The test is phrased in the present continuous ('is suffering') so that a person who has been but is no longer suffering from mental disorder is outside the scope of this section.

The section implies that this determination ought to be made prior to the confinement. This interpretation is given further credence by forms three and four of the regulations (SI 1983 No. 893), the medical recommendations upon which the confinement is based, which require the signing doctors to be of the opinion that the criteria of s. 2(2) are satisfied, including the existence of the mental disorder. This is at variance with the *obiter* view of Lloyd LJ in *R* v *Kirklees Metropolitan BC* (1993) (see 4.2) that because the definition of 'patient' in s. 145 includes a person who *appears to be* suffering from a mental disorder, admission under s. 2 would be lawful if the assessment subsequently revealed that the patient is not mentally disordered (p. 190). His Lordship held that 'Any other construction would unnecessarily emasculate the beneficial power under s. 2 and confine assessment to choice of treatment'. This is not necessarily correct, since the purpose of assessment is also, and as a prior requisite for the administration of treatment, to attain with greater precision the nature of the particular patient's mental disorder or explore avenues of treatment (Code of Practice, para. 5.2; Department of Health and Welsh Office, 1999). Many patients are in fact rediagnosed shortly after admission (Bean, 1980).

The mental disorder must be of 'a nature or degree which warrants the detention of the patient in a hospital for assessment (or for assessment followed by treatment) for a least a limited period'. The clear implication is that some types of mental disorder are *not* of a nature or degree that requires hospitalisation. However, and typically, the Act does not specify with any precision the limits of the powers given to those charged with its operation (Bean, 1986, p. 39). Nonetheless, the remainder of the section provides some guidance as to how this might be understood. Clearly, the provisions reflect a concern to safeguard the rights of mentally disordered persons from unwarranted compulsory hospitalisation. By the same token, they mean that the decision whether a patient should be admitted under s. 2 is not simply a clinical, medical one. It should also incorporate an assessment of the prospects for the patient if *not* hospitalised. Issues relevant to this assessment include the individual's home environment and the accessibility of other support networks, whether the formal provision of 'care in the community' or networks of friends and family. This is further reflected in the requirement that the ASW certify that 'detention in hospital is in all the circumstances of the case the most appropriate way of providing the care and medical treatment of which the patient stands in need' (Form 2, SI 1983 No. 893). Even if hospitalisation is required, an assessment must be made as to whether 'detention' is justified. Thus the doctors providing medical certificates in support of the application are required to provide reasons as to why informal admission is not appropriate in the circumstances (Forms 3 and 4, SI 1983 No. 893).

Under s. 2(2)(b), an individual can only be admitted if he or she 'ought to be so detained in the interests of his own health or safety or with a view to the protection of other persons'. The interpretation of this section is problematic. On the one hand, the structure of the paragraph as one continuous phrase suggests an intent that it should be read as a coherent whole. On the other, as we have seen, it is a simple disjunction of two separate justifications of confinement, beneficence and dangerousness, making such a coherent reading problematic. The difficulty becomes apparent in assessing how broadly the term 'health' is to be read. The gloss in the Code of Practice divides the health, safety and protection into three paragraphs, and italicises the 'or' between them, creating an impression that a very wide view of the health grounds would justify confinement (para. 2.6). The section itself does not do that, however. While it would be incorrect to read a dangerousness requirement as pervading all terms in the paragraph, it remains appropriate to follow the standard rule of statutory construction that items in a list modify each other to some degree. In that event, a reasonably serious risk to health would be required to justify confinement. That seems appropriate: confinement is an extreme mechanism, and ought only to be used for serious threats to the health of an individual.

The importance of this approach can be seen in considering the glosses placed on the criteria. The view of the Mental Health Act Commission, the Law Society Mental Health and Disability Committee, and the Department of Health are all that the section is broad enough to include a risk to mental health of the individual (Jones, 1999, p. 23–4). In the event of real and serious risk to the mental health of an individual, this may be a defensible position. The risk is that it will be over-used. Thus it would, for example, be a serious violation of an individual's right to make treatment decisions, if failure to take psychiatric medication routinely triggered these criteria.

4.4.2   Admission for treatment under s. 3

The criteria for admission for treatment are contained in s. 3(2):

3(2) An application for admission for treatment may be made in respect of a patient on the grounds that—

(a) he is suffering from mental illness, severe mental impairment, psychopathic disorder or mental impairment and his mental disorder is of a nature or degree which makes it appropriate to receive medical treatment in a hospital; and

(b) in the case of psychopathic disorder or mental impairment, such treatment is likely to alleviate or prevent a deterioration of his condition; and

(c) it is necessary for the health or safety of the patient or for the protection of other persons that he should receive such treatment and it cannot be provided unless he is detained under this section.

The structural similarities to s. 2 will be immediately apparent. As under s. 2, the patient must at the time of the application actually be suffering from the mental disability; but here unlike that section not any mental disability will do. Section 3 instead requires that the patient be suffering from one of the four specific sorts of mental disorder identified by s. 1(2) and, pursuant to s. 3(3)(b), each medical certificate must identify the same s. 1(2) category. It is not possible to admit a person under s. 3 on the grounds that he or she is suffering from 'any other disorder or disability of mind', as is possible under s. 2. The mental disorder must be of a nature and degree which makes it appropriate for him to receive treatment in a hospital. Analogous to the discussion of the criteria in s. 2, this would suggest that some disorders are inappropriate for hospital treatment; and as with s. 2, the assessment must be made on the basis of both clinical and social factors. It must be 'necessary' (perhaps a slightly higher threshold than 'ought' in s. 2) for the health or safety of the patient or for the protection of other persons that the treatment be given, with the attendant difficulties on how these substantive criteria are to be read. Unlike s. 2, s. 3 requires that the treatment in question could not be provided without detention under the section, and the medical certificates require reasons to be given why this is the case (Form 11, SI 1983 No. 893).

To what degree must the treatment be effective? For those with psychopathic disorders or (non-severe) mental impairment, the statute prescribes that the treatment be likely to alleviate or prevent a deterioration of the patient's condition. This has come to be known as the 'treatability test'. However, it is not clear that many psychopathic or mentally impaired individuals can be 'treated' in any conventional sense. How can treatment be expected to affect an 'arrested or incomplete development of mind', as required for a finding of mental impairment?

A similar issue arises regarding psychopaths where, as noted in Chapter 2, there is considerable dispute among doctors as to whether the condition is treatable. This divergence of opinion was noted by Lord Hope in *Reid* v *Secretary of State for Scotland* [1999] 1 All ER 481 at p. 493, a case decided under Scots law, but on principles held by the House of Lords also to be applicable to England:

Medical opinion which says that this condition is not susceptible of treatment in a hospital may be capable of being reconciled with the statute in a practical way, because those who hold to this opinion will refrain from recommending that a hospital order should be made in cases of this kind.

This is no doubt correct; but it is at best a sorry attempt to justify the statute, since it suggests that the decision as to whether an individual will be confined under the MHA 1983, or released (often to face criminal sanctions) is a function, not of the characteristics of the individual or the disorder, but instead of the doctor's belief about the treatability of psychopathy. As the patient has no right to choose a doctor upon assessment, but is instead assigned the doctor on duty, this turns basic decisions about the individual's civil rights into a lottery. It is difficult to see this as a justifiable situation.

The clearest exposition of the treatability test may be found in *R v Canons Park Mental Health Review Tribunal, ex parte A* [1994] 2 All ER 659 (CA). That case revolved around a person with psychopathic disorder, where the proposed treatment was group therapy. This of course requires the cooperation of those participating to be effective, and A refused to participate. Roch LJ, dissenting on other grounds, provided the following principles as a guide to treatability (at pp. 679–80):

First, if a tribunal were to be satisfied that the patient's detention in hospital was simply an attempt to coerce the patient into participating in group therapy, then the tribunal would be under a duty to direct discharge. Second, 'treatment in hospital' will satisfy the 'treatability test' although it is unlikely to alleviate the patient's condition, provided that it is likely to prevent a deterioration. Third, 'treatment in hospital' will satisfy the 'treatability test' although it will not immediately alleviate or prevent deterioration in the patient's condition, provided that alleviation or stabilisation is likely in due course. Fourth, the 'treatability test' can still be met although initially there may be some deterioration in the patient's condition, due for example to the patient's initial anger at being detained. Fifth, it must be remembered that medical treatment in hospital covers 'nursing and also includes care, habilitation and rehabilitation under medical supervision.' Sixth, the 'treatability test' is satisfied if nursing care etc. are likely to lead to an alleviation of the patient's condition in that the patient is likely to gain an insight into his problem or cease to be unco-operative in his attitude towards treatment which would potentially have a lasting benefit.

In *Canons Park* itself, Roch LJ held that the treatability test had been satisfied.

While the principles enunciated by Roch LJ appear innocuous enough at first glance, they are problematic. The first principle holds that detention should not be used in order to coerce consent to treatment; yet the fourth principle acknowledges that there may be an initial reluctance to consent based for example on anger at admission, and the sixth principle holds that rendering the patient cooperative in attitude toward treatment is a therapeutic objective. It is, on a practical level, difficult to see how confining a patient through the period of their initial anger with the hope of rendering them cooperative is different from the coercion prohibited by the first principle.

The breadth of 'treatment' under the 1983 Act will be discussed further in Chapter 7, but the court in *Canons Park* is not alone in adopting an expansive meaning to justify confinement. In *Reid*, the sheriff (the judicial officer hearing the case initially) held that in the structured and supervised setting of the state hospital, Reid's 'anger management' improved, and he became less aggressive. This allowed Lord Hutton to conclude that the treatability test was satisfied, on the basis that 'treatment which alleviates the symptoms and manifestations of the underlying medical disorder of a psychopath is "treatment" within the meaning of [the Act] even if the treatment does not cure the disorder itself.' (p. 514). A similar line of reasoning would, presumably, apply to those with mental incapacity.

While this escapes the difficulty of how a such a constitutional condition can be 'treated', it does so at some cost, for by focusing on symptoms and manifestations rather than the disorder itself, it emphasises the social control and policing functions of the statute.

For those diagnosed with mental illness or severe mental impairment, there is no express treatability test in s. 3. This is not an oversight. The Percy Commission had recommended that the treatability requirement apply across the board, but this suggestion was rejected on the basis that hospitalisation might offer asylum in times of crisis to some mentally ill or severely mentally impaired people, notwithstanding the untreatability of their condition (Royal Commission, 1957, para. 240). This is consistent with the conditions for renewal of s. 3 detentions, as they approach their expiry at the end of six months, where something analogous to a treatability test is included. The conditions for such renewals are contained in s. 20(4). While broadly similar to those in section 3, they do not restrict the treatability test to mental incapacity and psychopathy: s. 20(4)(b). For cases of mental illness or severe mental incapacity, however, an alternative is available to the requirement that treatment 'alleviate or prevent a deterioration' of the patient's condition (s. 20(4)):

> ... in the case of mental illness or severe mental impairment, it shall be an alternative to the condition specified in paragraph (b) above that the patient, if discharged, is unlikely to be able to care for himself, to obtain the care which he needs or to guard himself against serious exploitation.

On this reading, it would be possible to detain an individual who is not actually treatable. Particularly if an expansive definition of 'health' is adopted under s. 3(2)(c), as discussed above, these individuals will not necessarily be dangerous to self or others. While asylum may be an important option to leave open for individuals in this situation, it is less obvious that it should be imposed, using coercive powers.

There has, perhaps, been some retreat from that extreme position. In *R v Hallstrom, ex parte W (No. 2)* [1986] 2 All ER 306, the court held (at p. 315) that there must be some treatment to be given to the patient while confined in the facility:

'Admission for treatment' under s. 3 is intended for those whose condition is believed to require a period of treatment as an in-patient. It may be that such patients will also be thought to require a period of out-patient treatment thereafter, but the concept of 'admission for treatment' has no applicability to those whom it is intended to admit and detain for a purely nominal period, during which no necessary treatment will be given.

The phrase 'and his mental disorder ... makes it appropriate for him to receive treatment in a hospital' in section 3(2)(a) also leads to the conclusion that the section is concerned with those whose mental condition requires in-patient treatment.

Some hesitation may be appropriate in interpreting this case here, for the facts in that case are quite different from the current discussion. The case involved an individual detained under s. 3, on long-term leave of absence in the community. Renewal of the detention was sought to allow the mandatory treatment provisions of the 1983 Act to remain in effect in the community when the patient was, immediately, given a leave of absence. That is quite a different situation from admission to a facility where treatment is not available.

The argument based on *Hallstrom* may well be moot, for the expansive definition of treatment under s. 145 of the 1983 Act is open to be invoked: see further Chapter 7. If mere nursing constitutes treatment for purposes of ss. 3 and 20 (as it clearly does under that definition), confinement of the mentally ill or severely mentally impaired would be justified if it were appropriate that they receive some nursing care, and, if the detention is to continue beyond six months, that they are believed to be unable to care for themselves, or open to exploitation.

4.5   OTHER MECHANISMS OF CONFINEMENT: SUBSTANTIVE ISSUES

Sections 2 and 3 are the fundamental mechanisms of civil confinement under the MHA 1983. In support of them are a variety of other provisions to facilitate admissions under ss. 2 or 3 in difficult situations. These allow control to be taken of the individual, typically for up to 72 hours, to allow the processes leading to a ss. 2 or 3 admission to take place.

4.5.1   Admission of patients already in hospital

Section 5 allows an application under ss. 2 or 3 to be made in respect of an informal patient already in that hospital. In most cases, this will be used regarding an informal patient in a psychiatric ward, but the section is not formally restricted in that fashion, and it may be used to confine a patient in a different ward of the hospital, being treated for a reason other than mental disorder. The section is restricted to in-patients, however, and persons resident outside the facility but receiving treatment at out-patient clinics are beyond its scope.

The trigger of an application under s. 5 may well be the intent or attempt of an informal patient to leave the hospital. In these circumstances, there may well be insufficient time to follow the regular application processes before the patient leaves. To account for this problem, a 'holding power' is provided for doctors and nurses, giving authority to detain an in-patient who is not yet technically compulsorily admitted.

The provision relating to doctors is notably lax in its requirements. It is available only to the doctor in charge of the patient's treatment, usually a consultant psychiatrist, or in their absence, their named delegate, usually a junior doctor (s. 5(3); Hall et al, 1995). There is no separate substantive standard in the Act for the exercise of this holding power, except that the doctor thinks that an application under ss. 2 or 3 of the Act 'ought' to be made. Consistent with that, the doctor does have to provide reasons why informal status is no longer suitable: SI 1983 No. 893, form 12. The result is that the patient may be confined for 72 hours (s. 5(2)).

Nurses of the 'prescribed class' (s. 5(4),(7); see the Mental Health (Nurses) Order 1998 (SI 1998 No. 2625)), also have a holding power, of six hours' duration (s. 5(4)). Here, there are substantive criteria stated in the section. Unlike the remainder of the section, individuals subjected to this detention must actually be receiving treatment for mental disorder. In addition, it must appear to the nurse:

>   (a)   that the patient is suffering from mental disorder to such a degree that it is necessary for his health or safety or for the protection of others for him to be immediately restrained from leaving the hospital; and
>   (b)   that it is not practicable to secure the immediate attendance of a practitioner for the purposes of furnishing a report under subsection (2) above [the doctor's holding power].

Notwithstanding the similarity in wording between s. 5(4)(a) and ss. 2(2)(b) and 3(2)(b), there are significant differences. Section 5(4)(a) requires the necessity of immediate restraint, for the health or safety of the patient or the protection of others. The necessity of immediate restraint is on its face is a stricter test than 'ought' to be detained for assessment (s. 2(2)), and perhaps even than the necessity of treatment (s. 3(2)). It is certainly not a test which will be met simply because a mentally disordered patient wishes to leave the psychiatric ward at a time when no doctor is at hand. The nurse is placed in a position where he or she must make a decision on the criteria. Given the realities of hierarchy in the staffing of psychiatric wards, it may be optimistic to believe that this will be an effective decision on the criteria prescribed by the 1983 Act.

4.5.2   Emergency admission (s. 4)

Section 4(1) of the Act provides a reordering of the s. 2 process in cases of 'urgent necessity'. The application of the ASW or nearest relative requires medical certification from only one doctor, rather than two. This allows the individual to be detained in a psychiatric hospital for up to 72 hours. If a second medical certificate is provided in this period, the admission becomes a s. 2 admission.

The criteria for admission are as in s. 2, but in addition, the statement of the nearest relative or ASW must attest that the case is one of urgent necessity, and that resort to the processes of s. 2 would involve 'undesirable delay': s. 4(2). While the statute appears to place the responsibility for this matter in the hands of the applicant, the forms place it squarely on the doctor providing the medical certificate. Where the applicant's nearest relative or ASW must merely certify the urgent necessity, and the undesirable delay, the doctor must estimate the delay which would result from following the procedure in s. 2, and explain the harm which would result to the patient, those caring for the patient, or other persons (Form 7, SI 1983 No. 893).

The Code of Practice makes it clear that the provision is to be used for cases of 'genuine emergency' only, not 'administrative convenience' (para. 6.2). Interestingly, 'emergency' is understood by the Code as a function of carers to cope (para. 6.3). Evidence of an emergency includes the existence of significant risk of mental or physical harm to the patient or to others, the danger of serious harm to property, and the need for physical restraint of the patient. The Code actively discourages the use of this provision for convenience of doctors to examine the patient inside rather than outside hospitals, and ASWs unsatisfied with the unavailability of second doctors in these contexts are told to take the matter up with the relevant health authority (paras. 6.4, 6.6).

4.5.3 Powers of justices of the peace in s. 135

Section 4 will be effective in cases of urgency, when an approved social worker or nearest relative feels it necessary to act quickly. It will not be successful if an ASW lacks the information required for an application under ss. 2 or 3, nor if doctors are not given access to the patient, so as to provide the required medical certificates. In such situations, reference should be had to s. 135(1).

The substantive provisions of the subsection allow an ASW to make an application to a justice, if:

> there is reasonable cause to suspect that a person believed to be suffering from mental disorder—
> (a)   has been, or is being, ill-treated, neglected or kept otherwise than under proper control, in any place within the jurisdiction of the justice, or
> (b)   being unable to care for himself, is living alone in any such place.

On these grounds, the justice may issue a warrant for a constable, accompanied by an approved social worker and, if desired, a medical practitioner (s. 135(4)), to enter specified premises by force if necessary and, if thought fit, to remove the subject of the order to a place of safety for up to seventy-two hours, with a view to an application under part II of the Act.

The 'reasonable cause' standard in the subsection harkens back to standards of criminal law for search warrants. The social worker's belief need only be that the individual is suffering from 'mental disorder', not one of the specific types required for a s. 3 admission. It is clear from the subsection that the justification for the intervention must be protection of the subject from ill-treatment or neglect by others or by himself or herself, but the statute offers no further express guidance as to the degree of harm required to justify the order. A justification for intervention based on dangerousness here is likely to yield quite a different standard from one based on benevolence.

It is clear that removal to a place of safety will only be justified with a view to commencing proceedings under part II of the Act. Should that standard inform the degree of harm or neglect which ought to be required by the justice of the peace, prior to granting the order? The argument against such a standard would be that social workers ought to have access to people at risk of harm or neglect, even if the risk is insufficient to warrant confinement under part II, in order to inform those people of options other than involuntary hospitalisation, including home support services such as Meals on Wheels, or community care. Early intervention through this mechanism might allow the implementation of such programmes with the patient's consent, and minimise the risk of hospitalisation in the future. The argument against is that, as we have seen, coercion operates in many ways, and a forced entry to the individual's home, for example, such as might be justified by this sort of order, is bound to create an effect on the individual. There is no doubt a risk that intentionally or otherwise, an individual may feel pressured into adopting a programme which they would prefer, without the coercion, to avoid. In the event that this resulted in an informal hospital admission, the result would be a coerced hospitalisation without the criteria of part II being met, and a resulting circumvention of the safeguards of the 1983 Act.

It would appear that ss. 15 and 16 of the Police and Criminal Evidence Act 1984 (PACE) apply to warrants under this section (Jones, 1999, pp. 394) Indeed, the police powers of entry under s. 17(1)(e) of PACE 1984 provide an alternative although similar mechanism. Under this subsection, a constable may lawfully effect entry for the purposes 'of saving life or limb or to prevent serious damage to property'. Although it is clear that warrants are rarely issued under this section, it is not known how often the police are called in to use these alternative powers of entry.

4.5.4   Police powers under s. 136

As we have seen, the emergency provisions of the 1983 Act allow an expedited process on application by the nearest relative or an approved social worker. Section 135 allows access to people at risk in private places, in the event that there is no carer, or where the carer/nearest relative is being uncooperative. Section 136, by comparison, provides for situations in which intervention may be required concerning people found in public places:

> If a constable finds in a place to which the public have access a person who appears to him to be suffering from mental disorder and to be in immediate need of care or control, the constable may, if he thinks it necessary to do so

in the interests of that person or for the protection of other persons, remove that person to a place of safety within the meaning of section 135 above.

Due to the immediacy of the need to act in some situations, but unlike the other situations considered so far, there is no application process prior to intervention. Instead an on-the-spot assessment is made by the constable.

There are nonetheless standards which must be satisfied. Any mental disorder will suffice, but the individual must also be 'in immediate need of care or control', and arrest (for so it is, and therefore subject to PACE 1984: Jones, 1999, p. 398) must be 'necessary . . . in the interests of that person or for the protection of other persons'. Once again, these sections are a peculiar combination of dangerousness and beneficence themes. The requirement of immediacy of need suggests the impracticability of using one of the other admission mechanisms in the 1983 Act; it may or may not import to the standard a sense of gravitas. The requirement that arrest be 'necessary', rather than merely potentially beneficial, reflects the intrusiveness of the intervention. The clause regarding 'protection of others' (although presumably not protection of their property) resonates in a dangerousness framework, where the clause referring merely to the 'interests of the person' suggests a very wide beneficence theme, not obviously consistent with the seriousness suggested by the earlier language.

The result of intervention does little to clarify the situation. The result is detention in for up to 72 hours 'for the purpose of enabling him to be examined by a registered medical practitioner and to be interviewed by an approved social worker, and of making any necessary arrangements for his treatment or care' (s. 136(2)). Unlike the s. 135 intervention, there is no express expectation that an application under part II will be pursued.

The powers of intervention are given specifically to constables, and the ability of the police to make these decisions, and specifically to diagnose mental disorder, has been subject to strong criticism (Thomas 1986, Gostin, 1986). The concerns regarding diagnostics appear not to have been well-founded. Despite the fact that individual officers have very little training for or experience of s. 136 (Rogers, 1990), and typically have to make judgments about mental disorder on the spot with 'no advance warning' and 'little organisational back-up' (Rogers, 1990, p. 229), the evidence shows that 'the vast majority of police referrals are mentally ill and in need of treatment' (Fahy, 1989, p. 320). For example, Rogers found a 95 per cent correlation rate between assessments by the police and later professional assessments (1990, p. 232), whilst Bean (1980) in his research found that only one patient detained by the police was *not* compulsorily admitted into hospital. While these findings suggest considerable congruence between police practice and psychiatric practice, they do little to advance discussion on the appropriateness or legality of police actions with reference to the non-diagnostic criteria of the section.

Police intervention under this section is restricted to any 'place to which the public have access'. This has been given a relatively wide reading by the courts. Thus it includes the communal areas in a tenement block (*Carter v Commissioner of Police for the Metropolis* [1975] 1 WLR 507 (CA)). With this criterion, there is evidence that the use of the Act may be being extended. Rogers (1990) for example, found that 19 per cent of 'removals' made under s. 136 were not from public places.

The 72-hour detention period is a *maximum* and the detention should cease as soon as possible after the examination (which should preferably be carried out by an 'approved' doctor under s. 12(2), see Code of Practice para. 10.12), interview and necessary arrangements have occurred. The appropriate maximum for detention under this section was the subject of considerable controversy before the passage of the 1983 Act, with some (Gostin, 1975) arguing for a much shorter maximum period of detention. That it was decided to retain the 72-hour period that had pertained under the 1959 Act means that the falliblities of the system were accommodated by the legislation, at the expense of a concern for the rights of persons so detained. The present law gives rise to the fear that the need for prompt medical examination once detained is capable of being undermined; so that it is possible to be held for a considerable period of time in a police cell on the basis of a constable's 'diagnosis' of mental disorder.

Removal is, in theory to a 'place of safety' as defined by s. 135, above. As Bean has pointed out, this 'For all practical purposes . . . means a police station, for very few hospitals will accept patients on the recommendation of a police constable, and there are few "other places where the occupier is willing to temporarily receive the patient"' (Bean, 1986, p. 56, Rassaby and Rogers, 1987; Mokhtar and Hogbin, 1993).

4.6   THE CRITERIA IN ACTION

For most of the lifespan of the MHA 1959 the emergency admission section was the most frequently used compulsory power of admission. Its usage began to decrease in the 1970s (from 60 per cent of all compulsory admission in 1972 to 29 per cent in 1984), mainly as a result of implementing policies at local level to ensure the involvement of a psychiatrist in the admission procedure (Beebe, Ellis and Evans, 1973), and this decrease was given extra impetus by the passage of the 1983 Act, as the architects of that Act had intended (Barnes et al, 1990, p. 61). The latest statistics from the Department of Health (1998d) reveal that s. 4 was used in less than 7 per cent of compulsory admissions in 1996-7. It is now s. 2 which is most frequently invoked (52 per cent of admissions in 1996–7), the remainder (42 per cent) being admissions for treatment. The statistics for the use of s. 3 are significant, having risen continuously over the past decade, from 15 per cent in 1986, to 31 per cent in 1992 (Department of Health, 1998d, Table 1). In real terms, this is an increase from 2012 admissions in 1986, to 5653 in 1992, to 9247 in 1996-7.

These bare statistics hide a number of factors as Barnes, Bowl and Fisher's nationwide survey (1990) demonstrated. The most significant finding was widespread regional variation in the use of the various sections (pp.75-91). Further, Barnes, Bowl and Fisher found that the statistics for *out-patient admissions* understated the level of compulsion by around 50 per cent, as for every two out-patient admissions, one person already in hospital is either sectioned or 'promoted' from s. 2 to s. 3 status under s. 5 (p.61). To add to the confusion, Bean (1980) and Cavadino (1989) found that those operating the system (principally, psychiatrists and social workers), develop their own idiosyncrasies and preferences for the uses of a particular section, which can have little relationshipo to the formal criteria. Hence, any generalisation must be treated with caution.

Detention pursuant to s. 5(2) of patients informally in hospital was used on 9231 occasions in 1996-7, and the nurse's holding power in s. 5(4) on 1505 occasions. (Department of Health 1998d). In a variety of studies in different hospitals, s. 5(2) accounted for between 3 and 7 per cent of all compulsory admissions (see Brown, 1991; Pourgourides et al 1992; Hall et al 1995). However, it is not so much the incidence *per se* as the manner in which s. 5(2) is used which is controversial. Bean (1980, p. 147) found evidence that patients would be admitted informally and then quickly placed on a 'section 30' (now s. 5(2)). More recent research indicates that this practice continues fairly unabated, despite the clear advice of the Code of Practice, para. 8, and especially para. 8.9. In Hall et al's recent year-long study of 61 consecutive admissions under s. 5(2) at one hospital, on 23 occasions (38 per cent of the total) the holding powers were invoked within 24 hours of the patient's informal admission (1995, p. 233). Similar findings were made by Joyce et al (1991) (38 per cent within 24 hours) and Brown (1991) (33 per cent within 24 hours). Of those held under s. 5, 43 per cent revert to informal status at the end of the 72-hour period, and the remainder divide roughly evenly between s. 2 and s. 3 admissions (Department of Health, 1998d, Table 7)

These figures are of course open to interpretation. Hall et al (1995) argue that the high incidence of the use of these powers following the admission of informal patients 'may indicate, for example, that there is a genuine clinical need for a short period of detention at times of particular crisis in some conditions' (p. 235). Concern has been registered elsewhere, however, that the doctor's confinement power under s. 5 is a 'trial period' of compulsory detention (Bean and Mounser, 1993). That is clearly an abuse, since the subsection is expressly intended to provide a window to allow an application elsewhere under the 1983 Act.

The incidence of coercion in informal confinement has been discussed. Even for those persons who remain in hospital on an informal basis at the expiry of the 72 hours, it is reasonable to speculate that the use of the s. 5(2) or s. 5(4) power might well be perceived by the patient as a coercive act, severely restricting the reality of their option to leave the facility. Much research has shown that around 50 per cent of in-patients are unaware of their legal status (see Monahan et al, 1995, for a review), and thus the voluntary nature of the informal status of many of these patients is rendered suspect.

Although numbers are now declining, about 10 per cent of compulsory confinements result from the police powers in s. 136 (Department of Health, 1995d). These official statistics must be treated with caution for at least three reasons.

First, as there is considerable variation between jurisdictions and practitioners regarding ss. 2 and 3, there is similarly vast regional variation in the use of s. 136. In particular, recourse to s. 136 in Greater London is markedly greater than elsewhere. The Thames Regional Health Authorities were responsible for 90 per cent of s. 136 assessments in 1984 (Spence and McPhillips, 1995, p. 48). Bean (1986, p. 58) says that if one goes by official statistics, 'the use of section 136 is almost confined to the Metropolitan District in London'. As long ago as 1965 Rollins claimed that London was 'the sump into which the chronic psychotics from all over the United Kingdom, and indeed, farther afield, [were] drained' (cited in Spence and McPhillips, 1995, p. 48). By the same token, in many police areas s. 136 powers seem to be virtually obsolete.

Secondly, the official statistics may obscure the fact that some police forces act in the manner contemplated by s. 136 without actually invoking the section or making a record of its use (Fahy, 1989). It is not known how many persons arrested by the police are subsequently released without being admitted to hospital under part II or s. 131 of the Act (Bean, 1986, p. 58). The relationship between the police, social services and psychiatric professionals seems to be negotiated locally. Bean recounts how in Nottingham in the 1980s the practice was that the police, on arresting a person suspected to be suffering from mental disorder, would first contact a psychiatrist. Whether an ASW was contacted depended on the psychiatrist's diagnosis. If the psychiatrist decided against compulsory detention, the patient was either charged (usually with a minor offence) or released. As Bean says, 'Section 136 was being used — but not in the manner prescribed by legislation. No patient was officially recorded as being detained yet, in all other respects, section 136 was used in the manner legally prescribed' (Bean, 1986, p. 56).

Given the potential for wide regional variation (further examples are documented in Bean, 1986, Chapter five), then, it is virtually impossible to decide with any certainty how the police do in fact deal with mentally disordered persons 'found' in public places. However, from the fact that there is widespread regional variation, coupled with research which shows that it is common police practice to carry out stop and search procedures that are not 'officially' recorded as required by PACE Guidelines (McKenzie et al, 1990), it *can* be stated with a fair degree of certainty that the official picture will be under-representative of the actual use of these powers. This in turn problematises *any* finding derived from the recorded use of s. 136: things may be worse (or better) than they appear to be.

Thirdly, the use of s. 136 is in any event somewhat arbitrary, in the sense that its invocation does not depend solely on the officer's assessment of the mental health of the person in question, but rather this consideration is weighed against the behaviour of the person in question. In general terms, if a criminal offence has been committed the officer is less likely to invoke the section, and the more serious the offence, the less likely is it that s. 136 will be used (Bean, 1980). Other factors, such as the relationship between the police and the other relevant agencies at the local level, and the alternatives to use of s. 136, both formal and informal (availability of family members to take care of their relative and so on), also affect the decision whether to take the person into custody. Rogers (1990, p. 231) found that police stations in neighbouring areas responded to the attitude of their local magistrates' court, so that in an area in which magistrates disapproved of the bringing before a court of an obviously mentally disordered person, s. 136 was much more frequently used (Rogers, 1990, p. 231).

Many comparable factors apply, of course, to other compulsory admission powers, and specific extraneous factors seem to have an effect in determining the method of admission. Mokhtar and Hogbin (1993, p. 192), for example, found that if family members were involved, admission was by s. 4 or s. 2; but in no s. 136 arrest situation was a relative present.

4.6.1 Race and psychiatric detention

The detention criteria and their application have different impacts on different segments of the population. Black people from the Caribbean, and particularly men of this group, are statistically over-represented in the detention statistics, and the disparity increases with the level of coercion. Flannigan et al's (1994) study of inner London in the early 1990s, found that black Caribbean people comprised 23 per cent of the hospital psychiatric population in South Southwark, and 16 per cent in Hammersmith and Fulham, being respectively 2.1 and 2.9 times their prevalence in the population of those districts as a whole. Both white people, and persons of other ethnic backgrounds were confined in smaller percentages than their prevalence in the population. Where white people were admitted informally in 80 per cent of cases, black people from the Caribbean were admitted informally only 55 per cent of the time. Instead, they were compulsorily detained under ss. 2 or 3 twice as frequently as whites (35 per cent as compared with 17 per cent for whites), and under the emergency power of s. 4 three times as frequently (10 per cent rather than 3 per cent for whites: Bebbington et al, 1994; see also Pilgrim and Rogers, 1993).

These findings are consistent with other research. Bean et al (1991) found that people of Afro-Caribbean origin were two and a half times as likely to be the subject of a s. 136 arrest as others living in the same area, and that this likelihood was increased for young males. In Rogers's research (1990) Afro-Caribbean people were twice as likely to be referred under this section as others, and again the discrepancy was greater still for young males (p. 233). These findings are further consistent with research carried out into the use by the police of their stop and search powers under PACE and other legislation (Jefferson, 1988, Norris et al, 1992), and taken at face value would seem to be good evidence of discriminatory police practice.

Predictably, this disproportion has generated considerable controversy. It has been alleged by some that the police use s. 136 as a 'mental health sus law' (Black Health Workers and Patients' Group, 1983); that it is used in a discriminatory fashion; and that although the section repeats the *parens patriae* police powers pattern of the part II admission sections, its purpose is social control rather than assistance for persons with mental health problems. Similar arguments are made, although generally with somewhat less vehemence, about admissions under the other detention sections of the 1983 Act.

Certainly, express or implied racial bias in the mental health and law enforcement systems is one possible explanation for the over-representation of black people, but there are others. If one adopts a medical model, specific types of mental illness may be particularly prevalent in black communities, as are certain types of physical illness such as sickle cell anaemia. Even if one does not adopt a medical model, other factors such as pressures related to minority status might well be expected to increase mental disorder. Alternatively, cultural factors which minimise health care facilities for black people, or trust in health care professionals by black people, might be expected to result in a move away from informal admission toward confinement, and confinement through police intervention rather than GP or other medical route. Predictably, these bases are hotly disputed (see Littlewood, 1992 for a summary of the literature).

There is certainly evidence that race can be a factor in how doctors perceive patients. Using standardised case-vignettes with the race of the subject varied, a study by Loring and Powell in America showed a marked increase in willingness of American psychiatrists to diagnose schizophrenia, predict dangerousness and advocate confinement in the cases of black people than of white people in otherwise similar scenarios. While the rate of diagnosis of schizophrenia per 100,000 population for black people is almost double the rate for white people, (Bebbington et al, 1994, p. 743), English studies would suggest that this is not a function of race, but of other factors (Littlewood, 1992; Lewis et al, 1990) Other aspects of the American study have been replicated here, however. Lewis et al used a similar methodology to the Loring study, concluding that the race of the patient influenced clinical predictions and attitudes of British psychiatrists, to the degree that a stereotype could be extracted (1990, p. 413):

> This stereotype consists of an illness of short duration, more likely to lead to violence, in which criminal proceedings are slightly more appropriate, and in which neuroleptic medication is less likely to be necessary. It most easily fits the rubric of brief/acute reactive psychosis and may be especially strong in a male patient.

Such a finding is perhaps unsurprising. Similar stereotypes unfortunately exist more broadly in society; there is no obvious reason to suspect that psychiatrists will be mystically immune to such influences.

These broader biases may be significant in the apparent over-use of s. 136. In Rogers's survey, police initiated contact in only 8 per cent of the cases where the individual was subsequently arrested. Instead, the process was instigated in 42 per cent of instances by passers-by, in 15 per cent by neighbours and 13 per cent by members of the referee's family (1990, p. 228). The police, in other words, are cast in a *reactive* role, and so cannot be held responsible for the characteristics of those detained. Consistent with broader social prejudice, Rogers (1990, p. 233) also found that Afro-Caribbeans were more often referred by strangers and passers-by, and less often referred by friends or relatives, than other groups. Rogers concludes that 'this entails the police acting as a "conveyor belt" for community prejudices due to public perceptions of black people's deviant behaviour constituting a threat to public law and order'.

Similar complicating factors exist for other civil confinements. The study of Soothill et al of compulsory admissions in Birmingham and Lancaster show well over half as originating in the home (Soothill et al, 1990, p. 183). While this study is not restricted to black patients, it does serve as a reminder that doctors are not the only actors in the system.

There are other indications that simple medical bias may not be central to the disproportion of admissions of black people. The Bebbington study of inner London did not support that ethnicity *per se* was a factor in confinement, instead finding that 'the two major factors independently associated with compulsory admission are diagnosis of schizophrenia and challenging behaviour' (Bebbington, 1994, p. 748). This study, like the ones cited above, does not support a claim of misdiagnosis based on racial factors.

The reasons for the high diagnosis rate for schizophrenia have been the subject of considerable discussion. Some of these explanations place the social understanding of race as a factor both in the definition and prevalence of the diagnosis. Others do not. Eagles (1991) provides an array of medical alternatives to psycho-social models. Of particular interest for current purposes, the over-representation of cases is, according to some research, based in a specific subcategory. The study by Thomas et al shows that Afro-Caribbeans born abroad were in fact less likely than whites to be confined. The disproportion was in black people born in this country (Thomas et al, 1993, p. 94). This is significant not merely for epidemiological reasons, but also because of the implications for theories centred on racist practice: it is difficult to believe that racially discriminatory attitudes on the part of doctors, social workers, and the police would distinguish between individuals of the same race born in the UK and those born abroad.

In this context, the difference in admission mechanisms and the apparent over use of s. 136 might be seen to relate not to behaviour of doctors, but cultural factors among black people, and particularly black men. A hesitation to approach existing medical services, for example, might reasonably be expected to create a shift away from physician-led admission to police-led processes. Only 41 per cent of those in Spence and McPhillips's study were registered with a GP, for example (1995, p. 49). In Mokhtar and Hogbin's study s. 136 admissions were less likely than s. 4 admissions to have previously used social and community mental health services. The introduction of a physician at the relatively late stage of hospitalisation may limit the possibilities of negotiation and extra-legal coercion which, as we have seen, can result in informal admission. Consistent with this model of black people avoiding the system, Mokhtar and Hogbin defend s. 136 as 'a valuable "back up" for those who would otherwise fall through the net and fail to benefit from the Mental Health Act'. They call for an expansion of its use on the grounds that there is a 'hidden group' who are not using mental health community services and who are not being picked up by the police (1993, p. 195).

The over-representation of black people is thus problematic. Certainly, on therapeutic bases, it does seem that the typical s. 136 'customer' does seem in need of some help, and that as a group such people are typically reluctant to seek help at an early stage. At the same time, the failure of black people to make contact with existing medical and community mental health services voluntarily seems to suggest that current society has not yet found a selection of services which this community considers appropriate. That suggests a failure in health care policy, and it would seem deeply offensive to use the rather crude power of civil confinement rather than address that systemic problem.

Issues of race have attracted considerable discussion in a mental health context not merely because of the political and social implications that are contained in those arguments, but also because of the broader social attention to issues of racism. This does not mean that Afro-Caribbean blacks are the only people who could raise challenging questions about the system of confinement. The Irish, for example, are confined twice as frequently as black people (Pilgrim and Rogers, 1993). This has attracted minimal academic attention, presumably in part because issues of discrimination against the Irish do not have the political cachet of racial issues. The issue here is not to minimalise the importance of the racial questions; it is rather that the field must be expanded to ask comparable questions in the system more broadly.

The typical profile of the person detained in psychiatric facilities straddles a number of 'problem populations' who have historically been the target of social control strategies. The probability of detention is heightened by being young, male, unemployed, single and homeless (see e.g., Rogers and Faulkner, 1987; Spence and McPhillips, 1995; Thomas et al, 1993). There is a real sense in which the problems discussed here raise questions of housing and social policy (see further the discussion of community care provision in Chapter nine) as much as of mental health policy. To advocate increased use of the police as the appropriate response is therefore deeply problematic.

These additional factors are particularly problematic when, like race, they do not have an obvious justification under criteria such as dangerousness, therapeutics, or beneficence. Thus in Spence and McPhillips's research into assessments under s. 136 carried out at the Gordon Hospital at Westminster, it seems as though the police had a more pro-active policy towards s. 136 than that found by Rogers (in North East London). In their research 9 per cent of arrestees were taken from Thames bridges and 17 per cent from central London railway stations (p. 49), suggesting that the police in this area use s. 136 as one mechanism for keeping central London 'presentable' to tourists (p. 50). Westminster is also unusual in that the Gordon Hospital, unlike many other hospitals which refuse so to be designated, is the 'place of safety' for London SW1. Yet to implicate this area goes some little way towards implicating the use of s. 136 in general, given that it is London that sees most use of the section.

4.7   OTHER OPTIONS?

The English Act has its problems. As we have seen, the criteria reflect divergent and conflicting theoretical bases. There is no over-riding theoretical justification provided for confinement, but instead a collection of two centuries of statutory tinkering. Its apologists would argue that it works, at least most of the time. Its detractors would point to its lack of clarity: that it is difficult to tell whether it works, since it is difficult to tell what it is intended to do.

Arguments either way must be taken in the context of other options. It is not possible here to provide a detailed survey and analysis of hospitalisation world-wide. Instead, brief discussions will be presented of other approaches to confinement of the insane.

4.7.1 Dangerousness

Many North American jurisdictions have essentially admitted the policing function of civil confinement, with the adoption of a dangerousness standard. The Ontario legislation provides a particularly good example of such an approach (R.S.O. 1990, c. M-7):

15(1)   Where a physician examines a person and has reasonable cause to believe that the person,
   (a)   has threatened or attempted or is threatening or attempting to cause bodily harm to himself or herself;
   (b)   has behaved or is behaving violently towards another person or has caused or is causing another person to fear bodily harm from him or her; or
   (c)   has shown or is showing a lack of competence to care for himself or herself,
and if in addition the physician is of the opinion that the person is apparently suffering from mental disorder of a nature or quality that likely will result in,
   (d)   serious bodily harm to the person;
   (e)   serious bodily harm to another person; or
   (f)   imminent and serious physical impairment of the person,
the physician may make application in the prescribed form for a psychiatric assessment of the person.

The specificity of the subsection is significant: it tells the doctor specifically what to look for, as compared with the much vaguer set of English criteria. It is only likelihood of bodily harm or impairment which will justify confinement, and an express causal relationship is included between the mental disorder and the harm in question. The first half of the subsection further requires some concrete reason to believe that such harm or impairment is likely to occur: a diagnosis on its own will not suffice. Beneficence and possibility of treatment are conspicuously absent.

While the criteria, apart from the requirement of a diagnosis of mental disorder, appear untherapeutic, the process in Ontario as in most North American jurisdictions is doctor-driven: there is no role in confinement for the nearest relative, or a non-medical expert such as a social worker. Consultation with such individuals is usual as a matter of policy at some time prior to or during the confinement, but it is not required. In addition, only one medical certificate is required for confinement. Thus while the criteria appear complex, the process is arguably less bureaucratic than its English counterpart; and while they appear less medical, they are still essentially doctor-centred.

Unlike England and most jurisdictions in the United States, the Ontario criteria have no effect on treatment: in Ontario, legal ability to consent to or refuse treatment and selection of a substitute decision-maker in the event of incapacity are based on mental capacity, irrespective of status in or out of hospital. The state police interest in confinement is thus separated from therapeutic matters. The Ontario system in this regard seems more theoretically satisfying than the American norm. The justification for confinement is protection from dangerousness; once that purpose is met through the confinement, there is no obvious justification for further violation of rights through denial of treatment rights.

The Ontario system, like most North American systems, further requires renewal of the confinement more frequently. The initial certificate is valid for 72 hours, (s. 15(5)(b)) and subsequent certificates for periods from one week to three months (s. 20(4)). This is significant since in Ontario as in England, only one challenge of each certificate may be made to the review tribunal, so the frequency of renewal dictates the frequency of rights to review. In practice, psychiatric drugs have remarkably speedy efficacy, suggesting that the Ontario legislation may be more defensible than the English in this regard.

As a theoretical matter, the Ontario system has much to recommend it. The legal justification of confinement is generally clear — the state's police interest, with admittedly some beneficence encroachment with the provisions regarding self-harm by the patient — and the standards are similarly unambiguous. Unfortunately, there are practical problems with the implementation of this sort of system.

The clearest problem is that dangerousness is notoriously difficult to predict, particularly beyond the short term. Studies generally find that between one-half and three-quarters of those identified as dangerous by psychiatric professionals do not, in the end, turn out to be violent (studies are surveyed in Bowden, 1996, Monahan, 1988, Monahan, 1981). The civil liberties difficulties are apparent. With other police powers of the state, criminal law being the obvious example, it would be simply unacceptable that the detention of more than half the people confined turned out to be unwarranted. If the justification for psychiatric confinement, as in the dangerousness model, is a similar police power of the state, it is not obvious why a different standard ought to apply (see generally Dershowitz, 1970, Crawford, 1984).

This difficulty of prediction explains the two-step criteria in the Ontario legislation, which requires some behaviour to justify the belief in the risk to the patient or others. The initial set of criteria is to protect against such over-prediction.

Some more recent studies would indicate that various actuarial factors may improve predictive abilities somewhat (see Monahan and Steadman, 1994). The difficulty is that many of these factors are divorced from mental illness. West for example concludes that actuarial evidence based on factors such as sex, age, marital status, and criminal record are 'generally more efficient than clinical judgments of attitude, personality or mental state' at predicting future crimes involving sexual molestation (West, 1996, p. 55). Yet the premise of mental health legislation is that confinement prior to criminal act is justified by issues of mental disability, not demographic characteristic. In the Ontario legislation quoted above, for example, an express causal connection is included between the mental disorder and the bodily harm or impairment predicted, and the move from that nexus to the inclusion of other factors is problematic. Men are statistically far more violent than women, but it creates considerable civil rights difficulties to use gender as a predictive variable to justify psychiatric confinement, even in conjunction with other factors.

The expansion of factors further highlights the question of whether prediction of dangerousness is an appropriate medical function. This has always been an issue: it seems clear that doctors are no better at predicting dangerousness than other people, nor do they restrict themselves in this regard to medical criteria (see, e.g., Montadon and Harding 1984, and studies cited therein). The use of doctors to administer the confinement processes in North America is thus suspect. The issue is not simply one of expertise, but also conflict of interest. Doctors are trained to work in a therapeutic frame of reference. It is difficult to see that such a framework could fail to influence their decisions regarding confinement, undercutting the implementation of the dangerousness standard. While symbolically significant in distinguishing mental health law from other state police functions, the use of doctors to administer the confinement process may thus serve to undercut the dangerousness standard which serves as the justification of confinement.

It must also be said that the results are not problem-free. In so far as the over-representation of black people in the civil confinement structure is understood as a civil rights issue, for example, it is equally an issue in American jurisdictions (see, for example, Lawson et al, 1994 and studies cited therein) This is unsurprising, given the findings discussed above that psychiatrists are more likely to perceive black people as dangerous; but it does mean that the civil rights problem does not disappear due to a change in the criteria.

Finally, it is appropriate to acknowledge the symbolic importance of dangerousness as the confinement criterion. Notwithstanding public perceptions to the contrary, the mentally disordered as a whole are not much more likely to be dangerous than the remainder of the population. Confinement criteria arguably have a symbolic effect well beyond their proportion of those confined. Would the use of the dangerousness standard re-enforce the incorrect public stereotype of the mentally disordered as actually dangerous?

4.7.2   The Stone system

North American psychiatrists are not unaware of the contradictory roles they are expected to perform when dangerousness is the criterion for admission (see, e.g., Roth, 1979). Their concern tends to be less with the integrity of the dangerousness criteria themselves, than with their role as therapeutic professionals. They dislike being recast in a police function, arguing that this undermines both professional dignity and the therapeutic relationship with their patients. Rather than arguing for their removal as administrators of the confinement process, however, these psychiatrists tend to argue for a different standard, based on therapeutic criteria.

Therapeutic justifications for confinement import quite a different theoretical framework, with different corollaries. Most significant for present purposes, confinement on therapeutic criteria is generally seen to go along with forced treatment during confinement, since it seems bizarre to confine on the basis of treatability, and then not treat. This is a clear difference from a dangerousness standard where, as we have seen, enforced treatment does not necessarily flow from confinement.

The challenge in this context is to develop criteria which, while therapeutic, are justifiable violations of the rights of the person confined. We do not impose treatment on people for physical disease or disorders; without reference to the police power of the state, why should we impose psychiatric treatment?

One justification is found in the attitudes of the patients after the fact. A significant proportion of civilly confined patients, even if objecting to confinement when it occurred, reported finding the confinement broadly beneficial following discharge. In a study by Edelsohn and Hiday (1990), 55 per cent of civilly committed patients objected at the time of admission, but after the fact only 31 per cent felt the confinement unjustified. In a study by Kane in 1983, roughly two thirds of the civilly confined people who objected to confinement at the time, reported at discharge that their commitment was fortunate. (For further discussion of these and similar studies, see Monahan et al (1995) and Hiday (1992).) If intervention were able to be restricted to these individuals who subsequently agreed with its appropriateness after the fact, surely that would not violate civil rights?

American psychiatrist Alan Stone attempted to develop a therapeutically based, but rights aware, set of admission criteria in the mid-1970s. Under Stone's criteria, confinement would be justified only if all the following criteria were met:

(a)   a reliable diagnosis of severe mental disorder must be made;
(b)   the immediate prognosis must be one of major distress;
(c)   an effective treatment must exist;
(d)   the patient must offer incompetent refusal of treatment;
(e)   the proposed treatment must be reasonable (i.e., the reasonable patient would consent).

The criteria are designed to mix the gravitas which is appropriately a prerequisite for state intervention (severe mental disorder, immediate major distress), with selection of individuals who can actually be assisted by the mental health system (effective treatment must exist). The treatment refusals of mentally competent patients are to be respected and will serve as a bar to confinement; and there is a reality check to treatment desirability in the objective 'reasonable patient' test.

Stone's criteria, like the dangerousness test, are problematic in practice. Psychiatry is not an exact science, and reliability of diagnosis occurs only in a minority of cases (Crawford, 1984, p. 143, and studies cited therein). Equally problematic in practice are the value judgments contained in the conditions.

'Severe' disorders, 'major' distress, and 'effective' treatment are all highly subjective, and thus militate against patient challenge and correspondingly against patient rights. 'Incompetent' refusal and 'reasonable' consent as concepts have large legal and medical literatures of their own. They are thus more readily assumed into a patient rights framework; but they are also highly problematic in application.

Many of these problems are more appropriately discussed elsewhere in this volume; suffice it here to say that for the apparent protections to patient rights to be real, the administration of the system might become unwieldy. Enforcement of the criteria cannot depend on patient intervention, since the patient is expected to lack treatment capacity. It therefore cannot be assumed that the patient is in a position to press for his or her rights. Protections must be built in, to ensure the criteria are met as a matter of routine. Truly independent medical diagnoses would be necessary to ensure the reliability of the diagnosis. The doctor(s) recommending treatment would presumably not do so unless they thought a reasonable patient would consent to it. Consistent with this, in Hoge et al's study (1989, p. 172) of implementation of Stone, in a sample of 483 treatments, not a single doctor recommending treatment thought a reasonable patient would refuse it. Independent involvement would also be necessary at this stage, if the criterion is to provide meaningful protection. As will be seen below, a similar argument can be made regarding determination of treatment competence. The result is likely to be a highly complex administrative structure. That may be appropriate: civil confinement is a serious intervention, after all. It is not, however, likely to meet with political success in times of economic restraint; nor is it likely to meet with the approval of doctors, who tend to prefer the practice of medicine to administration.

Interestingly, the studies would suggest that it would result in a decrease, rather than an increase, in confinements, relative to the dangerousness test. Hoge et al (1989, p. 173) found that barely more than half of the people who would be likely to be confined under Massachusetts' current dangerousness standard would be confined under Stone. Their study did not include the procedural protections of various administrators assessing for the different criteria above, suggesting that with appropriate safeguards, the numbers might be even lower. Again, this is not necessarily a problem, since there is no reason to believe that the success of a model is directly proportional to the number of people confined under it; it does suggest that one cannot assume that therapeutic criteria, when civil rights protections are included, will result in high committal rates.

More problematic is that no study seems to have assessed whether the persons who would be confined under the Stone system are the patients who would go on to believe that their confinement had been beneficial. The structure of the criteria seem designed to select out these individuals, making this a reasonable speculation; but hard evidence is currently lacking.

4.8   CONCLUSIONS

Our discussion of the issues raised in this chapter reveals the complexity of the issues involved. Various points, however, do emerge. First, there is no rigid distinction between the informal and the compulsorily detained patient. Whether one is admitted under a 'section' or informally is dependent on a whole host of variables, to do with issues of time and resources, social status, age, gender and race, the power dynamics of the relationship between the patient, psychiatrist, second opinion doctor, ASW and the patient's relatives (we examine further some of these relationships in the next Chapter). Informal admission does not necessarily imply the patient's consent, nor does compulsory admission necessarily imply the patient's refusal to consent (although this is more often the case). Bean found that 'Most of the compulsory patients gave passive resistance, and most of the voluntary patients actively or passively surrendered' (1980, p. 120). The majority of patients who are compulsorily admitted (certainly under ss. 2 and 4) stay in hospital after the expiry of the section, although compulsory powers will often come back into play if the patient attempts to leave hospital. The legal status of the patient is in practice virtually an arbitrary factor.

The foundation of this edifice of ambiguities is similarly uncertain. The legal standards of confinement offer no clear interpretive framework, and the courts in this century have adopted a remarkably *laissez-faire* attitude to interpretation. Standards have in practice moved out of the legal arena, into the professional realm, raising considerable questions about the rule of law in this area. These questions are particularly important, given the civil rights implications of confinement.

It is to professional practice that we must turn to understand the application of the 1983 Act; yet it is very hard to generalise about this area of law. Widespread regional variation in application and idiosyncrasies of the actors involved defy any attempt to theorise in a predictive sense. The very notion of 'a system' does not capture sufficiently the federal nature of mental health provision. Each location in which services are provided or in which the 1983 Act operates is itself a fairly autonomous system in numerous ways (in the power given to consultant psychiatrists and the discretion given to ASWs for example), even if these micro-systems are subject to 'interference' from each other and to restraint from outside in the form of central policy and resourcing, or its absence.

It is to these relationships, both as prescribed in the 1983 Act and in so far as possible as they operate in practice, that we turn in the next chapter.

FIVE

The process of civil confinement

5.1 INTRODUCTION

The compulsory admission of a person into a psychiatric facility is not only a question of diagnosis or of moral justification for the confinement of the dangerous. It is also a matter of compliance with a detailed legal process. On its face, the MHA 1983 sets up a relatively straightforward scheme. An application for admission to hospital must be addressed to the managers of the hospital in question, and can only be made by an 'approved social worker' (ASW) or the 'nearest relative' (NR) of the person to be confined. Such applications must be 'founded on' two medical recommendations, although one will suffice in an emergency. Completion of the necessary paperwork gives legal authority to the applicant to convey the person to be admitted to the hospital in question, and provided that the receiving officer of the hospital is satisfied that the relevant paperwork appears to be in order, the hospital is then legally empowered to detain the subject of the application in the hospital.

The practice is not quite so straightforward. The Court of Appeal has held that as long as the various requirements of the admissions process have been complied with, an admission will not be unlawful if compliance was not in the chronological sequence implied in the statute. Hence, although an application must be 'founded on' the necessary medical recommendations, the application documents can be completed before the medical recommendations have been given: *Whitbread* v *Kingston and District NHS Trust* (1997) *The Times*, 14 July. This is a problematic reading of the MHA 1983, as 'founded on' does seem to imply that the application should follow the necessary medical recommendations. It also raises due process considerations, as it allows the possibility that an applicant for admission can certify that the *medical* criteria for admission are met without first having that opinion corroborated by doctors. Yet it also reflects the fact that the social processes that lead to the compulsory confinement of a person in a psychiatric hospital are dynamic rather than linear, and the various actors involved may inter-relate in a variety of ways. Moreover, there are more potential actors involved in the admissions process than indicated on the face of the MHA 1983. An admission to hospital under part II will involve some combination of: the patient; his or her relatives, carers, friends and neighbours; ASWs or other social workers; community psychiatric nurses (CPNs); psychiatrists and other doctors, particularly GPs; and police officers. The MHA 1983, the accompanying Code of Practice (Department of Health and Welsh Office, 1999) and the Memorandum on the Act (Department of Health and Welsh Office, 1998), contemplate that it will be possible for those involved to work together effectively. Yet there is reason to think that this is not always easily possible. The various professionals involved will each, to some extent at least, be a product of their professional training and this will be reflected in the perspective through which the admissions process is viewed. The attitude of relatives, friends and other non-professionals will also vary according to numerous factors. Some NRs, for example, may actively seek hospitalisation while others may oppose it. Some may act in what they believe to be the best interests of the patient; others may not. Those to be admitted will also vary in their attitude to that prospect. Of course the consent of the patient is not required for an admission under part II, and from a civil libertarian perspective, there is a risk that the voice of the patient will be drowned out by those of the others involved. Given all of the permutations which this dynamic process allows, and add the fact that such tensions are set within a broader framework in which control of both personal freedom and professional territory and status are at stake, it is apparent that there is as much likelihood of discord as there is of harmony.

In seeking to work through these issues, this Chapter will open with a brief consideration of the background against which the formal admissions process must function. It will then turn to the role given by law to ASWs and NRs, before considering how the admissions process is intended to work, how it does in fact work, and how it is limited in its effectiveness by its multidisciplinary nature. Finally, some space is given over to the question of how a legally flawed admission may be challenged by or on behalf of the patient.

5.2 THE CONTEXT OF ADMISSION UNDER PART II

5.2.1 How do its patients come to the attention of the mental health system?

Soothill et al concluded from their international survey into the source of referral for mentally disordered patients in six countries that 'a picture emerges of individuals troubled by mental illness over a considerable period, in whom a crisis or breaking point is reached in their own homes, and who are admitted to hospital for several weeks' (1981, p. 343). In a later replication study analysing data from two hospitals in a seventh country (England) this conclusion was fortified (Soothill et al, 1990a). Of 103 compulsory new admissions analysed in the English study, around 55 per cent of referrals in both hospitals (which covered very different catchment areas in socio-economic terms) were from the patient's home. This was lower than the international survey (69 per cent) but was still easily the most frequent source of admissions. Of the remainder, just under 20 per cent were referred from another hospital; just over 20 per cent from the police and courts (although this was more marked in one hospital, at 22 per cent, than the other, at 13 per cent). One person in each hospital was referred from a public place (1990a, p. 183). These findings are broadly in line with those of from number of other studies (Huxley, 1985, Chapter 1).

Of those patients referred from their own homes, a number initiate the admission process themselves by self-referral to their GPs, even if this is not always with a formal psychiatric complaint (Huxley, 1985, p. 9). It is a common research finding that GPs vary in their knowledge of psychiatry and ability to detect mental health problems (see Bean, 1980). In Goldberg and Huxley's research (discussed in Huxley, 1985, p. 9), GPs' non-detection of mental disorder, and decision even when a disorder was suspected not to refer the patient to a psychiatrist, constituted the largest filter of potential compulsory admission, with 230 consulters being reduced down to only 17 referrals. If following a GP's referral a psychiatrist takes the view that the patient should be compulsorily detained, then an ASW will become involved and the formal process of application for admission will begin.

Other sources of first referral are the family and relatives of the patient, and, less frequently, neighbours and friends. These, put together with self-referrals, either via a GP and psychiatrist or, less often, straight to a local authority social services department (SSD), tend to account for 40 to 50 per cent of patients brought to the attention of an ASW, although in some studies self-referral is more common than referral by relatives, in others the reverse is true. There are examples in the research of fairly low referral rates from these 'informal' sources, according to variables such as whether the person referred lived alone or not, and whether the process was initiated as a result of violence on behalf of the person to be admitted (Gondolf et al, 1991), with a correspondingly higher referral rate through the primary and secondary health care systems, or from the police. The rate of self-referral would seem, as Soothill et al (1990b) argued, to render problematic the claim that compulsory detention is 'about' social control. For such persons, the picture here accords much more closely with the medical model, of persons recognising themselves as 'ill' and seeking treatment from the 'health' services. Indeed, it is no easy matter to be detained. Barnes, Bowl and Fisher (1990, p. 13) found that 'for every 7 people detained, 3 are referred for the use of compulsion but not so detained'. In Bean's study there were 125 non-admissions out of 325 cases considered for admission (1980, p. 174). However, although in one study self-referral accounted for 33 per cent of the total, the more usual figure is around 12 to 18 per cent (see Appelbaum, 1985). This means that around 80 per cent of compulsorily admitted patients are admitted as a result of some other person taking the initiative in seeking 'help'.

5.2.2 Who is Admitted?

Not surprisingly, it is those who show obvious signs of severe disorder who are most likely to be 'diagnosed' as mentally disordered by laypersons (including GPs), to be referred by a GP, to be recommended for compulsory admission by a psychiatrist, and to be admitted under s. 2 (Huxley, 1985). Soothill et al (1990b) found in their study of 53 consecutive compulsory admissions into a hospital in Birmingham that 27 of those admitted (51 per cent of the total) posed no significant danger to themselves or other persons, a similar finding to that made by Bean in his larger study (1980). On this basis they argue that 'the 1983 Act allows the professional judgment of the clinician to remain paramount. The essential focus remains as a psychiatric question with the dangerousness issue as of only residual concern ... quite simply, dangerousness is not the primary issue of concern in terms of compulsory admission' (1990b, p. 24). As we saw in the last Chapter, this is controversial in that diagnostic techniques are a long way from scientific. Research has found that a variety of other factors are also relevant. A key indicator, not surprisingly, is previous admission. Being 'socially isolated', single, divorced or separated and female, or unemployed also render a person more likely to consult. The middle-aged, and separated, divorced or widowed persons were more likely to be diagnosed by a GP as mentally disordered, although young, single men were more likely to be referred by GPs, along with separated, divorced and widowed females. Those more likely to thought by the psychiatrist to be in need of hospitalisation were single, male and of social class V (Huxley, 1985, p. 10). These findings echo across a range of other studies. For example, as far as social class was concerned, Bean (1980) found that, out of 200 patients admitted under part II *and* s. 131, none were of social class I and few (5 per cent) were of social class II, whereas 61 per cent were from social classes IV and V (1980, p. 111). Only in social class V was the likelihood of being admitted under part II equal to that of being admitted informally, and this perhaps goes some, but not all, of the way to explain the high incidence per capita of the population of persons from ethnic minorities amongst those compulsorily admitted (see 4.6.1, and Moodley and Thornicroft, 1988).

Summarising this information, it can be said that although the admissions process is very often prompted by therapeutic considerations, it is focused on socially rather than medically problematic individuals. The above research also shows that often, although others involved are important filters, it will be a psychiatrist who is the main instigator of the admissions process. Yet as far as the law is concerned, only an ASW or an NR may be the applicant. Thus it can be seen that the way in which potential in-patients come under consideration for confinement contains the potential to undermine the legal conceptualisation of that process and who should drive it forward. This is of course all the more true when, as in 11,189 of the 20,561 uses of s. 3 in 1997-8 (Department of Health, 1998a, table 8), the patient is already in hospital.

5.3 NEAREST RELATIVES AND APPROVED SOCIAL WORKERS

Under the Victorian procedure, admission of paying patients to psychiatric facilities was on the application of a relative, and admission of pauper patients was on the application of poor law officials, with the proviso that the nearest relative of such paupers could generally obtain their discharge, on the undertaking that the individual would no longer be a drain on public funds. Medical certificates in a form noticeably similar to those under the current Act (one for paupers, two for private patients) were also required. Pauper patients, who constituted the vast majority of patients in Victorian asylums, always had their admission subject to the scrutiny of a justice of the peace, and this safeguard was extended to private patients under the Lunacy Act 1890.

The routine involvement of justices of the peace was removed for all confinements in 1959. Otherwise, the remnants of the Victorian processes can still be seen in modern admissions, although with the fusion of private and pauper status following the introduction of the National Health Service in 1948, statutory change has resulted at least in theory in involvement of both nearest relatives (now more closely defined than in Victorian times) and social workers (the modern inheritors of traditional poor law roles) in all confinements. Under the law since 1959, now the MHA 1983, the patient's NR, and ASWs have coexistent powers to make an application for compulsory admission. It was hoped by the Percy Commission (Royal Commission 1957, para. 403) that the majority of applications would be made by NRs, with help from an ASW only if necessary, although, as the Commission suspected, this is not how the system has subsequently proven to operate. At least in theory, the choice between the two applicants is not necessarily important anyway, since unlike Victorian law, the modern Act requires, whoever is the applicant, that the other of these figures be consulted in the process.

The existing process is thus very much the vestige of its nineteenth-century predecessors. The role and power of the family throughout the admission flows from middle class Victorian ideologies of public and private life; the role of doctors reflects both the gradual occupation of medicine as expert in the field of madness in the eighteenth and nineteenth centuries and the reality of doctors being the only reliably educated professionals in the poor law administrative system; and the social workers represent the municipal need to regulate relations between society and the asylum. The political justifications for the continued roles of these actors have changed over time. Thus modern arguments for the involvement of NRs are likely to focus on the knowledge of that individual of the specifics of the patient's life. The new justifications do not necessarily correspond to the roles prescribed in the 1983 Act, however, which were framed based on earlier justifications. The tensions between the roles of the various actors are amongst the key themes in this Chapter, and that the historical justifications for these roles is at odds with the contemporary reality is at least part of the explanation of those present tensions.

With the abolition of the hearing before the justice of the peace, an expressly legal voice was removed from the admission structure. The late Victorian introduction of this safeguard had been based in part on concerns regarding civil rights and wrongful confinement. The removal of this voice thus raises the question of where, if at all, in the current system, these issues will be raised. In addition, a traditional focus of legal hearings had been to serve as clearing house for divergent discourses. The efficacy of these legal hearings in this regard is dubious; certainly the Percy Commission saw them as a mere formality. The problem of mediation between the divergent discourses is real, however, as will be discussed later (see 5.4.2.1). The abolition of these hearings, while simplifying the system and perhaps rendering it less intrusive on patients, removed the chance to use them as a way of mediating between the divergent discourses.

The legal definition of an NR is found in s. 26(1), MHA 1983. The NR of a patient will be the person nearest to the beginning of the following list: (a) husband or wife; (b) son or daughter; (c) father or mother; (d) brother or sister; (e) grandparent, (f) grandchild; (g) uncle or aunt; (h) nephew or niece. Other persons with whom the patient had been residing for at least five years at the time of admission to hospital are added as a final class on this list by s. 26(7). Those entitled include relatives of both 'the whole blood' and half blood: s. 26(2). If there is more than one person of the relevant class, the elder will be the NR, and relatives of the whole blood are preferred over those of half blood: s. 26(3). Relatives living abroad, separated spouses, and relatives under age 18 other than parents or spouses are discounted: s. 26(5), but common law spouses of at least six months' standing are included so long as the patient is separated from anyone to whom the patient is married. Carers are given priority over other members of the same class: s. 26(4).

Even with the clarifications, the provisions are problematic if the objective is to select what would commonly be understood as the 'nearest' relative. For example, 'father' includes an unmarried father only if he has parental responsibility acquired in accordance with the requirements of s. 4, Children Act 1989, and members of the father's family similarly can only be the patient's nearest relative if the father has parental responsibility: s. 26(2)(b). Statutory responsibility acquired under the Children Act 1989 terminates on the child's eighteenth birthday, and so it would seem that all paternal 'relatives' of the adult offspring of unmarried parents are debarred from NR status, even if, for example, the unmarried parents do not cohabit and the adult patient is (and may perhaps have been since childhood) cared for by the father or his family. Similarly, gay or lesbian partners are not included in this provision, unless covered by s. 26(7), but even so this will be of no practical effect if the patient has any other relative in the s. 26(1) list. It is possible for an NR to delegate his or her functions, and there can be an application to a county court to remove and replace an NR (under s. 29, see below), but the former depends on the agreement of the existing NR and the latter is only used when there is concern about the abilities of the existing NR to perform his or her duties satisfactorily. Neither option is likely to afford much assistance to a *de facto* but not *de jure* NR.

The NR of the patient as defined by statute is thus not necessarily the nearest relative as understood either by the patient, or by the colloquial use of that phrase. References to age and legitimacy may have been justifiable under the Victorian family ideology; they are not obviously appropriate if the concern is to identify the person best placed to know and act upon the patient's wishes and best interests. At the same time, it could be questioned whether the NR as popularly understood is in the best position to act in this way in any event. The position of an NR serving as carer is bound to be fraught with conflicts of interest in this regard, in the event that the patient presents antisocial, but not dangerous behaviour. This can unquestionably be stressful for the carer, and it is difficult to see that it is a reasonable expectation for the carer to put these legally irrelevant issues to one side, when their life is being made difficult.

A person does not require any specialist training or knowledge to be a patient's NR under the 1983 Act. However, the other possible applicant, the ASW, is required to have 'appropriate competence in dealing with persons who are suffering from mental disorder': s. 114(2). Local SSDs 'shall appoint a sufficient number of approved social workers for the purpose of discharging the functions conferred on them [i.e. ASWs] by this Act': s. 114(1), and in so doing authorities 'shall have regard to such matters as the Secretary of State may direct': s. 114(3) by way of training and qualifications. As such, ASWs are constructed by the 1983 Act as specialists with autonomous decision-making capabilities. This, however, has not been without controversy. For the equivalent post under the 1959 Act (the 'Mental Welfare Officer' or MWO) there was no requirement for the possession of any special skills or training over and above that required to undertake social work, and appointment policy was a local matter. Bean's research (1980) found numerous examples of inefficiency, lack of expert knowledge, and actions of dubious legality by MWOs, and constituted a strong argument for the introduction of specialist training. Such factors dovetailed with the views of MIND, who saw a specialist social worker as a potentially powerful advocate for patients *vis-à-vis* the psychiatric profession (Gostin, 1986a), and of the British Association of Social Workers (BASW) which was keen to reconstruct mental health within a discourse founded on a welfarist rather than medical foundation and so enhance their claim to professionalisation, in juxtaposition to the medical profession in general and psychiatry in particular. As Prior (1992, p. 111, giving examples) notes, '[p]rofessional aggrandisement, using mental health legislation as the lever, was clearly evident in the social work press during the period 1981 to 1983'. The case for 'welfarisation' was also strengthened by the attacks on psychiatry coming from the antipsychiatry movement, which itself was bolstered by empirical research casting doubt on the claims to expertise of psychiatrists (e.g., Cocozza and Steadman, 1978), and the scandalous conditions revealed to exist in some hospitals (Barnes et al, 1990, pp.19-23).

There was, however, much opposition to the specialisation of mental health social work from within the social work profession, from local authorities, and from psychiatrists. For psychiatry, the problem was one of professional control of territory, both in terms of geography (for the emergence of welfarism as an alternative discourse was part of the wider shift out of the asylum (see 3.3)) and in terms of client base, coupled with a general low regard for the capabilities of social workers and a concern that the power given to ASWs is such that on occasion acute patients may be denied the treatment they need (Bluglass, 1987). For local authorities the problem was that the government expected the implementation of training for approved social workers to be implemented without an increase in central funding (Prior, 1992, p. 111). Finally, although the BASW was in favour of professionalisation, NALGO, the social workers union, objected to specialisation in principle, and to the fact that the ASW requirements placed new conditions of service on social workers if they were to continue to carry out the work they had been doing since 1959. Alternatively, if ASW status entailed new responsibilities, then a salary increase should be forthcoming to reflect this fact. NALGO also argued that social workers who had been carrying out the functions of the new ASW prior to the implementation of the 1983 Act should not be required to undergo training. The government eventually accepted this argument, so that those who had been in post as an MWO immediately prior to the Mental Health (Amendment) Act 1982 (that is, 27 October 1982) or had 'gained substantial experience' as a MWO in the period 1975-82 need not hold the Certificate of Qualification in Social Work (CQSW) or Central Council for Education and Training in Social Worker (CCETSW) equivalent; that is, they need not be qualified social workers (Department of Health, 1986, cl. 7(a)).

But in the long run, it was the pro training/specialisation viewpoint that, as we have seen, now represents the letter of the 1983 Act. The CCETSW set up an examination for qualified social workers. In directions made pursuant to s. 114(3) (Department of Health, 1986) it is provided in cl. 7(a) that in order to be eligible for approval by a local authority a person should: (a) be a qualified social worker (unless exempt under the deal worked out with NALGO); *and* (b) have received appropriate training for mental health work *and* have appropriate professional experience and have demonstrated 'an appropriate level of professional competence'. Approval should be for a period not exceeding five years: cl. 7(b)(iii). In order to deal with the problems of funding specialised mental health training, and to cope with the fact that NALGO boycotted the examination for post-qualification mental health training, cl. 7(c) provided that until 27 October 1988 local authorities could make 'transitional approvals' as ASWs of social workers of at least two years who had carried out the duties of an MWO or had acted under the supervision of an ASW in the execution of duties under the 1983 Act. This latter provision reflects the fact that although the new enhanced role for social workers appeared on the face of the new legislation, the politics of the Act's implementation meant that the putting into practice of the new scheme had effectively floundered. Four thousand social worker were approved under cl. 7(c), which was approximately 80 per cent of those operating in the mid 1980s (Prior, 1992). In practice, therefore, the professionalisation and specialisation of mental health social work took off only very slowly.

Even now, it is not apparent that the 1983 Act is working as intended. The issue of funding training has never been resolved to the satisfaction of local authorities, leading to continued infighting involving central and local government, NALGO, MIND and BASW, and concessions from the Department of Health, allowing cheaper training programmes to run with a consequent dilution of the extent of professional education which ASWs receive. The situation now is that to attain ASW status, a social worker must undergo around 12 weeks of training, and attend refresher courses at regular intervals (Central Council for Education and Training in Social Work, 1993). Nevertheless, as Prior points out, the low number of compulsory admissions as a percentage of the whole makes it difficult for an individual to build up an expertise in the compulsory admission process, and the situation is aggravated by low status of mental health work in social service departments (1992,

p. 113). It is easy to understand why many argue that the ASW has not emerged as a figure able to act as patient advocate in dealings with psychiatrists in the context of compulsory admission to hospital (Sammut, 1993). Against this, more recent research seems to indicate that ASWs are sometimes able to make a better judgment about the need for hospitalisation than are psychiatrists, and it is claimed that this is because of the training in issues such as discrimination and disadvantage that ASWs receive (Hatfield, Huxley and Mohamad, 1997). It must be said, however, that there is a dearth of contributions to this debate from those outside either social work or psychiatry.

It seems odd, given this protracted and complicated battle over the nature of ASW status, that an NR, who need have no professional training whatever, is equally able to make an application for admission of the patient (s. 11(1), MHA 1983). The reason, as we have seen, flows from Victorian processes, and Victorian ideologies of the family and local government. Now, both are to be involved in all compulsory admissions. An ASW must, prior to making the application, consult with the nearest relative, who may block an application for admission under s. 3. Upon admission following an application by an NR, the receiving hospital must contact the patient's local SSD which must then detail a social worker (although not necessarily an ASW) to interview the patient and provide a report on the patient's circumstance to the hospital: s. 14.

Whoever the applicant is, the application must be made to the hospital managers of the receiving hospital: s. 11(2), and must be made on the correct form (SI 1983 No. 893, reg. 4 and forms 1, 2, 4, 5, 8, and 9). In practice, the vast majority of applications for admission are made by ASWs, and even when an NR is nominally the applicant, it is usual for the ASW to play a significant role. Cavadino (1989) for example found that only three out of 47 applications for compulsory admission were made by the patient's NR, and an ASW was involved in all three (see also Bean, 1980; Barnes, Bowl and Fisher, 1990). It is to be expected that ASWs would predominate in the application process. It will be a rare NR who has the legal and procedural knowledge to make an application without help. According to Cavadino's research, ASWs tend towards the view that it is inappropriate for the patient's relatives to make the application as this may harm relationships within the family. This view is echoed in the Code of Practice (para. 2.35), and it has been the policy of MIND and the BASW for the last two decades that the role of NR should be abolished completely (Cavadino, 1989, p. 117). This would also enhance the position of social workers in the system, who may need to protect their area of expertise and professional power from encroachment by laypersons, and to assert their role in the admission process *vis-à-vis* the medical professionals (see below). It is nonetheless not obvious that the role of the NR should be removed completely. There may well be cases where the relative is aware of realities of the patient's life relevant to admission, and of wishes of the patient that may warrant respect. It is not obvious that professionals have access to this sort of information, and without such consultations being legally mandatory, they may not occur in a system facing continual cutbacks and where administrators are under increasing stress.

Whether the NR ought to have *control* of the situation is of course a separate question. As noted above, an NR will quite understandably often have needs and concerns which conflict with those of the patient, and it would be a superhuman expectation that they would keep these separate from the decision-making process regarding the patient. These separate needs and agendas may serve as an additional reason for their involvement, however. In a system based increasingly on community care, support structures in the community are increasingly important; and those structures will often be based in the family. To marginalise involvement of the family in the hospitalisation process arguably puts the continued set of relations between the medical professionals, the family, and the patient at risk, thus threatening the community support which the patient will need upon discharge.

This of course risks conflict with the civil rights of the patient. A civil libertarian is unlikely to see how it is justifiable that a patient be admitted for 'relief of carers', notwithstanding that this was the most frequent major reason cited for acute admissions to hospital in an Inner London study (Flannigan et al, 1994, p. 752), and the Code of Practice does include 'the needs of the patient's family and others with whom he or she lives' as a relevant factor to be taken into account by an applicant in assessing whether an application for admission should be made (Department of Health and Welsh Office, 1999, para. 2.6). Equally of concern here is the revival in the last twenty years of the ideology of the family, a belief in family involvement as a cornerstone of social policy, whether or not the family implied by the ideology bears any relation to the relations of people in individual cases.

This last factor suggests we may not have moved as far as we might have thought from the original Victorian issues regarding family involvement. Under the current regime the role of the NR is not simply that of alternative applicant for admission. In respect of admission under s. 2, s. 11(3): provides that:

> Before or within a reasonable time after an application for the admission of a patient for assessment is made by an approved social worker, that social worker shall take such steps as are practicable to inform the person (if any) appearing to be the nearest relative of the patient.

Under s. 13(1) the ASW must do so 'having regard to any wishes expressed by relatives of the patient'. This does not give the NR a power of veto (although he or she must also be informed, under s. 11(2), of their powers of discharge in s. 23: see 8.3.2), but it does give the NR, and by virtue of s. 13(1) other relatives of the patient, including those so defined by operation of s. 26(6) and (7) (see above), a right to be consulted.

The 1983 Act gives NRs rather more power in respect of an application by an ASW for admission for treatment. Section 11(4) states that an application for admission under s. 3:

> shall not be made by an approved social worker if the nearest relative of the patient has notified that social worker, or the local social services authority by whom that social worker is appointed, that he objects to the application being made and, without prejudice to the foregoing provision, no such application shall be made by such a social worker except after consultation

with the person (if any) appearing to be the nearest relative of the patient unless it appears to that social worker that in the circumstances such consultation is not reasonably practicable or would involve unreasonable delay.

If admission for treatment is contemplated, therefore, the ASW *must* consult with the person appearing to be the NR prior to making the application, unless this is not reasonably practicable or would involve unreasonable delay. As a s. 3 admission is by definition not an emergency, practicability and unreasonableness should be interpreted so as to allow consultation if at all possible.

The courts do not view this as a mere formality. In *R* v *South Western Hospital Managers and Another, ex parte M* [1994] 1 All ER 161 (HC), a patient, M, had been admitted under s. 3. The ASW involved in the case had consulted as NR the patient's mother, a resident of Eire, and had also discussed the situation with the patient's uncle, resident in the UK, who was not opposed to the admission. Laws J held that there had been a failure to comply with s. 11(4) because M's mother was disbarred from acting as NR by operation of s. 26(5)(a)(see above), and this was so notwithstanding that s. 11(4) requires the ASW to consult the person 'appearing to be the nearest relative'. He held that a person could not appear to be the patient's NR 'where, on the facts known to the social worker, the person in question is legally incapable of being the statutory nearest relative'. This seems to imply that if an ASW consults a person as NR who could be so in law but is not (which means, in essence, a person not disbarred by s. 26(5) or a father without parental responsibility and relatives of the father under s. 26(2)), then as long as this is done in good faith, s. 11(4) is complied with. On the other hand, this case shows that the consultation with the NR must proceed on the basis that that person is aware that he or she is the statutory NR, with all that this entails. To consult that person defined as the NR but only in the capacity of a 'mere' relative, as happened here, will not suffice: of particular importance is the need to explain the powers to object to the patient's admission and those of discharge available to the NR under s. 23: *In the Matter of Briscoe* [1998] COD 402 (HC). It is possible to delegate the duty to consult, but 'it remains throughout the approved social worker's responsibility' to ensure that the consultation is 'full and effective': *ex parte M*. Jones (1999, p. 63–4) suggests that for this to be the case the delegate must also be an ASW. This is perhaps doubtful, as it will be a question of fact whether a delegated consultation is 'full and effective'; and provided that it is, it seems unlikely that a court would find that a consultation had not taken place.

Section 11(4) further provides the NR with a power of *veto* over the making of an application, which is effective as soon as communicated to the ASW or the relevant SSD. The two elements in s. 11(4) are freestanding, so that the power of veto will be effective even if the ASW has not consulted the NR. As will be discussed in more detail in 8.3.2, the NR also has a continuing power to order the release of the patient at any time in a s. 2 or s. 3 detention, subject to an overriding authority of the hospital to detain the patient if 'dangerous': ss. 23(1), 25. The authority of the NR over the confinement therefore remains throughout its full duration.

The MHA 1983, then, gives the patient's NR a good deal of power. However, the person who is the patient's NR by operation of s. 26 may not always be in the best position to act. This possibility is anticipated by various provisions. First, an NR can delegate the power to act to any other person, other than one prohibited from so acting under s. 26(5), or under reg. 14, Mental Health (Hospital, Guardianship and Consent to Treatment) Regulations 1983, SI 1983/893. This must be done in writing: reg.14(1) and communicated to the local SSD, or hospital if the patient has already been admitted: reg.14(2). It is the responsibility of ASWs to suggest that a delegation be made in appropriate circumstances (Department of Health and Welsh Office, 1999, para. 2.17). But on occasion an ASW and an NR will be unable to agree about the need for hospitalisation, and as an NR has a power of veto over an application for treatment, an impasse may be reached.

Secondly, for this reason (and others), s. 29 allows a county court, on the application of any relative, an ASW, or a person with whom the patient was residing prior to hospitalisation, to substitute an individual to act in place of the nearest relative defined by statute. While the court has near infinite discretion as to whom to appoint, the grounds for the application are limited. They are contained in s. 29(3). Either there must be no NR under s. 26; or the prescribed NR must be incapable of acting due to mental illness or other disability; or the prescribed NR 'unreasonably objects' to an application for treatment or assessment; or the NR has exercised 'without regard to the welfare of the patient or the interests of the public', his or her power to order the discharge of the patient from hospital or guardianship. The powers accorded to the NR require his or her continuing involvement in the detention and treatment of the patient, and it is obviously important in that regard to ensure that the most appropriate person is exercising that authority on behalf of the patient.

As far as disputes between an ASW and an NR are concerned, it is the power of the courts to remove an 'unreasonable' NR that is most important. It has been held that this is an objective test, analogous to the welfare test in child law: *W* v *L* [1974] QB 711 (CA), so that the question for the court, when deciding whether to make an order under s. 29, is whether the actions of the NR whom it is sought to have displaced can be said to be reasonable or not. The court must also be given evidence that the proposed application for admission is necessary: *B(A)* v *B(L)* *(Mental Health Patient)* [1980] 1 WLR 116 (CA). In cases after the coming into force of the MHA 1983 the test in *W* was not applied, and instead the approach was that an NR was *prima facie* acting unreasonably if the criteria for compulsion under the 1983 Act were met: *Re B* (1985) (County Court), unreported. However, the *W* test was reasserted by the Court of Appeal in *Manchester City Council* v *Merceda Ingram* (1999) (CA) unreported, 25 June. This case, and that of *Merrill* v *Herefordshire District Council* (1999) (CA) unreported, 27 July, illustrate that the Court of Appeal takes a similar approach to appeals against the making of a s. 29 order, and will only allow an appeal if the first instance decision to make the order can be shown to be wholly unreasonable. It is rare that an NR will be able successfully to resist displacement, but it does happen. An example is *H* v *Essex County Council* (1997) Legal Action 24 (county court). Mr H, who had been detained under s. 3 with the consent of his mother and NR, Mrs H, had been discharged by a review tribunal on the basis that his illness was not of a nature or degree that warranted detention in a hospital. Mr H's doctor, unable to accept the decision to discharge his patient, had contacted an ASW, although not the one who had dealt with Mr H's initial admission, and the admissions process was put into motion. It was brought to a halt when Mrs H objected to her son's proposed readmission. The ASW's application to have Mrs H removed was dismissed by the court on the basis that in such circumstances — which clearly amounted to an attempt by the doctor in question to circumvent the authority of the tribunal and, so it seems, that of the ASW who had been the applicant for Mr H's initial admission — it was not unreasonable for Mrs H to withhold her consent to the admission. From one point of view, the degree of latitude that the s. 29(3) criteria accord to an NR severely limits the discretion of the court to appoint a more able or appropriate decision-maker, over one who is prescribed but relatively less appropriate. The limitations contained in these grounds mean that s. 29, while useful for other purposes, cannot correct the difficulties contained in s. 26. On the other hand, it could equally well be said that in cases like Mrs H's the criteria proved their worth, enabling an NR to have an effective power of veto over the arguably inappropriate plans of the professionals concerned for the readmission of her son.

If an NR objects to the admission for treatment under s. 3 of a patient already detained for assessment under s. 2, the 28-day period of detention under s. 2 may be extended until the application under s. 29 is heard, and for a further seven days if that application is successful: s. 29(4), to allow the formalities of a s. 3 admission to be complied with. It has also been held that it an interim order can be made under s. 29, and that a patient may be admitted under s. 3 during the currency of such an order if there are cogent reasons to admit the patient before the s.29 application can be finally determined: *R v Central London County Court and another, ex parte London* [1999] 3 WLR 1 (CA). The Court of Appeal rejected the submission that if, in on the subsequent full hearing of the application under s. 29 the interim order were to be discharged and no other order made, the patient would have been disadvantaged unfairly by the making of an interim order. But in such a case the patient will have been lawfully admitted under s. 3 over the objections of the (now reinstated) lawful NR, and although the NR will then have a power to discharge the patient under s. 23, that power can be vetoed by the RMO if the patient is thought to be dangerous (see 8.3.2). In any case, a power to discharge is a poor replacement for a power to prevent admission. It is to be hoped that courts will use the power to make an interim order sparingly. It can be argued that the decision of the Court of Appeal in this case is unfortunate in providing a mechanism by which those seeking to admit may on occasion be able temporarily to side-step the legitimate objections of a NR. The MHA 1983 might seem to provide an ASW who fears that the NR will in fact veto the making of the application under s. 3 with an avoidance strategy, that is, to apply instead under s. 2, thus bypassing the power of veto altogether. The Code of Practice states that this is not an acceptable reason to make an application under s. 2 rather than s. 3 (Department of Health and Welsh Office, 1999, para. 5.4.d). However, given that many patients admitted under s. 2 stay on in hospital following the expiry of their 'section' — 14,438 in 1997-8 (Department of Health, 1998a, table 7) — this option must be tempting to an ASW in this situation.

5.4   THE MECHANICS AND DYNAMICS OF ADMISSION

5.4.1   Prerequisites for the making of an application for an admission

It is the responsibility of the applicant to ensure, if compulsory admission is warranted, that all the requirements for a valid application are satisfied. Although in general the decision whether or not to make an application is in the discretion of the potential applicant (whether ASW or NR), s. 13(1) places a duty to make an application on an ASW 'in any case where he is satisfied that such an application ought to be made and is of the opinion ... that it is necessary or proper for the application to be made by him'. In making this decision an ASW must also consider the options for treatment or assistance without hospitalisation, and an assessment pursuant to s. 13, MHA 1983 may double as an assessment for entitlement to community care services under s. 47, National Health Service and Community Care Act 1990 (see 9.2, 9.3). An NR can initiate the assessment process under s. 13(4), MHA 1983, which gives an NR the right to request an SSD to 'direct an approved social worker as soon as practicable to take the patient's case into consideration under [s. 13(1)] with a view to making an application for his admission'. A request under s. 13(4) places the SSD under a duty of care towards the patient. The ASW may well also owe a duty of care to the patient in these circumstances: *Harnett* v *Fisher* [1927] AC 573. If the ASW after consideration decides that an application is not required, his or her reasons must be supplied to the NR in writing: s. 13(4).

5.4.1.1   The medical recommendations   An application for admission under part II must be 'founded on' the necessary medical recommendations: ss. 2, 3, 4. Under the terms of the statute the medical recommendations 'shall be signed *on or before the date of the application*': s. 12(1), but, following the decision in *Whitbread* (1997) *The Times*, 14 July, this does not mean that the medical recommendations must precede the making of the application. The Code of Practice states that medical and social work assessments should be carried out jointly unless there are good reasons for separate assessments (Department of Health and Welsh Office, 1999, para. 2.3). If it is not possible to gain access to the patient in order to carry out an assessment, recourse should be had to s. 135(1) (see 4.5.3) or to any powers of forced entry that the police may lawfully use (Department of Health and Welsh Office, 1999, para. 2.24).

For ss. 2 and 3 there must be two medical recommendations: ss. 2(3), 3(3). The two doctors may examine the patient together or separately: s. 11(7), but where separate examinations take place, they must not be more than five days apart: s. 12(1). The practice of requiring the agreement of two doctors is a function of a Victorian fear that doctors are easily corruptible, the idea being that each would police the actions of the other (Bean, 1986, p. 43). The 1983 Act, like its Victorian antecedents, also includes additional safeguards against potential collusion or improper use of medical recommendations. Section 12(5) disbars the following persons from acting as the second opinion doctor: the applicant for admission (some ASWs or NRs may be doctors); the professional partner or assistant of the first recommending doctor; any practitioner who has a financial interest in the hospital to which the patient is to be admitted; and close relatives of the patient.

Today, since doctors are normally salaried and have little financial motive for the confinement of patients, the argument about corruption seems unpersuasive. The requirement is instead better understood as a civil rights protection, ensuring a reasonable degree of medical certainty and consistency before confinement may occur. Reflecting that, while each recommendation may contain diagnoses of more than one of the specified forms of mental disorder, there must be agreement on at least one form of mental disorder if any subsequent application is to be effective: s. 11(6). As we have seen, however, a joint examination is possible, and even if examinations are performed separately, the Code of Practice requires the two doctors involved to discuss the patient with each other (para. 2.25). This on its face would undercut the civil rights protection, which would be strengthened if each doctor were required to reach an independent judgment. In the view of the Code of Practice, good practice also dictates that the recommending doctors discuss the situation with the applicant (para. 2.26), although there is no legal duty in the MHA 1983 to do so.

Of the two medical recommendations, one 'shall be given by a practitioner approved for the purposes of this section by the Secretary of State as having special experience in the diagnosis or treatment of mental disorder': s. 12(2). This person will usually be a professional psychiatrist, although the Code of Practice now encourages SSDs to take steps to encourage other doctors including GPs to apply for approval (para. 2.41). The power to approve practitioners under s. 12(2) has been delegated to health authorities (SI 1996 No. 708). The second recommending doctor must be a registered medical practitioner who has previous acquaintance with the mentally disordered person, unless the approved doctor already has such previous acquaintance: s. 12(2), or unless this is not practicable. This typically means that the second doctor will be the patient's GP.

The balance contemplated by the 1983 Act, then, is a mix of substantive expertise, and experience with the particular patient. There are a number of reasons, however, why the system has a tendency to break down in practice. First, not everyone will have a GP (Spence and McPhillips, 1995), although a high number of those admitted compulsorily have been admitted before (ibid.), so there may well be someone available who has previous acquaintance with the patient. If the patient has no GP or the GP cannot practicably be contacted, the Code of Practice takes the view that the second recommending doctor should also be 'approved' (para. 2.29). Secondly, when GPs are involved in the admission process it tends to be very much in a subordinate role to the appointed psychiatrist. Bean (1980, pp.162, 163) found that 'GPs, generally speaking, knew little of the [Mental Health] Act, and knew little of psychiatry'. Consequently, and also because of the hierarchy within the medical profession between generalists and specialists, the GPs did what the psychiatrists told them to do (Bean, 1986, p. 44). The hopes for balance and mutual restraint, then, have not been realised. Not more than one of the medical recommendations may be given by a practitioner on the staff of the receiving hospital: s. 12(3), unless to delay on these grounds would involve 'serious risk to the health or safety of the patient': s. 12(4)(a); *and* one of the practitioners works 'for less than half the time which he is bound by contract to devote to work in the health service' in the receiving hospital: s. 12(4)(b); *and*, where one of the recommending doctors is a consultant, the other does not work in a grade under that consultant's directions: s. 12(4)(c).

For admission under s. 4, the situation is different. Here there need be only *one* medical recommendation which need not be made by a psychiatrist, but should be made by a doctor with previous acquaintance with the patient if practicable: s. 4(3). Section 4 should only be used in cases of 'urgent necessity', and the Code of Practice (para. 6.2) states that s. 4 should never be used for administrative convenience. In particular patients 'should not be admitted under section 4 rather than section 2 because it is more convenient for the second doctor to examine the patient in, rather than outside, hospital' (para. 6.4). If as this implies, medical convenience does not render the situation one of urgent necessity, the use of s. 4 for this reason would render the confinement illegal. This argument has yet to be tested in the courts.

5.4.1.2 The Approved Social Worker Interview

The applicant, whether ASW or NR, must have personally seen the patient no more than 14 days prior to the date of the application for admission: s. 11(5). If the intending applicant is an ASW, he or she 'shall interview the patient in a suitable manner and satisfy himself that detention in a hospital is in all the circumstances of the case the most appropriate way of providing the care and medical treatment of which the patient stands in need': s. 13(2). The patient should be given the option of this interview being conducted in private (unless the ASW has reason to fear physical harm) or in the presence of some other person such as a friend: (Department of Health and Welsh Office, 1999, para. 2.13). An interpreter trained to act in a psychiatric context should be present if the patient and ASW do not speak the same language (para. 2.14), a relative, friend or neighbour of the patient should only be used as a last resort. The Code of Practice advises that 'it is not desirable for a patient to be interviewed through a closed door or window except where there is serious risk to other people' (para. 2.12.a). Instead the powers of intervention accorded to the justice of the peace under s. 135 (see 4.5.3) should be used.

One function of this interview should be to ensure that the legal grounds of confinement, as discussed in the previous chapter, are satisfied before an application is made. It was said in *St George's Healthcare NHS Trust* v *S* [1998] 2 FLR 728, 3 All ER 673 (CA) that for an admission for assessment, an ASW is not required to be certain that the patient definitely is mentally disordered. Indeed, it 'cannot be a final diagnosis. [An ASW] is entitled to be wrong: so are the medical practitioners on whose medical recommendations her application is based' (per Judge LJ at p. 690). But his lordship made clear that an ASW is required to 'believe' that the person to be admitted for assessment is mentally disordered. This is logical: more precise diagnosis may constitute the need for assessment in hospital. The same reasoning does not apply to admissions under s. 3, however, which would seem to imply that an ASW or the recommending doctors are *not* entitled to be wrong for such admissions. In practice the question is largely irrelevant, however, as a person who is found not to be mentally disordered after admission should be discharged, and if not is entitled to apply for *habeas corpus* (see 5.5.2) in either case.

Section 13(2) is not concerned solely with medical questions, however, but rather with the broader question of the 'appropriateness' of confinement. The BASW has taken the view that, in addition, the following constitute the role of the social worker in the admission process:

(a)   to investigate the client's social situation and how it has developed; and to estimate, in consultation with others involved, the extent to which the social and environmental pressures have contributed to the client's observed behaviour;

(b)   to apply professional skill to help modify any contributory personal relationship or environmental factors;

(c)   to mobilise the resources of the health service, the community service and acknowledge and use the community as a therapeutic resource;

(d)   to ensure that any intervention is the least restrictive necessary in the circumstances;

(e)   to ensure strict compliance with the law (BASW 1980; quoted in Jones, 1999, p. 73).

The emphasis of these criteria would ensure that confinement is the least restrictive option. While that is unquestionably desirable, training and expertise in the application of these criteria may, as we have seen, remain problematic. Equally problematic is the reduction of the legal standards of admission to merely one of a list of social work responsibilities in the area. The risk is that the provisions of ss. 2 and 3 will be seen merely as factors in admission policy, rather than legal standards that are *sine qua non* of confinement.

This mandatory requirement to interview the patient will often be straightforward, in the sense of the patient not actively resisting the process of hospitalisation, but not infrequently there is resistance. A prospective inpatient may refuse to speak to the ASW or to allow the ASW access to the patient's home, or may be verbally or physically violent towards the ASW or others involved in the admission process such as psychiatrists (Dean and Webster, 1991). The medical model approach for compulsory admission is backed up by a system of graduated coercion to ensure that hospitalisation is not thwarted by the patient's lack of cooperation. An ASW has powers of entry and inspection under s. 115, MHA 1983, which are exercisable 'at all reasonable times' in respect of premises (other than hospitals) 'in which a mentally disordered patient is living, if he has reasonable cause to believe that the patient is not under proper care'. However, s. 115 does not permit forced entry, and so is of little use if consent to enter the premises in question is not forthcoming. Under the 1983 Act it is an offence for a person 'without reasonable cause' to refuse to allow an inspection of any premises: s. 129(1)(a), as it is to 'refuse to allow the visiting, interviewing or examination of person by a person authorised in that behalf by or under this Act': s. 129(b) and to 'otherwise obstruct any such person in the exercise of his functions': s. 129(d). But, whilst an ASW who is refused entry to premises may use the fact that an offence or offences has or have thereby been committed as a bargaining chip, this is unlikely to be the appropriate course of action on many occasions. In particular, this does not address the question immediately at hand, of the need to interview the patient.

As we have seen (see 4.5.3, 4.5.4), powers of intervention are also given to justices of the peace and police, under ss. 135 and 136. These allow the person to be kept in a place of safety for up to 72 hours. This is not necessarily a guarantee that an interview will take place, if an interview is defined to mean a conversation to which both or all participants contribute. The patient may refuse to speak. If this occurs the ASW's assessment 'will have to be based on whatever information the ASW can obtain from all reliable sources'. If all else fails, therefore, the patient can seemingly be admitted into hospital in the absence of an ASW interview. The use of 'reliable sources' (whatever that means) is not an *alternative* to interviewing, as an ASW is required to make such enquiries in any case under s. 13(1).

5.4.1.3   The execution of an application   Execution of the application is pursuant to s. 6(1):

An application for the admission of a patient to hospital under this Part of the Act, duly completed in accordance with the provision of this Part of this Act, shall be sufficient authority for the applicant, or any person authorised by the applicant, to take the patient and convey him to the hospital.

This authority subsists for 14 days from the date of the last medical recommendation in the case of s. 2 and s. 3 admissions: s. 6(1)(a), and for 24 hours in the case of s. 4 admissions: s. 6(1)(b), after which time it will lapse.

Once the application is executed in this fashion, the patient is deemed to be in legal custody: s. 137(1). By s. 137(2), the person responsible for conveying the patient to hospital 'shall . . . have all the powers, authorities, protection and privileges which a constable has within the area for which he acts as constable'. This includes the right to use reasonable force, to sedate the patient (in which case a nurse, doctor or specialist ambulance person should accompany the patient to hospital (Code of Practice, para. 11.14)), and the power to arrest any person obstructing the execution of the application.

If access to the patient is denied, s. 135(2) allows a justice of the peace, at the instigation of the applicant for committal or a constable, to issue a warrant authorising a constable to enter the premises. The justice must be satisfied that the patient is to be found on the premises in question: s. 135(2)(a), and 'that admission to the premises has been refused or that a refusal of such admission is apprehended': s. 135(2)(b). It has been argued that the general requirements in relation to the execution of warrants for entry and search by police constables, contained in ss. 15 and 16 of PACE 1984 also apply here (see Jones, 1999, p. 394). The most important of these requirements for present purposes are that the warrant authorises entry on one occasion only: s. 15(5), and that the warrant has a life of one month from the date on which it is made: s. 16(3), and must be executed at a reasonable time unless there is reason to believe that the search would thereby be frustrated: s. 16(4). However, as Jones notes, s. 15(4), PACE states that the *constable* [making the application for the warrant] shall answer any questions that the justice of the peace hearing the application ... puts to him', which seems to imply that ss. 15 and 16 are relevant only when the applicant for the warrant is a constable. This is probably the strict legal position. Further evidence that the drafters of ss. 15, 16, PACE did not have s. 135, MHA 1983 in mind is that by s. 15(6), PACE the identity of the person sought should, so far as is practicable, be specified on the warrant, whereas s. 135(5), MHA 1983 provides that the name of the patient need not be given either in the information laid before the justice or the warrant. If this is correct it would mean that only warrants applied for under s. 135 by police constables are covered by these provisions, with warrants applied for by an ASW not being covered.

5.4.1.4 Taking the patient to hospital The applicant remains personally responsible for the proper conveyance to hospital of the patient, but may delegate the power to convey the patient to another person: s. 6(12). Conveyance is to be the 'most humane and least threatening' method consistent with the safety of the patient and others, taking into account the patient's preferences, the views of friends and relatives involved with the patient, the views of the professionals involved in the application, any potential violence on the part of the patient, and the impact of particular modes of conveyance on the patient's relationship with the community to which he or she will return (Department of Health and Welsh Office, 1999, para. 11.3). The police should usually be asked to help if the patient is likely to be violent or dangerous (para. 11.7). Dean and Webster (1991, p. 190) found that 15 per cent of compulsory admissions involved the use of 'restraint' by the police, and 55 per cent involved either verbal or violent resistance to the conveyance and admission. In such circumstances the preferred mode of transport remains by ambulance, although if this is not possible a suitable police vehicle may be used (para. 11.7). A violent or dangerous patient should never be conveyed by car (para. 11.6).

5.4.2 Is multidisciplinary teamwork possible?

The assumption behind the compulsory admission procedure is that the various persons involved can act effectively in tandem. The Code of Practice contemplates an approach based on teamwork and a 'framework of cooperation and mutual support' (Department of Health and Welsh Office, 1999, para. 2.3). The reality can be somewhat different. As already discussed, for example, GPs tend to accept that in matters of psychiatric expertise they are outranked by specialist psychiatrists, and the contemplated partnership between the specialist and the person with knowledge of the particular patient often fails to materialise. It is not unreasonable to conclude that the 'safeguard' of requiring two medical recommendations, apparent on the face of the 1983 Act, frequently does not exist in practice. This discrepancy between theory and practice can be seen in other aspects of the operation of the MHA 1983, such as the high number of s. 136 arrests that are not made in 'a place to which the public has access' (Rogers, 1990) or unlawful admissions that occur as a result of breaches of the letter of the 1983 Act by ASWs (Bean, 1980). However, the above examples are of improper uses of the 1983 Act *within* agencies or professions. Whilst here it is sufficient to say that the agency or profession does not always do what in law it should, a simple theory/practice opposition is not a sufficiently rigorous analytical model to understand compulsory admission as a dynamic process involving inter-agency cooperation.

A potential in-patient may be seen differently by each of those involved in the admission: as at once a legal actor with legal rights; a 'medical case'; a 'social work problem'; an actual or potential threat to public order; and a family member. It is worth pointing out that all of these perspectives are applied to the patient; and offer solutions defined by their understanding of the patient's problem and into which the patient is expected to fit himself or herself. The patient's own understanding of his or her problems is at risk of disappearing in the clash of the professional titans. These discourses may well offer competing rather than complementary interpretations of the situation at hand, each grounded in its own particular context and subject to its own imperatives and agendas, as well as the need to maintain, enhance, or acquire professional standing. To illustrate this argument, we shall look at the relationship between ASWs and psychiatrists, although similar sorts of argument may apply between any of the actors, both in informal and involuntary admissions. The relative importance of the discourses, and the nature of the tensions that result, will be a function of the individual case.

5.4.2.1   The interaction of doctors and social workers   The Percy Commission framework, intended to engender harmonious cooperation between ASWs and doctors, seems instead to have put into legislative form a relationship based on friction. In part this can be put down to the low esteem in which the two professions seem to hold each other (Cavadino, 1989, p. 114); in part also it is a question of territory and power. For those who are medically qualified the decision to admit is primarily a medical one, but the law usurps their clinical autonomy by giving ASWs a power of veto over the admission process. Moreover, under the terms of reference of the admission process the recommending doctors are required to stray into the professional territory of the ASW, whilst the applicant is also required to state that the patient is suffering from mental disorder, notwithstanding that the applicant will not be trained in psychiatry. In addition, there do appear to be significant differences between ASWs and psychiatrists that are likely to exacerbate tensions. Bean (1980, p. 157), for example, found that social workers tend on the whole to rate patients lower in terms of dangerousness to others than do psychiatrists. For the psychiatrist this displays either a lack of skill at diagnosis or a lack of realism in the social worker's assessment. For the ASW it is more likely to be seen as the manifestation of civil liberties-based concerns, coupled with scepticism about the professional abilities of psychiatry to 'cure' patients.

However, it is important to realise that such differences are more than of view; they are of perspective. ASWs bring a social work standpoint that may well be more influenced by concerns about autonomy and coercion, and even theses such as those of Szasz, Goffman and Foucault (Cavadino, 1989, p. 116). The hope of the Department of Health that a multi-agency approach to admission would work effectively fails to appreciate the non-transferability of knowledge or information across discursive contexts. There is a real sense in which doctors and ASWs in their professional roles do not talk the same language. Research shows that the two professions do indeed bring different 'models' of mental disorder to their task (Bean, 1980, p. 167) and this brings with it the risk of what Bean calls 'unstable interaction' (p.168), making the rule enforcement procedures unpredictable; which instability, Bean found, was lessened to the extent that the approved doctor took control of the situation, interviewing the patient with the GP and social worker and supervising the transfer to hospital (ibid.). The role of the ASW was reduced to no more than a rubber stamp. Psychiatrists do indeed view themselves as the senior professionals involved, with ASWs occupying a subordinate role. Here is the dilemma for ASWs: either accept a subordinate role which is a dereliction of the duty imposed under s. 13(1), and which in autopoietic terms reduces the ASW to the role of 'social worker-within-psychiatry' (King, 1991), but which may well mean that the admission process works relatively smoothly (if not always lawfully); or assert the independent nature of the social work role and both risk an unhappy working relationship with the psychiatrist and accept the resulting tensions and doctrinal inconsistencies in the admission process.

Cavadino (1989, p. 117) notes that the relatively new and not yet widespread practice of the ASWs being based in hospitals, might facilitate a better working relationship. This might indeed be the appearance of such a development, but from a perspective informed by autopoietic theory, which holds that knowledge generated within one professional paradigm cannot simply be transported to another without also in the process being 'translated', this represents the capitulation of social work to medical discourse and the latter's construction of the function of social work (Webb and Hobdell, 1980). Some in social work argue that a greater commitment by all involved parties to the concept of teamwork is the only way to rescue social workers from their secondary status in the compulsory admission process (Huxley, 1985), whilst others think that social work should strive to attain a position of professional status equal to that of psychiatrists by adopting an attitude of greater assertiveness in dealings with other professionals (Rabin and Zelner, 1992). We would argue that both strategies will be thwarted, not so much because the psychiatrist is on 'home turf' and in the dominant position (although this is of course important, as

Rogers (1993) found in her research into the relationship between police officers and psychiatrists), but because the ultimate goal — of an effective working relationship — is simply not possible to achieve. If, however, this would seem to be the case in any particular instance (and the empirical literature throws up no examples) then we would suggest that, in the terminology of autopoiesis, it is the 'psychic' rather than 'social' actors who are communicating effectively, which means that the professionals involved abandon their occupational discourses and interrelate instead as citizens. This would also seem to indicate that common ground is only found when professional perspectives and roles are abandoned in favour of a shared 'common sense' perspective, a 'common sense' language in which communication is possible.

5.4.3   Scrutiny and rectification of documents on arrival at hospital

A hospital may accept a patient if the application 'appears to be duly made and to be founded on the necessary medical recommendations': s. 6(3), MHA 1983, and this will involve the formal receipt of the various documents connected with the admission. Again following Victorian precedent, admission documents are to be routinely scrutinised, with rectification of some defects possible in some circumstances. The Victorian justification for this process was to ensure both the civil rights of those unjustifiably confined, but also to avoid the release of those appropriately confined, but by documents with technical defects. Without these provisions, such technical improprieties might in Victorian times allow parishes or poor law unions to escape payment of maintenance fees to the county asylum. In modern times, the process serves to protect the hospital from litigation flowing from the confinement, a function also served in Victorian private sector care.

The receipt, scrutiny and rectification of admission documents should be conducted by staff specifically delegated for the purpose and knowledgeable about the relevant law (Department of Health and Welsh Office, 1999, para. 12.1). As 24-hour cover is required for this function, it may in appropriate circumstances be delegated to senior nursing staff. The function of the receiving officer is specifically phrased in juxtaposition to rectification: 'to detect errors which cannot be corrected at a later stage in the procedure' (para. 12.3(b)). Accuracy is to be checked with the applicant, if an ASW. The Act allows a 14-day window for this purpose at the beginning of the confinement: s. 15(1), but the Code of Practice makes it clear that it should occur either immediately upon admission, or on the next working day, if admission occurs at night, on weekends or public holidays when appropriate staff are unavailable (para. 12.4.a) The medical certificates are to be scrutinised medically, to ensure that they show adequate grounds for confinement (para. 12.4.b).

The powers to 'rectify' a document authorising the admission and detention of a person under part II are contained in s. 15(1), and seem broad on their face. An application form, or any documentation relating to the medical recommendations upon which the application in question is founded, which 'is found to be in any respect incorrect or defective' may, with the consent of the hospital managers, be amended by the person who signed it. In addition, if a medical certificate is found wanting in either form or substance, it may be replaced with a fresh and proper one: s. 15(2), with the exception that s. 15(2) may not be used when medical certificates identify different mental disorders in violation of s. 11(6), in documentation in support of a s. 3 admission for treatment: s. 15(3).

The powers in s. 15(1) have, however, been interpreted fairly restrictively by the courts. In *R* v *South Western Hospital Managers, ex parte M* [1994] 1 All ER 161 (HC) it was said (at p. 177) that the rectification process is limited to errors or omissions on the face of the various documents. This means for example that s. 15(1) could not be used if the social worker or doctor did not have legal status to sign the certificate. In the case of the doctor, of course, a new certificate could be sought from a different doctor under s. 15(2); but this option would not be available if the social worker were not 'approved', as defined by the Act. Jones (1999, p. 82) suggests that an unsigned admission document cannot be rectified, and this is also the view of the Department of Health (Department of Health and Welsh Office, 1998, para. 46) as an unsigned document 'cannot be regarded as an application or medical recommendation' (ibid.). By extension, rectification could not cure a failure to include one of the required forms, so that for example a purported admission for treatment supported by only one medical opinion could not be saved since it requires two such opinions. Finally, rectification is unable to cure a defect which has arisen because a necessary event in the procedural chain has simply not taken place: *ex parte M*. Thus in that case, consultation with the wrong person as the NR could not be rectified. A similar reading of rectification was reached in *Re S-C (Mental Patient: Habeas Corpus)* [1996] 1 All ER 532 (CA) by Bingham MR, who held (at p. 537) that the rectification procedure cannot be used to correct 'a fundamentally defective application' . This would seem to limit rectification to cases of inaccurate record taking, and not to papering over procedural improprieties. The Memorandum gives examples of the sorts of defects that can be rectified. These are: the leaving of blank spaces or the failure to delete inapplicable alternatives (relating for example to the particular ground in ss. 2 or 3 upon which the admission is based); or inaccuracies in recording the name of the patient (Department of Health and Welsh Office, 1998, para. 48).

The receiving examination may be successful at identifying this type of defect, but it is difficult to see that it will be successful at identifying defects not apparent on the face of the documents. It would not, for example, have identified the deficiency in consultation with the NR, which was the issue in *ex parte M* (see 5.3). The result places admission staff in a difficult position. It is perhaps for this reason that in *ex parte M* Laws J held that although the conveyance to hospital in that case was not lawful as there had been a failure to consult the patient's NR, and the test in s. 6(1), being objective, so that for a conveyance to be lawful the application must be 'duly completed', this did not affect the legality of the patient's subsequent detention, which requires only that the application '*appears to be* duly made': s. 6(3). The Court of Appeal in *Re SC* held that Laws J had been wrong to hold that if s. 6(3) is complied with the patient's detention is lawful, notwithstanding a failure to comply with

s. 6(1), as this involved a *non sequitur* (the assumption that because there was a power to detain an unlawful admission was rendered lawful). However Laws J's analysis was in all other respects explicitly approved by Bingham MR (at p. 156), and by a unanimous Court of Appeal in *St George's Healthcare NHS Trust* (see 5.4.1.2). Thus there is nothing in any of these cases to contradict the view expressed in the Memorandum (para. 46) that 'the officer scrutinising the form may take statements at face value', and as long as this is done the hospital will be protected from any liability if it is subsequently shown that the admission was flawed in some way. This raises the question of how a patient is able to challenge detention on grounds that it is in some, less than obvious, way unlawful.

5.5 CHALLENGING THE LEGALITY OF ADMISSION UNDER PART II

5.5.1 Challenging the legality of admission by way of an application to a mental health review tribunal

The main mechanism in the MHA 1983 by which patients may challenge the legality of their detention in hospital is the Mental Health Review Tribunal (MHRT) (for detailed discussion of the tribunal system see 8.4). Tribunals *must* order the immediate discharge of any patients detained under part II of the Act if the criteria for admission cannot be made out to the satisfaction of the tribunal. There is also a general discretion to order the discharge of a part II patient 'in any case': s. 72(1). However the established wisdom is that MHRTs do not have jurisdiction to hear applications relating to the admission of a person into a hospital, but instead are limited to considering whether the grounds for continued detention exist. This is because s. 72(1) limits the consideration of an MHRT in the exercise of its *duty* to discharge to the situation 'then' pertaining. This reading of the power of MHRTs is based on dicta of Ackner LJ in *R v Hallstrom and another, ex parte W* [1985] 3 All ER 775 (CA) at pp.784-5. Ackner LJ based his view on two distinct elements: as well as the relevance of the use of 'then' in s. 72(1), it was also the case that an MHRT, because it must hear applications from persons 'liable to be detained', is not competent to hear an application from a person whose detention is defective.

However, as Eldergill (1997, p. 575) has pointed out, Neill and Glidewell LJJ expressly declined to express an opinion on the point in that case, which was in any case only of *obiter* status, and in the earlier case of *Re VE (mental health patient)* [1973] 1 QB 452 the Court of Appeal held that an MHRT should discharge a patient if the initial admission had been flawed. It must be conceded that *Re VE* is not on all fours with the situation under discussion here. That case was decided under the 1959 Act, which contained the rather strange rule, based on the view that psychopathy could only be treated if caught early enough, that no application for admission for treatment could be made in respect of patients over the age of 21. V, a 40-year-old patient, had been admitted for treatment diagnosed as suffering from mental illness. On her application to an MHRT for discharge, the tribunal declined to make the order sought but came to the opinion that she had been wrongly diagnosed and the correct diagnosis was psychopathy. The question arose whether, given that if V had been so diagnosed initially she would not have been liable to be detained, the tribunal should have ordered discharge consequent upon reclassifying her mental disorder. The Court of Appeal decided in such a situation the patient must be discharged. There is no scope under the 1983 Act for holding that a patient in such a situation 'must' be discharged, as the criteria for mandatory discharge are closely defined by that Act (and the Mental Health (Amendment) Act 1975 was enacted to overrule *Re V* to the extent that it placed an *obligation* on MHRTs to discharge in similar circumstances). But to put the case at its lowest, *Re V* arguably supports the view that such issues may be considered by an MHRT considering whether to exercise its discretion to discharge. On the other hand, as Eldergill concedes, a narrow reading of *Re VE* would find it consistent with the conventional view, that discharge may be ordered when a patient's detention is *no longer* justified, as opposed to it being authority to examine the initial admission, which is thought to be confined to the High Court in the exercise of its powers of judicial review and habeas corpus (see below).

Yet there is nothing in the MHA 1983 that limits the *discretion* of MHRTs to discharge; and to concede that only the High Court may quash an admission does not mean that an MHRT may not order discharge, as this is not the same thing at all; and that a patient may not in law be 'liable to be detained' because of some flaw in the admission process does not mean that a person *in fact* detained is not liable to be detained by the hospital managers at that point, on the basis of s. 6(3) (see 5.4.3). Eldergill concludes on the basis of these and other less substantial points that there is no reason why a tribunal should not be able to consider the legality of an admission to hospital in the context of its discretionary powers of discharge; but that the views of Ackner LJ are now so well established, if 'unconsidered' that the best practical advice is that it is this view which prevails, so that 'the tribunal must confine its attention to those matters expressly referred to in section 72' (1997, p. 591). This is an unfortunate conclusion: to limit the discretion of a tribunal is also to limit the chances for release of detained patients. Elsewhere in the Act — in the powers of hospital managers and doctors to make an order for discharge, for example (see 8.3.2) — discretionary power to release is not fettered in this way. Moreover, as a technical legal matter, where, as here, there seems to be some ambiguity about the scope of a statutory provision, it should be resolved in favour of the liberty of the subject. Technical arguments should not be employed to defeat this principle, even if they can 'technically' be made.

Nevertheless, such an argument has not yet been accepted by a court, and until such time as it is, the only option open to a patient to challenge the legality of his or her admission, short of absconding, is to look to the High Court, and request it to exercise its (discretionary) powers of judicial review or to issue a writ of habeas corpus. The difference between the two, although there is an area of potential overlap, is essentially that judicial review is the appropriate avenue by which to challenge a decision that its maker was lawfully empowered to make but which has been made unlawfully, for example by taking into account some irrelevant factor, whereas habeas corpus should be used when the claim is that there was no jurisdiction for a decision to hold a person in custody. The similarity between them is that neither is an appeal against the *merits* of a decision. Rather, the focus is on the procedures that must be gone through in decision-making, or on the accuracy of facts upon which an admission is based.

5.5.2   The writ of habeas corpus

'Habeas corpus' approximates to 'you must have the body', and is an ancient prerogative writ, which can be found in Magna Carta, designed to protect persons from illegal detention, whether in prison, hospital or some other place. It requires the person having custody of the applicant to present the body of that person before a court and show legal cause for the detention. An admission will be unlawful if some condition precedent is not satisfied. An example is provided by *St George's Healthcare NHS Trust* (see 5.4.1.2). S had been admitted under s. 2 after presenting at a primary health care centre to register with a GP. S was 36 weeks pregnant. Pre-eclampsia was diagnosed and S was advised that there was a risk to herself and to her baby and that a Caesarean section operation was indicated. However, S refused to give her consent to this procedure. She was seen by an ASW and two doctors and quickly admitted to a mental hospital, then transferred to another hospital, at which the operation was performed and a child delivered. A week later, having returned to the mental hospital, S's detention under s. 2 was terminated and she immediately discharged herself. The Court of Appeal held that S's admission to hospital had been unlawful because it had been prompted by concerns about her pregnancy and not the question of whether or not she warranted hospitalisation for any mental disorder. The ASW and recommending doctors had not turned their minds to that question. Therefore, it could not be shown that S was suffering from mental disorder. This was a precedent fact that had not been established and, had S not already been discharged, she would have been entitled to apply for a writ of habeas corpus which, according to Judge LJ 'would have led to her immediate release'.

The applicability and scope of an action for habeas corpus was discussed by the Court of Appeal in *Re S-C* (see 5.4.3). S-C had been admitted to hospital under s. 3 pursuant to an application for admission made by an ASW who had consulted S-C's mother as NR, knowing that in law her NR was actually her father, and that he objected to her admission. Bingham MR held that in such a case a writ of habeas corpus could be made. Although hospital managers are entitled to rely on an application for admission which 'appears to be duly made' by virtue of s. 6(3), and are therefore protected from a claim of false imprisonment, the initial admission remained unlawful. As mentioned above (see 5.4.3) the contrary view of Laws J in *ex parte M* was explicitly overruled on this point as, presumably, by implication were other cases inconsistent with this ruling, such as *R v Governor of Broadmoor, ex parte Argles* (1974), unreported (see Gunn, 1986a, p. 295). The Master of the Rolls held that were it otherwise, the 'horrifying' result would be that as long as an application for admission *appeared to be* lawful it would be so whatever failures or omissions lay behind the face of the document. Even so, a writ was not issued in *Re S-C*, as the hospital managers were not before the court and the case was adjourned for a week to allow them to appear and show cause for S-C's continued detention (in the event, S-C was discharged in the interim and the court made no order).

Thus, although *Re S-C* on one level amounted to a reassertion of the applicability of habeas corpus to unlawful detention in a hospital, it also demonstrates that even on a successful application it does not necessarily follow that the patient's immediate release will be forthcoming. Later cases have followed this pattern. In *Re John (Julie)* [1998] COD 306 (DC) a patient, J, had been detained under s. 3 although her NR had not been consulted. When J's solicitor questioned the legality of her detention, the s. 3 detention was discharged, and she was held under s. 5(2) before being 'readmitted' under s. 2. It seemed clear that the reason for the admission under s. 2 was that J's NR was known not to be prepared to consent to her admission, and so the use of ss. 5(2) and 2 was in the manner of a holding operation until J's NR could be replaced. It was held that her detention under s. 2 was *prima facie* lawful and as those who had engineered it were not available to be cross-examined as to their motives, J's application for habeas corpus had to be dismissed. The judgment carries the danger of implying that as long as those who play fast and loose with the statutory scheme stay away from court there will be no effective (that is, immediate) sanction. In another recent case, in which an application was, in theory at least, successful, the court followed *Re S-C* in allowing the hospital managers in question two days to show why the writ should not be made, as the court was concerned that immediate release would be antitherapeutic: *In the Matter of Briscoe* [1998] COD 402 (HC). Thus habeas corpus, even when successfully pleaded, cannot be relied upon as a mechanism to secure immediate release even if it is clear that a precedent fact, such as the duty to consult with the patient's NR prior to making the application, has not been satisfied. More recently still, the Court of Appeal in *Re Barker* v *Barking Havering and Brentwood Community Healthcare NHS Trust* [1998] 1 FLR 106 has sought to limit the use of habeas corpus in this context (see 5.5.4).

5.5.3 Judicial review

The basis of the High Court's contemporary powers of judicial review is also to be found in the ancient prerogative powers of the Crown. In essence, 'judicial review' refers to the High Court's powers to examine decisions taken on behalf of the state (in the broadest sense of that word), in order to determine whether such decisions have been properly made. One ground for judicial review is that some quality in the decision-maker was defective, such as a lack of appropriate qualifications, an inappropriate delegation of the power in question, or that the decision exhibits bias. However, in *Council of Civil Service Unions* v *Minister for the Civil Service* [1984] 3 All ER 935 Lord Diplock said (at p. 950) that the main three heads of judicial review, which are neither discrete nor necessarily exhaustive, are:

Illegality: the decision-maker does not have the legal authority to make the decision, or has failed to exercise a discretionary power.

Irrationality: a decision-maker cannot use a power, given for one purpose, for another purpose, and cannot consider irrelevant, or fail to consider relevant, information, or make a decision which is so unreasonable that no other decision-maker in a similar situation could make it (this test is known as 'Wednesbury unreasonableness', after the case, *Associated Provincial Picture Houses Ltd* v *Wednesbury Corpn* [1948] 1 KB 223).

Procedural Impropriety: if the statute giving the power or duty in question prescribes procedures, a decision will be reviewable if those procedures are not followed; and decisions must accord with the principles of natural justice, such as the right to a hearing, the right to impartiality in decision-making, and a (circumscribed and far from general) right to know reasons for a decision.

The remedies on a successful application for judicial review are technically discretionary, but there is a 'very limited ambit [to] that discretion in practice when the liberty of the subject is at stake' (per Bingham, MR in *Re S-C* at 539), and the High Court must now give reasons for refusing to grant relief on a successful application: s. 31(6) Supreme Court Act 1981. The remedies are:

Certiorari: the power to quash (nullify) a decision.

Mandamus: the power to compel a public authority to perform a public duty, to consider a matter which does fall within its remit, or to reconsider a matter in which it has been judged to have acted unlawfully.

Prohibition is a lesser used, but sometimes extremely useful, power to prevent an unlawful action by way of an *injunction*.

As Gunn (1986a) notes, that decisions relating to the compulsory admission of a person into a mental hospital are amenable to judicial review seems simply to have been assumed by the courts. But that assumption is not contentious, as decisions taken under the authority of the MHA 1983 are, as is normally required, administrative decisions grounded in statutory power (*Council of Civil Service Unions* per Lord Diplock at p. 949). The leave of the High Court must be sought under RSC Ord 53 (now to be found in Civil Procedure Rules 1998, sch. 1) and s. 31(3), Supreme Court Act 1981 before an application for judicial review can be brought. The purpose of the requirement of seeking leave is to screen out 'groundless, unmeritorious or tardy harassment' (*O'Reilly* v *Mackman* [1982] 3 All ER 1124 per Lord Diplock at p. 1133) of those charged with exercising statutory responsibilities. Leave will be granted if the patient can show that his or her complaint is worthy of fuller investigation: see *IRC* v *National Federation of Self-Employed and Small Businesses Ltd* [1981] 2 All ER 93 (HL). In addition, there is the hurdle presented by s. 139(2), MHA 1983 which provides that no civil proceedings may be brought without the leave of the High Court, and, by s. 139(1), that if leave is given liability can only be established if bad faith or lack of reasonable care can be shown (see 12.2).

However, in *R v Hallstrom and another, ex parte W* (No.1) [1985] 3 All ER 775 (CA) it was held that judicial review did not constitute 'civil proceedings' and therefore s. 139 did not apply. Hence a patient will only need to seek leave once and will not need to show bad faith or negligence (as would be the case under s. 139(2): *Kynaston v Secretary of State for Home Affairs* [1981] 73 Cr App R 281 per Lawton LJ at p. 285), to succeed on the substantive application. An example of a successful challenge to the legality of an admission under s. 3 is provided by *Hallstrom* in which a patient's detention was renewed only in order that immediate leave of absence be given, as a device to get around the embargo on treatment without consent in the community (see 8.2). Gunn (1986a, p. 293) gives the example of an application for admission made by an NR, the main purpose of which was to get the patient out of their house for the NR's benefit as another situation in which an order for certiorari might properly be made.

5.5.4 The relationship between habeas corpus and judicial review

It is easy enough to specify the difference between habeas corpus and judicial review in theory, but in practice the two tend to overlap. For example, a failure to consult with the NR or obtain the necessary medical recommendations can be viewed either as failure to comply with a condition precedent to lawful detention that gives rise to an application for habeas corpus, or as a procedural impropriety open to judicial review. There has long been academic debate about the appropriate cause of action in cases where there is overlap. Judicial review has the advantage of a wider range of remedies, including damages as well as the range of orders set out above, yet to be successful on an application for habeas corpus all that needs to be shown is a *prima facie* case of unlawful detention, which seems easier to satisfy than the requirements of judicial review, particularly with respect to irrationality. Moreover, leave is not required for an application for habeas corpus. Which course to opt for, then, is a tactical question.

But although there is a degree of overlap between the two actions it is important that this is not overstated. In *Re John (Julie)* (see 5.5.2) the application for habeas corpus failed because, having 'gone behind the document' to ascertain whether a precedent fact existed, as the Court of Appeal in *Re S-C* had done, the court in that case could find no obvious defect in the patient's admission, as there had been in *Re S-C*. And because it is not possible to make an order that would be possible under judicial review powers on a habeas corpus application, or an order for habeas corpus on an application for judicial review, the court could offer no remedy. In *Whitbread* (1997) *The Times*, 14 July (CA), a patient sought a writ on the grounds that the consultation that an ASW must have with the patient's NR before making an admission for treatment (s. 11(4)) must, as had not happened in this case, follow the interview with the patient required by s. 11(5). The Court of Appeal held that there was no necessary chronological sequence to which the various requirements of a compulsory admission must adhere. It is enough that they are all complied with. The court emphasised that it is only when there has been some non-compliance (or fraud) that a writ for habeas corpus will be appropriate.

There is, however, no intrinsic point at which habeas corpus stops and judicial review starts, and in *Re Barker* (discussed in greater detail at 8.2) the Court of Appeal played down the advantages of habeas corpus and emphasised the wider range of remedies available by way of judicial review, and withdrew somewhat from the position that had been taken in *Re S-C*, in which the ground that was 'appropriately' covered by habeas corpus had been drawn fairly widely. Lord Woolf MR referred to the dangers of duplication of proceedings, and expressed a strong preference that wherever possible actions should be commenced by way of an application for judicial review unless it was clear that an action for habeas corpus was the only appropriate action. Such situations will be rare. Habeas corpus has always been a remedy of last resort, to be used only when all avenues have been exhausted. Although the point about duplication is valid, and although Lord Woolf held that if both actions were commenced their progress should be harmonised, the practical effect of *Barker* is that, because of the need to seek leave, the judiciary have greater control earlier in the process than would be the case if an expansive attitude to the availability of habeas corpus were to be adopted. This means that in future situations like that in *Re S-C*, cases should be argued on the basis of procedural impropriety rather than unlawful detention. It remains to be seen whether this advice is heeded by advocates. Even if the range of remedies is in practice of little consequence, some may feel that to have to surmount the additional hurdle of seeking leave will delay, and hence deny, justice to their clients. It is also interesting to speculate what impact the Human Rights Act 1998 and its incorporation into domestic law of the right under art. 5(4) ECHR) to have the lawfulness of one's detention 'decided speedily by a court', will have on the way that applications to the High Court for release are framed.

5.6   CONCLUDING COMMENTS

As the discussion in this Chapter shows, at its worst the process of admission under part II can be little more than 'legalism' in its entirely negative sense; a set of tiresome bureaucratic requirements that are a source of irritation for, but do not actually impede, those who control admissions 'on the ground'. Even when the courts have found that an admission to hospital is unlawful, therapeutic considerations are, as in the habeas corpus cases, frequently allowed greater weight than a civil libertarian might wish to see. It does seem innocuous that the courts espouse a rhetoric of individual freedom, find that it has been infringed in the case before them, and then decline to grant the order sought. In other cases, those of *H* and *Hallstrom* provide examples, law has proved able to allow patients and their relatives a means by which successfully to challenge the exercise of power by professionals.

But successful challenges are conspicuous by their rarity. It is important to remember that many, although by no means all, admissions under part II proceed with the consent and agreement of all those involved, with the exception of the patient, as by definition the compulsory powers of confinement should not be used if the patient consents to hospitalisation; and the paperwork involved provides a positive incentive to avoid the use of the compulsory powers. Yet consent may not of course always be genuine, and this is true of those involved in the admissions procedure as it is of patients. The evidence suggests that the admissions procedure is driven principally by psychiatrists. Although ASWs are in the role of applicant, an application must be accepted by the hospital and so there is in practice a power of veto reserved to psychiatrists over the decision-making abilities of ASWs. Of course there will be cases, perhaps the majority, in which there is little scope to disagree that hospitalisation is required, whatever perspective one brings to that question. But on occasion differences in perspective will matter. It will be a strong minded ASW who resists making an application when requested to do so by a psychiatrist. Conversely, without the requisite medical recommendations an ASW cannot make an application. GPs are similarly likely to endorse the views of the specialist. In practice there are various ways around an impasse: find another doctor, find another ASW, remove a recalcitrant NR under s. 29, and so on. But it remains the case that despite the strict legal situation, admission to hospital is under the control of the psychiatric profession, and that control is inhibited more by questions of resources than by legal restraints. Against the broader background of the 'medicalisation of mental disorder', however, such a conclusion is perhaps not surprising.

SIX

Mental disorder and criminal justice

6.1 INTRODUCTION

Mental disorder and criminality are often viewed by the general public and the media as 'natural' bedfellows (Health Education Authority, 1997). This view is built into the fabric of the powers of civil confinement under the MHA 1983, which inscribes 'abnormally aggressive or seriously irresponsible conduct' into the definitions of mental impairment, severe mental impairment and psychotic disorder (see 2.2), 'dangerousness' into the powers of a responsible medical officer (RMO) to veto an application for discharge made by a nearest relative of the patient (see 8.3.2), and so on. Yet there is much reason to think that, although these two concepts clearly overlap, the extent of the linkage of mental disorder with criminality is, at root, dictated more by the way in which each is constructed and responded to, both by the state and the public at large, than by any innate qualities of the concepts themselves. As Peay (1997, p. 687) has pointed out, for example, 'the overwhelming correlates of violence are male gender, youth, low socio-economic class, and the use/abuse of alcohol or drugs, and not the diagnosis of major mental disorder'.

Long and Midgely (1992) trace the linkages made in professional and popular understandings of these two concepts in the nineteenth century. The causes of each were understood in much the same way, which meant that the 'two could be viewed together, two sides of a common problem' (1992, pp.64-5). At the same time, the problem of 'criminal lunatics' was very much in the public eye (see 1.4). When professional disenchantment with the potential to cure either the insane or the criminal set in, towards the end of the century, the view of the 'incurable criminal lunatic' as the archetype of both mental illness and criminality gained ground accordingly, in popular as well as professional discourses (Foucault, 1988). In part this mythology (for mythology it largely is) has been maintained through to the present day through a series of folk devils with a roll call that begins with Jack the Ripper, and includes Crippen, Hindley and Brady, Sutcliffe, Nielson, and which in recent years has taken on a broader complexion with homicides and other crimes committed by persons released from hospitals into care in the community (see 9.5). The 'criminal lunatic', and the conflation of the two concepts which such a person is set up to represent, is part of our cultural furniture, a staple in drama, from Hammer Horror to Fatal Attraction. In part also, though, it can be argued that this linkage is a professional tactic or technology of professional dominance. Szasz (1970), for example, has famously argued that the emergent profession of psychiatry campaigned successfully for a strategic linkage of the concepts of criminality and madness in the nineteenth century in order to stake out a professional stamping ground for themselves within the asylum and the prison, and since then has protected that linkage from attempts to separate it. It is certainly the case that the modern prison has been a continuous home for psychiatry. As Long and Midgely point out, right from the start of its life in 1842 Pentonville prison's inmate population featured an over-representation of lunatics by almost ten times more than would have been expected; a feature of imprisonment which as will be seen has changed little today.

Yet the 'official' state response to crime and mental disorder is structured around the supposition that there should be a separation rather than a conflation of criminality and madness. The health care system and the criminal justice system are, in theory at least, distinct systems pursuing different goals. Mentally disordered offenders, however, render that distinction problematic, and when a person who is, or is suspected to be, mentally disordered, comes into contact with the criminal justice system, the appropriate state response is far from clear. Each such individual represents in microcosm the dilemma of policy: treatment or punishment? Ironically there is in fact a certain ambiguity in the response of the state; an ambivalence about whether a mentally disordered offender should be treated or punished, which can be found also in the way in which the relationship between the health care system and penal system is formulated in law and policy, and in how that relationship is actually negotiated in practice. According to a government circular (Home Office, 1990, para. 2), 'it is government policy that, wherever possible, mentally disordered persons should receive care and treatment from the health and social services'. The circular proceeds to outline, and encourage the use by the various agencies of the criminal justice system of, the various legal mechanisms that are available to 'divert' mentally disordered offenders and suspects into the mental health system. In general terms the policy, then, is one of *diversion*. But the reference to 'wherever possible' makes clear that this is not a blanket policy, and in practice we are a long way from the full realisation of such a policy, for a number of reasons. Chief amongst these is the fact that the MHA 1983 functions more as a *threshold* than as a simple gateway between the two systems. Not all those who can be *clinically* classified as mentally disordered will meet the criteria for diversion out of the criminal justice system under the terms of the 1983 Act. For example, the exclusion from the mental health regime by s. 1(3) of the 1983 Act (see 2.2) of those whose disorder only manifests in the form of the misuse of drugs or alcohol explains a sizeable proportion of the mentally disordered, sentenced prison population as measured by clinicians (see Brooke et al, 1996, and below). There are other varieties of diversion, for example a decision by the police or the CPS not to proceed with a prosecution, which are not governed by such strictly defined criteria, but it is nevertheless the case that the 1983 Act does not attempt, nor should the Home Office be thought to advocate, a policy of diverting *all* people who could be said to be mentally disordered in some way. Even when it can be shown that an individual does satisfy the criteria for diversion required by the 1983 Act there is usually a discretion whether to act on that evidence. This is because the well-being of the offender is not the only concern, which must be balanced against the need to protect the public and to punish the culpable. And within the framework of the criminal justice system there may well be other options open, such as opting for a non-custodial criminal disposal, which can amount to a *de facto* diversionary measure.

These issues are controversial, and they raise the practical problem, both for operatives of the system as well as commentators on and students of it, of trying to gauge how well it is working, since which individuals should be diverted, at what stage of the process, and what form that diversion should take, are questions which do not permit of any easy or completely satisfactory answers. It will inevitably be to some extent at least a matter of opinion, comprising both clinical and moral considerations, whether or not a particular individual is a suitable candidate for diversion. It can be said that in principle a person who is mentally disordered but not sufficiently so as to satisfy the strict legal requirements for diversion should not be diverted. But it cannot be said that a person who does satisfy the criteria should be diverted: and it is this second scenario which in practice is most relevant.

The preference for a policy of diversion depends on the view taken of mental disorder and criminality. Szasz, for example, holds that there should be no diversion, that hospitals should not be places of compulsory confinement; and that follows from his understanding of mental disorder as a construction of the psychiatric professions. If, on the other hand, one concedes that on occasion at least the presence of mental disorder negates *mens rea*, then there can be no guilt and therefore no punishment. Rarely if ever is the situation so straightforward in practice. Even if a person can be shown to be mentally disordered, to show that there is a relationship between his or her disorder and offending is quite another question. By and large the current regime avoids these difficulties altogether, and makes diversion dependent solely on the presence of mental disorder (in fact, specific forms of mental disorder are usually required) without attempting to link that disorder with the offending behaviour, preferring rather to balance the two factors when deciding on disposal. Nevertheless it has been the established orthodoxy throughout the last decade that diversion is a 'good thing'. This Chapter does not seek to challenge that assertion, although this does seem to be the policy of the present government (see 6.7). Instead, the aim is to evaluate diversion on its own terms: does the law, policy and practice of diversion actually work?

6.2 DIVERSION FROM PROSECUTION

6.2.1 Early diversion from the criminal process

Police officers are empowered by s. 136, MHA 1983 to remove to a place of safety a person found in a public place who appears to be mentally disordered and in need of care or control (see 4.5.4). This in itself may function as a diversionary measure, as the s. 136 powers may be used even when the person in question has or may have committed an offence. There is research evidence to suggest that in deciding whether to proceed, factors such as the practicalities of pressing charges and the perceived seriousness of an individual's mental state are taken into account (Rogers, 1990). A decision not to proceed with criminal charges will often involve officers in negotiation with hospitals or social service departments. As was discussed at 4.6, around one in ten of hospital admissions are consequent upon the use of s. 136 powers, but in practice early diversion is something of a lottery, as much will depend on the availability of local alternatives that satisfy the officer in question that a decision not to proceed can be taken. Rowlands et al (1996) found that the most common form of diversion used by the police is to grant bail to a suspect after having arranged for an outpatient psychiatric assessment, although there was a high rate of failure to attend for such an assessment, particularly amongst substance abusers. Psychiatric services were able, however, to maintain contact with a sizeable number of persons, although most were not formally diverted until the stage of court disposal, when probation orders and discharges were reasonably common.

All of this depends on the abilities of police officers to detect the presence of mental disorder. This issue will be discussed in more detail below, but it is worth pointing out here that, as Laing (1995) documents, schemes in magistrates' court to identify and if appropriate divert those with mental disorders (see further below, 6.3.1) have begun to spread to police stations; and the process seems to have gathered momentum following the proposal to that effect made by the Royal Commission on Criminal Justice (1993, para. 92). An early and seemingly successful diversion scheme has been running in Birmingham since 1992. The scheme involves a Community Psychiatric Nurse (CPN) being present at police stations to screen for mental disorder problems and arrange for care to be given where necessary. In the first six months of this scheme (which began in 1992) only one individual identified as requiring psychiatric intervention by the CPN eventually went to court to face the criminal charges in question (Laing, 1995, p. 372). Nationally, however, such findings are unusual, and the preponderance of research shows that s. 136 is 'unlikely to be used when evidence of a notifiable crime is present' (Robertson et al, 1996, p. 176). The police, most often, prefer to leave the decision as to diversion to the court. There is of course the intermediary stage, at which a case put forward by police will be reviewed by an officer of the Crown Prosecution Service (CPS). The task of the CPS is to establish both that there is sufficient evidence for a case to proceed, and that it is in the public interest that a prosecution should be brought. One factor that should incline against proceeding is 'significant' mental illness, although this has to be balanced against the likelihood of repetition of the alleged offence. For some, it is not obvious that diversion on grounds of mental illness is to be encouraged, as it can amount to a denial of an accused person's right to test the evidence against him or her in a court, and so be seen to treat mentally ill persons as second class citizens (Carson, 1989b). There is little evidence on how these tasks are discharged by the CPS, but such evidence as there is (Cooke, 1991) suggests that, like the police, the CPS prefers to let evidentially strong cases proceed, and leave the diversion decision to the courts.

6.2.2   Diversion within the criminal process

Most mentally disordered persons who enter police custody are not immediately diverted out of the criminal process, but instead are funnelled into a second variant of diversion, which is found in Code of Guidance C, Police and Criminal Evidence Act 1984 (PACE). This is concerned with the diversion of mentally disordered criminal suspects, along with other 'vulnerable' detainees such as juveniles, into an investigative regime with greater safeguards than are ordinarily implemented. Code C was introduced in response to a highly publicised litany of miscarriages of justice involving mentally handicapped or mentally ill persons based on confession evidence given in police interviews. The Royal Commission on Criminal Procedure was set up in 1978 following the case in which an eighteen-year-old man with learning disabilities was, with two others, convicted of the murder of Maxwell Confait on the basis of confession evidence later shown not to have been true. Other notable appeals based on pre-PACE practice include those of Stefan Kiszko and Judith Ward. PACE extended the existing system of safeguards to cover mentally ill as well as mentally handicapped criminal suspects. The introduction of Code C has not, however, ameliorated concerns about miscarriages: in 1994 the pressure group, Justice reported 89 suspected miscarriages by reason of disputed confession evidence (Justice, 1994).

Continued concerns about the treatment of mentally disordered persons in police custody are partly explicable in terms of uncertainties and gaps in the regime laid out by the Code, as will be discussed below (see 6.2.2.1). But part of the explanation lies in the fact that Code C is targeted at police officers and has as its primary aim to ensure that evidence gathered in police interviews can survive challenge under ss. 76, 77 and 78 of PACE. Section 76(2)(a) requires a court to exclude evidence obtained by oppression, and s. 76(2)(b) requires that evidence obtained in circumstances likely to render any confession unreliable be excluded, unless the prosecution can prove beyond reasonable doubt that it was not in fact so obtained. Section 78(1) gives a discretion to exclude evidence which would adversely affect the fairness of the proceedings if admitted. Section 77(1) places a duty on a trial judge to warn a jury of the dangers of relying solely on the uncorroborated confession evidence of a mentally handicapped (but not mentally ill) person obtained in the absence of an independent third party. Code C, therefore, is, in a sense, only incidentally concerned to protect the rights of mentally disordered suspects and it is not concerned to divert offenders away from prosecution on grounds of mental disorder. This is a good example of the point that at the general level the policy is not diversion *per se*. Section 77(1) contemplates that a prosecution of a mentally disordered offender should go ahead, as long as the safeguards therein are adhered to, even if there has been a breach of the Code, and not that there should be no prosecution. In effect, the diversion question is then passed to the court.

6.2.2.1   The operation of the 'appropriate adult' scheme

6.2.2.1.1   The role of the 'appropriate adult'   When a vulnerable suspect is detained or interviewed by police officers in connection with an alleged offence, Code C of PACE prescribes a regime designed to ensure that the interests and rights of detainees are protected by the presence of an independent third party known as the 'appropriate adult' (AA). In general terms, the function of an AA is 'to befriend, advise and assist' the detainee (RCCJ, 1993, para. 4.103). More precise guidance is found at para. 11.16 of Code C:

> The appropriate adult is not expected to act simply as an observer. The purposes of his presence are first to advise the person being questioned, and to observe whether or not the interview is being conducted fairly; and secondly, to facilitate communication with the person being interviewed.

The presence of an AA does not depend on whether or not a mentally disordered suspect is to be interviewed. An AA should be asked by the custody officer to attend at the police station in any case (para. 3.9 Code C). If the detainee is not to be interviewed, that may well be the extent of the AA's involvement. Most persons — around 70 per cent (Robertson et al, 1996, p. 299) — detained at a police station are not in fact interviewed. When interviews do occur, they tend to be of short duration, with half being conducted within 20 minutes and 75 per cent within half an hour (Robertson et al, 1996; McConville and Hodgson, 1993).

If there is to be an interview, para. 11.14 of Code C provides that a mentally handicapped or disordered person 'whether suspected or not, must not be interviewed or asked to provide or sign a written statement in the absence of the appropriate adult'. There should be the opportunity for private consultation between the detainee and the AA before the start of a formal interview (para. 3.13), and at its commencement the AA should explain his or her role to the detainee while the tape is running. In this way the role of AA is reminiscent of that of attending solicitor, and in *R v Lewis* (Martin) [1996] Crim LR 260 (CA), it was said that the functions of each were essentially similar. However, lawyers do not necessarily have training in mental health matters and legal advice at police stations can be of low quality (Hodgson, 1997, pp.787, 794). Surely, the reason that a suspect should have the services of an AA in addition, if wanted, to those of a solicitor, is that it is intended that the AA will bring special knowledge of the particular suspect or expertise in dealing with persons who are mentally handicapped or mentally ill that, by implication, a solicitor is not expected to have. Moreover, it is not obviously the responsibility of a solicitor to 'facilitate communication' with the suspect. In a recent Court of Appeal decision, *R v Aspinall* (1999) *The Times*, 4 February, this sort of argument was accepted, and the court emphasised that the role of the AA, in safeguarding the interests of the interviewee, is broader than and distinct from that of an attending solicitor.

However, the detail of the role remains unclear. For example, a solicitor might advise a 'no comment' interview: should an AA still attempt to 'facilitate communication'? As Fennell (1994, p. 67) has said, the 'danger is that the role of facilitating communication may be over-emphasised to the extent that the [AA] becomes an agent of the interrogating officers'. The situation in *R* v *Jefferson, Skerritt, Readman and Keogh* [1994] 99 Crim App R 130 (CA) came very close to realising this concern. In this case the Court of Appeal upheld a decision not to exclude confession evidence obtained by interview of a juvenile suspect in the presence of his father as AA, on the grounds that the father had on occasion robustly joined in the questioning of his son, as this, it was held, had not impeded the father's ability to perform a protective role. Given what is known about the suggestibility or the urge to confess or to please others that some vulnerable persons exhibit (Royal Commission on Criminal Justice, 1993, p. 57), this in itself is a questionable decision. However, it also points to the broader uncertainties about the function of the AA and the interrelationship of that role with that of legal representative: should an AA take an 'interventionist' or a 'passive' role? If it is the former, how should the demarcation of the role of AA from that of legal advisor be expressed? What if there is no legal representative? AAs have an independent right to request the presence at the police station of a solicitor (Code C, para. 3.13), although this fact does not seem to be well known and, as in *R* v *Morse* [1991] Crim LR 195 (see 6.2.2.1.2) an AA may decline legal advice. How does this affect the role of the AA? What are the implications of the truncation of the 'right to silence' by ss. 34, 36 and 37 of the Criminal Justice and Public Order Act 1994 (see Fennell, 1994a, pp.58-60) for AAs? A key distinction between the situation of a solicitor and that of an AA is that there is no privilege in any statements made by the detainee to the AA. This can create a dilemma for an AA charged on the one hand to protect the rights of the detainee and on the other having no legal right to withhold information from the police, even if the detainee assumed that any information disclosed to the AA would remain confidential. Is it possible to 'befriend' a detainee and pass on his or her confidences to the investigating officers? In summary, although it is possible to give an account in broad terms of the appropriate role of an AA, the more the detail is examined the less clear the appropriate role becomes; and the more clear it becomes that to act as an AA is potentially extremely difficult.

    6.2.2.1.2 Who should act as AA? Despite the apparent complexities of the role of the AA, there is no requirement that an AA be given suitable training. For mentally disordered suspects, Code C provides that the AA should be a relative or guardian of the suspect, or a person with experience of mental handicap or mental illness, or failing that some other responsible person (para. 1.7(b)). A police employee may not act as an AA, nor may a lawyer attending the police station in a professional capacity, nor a probation officer (unless specifically requested by the detainee): *R* v *O'Neill* (1990) 16 October, unreported (Crown Court). An AA must be an adult: *R* v *Palmer* (1991) *Legal Action*, 21 September) (Crown Court); who is able effectively to communicate in English: *H & M* v *DPP* [1998] Crim LR 653 (CA); and who is able in fact to empathise with the suspect: *DPP* v *Blake* [1989] WLR 432 (CA). An AA should take an active role in events and so needs the mental capacity to fulfil the role. In *R* v *Morse* [1991] Crim LR 195 the father of a juvenile suspect acted as the AA during a police interview, but a psychologist later gave evidence that the father was of low IQ and was probably unable to appreciate the gravity of the situation and what was expected of him as an AA. The confession evidence obtained in the interview was excluded by a Crown Court under s. 76(2)(b), PACE, holding that the prosecution had failed to discharge its burden of proving that the unsuitability of the father to act as the AA had not raised doubts about the reliability of the evidence.

There are cases going the other way. In *R* v *W and another* [1994] Crim LR 130 (CA) the Court of Appeal emphasised that it is concern about the manner in which evidence was obtained, and not about the truth of the evidence, that triggered consideration of s. 76 (see also *R* v *Cox* [1991] Crim LR 276 (CA)). The court nevertheless upheld a decision to admit evidence obtained by way of police interview of a juvenile suspect in the presence of her mother acting as an AA, even though the mother herself was a person who, if detained, would require the presence of an AA, being mentally handicapped and suffering from psychosis. This was on the basis that the mother's psychotic thoughts were apparently concerned exclusively with her neighbours, and she was in fact capable of acting rationally in connection with the events in question. This is perhaps an unfortunate decision. It seems wrong in policy terms that a person whom the AA regime is intended to protect can herself act as an AA for a third party. Other worrying decisions include *Jefferson, Skerritt, Readman* and *Keogh* (discussed in 6.2.2.1.1), on the facts of which it is doubtful that the detainee would have felt befriended by his AA. These cases show the Court of Appeal being prepared to sanction an AA in situations that seem to depart from the spirit of protection behind the scheme, and that the courts have been satisfied with a bare minimum in terms of what is required of an AA. It may be that the trend has been bucked by *Aspinall* (see 6.2.2.1.1), insofar as the court emphasised the importance attached by the statutory scheme, not only to the attendance of an AA, but to that person's active involvement and active pursuance of his or her responsibilities towards the detainee.

Although parents most commonly act as AAs in respect of juvenile detainees, there is in fact a preference amongst police officers for social workers to be used for adult detainees (Brown, Ellis and Larcombe, 1993), although Bean and Nemetz (n.d) found that in one Midlands area victim support volunteers were preferred. Code C, in Note of Guidance 1E, advises that a trained AA is to be preferred to a relative of the suspect, and it is clear that an untrained AA may do more harm than good, by giving the appearance, but not the reality, of third party protection. But to secure the services of an AA who is not a member of the detainee's family is not to guarantee that that person has suitable training. For example, some local authorities, unable through pressure of resources to spare full time staff for this work, use social work volunteers who may well have no specialist training. Some ostensibly suitable providers of AAs, such as MENCAP, decline to cooperate with the AA scheme, precisely because in the past volunteers have experienced difficulties of the type discussed above with the role (Fennell, 1994a, p. 67). Suitable AAs can be hard to find, as Robertson and his colleagues discovered when researching the use of AAs in London: the researchers were coopted to act as AAs during their fieldwork 'to avoid lengthy delays for police and detainee' (1996, p. 309).

6.2.2.1.3   Detecting the need for an 'appropriate adult'   As with diversion out of the criminal justice system altogether, the efficacy of this scheme depends on the ability of police officers to detect the presence of mental disorder. Key to this is the role of the custody officer, usually a sergeant, who has a general responsibility for the welfare of detained persons and to ensure that no person is detained longer than is necessary. It is also the duty of the custody officer to inform an AA if a detainee is mentally handicapped or appears to be mentally disordered (Code C, para. 3.9), and to arrange for a Forensic Medical Examiner (FME, or police surgeon) to examine the detainee if it appears to the custody officer that the detainee is suffering from mental disorder (Code C, para. 9.2). In research carried out for the Royal Commission on Criminal Justice (the Runcimann Commission), Gudjonsson et al (1993) found that very often the presence of disorder is missed by custody officers, with AAs being present at 4 per cent of all interviews of adult suspects, yet being required in around 15 per cent. Other research reports even lower AA attendance rates (Bean and Nemetz, n.d.). This situation is perhaps not surprising. Police custody suites can be very busy places, and individuals with no history of mental disorder can react in a bizarre manner to the fact of arrest and detention (Gudjonsson, 1992). The influence of alcohol or drugs can be confused with the presence of mental disorder (Palmer, 1996, pp.634-5), and there is evidence to suggest that persons with learning difficulties or who are otherwise vulnerable, for instance by reason of illiteracy, may try to disguise their difficulties (Hodgson, 1997, p. 787). There is evidence to suggest that custody officers in London are more adept at detecting the need for an AA than their colleagues elsewhere (Roberston et al, 1996).

Palmer's (1996) study of police practices in Yorkshire confirmed the findings of earlier research that, although major disorders may be detected, minor disorders frequently are not. Palmer's research also highlighted the frequently made point that the lack of assistance given to police officers by way of a definition of mental disorder results in officers applying their own definitions. As one interviewee said: '[t]here is no test really as far as I can work out' (cited in Palmer, 1996, p. 634) and so some officers interpret the need for an 'adult' to indicate that it is detainees who exhibit 'childlike' behaviour who are to be defined as mentally disordered. In *Aspinall* (see 6.2.2.1.1), the detainee, who was in receipt of medication for schizophrenia, was adjudged by all concerned not to need the presence of an AA, as his illness was not then acute. He was also convicted in the Crown Court and it took the Court of Appeal to affirm that an AA should be called to attend, even if the detainee appeared to be lucid. It is not surprising, then, that the constant refrain of commentators is to emphasise the need for more and better training of police officers, and custody officers in particular, in matters of learning disability, mental health and illness.

6.2.2.1.4   The role of the forensic medical examiner and the question of 'fitness for interview'   Code C of PACE 1984 requires that before a mentally disordered person can be interviewed, he or she must be examined by an FME. FMEs are often GPs who work on a part-time basis for the police, attending to the injuries that police officers sustain in the course of their duties, as well as carrying out physical and mental health checks on detainees when required. There have long been concerns about the suitability of GPs (Royal Commission on Criminal Justice, 1993, para. 90), and although some forces, including the Metropolitan police force, do require FMEs to undertake relevant training, in other areas of the country FMEs will not necessarily have any specialist training in recognising mental disorder. A further cause for concern is that it is apparently the practice in some police forces not to call an AA until a suspicion of mental disorder has been confirmed by an FME examination (Palmer, 1996, p. 638). Yet it is clear from Code C of PACE that an AA should be contacted at the same time as the FME, and the task of the FME is to report on fitness for interview, and not the need for an AA.

There are three possible conclusions that an FME may reach on examining a detainee: that he or she is not fit for interview; is fit if there is an AA present; or is fit without the presence of an AA. What is not clear is *how* any conclusion should be arrived at. Before 1994 the decision was left totally to the FME concerned, but in that year the British Medical Association and Association of Police Surgeons issued guidance on the meaning of 'fitness for interview' (British Medical Association and Association of Police Surgeons, 1994). This guidance advised that fitness for interview should be assessed by reference to: an assessment of the detainee's competence to understand the situation and questions to be put to him or her; whether there was a need for an AA to be present; the expected length and conditions of the intended interview; and recommended also that the detainee be reassessed after interview. However, this guidance is less helpful than it might be because it does not discuss yardsticks, or how to discern into which of the three categories any given individual fits (Norfolk, 1997). It is clear that on occasion there is a failure to identify the presence of mental disorder, an infamous example being that of Travis Clarke (Laing, 1995, p. 374), who took his own life only hours after having been judged at no risk of suicide by an FME. Gudjonsson (1995) has suggested an approach which asks whether any statement made by the interviewee would be 'necessarily reliable', and if the answer to that question is 'no', then the detainee is not fit to be interviewed. Norfolk similarly advocates a functionalist approach, such that a person should be regarded as unfit if there is a 'substantial risk' that any statement made is likely to be unreliable, and where there is a 'significant risk' any interview should only proceed in the presence of an AA (Norfolk, 1997, p. 231). Although there will be problems with any chosen form of words, it is surely correct to emphasise that fitness for interview is concerned with the reliability of any information gathered, rather than the abilities of the interviewee to 'cope with' the experience of being interviewed. It seems that in practice, custody officers are on occasion more cautious than FMEs and, no doubt with at least one eye on the requirements of ss. 76 to 78 PACE, will bail a suspect to return to the police station at a later date if the officer feels that he or she is not at that time fit for interview, or will contact an AA to be present during interview, even if the FME states that the suspect is fit to be interviewed (Robertson et al, 1996). As *Aspinall* shows, however, this will not always be the case.

6.2.2.1.5 Should 'appropriate adults' be retained? There are examples to be found, *O'Neill* (see 6.2.2.1.2) is one, of police officers actively impeding a person attempting to assume the role of AA. But it is by far more common to find that persons called on to act in that capacity in fact do very little other than observe the proceedings (Littlechild, 1995, p. 541; Palmer, 1996, p. 641; Hodgson, 1997, p. 790). This is perhaps not surprising, given the difficulties of trying to determine exactly what is expected of an AA, and the fact that the AA has trespassed into the heartland of police territory, described by Simon Holdaway as 'an "inner sanctuary" of police stations where police are in total control, and social workers (and others) are potential challengers' (Holdaway, 1983, cited in Littlechild, 1995, p. 542). The police station and in particular the interview room can be a daunting and disempowering environment for those not accustomed to it.

And yet the presence of an AA is constructed in the current scheme of things as a vital mechanism by which the interests of the detainee are protected. There are many reported cases in which evidence obtained at interview has been held inadmissible by a court for want of the presence of an AA (see for example *R* v *Maloney and Doherty* [1988] Crim LR 523; *Palmer, Blake, O'Neill* and *Aspinall* discussed above). But the courts have also consistently held that the absence of an AA at the interview of a mentally handicapped suspect is not sufficient *per se* to render the suspect's confession inadmissible. Instead, the court should look to the circumstances of the interview and form a view of the effect of the absence of an AA on it: *DPP* v *Cornish* (1997) *The Times*, 27 January (CA). Quite how a court is to ask this hypothetical question of itself is far from clear — does it imply a 'reasonable AA' for example, or should the court consider what the effect of the absence of a *particular* AA may have been? Nevertheless, in *R* v *Law-Thompson* [1997] Crim LR 674 and in *Aspinall*, the Court of Appeal reiterated the stance in *Cornish*.

By the same token, in cases like *Cox* and *Jefferson*, when there is an AA present, the courts have been reluctant to exclude evidence, even if the AA seemed in fact to do very little or even 'sided with' the investigating officers, or there has been a breach of Code C of PACE. In the *H & M* case, for example, the Court of Appeal decided that although there had been a breach of para. 11.16 of Code C, as an AA had not been identified formally and the person who acted as *de facto* AA was unaware of the responsibilities attendant on the role, there had been no substantive injustice as a result and the interests of the vulnerable persons (in that case juveniles) had in fact been protected and there was no reason therefore to exclude evidence obtained in interview.

The message from the Court of Appeal in these cases is twofold. First, it is that when there is an independent third party present, he or she will only be judged not to be an AA if the standard of assistance to the detained person is very poor indeed. Secondly, even when there is no AA, evidence will only be excluded if, in the opinion of the trial court, there is good reason to think that the evidence *is in fact* unreliable. This marks a shift away from the approach taken by the Court of Appeal in cases like *R* v *Kenny* [1994] Crim LR 284, where it was emphasised that the issue for the court was whether the breach of the Code made it *likely* that evidence obtained was unreliable. Both elements of the message give cause for concern, since the Court of Appeal is seemingly prepared to endorse the provision of a low or at least variable quality service to mentally disordered detainees, the long history of miscarriages involving such persons notwithstanding.

It is a live question, given the review of mental health law, whether the AA system should continue in its present form. Fennell for one has suggested that the way forward is to abolish the role of AA, and instead put in place a scheme which ensures that mentally disordered suspects are automatically attended at the police station by 'fully qualified solicitors with special training in advising mentally disordered clients' (1994a, p. 67). This has the merit of avoiding the existing overlap in terms of personnel but it does not necessarily mean that the fundamental tension between the protective and facilitative elements of the role of legal advisor and AA will be any better reconciled. There seems to be a consensus that the key is effective training, but not all think that it is members of the legal profession who should be trained. Hodgson (1997) for example has pointed out that the term 'vulnerable' covers a wide range of conditions, even excluding consideration of juvenile suspects, and so there should be a variety of professionals — social workers, community psychiatric nurses — who would be recognised, on completion of both a generic and specialist training programme, as 'authorised' AAs, available to the police in need of the particular type of specialist help.

But trained personnel would not answer all the problems of the current system. There is, as Palmer (1996, p. 643) notes, a lack of strategic planning, and if the commitment is towards developing a nationwide, 24-hour responsive scheme, then some sort of national framework is required to deliver it. There are considerable resources implications attached to any set of proposals for change which would in effect professionalise what has hitherto been a largely voluntary, shoestring operation. Parents and relatives may attend at police stations free of charge but the quality of service which such persons can realistically be expected to provide by way of safeguarding the position of the detainee is low. Other substantive changes are required — for instance the limitation of s. 77, PACE to mentally handicapped persons is anomalous. The protection offered by the section should be extended to all vulnerable interviewees. And if there are to be trained specialist AAs then it behoves the courts to recognise their worth and vigilantly to exclude evidence obtained in the absence of the detainee's advocate. Even with all this done, it would still be necessary to clarify the nature of the role of advocate, which means not only providing internal coherence but also some guidance on its relationship to that of attending solicitor. Perhaps the real virtue of Fennell's suggestion is that it offers a solution that simply avoids this latter problem.

6.3 COURT BASED DIVERSION BEFORE THE SENTENCING STAGE

Virtually all criminal prosecutions open in a magistrates' court. Much of the throughput of magistrates' courts is in terms of one-off court appearances at which the case against the defendant is proven, or, more commonly, there is a guilty plea, and the defendant is convicted and sentenced immediately. Such cases are typically trivial in nature and most are dealt with by way of a fine. It is very rare that the defendant will have any further contact with officers either of the criminal justice system or the mental health services after conviction. However, in a significant minority of cases, progress through the system is less rapid. More serious offences, known as 'indictable offences', can only be heard by the Crown Court and require that the defendant is remanded, on bail or in custody, for considerable periods of time. For middle order ('either way') offences, either the defendant or the bench may elect for Crown Court trial. In some cases, magistrates will convict but then pass the case to the Crown Court for sentencing. In others, for example if a court is considering passing a prison sentence in certain circumstances, or is dealing with a member of a class of offenders, reports of various types, including psychiatric reports, must be called for (ss. 3,4, Criminal Justice Act 1991), and cases adjourned for that purpose. This means that the engagement with the trial process can for some be a protracted experience.

There are a number of legal mechanisms for the diversion of mentally disordered suspects from the judicial process before conviction and sentencing, although these are in the main intended to facilitate either the trial — for example by providing the accused person with treatment to allow the trial to proceed — or the sentencing process — by gathering information relevant to that process — rather than to divert the accused person out of that process. Nevertheless, on occasion a defendant may never become fit to be tried, or reports may lead to a more informally engineered diversionary disposal. It is also possible in certain circumstances for a court to make a long-term diversionary order for the hospitalisation of an accused person by way of final disposal of the case, without convicting the defendant.

6.3.1   Bail or remand? Questions of policy, practice and resources

In strict theory, remand in custody is the exception not the rule. Virtually all accused persons have the same entitlement to bail. Section 4(1), Bail Act 1976 introduced a statutory presumption in favour of granting bail to accused persons, including persons whose case is adjourned after conviction to enable reports to be made: s. 4(4). The presumption can be rebutted for various reasons, to do with the likelihood of reoffending, absconding or interfering with witnesses: sch. 1, part I, paras. 2, 2A, Bail Act 1976. It is possible to attach conditions to a bail order, relating for example to attendance for medical report or treatment, place of abode and so on: s. 3(6),(6)A, Bail Act 1976. Home Office guidance (1990) urges magistrates to work in cooperation with health authorities, and para. 8(1) requires magistrates to give consideration to alternatives to remand in hospital, such as the attachment as a condition to an order granting bail that the defendant stay in a hospital or attend as an out-patient. Moreover, according to para. 7 'a mentally disordered person should never be remanded to prison simply to receive medical treatment or assessment', and the power to remand instead to hospital rather than to prison 'should be used wherever possible to obtain a medical report on an accused person's condition': para. 8(2).

However, the remand prison population has continually been found to contain a high number of mentally disordered persons (Taylor and Gunn, 1984). A recent survey which sampled 9.4 per cent of the male unconvicted prison population of England and Wales (Brooke et al, 1996) found that 63 per cent had some form of psychiatric disorder. The largest diagnostic group was 'harmful drug or alcohol misuse', which is defined as a form of mental disorder by the psychiatric profession but is excluded from the ambit of the 1983 Act by virtue of s. 1(3). Research carried out by Birmingham et al (1996) at Durham prison, which did exclude substance abuse, found that 26 per cent of remand receptions had a form of serious mental disorder. Brooke et al (1996) are quick to point out that, although 55 per cent of their sample was in immediate need of medical treatment '[m]ost ... could be provided by health services in prison'. Yet in the view of the researchers 9 per cent of the sample (64 individuals) should have been in hospital (1996, p. 1526), which, extrapolating to the remand prison population as a whole (8,550 on 30 June 1997: Home Office Research and Statistics Directorate, 1998b, p. 2) suggests that, on any one day, there are several hundred persons remanded into custody who need to be in hospital.

Part of the reason for this is that power to do it exists. Further reasons for refusing bail are to be found in sch. 1, part I, Bail Act 1976. An accused person may be remanded to prison if the court is satisfied that this is required for his or her 'protection' which is capable of wide definition: para. 3; if it has not been practicable to carry out reports so as to enable a decision about bail to be made: para. 5; or if it appears to the court that it would otherwise be impracticable to complete any necessary inquiry or report: para. 7. Dell et al (1991) found that remand in custody for psychiatric reports was common. Of course, the courts do not remand defendants, mentally disordered or not, in custody simply because they can. A key problem is the lack of access to information that would enable a diversionary measure to be adopted *before* a defendant is remanded in custody. A number of 'bail information schemes' have been set up since the mid 1980s, totalling over 200 by 1993 (Cavadino and Dignan, 1997, p. 80). However, detecting persons suffering from mental disorder, out of the constant stream of people who pass through the court system, can be like looking for a needle in a haystack (Brabbins and Travers, 1994). Accordingly, the spread of court-based diversionary schemes specifically aimed at mentally disordered defendants has also been a noticeable development in recent years. In the mid 1980s such schemes were relatively unknown. By the turn of the decade 48 schemes were in existence (Blumenthal and Wessely, 1992), increasing to more than 100 by 1995 (Department of Health, 1995c, cited in Peay, 1997).

One such scheme is described by James et al (1997). This scheme operates across several central London boroughs and five magistrates' courts. Accused persons suspected to be in need of psychiatric attention are cross-remanded to one of the courts, at which a team comprising two consultant psychiatrists, an ASW, a senior nurse, a research worker and an administrator have office and interview accommodation. Assessments are requested by the defence and by the court, and assessment takes place in the court building, reports to the court are immediately available, and team members have access to in-patient hospital beds, including those in a secure unit. There are many variations on schemes such as this (see for example the scheme which operates in Leeds, described in Greenhalgh et al,1996). Although there are divergent findings about the impact of such schemes, and numbers diverted are typically modest (see Cooke, 1991; Evans and Tomison, 1997; Exworthy and Parrott, 1997; James et al, 1997), there is more agreement that the availability of a court-based diversion scheme can impact considerably both on the time taken for reports to be compiled and made available to sentencers and on the interval between initial arrest and arrival in hospital: in one study this latter figure was reduced from an average of 50 to 8 days (James and Hamilton, 1991).

Even when a defendant has been identified as a potential candidate for bail or some other form of diversion by a court-based scheme or otherwise, the Bail Act nevertheless requires the balancing of the needs of the individual concerned for treatment with the considerations in the Act. The experience of James et al (1997, p. 39) was that '[t]he most serious cases of violence would in any case be remanded into custody for reasons of public safety'. It is not possible to grant bail where a defendant, having a similar conviction or one for culpable homicide, is charged with murder, attempted murder, manslaughter, rape or attempted rape: s. 25, Criminal Justice and Public Order Act 1994, nor is it possible to remand a person accused of murder to hospital: ss. 35(3), 36(2), MHA 1983. In cases where the decision as to bail is one for the court, the factors to be considered include the nature of the offence, the strength of the evidence, and the strength of the accused person's community ties: sch. 1, part I, para. 9, Bail Act 1976, and it is easy for these factors to conspire in the direction of remand to prison for mentally disordered suspects. The net effect of this is that diversion schemes tend to operate around an axis governed by the seriousness of the alleged offending behaviour, focusing on the less serious offences, which, it can be suggested, is not sufficiently sensitive to the need for treatment.

Perhaps the main limitation of court-based diversion at present is the lack of resources, both in the courts and in terms of medical facilities. In 1996 the National Association of Probation Officers brought it to public attention that there had been 'a number of instances where adjournments have been refused to avoid an additional costly hearing' (Harry Fletcher, NAPO General Secretary, in Campbell, 1996). The ability of an advocate to suggest remand to hospital rather than prison is constrained by the fact that it is not always easy to find a hospital place, particularly if secure hospital accommodation is required, as Greenhalgh et al (1997) amongst others have discovered. Partly this is because there is a general shortage of beds, but in addition there is a certain degree of resistance within the mental health system towards accepting offender patients, partly because such patients tend to be more 'difficult' than others (Coid, 1988), and partly because of the pressure that criminal justice admissions place on already over-subscribed local hospital accommodation (James et al, 1998). At present, the efficacy of court-based diversion depends on local initiatives and must be funded out of local budgets. Although there is national guidance, there is little in the way of national strategy and structure. As a consequence, many in need of treatment slip through the net, and must take their chances at the next stage of the process.

6.3.2   Remand to hospital: the law

Section 35 of the MHA 1983 provides a general power to remand a defendant in a magistrates' court or the Crown Court to hospital 'for a report on his mental condition'. Section 36 confers a power, exercisable only by the Crown Court, to remand to hospital for treatment. In many ways the two sections are similar. In either case, a court shall not remand an accused person to hospital unless satisfied on the written or oral evidence of a doctor or manager at that hospital, that a bed will be available within seven days and that the accused can be detained in a place of safety in the meantime: ss. 35(4), 36(3). A period of remand may not last more than 28 days (ss. 35(7), 36(6)), but may be renewed if evidence is provided of the need to remand further to complete the process of assessment (s. 35(5)), or treatment (s. 36(4)); and the accused person need not be brought back before the court on such occasions provided that he or she is legally represented: ss. 35(6), 36(5). No person can be remanded for longer than 12 weeks in total: ss. 35(7), 36(6). However, there are also significant differences between the two sections, although the import of these has been lessened by recent decisions of the Court of Appeal.

6.3.2.1   Remand of an accused person to hospital for treatment under section 36
Section 36 is only applicable to an accused person in respect of whom the Crown Court is satisfied, on the written or oral evidence of two doctors, at least one of whom must be 'approved' under s. 12 (s. 54(1)), that he or she 'is suffering from mental illness or severe mental impairment of a nature or degree which makes it appropriate for him to be detained in a hospital for treatment': s. 36(1). The wording of this test is identical to that to be found in relation to civil detention for treatment under s. 3. However, a person in need of treatment by reason of mental impairment or psychopathic disorder cannot be remanded under s. 36, apparently because of the view that persons suffering from these conditions would be of problematic treatability. As one might expect given that this is remand for treatment, a patient detained under s. 36 is subject to the powers of compulsory treatment without consent contained in Part IV of the 1983 Act: s. 56(1). Section 36 is used relatively infrequently: 33 occasions in England in 1996-7, this being fairly typical of the pattern over the last decade or so, although there were 65 s. 36 admissions in 1993-4 and 18 in 1994-5 (Department of Health, 1998d, table 1). This seems to be because s. 36 is being squeezed by, on the one hand, the increased use of the Secretary of State's powers in s. 48 to transfer unsentenced prisoners from prison to hospital (see 6.6), and on the other, the tendency of court-based diversions schemes to come into play somewhat earlier in the process, in magistrates' courts (Blumenthal and Wessely, 1992), when it is s. 35 which is the relevant provision.

6.3.2.2   Remand under section 35
Section 35 is indeed used more frequently than s. 36, although the number of orders made in 1996-7, at 267, was lower than any previous year in the decade (Department of Health, 1998d, table 1). The powers contained in s. 35 are exercisable in respect of an 'accused

person', defined in s. 35(2). In respect of the Crown Court an accused person is one who is awaiting trial or has been arraigned for trial for 'an offence punishable by imprisonment' (s. 35(2)(a)) with the exception of the offence of murder. So far as magistrates' courts are concerned, an accused person is defined in s. 35(2)(b) to include:

> any person who has been convicted by the court of an offence punishable on summary conviction with imprisonment and any person charged with such an offence if the court is satisfied that he did that act or made the omission charged or has consented to the exercise by the court of the powers conferred by this section.

Thus, a person may be remanded to hospital by magistrates without the bench being satisfied that he or she did the act alleged if that accused person consents to the remand. If the defendant refuses to or lacks capacity to consent, a magistrates' court may, when there is a firm diagnosis by two s. 12 'approved' doctors that the defendant is suffering from mental illness or severe mental impairment, make a hospital order (see 6.5.1) under s. 37 instead of remanding the defendant to hospital under s. 35. This may be done without convicting the offender if the court 'is satisfied that the accused did the act or made the omission charged' (s. 37(3)), and does not require the consent of the offender: R v Lincoln (Kesteven) Justices, ex parte O'Connor [1983] 1 WLR 335 (DC). This mechanism can achieve the same effect as an order made under s. 35, with the important differences that a s. 37 order will not be time-limited and a patient detained under s. 37 is subject to the powers of treatment without consent contained in part IV of the 1983 Act.

Notwithstanding that the medical criteria for remand under s. 35 are similar to those for civil commitment for treatment under s. 3, and that the court must be satisfied, on the basis of the evidence of one doctor (who must be 'approved': s. 54(1)), that there is reason to suspect that the defendant is suffering from one of the four specified types of mental disorder required for admission under that section, remand under s. 35 does not allow the treatment without consent of the remandee under the provisions of part IV of the 1983 Act, as this is expressly excluded by s. 56(1)(b). It has long been the practice that where necessary to treat such persons without their consent then they would, during the duration of the remand, also be sectioned under ss. 2 or 3 of the Act, despite long-standing doubts about the legality of such 'double detention' (Fennell, 1991b). However, in *Dlodlo v Mental Health Review Tribunal for the South Thames Region* (1996) 36 BMLR 145 and *R v North West London Mental Health NHS Trust and Others, ex parte S* [1998] 2 WLR 189 the Court of Appeal decided that there is no embargo on the application of the provisions of one part of the 1983 Act to a person already detained under another part. Jones (1999, pp. 175–6, see also Fennell, 1991b) has laid out a number of strong arguments against the holding in this case, which include:

• this defeats the clear intention of Parliament that there should be no compulsory treatment of persons remanded for reports, as evidenced by s. 56(1)(b);

- why is there a separate provision — s. 36 — that provides for remand for treatment to a more limited category of patient (only the mentally ill and severely mentally impaired)?
- a person detained under part II could be 'discharged' by a tribunal (see 8.4) but would still be liable to be detained under s. 35;
- the powers of RMOs, for example to grant leave of absence, in respect of patients detained under part II would not in fact be exercisable;
- the duty of hospital managers under s. 132(1) to ensure that the patient understands the legal basis for detention and the avenues open by way of challenge to continued detention could only with difficulty be carried out.

In short, the argument is that the 1983 Act is clearly not set up to contemplate all the myriad complications relating to the legal status of a patient subject to 'dual detention'. Nevertheless the Court of Appeal has ruled in favour and there is little objection from within psychiatry (Gunn and Joseph, 1993). It is to be hoped that this is one matter that will be considered in the ongoing review of the MHA 1983.

Another matter might well be what appear to be serious problems with the drafting of s. 35. The general thrust of s. 35(2)(b) is to allow magistrates to remand to hospital both convicted, and in the circumstances detailed, unconvicted defendants. However in one important respect it seems that the wording of the provision frustrates that intention. The problem is with the reference to 'an offence punishable on *summary* conviction' as this comprises only summary offences (triable only in a magistrates' court) and offences which are 'triable either way' (which may be dealt with in either a magistrates' court or the Crown Court), which comprise petty and moderately serious offences. The most serious of offences are triable *only* 'on indictment', that is, only in the Crown Court. Such offences as a matter of law simply *cannot* result in a 'summary conviction', which means that a person charged with such an offence cannot be remanded to hospital by magistrates. This was the view of the law taken in *R v Chippenham Magistrates' Court, ex parte Thompson* (1995) *The Times*, 6 December (DC), in which it was held that a 'hospital order' in s. 37, which uses the same phraseology as s. 35, could not be made by magistrates in relation to an indictable offence. There would seem to be no good reason for the narrow scope of this provision as a matter of policy and it may well be explicable as clumsy drafting.

As this discussion shows, the area of remand into custody and the question of remand to hospital is beset with difficulties both in terms of resources and frameworks, and in terms of the detail of the legislative scheme. It is submitted that a sensible option would be to abolish s. 36, and redraft s. 35 so that the scope of that section is delineated with greater precision but, as always, meaningful reform is contingent on coherent policies and adequate funding.

6.3.2.3 Fitness to stand trial Remand to hospital is not the only pre-trial diversionary mechanism available for consideration. An alternative is to find that the accused person is not fit to be tried. It has long been the accepted wisdom of common law that there should be no trial of a person who is unable to understand the proceedings, and so cannot respond to the charge against him or her 'with that advice and caution that he ought' (Blackstone, 1793, in Mackay, 1995, p. 216). Section 2 of the Criminal Lunatics Act 1800, which put this view on a statutory basis, provided that a person found to be insane, by a jury empanelled for that purpose, should not be tried but instead 'kept in strict custody'. This was more or less the position until recently, with the caveat that the triggering concept was subsequently widened and is now that of 'disability' rather than 'insanity': s. 4, Criminal Procedure (Insanity) Act 1964 ('the 1964 Act') as substituted by s. 2, Criminal Procedure (Insanity and Unfitness to Plead) Act 1991 ('the 1991 Act'). The 1991 Act brought about significant changes to this situation, although the view that the 1991 Act does not go far enough is widespread (see below). The possibility that a defendant is under such disability as prevents him or her being tried may be raised by the defence 'or otherwise': s. 4(1), 1964 Act, in any case before a Crown Court. Recourse to the Acts of 1964 and 1991 is not possible in a magistrates' court (s. 5, 1991 Act), although as discussed in 6.3.2.4 magistrates may use their powers in s. 37(3), MHA 1983 to achieve much the same ends.

There is no statutory definition of the concept of 'disability' or 'unfitness to plead' as it is commonly but misleadingly described. The leading case remains R v Pritchard (1836) 7 C & P 303, in which it was held, per Baron Alderson, that a defendant is unfit for trial if not 'of sufficient intellect to comprehend the course of the proceedings in the trial so as to make a proper defence, to challenge a juror to whom he might wish to object and to comprehend the details of the evidence'. That this 'cognitive' test is capable of allowing departures from its spirit is evident from R v Podola [1960] 1 QB 325 (DC), in which a person suffering from amnesia about the events relevant to charge was held not to be unfit. It may well be that such a person can understand the proceedings, and so on, but without a memory of the relevant events, it is not clear how he or she could decide on a plea, instruct a lawyer effectively, provide evidence or testimony to contradict that of the prosecution and its witnesses, or make any number of other decisions that are required of a defendant in a criminal trial. This had led some commentators (Duff, 1986; Grubin, 1993; Mackay, 1995) to argue for a broader test of unfitness, which would include some assessment of the defendant's ability not merely to understand but to make relevant decisions before and during the process of trial. There is a good argument that the notion of capacity that has been proffered by the Law Commission, and has been adopted, for example, in the context of consent to medical treatment at common law (see 11.2), would be preferable to the test that is currently employed, all the more so as research has shown that there is 'some ignorance and confusion in many of the cases about the criteria [in Pritchard]' (Mackay, 1995, p. 225).

It is for a jury to determine whether a defendant is unfit: s. 4(5), 1964 Act. The issue is usually raised early in the trial process, at arraignment. If the case subsequently proceeds to trial, a different jury must be sworn in: s. 4(5)(a), 1964 Act. If unfitness is raised at any later stage, such as in the course of trial, it may be decided by a jury other than that which is concerned with the substantive issue, but need not be, at the discretion of the judge: s. 4(5)(b). The presumption is that the question of unfitness shall be determined as soon as it arises (s. 4(4)), but there is a discretion in the court to delay consideration of the issue until the opening of the defence case: s. 4(2). This may be a suitable option if there is reason to believe that the prosecution case is weak, such that the court may direct, or the defence submit, that there is no case to answer. In such circumstances the defendant must be acquitted and the question of unfitness 'shall not be determined': s. 4(3).

Until the reforms introduced by the 1991 Act, the consequences of a determination of the question of unfitness were straightforward. If fit for trial the defendant was tried in the normal way. If not, the court was required to make an order committing the defendant to hospital (a 'hospital order') without limit of time, coupled with a 'restriction order' (see 6.5.2), which effectively gives to the Home Secretary power to determine when, if at all, the defendant would be released from hospital, or be remitted to prison to stand trial. The prospect of indefinite detention meant that the question of unfitness was rarely raised, and increasingly so through the 1980s until by 1989 there were only 11 such cases nationally (Mackay, 1995, p. 222). This meant, in practice, the failure of this mechanism as a diversionary measure and, by implication, also that the rules of natural justice were often not observed. Moreover, as it was usual for a finding of unfitness to be made before the defence case had been put, there was the possibility that an offender found unfit to plead may have been acquitted had that case been heard, which, according to Grubin (1991, p. 543) was indeed the situation in 7 of the 295 cases of persons found unfit between 1976 and 1988.

The 1991 Act introduced two main innovations to address these concerns. First, s. 2 inserted a new provision, s. 4A, into the 1964 Act. This provides that, if a jury has determined that the defendant is under such disability that he or she is unfit for trial, the trial will halt. Then, a jury, which must be a different jury from that making the assessment of unfitness if that assessment was made at arraignment but need not be if that assessment was made after a trial had commenced (s. 4A(5), 1964 Act), will determine whether or not it is satisfied that the defendant did the act or made the omission with which he or she is charged: s. 4A(1),(2). This is to be done either on the evidence that has already been heard, or on the prosecution evidence and that given by a person appointed by the court to act for the defence: s. 4A(2)(a),(b). This is described in the long title to the 1991 Act as a 'trial of the facts'. Its purpose is to divert from the consequences of a finding of unfitness defendants who would not have been found guilty of the offence charged. A jury which is not satisfied — and the test seems to be that which is usually applied in criminal courts, of 'beyond reasonable doubt' (Home Office, 1991, para. 9) — that the defendant did the act or made the omission in question must acquit: s. 4A(4).

The view of the government at the time the 1991 Act was passed, was that a trial of the facts should be limited to an inquiry into whether the defendant had committed the *actus reus* of the offence in question, as otherwise there would be little to distinguish a trial of the facts from a full trial, for which the defendant is not meant to be fit (Mackay and Kearns, 1997, p. 650). However, as White (1992) pointed out, the *actus reus* of some offences — he gave the example of theft — embrace notions of intention. This very point arose in *R* v *Egan* [1997] Crim LR 225 (CA). The court held that 'did the act or made the omission' meant *all* the ingredients of the offence, so that on a trial of the facts on a charge of theft, a defendant is entitled to be acquitted unless the prosecution can show both that he or she took the property in question, and that this was done dishonestly and with an intention permanently to deprive. Although this means that a trial of the facts is in fact barely distinguishable from a full trial, and so raises the conceptual problems referred to above, it was the view of the court in *Egan* that to hold that 'act' should be defined narrowly risks subverting the underlying intention behind s. 4A(4) of the 1991 Act, because it would leave open the possibility that a defendant, who would have been acquitted had the case gone to trial, would not be acquitted on a trial of the facts. However, *Egan* is not likely to become an authority of any longevity. In *Attorney-General's Reference (No. 3 of 1998)* [1999] 3 ALL ER 40 (CA) a differently constituted Court of Appeal held that *Egan* 'appears to have been decided per incuriam' (per Judge LJ at p. 48). This view is, strictly, *obiter*, as the court in *Attorney-General's Reference* was concerned with the question of the 'special verdict' of insanity rather than with the issue of fitness to plead. However, as Judge LJ pointed out, in both contexts a 'trial of the facts' is required, which is identical and the product of the same legislative history, and hence 'whether the case is proceeding on the ground of insanity or unfitness to plead . . . the issue is identical, that is, whether or not the defendant did the act or made the omission alleged, but nothing in the legislation suggests that if the jury has concluded that the defendant's mental state was such that . . . his mental responsibility for his crime was negatived, it should simultaneously consider whether the necessary *mens rea* has also been proved' (at p. 47). Thus, in reality, *Egan* has been overruled.

With this decision, the Court of Appeal has restored the commonly understood pre-*Egan* position, that on a trial of the facts, whether following a finding of unfitness to plead or of insanity, all that is at issue is whether or not the defendant committed the *actus reus* of the offence charged. And there is a certain logic in the argument that when a defendant has been found not guilty by reason of insanity, as required by the special verdict, it is perverse to investigate his or her *mens rea* at the time of the offence. But the argument is perhaps less persuasive in the context of unfitness to plead. This is because such a finding carries no implications about the defendant's state of mind at the time of the offence, but only at the time of trial. Thus there remains the possibility that a defendant will be subject to a disposal under the 1964 and 1991 Acts who would, had his or her *mens rea* been investigated, have been entitled to an acquittal. There is also, as will be discussed below, a particular problem when the offence charged is murder. Mackay and Kearns (1997, pp.650-1) suggest that the approach taken in Scotland has the potential to provide both conceptual clarity and substantive justice. Section 174ZA, Criminal Procedure (Scotland) Act 1975, which came into force on 1 April 1996, requires that as part of a trial of the facts, the court must be satisfied that there are, on a balance of probabilities, no grounds for acquitting the defendant: *mens rea* must therefore be considered, but the court need not be satisfied beyond reasonable doubt that there are no grounds for acquitting the defendant, so less than a full trial will be required. It can be argued that this is splitting hairs — either a trial court does consider the state of mind of the defendant or it does not — or alternatively, if *mens rea* is to be an issue it should not be in this watered down version, which can still lead to a finding against the defendant in circumstances which, on a full trial, would have led to acquittal. Perhaps there is no way completely to reconcile the requirements of conceptual clarity and those of substantive justice to the defendant, in which case the latter should prevail.

The second main reform introduced in 1991 concerned choice of disposal following a finding of unfitness and that the defendant did the act in question. Until this Act, there was no choice: a defendant had to be sent to hospital indefinitely and placed under restrictions. Section 3 of the 1991 Act changed this situation by introducing a range of disposals (as s. 5 of the 1964 Act). A court may still make a hospital order (s. 5(2)(a), 1964 Act, sch. 1, para. 1(1), 1991 Act), but now with or without restrictions: sch. 1, para. 2(1)(b), 1991 Act. The making by a Crown Court of an order for admission to hospital gives authority for the defendant to be conveyed to and detained in the hospital in question (sch. 1, paras. 1(2), (3)), provided that this is done within the 'relevant period', which is two months from the making of the order: sch. 1, para. 1(4).

There are no criteria governing the making of a restriction order in addition to a hospital order. Presumably the court should apply the provisions of s. 41 of the 1983 Act and the relevant case law (see 6.5.2). Whether or not a restriction order is made is crucial to the defendant not simply because such defendants will be subject to a more restrictive hospital regime and to greater restrictions on release, but also because it is *only* when a court makes a restriction order in addition to a hospital order that the defendant can be remitted direct to court, or to a prison or remand centre, for trial, if following treatment he or she is well enough to stand trial. In all other cases, the disposal made by the court is treated as final: sch. 1, paras. 4(1), (2), 1991 Act. This power to remit is vested solely in the Secretary of State, and may only be exercised if, after consultation with the defendant's RMO, he or she 'is satisfied that that person can properly be tried', which, presumably, should involve a reapplication of the *Pritchard* test.

If the offence which the defendant is found on a trial of the facts to have committed is murder, there is no option but to make a hospital order and a restriction order without limit of time: s. 5(3), 1964 Act, sch. 1, para. 2(2), 1991 Act. There was long concern that if the offence charged is murder, then the question on a trial of the facts is limited to whether the defendant committed the *actus reus* of that offence or not, and not whether, if the case had proceeded to full trial, a verdict of manslaughter, which requires the same *actus reus* as murder, might properly have been returned. It seemed as though the decision in *Egan* has ameliorated these concerns to an extent, but in *R v Antoine* (1999) *Independent*, 12 May (CA) the decision in *Attorney-General's Reference* was applied in precisely this situation. The defendant had been found by a jury to be unfit to plead to charges of murder and manslaughter. A trial of the facts for the charge of murder had followed and the defendant was found to have committed the *actus reus* of that offence. The court consequently made a hospital order of unlimited duration and a restriction order. The trial judge, Van der Werff J, also refused to hear argument that the defendant was suffering from diminished responsibility since that went to the question of *mens rea*, which is not at issue on a trial of the facts. The Court of Appeal upheld the decision. There is thus, on the law as it stands at present, no way for a defendant charged with murder and subsequently found to be unfit to plead to access the defence of diminished responsibility. There is currently no *charge* known to law of diminished responsibility manslaughter. Given the harsh consequences of a finding that the defendant committed the *actus reus* of murder following a finding of unfitness to plead, it is to be hoped that prosecutors keep the possibility of injustice in mind when laying charges, and that a charge of manslaughter rather than murder is brought in appropriate cases. This would allow the courts access to a broader range of disposals.

For offences other than murder, the court may, instead of making a hospital order, make an order for guardianship within the meaning of the 1983 Act; or a 'supervision and treatment order' as defined in sch. 2 of the 1991 Act or discharge the defendant absolutely: s. 5(2)(b), 1964 Act. The choice between these disposals is for the court, according to what is deemed 'the most suitable in all the circumstances of the case' (s. 5(2)(b), 1964 Act), although there is no guidance about when a community-based disposal is to be preferred over the making of a hospital order.

Supervision and treatment orders are only available under the Acts of 1964 and 1991. The details of the scheme are found in sch. 2 to the 1991 Act. Such orders are similar to guardianship orders (see 9.5.2) in some respects, but provide for considerably more control over the subject of the order. That person will be under the supervision of a social worker or probation officer for up to two years (para. 1(1)(a)), and must submit to treatment by or under the supervision of a doctor for all or part of that period, as specified in the order (para. 1(1)(b)), 'with a view to improvement of his mental condition'. Such an order may not be made unless at least two doctors, one of whom must be 'approved', have given written or oral evidence that the mental condition of the defendant is susceptible to treatment, and that a hospital or guardianship order is not suitable: para. 2(1)(a), (b). This is far from straightforward. It may be thought that a hospital order will not be suitable if the defendant does not require hospitalisation for treatment to be effective, and a guardianship order may not be suitable if there are concerns that the defendant may not consent to medical treatment if not in hospital, because a guardianship order does not provide a power to impose treatment, whereas a supervision and treatment order not only can but 'shall include a requirement that the supervised person shall submit ... to treatment': sch. 2, para. 4(1). However, although this provides a point of distinction between a supervision and treatment order and a guardianship order, it blurs that between a supervision and treatment order and a hospital order. A supervision and treatment order may, like a guardianship order, specify the place of residence of the subject of the order: sch. 2, para. 5(1). And sch. 2, para. 4(2) provides that the order may specify the place and type of treatment, and includes the option of in-patient hospital treatment. It may therefore be a close call whether a hospital order or a supervision and treatment order specifying that the patient submit to in-patient hospital treatment should be made. The key difference is the two year limitation on the duration of supervision and treatment orders.

These reforms do seem to have encouraged the increased use of the 1964 Act, although the increase has in absolute terms been fairly minimal. As mentioned above, in 1989 there were only 11 cases of unfitness to plead. Initially, the enactment of the 1991 Act seemed to make little difference, but there were 28 cases in 1994 and 27 in 1995 (Mackay and Kearns, 1997, p. 645). More recent statistics on all cases of unfitness have yet to be published, but in 1997, 16 restriction orders were made following a finding of disability (Home Office Research and Statistics Directorate, 1998a, table 3). A similar number of orders were made in 1994 and 1995, which would seem to suggest that the rise has levelled off at 1994-5 rates.

One final development introduced by the 1991 Act was to provide that a jury may not find a defendant unfit to plead except on the written or oral evidence of two or more doctors, at least one of whom must be 'approved': s. 4(6), 1964 Act, as inserted by s. 2, 1991 Act. There had been cases under the 1964 Act in which a defendant had been sentenced to hospital in the absence of medical evidence (Mackay, 1990, p. 251). Fennell (1992, p. 549) has suggested that '[t]his is an effort to introduce greater congruence' between the 1964/1991 Acts regime and the MHA 1983, as under part III of that Act any disposal by a criminal court must also be made on the evidence of at least two doctors. However, Baker (1994, p. 86) points out that there is good reason to think that this innovation is purely procedural, in answer to the concerns raised by Mackay. This view is perhaps strengthened by the point that the wording of s. 4(6) of the 1964 Act (and its counterpart, in s. 1(1) of the 1991 Act, in relation to the insanity defence, see 6.4) mirrors that for the making of a restriction order in s. 41, MHA 1983, and in *R* v *Birch* (1989) 11 Cr App R(S) 202 (CA), it was held that the requirement was only to *consider* the evidence and not necessarily to be bound to follow medical recommendations.

It is perhaps inappropriate to criticise the 1991 Act for not effecting more fundamental reform, given that it started life as a Private Member's Bill, albeit with government support, but nevertheless one problem which was apparent before the passage of the 1991 Act has not been addressed. This is the mismatch between the criteria for unfitness to plead (and for finding a defendant 'not guilty by reason of insanity', discussed at 6.4) and those applicable to admission to and detention in a hospital. As things stand now, a person who on an application of the *Pritchard* test is found unfit, can be placed on a hospital order, only to be discharged by the RMO, hospital managers or a tribunal (see Chapter 8) because the criteria for continued detention under the 1983 Act — which are narrower than the *Pritchard* test — are not met, as happened in the case of Glenn Pearson in 1986 (Emmins, 1986). It is a matter for concern if the 1964/1991 Acts regime is capable of undermining the strict criteria for the detention in a hospital set by part III of the 1983 Act, as it is that the intention of a court, that a defendant should receive treatment in hospital, can be thwarted by the operation of the 1983 Act. Of course, the wider range of disposals available since January 1992 (when the 1991 Act came into force) may well obviate this problem if the court takes cognisance of the medical evidence and that evidence contains a view as to whether the criteria for detention under the 1983 Act are satisfied. However, this would be effectively to overrule the common law test for disability, and there is no reason to think that this is what the 1991 Act intended; and in any case this should not be left to chance. One solution may be to write the 1983 Act requirements for the making of a hospital order into what is currently s. 5(2)(a) of the 1964 Act. The more radical option, discussed further at 6.4 in the context of the insanity defence, would be to abolish the common law definitions, both of 'unfitness to plead' and 'not guilty by reason of insanity', and allow the 1983 Act definitions to fill the field, so that 'unfitness to plead' would be coterminous with the four specified forms of mental disorder contained in s. 1(2) of the 1983 Act. Although perhaps initially attractive, this option, as will be seen, has problems of its own.

6.3.2.4 Magistrates' courts and unfitness to plead   Although the Acts of 1964 and 1991 are not generally applicable in magistrates' courts, it is only a magistrates' court that can revoke or amend a supervision and treatment order: sch. 2, part III, 1991 Act. An application for an order to be revoked can be made by a supervising officer or a supervisee, and may be revoked if 'having regard to the circumstances which have arisen since the order was made, it would be in the interests of the health or welfare of the supervised person that the order should be revoked': sch. 2, para. 6, 1991 Act. It is difficult to know what a magistrates' court would make of this provision, as there are so few cases, but it is likely that in practice the opinion of the supervisor would be determinative, whether the application was for a revocation or an amendment. An order cannot be 'amended' to extend its duration beyond two years from the date on which it was made: sch. 2 para. 8(2).

Magistrates can in fact achieve much the same effect as an order made under the Acts of 1964 and 1991. This is because magistrates may make a hospital order under s. 37(3) of the 1983 Act without convicting the defendant if, on a trial of the facts identical to that contained in s. 4A(2) of the 1964 Act, the bench is satisfied that the defendant did the act or made the omission which constitutes the *actus reus* of an offence punishable on summary conviction with imprisonment, which includes offences triable 'either way' even if the defendant wishes to elect for Crown Court trial: *R v Ramsgate Justices, ex parte Kazmarek* (1985) 80 Cr App R 366 (DC), but not offences that are triable only on indictment, since such offences are not punishable on *summary* conviction: *R v Chippenham Magistrates' Court, ex parte Thompson* (1995) *The Times*, 6 December (DC). It has been said that magistrates will only very rarely have need to use this power: *R v Lincoln (Kesteven) Justices, ex parte O'Connor* [1983] 1 WLR 335 (DC). Nevertheless it is noteworthy that, when it is used, it must be used in accordance with the diagnostic criteria employed by the MHA 1983 rather than the *Pritchard* test, and although a court using s. 37 can make a guardianship order it cannot make a supervision and treatment order, and so cannot access the powers of compulsory treatment in the community; all of which adds a further layer of incongruity to this area of law.

6.4 THE SPECIAL VERDICT

The equivalent provision of the 'special verdict' offers an alternative to conviction. The legal basis of the special verdict remains s. 2, Trial of Lunatics Act 1883, which now provides that a person who was insane at the time the alleged offence was committed may be found 'not guilty by reason of insanity'. Like the law relating to disability to stand trial, the special verdict is subject to the regimes laid down by the Acts of 1964 and 1991; and as with unfitness, before the 1991 Act the only disposal available was indefinite detention in a hospital. The situation now is that the range of disposals discussed in 6.3.3.2 in the context of unfitness are also available if a special verdict is returned (s. 5, 1964 Act), again with an exception that only an order committing the defendant to hospital with restrictions can be made if the offence in question is murder: s. 5(3), 1964 Act, sch. 1, para. 2(1)(b), (2) 1991 Act. As with unfitness the issue of insanity may be raised by defence, prosecution or the court, and it is now established that the defence is available both in the Crown Court and on summary trial in magistrates' courts: *R* v *Horseferry Road Magistrates' Court, ex parte K* [1996] 3 All ER 733 (CA).

However, the 'insanity defence' does differ from the situation relating to unfitness in two ways. First, in terms of definition. The 1991 Act did nothing to change the definition of insanity for these purposes, and the leading authority remains the infamous *M'Naghten's Case* (1843) 10 C & F 200, in which Tindal CJ (at p. 210) laid out the 'M'Naghten rules'. That is, to establish the defence of insanity:

it must be clearly proved that, at the time of the committing of the act, the party accused was labouring under such a defect of reason, from disease of the mind, as not to know the nature and quality of the act he was doing; or if he did know it, that he did not know that what he was doing was wrong.

These words, which have since set as firm as any statutory provision, set up a similar mismatch with the criteria for admission and detention under the MHA 1983 as that discussed in 6.3.2.3 in the context of disability; and in so far as this test is also inconsistent with that in *Pritchard*, there is in fact a three way mismatch between the relevant legal regimes. This means that the problem identified in relation to unfitness to be tried applies here too, so that the possibility that a defendant may be sent to hospital but not detained there is also relevant here.

The second point of distinction between the insanity defence and the law relating to unfitness to plead is that the relaxation of the restrictions on disposal options in 1991 has not increased the use of the insanity defence. In 1997 only two individuals were admitted to hospital with restrictions in consequence of its use (Home Office Research and Statistics Directorate, 1998a, table 3). Mackay (1990) has pointed out that the above statistics refer only to the use of the defence in cases where the charge is murder, and that over the period 1975 to 1988 approximately two further uses were made of the insanity defence for each use in a murder case. But unlike the comparable statistics for those admitted to hospital by reason of being unfit to plead, which as discussed in 6.3.2.3 show an upwards trend following 1991, the numbers admitted as a result of the special verdict fell from nine to one, with seven in 1994 and five in 1996. The numbers involved are so small that it is difficult to talk of trends; but in any case it is clear that the use of the special verdict is a rare event.

The reasons for this are well known. To a large extent, the function of the special verdict in murder cases has been superseded by the defence of diminished responsibility that was introduced in 1957; and the abolition of the death penalty in 1965 meant that it was no longer clear that indefinite detention in a psychiatric hospital was preferable to a criminal disposal from the point of view of the accused. In cases involving offences other than murder, such evidence as there is suggests that fears of indefinite hospitalisation are largely unfounded, as discharge from hospital will be rapid in appropriate cases (Mackay, 1990). Yet this does not mean that there is no reason to be concerned about the operation of the special verdict, for three reasons in particular. The first, already mentioned is the mismatch between the criteria applicable for the special verdict and those for continued detention under the MHA 1983, notwithstanding the requirement that a disposal must be made after hearing medical evidence. Secondly, the M'Naghten rules are capable of producing manifest injustices, such as that in *R* v *Sullivan* [1984] AC 156 (HL), in which it was held that psychomotor epilepsy came within the *M'Naghten* definition of insanity (bizarrely, the courts have always insisted that the definition of insanity to be used in criminal trials is a matter of law, yet of course in reality *M'Naghten* constitutes the legal 'freezing' of a particular phase in the development of *psychiatric* knowledge and theory). Thirdly, despite the requirement of hearing medical evidence, the special verdict allows hospitalisation that is not based on 'objective medical expertise' required by art. 5(1)(e), European Convention on Human Rights, as interpreted in *Winterwerp* v *The Netherlands* (1979) 2 EHRR 387.

There is therefore good reason to suggest that the definitions employed for both the special verdict and in the context of a determination of fitness to stand trial should be redrawn. The suggestion of the Butler Committee was that the definitions of insanity and unfitness be abolished and replaced with the criteria used for detention for treatment under s. 3, MHA 1983 (Home Office and Department of Health and Social Security, 1975, para. 18.37). It was felt, however, that this would be to widen the criminal law definition to an unacceptable extent, allowing an escape route for many who are in fact culpable, or demeaning to the dignity of persons with mental disorders by denying them the right to a trial, depending on the perspective taken (Carson, 1989). In fact, the relation between the insanity and unfitness criteria on the one hand, and the MHA 1983 criteria on the other, turns out to be a conundrum. Either the terms of the former are widened to be compatible with those of the latter, with the above problems, or they are not, in which case the incompatibility remains. Furthermore, to shift from a legal to a medical definition of 'cause' in a criminal law context is problematic. It is not the task of the psychiatrist to diagnose 'responsibility'. Nor is it clear that psychiatry could provide answers that law could accept. Law insists that events be placed within a relatively narrow time frame, whereas psychiatry tends to look over a much broader period for the causes of an individual's present disorder. And law tends to view an individual without reference to his or her social context to a much greater degree than psychiatry, and therefore functions within a different paradigm of 'cause'.

Yet, if the function of the M'Naghten test is to differentiate the dangerous (in need of detention in a hospital) from those who are not (and so are able to access the alternative of non-insane automatism, which provides a complete defence), or the morally blameworthy from those who are not, there is general agreement that it fails (Baker, 1994). The preferred reconciliation of these competing considerations has taxed the minds of jurists on both sides of the Atlantic over much of the second half of this century if not before (Clarkson and Keating, 1990, pp.345-70), but this is not the place to rehearse the detail of those debates. What can be said is that, first, it is undesirable that the M'Naghten test continue to be used, and that secondly, the preferred solution should not be to attempt to reconcile the differences between the various sets of criteria — they are not, after all, concerned with the same issue — but rather focus on bringing the insanity defence up to date so that it is both morally and medically credible.

6.5 SENTENCING AS DIVERSION

The relevance of mental disorder to the substantive criminal law is beyond the scope of this text, as is detailed discussion of the sentencing options open to a court on convicting an offender. Nevertheless, it is appropriate to point out that *prima facie* at least the principles of desert, proportionality and protectionism that are to be found in the Criminal Justice Act 1991 apply to all offenders, mentally disordered or not. That Act introduced a graded system of sentencing, in an attempt to engender proportionality in sentencing practices. A prison sentence, and a community sentence, cannot be passed unless the court is satisfied that the offence committed is serious enough to warrant it, and the sentence passed must be commensurate to the seriousness of the offence: ss. 1(2), 6(1), 2(2)(a), Criminal Justice Act 1991. A person who appears to be mentally disordered cannot be imprisoned unless the court has first obtained a medical report: s. 4(1). However, there are exceptions to these general rules, and in particular s. 2(2)(b) provides that a prison sentence of longer duration than strictly deserved for the offence in question may be given on conviction of a violent or sexual offence, if in the opinion of the court this is required in the interests of protecting the public from serious harm.

Concern has been voiced that longer than normal sentences are being passed disproportionately in cases involving mentally disordered offenders. Solomka (1996, p. 241) found that 65 per cent of all cases heard by the Court of Appeal over a five month period involved a psychiatric report. Not surprisingly, in around 40 per cent of those cases where a report was called for, a personality abnormality or disorder ('psychopathic disorder' in legal terms) was identified. The treatability of psychopathically disordered offenders has long been a matter of concern, which means that hospitalisation is often not an option. Once consigned to passing a prison sentence for an offence of sex or violence, s. 2(2)(b) of the 1991 Act applies and Crown Court judges are obliged to push offenders 'up tariff'. This provision does not impact solely on mentally disordered offenders. In 1997 the average prison population of England and Wales was 61,114, a 37 per cent increase over the 1993 figure of 44,570. The main reasons for the increase are a greater use of custody and an increase in the average sentence length (Home Office Research and Statistics Directorate, 1998b, p. 1). The trend is likely to be exacerbated by the bringing into force of those elements of the Criminal Justice Act 1997 which relate to mandatory minimum sentences for specified repeat offenders. Section 2 of the 1997 Act introduces mandatory life sentences for those convicted of a second serious violent or sexual offence without 'exceptional circumstances', which are not intended to include mental disorder (Laing, 1997, p. 507). Other sections introduce mandatory minima for third time drug trafficking and domestic burglary offences. Laing (1997, p. 506) has speculated that, in an attempt to avoid the consequences of the 1997 Act, mentally disordered offenders may be more inclined than has been the case in the past to rely on the provisions of the Acts of 1964 and 1991 which deal with unfitness to plead.

In addition to the standard sentencing options, the courts can send a mentally disordered person to hospital instead of prison by making a 'hospital order', which can be given additional bite by the addition of a 'restriction order', or to prison with immediate reception into a hospital, in the form of a 'hospital direction' coupled with a 'limitation direction'. There are also proposals to introduce a new option of a 'reviewable detention order' permitting the incarceration of severely personality disordered persons who have not committed a criminal offence but are thought to constitute a risk to the public (see 6.7). In absolute terms, these orders are rarely used: less than half of one per cent of all disposals between 1992 and 1996 were hospital orders, and of these only a quarter had restrictions attached (Street, 1998, p. 101).

6.5.1 Hospital orders

The power to make a 'hospital order' is contained in s. 37 of the 1983 Act. The order is an alternative to imprisonment. Whenever a s. 37 order is made the defendant passes out of the criminal justice system altogether, and cannot be brought back into that system. In the leading case on the use of hospital and restriction orders, *R v Birch* (1989) 11 Cr App R(S) 202 (CA), Mustill LJ explained (at p. 210) that the option for sentencers of being able to sentence an offender to hospital:

> is intended to be humane by comparison with a prison sentence. A hospital order is not a punishment. Questions of retribution and deterrence ... are immaterial. The offender who has become a patient is not kept on any kind of leash by the court.

Nor does the Home Office monitor the subsequent history of patients sentenced to hospital under s. 37 if restrictions are not also imposed under s. 41 (Home Office Research and Statistics Directorate, 1998a, n.1, p. 24). The criteria for making an order under s. 37 (which may be for guardianship as an alternative to detention in a hospital, although guardianship orders are almost never made under this section), are substantially the same as for civil confinement under s. 3, and psychiatrists and review tribunals have similar powers to discharge hospital order patients as apply to patients detained under part II of the 1983 Act (see Chapter 8).

Unrestricted hospital orders were made on 701 occasions in 1997 (Home Office Research and Statistics Directorate, 1998a, table 18). This compares with 717 in 1996 and 649 in 1995, this being the fewest number of orders made in a year in the last decade, the highest number being 789 in 1990. By contrast 211 hospital orders coupled with restriction orders were made in 1997 (ibid., table 3). Of those persons in respect of whom a hospital order without restrictions was made by a court in 1997, 233 had been convicted of a violent offence, including 12 convictions for manslaughter (ibid., table 18). It is not possible to make an unrestricted hospital order in respect of a conviction of murder: s. 37(1). A sizeable number — 115 — had been convicted of criminal damage including arson. A further 42 had been convicted of a sexual offence. A similar number had been convicted of burglary, slightly more for theft or handling, and slightly fewer for robbery. Of the rest, 74 had been convicted of other indictable offences, and 104 of summary offences (ibid.). Thus, although, as might be expected, a good number of persons in respect of whom hospital orders are made have been convicted of an offence with an element of actual or potential dangerousness to others, the range of offences in respect of which hospital orders are made is relatively broad. This seems to imply that the courts do see the order as a therapeutic response, and its use is not linked to the offence but the need for hospital treatment. The profile of offending of those given a hospital order with restrictions leans more noticeably towards the more serious offences than the profile laid out above. The number of persons convicted of a summary offence who are given a hospital order is a potential cause for concern, as it is likely that many of this group will spend more than six months — the maximum prison sentence that may be given in a magistrates' court on conviction for a summary offence — in hospital. In 1997 104 hospital orders were made by magistrates' courts in proceedings relating to summary offences (Home Office Research and Statistics Directorate, 1998a, table 18). Although information on the average period spent by hospital order patients in hospital is hard to come by, it is unlikely that all are discharged within the first six months following the making of the order by the court.

Before making a hospital order the court must be satisfied, on the written or oral evidence of two doctors, one of whom must be approved (s. 54(1)), that the defendant is suffering from one or more of mental illness, psychopathic disorder, severe mental impairment or mental impairment of a nature or degree which makes it appropriate for him or her to be detained in a hospital for treatment: s. 37(2)(a). It is not necessary that both doctors agree that one of these disorders is all that the defendant is suffering from, although they must both diagnose the presence of the same disorder: s. 37(7). As with admission under s. 3, there is a treatability requirement in respect of psychopathic disorder and mental impairment: s. 37(2)(a)(i). There have long been concerns about the treatability of persons diagnosed as suffering from psychopathic disorder, with the result that many such persons have received a prison sentence rather than a hospital order. It is this perceived problem with the operation of s. 37 that provided the initial impetus to introduce in 1997 what are now known as 'hospital and limitation directions', discussed further below.

As with orders made under ss. 35 or 36, an order under s. 37 'shall not be made' unless the court is provided with evidence (which may be written or oral) from the doctor who will be in charge of the patient's treatment (the 'responsible medical officer' or RMO) or the managers of the intended recipient hospital that arrangements are in train for the admission of the defendant within 28 days of the making of the order: s. 37(4). If the admission cannot occur immediately, the defendant may be conveyed to and detained in a 'place of safety' (defined in s. 55(1) to include a police station, prison, remand centre or other hospital). A practical problem may arise if, after an order has been made, the assurance of a hospital place having been given, it is then withdrawn. In such a situation the Secretary of State may direct that the patient be admitted to another specified hospital (s. 37(5)), or the sentencing court may substitute a sentence under s. 11(2), Crown Court Act 1971 or s. 142, Magistrates' Courts Act 1980. There has been an acknowledged problem since at least the mid 1970s of hospitals refusing to take some hospital order patients (see *R* v *Officer* (1976), *The Times*, 20 February; *R* v *Gordon* (1981) 3 Cr App R(S) 352 (HC); *R* v *Harding* (1983), *The Times*, 15 June (CA), which does not appear to have abated in the 1990s (Ashworth, 1996), as despite the expansion in medium secure provision over the last decade and a half, the pressure on beds both in medium security and high security accommodation remains at crisis point (see 3.4).

In addition to the requirements of s. 37(2)(a) being met, s. 37(2)(b) provides that before a court may make a hospital order it must be 'of the opinion, having regard to all the circumstances including the nature of the offence and the character and antecedents of the offender and to the other available methods of dealing with him' that a hospital order is the most suitable disposal. In *Birch* the Court of Appeal suggested the following order of deliberations. First, a sentencing court should decide, on normal sentencing principles, whether the defendant should be compulsorily detained or whether some form of community-based sanction such as probation with treatment-related conditions would be more appropriate. If it is decided that detention is required, the second question is whether the conditions contained in s. 37 are satisfied and, if so, whether the making of such an order is preferable to the imposition of a prison sentence. According to the court in *Birch*, there are only two reasons for sending a mentally disordered person in respect of whom the conditions in s. 37 are satisfied to prison: (1) 'the offender is dangerous and no suitable secure accommodation is available' (Mustill LJ at p. 215) and; (2) where 'notwithstanding the offender's mental disorder there was an element of culpability in the offence which merits punishment' (ibid.). In short, the court must decide whether the offender perpetuated a crime primarily 'of illness' or 'of wicked-ness' (ibid.); of madness or badness. The thrust of the court's approach, though, was in favour of diversion from prison, Mustill LJ holding that 'even where there is culpability, the right way to deal with a dangerous and disordered person is to make an order under section 37 and 41' (s. 41 is considered below), and that it is inappropriate to pass a prison sentence out of a concern that the defendant will be released earlier from hospital than would be the case if sent to prison. In this the Court of Appeal in *Birch* was following its own earlier authorities, *R v Howell* (1985) 7 Cr App R(S) 360 and *R v Mbatha* (1985) 7 Cr App R(S) 373, which are to the same effect.

The more recent case law indicates that the Court of Appeal has maintained this stance. In *R v Fairhurst* (1996) 1 Cr App R(S) 242 the trial judge decided, in a case in which the defendant had been convicted of manslaughter by reason of diminished responsibility, that the defendant's culpability was nevertheless such that a prison sentence should be passed on him. The defendant was sentenced to life imprisonment with a recommendation (as required by s. 34, Criminal Justice Act 1991) that he should serve at least eight years. The judge did recommend, however, that the Secretary of State should consider using his powers to transfer the defendant from prison to hospital (see 6.6). The Court of Appeal held that the defendant's culpability was not sufficient to depart from the normal preferred practice, and substituted a hospital order with restrictions. The same approach was also taken in *R v Mitchell* (1997) 1 Cr App R(S) 90 (CA) and *R v Hutchinson* (1997) 2 Cr App R(S) 60 (CA).

One exception to the consistency of this line of cases is *R v Fleming* (1993) 14 Cr App R(S) 151 (CA), in which it was held acceptable to pass a sentence of life imprisonment rather than make a hospital order on the basis that, in that case, the ultimate decision about the release of the defendant would be one for the Home Secretary, rather than, if a hospital order was imposed, for a tribunal. Clearly the court felt that in some situations tribunals could not be trusted not to release dangerous offenders prematurely. However, in *Mitchell* Otton LJ pointed out that this was wrong in law — it is the discretionary lifer panel of the Parole Board which decides whether lifers should be released, by virtue of s. 34(4), Criminal Justice Act 1991, and not the Home Secretary — and held that *Fleming* 'is better disregarded' (at p. 93), a view endorsed by Rose LJ in *Hutchinson* (at p. 63). Nevertheless, the approach in *Fleming* finds support in *Birch*, in which Mustill LJ (at p. 214) held (seemingly inconsistently with the general tenor of his judgment in that case) that the sentencing court could properly consider 'the practical effect of all the orders'. This, as Baker (1992, p. 48) argued, could be seen as 'an invitation to disposing courts to impose prison sentences on offenders whom they believe to pose a risk, no matter how badly in need of treatment they are and, presumably, to rely on the Home Secretary's discretion to transfer them to hospital afterwards if necessary', which is precisely what was done in *Fairhurst*. A patient transferred to hospital from prison can be returned to prison if treatment given in hospital is successful or of no beneficial effect. A patient discharged by a tribunal may be released straight into the community, and it is not surprising that some trial courts are uneasy about the latter prospect. The point as a matter of law must, as a result of the inconsistency between *Birch* and *Fleming* on the one hand and *Fairhurst*, *Mitchell*, *Hutchinson* (and *Birch* itself) on the other be classified as uncertain. But in so far as *Birch* and *Fleming* do allow a therapeutic disposal to be rejected because of such concerns about tribunal system, their authority on this point is properly disregarded, not so much because (in *Fleming* at least) the decision is *per incuriam*, as Otton LJ held in *Mitchell*, but on the grounds that concerns about the laxity of the tribunal system are largely without foundation. It can be no easy feat to leave hospital for those sent there by a court, particularly if, as is usual in cases in which the defendant is perceived to constitute a risk to the public, a restriction order is appended to the hospital order (see 8.5).

6.5.2 Restriction orders: s. 41

In *Birch* Mustill LJ explained (at p. 211) the effect of a 'restriction order' being added to a hospital order:

> No longer is the offender regarded simply as a patient whose interests are paramount ... Instead, the interests of public safety are regarded by transferring the responsibility for discharge from the responsible medical officer and the hospital ... to the Secretary of State and the Mental Health Review Tribunal. A patient who has been subject to a restriction order is likely to be detained in hospital for much longer than one who is not, and will have fewer opportunities for leave of absence.

Even when a restriction order patient leaves hospital, it is overwhelmingly likely that that discharge will be conditional in the first instance, and a conditionally discharged restriction order patient remains liable to recall to hospital (see Chapter eight). A s. 37 order coupled with a restriction order made under s. 41 can therefore be understood as the conceptual intersection between treatment and punishment or protective custody. This option is designed to accommodate those who are both mad and 'bad', or dangerous.

An order under s. 41, which cannot be made by a magistrates' court (s. 41(1)), is not freestanding, but must be attached to a s. 37 order. The requirements of s. 37 must therefore be met as a prerequisite to the making of a s. 41 order. In addition, a s. 41 order can only be made where the court is of the view, given the nature of the offence, the history and antecedents of the offender, and the risk of reoffending, that 'it is necessary for the protection of the public from serious harm': s. 41(1). The meaning of this phrase was considered in *Birch*. Mustill LJ held that 'harm' here is 'not limited to personal injury. Nor need it relate to the public in general' (p.213). The condition may be met where there is a risk of serious harm to 'a category of persons, or even a single person ... Nevertheless, the potential harm must be serious, and a high possibility of a recurrence of minor offences will no(t) ... suffice' (p. 213). The court overruled earlier cases where orders had been made on this basis, but did approve the case of *R* v *Khan* (1987) 9 Cr App R(S) 455 in which, although the offences in question were fairly minor (reckless driving) the risk that was thereby posed to the public was serious. In *R* v *Pemberton* (1996) 24 June, unreported (CA) an appeal was allowed against the making of a s. 41 order because the trial judge had considered there to be a 'serious risk' of harm. The Court of Appeal, citing *Birch*, pointed out that it is the potential harm and not the risk of its occurrence which must be serious. Nevertheless, as Street (1998, p. 14) found in his analysis of all restriction orders made in 1992 and 1993, there do appear to be cases, which are not appealed, in which a s. 41 order has been made although 'the risk of serious future harm was not readily apparent'.

In arriving at its decision, s. 41(2) requires that the court hear oral evidence from at least one of the doctors who have already given evidence about the suitability of a s. 37 order, and although this need not as a matter of law be a s. 12 approved doctor it should as a matter of good practice be a doctor on the staff of the hospital at which the defendant will be detained if the order is made: *R* v *Blackwood* (1974) 59 Cr App R(S) (CA). As Akinkunmi and Murray (1997, p. 55) note, however, this is not always easily possible. For example, staff at the Bentham Unit (a specialised unit designed to accept persons remanded to hospital by a court under ss. 35 and 36) have found that a problem has arisen on sentencing subsequent to a period of remand, as only they have the expert medical knowledge of the patient which the court needs to decide whether or not a hospital order should be made but they do not intend to accept a patient on a long-term basis under a hospital order.

It is the responsibility of this doctor or doctors (it is unusual in practice for a sentencing court only to hear the evidence of one doctor) to advise the court on the question of risk. Although risk assessment is a technical matter, Street found that 'psychiatrists largely took the straightforward view that those offenders who committed the most serious offences were the most likely to pose a risk to others in the future' (Street, 1998, p. 24). Recommendations to the court come in various shades, from a firm recommendation that a restriction order is required, through a recommendation that a hospital order be made with no opinion expressed about a restriction order, although it is rare for psychiatrists who recommend a hospital order positively to oppose the making of a restriction order. In a number of cases there will be no express recommendation, as some psychiatrists feel that it is not the role of the doctor to become too closely associated with the sentencing process. But in the majority — 70 per cent — of cases in which a restriction order is made there had been a preponderance of medical evidence to the effect that the defendant did pose a risk of significant harm to others, even if there was not always a positive recommendation that a s. 41 order be made (Street, 1998, p. 28). This still means, however, that 30 per cent of restriction orders are made even though there is no consensus amongst medical witnesses that the defendant poses a significant risk. As the facts of *Birch* demonstrate, medical evidence does not need to be followed by the sentencing judge. In that case, three approved doctors gave evidence that the defendant who, acting under diminished responsibility as a result of her mental disorder, had killed her husband, did not present a danger of significant harm to the public or any individual. Nevertheless the trial judge made a restriction order and his decision was upheld by the Court of Appeal, where it was pointed out that under the terms of s. 41, unlike those of s. 37, the trial judge need not follow any medical recommendations that are made. The decision, ultimately, is one for the court. This may mean that on occasion a sentencing court, having rejected imprisonment in favour of a s. 37 order, nevertheless passes a prison sentence because of a decision not to use s. 41.

In *Birch* the Court of Appeal approved as good law under the 1983 Act the dicta of Parker CJ in *R* v *Gardiner* (1967) 51 Cr App R 187, that for crimes of violence, particularly where there is a prior history of such offending, or of mental disorder manifesting as violence 'there must be compelling reasons to explain why a restriction order should not be made'. Each case, however, must be decided on its own circumstances, including the seriousness of the offence, the medical evidence and prognosis, and any other relevant factors. It would seem to follow that, because there is a general discretion to ignore medical advice in the interests of public safety a decision to add a restriction order will be harder to appeal than the making (or not making) of a s. 37 order in the first place, and indeed this is generally the case. The Court of Appeal has, however, made plain that it will allow an appeal if the trial court falls into error on the law (*Pemberton*), and in *R* v *Slater* (1996) 7 October, unreported (CA) an appeal was successful as the Court of Appeal was satisfied that there had not in fact been a serious risk of harm if the order were not made.

As already mentioned, 211 restriction orders were made by a court in 1997 (Home Office Research and Statistics Directorate,1998a, table 3). Although down from 1996 figures, when 243 such orders were made, the trend over the last decade is of a steady increase in the number of restriction orders imposed by the courts. The vast majority — 168 — of defendants who were made subject to a restriction order in 1997 was diagnosed as suffering from mental illness. Numbers for psychopathic disorder and mental impairment were barely in double figures, and only three orders were made in respect of severely mentally impaired defendants (ibid., table 4). As with hospital orders, both property offences and offences of violence feature in the statistics, although the latter are more prominently represented here, with 27 offences of manslaughter and 85 of 'other violence' amongst the 211. There were 14 restriction orders made following conviction of a sexual offence and 23 following conviction for arson. Restriction orders following property offences were rare, although 35 orders were made following a conviction for other offences, which would no doubt include some of a minor nature (ibid., table 5).

Street (1998) found that, apart from restriction order patients being more likely to have committed a dangerous offence and more likely to have, or likely to have more, previous convictions than hospital order patients, there was very little to distinguish the two groups in terms of age, sex or age at first conviction. The majority of all patients are in the 21 to 39 years age range (Home Office Research and Statistics Directorate, 1998a, table 11), and 90 per cent were male, being first convicted at around 20 years of age (Street, 1998, p. 31). However, *within* the group of restriction order patients there were significant variables. Men are much more likely to be sentenced to a restriction order than women but women were twice as likely as men to have a main diagnosis of psychopathic disorder, and less likely to be diagnosed as mentally ill (which echoes the finding of Milne et al, 1995). Black defendants were nearly all (96 per cent) diagnosed as mentally ill, compared with 69 per cent of white defendants (Street, 1998, p. 10). Other research has found a wide discrepancy in the frequency with which black defendants have a diagnosis of schizophrenia (see 4.7). In general terms Street found a significant over-representation of black African or Caribbean people (21 per cent of those given a restriction order) compared with the population as a whole (at around 2 per cent). The reasons for this are complex and disputed, and the arguments have been rehearsed at various points throughout this text. Street did find that white defendants made subject to a restriction order were less likely than black defendants to have committed a crime of violence, at 75 per cent compared with 85 per cent, although this hardly explains the width of the discrepancies which exist; and other studies, such as that carried out by Shubsachs and colleagues (1995) at Rampton found no significant differences on a number of indicators, including offence. In a helpful review of the literature and issues, Boast and Chesterman (1995) conclude that the high incidence of black people at the deep end of mental health services represents the outcome of social disadvantage, and both direct and indirect discrimination at various decision-making points 'lower down' the system, from the diagnosis of disorder to the perception of the police and the courts of the (perceived) relation between ethnicity, dangerousness and risk. Equally depressing statistics, however, cut across barriers of race. Street found that the typical recipient of a restriction order is long-term unemployed (90 per cent of all orders made in 1992 and 1993), long-term single (68 per cent) and, with the exception of mentally impaired persons, a high percentage (41 per cent) lived alone. Around 20 per cent, rising to almost 40 per cent of mentally impaired defendants, lived in hostels, bed and breakfast establishments or were homeless (Street, 1998, p. 12). Restriction orders, in short, are overwhelmingly made in respect of some of the most economically and socially disadvantaged in society.

6.5.2.1 The nature of the restrictions and the restricted patient regime

There are few restrictions on the way in which a restricted patient is treated (in the broad sense of this term) when in the hospital system (Baxter, 1991). Until recently, for example, there was no legal requirement that a s. 41 patient be held in secure accommodation such as a special hospital, although the situation now is that the court may specify not merely the hospital but also the unit within the hospital in which the subject of the order is to be detained: s. 47(1), Crime (Sentences) Act 1997. In a sense, therefore, a restriction order is not aimed so much at the restricted patient as at the medical professionals responsible for his or her care (Baker, 1992, p. 32). It is the clinical freedom of the RMO to discharge his or her patient, or to organise transfer, when satisfied that treatment is no longer required, or in such secure conditions, that is curtailed by a restriction order. As such the restriction order is one of the best examples of the legal institutionalisation of a hierarchy of concerns that places control above treatment. The restrictions are set out in s. 41(3), and s. 41(3)(a) provides that 'none of the provisions of part II of this Act relating to the duration, renewal and expiration of authority for the detention of patients shall apply'. There can be no application to a tribunal except in circumstances specified: s. 41(3)(b) (see 8.4.2.1.2). The patient cannot be given leave of absence, or be transferred, or discharged, by the RMO without the consent of the Secretary of State: s. 41(3)(c). If leave of absence is granted the patient can be recalled to hospital at any time by the Secretary of State: s. 41(3)(d) (see 8.2). Whilst a restriction order is still in effect any hospital order will also continue (s. 41(4)), although the bringing to an end of a restriction order (by the Secretary of State or a tribunal) does not mean that a patient is no longer liable to be detained. Instead such a patient is treated as though on a s. 37 order from the date of the cessation of the restriction order: s. 41(5).

It is perhaps misleading, however, to explain the effect of a restriction order simply in terms of a list of restrictions. Restricted patients do tend to begin their time in hospital at the deep end of the hospital system, and are for the most part keenly aware of their status. Restricted patients are subject to ongoing monitoring by the Mental Health Unit (MHU) of the Home Office, by way of mandatory annual reports that must be made to the MHU by each patient's RMO (s. 41(6)), and the MHU and the Home Secretary tend towards caution in their attitude to the release of restriction order patients. A restricted patient will feel the state breathing down his or her neck much more keenly than other detained patients. Moreover, the effects of a restriction order continue after release from hospital, as most restricted patients are in the first instance discharged conditionally, and unless and until discharge is made absolute, are liable to recall to hospital (see 8.3.4).

The restricted patient regime does not only apply to those sentenced to a restriction order by a court, but also includes patients transferred to hospital from prison, and those found unfit to be tried, and those found not guilty by reason of insanity (always if the charge is murder, possibly otherwise). Many can expect to spend long periods in hospital before being considered for release. Of the 2694 restricted patients detained in hospital in England and Wales on 31 December 1997, 58 had been in hospital for more than 30 years, 243 for between 20 and 30 years, 481 for between 10 and 20 years, 476 between 5 and 10 years, 650 between 2 and 5 years and only 786 (including 228 remand prisoners) less than two years (Home Office Research and Statistics Directorate, 1998a, table 14). Of those detained for long periods, a numerically small but statistically significant number of patients with psychopathic disorder — 17 out of a total of 398 — had been detained for more than 30 years. By way of comparison, 18 mentally ill patients had been detained as long, but this was out of a total of 1820 (ibid., table 15). Another 115 psychopathically disordered patients had been detained for between 10 and 20 years, and 73 for between 20 and 30 years. Yet what is more remarkable is many patients in all disorder categories spend a considerable number of years in hospital. It is clear that a restriction order is by no means a 'soft option' compared with imprisonment, at least in terms of time served.

6.5.2.2 Restriction orders of limited duration An order under s. 41 may be made 'either without limit of time or during such period as may be

specified in the order': s. 41(1). In the early years of the regime inaugurated by the passage of the MHA 1959, almost half of restriction orders made were of limited duration, but the Court of Appeal turned its face against limited duration orders in *Gardiner* (see 6.5.2), given that prognosis is usually uncertain at the time of sentencing. From 1968 onwards such orders became much rarer (Robertson, 1989), as remains the case. Limited duration orders now account for around 5 per cent of all restriction orders: 72 out of 1448 s. 41 orders made in the decade 1983-93 (Romilly, Parrott and Carney, 1997, p. 564). It seems likely that this pattern will not change in the foreseeable future. The Court of Appeal has reiterated the view taken in *Gardiner*, *Birch*, and *R* v *Nwohla* [1995] Crim LR 668.

An analysis of the use of limited duration restriction orders in the ten years following the passage of the MHA 1983 (Romilly, Parrott and Carney, 1997) found, perhaps not unexpectedly, that the profile of offenders for which such orders are made was less serious than that of those sentenced without limit of time. Of more interest, when a limited duration order was made, it was often on the initiative of the trial judge acting against (11/72) or without (30/72) medical opinion as to the suitability of such an order. Firm medical recommendations leading to an order being of limited duration were relatively rare (26/72); and it was rarer still that the reason for the medical recommendation for a limited duration order was a firm prognosis for effective treatment within the specified time period, which forms the basis of the stance taken by the Court of Appeal. Often, such a recommendation was made in an attempt to dissuade the judge from making an order that in the opinion of the doctor in question would have been even more undesirable — whether that be an unlimited s. 41 order or a prison sentence. Romilly et al conclude that, as far as generalisation is possible, when a limited duration s. 41 order is made it reflects a judicial desire to pass a sentence which in terms of time in confinement is commensurate to the tariff. The guidance of the Court of Appeal in *R* v *Hayes* (1981) 3 Cr App R(S) 330, that this practice is inappropriate, seems to have gone unheeded by the lower courts.

The Butler Committee recommended the abolition of limited duration restriction orders when the law was reformed in 1983, but that view was rejected on the grounds that the order was useful when a firm prognosis was possible at the time of trial. The evidence is strong, though, that the order is used in this way only rarely, and is used more often as a covert way to introduce a punitive element into a treatment order in a way which departs from the spirit of the general policy of diversion. The argument for abolition, therefore, is now that much stronger than it was in the early 1980s.

6.5.3   Hospital and limitation directions

Under the regime contained in part III of the 1983 Act, as initially enacted, a patient sentenced to hospital could not be transferred to prison at a later date. Although s. 38 provides for interim hospital orders (see below) this provision, as the Court of Appeal noted in *Birch*, has not been popular with sentencers. There have been calls for a number of years for greater flexibility to be crafted into the system. In addition, there has long been concern about the particular problem of psychopathically disordered offenders, given the dubious treatability of this condition, making it unclear that a hospital order under s. 37 was always appropriate. In such cases, the accused person would on conviction receive a prison sentence, and although there is the possibility of transfer to hospital from prison, this is not a realistic prospect for the majority of offenders; and transfer may happen late into the sentence of imprisonment, with the consequence of the offender continuing to be detained in a hospital after the expiry of the sentence given, which raises its own set of ethical problems (see below). Conversely, in some cases s. 37 orders have been made, only for those charged with treating the subject of the order to discover that he or she is not in fact treatable, with the consequence that the function of hospitalisation, in practice, is purely custodial. Hospital orders are made rarely in cases involving psychopathic disorder — only 20 patients diagnosed as psychopathic were admitted to a hospital under ss. 37 and 41 in 1996, compared with 178 mentally ill offenders (Home Office Research and Statistics Directorate, 1997, table 4). Psychopathically disordered offenders are also more likely to be recalled after discharge than other categories of mentally disordered offenders. In practice, most psychopathically disordered offenders are given a punitive disposal that frequently means that there is no further involvement by the mental health services, during or after custody, until, in those few cases where it does, disaster strikes.

The White Paper, *Protecting the Public* (Home Office, 1996) and an ensuing consultation document (Department of Health and Home Office, 1996) signalled governmental acceptance of, at least some version of, these arguments, and s. 46, Crime (Sentences) Act 1997 inserted new sections — ss. 45A and 45B — into the 1983 Act which now provide for 'hospital and limitation directions' to be made by a sentencing court. Now, a court is not faced with a stark choice between sending a defendant either to prison or to hospital, but may instead direct that the disposal is initially to a hospital, but with imprisonment as a backstop. A 'hospital direction' is defined in s. 45A(3)(a) as 'a direction that, instead of being removed to and detained in a prison, the offender may be removed to and detained in such hospital as may be specified in the direction'. A hospital direction can only be made following the conviction of the defendant in a Crown Court: s. 45A(1), and in circumstances in which the court has considered making an hospital order under s. 37 but has decided that a sentence of imprisonment would be more appropriate: s. 45A(2)(b), because a hospital order will not be sufficient to protect the public from harm, or because of the operation of s. 2 of the 1997 Act under which a mandatory life sentence must be passed (Home Office, Mental Health Unit, 1997).

However, and confusingly, the conditions that must be met before a hospital direction can be made are the same as those relevant to the making of a hospital order under s. 37. As under that section, a court contemplating making a hospital direction must be satisfied on the written or oral evidence of two doctors (who need not be 'approved' nor even psychiatrists) that the mental disorder from which the defendant is suffering is of a nature or degree which makes it appropriate for him to be detained in a hospital for medical treatment (s. 45A(2)(b)) and that 'such treatment is likely to alleviate or prevent a deterioration of his condition': s. 45A(2)(c). Section 45A also introduces the 'limitation direction' which is 'a direction that the offender be subject to the special restrictions contained in s. 41'. It seems that there is no scope to make a hospital direction without also making a limitation direction. The court must hear oral evidence from at least one of the two doctors who gave evidence under subsection (2) before making the two directions, but as the wording of s. 45A(4) is similar to that of s. 41(2) (see 6.5.2), it would seem clear that, as under that section, the final decision is for the court.

It may well be asked what difference there is between directions made under s. 45A and orders made under ss. 37 and 41. It is certainly the case that the new sentencing option has ended up being closer to that which was already available to a sentencing court than was originally envisaged. There are, however, two significant differences. First, a hospital direction can only be made if 'the offender is suffering from psychopathic disorder': s. 45A(2)(a). As mentioned above, the new powers were born out of a perceived need for flexibility in the sentencing of psychopathic offenders in respect of whom there was uncertainty about the efficacy of treatment (Reed, 1994), and resurrected an earlier proposal along the same lines (Peay, 1988). The 1996 consultation document retained this rationale, explaining that a hospital direction and limitation direction would be appropriate where the outcome of treatment was uncertain, but as seen above, in the new powers as actually enacted, there is a treatability requirement identical to that imposed under s. 3. At some point in the transition to the statute book, the initial justification for the new directions has been lost.

The consultation document also explained the need for the new directions in cases where it was not clear that the making of a hospital order, with or without restrictions, would 'sufficiently address the risk to the public posed by the defendant' (Department of Health and Home Office, 1996, para. 1.4). This is because on discharge from hospital a patient detained on a s. 37 order, even one with restrictions attached, has to be discharged into the community; and even though such discharge can be conditional in the case of restricted patients, and even though there is a certain logic in the discharge of patients from hospital who have apparently responded successfully to treatment or are found not to be treatable, the concern about the presence of known dangerous psychopathically disordered persons in the community is such that, in political terms, something had to be done. Accordingly, the second main difference between the new directions and the existing orders is that by s. 45B(2), a hospital direction is to have effect as a transfer direction and a limitation direction as a restriction direction, which means that on discharge a s. 45A patient will be transferred to prison to serve out his or her sentence: s. 50(1). Laing (1996, p. 138) has argued that this may undermine the doctor/patient relationship for s. 45A patients, either by offering patients who do not wish to confront their problems an escape route from hospital (Mental Health Act Commission, 1995, p. 72) or by providing a disincentive to respond as well as might otherwise have been the case for patients who do not wish to return to prison.

But within the frame of reference in which the new directions were concocted — the need to convince sentencers that detention in a hospital would not increase the chances of early release back into the community — this problem seems to be unavoidable. Simply, without the backstop of prison, there would be no meaningful distinction between the new powers and the established orders, and so no encouragement for sentencers, who have been reluctant to make hospital orders in cases involving psychopathically disordered offenders, to make hospital directions.

The final justification for the new directions that is made in the consultation document is that hospital and limitation directions would be appropriate in cases where 'a punitive element in the disposal is required to reflect the offender's whole or partial responsibility' (para. 1.4). Subsequently, however, the reference to 'responsibility' was conspicuous by its absence from the Home Office Circular that accompanied the 1997 Act (Home Office, Mental Health Unit, 1997). This may be because the possibility that hybrid orders should be used to denote the offender's responsibility was heavily criticised (Eastman, 1996; Laing, 1996), as it had been in earlier forms (Peay, 1988; Home Office and DHSS, 1975, para. 19.5) and in other contexts (Dell, 1982), on the grounds that it seeks to draw psychiatrists into the sentencing process, notwithstanding that 'psychiatrists are likely to resist such direct involvement in sentencing decisions, both on ethical grounds and because there is no scientific basis upon which such advice could be given to a court' (Eastman, 1996, p. 488), which is to say that criminal responsibility is not a medical concept.

It may not, however, be so easy, in practice, to expunge consideration of 'responsibility' from the sentencing decision-making process. In order to get to the point at which it is proper to consider making a hospital direction, the sentencing court must first go through the process laid down by the Court of Appeal in *Birch*. As discussed in 5.5.1, this requires the judge to consider, first; the making of a non-custodial disposal; secondly, if detention in some form is required, whether a hospital order can and should be made. And the only reasons to decide against making a hospital order when the criteria are satisfied are to protect the public when there is no secure hospital accommodation available, or to recognise the culpability of the offender when punishment is warranted. Thus, considerations of culpability will be firmly to the fore when the judge is at this stage of the reasoning process. Hospital directions, therefore, which should not be considered until this point as an alternative to imprisonment after it has been decided that for the reasons outlined above a hospital order — even coupled with a restriction order — is not appropriate, are reserved for dealing with those (psychopathically disordered) offenders who by definition are either particularly dangerous or particularly culpable (as discussed in 6.5.1; in *Birch* Mustill LJ held that orders under ss. 37 and 41 are 'even where there is culpability, the right way to deal with dangerous and disordered persons. . . .').

Moreover, having rejected a non-custodial disposal, or as part of that decision, the court is required to obtain and consider a report on a mentally disordered offender under s. 4 of the Criminal Justice Act 1991 and, having rejected the option of a hospital order, the court must go on to consider, either before or as part of the deliberations concerning whether to make a hospital direction, the appropriate sentence length. Given that, by this stage of the process, the number of offenders under consideration will have been whittled down to a problematic core of particularly dangerous and/or culpable psychopaths, it may be that the court will consider it appropriate to use its powers in s. 2(2)(b) of the 1991 Act to pass a 'longer than normal' sentence. But as future dangerousness *per se* is peculiarly difficult to predict, let alone its expected longevity, the temptation to fix sentence length by reference to 'responsibility' will be virtually overwhelming (Eastman and Peay, 1998, p. 100).

This means that the psychiatric profession will be drawn into the sentencing process by the new directions. Eastman and Peay see this as 'a fundamental shift in thinking which will have a radical impact on the relationship between courts and psychiatrists' (1998, p. 105), in that involvement in the sentencing process is being foisted on psychiatric professionals against their wishes. From a more theoretical perspective, the reasoning process attendant on making hospital and limitation directions attests to a particularly graphic example of the complexity of the fusion of psychiatric and jurisprudential discourses which constitutes a new density to the 'micropractices' of power/knowledge. There are other reasons to be concerned about the new directions. For instance, how is it possible to justify the applicability of the new directions solely to psychopathic offenders who, although likely to be culpable to a greater or lesser extent for the crimes that they commit, are not necessarily more likely to be culpable than other mentally disordered offenders? Part of the answer, no doubt, is that in *political* terms psychopathic offenders are perceived to be a particularly problematic group, about whom 'something must be done', but this is akin to saying that the 1997 Act provisions can be read as the latest instalment in the historical project of demonising the criminal psychopath as the epicentre of both badness and madness.

It may be that it is not long before the availability of hospital and limitation directions is extended to other forms of mental disorder. The equivalent Scottish legislation (s. 59A Criminal Procedure (Scotland) Act 1995, as inserted by s. 6, Crime and Punishment (Scotland) Act 1997) from the outset has been available for all forms of mental disorder, and there is provision in s. 45A(10) of the 1983 Act for the English and Welsh legislation to be similarly extended. Indeed, it seems that it was only financial and resources reasons that explain the current limitation to psychopathic disorder (Eastman and Peay, 1998, p. 98). At present, the combination of s. 2(2)(b) of the Criminal Justice Act 1991 and the availability of hospital directions risks pushing psychopathically disordered offenders 'up tariff' by attaching the hospital direction to a 'longer than normal' sentence. If this situation is extended to all categories of mentally disordered offenders, although it will mean that psychopathy can no longer be singled out as a particular human rights concern, it will constitute an important shift in diversion policy at the general level, as the balance between treatment and punishment will move significantly towards the latter. It is at present too early to tell, but it may be that sentencers will be greatly attracted to the 'added ingredients' that distinguish hospital and limitation directions from hospital and restriction orders.

In lieu of the failure of the 1997 Act to provide for the originally intended target population of patients of uncertain treatability, sentencers should be encouraged to make greater use of their powers, contained in s. 38, MHA 1983 to make an interim hospital order. A sentencing court in need of information to enable it to make a hospital order may, in addition to the reports discussed above, request that a health authority provide information about the availability of hospital accommodation: s. 39. Where the issue is not availability of accommodation but the treatability of the offender, it may make an interim hospital order, provided that an offender is suffering from one of the four specified forms of mental disorder (s. 38(1)(a)), and two doctors, one of whom is employed at the hospital to be specified in the order (s. 38(3)), have given evidence to the court's satisfaction that there is 'reason to suppose that the mental disorder from which the offender is suffering is such that it may be appropriate for a hospital order to be made in his case': s. 38(1)(b). An order under s. 38 can only be made by a court on convicting a defendant of an offence punishable with imprisonment. As with an order under s. 37, it must be certified that the arrangements have been made for the reception of the defendant into hospital within 28 days of the making of the order and that there is a place of safety available if necessary: s. 38(4).

The idea of the interim order is to give adequate time to assess the treatability of the defendant's disorder, which may not be available under the remand powers. If judged suitable, a full hospital order may be made without the defendant being brought back before the court provided that his or her legal representative has the opportunity to be heard: s. 38(2). If not, the defendant may be sentenced to a term of imprisonment. Until recently the maximum duration of an interim hospital order was six months (s. 38(5)), but this was extended to 12 months by s. 49(1) of the Crime (Sentences) Act 1997 — the same legislation which introduced the new directions. In view of the fact that an order under s. 38, as amended, should be able to deal satisfactorily with the initial justification for the introduction of hospital and limitation directions, any suspicion that the main function of the new directions was really to constitute a general toughening up of hospital orders, so that such orders can be replaced rather than augmented by hospital directions, is given additional credence.

The reforms introduced by the 1997 Act, as mentioned above, were limited in their scope by reason of the limitation of resources; and the reforms do nothing to address this underlying issue of shortage of hospital accommodation (Fennell, 1991a). It can be forcibly argued that the 1997 reforms hint at an impending, more wholesale, sea change in diversion policy, suspicion of which is greatly increased by the current proposals for 'reviewable detention' (see 6.7). But perhaps of equivalent significance is that they point to the practical limitations to any policy of diversion that is not adequately funded.

6.6   TRANSFER FROM PRISON TO HOSPITAL

If the measure of the success of the policy of diversion is the numbers of mentally disordered persons who end up in prison, then there is a good argument to say that the policy has failed. As Peay (1997, p. 668) succinctly states '[m]any, if not most, 'disordered' offenders do not receive the therapeutic 'hospital order' disposal, even though their culpability may be mitigated, if not absolved, by their mental state'. Despite the policy of, and the numerous mechanisms to secure the practice of, diversion of offenders suffering from mental disorder from the penal to the hospital system, the numbers of such persons amongst sentenced prison populations has been consistently well documented (see 6.3.1). In some instances this will be because an offender's mental health is negatively affected by prison conditions, but there is little doubt that some of those in prison suffering from mental disorder were suffering at the time of conviction. Research has shown that prison screening programmes can fail to detect mental disorder (Birmingham et al, 1996), although it has more recently been suggested that screening programmes have a reasonable detection rate (Hardie et al, 1998). Gunn et al (1991) found that 3 per cent of prisoners required transfer to hospital, which amounts to several hundred individuals. Mechanisms for the transfer of such persons from prison to hospital have long been a feature of mental health legislation. Although it is possible to transfer *such persons* back to prison from hospital, there is no mechanism to transfer a person initially sentenced to hospital to a prison; as we have seen above, persons sentenced to hospital pass out of the criminal justice system once and for all. It was this gap that the reforms introduced by the Crime (Sentences) Act 1997 attempted to plug.

The current law with respect to the transfer of a person from prison to hospital is to be found in ss. 47 to 49 of the 1983 Act. Section 47 provides for the transfer of sentenced prisoners. The medical criteria to be satisfied are identical to those contained in ss. 3 and 37. Two doctors, at least one of whom must be 'approved', must examine the patient and agree that he or she is suffering from one of the four specified forms of mental disorder (s. 47(4), although it is not necessary that they agree that this is all that the patient is suffering from), to a nature or degree which makes it appropriate for him or her to be detained in a hospital for treatment. There is also a treatability test in respect of psychopathic disorder and mental impairment: s. 47(1). The decision whether to transfer a prisoner lies with the Secretary of State who 'may, if he is of the opinion having regard to the public interest and all the circumstances that it is expedient to do so direct that the person is question be transferred to a specified hospital': s. 47(1). This provision is very widely worded. It is clear for example that 'all the circumstances' includes such things as the availability of a hospital bed. In *R v Secretary of State for the Home Department, ex parte K* [1990] 1 All ER 703 (DC) McCullough J, in a wide ranging discussion of the powers given to the Secretary of State by part III of the Act, said, *obiter*, that 'the Secretary of State is never obliged to act under s. 47, even if he thinks that the necessary preconditions are fulfilled' (p.716). This does not mean that the Secretary of State is immune from judicial review, though. When he or she does act under this section, it must first be decided in good faith that a proposed transfer is expedient (*Birch* per Mustill LJ at p. 210; see 6.5.1). A transfer direction made under s. 47 is deemed to have the same effect as a hospital order: s. 47(3). An order made under s. 47 can be accompanied by an order made under s. 49, by which the restrictions contained in s. 41 may apply to a transferee: s. 49(1), (2). It is the norm that restrictions be imposed. In 1997-8, of 247 orders made under s. 47, only 31 were unrestricted (Department of Health, 1998d, table 1). If a restriction direction is made, it will automatically cease to apply 'on the expiration of the sentence' (s. 50(2)), at which point the patient, if still in hospital, will be detained as if held under s. 37.

There is also provision for the transfer of other than sentenced prisoners under s. 48, defined to include: remand prisoners, civil prisoners and those held under the Immigration Act 1971: s. 48(2). Section 48 applies only to prisoners suffering 'from mental illness or severe mental impairment of a nature or degree which makes it appropriate for him to be detained in hospital for medical treatment and is in urgent need of such treatment'. A patient so transferred is treated as though transferred under s. 47 (s. 48(1)), which means that the patient is treated as though on a hospital order (s. 47(3)), although again it is unusual for an order to be made under s. 48 without an accompanying direction being made under s. 49(1). The use of s. 48 has increased markedly between 1987, when 77 untried or unsentenced prisoners were transferred to hospital, and 1994, when there were 536 such transfers. Over recent years the rate has settled at a little under 500 transfers annually; there were 494 in 1997 (Department of Health, 1998d, table 3).

For all transfers the receiving hospital must be specified in the direction (s. 47(1)) and although it does not follow from this that the agreement of that hospital must be obtained before a direction is made, this has been the normal practice of the Secretary of State: see *R* v *Secretary of State for the Home Department, ex parte T* [1994] 1 All ER 794 (DC). The Butler Committee (Home Office and DHSS, 1975, para. 2.29) noted the practice without comment. This is understandable, particularly as under the terms of s. 47(2) a transfer direction will cease to have effect if the person named in the direction has not been transferred within 14 days of its making. Under the 1959 Act regime, the delay in the time from when a prisoner was first referred for transfer to the actual transfer increased steadily. Grounds (1990) found that in the decade 1974-83 the mean wait was 7.5 months, with a quarter of patients waiting a year or more. This increase took place against the backdrop of a fall in the number of prisoners recommended for transfer by prison service doctors, despite an ever-increasing prison population. The reasons for this fall include the introduction of waiting lists at Broadmoor for transfer patients; a disinclination on the part of psychiatrists to accept chronic patients (Dolan and Shetty, 1995; Cheadle and Ditchfield, 1982; Tidmarsh, 1978, cited in Grounds, 1990) and those diagnosed as having personality disorders (Hargreaves, 1997); and the difficulties experienced by special hospitals when trying to secure a bed for patients able to move into less secure accommodation (see 3.4). From the late 1980s, with the introduction of more secure provision in the form of regional secure units and medium secure units, the numbers of prisoners being transferred to hospital after sentence, as with those transferred before sentence, rose dramatically from 103 in 1987 to 251 in 1997, the highest annual figure being 284 in 1993 (Department of Health, 1998d, table 3).

Yet according to some recent research (Huws et al, 1997) the average wait from the initial request from a prison doctor for a second opinion to the actual transfer has fallen throughout this period and is now less than two months. It is hard to generalise in this area, though. Hargreaves's (1997) experience in Wakefield is that waiting times remain high. For transfers out of Wakefield prison the mean wait is around six months. As Larkin and Close (1996) have pointed out, the mean waiting times obscure the fact that referrals are classified as either urgent or routine, with the former being processed in around one-third of the time of the routine referrals. In their audit of the referral system as it operates at Rampton hospital, a mean waiting time of 41.4 days disguised the fact that urgent cases were admitted within 20.6 days, compared with a mean of 61.5 days for routine cases.

A transfer direction need not be signed until a bed has been found and the purpose of s. 47(2) is, therefore, not clear. Worse, as Grounds pointed out, under the 1959 regime it was, and still is under the 1983 Act, possible for transfers to take place 'on the basis of out date medical reports, long after the initial recommendation' (1990, p. 548), although it has recently been held that, if there is fluctuation in the medical condition of the person in respect of whom transfer is being contemplated, it is unreasonable of the Home Secretary to rely on dated medical reports (*R v Secretary of State for the Home Office, ex parte Gilkes* (1999), unreported (HC)). More recently, Hargreaves concluded that 'the process of transfer for mentally ill prisoners remains slow and characterised by unacceptable delays at each stage of the process. In essence, it remains possible for a severely ill and behaviourally disturbed prisoner to remain untreated for a period of months before transfer is effected' (1997, p. 70). In addition, it can be said that, to the extent that there has been some improvement in the overall performance of the transfer system in this regard in recent years, this cannot be credited to the wording of the Act, which has not changed throughout this period. On the contrary, the 1983 Act here, as in many other places, provides a 'safeguard' provision that in practice is of no relevance whatever. It is instructive to compare s. 47(2) with s. 11(5), which provides that no application is to be made under ss. 2, 3 or 7 unless the applicant has personally seen the patient within the previous 14 days.

There are other concerns with the operation of the transfer provisions. The most significant is the effect that a transfer to hospital has on the length of time that the individual spends in custody. Grounds found that one consequence of the reduction of the availability of hospital beds for transferees was that transfers took place at a later stage in the prisoner's sentence. One consultant at Broadmoor gave evidence to the Butler Committee that, because of the difficulties, some prison doctors had given up trying to get patients onto the Broadmoor waiting list for transfer and that '[b]ecause of the waiting list we have had to admit patients very near the end of their sentences' (para. 3.41 cited in Grounds, 1990, p. 57). In consequence there was a risk that patients would be detained in hospital beyond the date at which they would otherwise have been released from prison. This will usually be the earliest release date (ERD), although it could be the latest date of release (LDR), that is, the last date of a determinate sentence served in full, with no remission or parole. The

Butler Committee dismissed these concerns as 'almost entirely theoretical' (Home Office and DHSS, 1975, para. 3.42). Others argued that a transfer direction should not survive the patient's ERD, and that further detention past that date should be permissible only if that patient was first sectioned under s. 3 (Gostin, 1977). The 1983 Act took a middle course. Now, under s. 50(2),(3), where a restriction direction is made it must not survive the ERD, rather than subsisting until the LDR, as was the case under the 1959 Act. The practical effect of this is that a transferee remaining in hospital at the ERD may apply to a Mental Health Review Tribunal for discharge from that date.

Nothing was done in 1983, or since, however, to prevent the transfer of a person from prison shortly before that person's ERD. Despite the confidence of Butler, it seems clear that late transfer was and continues to be a problematic issue. Grounds found that in the 1960s transfers were typically 23 months before ERD; in the 1970s this had fallen to 10 months, a change 'not due to any significant reduction in the mean length of their sentences' (1991, p. 59). In addition, length of stay in hospital after transfer (4 years mean, with 7.4 years mean for sex offenders) meant that '[m]ost [62 per cent] of the patients transferred to Broadmoor ... continued to be detained in the hospital well beyond their LDRs — in some cases for many years' (p.62); and this 'extra' period of detention bore a 'strong relationship' to the gravity of the offence. There is evidence to suggest that the situation has changed in the last decade. In Huckle's study of transferees to hospitals in South Wales over the three year period 1992-5, 66 per cent of transfers took place within three months of the offender's arrival in prison (1996, p. 39). Huws et al's research into the operation of the 1983 Act in special hospitals in the period 1984-1 found no correlation between time in hospital and the gravity of the offence (1997, p. 81), although that 44 per cent of transferees were detained beyond their LDR, with 59 per cent held beyond their ERD. Compared with the earlier figures this seems to be an improvement, yet the numbers detained in hospital longer than they would otherwise have been had they not been transferred, remains disquietingly high. In addition, Huws et al's results are not strictly comparable with those of Grounds, as a high percentage — 81 per cent of the latter's sample — had left hospital by the end of the study period, whilst in Huws et al's research only 56 per cent had left the hospital (p. 81). The arguments made two decades ago by Gostin, that there should be a require-ment that detention post–ERD should have to be justified on medical grounds, such as in the form of a s. 3 admission at that point, seem to be as strong as ever; particularly as the making available of a right to apply to a tribunal for discharge post-ERD seems to have had little impact (only 17 out of 351 transferees to special hospitals in the period 1984-91 were discharged by a tribunal: Huws et al, p. 81). Of particular concern is Huws et al's finding that 6 per cent of transferees (21 individuals) were transferred late into their sentences — within six weeks of ERD — on grounds of 'worry about their release' (p. 77); and 4 per cent (15) of transfers took place within one week of ERD. Of these patients 66 per cent (14) were suffering from a personality disorder. Their mean sentence length was 3.7 years and mean time in hospital 2.8 years (p. 78). The period in hospital does not differ significantly from the mean time in hospital of those transferred earlier in their sentence, but of course for the late transferees virtually all of this period was in excess of the sentence given by the court at the time of conviction. It may well be, as Huws et al suggest, that prisoners suffering from a personality disorder, unlike mentally ill prisoners, do not come to the attention of prison medical services until they are assessed prior to their proposed release from prison (p. 82), since those suffering from such disorders do not necessarily appear to be 'mad'. But this does not detract from the crucial point here, which is that transfers should, under the terms of s. 47, only take place on medical grounds. 'Concerns about release' that are not concerned directly with the need for treatment to improve or prevent a deterioration in the patient's state of mental health, are not *per se* a good enough reason for transfer. It seems odd that psychopaths feature so largely in this group, when elsewhere their treatability is at best suspect. It is difficult not to feel a lurking sense of unease that, when release is imminent, psychopaths are suddenly deemed treatable, albeit not in large numbers.

6.7   CONCLUDING COMMENTS

The stated aim of this Chapter was to evaluate the policy of diversion on its own terms, to ask 'does diversion work?' It can now be seen that there can be no easy or unqualified answer to that question. The policy of diversion *does* work, but only imperfectly. The system as a whole is shot through with some common problems. Foremost amongst these are: a shortfall in funding; lack of coherent central guidance; and effective training of criminal justice personnel and others, such as persons to act as AAs. Diversion *practice* has been left to a large extent to those working at local level, and the result is service provision that is patchy both in terms of geographical spread and of quality. There is also uncertainty, amongst police officers, lawyers and courts, as to the appropriate scope and target population of the policy of diversion.

Added to these considerations, the MHA 1983 at various points — notably the powers to remand to hospital — places legal limitations on the potential of early diversion, although for reasons that are not readily apparent. The removal of these legal–structural limitations on diversion should be of pressing concern to those involved in the review of mental health law. Even so, the limited time, resources and information available to sentencing, particularly magistrates', courts makes it likely that the remand prison population will continue to feature large numbers of persons who are mentally disordered. Ultimately, the extent to which this is an acceptable feature of our criminal justice system is a political, rather than a legal, medical, or even philosophical question. And that we seem, as a society, to be equivocal in our response is possibly the most fundamental limitation on the potential for diversion.

One way in which this ambivalence manifests itself is as a reluctance on the part of sentencers to make full use of the range of options available under the MHA 1983. In part this seems to be because of a perception that defendants sentenced to hospital will be released inappropriately early. Such fears are largely unwarranted; and for some, mainly personality disordered, defendants 'diversion' can mean a much longer period of incarceration than would otherwise have been the case, with hospitalisation late in a prison sentence being used as an *extension of*, rather than an *alternative to* imprisonment. Such factors speak in turn of the more deeply seated tension between treatment and control, and it is clear that diversion policy has always been circumscribed, not so much by moral or philosophical questions of criminal responsibility and desert, but by more pragmatic considerations of public safety. But perhaps the most important of current developments is the possibility that a fundamental policy shift is underway. This has been signalled by the new sentencing options introduced by the Crime (Sentences) Act 1997. These measures were, as has been seen above, originally aimed at psychopathically disordered persons of uncertain treatability. Yet hospital and limitation directions as enacted have systematically excluded this target group by the insertion of the treatability requirement. This goes a long way to explain the indifferent reception that the new orders have received from the courts. If their introduction is to have any impact it will be necessary to extend their reach to all those currently eligible for hospital and restriction orders under ss. 37 and 41, as has already been done in Scotland. In the worst case scenario, the way is now clear for the abolition of ss. 37 and 41; but this would of course constitute a general harshening of our attitude to mentally disordered offenders as a class.

It would also leave the original target group of the 1997 reforms unaffected. It is for this reason that the government has proposed that a 'reviewable detention order' be introduced for untreatable but dangerous personality disordered persons, and 'admission to the new regime will not be dependent upon the person having committed an offence, nor whether they are treatable under the terms of the current Mental Health Act' (Department of Health, 1998a, para. 4.33; see also Home Office and Department of Health (1999)). It is difficult not to have some sympathy with this proposal, in the light of cases such as *R v Swindon Borough Council, ex parte Stoddard* (1998) 2 July, unreported, (DC). S was at the end of a prison sentence, passed for an offence of violence. S was suffering from an untreatable personality disorder, which by common opinion, including his own, rendered him at significant risk of violent reoffending. The case arose because S was unable to obtain secure community care accommodation from his local authority, even though it had assessed him as being in need of such provision and it was accepted that the duty of the authority was to supply the accommodation under the relevant community care legislation (see 9.2 to 9.4). This was because the authority had been unable to find a provider of secure accommodation that would agree to take a patient who was not 'sectionable'. Moses J held that there could be no breach of duty by the local authority or providers of accommodation in such circumstances. The judgment means that local authorities and health authorities, and the providers of services to those authorities, can avoid responsibility for persons such as S. Moreover, the court also accepted the view of the Home Office that the powers of the Secretary of State to recall prisoners released on license, contained in s. 39, Criminal Justice Act 1991, can only be used to recall a prisoner on the basis of behaviour *after* release, and cannot be used to *prevent* release, however great the perceived risk.

Individuals like S fall between the mental health and criminal justice regimes. But it is clearly highly controversial to act on risk alone. The government view is that any new powers of reviewable detention will not infringe the European Convention on Human Rights (Department of Health, 1998a, para. 4.33). It may be that, if detention were based on 'objective medical evidence', there would be compliance with the Convention, notwithstanding that there is no requirement that a crime be committed. Preventative detention is permissible under part II of the MHA, after all. However, it seems that if such an order were to be made, it would only be on the basis that the objective medical evidence was that there was *no* medical justification for detention. It is difficult to see, therefore, how greater powers than are already available, either to incarcerate a person or to provide supervision in the community would be able to avoid falling foul of the Convention. It is perhaps more difficult still to accept that such a significant inroad into civil liberties can be morally justified, particularly as the policy is driven by widespread but inaccurate public conceptions and media distortions of the risk posed (Health Education Authority, 1997).

Moreover, it is not merely the fate of this relatively small group of problematic individuals that is at stake in these developments. The risk is, as mentioned above, that the 1997 reforms, targeted initially at this group, will be inherited by those currently eligible for a hospital order, whilst even more intrusive powers are developed for the original target group. The point here is not merely that this would constitute a significant shift in the balance between treatment and control, but that the 'dangerous psychopath' would have become the axis around which mental health policy more broadly is being reconstituted. There is of course a certain irony here, in that the mental health regime, if these fears prove founded, would be in the situation in which policy towards those that the mental health services do want to treat is propelled by policy towards those that they do not. If this is social control then it also looks a lot like 'social control' of medical professionals, and conspiracy theorists perhaps need to look elsewhere for the prime instigator of these measures. Perhaps we should all look, ultimately, at our own views and their implications.

SEVEN

Treatment in hospital

7.1 INTRODUCTION

The medical treatment of many mentally disordered persons in hospital now corresponds closely to the medical treatment of other patients in numerous ways. They are likely to be admitted to the same district general hospital as patients with physical complaints. In either case, the emphasis is on through-put, and hospitalisation is likely to be for as short a period as possible. For the vast majority of psychiatric patients, admitted 'informally' under s. 131, MHA 1983, the law applicable to their medical treatment is that relevant to all other hospital patients. An informal patient in a psychiatric facility may refuse treatment, leave hospital at any time, access the same complaints procedures, and so on, in exactly the same way as any other hospital patient.

For detained patients, the position is different. Part IV, MHA 1983 lays out a legal regime that allows for treatment without consent. Hence the policy behind the MHA 1983 is that it is justifiable to override the autonomy of detained patients and impose treatment, either for the good of the patient or of others. But part IV of the 1983 Act is double-edged. The libertarian critique of 'psychiatric treatment as social control' in its less radical form (Gostin, 1975) was a potent influence on the construction of the 1983 Act. Part IV also provides that even detained patients have an absolute statutory right to refuse the most invasive treatments of psychosurgery, which may change the personality of the patient through the destruction of brain tissue, and the surgical implantation of hormones to reduce male sexual drive. Such treatments are used relatively rarely. The main 'physical treatments' are drug therapies and electro convulsive therapy (ECT), and these too are subject to a system of safeguards, requiring either the consent of the patient or a second opinion. For ECT the safeguards system applies from the first administration of the treatment to a patient, but it does not come into operation in respect of drug treatments until three months after such treatment has first been administered. Once three months have passed, drug treatments may only be given without consent if a second opinion that it is desirable to do so is provided, by one of the doctors appointed for this purpose by the state. In turn, the whole system is overseen by the Mental Health Act Commission (MHAC). The safeguards are designed to compensate for the removal of the patient's right to refuse treatment.

Part IV of the MHA 1983 can be read as a truce between two competing models of psychiatric treatment: as 'medicine' and as 'control'. Its detail weaves notions of treatment and control, autonomy and beneficence, rights and their overriding, together in complex and sometimes perplexing patterns. For example, it is not clear why the equation between detained patients and restrictions on medical treatment is made. Do the same concerns about inappropriate treatment not apply to informal patients? Perhaps not, if informal patients are able in fact to exercise their legal rights; but as was seen in 4.2, 'informal' does not necessarily mean 'voluntary', and capacity will often be an issue. There is a risk that, if law sees only its own inventions (here 'the autonomous individual') rather than real people, some of whom will be far from autonomous, there may be no real protection of their interests, whatever the law says. Similarly, one might question whether 'detained patients' are properly seen as a homogenous class, given the range of accommodation in which such patients may be held, from open wards in district hospitals to high security intensive wards in the special hospitals. Although the primary concern of this Chapter is to detail and analyse the legal rules that are relevant to the medical treatment of both informal and detained patients, considerations such as this underline the importance of studying those rules in their context, asking not merely 'what are the rules?' but also 'do they work, and if so, how?'. It also means that an informed legal debate must rest on at least a basic understanding of the medical practices that law seeks to regulate.

Hence, this Chapter opens with a consideration of the range of interventions that come under the heading of medical treatment for mental disorder. The extent to which treatment can be seen as beneficial or benevolent, and indeed as 'medical' at all, is unavoidably put into question by such a discussion. Secondly, the law and practice of treatment in hospital will be examined. Here the main subtheme is the relation between 'medicalism' and 'legalism'. As will be seen, the provisions of the common law as well as the mechanisms in the 1983 Act, designed to protect the rights of patients, not only very often fail to do so but arguably also reveal that the view of some — that 'medicalism' and 'legalism' are opposites; that beneficence and autonomy are the natural province of each respectively; and the tension between them is inherent and inevitable (see, for example, Richardson, 1993, p. 238) — is incorrect and misleading. The third section of the Chapter considers the relevance of the emergency measures used when a patient's behaviour is risking harm to self or others. These measures occupy a sort of conceptual hinterland between the poles of treatment and control, and an analysis of them helps to facilitate the development of a fairly sophisticated understanding of that relation. The Chapter concludes with a consideration of the implications for the broader questions, of how the mental health system should be conceptualised, and the relevance to its operation of legal discourses, particularly that of 'rights'.

7.2   MEDICAL TREATMENT FOR MENTAL DISORDER

The history, particularly the recent history, of treatment for mental disorder is one of change and innovation. Yet for all this, there is a remarkable degree of continuity in the way in which mental distress has been approached across time and space. So called 'non-psychiatrised' societies, for example, utilise practices of constraint and control in response to individuals deemed to be 'insane' which are familiar in design and intent to those practised elsewhere as psychiatric interventions (see Mason, 1993). At the Sanctuary of Asklepios at Epidauros in the Argolid, which was a sizeable healing centre by the end of the fourth century BC, the practices of the healer Asklepios were applied. It is said that Asklepios, when confronted by patients suffering from distress, hallucinations or delusions, would use one of two tactics. Either he would talk to the afflicted individual, trying to transmit the sense of calm that the Sanctuary insisted upon to that person, or he would throw snakes into patients' beds while they slept, the idea being that the patient, on waking to find himself or herself surrounded by snakes, would be shocked out of his or her condition. A similar bifurcation is noted by Sedgwick (1982) in ancient Rome. In India, there are textual references dating back even further, to 1500 BC, which recommend the root of the plant *Rauwolfa serpentina* as a remedy for what would now be called psychiatric disturbance, which as Silverstone and Turner (1995, p. 4) note 'was found in the 1950s to be soundly based, and resperine was among the first of the newer 'antipsychotic' drugs'.

It is altogether too neat to suggest that these three approaches continue in an unbroken line to the present. Asklepios's 'talking cure' is not the forerunner of modern psychoanalysis or of psychotherapy, although these two interventions are known today as the 'talking cures'. Similarly, it would be inaccurate to suggest that modern ECT techniques are the descendants of Asklepios's 'snake treatment', since ECT, although the administration of an electric shock, does not attempt to 'shock' the patient out of his or her disorder. It is, however, only fairly recently that such 'shock treatments' passed out of common usage. Even in the 1930s, paraldehyde, laxatives and cold baths were being prescribed for psychotic patients. ECT today is often bracketed together with the use of drugs, under the heading of 'physical treatments'. Talking cures and physical treatments are the two main typologies of treatment for mental disorder. Although all treatments are used in hospitals, drug treatments are the main plank of treatment provision within mental health. One survey found that 98 per cent of patients in hospital were given drug treatments, with 60 per cent given psychotherapeutic treatments (Rogers et al, 1993).

7.2.1   Physical treatments

7.2.1.1   Drug treatments   As mentioned in Chapter two, psychiatric drugs constitute around one-quarter of all prescriptions dispensed by the National Health Service. The treatment of schizophrenia alone, involving some 185,000 patients annually, costs £396 million per annum or 1.6 per cent of the total health budget (Howlett, 1998, p. 97). Silverstone and Turner (1995) provide a useful typology of psychiatric drug treatments (at pp. 7, 8):

(a) *Antipsychotics*: drugs with therapeutic effects on psychoses and other types of psychiatric disorder. In addition they frequently produce extrapyramidal effects, such as tremor and rigidity.

(b) *Antidepressants*: drugs effective in the treatment of pathological depressive states.

(c) *Antianxiety drugs*: substances that reduce pathological anxiety, tension and agitation, without therapeutic effect on disturbed cognitive or perceptual processes. These drugs usually raise the convulsive threshold and do not produce extrapyramidal or autonomic effects. They may produce drug dependence.

(d) *Psychostimulants*: drugs that increase the level of alertness and/or motivation.

(e) *Pyschodysleptics*: drugs producing abnormal mental phenomena, particularly in the cognitive and perceptual spheres.

(f) *Nooceptive drugs*: drugs that improve cognitive function and memory.

Antipsychotic drugs are also known as 'neuroleptics' or 'major tranquillisers', antianxiety drugs as 'minor tranquillisers', although the latter term is something of a misnomer as these drugs can have effects that are far from minor. The 'official' typology of psychiatric drugs is found in the British National Formulary ('BNF'). The BNF, which is published twice annually by the BMA and the Royal Pharmaceutical Society of Great Britain, lists drugs by category and provides information on side effects and gives advisory maximum doses for most drugs. Within each BNF category there is a surprisingly wide range of drugs available. According to Silverstone and Turner (1995, p. 7) there are currently available in the UK 22 antipsychotic compounds, 20 antidepressants and 12 antianxiety compounds, and these figures are already out of date, as at least three new antipsychotic compounds have become available since 1996 (Howlett, 1998, p. 100). This in itself indicates that existing drug treatments are problematic, as the search continues for better acting drugs with fewer side effects. Nevertheless, there is support from randomised clinical trials for each of these drug treatments, as indeed there is also regarding ECT and various forms of psychotherapy (Rogers and Pilgrim, 1996, p. 125); and there is something approaching a consensus that the new drug treatments that appeared in the second half of the twentieth century 'have improved the quality of life for many hundreds of thousands of seriously distressed people' (Lacey, 1996, p. 80). It is not a matter of controversy, then, that psychiatric drug use can produce beneficial effects. Yet such drugs invariably also carry the risk of detrimental effects that may outweigh any benefits gained. In a purely clinical sense, the skill consists in getting the balance between benefits and disbenefits to the optimum level, although this does nothing to address the moral–political questions surrounding drug treatments, particularly when given without full and informed consent.

The benefits to be derived from drug treatments are by no means universal. The treatment of schizophrenia is a case in point. Antipsychotic medicines have, since the introduction of Chlorpromazine (known in the UK as 'Largactyl') in the 1950s, become established as the main treatment of this condition: 'with the honourable exception of the work of a few multidisciplinary teams, the treatment of schizophrenia in Britain is limited to the use of drugs to control its symptoms' (Lacey, 1996, p. 89). Antipsychotic drugs cannot 'cure' schizophrenia, although it is unusual that symptoms will remain acute. When a person suffers the acute onset of a bout of schizophrenia of short duration, Silverstone and Turner recommend the gradual reduction of medication, beginning one year after the illness goes into remission (1995, p. 119), on the basis that around 50 per cent of such patients 'do well' without long-term drug treatment. It has also been suggested that early intervention increases the likelihood of a satisfactory outcome (Birchwood, McGorry and Jackson, 1997). But for some it will be necessary to take medication, if intermittently, over a number of years, possibly for life. Much seems to depend on the 'type' of schizophrenia. Positive (extrovert) symptoms seem to respond better to drugs than negative (introvert) symptoms. In cases of chronic schizophrenia, drugs are often administered in depot form. Depot preparations are slow release and long-lasting, and so reduce the frequency of injections needed. Administration by depot allows a lower total dose and appears to be a more successful approach for patients who require drug treatments over long periods (Johnson, 1990). Despite these advantages, though, there are concerns about the heightened risk of some side effects, particularly impotence and other sexual dysfunction, estimated by Stone (1992) in a review of the literature to stand at 50 per cent.

Some patients report total satisfaction with drug treatments. Jameson (1996, p. 54), for example, receiving ongoing drug treatment for schizophrenia, has written that he is 'profoundly thankful because now I can get on with my life . . . the state I am in at present is, I am convinced, as good as cure'. For others, though, symptoms are *not* relieved by antipsychotic medicine, or are only kept at bay for relatively short periods. One survey (Crow et al, 1986) found that 58 per cent of patients had relapsed within two years. Nor does the prescription of higher doses produce a more favourable outcome (Royal College of Psychiatrists, 1993). Indeed, higher doses are, not surprisingly, associated with increased risks of side effects, as is polypharmacy — the prescription of two or more drugs simultaneously — and research has shown that both are widely practised (Fennell, 1996, see below 7.3.3), whilst 'megadosing' is not unusual for patients unresponsive to lower dosages (Royal College of Psychiatrists, 1993). The side effects of antipsychotic medicine are potentially manifold, and include, amongst many others, lethargy, blurred vision, impotence, nausea, constipation, reduced sexual arousal, sterility, skin disorders, and an increased propensity for violence. Very rarely, patients die as a result of the drugs they are prescribed. Other serious iatrogenic effects are 'pseudoparkinsonism' , known colloquially as the 'Largactyl shuffle', with symptoms including shaking hands, difficulty in maintaining balance, a shuffling walk, lack of facial expression, which in its worst manifestations 'may progress to a complete seizing up with a virtual absence of movement' (Silverstone and Turner, 1995, p. 122). The condition affects 20 to 40 per cent of patients prescribed antipsychotic medicine (ibid.), and patients often require antiparkinsonian medication. This feature of medication for schizophrenia — that medication aimed at primary symptoms will often require further medication to suppress the side effects of the initial medication — is by no means an issue that is limited to medical treatment for mental disorder, but it is arguably an issue of particular importance here, given that the client population will contain many who are either vulnerable by reason of their mental disorder, or detained under the MHA 1983, or both.

The condition known as tardive dyskinesia may develop after prolonged use of antipsychotics and, very rarely, after a small number or even a single dose. The symptoms of tardive dyskinesia are, ironically, those perhaps most closely associated in the popular mind with the symptoms of madness: 'hyperkinetic involuntary movements which are most frequently limited to the face, lips, tongue, jaw and neck, but which can involve the trunk, arms and hands' (Silverstone and Turner, 1995, p. 124). The 'mad person', rocking ceaselessly, puckering cheeks, and engaging in other compulsive, repetitive movements is often exhibiting, not symptoms of his or her illness, but of its treatment. Tardive dyskinesia, which affects between 10 per cent and 30 per cent of those treated (Silverstone and Turner, 1995, p. 125), can be a permanent consequence of antipsychotic drug treatment, and may not be apparent until medication is stopped. Even then, it may not be clear that the condition is a side effect; it has recently been suggested (although very much against the grain of conventional wisdom) that tardive dyskinesia may be a symptom of schizophrenia (Fenton et al, 1997). In any case, the problem of separating symptoms from side effects, particularly when patients, as they often are, are receiving more than one antipsychotic compound, is another issue common to many psychiatric drug treatments.

It is a feature of medicine generally that for a number of reasons many patients are unwilling to take their drugs. The issue has a particular resonance in the context of psychiatric treatment however, as discontinuance by patients in the community is a major factor in the debate over community care (see 9.5). Patients in hospital are often similarly reluctant to take their medication, but in hospital situations, there is a temptation for staff to administer medication covertly. The *Sixth Biennial Report* of the Mental Health Act Commission gives an example of medication being covertly given to patients in tea (Mental Health Act Commission, 1995, para. 5.8) and expresses 'fears that such practices may be widespread in many nursing homes'. It is an open question whether such practices can ever be morally justified. As far as the law is concerned, covert administration is most probably lawful in the case of a detained patient if the requirements of part IV of the 1983 Act are complied with, but would only be so in the case of an informal patient if that patient lacked the capacity to give his or her consent and the treatment was in the best interests of the patient. Yet the MHAC (1995, para. 5.9) advises that 'professional judgment must be relied upon in making decisions on this important ethical issue'. This statement is not only potentially misleading as to the legal situation, but it also risks reinforcing the view amongst medical professionals that law is of merely advisory status and need not be adhered to if that is contraindicated by 'professional judgment'.

Professional judgment is not, however, the only factor which informs the use of drug treatments. A further issue is cost. Hogman (1996, cited in Howlett,

1998) conducted a survey of the prescribing practices of 761 members of the Royal College of Psychiatrists in the treatment of schizophrenia. It was found that a majority of respondents continued to prescribe Chlorpromazine, which costs eight pence for a daily maintenance dose, despite its well-known and significant side effects, rather than the newer drugs which according to Howlett (1988, p. 100) 'represent radical developments in the treatment of schizophrenia. These new, relatively non-toxic, compounds have a clinical profile in which extrapyramidal side-effects (tremor, rigidity, tardive dyskinesia, akathisia) are not usually seen at clinically effective doses' (even though there is a risk of fatal side effects with the best known of the newcomers, Clozapine, necessitating those prescribed it entering the national blood monitoring programme). A significant reason for the slow uptake in the prescription of these new alternatives to Chlorpromazine is that the cost of a daily maintenance dose is around £4 to £5.50 (Howlett, 1998, p. 101). The White Paper on mental health services (Department of Health, 1998a, para. 4.44) announces that extra resources will be available to 'assist in' funding the provision of new drug treatments, which is good news for the drug companies, which, as discussed in Chapter one, have a significant influence over treatment provision and a vested interest in the use of drugs in treatment. Whether it is also good news for patients remains to be seen.

7.2.1.2 Electro convulsive therapy Apart from drug treatments the main physical treatment given in hospital is ECT. The administration of electric shocks has a long history in psychiatry, but ECT in its present form was first used in the treatment of mental illness in 1938 and continued in fairly common usage, as a treatment for schizophrenia in the 1950s (Fennell, 1996, p. 140; it is still sometimes used for such patients if unresponsive to drug treatments) and now as an established treatment for depressive disorders and affective psychoses. Farrell (1997, p. 130) explains the procedure: 'ECT is carried out under anaesthetic, with the use of muscle relaxant, by placing electrodes on either temple and forehead and passing a small electric shock across the brain for approximately four seconds. This electric "shock" induces a short epileptic fit'. Quite how this affects the patient's disorder is not understood, but it is claimed that ECT can have a beneficial effect on mood and functioning, which can be extremely rapid, and ECT is sometimes used as an emergency treatment when a patient's depression is particularly acute and the patient is refusing food (Fennell, 1996, p. 200). A typical treatment plan consists of around twelve 'doses' of the treatment. It has been estimated that 'around 20,000 people have ECT every year' (Farrell, 1997, p. 130), with somewhere in the region of 85 per cent being informal patients in respect of whom, unlike detained patients, the MHA 1983 affords no special protection over and above those to be found in common law (see 7.3.1).

Despite its longevity, ECT remains intensely controversial. The beneficial effects of ECT often seem to be short-lived (Farrell, 1997, p. 130). Personal testimony from patients both for and against ECT can be found. Perkins, for example, details how her depression prevented her from functioning, as she was 'unable to think properly' (1996, p. 66) and yet, after receiving a course of six doses of ECT was back at work within a week. Perkins experienced little in the way of side effects although she did suffer from memory problems whilst having the course of treatment. In contrast, Taylor (1996) describes the course of 12 ECT treatments given to him as 'barbaric or inhuman'. Taylor experienced a number of side effects, including severe headaches, neckache, memory loss, disorientation, and 'total confusion and a confused sense of time and space', which left him in a 'vegetative, numb or stupefied condition' (1996, p. 64). Taylor reports that although the intensity of these effects lessened over time, memory problems, low self-esteem and a state of confusion were semipermanent effects of the treatment. Such stories are fairly common. Other potential side effects include heart problems, strokes and falls, of which the risks are greater for older patients; and this is a live issue given that in one survey in Sheffield, the findings in which are typical, the mean age of patients in receipt of ECT was 68.5 years (Openmind, 1995). In the same Sheffield study, women were twice as likely to be given ECT as men, which is to be expected as women are much more likely to be diagnosed as suffering from depressive or affective disorders than men, and this is even more the case amongst the elderly population (see further below 7.3.3). A Private Member's Bill to tighten the legal restrictions on the use of ECT was introduced into Parliament in December 1997, but was dropped early in 1998.

7.2.1.3 Psychosurgery The third type of physical treatment requiring a mention is psychosurgery. This was a common treatment before the advent of the 1950s drug revolution in psychiatry — 10,365 prefrontal leucotomies were performed in the decade 1942-52, as were several hundred operations utilising other psychosurgical techniques (Dally and Connolly, 1981, p. 68) — but psychosurgery is now practised no more than two or three dozen times annually. The way in which psychosurgical operations work is only imperfectly understood, but it seems that the creation of lesions separating the frontal lobe cortex from the limbic lobe may reduce unwanted emotions (ibid.). Thanks to the 'horror' films produced by Hammer studios and others, psychosurgery evokes images of surgeons far madder than any patient, gleefully sawing through patients' craniums. Modern techniques, still controversial in that brain tissue is destroyed with the intention of inducing permanent personality changes in the patient, use radioactive rods attached to a metal frame placed on the patient's head, from which they can be inserted into the brain to effect the lesion. According to the MHAC (1997, para. 5.3.3), a new technique which involves placing a sheath of electrodes in the brain, which are then progressively stimulated, perhaps over a period of months, until therapeutic effect is achieved, will soon be in operation.

Having been used for all manner of conditions in the past, psychosurgery is now only used as a last resort intervention in a small number of (mainly female) patients suffering from depression or obsessional disorders (MHAC, 1995, appendix 4.1). MHAC data, although involving small numbers, reveals that psychosurgery is often perceived to have a beneficial effect and only rarely a detrimental effect by both doctors and patients (MHAC, 1995, para. 5.1). There is evidence to show that it is only in very rare cases that a patient will be symptom free two years after the treatment has been given and for rather more patients than doctors, the treatment is felt to achieve no change in their condition (Dally and Connolly, 1981, p. 74). The view of the law is that psychosurgery is the most serious of all medical treatments for mental disorder, and its practice is made subject to a special legal regime which, unusually, applies to both detained and informal patients.

7.2.2   Non-physical treatments

It is rare to find hospital in-patients subject to a treatment regime that comprises only psychotherapy. Most often, psychotherapy or therapy involving psychoanalytical techniques will be given alongside drug treatments. Psychotherapy comes in various forms, from one-to-one sessions to various species of group therapy, as does psychoanalysis. The basic difference between them is that psychotherapy is led by the therapist, whereas psychoanalysis tends to be led by the patient and the analyst's role is more that of facilitator. Both are part of the larger group of 'non-physical treatments' which also includes such things as counselling and occupational therapy. There is in fact a somewhat bewildering array of types and subtypes of therapies, many of which are practised outside the hospital setting. Although, as seen above, talking cures have a long history, it is Sigmund Freud who is usually credited with the development of modern psychoanalysis. Freud viewed mental distress, in particular neuroses, as the manifestation of unconscious conflict between the 'id', the 'ego' and 'superego', representing innate sexual and aggressive drives and social rules respectively. The aim of therapy, therefore, is to draw out and verbalise the particular instance of this conflict which is distressing the patient or 'client', and this entails the exploration of the client's life, very often childhood, experiences. Freud's emphasis on the importance of the libido, as well as the normative assumptions, particularly relating to the gender relation, which underpinned his work, have been subject to much criticism from feminists (e.g. Firestone, 1971, chapter 3; Russell, 1995, pp. 22-4) and later psychoanalysts, and the result is that psychoanalysis is theoretically controversial, and there are now a number of neo- and post-Freudian schools. Other, less commonly practised psychoanalytical techniques include Jungian therapy, which draws on Durkheimian ideas about the 'collective conscience' as a context in which to situate individual episodes of mental distress, and Gestalt therapy which rejects the emphasis on past experiences in preference of an approach that allows clients to articulate present needs rather than past traumas.

Group therapies attempt to address problems that people experience in their relations with others, or to provide a supportive environment in which it is possible to divulge information about oneself and as such are broadly comparable with individualised talking cures. Again, there are various species of group therapy, ranging from self-help groups to closely supervised sessions, with groups typically comprising twelve or so patients and one or two therapists (Roberts and Pines (eds), 1991). Groups can be semipermanent institutions with a core of semipermanent members. If group therapy implicitly moves away from the medical model, the concept of 'medical treatment' is expanded further still by occupational therapy, which uses all sorts of everyday activities to accentuate positive and identify negative attitudes, engender feelings of self-worth through creative activity, and encourage patients to develop lasting interests and mechanisms for coping with stressful situations or relationships. At the extreme point of this way of thinking is the 'therapeutic community'; small wards or units in hospitals in which the whole regime is conceived of as therapeutic. Such units are uncommon, but not unknown. The best known example is probably the regime that operates at Grendon Underwood which, although in the prison system, specialises in the treatment of personality disordered offenders.

A more controversial psychotherapeutic intervention is behaviour modification (BM), which comprises a range of interventions designed to modify behaviour, essentially through a programme of rewards and deprivations. The use of techniques such as high decibel noise, drugs like anectine which cause loss of muscle control, as well as a host of other punitive techniques — cold baths, unpleasant tasting food, physical violence and electric shocks — is well documented to occur in prisons, juvenile correctional programmes and elsewhere as well as mental hospitals (Adams, 1998; Butler and Rosenthal, 1985, chapter 14), although it must be said that at least some of these practices were 'punishment' as distinct from 'deprivation' and therefore not strictly within the realms of BM. Nevertheless, BM is so potentially controversial that it merits its own Chapter in the Code of Practice, in which it is provided that '[n]o treatment should deprive a patient of food, shelter, water, warmth, a comfortable environment, confidentiality or reasonable privacy' (Department of Health and Welsh Office, 1999, para. 18.1). The Code of Practice picks out for particular comment the BM technique known as 'time out' — which excludes the patient in question from participation in some activity for a period of between seconds and fifteen minutes (the maximum period allowed under the Code: para. 18.10), in immediate response to inappropriate behaviour. Hospitals should have clear written policies on the use of time out (para. 18.10), which should be monitored, and the technique should form part of a programme and not be a spontaneous reaction to unwanted behaviour (para. 18.9). The aim of this advice is to attempt to delineate an area of lawful practice of this control technique, as distinct from its use as an act of abuse or punishment. It remains contentious, though, that such techniques are ever used as part of a treatment plan (Adams, 1998, p. 74).

The efficacy of psychotherapeutic intervention depends to a large extent on the attitude of the patient. Often, without the consent of the patient 'talking cures' cannot easily proceed. This is obviously less true of BM, although even here a recalcitrant patient may often be able to resist the attempted modification of his or her behaviour. On the other hand, as with physical treatments, patients may often consent with less than total willingness, for a variety of reasons. There is no doubt that the talking cures can have substantial beneficial effects, but side effects are also an ever present part of the package. These include the 'deterioration effect', when a patient's condition worsens whilst on a course of therapy; and therapy and therapeutic relationships are inherently double-edged. For example, negative stereotypes and power imbalances may be reinforced rather than challenged by therapy. Another potential 'effect' of the combination of a power imbalance between therapist and client, and the vulnerability of the latter, is sexual abuse (Garrett, 1994). In group therapy, individuals who stand out from the rest of the group in some way — presenting different symptoms from the rest, or being in a minority in terms of race, age, gender or IQ — may find therapy isolating or dispiriting rather than therapeutic (Manor, 1994). As *One Flew Over the Cuckoo's Nest* (Kesey, 1977) graphically illustrates, group therapy can inflict profound damage on the psyche of individual members.

The various talking cures are often delivered as out-patient services, but they do have a significant role to play in hospital, in the treatment of neuroses, as already mentioned; and psychotherapies grounded in learning theory, and BM techniques, are used in the treatment of mental impairment. A key contemporary issue here is the treatment of psychopathy. Although of problematic scope and treatability, in Tennent et al's research (1993), 61 per cent (267/435) of psychiatrists questioned took the view that psychopathy was sometimes treatable; fewer than 1 per cent thought it was never treatable. It cannot be said that drug treatments are never effective in the treatment of psychopathy (Stein, 1993), although there is general agreement amongst psychiatrists that drug treatments are the least effective of the options on offer (Tennent et al, 1993). Prins (1995) in a review of the literature reports that '[c]alm confrontation' of the unacceptable elements in the behaviour of psychopaths either in peer group contexts or one-to-one encounters may have some lasting beneficial effect, with some 'symptoms' (chronic antisocial behaviour, abnormal aggression and lacking control over impulses) being more amenable to talking cures than others (lack of shame, inability to experience guilt, and 'pathological eccentricity') (Tennent et al, 1993, p. 65). Prins emphasises the three therapeutic virtues of 'consistence, persistence and insistence' (1995, p. 313). Although there is as yet little more than anecdotal evidence of the success of this approach, it may well be that the success of the new 'hospital and limitation directions' (see 6.5.3) is intimately linked with the abilities of talking cures to prove their worth in this area, which is seemingly otherwise beyond the reach of the mental health services.

7.3   MEDICAL TREATMENT IN HOSPITAL: LAW AND PRACTICE

7.3.1   The position at common law

7.3.1.1   The right to refuse treatment   For detained patients, Part IV of the 1983 Act lays down a statutory regime to govern and regulate their medical treatment for mental disorder in hospital. Part IV of the Act, though, applies only to treatment for mental disorder (s. 63, see below, 7.3.2.1.1), and a detained patient's common law right to consent to or refuse other treatments is unaffected (for detailed discussion of the common law, see Montgomery, 1997). The vast majority of in-patients are informal. There are, with the exception of psychosurgery and certain types of hormone therapy (see below, 7.3.2.1.2) no special provisions in the 1983 Act in respect of their medical treatment, and the common law applies to treatment for mental disorder as it does to other forms of medical treatment. The basic rule is that no treatment may be given without consent; see Lord Donaldson in *Re T (Adult: Refusal of Treatment)* [1992] 3 WLR 782 (CA) at p. 799:

> Every adult has the right and capacity to decide whether or not he will accept medical treatment, even if a refusal may risk permanent injury to his health or even lead to premature death . . . it matters not whether the reasons for the refusal were rational or irrational, unknown or even non-existent.

A well-known illustration of the operation of the rule is provided by *Re C (Adult: Refusal of Treatment)* [1994] 1 All ER 819, [1994] 1 WLR 290 (HC). The case involved C, who had been a patient in Broadmoor from the early 1960s, diagnosed on admission as suffering from chronic paranoid schizophrenia. In 1993 it was discovered that C was suffering from a gangrenous infection in his right leg, which in the opinion of a consultant vascular surgeon would lead to imminent death if the lower leg were not amputated. C refused to consent to this treatment for a variety of reasons. The main issue in the case was the test of capacity to be applied in the context of medical treatment (see Chapter eleven), but the relevant point here is that the court, having decided that C did have the capacity to make his own treatment decisions, simply applied the general rule expressed by Lord Donaldson MR in *Re T*. In this case the treatment in question was not related to C's mental disorder, but, for informal patients, according to the strict letter of the law the outcome of the case would have been the same if it had been.

7.3.1.2 Problems with the right to refuse: information, coercion and capacity It is not so clear, however, that patient autonomy and the right to refuse treatment is always so well respected in practice. Three issues are of particular concern: information provision, coercion, and capacity or the mental ability to give or refuse consent. Questions of capacity are discussed in detail in Chapter ten. The focus here is on the first two factors, which are applicable to both informal and detained patients.

7.3.1.2.1 Information The common law requirements for the provision of information to patients about their proposed treatment and its attendant risks are governed by the *Bolam* standard laid down in the case of *Bolam v Friern Hospital Management Committee* [1957] 2 All ER 118 (HC), which essentially leaves the decision to the psychiatric profession. *Bolam* involved a patient who suffered physical injury as a result of being insecurely restrained whilst being given ECT. He sued for negligence and was unsuccessful, the court deciding that as the restraint that had been applied in this case was in line with common practice, no negligence had been committed. This approach was transposed to the provision of information by the House of Lords in *Sidaway v Board of Governors of the Bethlem Royal Hospital and the Maudsley Hospital* [1985] 1 AC 870. The general rule is that liability will not attach to a failure to divulge information to a patient concerning inherent risks or side effects if the person withholding that information (Lord Diplock at p. 893):

> acted in accordance with a practice accepted as proper by a body of responsible and skilled medical opinion.

Notice that it is a body of medical opinion. Lord Diplock said that 'there may be a number of different practices which will satisfy [the *Bolam* test] at any particular time', and as long as a respondent can produce evidence to show that non-disclosure of a particular risk is the practice of *one* body of responsible medical opinion, it is immaterial that another body of opinion does not share that view or practice. This obviously gives a considerable degree of latitude to the professional judgment of those charged with a patient's treatment. This, though, is subject to the caveat that Lord Bridge reserved to the courts a power of veto over the prevailing standards and norms of medical practice. He said at p. 900:

> the judge might in certain circumstances come to the conclusion that disclosure of a particular risk was so obviously necessary to an informed choice on the part of the patient that no reasonably prudent medical man would fail to make it.

He continued:

> The kind of case I have in mind would be an operation involving a substantial risk of grave adverse consequences, as for example, [a] 10 per cent risk of stroke from the operation ... In such a case, in the absence of some cogent clinical reason why the patient should not be informed, a doctor ... could hardly fail to appreciate the necessity for an appropriate warning.

It is a moot point as to when a risk becomes 'substantial', likewise what counts as 'grave adverse consequences'. Nevertheless, given the serious unwanted effects of much medical treatment for mental disorder, it could well be argued that the 'safety net' constructed by the House of Lords is of more relevance to mental patients than many others. The risk of tardive dyskinesia in long-term antipsychotic medicine use, for example, is somewhere between 10 per cent and 30 per cent, as seen in 7.2.1.1. Moreover, the *Bolam* approach is dictated by the standards of the professions involved, which can in turn be affected by the provisions of the Code of Practice, by pushing practice in the direction of full disclosure of information. In this respect, the Code is disappointing. It does repeat the more empowering aspects of *Sidaway* in requiring that patients' questions be answered 'fully, frankly and truthfully' (Department of Health and Welsh Office, 1999, para. 15.16). But it also echoes the language of the *Bolam* approach, stating that consent will be valid if given on the basis of an understanding in broad terms of the nature, likely effects and risks of the treatment, and '[a]dditional information is a matter of professional judgment for the doctor proposing the treatment' (para. 15.15). If this is 'legalism', then it is also an example of the tendency of 'legalism' to sanction 'medicalism'.

As far as the ethics of disclosure are concerned, Bean (1986, p. 134) points out that it is inevitable given the current state of knowledge, that full information cannot be given, but he goes on to argue that 'full information' is provided when the patient is told that there is a lacuna in the professional knowledge concerning the workings of the treatment. The argument that some knowledge is 'too technical' to allow it to be effectively imparted to patients is rejected by Bean, on the grounds that the important factor, given that 'consent is a moral commitment on behalf of the informer to provide information upon which the decision can be made' (1986, p. 136), is the way in which information is given, the environment created by that person — is it conducive to the patient feeling able to ask questions? — rather than a question of the accurate communication of technical and abstract details.

By whatever criteria, though, there seems to be a good deal of patient dissatisfaction with the information that is provided about the purpose and potential effects of treatments, particularly drug treatments (Rogers et al, 1993). In general terms there is a body of evidence which shows that patients are often unsure about their legal status and rights (Bean, 1980; Hoyer, 1986; Goldbeck, MacKenzie and Bennie, 1997). Goldbeck et al (1997) found that in a study of 111 detained patients only 32 per cent 'recalled having received verbal information about their detention and legal rights from medical staff' (1997, p. 577): the same number acquired the information from other patients, overall only 46 per cent believed that they had been given enough information (ibid.), although a sizeable proportion of patients had not correctly understood the legal relevance of the information they had been given. Monahan et al (1995) found that between 40 per cent and 50 per cent of involuntary patients did not appreciate their informal status. The latest *Biennial Report* from the MHAC reports that some patients, deemed by hospital staff to have consented to treatment 'have little awareness of the nature of the treatment' (MHAC, 1997, para. 5.2.1). Although the remit of the MHAC is limited to the treatment of detained patients, and the studies of patients' awareness of relevant information tend similarly to focus on detained patients, it seems reasonable to suppose that informal patients are no better off, and indeed may be worse off, since the law relevant to them, as case law, is if anything more opaque than the provisions of part IV of the 1983 Act.

7.3.1.2.2   Coercion   The law does not recognise that a prison environment may undermine an individual's freedom to give or refuse consent (*Freeman* v *Home Office* [1984] QB 524 (HC), and so it follows that the same is true of psychiatric hospital in-patients, particularly when 'informal' and, in theory at least, free to leave at any time. Yet there are various ways in which an informal patient may in reality feel coerced into consenting to treatment. It would follow from some of the arguments and research considered in Chapters two and three that the mere fact of being in hospital, assigned to the role of 'mental patient' is inherently coercive. Bean (1986, p. 139) defines coercion not as pressure but as the exploitation of vulnerability, and it takes little thought to appreciate that the status of informality means that a patient is always potentially vulnerable to pressure to conform to the wishes of his or her treatment providers. Indeed, this pressure may well be self-imposed: a patient does not need a naked threat to realise that lack of cooperation may lead to the use of the holding powers in s. 5 followed by 'sectioning' (see 4.6). Alternatively, informal patients who refuse to cooperate with the regime may be discharged, which may be an equally coercive prospect for some. Richardson (1993, p. 243) suggests that a patient may consent to treatment in order to appease the doctor or through a concern that refusal to cooperate will lengthen the time spent in hospital and Hart's (1996) personal testimony bears this view out.

Although there is a relative dearth of information on coercion and informal patients, Kjellin and Westrin (1998) found that 28 per cent of 99 voluntary patients reported coercive measures used against them, whilst in Finland Kaltiala-Heino, Laippala and Salokangas reported a figure of 23 per cent, using a rather tight definition of coercion which excluded support, persuasion and other milder interventions (1997, p. 318). In both cases, not unexpectedly, the figure was much higher for detained patients. Kaltiala-Heino, Laippala and Salokangas also found that the use of coercion in treatment negatively affects the therapeutic relationship and 'is related to poorer treatment outcome' (1997, p. 318). Winick argues that this is because a failure to include the patient in drawing up a plan of treatment denies the patient the opportunity to set a goal for the treatment to achieve, yet 'the conscious setting of a goal is virtually indispensable to its achievement' (1994, p. 102). Conversely, there is no evidence to suggest that the coercive administration of treatments as diverse as psychotherapy and antipsychotic medicine achieves beneficial results (1994, p. 107), and there is evidence to suggest that coercion in treatment has its own set of unwanted effects including severe somatic problems, 'learned helplessness' or institutionalisation, and even death in some rare cases (1994, p. 109).

Notwithstanding *Freeman*, it may perhaps be questioned whether consent to treatment obtained by coercion is valid in law. Consent is nullified, inter alia on grounds of duress. In the field of medical law, the leading case is *Re T (Adult: Refusal of Treatment)* [1992] 3 WLR 782 (CA) in which Lord Donaldson said (at p. 797) that to test for the presence of duress:

[t]he real question in each such case is 'Does the patient really mean what he says or is he merely saying it for a quiet life, to satisfy someone else or because the advice and persuasion to which he has been subjected is such that he can no longer think and decide for himself'?

It is only possible to speculate how many informal patients who complain of coercion in the administration of treatment would satisfy this test. We suspect that the numbers may be not inconsiderable. For detained patients, coercion may be even more difficult to spot. A detained patient may be treated for mental disorder with drugs for three months without consent, after which time treatment requires either consent or a second opinion. A patient may well consent to such treatment out of a view that the second opinion will inevitably authorise the treatment (as is indeed almost always the case), and so there is no point in refusing, which may only anger their doctor who will as a consequence then have to go through the whole second opinion procedure. If this is so, patients may consent feeling under duress to do so, although the coercion in

such a situation is virtually invisible (Richardson, 1993,
7.5).

7.3.1.2.3 Capacity Concerns about information
presume that the recipient is able to digest and act on
conscious will which is capable of being overridden
some patients, these presumptions will not hold, as the
treatment and other decisions will be lacking. In th
Bournewood litigation (see 4.2), it was estimated by the MHAC that, had the
judgment of the Court of Appeal been allowed to stand, the increase in
admissions under part II would have been increased by 48,000 a year, on the
grounds that such persons lacked capacity to consent to informal admission.
While capacity to consent to treatment is not the same as consent to admission
(see Chapter ten), the groups will have considerable overlap: clearly, capacity
is an issue in the treatment of many patients. The way in which capacity should
be evaluated, and its application in the context of medical treatment, are
discussed in Chapters ten and eleven respectively, but it is necessary to say a
few words here about the treatment of persons found to lack capacity.

When it has been found that a patient lacks capacity, it is lawful to treat for
his or her 'life, health or well being', as decided by the House of Lords in *F* v
West Berkshire HA [1989] 2 All ER 545. The case concerned a proposal to
sterilise a severely learning disabled woman on the basis that pregnancy and
childbearing would be contrary to her best interests. The House of Lords,
having held that the treatment was in fact in the best interests of the patient, but
also that there was no mechanism in English law to allow the authorisation of
the medical treatment of a person like Ms F to be given by a third party, found
a legal basis for treatment to be given in the doctrine of necessity, although the
concept in this situation is of wider than usual application. It is for the doctors
involved, guided by the standards of their peers, as required by *Bolam*, to
determine what this means in practice. Although the courts will entertain an
application for a declaration in such situations, it was made clear in *F* that there
is no legal duty to make such an application, nor any right in the court to give
permission for proposed treatment. All that a court can do is declare that the
treatment proposed will be lawful: and in *F* the House of Lords also made it
clear that such applications should only be made when the treatment in
question is particularly controversial. This means that the psychiatric treatment of persons in mental hospitals is regulated only by the standards of the
profession, and no legal mechanism currently exists to oversee the treatment of
informal patients.

7.3.2 Treatment under compulsion: detained patients

The MHA 1959 was silent on the question of patients' rights to refuse
treatment and the rights of doctors and nurses to impose it. It was a commonly
held view that the powers in that Act (s. 25(2)(a)) to detain patients for
treatment or for 'observation (with or without medical treatment)', necessarily
implied a right to treat detained patients with or without consent. This may
have been because it was assumed that mental patients lack capacity to consent

...ment by virtue of their condition (Hoggett, 1996, p. 133), although it ...s that this view was assumed rather than debated. As Fennell notes, ...questions of consent to treatment did not loom large in the Percy ...ommission's thinking' (1996, p. 168), working as it was on the underlying assumption that the function of the 1959 Act was to give statutory recognition to the 'transformation of the mental health services from an essentially custodial to a more dynamically therapeutic function' (Unsworth, 1987, p. 232) that had been made possible as a consequence of the development of the new treatments from the 1930s and in particular the 'drugs revolution' of the 1950s. As far as mental health professionals were concerned, their practices were by now fully 'medicalised' and '[t]herapeutics were not conceived as a potential source of antagonism between doctors and patients' (1987, p. 322). This view was in fact reflected in the composition of the Percy Commission, which as Unsworth notes, had 'no aggressive advocate of greater formal legal safeguards ... as a counterweight to the professional preoccupation with therapeutic goals' (1987, p. 267) which dominated the Commission's thinking.

A decade later, however, the dominance of therapeutic perspectives was increasingly under challenge for a number of reasons. The public outlook on madness was not in fact changed radically by the advent of the drug revolution, and media coverage of cases like that of Brady and Hindley, and Graham Young (Holden 1974, later to be the subject of the film 'The Young Poisoner's Handbook) bolstered the view of the mentally ill as 'other' and as dangerous. At the same time, the 'new legalism' began to develop out of concerns that hospital patients were being used as guinea pigs in the trial of new, potentially life-threatening drugs of unproven efficacy but with seriously problematic side effects; that 'treatment' was being used as 'punishment' in some instances (Fennell, 1996, pp.170-2); and that the implied right to treat which some detected in the fabric of the 1959 Act was at odds with the common law right to refuse treatment (Jacob, 1976). In consequence, although the Butler Committee rejected the need for general provisions relating to consent to treatment (Home Office and DHSS, 1975, para. 3.54), by the time of the debates leading eventually to the 1983 Act the arguments in favour of legislation on this question were in the ascendancy.

The chief architect of the 'new legalism' was Larry Gostin, then legal officer at MIND. Gostin (1975, 1983) promoted 'the ideology of entitlement', which comprised three strands:

(a)   that good health care is a right which service users should be able to enforce through the courts;
(b)   that legal constraints should be placed on the power and discretion of service providers; and
(c)   that hospitalisation should not affect the ability of patients to exercise general legal rights such as the right to vote or to go to court.

The second of these strands led to the requirement, that those wishing to treat nonconsenting detained patients must seek a second opinion before so doing, finding its way into the 1983 Act. The Act was in general terms seen as a return to 'legalism', with its provisions relating to the medical treatment of detained patients being seen as a key expression of this shift. However, the 1983 Act was never a simple shift from medical to legal control of in-patient treatment. There is no legal regulation other than that provided by the common law as far as the treatment of informal patients is concerned; and the common law inclination is to give control to the medical professionals. Moreover, to the extent that the 1983 Act does inaugurate a new era of legal controls over medical discretion, the substance of the procedures required by that Act nevertheless leave considerable power in medical hands. The second opinion scheme is the prime example of this. Gostin had argued that the second opinion should be provided by a multidisciplinary team or even by a court (1975, p. 120), but in the event, as Fennell (1990, p. 34) notes '[t]he political influence of the Royal College of Psychiatrists on the shape of the second opinion procedures was to ensure that the decision was taken by doctors on the basis of medical criteria'. Moreover, the type of 'rights' that the legislation, and part IV in particular, give to patients 'are public law, due process, rights; not rights to *deal*, but entitlements that certain procedural and substantive limits will be adhered to in the way that they are *dealt with*' (Fennell, 1986, pp.58-9, emphasis in original). Evidently, then, in turning to the detail of the law, there is the need for a more sophisticated analysis than is afforded by reliance on a simple 'medicalism or legalism?' conceptual model.

7.3.2.1 Part IV of the 1983 Act The powers of compulsory treatment contained in part IV of the 1983 Act apply to all patients who are 'liable to be detained' *except* patients detained under s. 4 (s. 56(1)(a)), and other short-term detentions under ss. 5(2), (4), 35, 135, 136, and 37(4): s. 56(1)(b). Part IV does apply, though, to patients on leave of absence under s. 17 as they remain 'liable to be detained' unless the section expires, but excluded from the ambit of part IV are restricted patients discharged by the Secretary of State or a tribunal (see Chapter eight) who have not been recalled to hospital: s. 56(1)(c). With one exception, part IV of the Act does not apply to informal patients, the position of whom is governed by the common law.

For every patient detained under the Act there will be a 'Responsible Medical Officer' (RMO), who must be a registered medical practitioner: s. 64(1). The main function of the RMO will be to supervise the administration of treatment to the patient: s. 34(1). An RMO has other specific duties and responsibilities concerning for example leave of absence and discharge. It is expected that RMOs will be consultants (Department of Health and Welsh Office, 1998, para. 61). If the RMO is not available when swift action is required, as for example when an application for discharge has been made by the NR of a patient under s. 23 (see 8.3.2) then 'the doctor who is for the time being in charge of the patient's treatment (who should normally be another consultant) should exercise the functions of the RMO' (Department of Health and Welsh Office, 1998, para. 61). The Memorandum gives the impression that ordinarily patients will have regular consultations with their RMOs, but in practice RMOs, who are allocated around 70 patients each (Peay, 1989, p. 64), will see their patients infrequently and patients will have much greater contact with nursing staff.

7.3.2.1.1   A general power to treat without consent   Section 145(1) defines 'medical treatment' for the purposes of the Act as that which 'includes nursing, and also includes care, habilitation and rehabilitation under medical supervision'. As it stands this definition is not limited to treatments for mental disorder, but it is modified in this regard for the purposes of part IV of the Act by the wording of s. 63, which provides that:

> the consent of the patient shall not be required for any medical treatment given to [him or her] for the mental disorder from which [he or she] is suffering, not being treatment falling within section 57 or 58 [. . .], if the treatment is given by or under the direction of the responsible medical officer.

It is important to understand, therefore, that the powers of compulsion authorised by part IV of the Act apply *only* to the medical treatment for the mental disorder from which the patient is suffering. These powers, in theory at least, cannot be used to force any other sort of treatment on a detained patient. On the other hand, it is noteworthy that s. 145(1) is inclusive rather than exclusive, and is therefore not necessarily an exhaustive definition; and the judiciary have taken full advantage of the expansive wording of the definition in s. 145(1) to license interventions which are distinctly controversial. In *Pountney* v *Griffiths* [1976] AC 314, a case heard under the 1959 Act but which is still relevant today, the House of Lords took the view that when a patient is detained under the MHA for medical treatment that 'necessarily involves the exercise of control and discipline. Suitable arrangements for visits to patients by family and friends are an obvious part of a patient's treatment' and this in turn licensed, as 'treatment', the restraint of the patient in the course of 'ushering him back to his quarters when permitted visiting time is ended' (per Lord Edmund-Davies at p. 335). *Pountney* was concerned with the legality of restraining practices and the scope of the bar on the bringing of legal proceedings in respect of acts done in pursuance of duties under the Act (now contained in s. 139, see 12.3), rather than the definition of treatment directly, and is considered further below (see 7.4.2.1). But more recent case law has followed the expansive tenor of the Lords' opinions.

In *B* v *Croydon Health Authority* [1995] 1 All ER 683 (CA), a 24-year-old woman, B, had been detained under s. 3 diagnosed as suffering from 'psychopathic disorder' in the form of a borderline personality disorder, coupled with post traumatic stress disorder arising from acts of sexual abuse which she had suffered over a prolonged period of time. B's condition manifested as depression and a compulsion to self-harm. As discussed earlier, the treatability of personality disorders is problematic, but in B's case it was thought that she would benefit from psychoanalytic psychotherapy. Once detained, B was prevented from self-harm and in response she started to refuse food. Her condition became so serious that it was not possible to provide her with psychotherapy sessions until she regained weight, and she continued to deteriorate until her life expectancy was estimated at two to three months. Threatened with being fed by nasogastric tube without her consent, B sought an injunction against the defendant health authority which was granted, but at a full hearing in the High Court it was held lawful to administer the treatment under s. 63.

On appeal Hoffman LJ (at p. 687) noted that 'a range of acts ancillary to the core treatment fall within the definition' in s. 145(1), and, although it is the case that the treatability requirement in s. 3(2)(b) prevents the compulsory admission into a hospital of persons suffering from psychopathic disorder unless their condition is treatable, in the view of Hoffman LJ (at p. 687), in which the other members of the Court of Appeal concurred:

> It does not, however, follow that every act which forms part of that treatment within the wide definition in s. 145(1) must in itself be likely to alleviate or prevent deterioration of that disorder. Nursing and care concurrent with the core treatment or as a necessary prerequisite to such treatment or to prevent the patient from causing harm to himself or to alleviate the consequences of the disorder are, in my view, all capable of being ancillary to a treatment calculated to alleviate or prevent a deterioration of the psychopathic disorder.

One should not, in the opinion of his lordship, take an 'atomistic' view of the treatment of a patient's condition. Hoffman and Neill LJJ both made reference to s. 62 (discussed further below, see 7.4.1) which permits controversial treatments, otherwise made subject to special restrictions by ss. 57 and 58, to be given without compliance with prior formalities in emergency situations. If the patient's life is at risk, or there is a need to prevent serious suffering to the patient, or to prevent the patient acting dangerously to himself or herself or others, treatment which is 'immediately necessary', subject to some limitations, may be given. As Hoffman LJ pointed out, the wording of s. 62 seems to contemplate the treatment of *symptoms* of the patient's condition — such as acting in a dangerous manner — as well as causes, and therefore it can be presumed that the intention behind the Act was that the treatment of such would be covered by the concept of 'treatment for the mental disorder from which the patient is suffering'.

There is force to these points, particularly the relevance of s. 62. Nevertheless, with respect to the Court of Appeal, it does not follow that, because it is difficult to delimit what is to count as medical treatment for mental disorder at its extremities, it is necessary to take such an expansive approach as was taken in this case. As so often in health care law, the truism that bad cases make hard law is lost on judges faced with life and death situations. This is understandable, but of course the approach taken here is not limited to those suffering from psychopathic disorder, nor to life and death situations; and the strategy adopted by the court means that the difficulty of deciding when there is a sufficient nexus between the intended treatment and the mental disorder has been abrogated by erring on the side of interventionism.

It is at least arguable that B's refusal to eat can properly be seen as a symptom of her disorder, but in the later case of *Tameside and Glossop Acute Services Trust v CH* [1996] 1 FLR 762 — in which *B v Croydon* was 'applied' — the concept of a 'symptom', and the nexus between the mental disorder in question and the proposed treatment, was arguably stretched beyond even the generous limits set by the Act. In this case CH had been detained under s. 3 suffering from schizophrenia, one manifestation of which was said to be psychotic paranoia manifesting *inter alia* as distrust of medical staff. She was in the thirty-eighth week of pregnancy and there were concerns that the foetus was not growing properly because it was not being provided with nourishment by the placenta. The likelihood was that without intervention the foetus would die *in utero*. Dr G, the consultant obstetrician and gynaecologist responsible for this aspect of CH's care, was concerned that CH, who had refused to cooperate with antenatal care in the earlier stages of her pregnancy might continue to do so, even though she had given her consent to a proposed induction of the birth. The Trust applied to the High Court for an order that it would be lawful to treat CH as necessary to save the life of the foetus, including the performance of a Caesarean section operation without her consent should that prove necessary.

The latest edition of the Code of Practice, citing *B* v *Croydon*, advises that treatment for physical disorder cannot be given under part IV for physical disorder 'unless it can reasonably be said that the physical disorder is a symptom or underlying cause of the mental disorder' (Department of Health and Welsh Office, 1999, para. 16.5). From one point of view, the situation in *Tameside* falls clearly outside of this situation: in no way could it be said that CH's pregnancy was a 'symptom or underlying cause' of her schizophrenia. On the other hand, there was evidence before the court from CH's doctor, Dr M, that the birth of a stillborn child 'will have a profound deleterious effect both in the short and the longer term' (at p. 767), confirming CH's paranoid delusions about those responsible for her treatment. An alarming picture of CH's future was painted: '[i]f she does not trust the services, she is likely constantly to relapse and not make a recovery with treatment. If she fails to recover she would be unable to care for the child. She would require constant readmissions' (at p. 767). If, on the other hand, the court authorised the proposed treatment '[t]he prognosis if she delivers a healthy infant is that she can recover from her psychosis and be able to provide care and support for her child. She will then be in a stable mental condition and rational and free from psychotic symptoms' (at p. 767). Essentially, the choice that CH's doctor presented the court with was between a psychotic patient and a dead child on the one hand and a mentally healthy mother and child on the other. Small wonder, then, that the judge chose the latter option. To do this he adopted the 'holistic' approach taken in *Croydon*, and held that the prognosis if the treatment was not administered to save the foetus was such that it would clearly be of benefit to CH's mental health for the treatment to proceed: 'It is not ... stretching language unduly to say that achievement of a successful outcome of her pregnancy is a necessary part of the overall treatment of her mental disorder' (at p. 773). Accordingly, the treatment fell within s. 63.

In their discussion of this and other recent forced Caesarean cases decided at common law, Widdett and Thomson (1997) take issue with the assumptions behind the assertion presented as incontrovertible fact that CH's disorder would vanish from view on the birth of a healthy child. As they say '[h]aving a child is clearly constructed as curative and normalising' (1997, p. 86). By the same token, the decision to intervene against CH's wishes 'may be located within broader stories regarding female instability during pregnancy' (1997, p. 85). Widdett and Thomson point to the orthodoxies of nineteenth century medical science which posited female health and ill health — both physical and mental — to be in a direct relation to the proper functioning of an individual's reproductive organs. The logic employed in *Tameside* is no different: 'the prognosis for her mental health was polarised by the possible outcomes of her pregnancy' (1997, p. 87). This is not merely some 'theoretical' point. It structures the judgment and outcome of the case precisely by overriding a different view of CH that emerged from a report produced by the Official Solicitor's agent at the request of CH's lawyers, which Wall J tells us, found her to be 'well oriented and clearly aware of the problems suffered by the foetus' (at p. 768). According to this report, CH claimed that it was *she* who had suggested the possible need for a Caesarean section operation, and had resisted the planned induction of the foetus only because it was her view that with antibiotics its health would improve, which it in fact did. In sum, this report portrays CH as rational and intent on saving her baby, yet its contents were rejected in favour of the evidence of Drs G and M. This, Widdett and Thomson suggest, demonstrates the pull of a particular, normative, ideology of femininity. (CH's capacity to consent, also at issue in the trial, is discussed in Chapter eleven).

One might ask at this point whether, on the basis of the holistic logic employed in these cases, it will *ever* be the case that *any* treatment of a detained patient will *not* be treatment for that patient's mental disorder, since any treatment is designed to make the recipient 'feel better' and therefore can be said to be of benefit to his or her mental health. In both the *Croydon* and *Tameside* cases the earlier decision of *Re C (Adult: Refusal of Treatment)* [1994] 1 All ER 819, [1994] 1 WLR 290 was distinguished. As discussed above, this case stands for the proposition that at common law a competent adult patient has an absolute right to refuse treatment, notwithstanding that the patient is suffering from a mental illness.

Although C suffered from schizophrenia and was a detained patient in a special hospital, the court in that case made no mention of s. 63 of the 1983 Act. According to the courts in *Croydon* and *Tameside* this was because in *Re C* 'the gangrene was entirely unconnected with the mental disorder' (per Hoffman LJ in *Croydon* at p. 688) so that 'Treatment of C's gangrene was not likely to affect his mental condition: the manner in which the delivery of the defendant's child is treated is likely to have a direct effect on her mental state' (per Wall J in *Tameside* at p. 773). The present authors' reaction to this point of distinction is mixed. Although pleased that the courts have attempted to define the limits of treatment of physical disorders under s. 63 — where the disorder is 'entirely unconnected with the mental disorder' — the distinction between those treatments which are and those which are not in some way 'connected' seems problematic, particularly in light of the 'holistic' attitude adopted by the courts in these cases. In *Re C* the relevance of s. 63 was not even argued, and so its positing as being on the 'other side of the line' can only be *ex post facto*.

More than this, though, had it been argued in *Re C*, it may well have been, *on the logic employed in Croydon and, particularly, Tameside,* that the treatment *could have been* carried out under s. 63. The court in that case was concerned only to examine C's capacity to take his own decisions and not the connection between his mental disorder and his refusal to consent. Even so, the court was presented with evidence relevant to this latter issue. Dr Nigel Eastman, a prominent figure in mental health law and policy, accepted instructions from C's solicitor to see and report upon C's ability to refuse consent. Dr Eastman gave evidence to the court that schizophrenia is an all-pervasive illness and manifested in C's case in the form of 'grandiose and persecutory delusions as well as ... [a] mismatch between words spoken and the accompanying emotional display' (at pp. 821-2). Dr Eastman considered that C was not competent to consent because although he understood the information that was given to him about the state of his leg, *as a result of his mental disorder* he did not believe it (at p. 822). In addition, we are told that C's schizophrenia manifested at this time in the delusions that he was a doctor, and that his carers were intent on destroying his body with their interventions (at p. 823). Although Thorpe J recorded that Dr Eastman 'did not find any *direct* link between C's refusal and his persecutory delusions' (at p. 823, emphasis added) the crucial point is that *a direct link is not required by the decisions in Croydon and Tameside.* In the holistic universe, all things are linked to all others.

Thus it could be argued that there *is* here a causal connection between the physical and mental disorders such that treatment under s. 63, as this section has been interpreted in *Croydon* and *Tameside,* would have been lawful. C's attitude towards the proposed treatment on his leg was a 'symptom' of his disorder in this broad sense. It may be possible to go further still, and argue that the leading House of Lords decision on the treatment of incapacitated patients at common law, *F* v *West Berkshire HA* [1989] 2 All ER 545 could, on the logic of *Croydon* and *Tameside,* have been lawfully performed under s. 63. As discussed at 7.3.1.2.3, the House of Lords held that the performance of a sterilisation operation on F was lawful by operation of the common law principle of necessity. In the opinion of Lord Brandon of Oakbrook in that case (at p. 550), with which Lord Griffiths (at p. 561) agreed (no other member of the House mentioning the MHA at all), it was not necessary to detail part IV of the 1983 Act as it clearly did not apply. But the fact is that the evidence in F that was used to demonstrate that treatment at common law without F's consent would be lawful because it was in her 'best interests', also shows clearly that the decision whether to treat or not *had a direct bearing on F's mental condition.* In the words of Lord Brandon 'it would, from a psychiatric point of view, be disastrous for her to conceive a child' (at p. 550). How is this different from *Croydon* or *Tameside?* Part of the answer is that F was not a detained patient, but this was not the point of distinction which Lord Brandon relied upon, holding (at p. 550) that part IV of the 1983 Act was not relevant because 'it does not contain any provisions relating to the giving of treatment to patients for any conditions other than their mental disorder'.

One is left, consequently, wondering where for the purposes of s. 63 the line is to be drawn. The above analysis of the jurisprudence on this question seems to suggest that the 'limit' of s. 63 has a decidedly 'postmodern' quality to it: that is, it is a limit which continually recedes as one approaches it (Cornell, 1992), rather like the end of a rainbow. On a less esoteric level, the conclusion must be that the Court of Appeal in *Croydon* was in error in adopting the 'holistic' approach. This is not only because to do so is to institutionalise a system whereby persons detained in hospital for treatment for mental disorder are placed in an inferior position in respect of their rights to refuse treatments for *physical* disorders purely on the fact of their detention, nor because of the more technical point that this implicitly goes against the decision of the House of Lords in *F* which is binding on the Court of Appeal, but because this effaces the distinction between treatment of physical and mental conditions. Even if this distinction is philosophically problematic (because it is not clear that a mind/body distinction can rigidly be drawn), it functions in practice as a protective barrier for the rights to autonomy of persons detained in hospitals. The approach of the Court of Appeal in *Croydon*, and the application of that approach in *Tameside* has effectively removed that protective barrier.

It is difficult not to notice that the gender of the plaintiff in *Re C* was male, and in the other cases female. The courts in both *Croydon* and *Tameside* could also have referred to *Secretary of State for the Home Department* v *Robb* [1995] 1 All ER 677 (HC), a case decided shortly before *Croydon*, in which it was held that a male prisoner, Robb, who was on hunger strike had the right to refuse food even if that were to lead to his death. Despite the fact that Robb had been diagnosed as suffering from a personality disorder, his capacity to consent to or refuse treatment was agreed by four psychiatrists and a psychologist. The court did not even consider the possibility that Robb's refusal to accept food could be seen as a manifestation of his psychiatric condition. If they had done so, it is possible that arrangements could have been put in train for his transfer to hospital for treatment (as was suggested by a psychiatrist employed by the Official Solicitor, acting as *amicus curiae*: see p. 680). Instead, in order to uphold Robb's right to refuse treatment, Thorpe J in the High Court was obliged to disapprove the earlier case of *Leigh* v *Gladstone* (1909) 26 TLR 139 — the only legal authority directly on the question of forced feeding — in which it had been held lawful to force feed hunger striking suffragettes, imprisoned for criminal acts carried out in pursuance of female suffrage, on the grounds that this was 'of little relevance or weight in modern times' (at p. 681). It is easy to see how, from a feminist viewpoint, this aspect of the case merely enhances the thoroughly patriarchal context of this body of law.

The treatment of mental disorder is shot through with gendered assumptions. Clearly the arguments of Widdett and Thomson are well made. However, the present authors do not subscribe to the thesis of gendered judicial conspiracy as being the determining factor in analysing the jurisprudence on the scope of s. 63. Looking more closely at the two cases involving male patients — *Re C* and *Robb* — it is clear that the court was not in fact dealing with life and death situations. C, although refusing to consent to the amputation of his leg, did consent to conservative treatment. By the time of the High Court hearing, C's gangrenous infection had cleared up and the wound was healing (p. 822) and there had been 'a dramatic aversion of the risk' (at p. 823). In Robb's case, the hunger strike that was the subject of the legal proceedings was only the latest in a history of such behaviour. On previous occasions Robb had 'achieved nothing' (per Thorpe J at p. 679), and on the instant occasion 'his determination to continue on his hunger strike to the end has wavered. On one occasion he began to accept nutrition and was transferred to a local hospital so that the return to nutrition could be overseen medically' (at p. 680). One cannot help but suspect that the view that Robb did not intend to refuse food to the point of death informed Thorpe J's ruling that he could lawfully do so. By contrast, in the cases involving female patients — *Croydon* and *Tameside* — the prospect of a death consequent upon the judicial decision was much more real. This analysis might seem to be upset by the ruling in *Re JT (Adult: Refusal of Medical Treatment)* [1998] 1 FLR 48, in which the court, following *Re C*, upheld the right of a young woman detained under s. 3 on grounds of mental impairment to refuse life-saving dialysis for kidney problems caused by renal failure, having judged her competent to make her own decision. But in that case the situation was that without cooperation from the patient the treatment could not be successful and so a court order that she comply would not have substantively altered the reality of the situation that JT was going to die. Here, s. 63 was barely mentioned, and then only to confirm its inapplicability (per Wall J at p. 51).

Thus it is possible to argue that the expansive reading of the scope of s. 63 is explicable in terms of a judicial wish to act so as to preserve life wherever possible. But the above discussion shows that the problems with this are manifold. Surely the better approach — and arguably the better reading of the provision — is to limit the reach of s. 63 to cover treatment of the 'core condition' and only those physical conditions which are either manifestations of an underlying mental disorder or which give rise *directly* to a mental disorder. One relevant authority, not referred to in any of the case law here under analysis, is *R v MHAC, ex parte X* (1988) 9 BMLR 77 (DC), in which it was held that if a 'sexually deviant' patient's sexual deviance is 'inextricably linked' with his or her mental disorder, so that treatment for one is treatment for the other, then it will be lawful to treat the sexual deviancy under the compulsory powers in part IV. This case, as a matter of law, seems to have it about right. This would mean that *Croydon* was correctly decided (although the product of rather loose and unhelpful judicial thinking) but *Tameside* was not. Even those who are apprehensive about the conceptualisation of eating disorders as mental illness agree that such disorders are the manifestation of some underlying aetiology which is psychological in character (Bordo, 1988, 1993, Orbach, 1993, Eckerman, 1997; Bridgeman and Millns (eds), 1998 at pp. 545-74) and can thus be said to be 'symptoms' of mental disorder in the sense meant by the 1983 Act. There is, on the other hand, no such relation between pregnancy and mental disorder: neither is per se causative of the other. The approach of the Court of Appeal in *St George's Healthcare NHS Trust* (for facts see 5.5.2) possibly comes close to endorsing this view. Judge LJ held that 'a woman detained under the Act for mental disorder cannot be forced into medical procedures unconnected with her mental disorder' ([1998] 3 All ER 673 at p. 693). However, the court in that case also emphasised that although pregnancy *per se* was not a reason for hospitalisation under the MHA 1983 it may be, as in that case, a relevant consideration. And although the Court of Appeal stated that it may well have been prepared to issue a writ of habeas corpus in this case, that was not on the basis that the patient was not mentally disordered, but only because mental disorder had not *in fact* been the reason for her admission. Nor is there any mention in this case of the line of authorities starting with *Croydon*. Therefore, the import of the judgment in *St George's Healthcare NHS Trust* should be treated with caution: it may be that it marks a reversal of the trend, but the evidence is in reality slight.

7.3.2.1.2   Restrictions on the general power   In legal terms the scope of s. 63 is not otherwise controversial. It covers the whole range of physical and psychotherapeutic interventions, as well as nursing care and restraint. However, there are some exceptions to this general position written into the scheme of the Act. Certain procedures — the physical treatments — are taken out of the ambit of the general authority to treat in s. 63 and made subject to specific safeguards in ss. 57 and 58. The backbone of the safeguards system is the regime of second opinions that must be obtained for the provision of the treatments in question, which is administered by the Mental Health Act Commission (MHAC). This section looks at the legal requirements that apply to this system. The following section considers how the scheme actually works in practice.

Section 57, because of the serious and controversial nature of the treatments in question applies both to patients who are liable to be detained *and* to informal patients, whether or not resident in hospital: s. 56(2). It does not, however, apply to detained patients excluded from the ambit of part IV by virtue of s. 56(1) (see above, 7.3.2.1). Jones (1999, p. 250) argues that there is no good reason for this omission, which appears to be an oversight. Section 57 covers surgical treatment which destroys brain tissue or the functioning of brain tissue (psychosurgery) (s. 57(1)(a)), and 'such other forms of treatment as may be specified for the purposes of this section by regulations made by the Secretary of State': s. 57(1)(b). To date, only one treatment has been so specified: 'the surgical implantation of hormones for the purposes of reducing male sex drive' ('chemical castration'), added by reg. 16, Mental Health (Hospital, Guardianship and Consent to Treatment) Regulations 1983, SI 1983 No. 893. There are powers to extend to ambit of s. 57 via the Code of Practice (s. 118(2)), but they have not been used.

Before either of these treatments can be given *it is necessary that the patient consent*: s. 57(2). This means that treatment under s. 57 cannot be given to patients who lack capacity to consent to the treatment and not just those who actively refuse to consent. Section 57(2)(a) further provides that before the treatment can be given an independent doctor (known as a 'second opinion appointed doctor' or SOAD) and two other persons appointed by the Secretary of State for the purpose certify that the patient has consented and understands the nature, purpose and likely effects of the treatment. The Secretary of State's powers have been delegated to the Mental Health Act Commission: s. 121(2)(a). The appointed persons need not be members of the Commission, but the Commission has stated that in cases of requests for second opinions under s. 57 they will be (Department of Health and Social Security, 1984, para. 8(i)). It is also required, by s. 57(2)(b), that the SOAD certify that the treatment should be given because it is likely to alleviate the patient's condition or prevent its deterioration. Before so doing, the SOAD 'shall consult with' two other persons who have been professionally involved with the patient's treatment, one of whom must be a nurse and the other of whom neither a nurse nor a doctor: s. 57(3).

Section 58 is concerned with two types of treatment: ECT (inserted by reg. 16 of the 1983 Regulations into s. 58(1)(a)), and the administration of medicine to a patient by any means at any time after three months has elapsed since the first time in that period of detention when the patient was given medicine for his mental disorder: s. 58(1)(b). Section 58(1)(b) is known as the 'three month rule'. Its purpose is to protect patients from the continual administration of drugs under the general power in s. 63 if there is no obvious benefit to the patient in so doing. There can be only one three-month period in any one period of detention, and a period of detention is not interrupted by a change in the section under which the patient is detained (Department of Health, 1995b para. 195) nor by the transfer or renewal of the authority to detain the patient (Department of Health and Social Security, 1984, para. 15). The Secretary of State has powers to extend the three-month period by s. 58(2), although these have not been used. The MHAC has recently recommended that forced feeding should be brought under s. 58 (1997, para. 5.2.8), and is it difficult not to support this proposal.

Before either of these treatments is given, it must be certified *either* that the patient has consented and the RMO or SOAD has certified in writing both that the patient has consented and understands the nature, purpose and likely effects of the treatment (s. 58(3)(a)), *or* that a SOAD (and not the RMO) has certified that the patient is not competent to consent or has refused to consent but that the treatment should be given because it is likely to alleviate the patient's condition or prevent its deterioration: s. 58(3)(b). In the case of treatment under s. 58(3)(b) the SOAD must also consult with a nurse and one other person being neither a nurse nor a doctor concerned with the patient's treatment before issuing the certificate: s. 58(4).

By s. 59 a patient who consents to treatment under ss. 57 or 58 may consent to more than one treatment under the respective section, and to a 'treatment plan' which does not need to have a specified end-point. Current MHAC policy is to limit all certificates given to two years, and to one year for patients in high security accommodation or in receipt of 'high dose or complex treatment plans' (MHAC, 1997, para. 5.2.3). A certificate signed by a SOAD following a request for a second opinion may be similarly open-ended, although the MHAC view is that a certificate authorising psychosurgery should be time-limited to eight weeks, and it has been said that time limitation is also likely in the context of drug treatments (Jones, 1996, p. 231). There is no definition of 'medicine' in the 1983 Act but the MHAC view is that it 'will broadly encompass any substance intended to influence the mental disorder' (Department of Health and Social Security, 1984, para. 15). In *Croydon* Hoffman LJ held that 'ordinary food in liquid form, such as would be used in tube feeding, is not a medicine within the meaning of s. 58' (at p. 687), although it is 'medical treatment' under s. 63.

Consent to treatment may be retracted at any time: s. 60. Treatment under s. 57 must then cease. Treatment under s. 58 may continue only if the safeguards in s. 58(3)(b) are first complied with, although there is a period of grace given by s. 62(2) during which treatment given under ss. 57 or 58 can continue even though consent has been withdrawn if the RMO 'considers that discontinuance of the treatment or of the treatment plan would cause serious suffering to the patient'. Section 61 provides that in respect of treatment given in accordance with ss. 57 or 58(3)(b) (that is, treatment under that section in respect of which the patient has refused or is unable to consent), the RMO must report on the treatment and the patient's condition to the Secretary of State as part of the requirement of reports required to renew the authority to detain under ss. 20, 41(6) or 49(3), as the case may be.

7.3.3 The operation of the scheme of second opinions and reports

The second opinion scheme was one of the major innovations brought in by the MHA 1983. It came as part of a compromise deal with the medical profession which gave psychiatrists an express legal right to treat without consent for the first time, at the expense of being 'encumbered' in the exercise of that right 'by the erection of a complex and intricate system of formal safeguards for the protection of patients which represents the high water mark of legalism in the Act' (Unsworth, 1987, p. 324). Section 57 in particular, which requires the RMO to seek a second opinion *even when the patient consents to the treatment* was seen as 'a significant intrusion into the doctor-patient relationship' (ibid., p. 325). There is no doubt that the regime is bureaucratic, and on the face of it at least, restrictive of the autonomy of the psychiatric profession.

Information for RMOs, SOADs and others with responsibilities for running the regime of second opinions and reports is to be found in the revised Code of Practice (Department of Health and Welsh Office, 1999), MHAC Guidance (Department of Health and Social Security, 1984, Circular DDL(84)4), and the *Memorandum* (Department of Health and Welsh Office, 1998) on various parts of the Act. The Code of Practice provides that (at para. 16.23), although overall responsibility for compliance with the requirements of the Act rests with hospital managers, '[t]he patient's RMO is personally responsible for ensuring that part IV procedures are followed in relation to that patient' (para. 16.24), including ensuring that requests to the MHAC for a SOAD visit are made, and making the arrangements for such visits. When an RMO is considering the use of any of the treatments to which ss. 57 or 58 apply, the first step is to consult the patient and seek his or her consent (paras. 16.7, 16.9, 16.11). The patient will only be able to give a valid consent if competent to do so. The phraseology used in the Act is that to be competent the patient must be 'capable of understanding the nature, purpose and likely effects' of the proposed treatment (ss. 57(2)(a), 58(3)(a)), to which the Code of Practice (para. 15.10) adds that the requirement is that the patient be capable of understanding the principal risks and benefits of the treatment and of not having it, and refers to the test for capacity laid down in *Re C*, see 11.1.2). MHAC Guidance (Department of Health and Social Security, 1984, para. 14) states that 'informed consent' is required for ECT, and the Code of Practice (para. 16.10) advises that patients should be provided with information leaflets in addition to the RMO personally seeking consent. It is not clear whether this would be enough as a matter of law to raise a greater entitlement to information in respect of ECT compared with other treatments; ECT is a serious intervention but not necessarily more serious than the other treatments covered by these sections. Consent of course depends on having the capacity to give it. Determination of capacity to consent to treatment will be discussed in detail in Chapters 10.4 and 11.1.3.

When a valid consent is forthcoming for treatments under s. 58 the RMO need not seek a second opinion. He or she must complete the appropriate form as required by reg.16, 1983 Regulations, which is form 38. This form requires the RMO to state that the requirements of s. 58(3)(a) have been met, namely that the patient has the capacity to consent and has in fact consented to the treatment, and to give a description of the treatment or treatment plan comprising either the proposed maximum number of doses of ECT (Department of Health and Welsh Office, 1999, para. 16.9a), or drugs proposed by British National Formulary (BNF) class rather than name, the method of administration (whether oral or depot antipsychotics, for example) and the dose range, including whether the proposed dosages are above BNF recommended maxima (para. 16.14). The MHAC reports (1997, para. 5.2.2) that its advice to SOADs, when a second opinion *is* required, is to specify on the appropriate form (form 39, see below) the number of preparations authorised from a BNF category and the upper dose limit, as this 'allows SOADs to set a clear ceiling on what is authorised' whilst still allowing scope for 'slight changes' to be made by the RMO (ibid.). When particularly problematic drugs are to be given - the MHAC refers to Clozaril (the trade name in the UK of the antipsychotic drug clozapine which carries a substantial risk of serious, even fatal, blood disorders; which cannot be given unless the patient's blood is tested on a weekly basis, and is only used when other antipsychotic medicine has been tried and failed: Lacey, 1996, p. 95), and newly available antipsychotic medicines not yet in the BNF — 'the individual name of the drug and a specific dose range must be recorded' (MHAC, 1997, para. 5.2.2). The clear implication of this no doubt good practice in relation to form 39 is that patients who consent and so are given treatment under form 38 do not have these protections. Moreover, as each BNF category includes a number of different drugs (see 7.2.1.1), under the current requirements the discretion of the RMO to switch drugs within a category, exceed recommended doses, practise polypharmacy or any combination of the three, is largely unfettered. There is force in Richardson's point that the Code of Practice at this point lets patients down by giving RMOs scope to adhere to the letter but not the spirit of the legislative scheme to the extent that it may be questionable whether a patient's consent can really be regarded as genuine (1993, p. 243).

Concerns about form 38 and treatment under s. 58(3)(a) are compounded by the fact that there is no statutory procedure for reviewing the use of form 38, and although the Code of Practice urges that its use be reviewed regularly at local level, with a new form being completed at each review, providing that it continues to be appropriate to do so (1999, para. 16.35), and although these forms are regularly examined on general MHAC visits (MHAC, 1997, para. 5.2.1.) there is an obvious temptation for an RMO to deem a consenting patient competent to do so, to avoid needing to instigate the SOAD procedure. In the case of s. 57 patients, as already mentioned, consent is a prerequisite to any treatment, but even when a patient does consent there will still be the need for a second opinion. This is not case under s. 58. The efficacy of judgments of capacity is therefore crucial. As Fennel puts it '[i]t scarcely upholds the principle of self-determination if a RMO accepts the consent of a patient who does not understand the decision being made, or who has not been given information about the treatment's nature, purpose and effects' (1996, p. 194). Although there has been no systematic research into the reality of these concerns, the most recent MHAC *Report* recounts that failure to comply with the Code of Practice in respect of form 38 is common, with forms not completed by the current RMO, and patients being given treatments not mentioned on the form. Pro re nata (PRN 'as required') medication is a particular concern as this can in practice mean regular high doses or 'cocktails' being given (1997, para. 5.2.1). In addition, there is often a lack of written evidence that patients have given consent based on discussions with the doctor, and there have been 'doubts about the authenticity of the consent certified' with Commissioners forming that impression that 'compliance has been taken as consent or that patients deemed consenting have little awareness of the nature of the treatment' (para. 5.2.1). A graphic example of the way in which institutional practices can conflate compliance and consent is provided by the relative dearth of requests for a SOAD emanating from Broadmoor hospital in two years after the implementation of the MHA 1983 (Richardson, 1993, p. 244). In this period 89 requests came from Broadmoor, with an average patient population of 494 individuals, compared with 413 requests from Rampton and 262 from Ashworth, with average populations of 590 and 562 respectively. It transpired that at Broadmoor a patient would only be considered for transfer or discharge if accepting treatment.

For treatment under s. 57 or under s. 58 without the consent of the patient, a SOAD team visit will be necessary. It is the RMO's responsibility to make or ensure the making of the arrangements for these visits, which entails contacting the MHAC, and making sure that the relevant information is available to the team on arrival. When the team arrives, the SOAD must first check that the patient's detention documents are in order (if the patient is not lawfully detained, treatment under part IV cannot be given), and review the patient's clinical notes and the treatment plan at issue. There should also be consultation with the patient and RMO, and others who have relevant information, before the treatment is authorised. Before an RMO can give treatment under s. 57, the SOAD and other MHAC appointees must fill in form 37: s. 64(2) and sch. 1, 1983 Regulations. Information required by this form includes the type of treatment which is to be given, the fact that the patient has given consent and has the legal capacity to do so, and that it is expected that the treatment will have a beneficial effect on the patient's condition. If treatment under s. 58 is given without the consent of the patient, the SOAD team must complete form 39. Similar information is required as with form 37, tailored though to the specific requirements of the relevant subsections of s. 58.

The completion of these forms provides the legal authority for treatment to be given. They require the signatories to certify that the requirements of ss. 57 and 58 have been complied with. Completed forms must be returned to the MHAC, irrespective of whether or not the SOAD authorises the treatment in question. A further level of paperwork has been instigated by the MHAC. Form MHAC 2 applies to treatment given under s. 58(3)(b). It must be completed and returned to the MHAC by the SOAD along with form 39. This form requires the provision of greater detail than the forms applicable under the 1983 Regulations, covering the case history of the patient; the opinions formed about the patient and the treatment by the SOAD; whether the patient consented to the treatment; whether the SOAD required the RMO to amend the proposed treatment or treatment plan in any way; approved dosages of drugs particularly if above normal levels (as set by the BNF); and whether emergency treatment has been given under s. 62 before the SOAD visit.

Finally, Form MHAC 1 must be completed by the RMO following treatment given under s. 58(3)(b) pursuant to the requirements of s. 61, which requires the RMO to report on treatment given under ss. 57(2) or 58(3)(b) and the patient's condition to the MHAC, in the case of restricted patients, six months after the commencement of the restriction direction or order and thereafter annually (s. 61(2)); and in the case of other patients, on the occasion of the renewal of the authority to detain: s. 61(1). The MHAC reviews the information provided and will organise a new SOAD visit when appropriate (Department of Health and Welsh Office, 1999, para. 16.36). The information required by form MHAC 1 largely duplicates that obtained from form 39, although in addition the RMO is required to detail treatments that have been given under s. 58(3)(b), progress made by the patient and the RMO's future intentions regarding further treatment under that section. Despite all this paperwork, though, the argument made out above in the context of form 38, is equally applicable to forms 37 and 39 and the MHAC forms; that is, it can be argued that the restriction which the requirements of these forms actually places on medical discretion to use potentially dangerous treatments is minimal. In any case, many MHAC1s are either not returned to the MHAC, or are returned with incomplete data (MHAC, 1997, para. 5.17), just as many forms 38 and 39 are also often deficient or confusing in a variety of ways (MHAC, 1995, para. 5.12).

Treatment is infrequently given under s. 57. There have only been four applications for a second opinion in respect of proposed hormone treatments under s. 57(1)(b) in the lifetime of the Act, only one of these has resulted in treatment, and there have been no applications since 1988 (Jones, 1999, p. 251). There is no mystery about why this is the case, however: the most commonly used sexual suppressant is given orally, not surgically (Fennell, 1996, p. 188), and in *ex parte X* it was decided that the section did not extend to hormone analogues but only to hormones and synthetic hormones on the grounds that the former are not composed of naturally occurring substances.

This left the hormone analogue Goserelin outside the scope of the section, even though it is one hundred times more powerful than the hormones and synthetic hormones that are covered by it. Memorably putting the letter of the statute before its spirit, Stuart Smith LJ held that '[i]f Parliament passes legislation on the control of leopards, it is not to be presumed that leopards include tigers on the basis that they are larger and fiercer'. The court also decided that there must be some sort of incision before it can be said that there has been a 'surgical implant' (Fennell, 1988). The practical result of this is that Goserelin and other powerful sexual suppressants can be given under s. 63 for three months after which time they are most probably covered by s. 58 as 'medicine' (*B* v *Croydon HA* (1995) (see 7.3.2.1.1)). Psychosurgery has continued to fill a residual place in treatment for mental disorder with around twenty-five to thirty applications for a second opinion being made each year throughout the 1980s and early 1990s, until 1993-5, when only thirty applications were received by the MHAC, apparently because of a shortage of yttrium rods essential for this treatment and the relocation of one of the main centres for the provision of this treatment (Fennell, 1996, p. 186; MHAC, 1997, para. 5.3). The treatment has since regained some ground, and in the 21-month period of the most recent MHAC *Report*, 30 SOAD visits were made in respect of psychosurgery (or 'neurosurgery for mental disorder' as the MHAC now wishes the treatment to be known: 1997, para. 53), all of which resulted in the treatment being given. Interestingly, s. 57 was first used in respect of a *detained* patient only within the period of the most recent *Report*.

Section 58 is much more frequently used, as might be expected. Between July 1995 and April 1997 there were 10,216 referrals for a second opinion for treatments under this section (MHAC, 1997, para. 5.2). The overwhelming majority of referrals (9,371) were made in respect of the treatment of mental illness. The numbers for mental impairment, severe mental impairment and psychopathic disorder were much lower (213, 113 and 116 respectively), and 403 patients had a dual diagnosis. Around 60 per cent of requests were for authority to administer drug treatments, and around a third for ECT. There were clear distinctions along the lines of gender. Women tended to be referred for ECT or drug treatments in equal numbers, whereas men were much more likely to be referred for drug treatments than ECT, which comprised only around 20 per cent of referrals of male patients. There was also a significant variation by the race of the patients. Black patients were 90 per cent likely to be referred for drug treatments whereas white patients were only around 60 per cent likely, Asian and others 70 per cent likely. It is probable though, that racial variations under s. 58 are a function of gender differences: 'over 70 per cent of Black patients referred for a Second Opinion were male' (MHAC 1997, para. 5.2); although of course this raises another set of issues about why it is that there are a high number of black men in mental hospitals (see 4.7).

MHAC Biennial *Reports* have continually referred to a number of practical problems with the operation of the second opinion scheme. The requirement to consult a non-medical person 'professionally concerned' (s. 57(3), 58(4)) with a patient's treatment, for example, is not always easy to satisfy. Social workers and occupational therapists are most frequently consulted, although on occasion inappropriate persons are consulted such as the 'ward domestic' (MHAC, 1995, para. 5.13) or a hospital secretary (MHAC, 1997, para. 5.2.2); or there is no consultation at all (Fennell, 1996, p. 206). The idea behind the consultation requirement was that it would bring a genuine multidisciplinary dimension to the second opinion process. The reality is that the requirement is little more than 'legalism' in the negative sense of a procedure without a purpose, 'seen as a tiresome formality' (Fennell, 1996, p. 208) by RMOs. It is not only these 'peripheral' consultations which are a cause for concern. The Code of Practice (Department of Health and Welsh Office, 1999, para. 16.33) provides that consultations should 'only in exceptional cases' be by telephone, and yet Fennell in an extensive piece of research found that as between RMOs and SOADs 'telephone consultation appeared to be more the norm than the exception' (1996, p. 204). This does not necessarily render the consultation process deficient, although it does help to raise the suspicion that those operating the scheme are prepared to cut corners on ground of convenience.

Fennell's research helps provide a more complete picture of the patterns of the SOAD system than that found in the MHAC Reports. Fennell analysed all MHAC2s (which must be completed when treatment is given under s. 58(3)(b)) in the period December 1991 to August 1992 and MHAC1s (which must be completed when an RMO reports on treatment given under ss. 57 or 58) returned to the Commission between January and March 1992, with totals of 1,009 and 232 respectively. This gave data about the practices of a large number (276) of hospitals of all types. The majority of applications for a SOAD visit were made in respect of patients held under part II (839 or 83 per cent, with 164 or 17 per cent of applications made in respect of patients held under part III). The overwhelming majority of part II patients were detained under s. 3 on grounds of mental illness (963 applications), of whom around half (445) had a diagnosis of schizophrenic psychosis, the other most common diagnoses being affective psychosis (277) and depressive disorders (216).

In terms of gender, race and age Fennell found much the same patterns within the treatment of detained patients within this period as we have discussed above. Women comprised 55 per cent of the sample (566) and men 45 per cent (443). Applications for drug treatment and ECT were about even but ECT was overwhelmingly a 'woman's treatment': 73 per cent of all requests for a second opinion for ECT were for female patients (1996, p. 197) diagnosed as suffering from affective psychosis or depressive disorder; and 77 per cent (167/216) of those diagnosed as suffering from depressive disorder were women, of whom almost all (93.4 per cent) were given ECT (p. 197). The gender differential was not just a function of diagnosis, however. Of men diagnosed as depressive 85.7 per cent were given ECT. A similar pattern emerged in respect of affective disorders and schizophrenia (p. 198). The differences became even more marked for elderly patients as, although ECT was the most likely treatment for both sexes, many more elderly women than elderly men were detained. Young males diagnosed as schizophrenic were, however, markedly more likely than older men to be given ECT: 63 per cent (22/35) of men receiving this treatment were in the 21-35 age group (p.198), and of the 17 men aged 21-30, 5 were Afro-Caribbean (ibid.), which tallies with the findings of earlier research that black people are more likely to be diagnosed as schizophrenic than white people (Lewis, Croft-Jeffreys and David, 1990; Berthoud and Nazroo, 1997; Cope, 1989). The overwhelming majority of males diagnosed as schizophrenic, though, were likely to be the subject of a second opinion for drug treatments (86.4 per cent or 241/279, p. 198). This reflects the general pattern that men are more likely than women to be given drug treatments: 61 per cent of all such requests for a SOAD, although younger patients of both sexes were more likely to be given such treatments, the 'vast majority' (p. 200) for antipsychotic medicines.

A worrying feature revealed by Fennell's research was the willingness of SOADs to certify drug treatment plans that exceeded BNF recommended doses or utilised polypharmacy. Both MHAC1s and MHAC2s showed that 'by far the most common prescribing combination was antipsychotics from both categories 4.2.1 and 4.2.2 together with anticholinergic drugs for side effects' (p. 202). Fifty-six per cent of all MHAC2 cases followed the above pattern, although more than one antipsychotic medicine was authorised by the SOAD in a higher percentage — 73 per cent — of cases (p. 202). In short, polypharmacy was the norm. No doubt there are variations in the prescribing practices of different hospitals and different doctors, although the evidence shows that such differences are relatively slight. Fraser and Hepple (1992) for example, found that psychiatric drugs are administered at similar levels at Broadmoor and at a hospital in Newcastle which provides non-secure accommodation: two-thirds of patients in both institutions were receiving two or more psychotropic drugs, although administration by depot was more common in Broadmoor. This research did show, though, that women diagnosed as psychopathic were more likely to be given drug treatments than their male counterparts, and patients in the special care unit at Broadmoor were prescribed higher dosages than patients housed elsewhere.

In Fennell's research it was unusual (eight cases) for a SOAD to express concern about polypharmacy, and in only two cases was approval time limited (1996, p. 203). Apparently, it was not until a treatment plan involved the use of drugs from four or five BNF categories that SOADs would raise a query. In only 36 (3.6 per cent) cases was form 39 withheld by the SOAD, either because the technical requirements of the Act had in some way not been complied with, or because of diagnostic concerns or, infrequently, because the SOAD took the view that the situation was not so serious as to warrant overruling the refusal to consent of the patient in question. In some 13 cases, the SOAD suggested a *more* interventionist plan than that proposed by the RMO. Overall, the RMO and SOAD were in agreement in around 96 per cent of cases (p. 211), a statistic which has been repeatedly given by the MHAC (1985, para. 11.4; 1987, p. 22, 1989, p. 5, 1991, p. 31). The most recent *Report* reports an 'amendment rate' of 15 per cent (1997, para. 5.2.4) but it is not clear what proportion of these included a refusal to authorise the treatment in question. The role of the SOAD is not to provide a 'second opinion' as such, but rather to decide in his or her opinion 'whether the proposed treatment is reasonable in the light of the *general consensus* of appropriate treatment for such a condition' (Department of Health and Welsh Office, 1999, para. 16.21, emphasis added). The responsibility of the SOAD, therefore, is not to 'agree' with the specific treatment plan in question but to be satisfied that it comes within the bounds of treatment that would be given in the circumstances in question by a responsible body of medical opinion. Although patients may make a complaint about their treatment (see 12.6), there is no appeal against the decision of a SOAD, and appointees are independent of the MHAC once appointed (para. 16.21). It is not clear how this scheme — which amounts to a statutory version of the *Bolam* approach — can be said 'to protect the patient's rights' as the Code of Practice claims (para. 16.20). Or at least, it seems to be the case that the psychiatric profession as a whole is prepared to accept that patients' rights are not detracted from by the administration of medication at levels at which there is an increased risk of harmful and unpleasant 'side effects', on the grounds of securing improvement in the patient's initial condition. Given the dubious efficacy of many treatments, however, at least when there is no suitable accompanying social support for the patient, it is by no means clear that patients' rights are protected by giving free reign to the psychiatric profession, which is arguably what the policing of RMOs by SOADs, and the limited remit of the MHAC, amounts to. SOADs are, after all, practising or retired psychiatrists, schooled in the same paternalistic ethos as those they police.

As far as the SOAD regime is concerned, then, it can be argued that 'the new legalism' appears to have been something of a chimera: in terms of the frame of reference set by the medicalism versus legalism debate, it can be said that medicalism remains dominant. As Fennell has put it '[a]lthough the 1983 Act is often described as representing a return to legalism, it builds on the basic framework of discretionary powers in the 1959 Act' (1996, p. 181). Moreover, as the system depends on psychiatrists to police psychiatrists, the issue is one not only of 'discretion' but *medical* discretion. How this was ever seen as 'legalism' is open to question (Rose, 1985) and in practice the SOAD system does little to protect patients from over-enthusiastic treatment regimes or abuses of their legal rights.

This is a gloomy conclusion for those who had hoped that legal rights would be an effective protection against inappropriate zeal or abuse. The new legalism, as explained above, found a legislative voice against the backdrop of jaundice about the curative potential of medicalised psychiatry and the failure of the benevolent aspirations behind the 1959 Act. Nowhere is this view to be found better expressed than in Jefferys and Blom-Cooper's oft-quoted foreword to Gostin's *A Human Condition* (1975, p. 6):

Optimism has given way to scepticism if not pessimism. We are more aware of the complexities of human behaviour, of the unintended and unwelcome side-effects of well-intentioned statutory provision, of the differences in interest and outlook that lie behind an apparent consensus of approach to the treatment of the mentally ill.

The new legalism was born out of this scepticism and pessimism. Ironically, there is today as good a reason to be sceptical about the solution as there was to be so about the original problem.

7.4   EMERGENCY MEASURES: TREATMENT OR CONTROL

There are relatively high levels of violence in psychiatric facilities, and to the extent that patient violence is predictable, attempts by nursing staff to administer medication is a key indicator. However, violence is not the only way in which an emergency situation may manifest. A depressive patient may refuse treatment to the point of putting his or her life in danger, for example. In addition to the administration of treatment, the range of emergency responses also comprises the practices of 'restraint' and 'seclusion'.

7.4.1   Emergency treatment

The MHA 1983 provides for the emergency treatment of detained but not informal patients in s. 62(1):

Sections 57 and 58 above shall not apply to any treatment—
  (a)   which is immediately necessary to save the patient's life, or
  (b)   which (not being irreversible) is immediately necessary to prevent a serious deterioration of his condition, or
  (c)   which (not being irreversible or hazardous) is immediately necessary to alleviate serious suffering by the patient, or
  (d)   which (not being irreversible or hazardous) is immediately necessary and represents the minimum interference necessary to prevent the patient from behaving violently or being a danger to himself or others.

The disapplication of ss. 57 and 58 means that treatment can be given as though under s. 63, that is, without the consent of the patient. However, the scope of s. 62 is limited to treatment which is *immediately* and *minimally* necessary, which has been defined tightly at common law in *Devi v West Midlands AHA* [1980] 7 CL 44 (HC). There is no other limitation on life-saving treatment, but for lesser emergencies the treatment must not be 'irreversible', or 'irreversible and hazardous', as the case may be. These terms are defined in s. 62(3). Treatment is classified as 'irreversible' if it has unfavourable, irreversible physical or psychological consequences and 'hazardous' if it entails significant physical hazard. Although all physical treatments potentially carry the risk of unfavourable irreversible consequences, it is unlikely that the emergency administration of drugs or ECT would be so classified by a court, or else s. 62 would be otiose. These treatments are hazardous in the sense that they may have unwanted detrimental effects, but the definition of this term is limited to *significant, physical* hazards. Treatments under s. 57 are more problematic in theory but in practice it is most unlikely that the treatments covered by that section would be given in an emergency: as we have seen, its application to hormone therapy is in reality nonexistent, and psychosurgery is relatively rarely practised, and never in an emergency situation. In their *Third Biennial Report* the MHAC stated that it was unusual for drugs to be given in an emergency situation, but more common for ECT to be given, usually pending a SOAD visit (MHAC, 1989, para. 7.6(j)). That this continues to be the case is borne out by more recent research, which found that the use of s. 62 to provide treatment prior to the giving of a second option is recorded on 11 per cent of MHAC 2s; of 116 such cases, 112 involved ECT (usually one dose), overwhelmingly for women patients suffering from depressive disorders (Fennell, 1996, p. 199), and the reason for the treatment was to save the life of the patient or prevent a serious deterioration in his or her condition (ibid, p. 200). Around 60 per cent of patients were given ECT within a week of detention under the Act, which seems to indicate that s. 62 is often used for informal, competent, refusing patients who are sectioned for this purpose. However, this is not always the case. The MHAC has long reported concern that s. 62 has been used to justify the emergency treatment of informal patients or those excluded from the ambit of Part IV by s. 56 (1993, para. 7.12; 1997, para. 5.2.7), but such treatment is unlawful unless covered by the common law.

The patterns of emergency treatment under the authority of common law are unknown, although it seems that antipsychotic medicine may be used relatively more frequently than under s. 62 (MHAC, 1995, para. 5.14). The general common law principles — that no treatment may be given to an adult without consent, unless the patient lacks capacity, in which case he or she may be treated without consent to protect life, health or well-being — have been discussed above (see 7.3.1.2.3). If the patient is temporarily incompetent, the principle of necessity is of more circumscribed application than it is in the treatment of permanently incapacitated patients, and will authorise only such treatment as is *immediately necessary*: *Devi*, *Re T*. These same principles apply in emergency situations, indeed cases like *Re T* did involve emergency situations. Moreover, it is clear that a refusal of treatment made by an adult when competent should continue to bind if the patient loses competence. In *Re T* the Court of Appeal accepted the validity of an anticipatory refusal and in the House of Lords decision in *Airedale NHS Trust* v *Bland* [1993] AC 789 Lords Goff and Keith (at pp. 864 and 857 respectively) all accepted that a health care provider would be guilty of battery if he or she treated a patient who had given a valid anticipatory refusal. If a competent patient refuses emergency treatment, the treatment cannot proceed and the proper course is to 'section' the patient and treat under part IV. Of course, the procedure may take some time, and the holding powers in s. 5 are no use here because they are excluded from the application of Part IV by s. 56. Nevertheless, the law is that any treatment not authorised by s. 62 will be unlawful. The law is not always observed, however. The sixth MHAC *Report* refers to 'anecdotal evidence that patients treated in emergency situations, often under common law and by inexperienced staff, are particularly subject to harm including collapse and death' (1995, para. 5.14). ECT carries a risk of death of 0.45 per cent (Fennell, 1996, p. 198) at the best of times, and the death rate from antipsychotic medicine is slightly lower. It is a real concern if it is indeed the case that these treatments are administered by underqualified staff as a heat of the moment response to difficult situations. Each detained patient will have an RMO and informal patients will be under the authority of a named doctor. The Code of Practice provides that emergency treatment of detained patients is the responsibility of the patient's RMO (Department of Health and Welsh Office, 1999, para. 16.40) which must be right as a matter of law as treatment under s. 62 is analogous to treatment under s. 63 which specifically provides that this is the case. The situation is perhaps not so clear at common law because as long as there is consent, or the patient lacks capacity to consent, treatment in accordance with the above principles will be lawful, whoever takes the decision to administer it. As a matter of practice though, this is clearly unacceptable, which provides yet another reason why the disapplication of the 1983 Act to informal patients should be reviewed.

7.4.2 Restraint and seclusion

The Code of Practice advises that ideally the causes of inappropriate behaviour should be investigated and preventative measures taken (paras. 19.4,5), for example by giving patients adequate explanation of their treatment and the reason for it, the provision of personal space and access to open space, the structuring of activity and allocating patients to particular nurses. There is reason to believe that such measures can prove effective. Adshead (1998) has argued that attachment theory — which holds, broadly, that mental health is improved by the formation of relationships of attachment between individuals — can be used to modulate anxiety or arousal in patients and so minimise or prevent the occurrence of violent or disruptive behaviour. A moving, first-hand account of such an attachment having a positive therapeutic value for the patient can be found in Lindsay (1996). On the other hand, however, as Adshead also points out, insecure or unhealthy patient-staff attachments can be a cause of such behaviour. Preventative measures, in other words, may on occasion be the cause of violence or disruptive behaviour. When this is the case, restraint and seclusion are the measures of last resort.

These practices are often described as 'management' in the literature (for example, Code of Practice, Chapter 19), but this description is arguably disingenuous. There is force in Cohen's point that 'social control', if defined too broadly, becomes a 'mickey mouse' concept (1985, p. 2); but the practices of restraint and seclusion, as is also the case with the medical practices of the mental health sector, fall comfortably within Cohen's truncated criteria of 'organised responses to crime, delinquency and allied forms of deviant and/or socially problematic behaviour which are actually conceived of as such, whether in the reactive sense . . . or in the proactive sense' (1985, p. 3). On this view, 'control' more accurately captures the reality of the situation. As far as the law is concerned, though, these interventions are to be seen as 'treatment'.

7.4.2.1 Restraint
The aim of restraint should be to minimise unacceptable behaviour and if used regularly as part of a treatment programme its use should be reviewed regularly (Department of Health and Welsh Office, 1999, para. 19.14). Staff should be trained in the use of restraint techniques (para. 19.9), and courses should be given by persons with a suitable qualification. According to the Code of Practice, physical restraint should be used 'only as a last resort and never as a matter of course' (para. 19.11), and the use of tying or hooking

a patient to a part of a building or a fixture should never be used (para. 19.10). If restraint is used on an informal patient, consideration should be given to the invocation of formal powers of detention (para. 19.8). The use of restraint is fairly common, and 'it appears that physical restraint is being used with increasing frequency' (MHAC, 1997, para. 10.2.3). Smith and Humphreys (1997) found that, of patients requiring transfer to intensive psychiatric care wards, 37 per cent were subject to physical restraint in the four hours prior to transfer, and that restraint was used most frequently on patients admitted under s. 4 who resisted admission and acted violently on detention. In practice, the formulation of a 'policy' on restraint means the appointment of three persons from amongst nursing staff to act as ward 'restraint teams'. The use of restraint has a chequered history, particularly but not exclusively in the special hospitals, and concerns continue to be expressed about the use of techniques such as the 'wristlock', which can be effective if applied correctly, but often staff fail to retain skills and techniques in which they have been trained (Gallon, 1999). The use of straitjackets remains common on the intensive care wards in the special hospitals (MHAC, 1997, para. 4.5.3). The MHAC report that there is a worrying number of complaints from patients that restraint is painful and causes injury (1997, para. 10.2.3). Most worrying of all, there have been a number of deaths following the application of restraint, the risk of which is greatly increased if the patient has recently been given more than a small dose of antipsychotic medicine. In combination, restraint and medication can cause acute stress and cardiac arrest (see *Buckley* v *UK* [1997] EHRLR 435). Those dedicated persons who perform to the best of their abilities in providing treatment to aggressive or disturbed patients deserve a vote of thanks for the difficult and sometimes dangerous responsibility that they shoulder for the general social good. But this does not detract from an argument that it is at this point that the credibility of the medical model of mental disorder begins to look *decidedly* problematic.

The law does not see it this way. The leading case on the use of restraint remains *Poutney* v *Griffiths* [1976] AC 314 (HL). A nurse physically restrained a patient, who had been transferred to hospital (the hospital in question being Broadmoor) from prison, when the patient did not respond to a request to return to his ward at the end of a visit from relatives. The patient alleged that the nurse had punched him, and the nurse was convicted of assault by a magistrates' court. This decision was quashed by the Divisional Court and the patient appealed to the House of Lords. Before the House it was accepted that 'a hospital's staff has powers of control over all mentally disordered patients, whether admitted voluntarily or compulsorily, though the nature and duration of the control varies with the category to which the patient belongs' (per Lord Edmund-Davies at p. 334). For detained patients, such powers are inherent in the fact of detention, and hence, in the MHA 1983. In *Tameside and Glossop* v *CH* (1996) (see 7.3.2.1.1), Wall J having held that the performance of a Caesarean section operation was lawful under s. 63 held that 'it follows that since the defendant's consent is not required, Dr G is entitled, should he deem it clinically necessary, to use restraint in order to achieve the delivery by the defendant of a health baby' (at p. 774). The 1983 Act also contains the latest version of the immunity from suit introduced by the Lunacy Act 1890, s. 139. In *Poutney* it was established that s. 139 protects staff who use reasonable restraint in the course of a patient's treatment (see further 12.3).

For informal patients, the legal situation is murkier. There is Crown Court authority that dealings with informal patients are not covered by s. 139 because such dealings are not conducted 'in pursuance of this Act' as that section requires: *R* v *Runighian* [1977] Crim LR 361. But there are a number of overlapping legal justifications for the use of restraint against an informal patient. There is a common law power exercisable by all citizens to prevent a breach of the peace, which is exercisable in hospitals and residential accommodation. There is a common law right to use force in self-defence, which includes the defence of others. There is also a common law right to confine a person who is insane, as demonstrated by the well known case of *Fletcher* v *Fletcher* (1859) 1 El & El 420. Finally, there is a generally available power in s. 3(1), Criminal Law Act 1967 to use force to prevent a crime or to arrest a person unlawfully at large. The precise nature of each of these powers is debatable (see Hoggett, 1996, pp.140-2), but the general thrust of the law is clear, which is that subject to requirements of reasonableness and proportionality, there will be little difficulty for a staff member in finding a legal basis for the restraint of an informal patient.

7.4.2.2 Seclusion Although the 1983 Act is silent as to the practice known as 'seclusion', the Code of Practice offers the following definition (para. 19.16):

Seclusion is the supervised confinement of a patient in a room, which may be locked for the protection of others from significant harm.

Hospitals are enjoined by the Code to draw up guidelines concerning the use of seclusion, and for the monitoring and review of practice, which should be carried out regularly by hospital managers (para. 19.23). The Code itself, however, also makes clear the Department of Health's view of best practice. Seclusion should only be used as a last resort for the shortest time necessary. It should not be used as punishment, threat, as a consequence of staff shortages or if there is a risk of suicide or self-harm (para. 19.16). The protection of other persons is the 'sole aim' of seclusion. It is the view expressed in the Code that seclusion can be ordered by the nurse in charge of the ward, a senior nursing officer, or a nursing officer as well as by a doctor, although if the initial decision is taken by someone other than a doctor, one should attend immediately (para. 19.18). Seclusion should only take place in a safe, secure and properly identified room, adequately heated, lit, ventilated, with seating, which provides a safe, private environment for the detainee, whilst also allowing complete observation. There should be a nurse within sight and sound of the room at all times (para. 19.19) and present if the patient has also been sedated. 'The aim of observation is to monitor the condition and behaviour of the patient and to identify at what time seclusion can be terminated' (para. 19.20). There should be a documented report every fifteen minutes, with a review by two nurses in the seclusion room and by a doctor every two and four hours respectively. If seclusion is to continue for more than eight hours consecutively or for twelve hours within a forty-eight hour period, there should be an independent review by a multidisciplinary team not involved in the patient's care at the time that the period of seclusion began (para. 19.21).

In most of its detail, the advice given in the Code reacts against previous scandals about the practice of, and concern about the reasons for, the use of seclusion. It can be suggested that in effect the Code attempts to paper over the cracks of controversy. As far as the Code is concerned, seclusion should not be considered as part of a treatment plan — as is implied by its emergency use status — but nevertheless falls within the definition of treatment in s. 145(1). Both elements of this view are debatable. As Mason (1992, 1993) discusses, at a theoretical level there are at least three possible explanations for the practice of seclusion, namely; therapeutic, containing and punitive, and ultimately however guidelines, in whatever form, are framed, it will always be an open and empirical question as to which explanation best fits the facts. There is also a lack of consensus as to how seclusion should be defined (Mason, 1992), but there is indisputably a sense in which seclusion that is *experienced* as punitive is punitive. In the year 1995-6 there were 5223 reported uses of seclusion involving 2450 patients, and an unrecorded number of other incidents of solitary confinement not amounting in the opinion of staff (although the MHAC did not always agree) to seclusion (MHAC, 1997, para. 10.1.2). A small number of patients had experienced seclusion for more than 24 hours continuously, and one individual, in need of unavailable secure provision, had been in seclusion for more than three weeks (ibid.). A patient died one week into seclusion at Ashworth hospital, and at Rampton reasons recorded for the use of seclusion included risk of self-harm or the patient's safety, even though such justifications are disapproved of in the Code (MHAC, 1997, para. 4.5.3).

7.5 CONCLUDING COMMENTS: BACK TO THE CRITIQUE OF THE MEDICAL MODEL OF TREATMENT FOR MENTAL DISORDER

That practices of restraint and seclusion come within the definition of medical treatment in s. 145(1) of the 1983 Act raises difficult enough questions about the 'medicalisation' of our response to mentally distressed or disturbed people. However, the critique of the 'medicalisation of madness', which now has a long history within the sociology of medicine, aims its criticism more broadly, to encompass not simply these ancillary aspects of treatment but also those at the core of the medical model — the physical and talking treatments. This body of literature was discussed at some length in earlier Chapters and will not be discussed again here. But having now looked in some detail at the law, policies and practices which structure medical treatment in hospital, it is worth pausing to consider whether such theoretical perspectives can throw any light on the limited ability of legal mechanisms to exert a significant degree of control over medical discretion. The suggestion here is that it is in the inter-relationship between the three structuring issues outlined at the start of this chapter, namely whether treatment in hospital can properly be called 'medical'; the relationship between 'medicalism' and 'legalism'; and the distinction between 'treatment' and 'control', that the most fruitful insights into this question are to be found.

Medical treatment for mental disorder, although now seemingly inescapably eclectic, continues to be dominated by the medical model of madness, which has been able to expand to accommodate psychological and environmental perspectives on questions of aetiology and treatment. As Pilgrim and Rogers (1993, p. 101) put it, even though these other aetiological factors are more often taken into account than previously, 'they still legitimize the disease model and the authoritative power of medicine in the diagnosis and treatment of people with personal and social problems'. And despite the current eclecticism, physical treatments continue to dominate. It may seem that drug treatments, in particular, are 'properly' medical, but the fact is that the medical model is a social construction. Medicine trades in what Berger and Luckman (1967) call our 'secondary reality', which comprises those elements of experience which are not explicable by recourse to common sense — concepts like justice, deity, death and madness, for example — for which there is a need to develop specialised knowledge and institutions to provide explanations. How these specialisms have developed and have annexed the social problems that constitute their particular domain is a question in need of an answer. The appropriateness of the medical model may seem to be a matter of common sense, but the key question is really how it has come to be so seen.

Given the dominance of physical treatments, the current state of psychotherapy has a particular relevance here. An umbrella organisation, the United Kingdom Council for Psychotherapy (UKCP) was established in 1993, replacing the United Kingdom Standing Conference for Psychotherapy which had been set up in 1989, which itself replaced earlier prototypes of self-regulation following a Private Member's Bill, initially if indirectly prompted by the practices of Scientologists, to regulate the practice of psychotherapy, which failed to get through Parliament in 1982 (Pokorny, 1994, p. 515). Also in 1993 a voluntary register of psychotherapists was established. According to Clarkson (1994) the purpose of the UKCP is 'to create a profession and a register so that the public can identify appropriately trained practitioners who are subject to an enforceable Code of Ethics', whilst the voluntary register 'will form the foundation of a statutory register of psychotherapists' (1994, p. 12). National vocational qualifications are also being developed, and 'it has now been agreed by all the organisations of the UKCP that entry to psychotherapy training must be at postgraduate level and have an academic content roughly equivalent to a masters degree' (Clarkson, 1994, p. 23). What can be seen here is the attempted professionalisation of this branch of medical treatment for mental disorder. The definitions generated from within the ranks of psychotherapists invariably emphasise training and professional status (see Freedman, Kaplan and Sadock, 1975, p. 2601; Wolberg, 1954, p. 118, cited in Clarkson, 1994, p. 12). According to Clarkson this project is for the benefit of the public, but it is difficult to believe that there are no other intended beneficiaries. The UKCP polices its boundaries (Pokorny, 1994, p. 515), and it would be naive not to realise that this is because the achievement of professional status is just that; a *status*, a source of empowerment, which is necessary if psychotherapy is to make any significant inroads into the professional dominance of the psychiatric profession and the Royal College of Psychiatrists — which has been influential in the shape of the Mental Health Acts of 1959 and 1983 — over the provision of in-patient treatment.

The relevance of this consideration of contemporary developments in the structure of psychotherapy is that, first, it reminds us that 'the medical' comprises that which is so called, nothing more nor less. There is no inherent defining quality to interventions that are or should be covered by the term. Rather, and this is the second point, it is a question of professional and political power plays. As far as psychiatry and physical treatment is concerned, it was the drug revolution of the 1950s that finally made the claims to medical status of the psychiatric profession plausible (see 3.2). From a perspective at the end of the century, though, the claims that sounded so plausible 40 or 50 years ago have been shown to be problematic. Drug treatments do have beneficial effects but the degree and longevity of those effects remains a matter of intense controversy, whilst concerns about side effects remains high, at least outside of professional circles. Pilgrim and Rogers see reliance on drug treatments and lack of concern about side effects as a function of psychiatry's relation with the other branches of medicine: '[a]n over reliance on drug treatment is inextricably linked to a professional strategy on the part of psychiatrists' (1993, p. 106). And just as psychiatry is parasitic on 'the medical profession', so the process is now being repeated, at one stage removed, in the relation between psychotherapy and psychiatry as it is currently being played out.

It is tempting to conclude on this basis that the treatment of mental disorder is more about power and control than beneficence, and that mental patients are objects in a power play rather than subjects, autonomous individuals with rights. On this view, patients are better understood as 'victims', or more neutrally as 'targets', simply the stock in trade, of medical intervention; and what is required is a disempowerment of psychiatry — a demedicalisation of madness — rather than a broadening of the psychiatric power complex through the establishment of new treatments and new professions to administer them. This caricature is in fact not too far removed from the position of the antipsychiatry movement and its champions, as Atkinson (1995, p. 33) has argued.

Moreover, it was something like this line of thinking which underpinned the pressures to introduce the legal safeguards for the protection of patients' rights now found in the 1983 Act. And yet, far from being an effective watchdog over the use of medical discretion, the 'return to legalism' has turned out in practice to be the medical model's 'alibi'. Part IV of the Act masks the reality of medical freedom with the appearance of legal control. It is at least arguable that part IV should be understood as a *colonisation* of legal language and concepts by medicalism. The law contained in part IV of the Act, and the common law for that matter, passes Hart's (1961/1994) test for identifying law, the 'rule of recognition', as it is discourse produced by particular bodies (the legislature and the judiciary) in particular places (Parliament, and the courts) in ways which we recognise as connoting its 'legal' character, and yet this law *constitutes a field of medical intervention.* As Fennell (1986, p. 36) puts it, '[l]egal rules provide the medium through which disciplinary power in general is both constituted and exercised, and in this context psychiatric interventions represent a specialised aspect of disciplinary power'. The theoretical flaw in the 'ideology of entitlement', from a legalistic point of view, is that it posits medicalism and legalism as a simple opposition, without appreciating this potential for colonisation.

Rose (1985) has argued, more sociologically, that the ideology of entitlement and the opposition of legal rights to medical discretion wrongly assumes that control and liberty are distinct concepts, when in fact '[t]he contemporary psychiatric system operates predominantly not by coercion but by contractuality' (p. 203), and when 'many modern psychiatric practices seek to promote autonomy' (p. 204), *using* control to help patients *gain* greater control over their own lives. In consequence, Rose argues, the ideology of entitlement is ill-equipped to assess the form that the control/liberty relation should take, and the practical effect is that legalism abdicates power to medical discretion.

This analysis of the reasons for the failure of legalism to deliver its underpinning policy of empowerment also informs the reasoning of those who reject what Lupton calls the 'orthodox' medicalisation critiques, on the grounds that it utilises an overly simplistic understanding of control. Lupton argues that (1997, p. 98):

[i]n their efforts to denounce medicine and to represent doctors as oppressive forces, orthodox critics tend to display little recognition of the ways that it may contribute to good health, the relief of pain and the recovery from illness, or the value that many people understandably place on these outcomes ... or the ways that patients willingly participate in medical dominance and may indeed seek 'medicalisation'.

Most hospital in-patients are not detained, and most consent to treatment, even if that consent is often ambivalent. By the same token, it is arguable that the case law discussed in this Chapter — *Tameside, Croydon, ex parte X* and so on — reveals not so much medical attempts to control patients as the absolute inseverability of control and beneficence, the ultimate aim of which is to restore autonomy. It is important not to overstate this point: on occasion, treatment *is* more about control than beneficence, and treatment without consent under part IV may of course be given to patients detained solely for the benefit of other persons. But to suggest that this is always, or even usually the case, or that control can be seen as some sort of 'bottom line' with beneficence a veneer, seems to us to impute to those providing in-patients treatment motives both more conspiratorial and sinister than are likely.

There is a need, therefore, to develop a theoretical understanding of the relations between coercion and consent, and between control and beneficence which does not structure them oppositionally, as alternatives, and this in turn requires one to think more carefully about what we mean by the phrase 'the medical model'. The present authors' suggestion, derived from Foucault, is that the power of this model should be seen in more 'fundamental' terms, as *the medical construction of social reality.* The power of psychiatry lies in its ability to produce a reality in which medical treatment for mental disorder is actively sought out. In other words, although coercion may be and not infrequently is present at the actual point of treatment, it is necessary to understand that its absence at this point and its substitution by an apparently consenting patient does not mean that coercion is radically absent. On the contrary, it may well be functioning at the 'deeper' level of constructing a reality, a coercive environment or backdrop against which consent 'seems natural'.

This criticism of the ideology of entitlement and antipsychiatry, then, requires attention to be given not only to the inadequate theorisation of control but also the inadequate theorisation of power. It is at this point that the various strands of this discussion converge, namely the medicalisation critique; the medicalism/legalism relation; and the socially constructed nature of the 'medical model'. Again that convergence is precipitated by the work of Foucault. There are two key innovations in Foucault's thought which are particularly pertinent for us. First, Foucault argued that power should be seen as a positive, productive force as well as a negative, prohibitory one; and secondly that the power of psychiatry, psychotherapy and so on should be seen more in terms of *discourses* than of *actors*. What this amounts to is a view of medical power as that which operates *through* medical professionals — as the discourses they expound and the discursive techniques or micro-practices (treatments) they apply — rather than this power being 'held' by them, with 'mental patients' as the 'products' of these discourses and as one measure of their power relations.

There are two key points to be taken from this. First, these power relations are of a particular order, the order of the medical discourses that produced them. Legal discourses are of a different order. Richardson (1993, p. 238) argues that legal discourse is structured around the organising principle of autonomy; medical discourse around beneficence. It may be that the distinction is not as neat as Richardson suggests. As already noted Rose has pointed out that medical beneficence aims to realise patient autonomy, and by the same token the legal positing of autonomous individuals is a beneficent act on the part of law and its framers. In other words, the beneficence/autonomy relation is deconstructable. But at the level of the production of discourse Richardson's point does hold good, and it follows from this that the two cannot operate in tandem, which is why it is necessary to speak of 'colonisation' rather than of 'fusion'. But there is *a priori* no reason why the colonisation must be *of* the legal *by* the medical. There is no reason, in other words, why the mechanism of legal rights should not operate more effectively than it seems to at present, to shut down areas of medical discretion as constituted by medical discourse (for example, that beneficent motivations justify the treatment of refusing patients without consent) by colonising that situation with autonomy. This would require not only the rewriting of part IV so that its inherent paternalism is 'de-inscribed' (Fennell, 1990) but also the extension of its mechanisms for the protection of autonomy — the system of second opinions and reports — to all patients, detained or not. Better protection of autonomy also requires a shift from one legal discourse to another, from, that is, rights conceived of as due process rights to rights as conceived in private law: 'rights to deal', as Fennell aptly describes them. The argument, in short, is for a 'return to legalism' of the type originally envisaged by Gostin, rather than the truncated, 'compromise' version now contained in the Act of 1983.

Secondly, however, Foucault shows us that we cannot expect the law in part IV, however framed, to be a panacea. This is because it is experienced by medical professionals as a set of negative prohibitions, which is to say that it relies on the weak model of power (as repressive) and as such it does not challenge the *production* of medical knowledge. Rose is sceptical of the ability of 'rights' to effect substantive change, for this reason and for two others, the first of which is that '[t]he doctrines of right and entitlements cannot resolve the issue of whose "rights" shall prevail; it merely dissimulates the grounds upon which choices are made' (1985, p. 213), and the force of these points must be accepted. The 'question of rights' has been a dominant intellectual problem for all types of jurisprudence and philosophy since at least the time of Plato, and the advent of postmodern thinking has given these debates a new vitality (Morrison, 1997). Rose does, however, concede that 'there might be an argument for the tactical use of rights' (1985, p. 214) and for us this is sufficient. Moreover, the impact of rights discourse is variable; it may be a set of negative impositions as far as those wishing to provide treatments are concerned but to the patient it can be a source of empowerment. Law like medicine is in the business of reality construction, and rights discourse at least constructs a reality in which the intended recipients of medical treatment for mental disorder are *a priori* autonomous agents.

The third strand of Rose's criticism of rights discourse is that it has a poor record 'when it comes to the positive changes upon which the strategy bases its claims for progressive mental health policy reform — improving buildings, staffing levels and proficiency, conditions, standards of conduct or treatment regimes, or providing alternatives to institutionalisation' (1985, p. 210). Again, we accept this point. But for us it is not *the* point. Rights discourse cannot be the total sum of any strategy of empowerment, and to identify its limitations in affecting policy and resources does not mean that it cannot be effective within these limitations. From a Foucaultean perspective, the list of 'real policy issues' given by Rose itself poses a set of limitations, in the form of the acceptance of the medical discourse on madness that is implied by arguments in favour of increasing the resources put into mental health services, or increased 'proficiency' in the delivery of treatments when it is not at all clear that it is lack of proficiency which is the problem. By the same token, if the ultimate aim of policy in this area is the empowerment of patients in the face of the constructive power of medical treatment, it is not clear that to shift towards alternatives to institutionalisation will necessarily achieve this, and to run the two concepts of demedicalisation and deinstitutionalisation together is problematic. For Lupton 'the move towards 'demedicalisation' may be interpreted paradoxically as a growing penetration of the clinical gaze into the everyday life of citizens' (1997, p. 107). This question has already been discussed in this text (see 3.3) and will be discussed further in a later Chapter (see 9.5), but its relevance here is as a further reminder that 'demedicalisation' can only really be challenged at the level of the production of discourse on madness. And despite all its faults and failings it can be argued that rights discourse, and with it proper, medically independent mechanisms for the enforcement and protection of those rights, may be the best practical way to pursue a strategy of demedicalisation, whether inside of hospital or out, at this discursive level.

EIGHT

Leaving hospital

8.1 INTRODUCTION

The contours of the context in which the issue of discharge from hospital must be situated have changed significantly over the last few decades. The shift from chronic to acute patients as the main 'clients' of in-patient services, together with the programme of closure of Victorian asylums and the relocation of psychiatric services into units within general hospitals and into 'the community', means that many patients who would previously have been hospitalised for periods of years if not decades now enter hospital, if at all, only for relatively short periods of time. Despite the change of policy, however, the MHAC has continually reported the pressure on in-patient services, one consequence of which is that patients are often discharged from hospital earlier than would otherwise have been the case (1997, para. 4.1). Yet mental health patients, as this book has been at pains to emphasise, are not a homogeneous group; and some patients, for example the elderly and institutionalised, continue to spend long periods in hospital. The plight of this group of patients attracts the attentions of the general media and public only rarely. The discharge of restricted patients and others considered or proven by subsequent events to be dangerous, by contrast, is rarely out of the news. In 1995 new statutory powers for 'supervised discharge', which allow for the continuing, and to an extent compulsory, treatment and supervision of patients in the community following discharge were introduced. These powers are considered in 9.5.3. They do not apply to restricted patients (s. 41(3)(aa), MHA 1983) in respect of whom there have long been powers to impose conditions on discharge, and these powers are considered in this Chapter.

There are various persons who may initiate or order the discharge of a sectioned patient: the patient's RMO, the managers of the hospital in which the patient is detained, a Mental Health Review Tribunal (MHRT), and in some circumstances the patient's nearest relative (NR). The Secretary of State has powers both to discharge and to veto proposals for the discharge of restricted patients that come from the RMO or hospital managers. These various possibilities will be considered in turn. However, for most patients discharge is not an event but a process, and before final discharge is agreed to there will be often be a trial period, during which the patient is given leave of absence, and so this Chapter opens with a consideration of this issue.

8.2   LEAVE AND RECALL

Leave is seen to have a therapeutic and rehabilitative effect and often features as part of a patient's treatment plan, in a variety of forms, including unaccompanied 'home leave' of various durations, or in the form of short trips alone or under the supervision of nursing staff. As far as patients detained under part II are concerned, s. 17 gives the non-delegable (Department of Health and Welsh Office, 1999, para. 20.3a) responsibility and power for granting and withholding leave to the patient's RMO, but it is likely that in practice RMOs give permission in general terms rather than for each trip outside the hospital (MHAC, 1991, para. 9.7). When a longer period of leave is contemplated, as a trial for discharge, the Code of Practice provides that an RMO should undertake 'any appropriate consultation' (para. 20.3.a) before granting leave to an unrestricted patient, although there should be 'detailed consultation' with community service providers, carers and appropriate friends and relatives, and patients themselves. Leave should not be granted if the patient refuses to consent to these consultations taking place (para. 20.5).

Leave may be granted for a limited or unlimited period and may be renewed in the absence of the patient (s. 17(2)), but a period of leave of absence will end on the expiry without renewal of the authority to detain: s. 17(5). This means that the maximum period of leave possible under s. 17 is one year (the period of detention for treatment of a renewed s. 3 admission). It has been accepted since the decision in *R v Hallstrom, ex parte W; R v Gardner, ex parte L* [1986] 2 All ER 306 (DC) that it is unlawful to renew the authority to detain a patient under the procedure found in s. 20 merely to extend a period of leave. The decision in *Hallstrom* put paid to attempts by doctors to find a way around the embargo on ongoing compulsory treatment in the community, but it must now be read in the light of the recent ruling of the Court of Appeal in *Re Barker; Barker v Barking Havering and Brentwood Community Healthcare NHS Trust* [1999] 1 FLR 106.

In *Barker*, the care plan of B, a patient detained under s. 3 was for graduated, supervised return to the community. She had been granted leave, which at the time that her detention was renewed allowed her to be absent from the hospital for a number of days each week. B complied with her treatment plan and on her days in hospital was assessed rather than treated. She sought judicial review of the decision to renew her detention, on the grounds that the requirements of s. 20(4) were not met. These are essentially a repetition of the grounds for initial admission under s. 3. A period of detention cannot be renewed unless the patient is suffering from one of the four types of mental disorder specified in s. 1(2) (see Chapter two) to a nature or degree which makes it appropriate that the patient receive medical treatment in a hospital (s. 20(4)(a)), and that it is necessary for the health or safety of the patient or others that the patient 'should receive medical treatment and that it cannot be provided unless he continues to be detained': s. 20(4)(c). There is also a treatability requirement, which applies to all detained patients, unlike its equivalent in s. 3(2)(b).

In *Hallstrom* McCullough J had held that these criteria were not satisfied if at the time of the renewal it was not in the opinion of the RMO necessary that the patient be hospitalised. The Court of Appeal in *Barker* agreed this, but added the gloss that, although it had to be necessary for the purposes of the renewal of a section under s. 20(4)(c) that a patient 'continue to be detained', this did not mean that it was actually necessary that a patient in B's position needed to be confined to a hospital. It was sufficient that detention would be used as a backstop if the care plan for graduated discharge ran into problems. This is debatable, as a matter of statutory interpretation (Eldergill, 1999), but its effect is reasonably clear. The law as it now stands seems to be that it is *only* when there is *no* intention of hospitalising a patient on leave, and the *only* reason for the extension of a period of detention is to permit continued treatment in the community, that the renewal of authority to detain will be unlawful. Perhaps this is what the MHA 1983 has always provided for, and the decision in *Hallstrom* has routinely been overestimated in its effect on clinical freedom. But, in any case, after *Barker*, which is clearly in step with the realities of the care programme approach (see 9.4), further debate on this point is merely academic.

Leave may be granted subject to conditions that the RMO 'considers necessary in the interests of the patients or for the protection of other persons': s. 17(1). One specific condition that is mentioned in the 1983 Act is that the RMO may direct that the patient remain in the custody of a nominated 'officer' on the staff of the hospital or any other person authorised in writing by the hospital managers, if it appears to him or her 'necessary so to do in the interests of the patient or for the protection of other persons': s. 17(3). 'Interests' is not defined further and is probably open to a broad definition, whilst 'necessary' is defined by the position as it appears to the RMO and not by some objective standard, giving wide scope to the exercise of an RMO's discretion. An 'officer', not defined by the Act, is presumably any employee. The Memorandum explains that s. 17(3) is intended, *inter alia* to 'allow detained patients to have escorted leave on outings, to attend other hospitals for treatment, or to have home visits on compassionate grounds' (para. 63), but might also include home leave under the custody of a relative, for example. As far as other conditions are concerned, requirements relating to residence and treatment are most common. The patient and other appropriate persons should be given a copy of any conditions (para. 20.6). A patient given leave remains 'liable to be detained' and therefore subject to the consent to treatment provisions contained in part IV (s. 56(1)), and the after care provisions in s. 117 (see 9.2.2.4, 9.3.2 and 9.5.3) apply to patients detained for treatment on leave: s. 117(1). Although this does mean that it is possible in theory to administer treatment without consent in the community, the Code of Practice (para. 20.7) advises that 'consideration should be given to recalling the patient to hospital' if treatment is refused.

The powers of recall are contained in s. 17(4). The patient's RMO must, by notice in writing to the patient or to the person 'in charge of the patient' (who will be a person appointed under s. 17(3)), revoke the leave of absence and recall the patient to hospital if 'it appears' to the RMO 'that it is necessary so to do in the interests of the patient's health or safety or for the protection of other persons'. Again, this form of words gives a good deal of discretion to RMOs. The Code of Practice directs RMOs to 'consider very seriously the reasons for recalling a patient' including the effects of revocation on the patient, and 'refusal to take medication should not on its own, for example, be a reason for revocation' (para. 20.11).

The MHAC has expressed concerns over the operation of s. 17, including the withholding of authorised leave by nursing staff as punishment or coercion, failure to appreciate the need for compliance with s. 17 for escorted or short trips out of hospital (MHAC, 1995, para. 9.4), no record of leave having been granted, unlawful delegation of an RMO's powers, failure to specify conditions or to consult, or to give the patient and other appropriate persons, such as relatives or professional carers a copy of the conditions of leave, as envisaged in the Memorandum, failure to obtain written permission from the hospital managers before the patient is placed in the custody of someone other than an officer of the hospital (MHAC, 1997, para. 3.4). A predominant concern in the *Sixth Report* was the use of s. 17 as an alternative to transferring the patient under s. 19, MHA 1983. A formal transfer under that section involves the transference of the authority to detain and all ancillary powers between the respective hospitals, but if a patient is transferred under s. 17 the various powers and duties remain with the first hospital. This means that those responsible for the patient's treatment in the hospital to which he or she has been transferred have no original authority over the patient, but the situation had arisen because transfers under s. 17 are typically used to remove acute patients from a district hospital to an RSU, and RSUs had insisted that such transfers occur under s. 17 rather than s. 19 as there were concerns that otherwise district hospitals would refuse to accept the return of patients from RSUs. Nevertheless, some patients had remained 'on leave' for many years in such cases (MHAC, 1995, para. 9.4). Subsequently Department of Health Guidance was issued on the use of s. 17 (Department of Health, 1996b), but this has not been enough to allay the concerns of the MHAC (1997, para. 3.4.1).

The provisions of s. 17 apply to patients detained under s. 37 without modification (sch. 1, part I, para. 1, MHA 1983), and to restricted patients with the modifications in sch. 1, part II, para. 3. A restricted patient may not be given leave of absence without the consent of the Secretary of State (para. 3(a)), and the Secretary of State has powers coexistent with the RMO to recall a patient under s. 17(4): para. 3(b). Paragraph 3(c) provides that s. 17(5) is modified so that a patient given conditional leave of absence either by the RMO or the Secretary of State cannot be recalled to hospital by the RMO after the expiration of twelve months from the day that leave of absence began, but can be recalled by the Secretary of State without limit of time. This does not mean, however, that at the expiry of the twelve month period an RMO can do nothing. There is always the option of admission of the patient under the *civil* law of compulsory admission, as happened in *R* v *North West London Mental Health*

NHS Trust and Others, ex parte S [1998] 2 WLR 189 (CA) (see 6.3.2.2). Street (1998) found that 93 per cent of restricted patients had unescorted leave of absence before final discharge, that in the great majority of cases leave passed without incident, and that around one-third of restricted patients discharged from hospital were on leave of absence and living away from hospital at the time (1998, p. 56). This does not mean that restricted patients are given leave freely, and unescorted leave in particular will only be granted very close to the end of a period of hospitalisation, during which the patient will have moved into increasingly less secure accommodation, but it does emphasise the widespread use of s. 17 leave.

8.3   DISCHARGE FROM HOSPITAL: THE LAW

8.3.1   Informal patients

There are no special provisions governing the discharge from hospital of informally admitted patients. In theory, informal patients are free to leave at any time, subject to the holding powers contained in s. 5 (see 4.2), and subject to having the mental capacity to reach a decision to leave the hospital, which a significant proportion of informal patients will lack. In evidence given to the House of Lords in the *Bournewood* (see 4.2) case, the MHAC estimated that if persons lacking capacity to consent to admission were all to be detained under part II, this would result in an increase in annual admissions of 48,000 with 22,000 extra detained patients being in hospital on any one day. The decision in *Bournewood* means that this group of patients will continue to be in some sense *de facto* detained, yet outside the scope of the statutory mechanisms to monitor continuing detention which apply to formally detained patients. This in turn means that informal but incapacitated patients rely solely on friends and relatives, and the professional ethics and good practice of hospital staff and managers, to protect them from unwarranted hospitalisation. Informal patients fall outside the remit of the MHAC. Why the concerns about psychiatry which explain the special legal status of detained patients do not apply to all in-patients is a question that has already been raised on more than one occasion in this text. But of course, to suggest that legal controls should be expanded is to challenge the 'medicalised' image of in-patient services which 'informal' status was introduced to reflect.

8.3.2   Patients detained under civil law

As far as patients detained under part II and s. 136 are concerned, the issue is discharge of the authority to detain rather than discharge from hospital. Whether or not a person discharged from a section subsequently leaves hospital is not a legal concern, as on the discharge of a section the patient acquires informal status and the above considerations apply. The Memorandum (Department of Health and Welsh Office, 1998, para. 301) does require, though, that on discharge of a section it should be made clear to the patient that the authority to detain him or her no longer exists. Sackett (1996) found that release from one hospital, of persons detained under s. 3, within three months of admission stood at 36 per cent in 1985 but had risen to 60 per cent by 1994, whilst the number of s. 3 detentions renewed over the same period has fallen from 10 per cent to 5 per cent.

Authority to detain a patient held under part II will cease automatically if the period of detention expires without it being renewed: ss. 2(4), 4(4), 20(1). It seems to be increasingly less likely that a detention will simply be allowed to lapse (Sackett, 1996, p. 65). A 'section' may be ended at any time by the making in writing of an 'order for discharge' (s. 23(1)) by the RMO, hospital managers or NR: (23(2)(a)), and in addition, if the patient is detained in a mental nursing home, by the Secretary of State; and, if in NHS Trust, health authority (HA) or special health authority (SHA) facilities, or if in a mental nursing home by virtue of a contract between that home and a HA, then by that Trust, HA or SHA: s. 23(3). Any body or Trust given powers to make an order for discharge may delegate them to a committee or subcommittee of at least three members: s. 23(4). In reality it is by far most common to find that a section will be ended by the patient's RMO — 81 per cent in 1991, 76 per cent in 1994 in Sackett's survey — and that of those left most will lapse. Most of the remaining orders are made by hospital managers. It is rare that an order for discharge is initiated by an NR.

There are no criteria governing discharge to be found on the face of the MHA 1983. In consequence, it seems that it is lawful to detain a patient for the full duration of a period of detention even if the grounds for admission could no longer be made out, and similarly to discharge a patient when they can be. Jones (1999, p. 115) has suggested that the criteria should be those which apply to the renewal of a detention for treatment in s. 20(4) (see 8.2). The latest edition of the Code of Practice endorses Jones's suggestion (para. 23.11), and advises that hospital managers should appoint review panels to consider the case for discharge, and that this should be done more frequently than required under s. 20; and that in cases where continued detention is contested, the decision should be made by a multidisciplinary team (para. 23.13).

In *R v Riverside Mental Health Trust, ex parte Huzzey*, *The Times*, 18 May 1998 (HC) Latham J held that, when carrying out a review of a patient's detention, hospital managers should consider the factors in s. 3 (the relevant section in that case) but are not limited to them, and could also consider the contents of a report recently made by the RMO (under s. 25, dealt with below) stating that the patient is dangerous. On this authority the criteria for discharge under s. 23 seem to comprise, at the least, both those relevant to admission in the first place and that mentioned in s. 25. As mentioned earlier, the difference between the criteria in s. 3 and those in s. 20 is that in the latter there is a treatability requirement in respect of mental illness and severe mental impairment in s. 20 but not in s. 3, but the tone of the judgment in *Huzzey* is very much that the managers can consider any factors felt to be relevant, subject only to the limitations imposed by judicial review. This is also logical as the decision to discharge is the flip side of the decision to renew detention, rather than to admit to hospital in the first place, and so it is the s. 20 criteria which are *prima facie* most relevant. The same logic applies to decisions made by RMOs.

Each person or body empowered to make an order for discharge can act independently of the others (Department of Health and Welsh Office, 1999, para. 102). The only exception to this is that an order for discharge is not to be made by an NR unless 72 hours notice has been given to the hospital managers: s. 25(1). In *In the matter of Gary Kinsey* (1999) 21 June, unreported (HC) it was held that the notice had not been given to the hospital managers by a NR who handed a letter requesting the discharge of her son to the hospital receptionist, as to be effective notice must be given to an officer of the hospital appointed for this task. The reason for the 72 hour delay is to give the RMO time to object to the making of the order in the form of a report to the managers 'certifying that in the opinion of that officer the patient, if discharged, would be likely to act in a manner dangerous to other persons or to himself': s. 25(1). If this is done, the NR may not apply again for the discharge of the patient for six months from the date of the report: s. 25(1)(b). This is one of the rare occasions when the word 'dangerous' actually appears on the face of the Act. This in itself is interesting, given the problems in accurately identifying future dangerous behaviour (see 4.3), but the more pertinent point here is that the effect of s. 25(1) is that a patient can be discharged by an NR, in the face of opposition from the RMO or others involved in the treatment and detention of the patient, if the patient is *not* 'dangerous', *even if* he or she is mentally disordered to a degree which makes hospitalisation appropriate, and even if discharge poses a risk to that patient's health or safety. This was the situation in *Riverside*. In a judgment which also makes it clear that the hospital managers must not simply accept a s. 25 report as accurate, but rather have an active, quasi-judicial role, of accepting or rejecting the RMO's view (see also Department of Health and Welsh Office, 1999, para. 22.2.d), Latham J held that under s. 25 dangerousness is the sole issue. There may well be contradictory views in front of the hospital managers as s. 24 gives a medical practitioner, acting on behalf of an NR considering making an order under s. 23, a right of access in private to the patient, and to records relating to the detention and treatment of the patient. However, the odds are stacked in favour of the RMO, because the hospital managers are, presumably, only required to ensure that the RMO's opinion is reasonable, and not necessarily one with which they agree.

8.3.3 Discharge from hospital: the practice

All patients should be subject to the 'care programme approach' (see 9.3.3), and there is specific guidance relevant to the discharge plan of a patient who is to be made subject in discharge to the available powers of continued supervision in the community (see 9.5.3). In its general guidance, the Department of Health (1989) advises that 'planning [for discharge] should start at an early stage', and if it is known in advance that support will be required on the discharge of non-emergency patients, planning should start 'before admission' (para. 2). The aim of the planning process is to restore the patient to independence in the community to the fullest extent possible (para. 3), and should involve both the primary care team and social services departments, and others who may have a role to play in the continued care and support of the patient (para. 2), such as relatives and GPs. Paragraph 5 provides that '[p]atients should not be discharged until the doctors concerned have agreed and management is satisfied that everything reasonably practicable has been done to organise the care that patient will need in the community', and the patient or his or her relatives should be given written guidance on medication, lifestyle, early indicators of relapse and sources of help. Responsibility for overseeing the making of these arrangements should be allocated to a named member of staff (para. 6).

There is more to discharge, though, than logistics. It seems that in practice a rehearsal of the criteria for admission will structure the consideration of discharge, of both detained and informal patients. This will entail the diagnostic considerations (see Chapter two); the vulnerability question, in particular the risk of suicide (see 3.4) and the dangerousness question (see 4.3). All of this must be considered in the context of the circumstances of the particular patient and so, as with admission, factors such as the patient's willingness to continue to be treated as an out-patient and home circumstances, and the availability of suitable accommodation more generally, will impact significantly on each of these questions (Dell and Robertson, 1988). The various issues to be considered have been structured in the form of 'readiness for release' scales such as that devised by Eisner (1989) and Hogarty and Ulrich (1972). Further guidance was issued by the NHS Management Executive (1994b) as part of the initiative to standardise and formalise care in the community. This provides that patients should be discharged 'only when and if they are ready to leave hospital', bearing in mind the availability of out-patient services and the attitude of the patient towards them; and spells out the 'fundamental duty' which those considering discharge have both to protect the health, safety and welfare of the patient and other persons (para. 2).

There is no legal duty on the face of the Act. It has been suggested that there is a common law duty of care placed on those taking discharge decisions (*Holgate* v *Lancashire Mental Hospitals Board* [1937] 4 All ER 294), but more recent decisions do not share this view. The Court of Appeal held in *Clunis* v *Camden and Islington HA* [1998] 2 WLR 902 that a person who had killed a third party shortly after being discharged from hospital, and after failing to keep out-patient appointments with his doctor, had no cause of action for negligence against his health authority, both on the grounds that he should not be allowed to profit from his own wrong, and that to find the existence of a duty of care in such circumstances would be counter to public policy.

Similarly, in *Palmer* v *Tees HA and another*, *The Times*, 6 July 1999 (CA), in which a psychiatric out-patient had abducted, sexually abused and murdered a four-year-old girl, it was held that there was no cause for an action for negligence brought by the child's mother. Relying on the policy arguments, that to find the health authority liable would not prevent further incidents of this nature and would detract from their primary functions, and that to issue warnings concerning risk to the public would breach confidentiality; and on the decision of the House of Lords in *Hill* v *Chief Constable of West Yorkshire* [1989] AC 53, that in order to be liable for negligence based on the actions of a third party it must be shown that the victim belonged to a special class of persons at risk, which was judged not to be the case here, it was held that there was no duty of care in such a situation. This is a difficult issue: if there is to be liability in a situation such as that in *Clunis* or *Palmer*, one inevitable consequence would be an increased reluctance to discharge at least some patients who are in fact fit for discharge. Yet it is perhaps hard to justify why normal principles of negligence should not apply here. After all, under such principles health care and social service professionals are judged by no harsher a standard than that set by their peers (see further 12.5).

8.3.4 The discharge of part III patients

The powers of discharge in s. 23 apply to patients detained in hospital under s. 37 although subject to the modifications in sch. 1; part I, para. 8, MHA 1983 which disapplies the power of the NR to order discharge. For patients subject to s. 41 restrictions, sch. 1, part II, para. 7 provides similarly, and also adds the requirement to s. 23(1) that any order for discharge can only be made with the consent of the Secretary of State. The powers given to the Secretary of State provide an example of the limitation of medical power and clinical discretion concerning restricted patients, with its implicit message that the clinical gaze fails to note all factors relevant to the discharge of presumptively dangerous patients.

The Secretary of State usually prefers, rather than ordering the discharge of a restricted patient under s. 23, to use the more sophisticated powers available in s. 42 to discharge the patient absolutely or conditionally. But here, as under s. 23, there are no detailed criteria on the face of the Act by which to make that decision. A restriction order may be ended 'if the Secretary of State is satisfied that … a restriction order is no longer necessary for the protection of the public from serious harm': s. 42(1) (in which case the patient is treated as though on a s. 37 order from the date of the discharge of the restrictions by virtue of s. 41(5)), but this wording is nowhere more closely defined, and, according to Stuart Smith LJ in *R v Parole Board, ex parte Bradley* [1990] 3 All ER 828 at p. 836, cannot be elaborated with any degree of precision. There is even less guidance on discharge, which the Secretary of State may do by warrant 'if he thinks fit': s. 42(2). In practice, these decisions are taken by the Home Secretary in consultation with various bodies. Section 41(6) of the 1983 Act requires the RMO of a restricted patient to make yearly reports to the Home Secretary, which must contain 'such particulars as the Secretary of State may require'. The purpose of these reports is to prevent the unwarranted detention of restricted patients (Jones, 1999, p. 206). The Home Office has issued Guidance (Home Office, n.d.) which requires that reports contain information relating to patients' attitudes and motivations, the effects of treatment, and the chances of reoffending, and give reasoned advice on the need for continued detention, and whether detention need be in a special hospital.

The Home Secretary may also call upon the Aarvold Advisory Board on Restricted Patients (AAB), set up in 1973, following the recommendation of the Aarvold Committee (Home Office, 1973), in the wake of the release and reoffending of the mass poisoner, Graham Young. The AAB draws its membership from the great and the good of legal, forensic psychiatric, probation, social service and criminal justice circles. Its role is to advise the Home Secretary about restricted patients in respect of whom the risks to the public are particularly difficult to predict, or where the case is otherwise potentially controversial. Around 50 cases are referred to the AAB by the Home Secretary annually, which constitute around 15 to 20 per cent of all discharge and transfer recommendations (Eldergill, 1997, p. 166). The main concerns of the Home Secretary and the AAB are essentially the same as those which feature in the discharge of patients not subject to restrictions, although, as might be expected, with the emphasis on the degrees of risk to other persons that the patient, if released, might pose (Green and Baglioni Jr, 1997).

The AAB reports to the Home Secretary, and to an RMO if his or her recommendation is not agreed with, but not, until recently, to the patient. It has long been thought that a patient has no right of access to the recommendations of the AAB, as the decisions of that body are not open to judicial review, as was held in *R* v *Secretary of State for the Home Department, ex parte Powell* (1978, unreported). But in *R* v *Secretary of State for the Home Department, ex parte Harry* [1998] 3 All ER 360 (HC), in which a proposal for a patient's transfer had been made by a Mental Health Review Tribunal (see 8.4) to the Secretary of State, who in turn had consulted the AAB, it was held to be a breach of natural justice if the patient is not allowed an opportunity to make representations both to the AAB and, following its recommendation, to the Home Secretary. Accordingly, the Home Office has changed its practice, and in future patients will be entitled to make representations, and to be given a copy of the AAB's report to the Home Secretary, and of the Home Secretary's reasons for his or her decision. As Horne (1999) suggests, however, it is important not to overestimate the importance of this victory for patients. *Harry* was also the latest in a long line of cases to confirm the width of the discretion available to the Home Secretary, both to consult whomsoever he or she thinks fit before consenting to a discharge, and to give full weight to considerations of public safety when arriving at a decision.

In practice what happens is this. The AAB meets monthly (see Egglestone, 1990) to consider the cases assigned to it by the Home Secretary, which will in turn have been recommended for discharge by the patient's RMO. If the patient is in a special hospital it is unlikely that he or she will be discharged into the community. It is more common that the RMO will recommend that he or she be transferred into increasingly less secure accommodation — RSUs and then general NHS hospitals — before final discharge. The Secretary of State may direct the transfer of any patient subject to a hospital order or a transfer direction either between special hospitals (in respect of which the patient has no right to be consulted: *R* v *Secretary of State for the Home Department, ex parte Pickering* (1990, unreported) (CA)), or from a special hospital into less secure accommodation: s. 123, reg. 7, 1983 Regulations, SI 1983/893. In either case, a positive RMO recommendation will entail a member of the AAB visiting the patient. In addition, the Special Hospitals Authority (SHA), which processes the RMO's recommendation, may also add its opinion to the documentation forwarded to the Home Secretary, even though the member of the authority may never have seen the patient. Clearly, much of the decision making process in respect of the discharge of restricted patients from special hospitals into less secure forms of compulsory detention is still carried out 'in private and with few procedural safeguards' (Richardson, 1993, p. 287).

There are also practical problems facing patients seeking transfer out of a special hospital. A substantial number of patients do not require the level of security maintained (Gostin, 1986a; Home Office and Department of Health, 1992), yet despite the increase in RSU provision, RSUs are often unwilling to accept patients who require more than two years care, whether dangerous or not (Dolan and Shetty, 1995), giving priority to admissions from the prison system or from local hospitals (Gostin and Fennell, 1992, p. 211), so that even when transfer has been approved, alternative hospital accommodation has long been hard to find (Dell, 1980; Smith, Donovan and Gordon, 1991). The mean wait in one study carried out at Rampton in the early 1990s was 425 days, with individual cases ranging from 149 to 824 days, which also found that delay was in part attributable to lags in the process of initiating transfer (Dolan and Shetty, 1995). The situation does not seem to have improved, as the most recent MHAC *Report* still records 'inordinate delays at every step in arrangements for transfers' other than to prison or between wards within each hospital (MHAC, 1997, para. 4.5.4). This can mean that what started as a recommendation by the RMO for transfer becomes a recommendation for discharge by passage of time. According to Gostin and Fennell (1992, p. 211) '[i]t is not uncommon for a patient on a transfer list to have improved to the point that discharge is appropriate rather than transfer'. Clearly this situation is less than satisfactory. It remains to be seen what effect the promised reforms of 'deep end' hospital provision to be found in the White Paper on mental health (Department of Health, 1998a) will have on this situation.

If a decision to discharge is made, the question arises of whether conditions should be attached. This, like the decision to discharge, is a matter of discretion (unlike in the case of discharge by a tribunal: see 8.5), but this does not mean that there are no limitations to its exercise. In *Kynaston* v *Secretary of State for Home Affairs* (1981) 73 Cr App R 281 (CA) Lawton LJ held that the Home Secretary should direct the absolute discharge of a patient if satisfied that he or she was no longer suffering from mental disorder, but this is perhaps doubtful, as in the later Court of Appeal decision in *R* v *Merseyside Mental Health Review Tribunal, ex parte K* [1990] 1 All ER 694 (discussed further below see 8.5.2.3) it was held that a tribunal can give a conditional discharge to a patient not then suffering from mental disorder, and it would be strange if this power were not also available to the Home Secretary, given that his or her margin of discretion is wider than that of a tribunal (see below). The weight of academic opinion is to the effect that a patient who is not mentally disordered cannot be detained because Art. 5(1)(e) of the ECHR requires that no person may be detained in hospital unless of 'unsound mind' and the European Court of Human Rights in *Winterwerp* v *The Netherlands* 2 EHRR 387 held that any such diagnosis must be reliable and show that the disorder is of a degree warranting detention, and detention is justified only so long as the disorder persists.

A conditional discharge will usually require the patient to reside at a particular location, to attend for treatment (although there are no powers to treat without consent: s. 56(1)(c)), and to consent to the supervision of a social worker or probation officer, for a period of five years in a typical case, after which time if progress has been satisfactory the supervisor will recommend to the Home Secretary that the discharge be made absolute (Baxter, 1991). Conditional discharge, in the first instance, is the norm (ibid.): the Home Secretary understandably takes a cautious approach. Only 28 discharges were ordered by the Home Secretary in 1997, all of them conditional, compared with the 160 ordered by an MHRT (see 8.6) (Home Office Research and Statistics Directorate, 1998a, table 16). In addition, s. 42(3) empowers him or her to recall the patient to hospital at any time unless and until absolutely discharged, at which point the patient will 'cease to be liable to be detained': s. 42(2). There are no criteria for the application of s. 42(3) and here as elsewhere the courts have been reluctant to fetter the discretion of the Home Secretary to act on the basis of considerations of public safety. A conditionally discharged patient can be recalled to hospital even if not then mentally disordered: *R* v *Secretary of State for the Home Department, ex parte K* [1990] 3 All ER 562 (CA), and although there are dicta to be found in the first instance decision in that case that it would be unlawful for a patient to be recalled by the Home Secretary under s. 42(3) shortly after discharge by a tribunal if there had been no change in circumstances in the intervening period ([1990] 1 All ER 703 (HC)), it is unlikely as a result of the later decision in *R* v *South Western Hospital Managers and Another, ex parte M* [1994] 1 All ER 161 (HC), discussed at 8.7.2, that a decision to recall taken in good faith would be found to be unlawful by a court. It has also been held that a restriction order is not discharged by implication if the Home Secretary allows the conditions of discharge to lapse: *R* v *Secretary of State for the Home Department, ex parte Didlick* [1993] COD 412 (DC). Although an RMO has no powers of recall, the decision in *ex parte S* (see 6.3.2.2) means that, if the grounds can be made out, there is always the option of sectioning a patient under s. 3 as an alternative to formal recall under s. 42(3); and such a patient remains liable to recall under s. 42(3) even after discharge from detention under s. 3.

An audit of all recalls to Ashworth hospital over the period 1981-91 (Dolan, Coorey and Kulupana, 1993) found that the most common reasons for recall were problems with the provision of suitable community services, especially for persons with alcohol and sexual problems, reoffending by patients, and concerns about public safety. Offending rates by discharged restricted patients are relatively low. Of those 135 discharged in 1995, only nine had been convicted of a standard list offence two years later, and only one of those of a grave offence; of those 147 discharged in 1992, 20 had been convicted of a standard list offence five years later, with seven of these being grave offences (Home Office Research and Statistics Directorate, 1998a, table 17). Street (1998, Chapter 8) found that the grave offences covered a wide spectrum of mainly violent offences, although the numbers were very low (one for manslaughter, three for rape) of all patients discharged in the four years up to 1994. There is evidence to suggest that psychopathically disordered offenders are markedly more likely to reoffend, and for a longer period after discharge, than persons diagnosed as mentally ill, and that conditionally discharged patients are less likely to reoffend than those who are absolutely discharged (Bailey and MacCulloch, 1992), which helps explain why so few absolute discharges are made.

8.4   MENTAL HEALTH REVIEW TRIBUNALS: PRELIMINARIES AND PROCESS

Mental Health Review Tribunals (MHRTs) were introduced by the MHA 1959 for the purpose of providing a mechanism to review the legality of the detention of detained but not informal patients, as well as those subject to guardianship, and now also compulsory after care (see 9.5.2 and 9.5.3). They were devised by the Percy Commission as a replacement for judicial commitment, which was abolished by the 1959 Act. As the admission process was handed over to ASWs and doctors, MHRTs constituted the structural downgrading of legalism, from main player in the admission process to *ex post facto* watchdog. Despite this, MHRTs continue to have significant legal powers to discharge patients. In the context of the 1959 Act, MHRTs could be seen as an oasis of legalism in a sea of medical power. The 1983 Act extended the legal powers of MHRTs further, largely as a result of the decision of the European Court of Human Rights in *X* v *United Kingdom* (1981) 4 EHRR 181, in which it was held that the situation under the 1959 Act regarding the discharge of restricted patients, who could not apply to a tribunal for discharge and whose release was at the discretion of the Home Secretary, violated Art. 5(4), ECHR. Under the 1983 Act *all* detained patients have a right to have their continued detention in hospital reviewed at periodic intervals by an MHRT with the power, indeed, the duty, if the prescribed criteria are met, to discharge the patient.

8.4.1   Constitution and appointment

The basis of the powers of MHRTs is currently s. 65, together with sch. 2, MHA 1983, augmented by the Mental Health Review Tribunal Rules 1983 ('the 1983 Rules'), SI 1983 No. 942 (amended by SI 1996 No. 314 and SI 1998 No. 1189), made by the Lord Chancellor under s. 78. There must be an MHRT for every region of England, and one for Wales (s. 65(1A)), and it is the duty of the Secretary of State to determine the regions and to ensure that they cover the whole of England: s. 65(1B). A pool of MHRT members must be appointed by the Lord Chancellor, and in each region must include a number of 'legal members', 'medical members' and 'lay members' (as they have come to be known), defined as persons with 'experience in administration ... knowledge of social services or such other suitable qualifications and experience as the Lord Chancellor considers suitable': sch. 2, para. 1. On 31 December 1996 the total membership stood at 617, of which 232 were legal members, 182 medical members, and 203 lay members (Department of Health, 1997, para. 3.2). In each region, a legal member will be the 'chairman of the tribunals' (sch. 2, para. 3), and it is the responsibility of that person to appoint the members for each proceedings or set of proceedings for which an

MHRT must be constituted: r. 8(1), 1983 Rules. Each MHRT must consist of at least three members (s. 65(4)), with at least one legal, one medical and one lay member, and the legal member is to be the president of the tribunal so constituted: sch. 2, paras. 4, 6. In practice, it is rare for more than three members to be present at an MHRT hearing. If the application is by a restricted patient, the president of the tribunal must be selected by the chairman from a list approved by the Lord Chancellor, and such persons will be those with experience in the criminal courts: r. 8(3), 1983 Rules. Fifty of the 232 legal members deal solely with restricted patients. The vast majority are circuit judges, although there are a couple of recorders and QCs (Department of Health, 1997, Appendix 1). To prevent a possible conflict of interests, members or officers of the management of the hospital or mental nursing home at which the patient resides, members of the HA or Trust with powers to discharge the patient under s. 23, and anyone with 'a personal connection with the patient or [who] has recently treated the patient in a professional medical capacity' are ineligible from tribunal membership: r. 8(2), 1983 Rules.

8.4.2   Applications and referrals

The process of making a tribunal application can be complicated, confusing and intimidating to patients. Hospital managers are under a duty to 'take such steps as are practicable' to inform detained patients about their right to apply to an MHRT 'as soon as possible after the commencement of the patient's detention' (s. 132(1)(b), MHA 1983), and a similar duty applies in respect of the patient's NR and his or her rights to apply to a tribunal: s. 132(2). All information must be given both orally and in writing: s. 132(3). The Code of Practice additionally requires that patients wishing to apply to MHRTs be 'given all the necessary assistance to progress with such an application' (Department of Health and Welsh Office, 1999, para. 22.17), including being told about the right to legal representation (see further below, 8.4.3) and how to obtain it. A member of staff, usually known as the Mental Health Act Administrator, should be designated by the managers as responsible for ensuring that patients are given this advice and assistance (para. 14.13.c).

8.4.2.1   Applications   When a patient is liable to be detained (except under the short term civil provisions in ss. 5, 135 and 136, or under a remand order or interim hospital order made by a court: ss. 35, 36, 38), the patient and/or the patient's NR have a right to test the grounds for the continued (liability to) detention by applying to an MHRT under s. 66. Basically, a fresh application may be made by the patient whenever a significant decision relating to the detention is made. An application must be made within the 'relevant period' (s. 66(1)), which varies according to the event triggering the right to apply. On occasion both the patient and his or her NR have a right to apply, but each can only make one application within each relevant period (s. 77(2)), and there can be no application except in accordance with the following provisions: s. 77(1). The detail of entitlement to make an application is as follows.

8.4.2.1.1 Patients not subject to restrictions The patient alone may make an application:

(a)   within 14 days of admission for assessment: s. 66(1)(a),(2)(a);
(b)   within 6 months of admission for treatment: s. 66(1)(b),(2)(b);
(c)   within 6 months of transfer from guardianship to hospital: s. 66(1)(e),(2)(e);
(d)   within the period of renewal (which will be 6 months in the first instance, 12 months thereafter: s. 20(2)(a),(b)) of the authority to detain: s. 66(1)(f),(2)(f).

The patient or (but not and: s. 66(1) (i)) the NR (provided that the NR was or was entitled to be informed of the report) may make an application:

(a)   within 28 days of a report reclassifying the patient's disorder being furnished under s. 16: s. 66(1)(d),(2)(d).

The NR alone (s. 66(1)(ii)), may make an application:

(a)   within 28 days of a report being furnished by the patient's RMO under s. 25 blocking discharge by the NR of a patient admitted for treatment: s. 66(1)(g),(2)(d);
(b)   within 12 months (and again in any subsequent period of 12 months during which the order continues in force) of an order made under s. 29 replacing the NR with an acting NR, whether made before or after the patient's admission: s. 66(1)(h),(2)(g).

Section 66 applies to patients placed under a hospital order by a court in much the same way (s. 40(4)), although with two modifications. First, there can be no application in the first six months of hospitalisation, but such a patient may apply within the second six month period of the order and thereafter annually. Secondly, an NR may make an application where there has been a report made under s. 16 reclassifying the patient but not otherwise in the first six months: s. 66(1)(f),(d), sch. 1, part I, paras. 2, 9, MHA 1983. An NR may, however, apply in the second six months and thereafter annually if the hospital order is renewed: s. 69(1)(a). If a person is treated by operation of s. 41(5) as being subject to a hospital order because a restriction order ceases to have effect, he or she may, however, apply within the first six months from the date on which the restriction order ceases to have effect: s. 69(2)(a). This is understandable because in the vast majority of cases s. 41(5) is triggered by the Home Secretary using his or her powers under s. 42(1) to end a restriction order, which is a good indication that the patient is no longer considered to constitute a serious risk to other persons. Also, as such patients will by definition have been in hospital for a considerable period of time, there is no reason why they should have to wait six months before making an application.

8.4.2.1.2 Patients subject to restrictions There is a different regime for restricted patients, defined by s. 79(1)(b) as including those subject to a restriction order, limitation direction or a restriction direction, as well as patients held under s. 5(1), Criminal Insanity (Procedure) Act 1964 or ss. 6 or 14(1) of the Criminal Appeals Act 1968 (who will be detained by reason of being unfit to plead or on acquittal on the grounds of insanity: see 6.3.2.3, 6.4). Section 70, MHA 1983 provides that a restricted patient as defined in s. 79 may apply to an MHRT, first, between six and twelve months into their detention (s. 70(a)), and thereafter in any subsequent twelve-month period: s. 70(b). However, s. 70 must be read together with s. 69(2)(a), which provides that a person held under s. 5(1) of the 1964 Act, or by virtue of a transfer direction, with or without restrictions, or by a hospital direction, with or without an accompanying limitation direction, may apply within the first six months beginning on the date that the order under that Act was made. The reason for this is that a person held under the 1964 Act can on discharge expect to face the criminal charges that were pending when the order was made, whilst the Home Secretary has the option, in the case of a person transferred from prison to hospital or subject to a hospital direction, to transfer that person (back) to prison if hospital treatment is no longer required: s. 50. Not all restricted patients will be in hospital, as a percentage will have been conditionally discharged. Patients in this category remain liable to recall until absolutely discharged, and consequently may apply to a tribunal once in the second twelve months following discharge, and thereafter, biennially: s. 75(2). If recalled to hospital following conditional discharge, the situation is as if a new order has been made and so s. 70 applies (s. 75(1)(b)), although the Home Secretary must refer such cases to a tribunal within one month (see 8.4.2.2).

8.4.2.2 Referrals The procedure for making an application to an MHRT is patient led, and not all patients, whether because of cynicism, fear, apathy, or disorder, will activate it. To ensure that all detained patients are subject to an independent review of the grounds for detention, the 1983 Act requires hospital managers, or the Home Secretary, according to the circumstances, to refer cases to an MHRT. It also gives the Secretary of State a wide discretionary power to make referrals.

Hospital managers must refer the case of a patient admitted under s. 3 or transferred to hospital from guardianship if the patient does not make an application, or makes but subsequently withdraws an application (s. 68(5)), and the patient's case will not otherwise come before an MHRT, by reason of an application made by the patient's NR or a referral by the Secretary of State under s. 67 (see below). This must be done, first, at the expiry of the first period in which an application could be made (that is, six months: s. 68(1)), and thereafter every three years, unless the patient is under 16 years of age, when the period is one year: s. 68(2). In addition to the powers of hospital managers, which do not extend to hospital order patients, the Secretary of State has discretionary powers 'if he thinks fit, at any time' to refer the case of any patient detained under Part II, or under a hospital order without restrictions made by a court, to an MHRT: s. 67(1), sch. 1, Part I, para. 1.

The Secretary of State also has discretionary powers to refer 'at any time' the case of patients subject to restrictions (s. 71(1)), whether actually 'detained' or not: s. 71(4). Detained restricted patients (rather than those 'liable to be detained', which would include conditionally discharged patients and those on leave of absence) whose case has not been considered by a tribunal for three years *must* be referred: s. 71(2). The Home Secretary is also under a duty to refer the case of a patient treated as though subject to a hospital order and restriction order under s. 5(1) of the Criminal Procedure (Insanity) Act 1964 who does not take the opportunity to apply under s. 66, once six months have passed since the order under the 1964 Act was made: s. 71(5), 1983 Act. If a conditionally discharged restricted patient is recalled to hospital by the Secretary of State, he or she must also refer that patient's case to a tribunal within one month (s. 75(1)(a)) so that the recall decision can be scrutinised by a tribunal in accordance with specific criteria, as a safeguard against the possible abuse of power by the Secretary of State, who, as seen above (8.3.4) may recall a patient on the basis of other than medical evidence. This, as Hoggett (1996, p. 180) notes 'is the answer to the precise problem raised by the case of *X* v *United Kingdom*'.

Although the general scheme of this process, as evidenced by s. 77(2), is that there should only be one application per patient per relevant period, the situation can arise when an application and a referral, or two applications, both fall due to be heard at the same time or in close succession. For example, hospital managers must refer the case of a s. 3 patient at the end of the first six month period of detention if the patient has not made an application during that period, even if the patient does decide to apply on the occasion of the authority for detention being renewed. Because of delays between application and hearing (see 8.4.4), or because both the patient and his or her NR have exercised a right to make an application, a situation may arise whereby two applications are pending. It is possible for an MHRT to conjoin two applications and hear them together (r. 18(1), 1983 Rules), although both applicants (if there are more than one) have full rights to be provided with documentation, representation, and so on: r. 18(2). Another option if there are two applications, or an application and a mandatory reference, pending, is to withdraw an application. An application may be withdrawn at any time by the patient in writing with the agreement of the tribunal (or the regional chairman), and will be deemed withdrawn if the patient is discharged before the hearing: r. 19(1), (2), 1983 Rules. If an application is effectively withdrawn another application may be made within the relevant period: s. 77(2). This allows the patient to 'bank' one application for use later in the same relevant period. In other circumstances it may be that the withdrawal of an application triggers the duty of the hospital managers or the Home Secretary to make a referral, which cannot be withdrawn. The permutations and possibilities open means that there is a tactical aspect to the timing of an application from a purely technical view, in order to ensure that maximum use is made of the tribunal system (Gostin and Fennell, 1992, p. 77).

8.4.3   Before the hearing

Rule 3(1), 1983 Rules requires that applications to tribunals must be in writing, and 'wherever possible' include the patient's name, address (home and hospital), section under which he or she is currently liable to be detained, whether on leave of absence or not, and any other relevant information. If the application is to be made by the patient's NR, his or her details must also be included: r. 3(2). The application must be signed by the applicant or 'any person authorised by him to do so on his behalf', who may be the member of staff designated to provide assistance, for example. The application must also include information about the applicant's intentions regarding representation. An applicant may represent him or herself (r. 3(2)(e)), or may authorise 'any person' to provide representation, except another patient who is liable to be detained (which includes patients on leave or conditionally discharged but not informal in-patients) or is subject to guardianship or after care under supervision: s. 78(2)(f), r. 10(1). If a patient does intend to be represented and the name and address of the authorised representative (AR) is known at the time of making the application, that information should be included (r. 3(2)(e)), and in any case an AR should on appointment notify the tribunal of his or her name and address: r. 10(2). If the patient makes no appointment, the tribunal has discretionary default powers to do so on his or her behalf: r. 10(3). The tribunal's powers under r. 10, and other rules dealing with preliminary and incidental matters (rr. 6, 7, 8, 12, 13, 14(1), 15, 17, 19, 20, 26 and 28) may be exercised by the chairman of the tribunal alone (r. 5), or by his or her deputy: s. 78(6) and sch. 2, para. 4, MHA 1983.

Most applicants appoint a lawyer as AR (Eldergill, 1997, p. 875). The Law Society has established the Mental Health Review Tribunal Panel which admits solicitors, solicitors' clerks and members of the Institute of Legal Executives (ILEX) on satisfactory completion of (it must be said, fairly minimal) training and practice in, and observation of, MHRT work. Both patients and NRs are entitled to advice and assistance under the 'Green Form' scheme, which is means tested, but since 1982 legal representation at an MHRT, as well as advice and assistance, has qualified for non-means tested Assistance by way of Representation (ABWOR) with the agreement of the Legal Aid Board (part III, Legal Aid Act 1988; part III Legal Advice and Assistance Regulations 1989, SI 1989 No. 340, SI 1994 No. 805). Agreement usually takes about a week, but can be done by telephone in emergency situations. Agreement can be refused if it is unreasonable in all the circumstances to grant legal aid. As only a relatively small percentage of all patients, and very few restricted patients, are discharged by a tribunal, a strict interpretation of the Regulations could see legal aid frequently being refused, and there are reports that this has happened in the past (Peay, 1989, p. 47), although it seems that legal aid is only routinely denied on financial grounds. Once appointed, an AR has the same entitlements as the patient to be supplied by the tribunal with 'all notices and documents' relevant to the application: r. 10(4), 1983 Rules.

The notification of an intention to make an application triggers the duty of the tribunal to contact the managers of the hospital at which the patient is liable to be detained (r. 2(1)(a)), the Secretary of State if the patient is subject to restrictions (r. 4(1)), and 'other persons interested': r. 7. This in turn triggers the duty of hospital managers to provide detailed and wide-ranging information about the patient (r. 6(1)(a), sch. part A), and to commission new medical and social work reports on the patient: r. (6)(1)(a), (b), sch. part B, para. 1. This must be done 'as soon as practicable', but in any case no more than three weeks after receipt by them of the notification of the patient's application. If the patient is subject to restrictions, the Secretary of State, subject to the same time limits as hospital managers, must send a 'statement of further information relevant to the application as may be available to him' (r. 6(2)), unless the patient has already been conditionally discharged (and will thus be seeking an absolute discharge under s. 75: see, 8.4.2.1.2), in which case the Secretary of State must, within six weeks, provide the information listed in sch., part C, which is similar to that in part A, although tailored to the fact that the patient is not in hospital, and so requests information, for example, about treatment provision or supervision by a probation officer or social worker rather than by an RMO: r. 6(3)(a). Medical and social work reports should be provided by the Secretary of State (sch., part D), but again only if it is 'reasonably practicable' to do so: r. 6(3)(b). Such reports are in fact routinely provided, particularly if the Secretary of State is opposed to discharge.

A copy of all this documentation must be forwarded to the patient or his or her AR (rr. 6(5), 10(4)), unless r. 6(4) applies. This allows a tribunal to withhold documents from the applicant, but only if 'disclosure would adversely effect the health or welfare of the patient or others'. The supplier to the tribunal of the documentation in question must state the grounds on which they rely, and it is then the duty of the tribunal to consider, applying the same 'adverse effect' test, whether the grounds are valid, and if it decides that they are, it must withhold the document in question and record the reasons for that decision: r. 12(2). The scope of the test in rr. 6(4) and 12(2) is nowhere closely defined. There is agreement amongst academic writers that it does not extend to protect damage to the therapeutic relationship (see Jones, 1999, p. 526, Hoggett, 1996, p. 189). But other boundaries are less clear: how great must the *risk* of adverse effects be? The word used is 'would' not 'might' which seems to indicate that there must be adjudged to be a fairly high degree of risk. A second issue is: how adverse must any effect of disclosure be? There is no modifier, so presumably *any* adverse consequence will suffice. If so, this is questionable in policy terms. Gostin and Fennell (1992, p. 122) suggest that all information should be disclosed to the patient unless there are 'clear and specific' reasons for non-disclosure. For some, the present authors included, it is arguable that even this does not go far enough. The right to know information relevant to a judicial decision concerning oneself is a requirement of natural justice, and it is hard to see how there can ever be a justification for non-disclosure, particularly to protect the welfare of others. Rules 6(4) and 12(2) were made in accordance with s. 78(2)(h), which provides that rules may be made allowing non-disclosure if considered to be 'undesirable in the interests of the patient or for other special reasons'. Although the words of the statute still of course have the force of law, the fact is that Rules do *not* allow non-disclosure for 'special reasons' (the phrase in s. 78(2)(h) was initially repeated in the Rules until the 1996 amendments) and as things stand at present, therefore, such should not form part of the reasoning of any decision whether or not to disclose. Whether or not this is the case in practice is difficult to discern. Eldergill (1997, p. 705) suggests that in so far as the Rules provide for non-disclosure in situations where that amounts to a denial of justice, provided that disclosure would have the effect on health or welfare required by rr. 6(4) and 12(2), when s. 78(2)(h) uses the broader concept of interests, such as the interest in being treated justly, or in being discharged, it may be that the rules are *ultra vires* as an unlawful fettering of discretion. The case has yet to be tested in a court but the argument is a strong one. Part of the problem with policing this power, however, is that these decisions may be taken in private, possibly by one individual: r. 5.

When there has been a decision not to disclose information to the patient, the status of the AR may prove crucial. By r. 12(3), if the patient has appointed as AR a barrister, solicitor, doctor or other 'suitable person by virtue of his experience or professional qualification', the information in question 'shall' be disclosed to the AR, as long as he or she undertakes not to disclose the information to the patient. This allows an AR access to the full information to ensure that the patient's case is heard and decided fairly and lawfully; and to argue an informed case for disclosure to the patient where a tribunal is 'minded not to disclose any document' to the patient. This is a pragmatic solution to a moral problem, but can place an AR in an impossible position *vis-à-vis* the patient (see further 12.2.1). In practice an AR will only rarely face this type of ethical dilemma as, after initial resistance to disclosure of medical reports, particularly from special hospital RMOs (Peay, 1989, p. 66), it is now rarely the case that all documents are not disclosed to patients, which provides further reason why the Rules should be amended.

An MHRT will not receive information solely from those exercising the authority to detain the patient. The patient is entitled under s. 76 to seek his or her own independent medical report. The purpose of such a report is to provide the patient with advice on whether to make an application to an MHRT, but of course if the report advises the making of an application the patient will want to present it to the tribunal. A doctor 'authorised by or on behalf of a patient' must be given access to the patient in private and may examine records relating to detention and treatment. Although a patient may be denied access to information under rr.6(4) and 12(2), he or she cannot prevent the disclosure of an unfavourable report that he or she has commissioned, if there is sufficient public interest to justify its disclosure (*W* v *Edgell and others* [1990] 1 All ER 835 (CA)), which means that a report that shows, for example, that a patient is more dangerous than thought to be by the RMO or hospital managers can, as in *Edgell*, be disclosed by the person making it.

Finally, information is also generated by the medical member of the MHRT. Rule 11, 1983 Rules requires the medical member, before the tribunal hearing takes place, to 'examine the patient and take such other steps as he considers necessary to form an opinion of the patient's mental condition'. For this purpose the medical member has rights of access to the patient and his or her records, similar to that of doctors authorised by the patient under s. 76. If the patient refuses to be examined a hearing can be postponed (r. 16(1)) or be deemed withdrawn: r. 19(2). The issue of due process is also to the fore here, as r. 11 casts the medical member as both 'witness' and 'decision-maker'. According to the Department of Health (1997, Appendix 13) the medical member should not give his or her opinion to the other members of the tribunal before the hearing, but the risk with this approach is that it is not then heard by the other tribunal members until *after* the hearing, with the applicant neither knowing about it nor having an opportunity to see it. In *R v Mental Health Review Tribunal, ex parte Clatworthy* [1985] 3 All ER 699 (HC) Mann J held (at p. 704) that it would be a breach of natural justice for a tribunal to reach a decision based on the opinion of the applicant's condition that the medical member had formed, without that reasoning being made available to the applicant. This does not necessarily mean that the medical member's findings should be made available as evidence and therefore subject to cross-examination. As Gunn (1986c, p. 251) has pointed out, Mann J referred to a tribunal resting its decision on the *opinion* of the medical member. Gunn suggests that this is to blur the opinion/evidence distinction, and it may be that it is only *facts* known to the medical member, rather than his or her opinions, which must be disclosed to the applicant. The point remains unclear.

8.4.4   Haste and delay in the application process

A truncated procedure applies in the case of applications or references by or in respect of patients detained under s. 2. As with other applications there must be a written, signed application containing the information discussed above (r. 30), but on receipt of an application the tribunal must fix the date of the hearing at not later than seven days after the application was received and give notice of the date, time and location of the hearing to all those involved and who in the opinion of the tribunal should have an opportunity to be heard: r. 31. The responsible authority, as soon as it learns that there is to be an application, must supply copies of the admission papers and such information, detailed in sch. parts A and B (see 8.4.3), as can reasonably be provided in the time available: r. 32. Documents can be withheld from the patient as in non s. 2 applications: r. 32(2). According to the Annual Report for 1991 (Department of Health, 1992, para. 6) adherence to this timetable can mean hurriedly prepared reports being made available to tribunal members in insufficient time to allow their contents to be digested. Indeed, in Milne and Milne's research into the operation of the MHRT system as it affected one northern hospital in 1988-92, all medical and social work reports bar one were submitted to the tribunal on the day of the hearing (1995, p. 95). It is unlikely that the situation has improved in the intervening years. The 1997 Annual Report (Department of Health, 1997) details a service in crisis. One main reason for this is the exponential increase in the rate of applications to tribunals over recent years. For all categories of patients, 1986 saw 5046 applications, by 1996 this had increased to 14,913. Applications by patients detained under s. 2 increased from 1503 to 4145 in the same period (1997, Appendix 3). There is a considerable falling off of applications — in 1996 only 49 per cent of all applications actually resulted in a hearing, although the rate had been higher at between 54 and 60 per cent over the previous decade (1997, Appendix 5), either because the patient is discharged before the hearing by the RMO or because the application is withdrawn for some other reason (see below) — but this is less of a feature in s. 2 cases than in other non-restricted cases, 58 per cent of which (2629 cases) proceeded to a hearing. This is no doubt a function of the seven day time scale which must be adhered to in these cases, as there is less time for the situation to change once an application has been made.

If haste is the problem with s. 2 applications, for other categories of patient it is delay. Although there is some regional variation, of the 951 non-restricted patients, excluding those detained under s. 2 or in special hospitals, who had applied to a tribunal in the last quarter of 1996, only 334 (35 per cent) waited less than eight weeks for a hearing; 411 (43 per cent) waited between 9 and 12 weeks and 206 (22 per cent) waited more than 12. Of the 46 applications by non-restricted patients detained in special hospitals, over half — 25 (54 per cent) — waited more than 12 weeks and only 1 (2 per cent) had to wait less than eight weeks. For restricted patients, particularly those held in special hospitals, the situation is even worse, with 87 (63 per cent) of the 137 special hospital applicants having to wait over 20 weeks (Department of Health, 1997, Appendix 9). These figures show a trend towards increased waiting times over previous years, as 'ever increasing applications for tribunal hearings has made it impossible to maintain the previous output rate for holding cases within the agreed deadlines' (1997, para. 7.1).

Applications by patients other than those detained under s. 2 have increased markedly over the past decade. Applications by restricted patients have increased, although relatively slowly, from 1134 in 1986 to 1752 in 1996. By contrast there were 2409 applications by non-restricted patients in 1986, rising to 9016 in 1996 (1997, Appendix 3); almost a fourfold increase. One reason for this rapid increase is the rise in the absolute number of formal admissions (from 14,780 in 1986 to 24,191 in 1996-7 (1998d, table 1); which itself reflects the shift in focus from chronic to acute care over this period. Another reason is the knock-on effects of the mandatory seven day timetable for s. 2 applications, causing other applications to be delayed (Wood, 1997, p. iii). A third cluster of reasons is concerned with the collation and distribution of paperwork and other preliminaries required by s. 78 and the 1983 Regulations. As well as complying with the procedures outlined above, an MHRT has a general discretion to give 'directions as it thinks fit to ensure the speedy and just determination of the application' (r. 13), and this power can be delegated to the chair of the tribunal or his or her deputy: r. 5. In practice it is the responsibility of the MHRT Secretariat, which operates out of offices in London, Nottingham, Liverpool and Cardiff, to set up hearings (which involves coordinating all the various witnesses, their legal representatives, as well as tribunal members and support staff), ensure that all necessary documents have been submitted and circulated, provide from its staff clerks for hearings, and generally ensure the smooth running of tribunals, as well as providing the administration of the MHRT regime more generally (Department of Health 1997, para. 3.6).

The Annual Reports of the MHRT regime are replete with attempts of the 15 or so staff in each of the five MHRT regions in England and Wales to cope with the massive workload that the increased number of applications has imposed on them. According to the report of the Cardiff office, the main reasons for delay are 'the patient either going awol or their solicitor requesting a postponement in order to obtain an independent medical report' (Department of Health 1997, para. 4.28). The latter of these reasons was also identified by Blumenthal and Wessely (1994). One long-standing problem, which the report of the Liverpool office specifically refers to as exacerbating the problem of delay, 'is the additional time and effort employed in pursuing overdue reports', which are often faxed to the secretariat office in the days immediately preceding the hearing date (Department of Health, 1997, para. 4.14). Blumenthal and Wessely found that it was the complexity of the process which explained most delays, although Milne and Milne (1995, p. 98) suggest that the main causal factor explaining delay in the process from application to hearing, given that the longest period within the process tends to be *after* the necessary reports have been submitted to the secretariat, is with the secretariats themselves. Another view would be that this is uncomfortably close to scapegoating the various secretariats, who are clearly understaffed. One delaying factor in restricted cases, for example, which is independent of the procuring of all necessary reports, is the limited availability of circuit judges to hear such applications, who must juggle the demands made on them by the tribunal system with the demands of the Crown Court system. MHRT secretariat staff may have little influence in the face of what are perceived to be more pressing concerns on the time of legal members. This is not to deny, however, that under resourcing *per se* is a substantial problem. In a number of MHRT areas, 1996 saw hearings proceed unclerked for the first time, as there are simply not enough secretariat staff to go around. This is unfortunate as there is evidence that tribunal clerks, as well as their other duties, are a source of valuable reassurance to patients waiting for an MHRT hearing to commence (Peay, 1989. p. 42). There is a clear and urgent need for substantially increased resources to be put into the operation of the tribunal system if the issue of delay is to be tackled effectively and the general quality of the service to patients is not to be significantly compromised. This is not a novel observation, having been made by the MHAC as long ago as its Report for 1985-87 (MHAC, 1987, para. 18.13). On present evidence, though, the indications are that the situation is set to worsen.

There is no mechanism in the Act or Rules whereby a patient can challenge the legality of such delays. It may be possible to seek judicial review on the grounds of unreasonableness or, more likely, that justice delayed is justice denied, according to the rules of natural justice that are applied on a judicial review application. However, to date applications for judicial review have been headed off by the rather disingenuous and ethically suspect method of allowing the patient in question to jump the queue (see Eldergill, 1997, p. 787), or have fallen away because the patient has been discharged (as in *Roux* v *UK* [1997] EHRLR 102). The other option open to an aggrieved patient is to challenge the legality of their detention by reference to Art. 5(4) ECHR, which gives any detainee the right to have the lawfulness of his or her detention 'decided speedily by a court'. In a friendly settlement agreed before the European Commission of Human Rights in *Barclay-Maguire* v *United Kingdom* December 1981, App. No 91/7/80 (discussed in Gostin, 1982), the UK government suggested 13 weeks as a reasonable maximum waiting time for MHRT applicants. Yet this time scale has been routinely exceeded particularly in the case of special hospital patients, a majority of whom in 1996, as in previous years, have had to wait more then 20 weeks for a hearing (see above). It is likely that this level of delay does constitute a breach of human rights. In 1990 the European Court of Human Rights held that a five month delay was 'excessive': *Van der Leer* v *The Netherlands* (1990) 12 EHRR 567. In September 1996 the Commission declared admissible the case of *Roux*, on the basis, *inter alia* of a six month delay between application and hearing, and in *Pauline Lines* v *UK* [1997] EHRLR 297 the Commission declared admissible the factually complicated case of L, a conditionally discharged restricted patient, who after discharge had been admitted under s. 3 six months before being recalled by the Home Secretary under s. 42(3) and referred to an MHRT, which heard the application seven months after L's admission under s. 3. In a friendly settlement which followed, L was paid £2,000 compensation, and the UK government undertook to amend the 1983 Rules to ensure that no recalled patient waited more than two months after recall for a tribunal hearing. Whilst this is welcome, the friendly settlement reached in 1981 in *Barclay-Maguire* has been more honoured in the breach than the observance. This is, of course, one of many issues that may be affected by the coming into force of the Human Rights Act 1998.

On the other hand, and whatever the Rules might say, without a commitment in the form of resources, or some reform of the system, real change is unlikely. Reforms that have been suggested include relaxing the requirement that all cases involving restricted patients must be heard by a judicial member (Eldergill, 1997, p. 786), or the introduction of a new intermediary section 'between' ss. 2 and 3 authorising detention for around six to eight weeks, which, it has been suggested, would reduce the pressure caused by the increase of time limited applications under s. 2, which should be retained only for patients on their first admission to hospital (Wood, 1997, p. iii). Although many s. 2 patients are not discharged by a tribunal, often on the grounds that insight into their condition has not returned and so cooperation with the RMO unless detained is unlikely, 'some tribunals discharge up to 40 per cent of [s. 2] patients' (Eldergill, 1997, p. 787), and so there must therefore be concerns about any measure which will reduce the availability of an early tribunal hearing to these patients, the relaxation of the rules concerning legal members is a suggestion worthy of serious consideration.

It may well be that delay in the process is a factor in explaining the surprisingly high number of applications that do not result in a hearing, with patients withdrawing applications in frustration (Milne and Milne, 1995, p. 98). Other patients might withdraw applications because of other events, such as a setback in their mental condition (Peay, 1989, p. 53). In addition, the fact that the system is logjammed means that applications made towards the end of a calendar year are unlikely to be heard by a tribunal in that year, which would also account for some of the shortfall. But the main reason is no doubt that patients are discharged by RMOs before an MHRT hearing can be scheduled. Eldergill (1997, p. 206) estimates that this explains 'almost all' of the fall off of s. 2 cases and 'about half' of it in other non-restricted cases. In restricted cases, for obvious reasons, a majority of applications do result in a hearing: 64 per cent in 1996, although the rate had been higher at 75-88 per cent over the previous decade (Department of Health, 1997, Appendix 5).

8.4.5   At the hearing

Neither the Act nor the Rules prescribe any formal procedural requirements for the conduct of tribunal hearings, except that the last word must be given to the applicant (or the patient, if not the applicant) if he or she wishes it: r. 22(5). This apart, each MHRT may conduct its own hearings as it sees fit, bearing in mind the health and interests of the patient and the desirability of minimal formality: r. 22(1). Tribunals may hear evidence which would not be disclosable in court proceedings, such as hearsay evidence (r. 14(2)), and will ordinarily sit in private (in a committee room in the hospital in question) unless the patient requests a public hearing and the tribunal is satisfied that to do so would not infringe the interests of the patient: rr. 21(1), 22(2). Although the patient may be accompanied by his or her AR and 'such other person or persons as he wishes' (r. 10(6)), a tribunal sitting in private has discretion as to who may be given access (r. 22(3)), and may exclude a person from any part of the hearing if information disclosable under r. 12(3) is to be discussed: r. 22(4). A tribunal must record its reasons for each of these decisions.

Other parties to the hearing will include the hospital managers and, in the case of a restricted patient, the Home Secretary. A failure to notify the Home Secretary is a breach of natural justice which will vitiate the hearing: *Secretary of State for the Home Department* v *Oxford Regional Mental Health Review Tribunal and another* [1987] 3 All ER 8 per Lord Bridge at p. 10. The Home Secretary will not usually be represented by counsel, but may well be in complicated or controversial cases, for example where the Home Secretary and the patient's RMO disagree about whether the patient should be discharged (Eldergill, 1997, p. 164). Richardson (1993, p. 288) has pointed out that in cases where the Home Secretary supplies only affidavit evidence, it will not be possible for that evidence to be cross-examined by the applicant. The evidence for discharge will, of course, always be cross-examined, if only by the MHRT members: r. 22(2).

The lack of a prescribed procedure results in 'stark differences ... in the format of hearings' (Peay, 1989, p. 95). Peay found that some tribunals would hear evidence from the patient, then cross-examination of that evidence by tribunal members and RMOs (if the RMO was opposed to discharge), followed by the case against discharge. Others did not provide RMOs with the same opportunities to cross-examine, others still heard the RMOs' evidence at a much earlier stage. The point here is not that 'justice by geography' *per se* is a bad thing; it is also that the order of proceedings can influence the weight given to the various elements of evidence that are presented, and so the chances of discharge. At the risk of undermining the policy that tribunals should be relatively informal affairs, there is a good argument to be made that tribunals should be required to follow what Peay calls 'standard criminal-court procedure' (1989, p. 95). It is easy for 'informality' to descend into a denial of the due process rights which have been devised as the best way in which to protect the interests of defendants in criminal trials; and MHRT applicants should be in at least as good a position as criminal defendants. An example of the dangers of informality is provided by *R v Mental Health Review Tribunal, ex parte Kelly* (1997) 22 April, unreported (HC). In this case a conditionally discharged restricted patient had been recalled to hospital by the Home Secretary under s. 42(3) following his arrest on allegations of criminal damage and assault. His case was referred to a tribunal under s. 75(1), but the tribunal declined to order discharge, pointing to the alleged criminal behaviour. On an application for judicial review the tribunal's decision was quashed as being in breach of the rules of natural justice, as it was found that the tribunal had proceeded on the basis that the patient had committed the criminal offences alleged against him, and had not cross-examined that evidence.

8.5   SUBSTANTIVE POWERS OF DISCHARGE

The substantive powers of MHRTs are found in ss. 72-75, MHA 1983. Section 72 applies to all patients, other than those subject to restrictions, dealt with by ss. 73-75. On hearing an application for discharge from a non-restricted patient, an MHRT has various options open to it. For most patients, an order for discharge is naturally the hoped for outcome. Discharge can be immediate or deferred to a future specified date: s. 72(3) and s. 73(7) (which applies only to the conditional discharge of restricted patients). A discharge will be deferred if there is a need to make arrangements for some form of care in the community or suitable accommodation. The Act places no limit on the length of time for which a discharge may be deferred. Gostin (1986b and supplements, para. 18.09), surely correctly, argues that it is not open to a tribunal to specify a date after the expiry of the authority to detain. It is not lawful to defer discharge in order to give time to consider whether there is any other lawful basis for the patient's continued detention: *Perkins v Bath District Health Authority* (1989) 4 BMLR 145 (CA).

If a tribunal decides not to discharge an unrestricted patient, it may recommend that he or she be transferred or given leave of absence (s. 72(3)), or that the patient's RMO consider making a supervision application (for the supervised discharge of the patient into the community (see 9.5.3)) in respect of the patient: s. 72(3A). If a recommendation is not taken up within a period specified by the tribunal the case will go back for further consideration, at which point the tribunal may discharge the patient: r. 24(4), 1983 Rules and *Mental Health Review Tribunal v John Hempstock* [1997] COD 443 (HC). The power to make recommendations can therefore be a powerful lever over the care of undischarged patients. An MHRT may also direct that a patient's disorder be reclassified: s. 72(5).

There is no power to make recommendations in respect of restricted patients. Richardson (1993) argues that this means that tribunals are of much less relevance to such patients, who are ordinarily held in special hospitals, and for whom the route back into the community is usually via RSUs and general NHS hospitals, because the amount of time spent in custody, as Goffman suggested (see 3.4), means that it can be hard to assess how the patient might behave outside the institution. As a consequence, special hospital patients are often not looking to the tribunal to make a direction for discharge but rather are hoping to speed up the process of transfer into conditions of lesser security, yet the tribunal cannot do this. Tribunals can and do make recommendations for transfer or leave of absence to be given to special hospital patients, but such recommendations have 'very little impact unless supported by the RMO' (Richardson, 1993, p. 294). In any case, a restricted patient cannot be transferred or given leave of absence without the consent of the Secretary of State: s. 41(3)(c). As with discharge under s. 42(2) (see above 8.3.4), the matter will be considered by the Home Secretary on the advice of the RMO, the AAB and the SHA, and the decision in *Harry* (see 8.3.4) has done nothing to limit the discretion of the Home Secretary to decline to act on any recommendations made by a tribunal concerning a restricted patient.

8.5.1 Patients not subject to restrictions

Section 72(1) lays out two avenues of discharge. The first of these is mandatory discharge, the second is discretionary discharge. In either case, discharge may be deferred: *R* v *Mental Health Review Tribunal, ex parte Pierce* (1997, unreported) (HC).

8.5.1.1 Mandatory discharge Section 72(1)(a), which applies only to patients detained under s. 2, provides that 'the tribunal *shall* direct the discharge of a patient', which means that there is no choice about it:

> If they are satisfied (i) that he is not then suffering from mental disorder or from mental disorder of a nature or degree which warrants his detention in a hospital for assessment (or for assessment followed by a medical treatment) for at least a limited period; or (ii) that his detention as aforesaid is not justified in the interests of his own health or safety or with a view to the protection of other persons.

Thus the criteria for discharge mirror those for admission in the first place, with the substitution of 'justified' in s. 72(1)(a)(ii) for 'ought to be detained' in s. 2(2)(b), although nothing seems to turn on this, and the addition of the word 'then' to the first, medical, limb of the test. This is what explains the conventional view that an MHRT is not concerned to judge the legality of an admission (see 5.5.1), but what other implications its use may have are debatable. Eldergill (1997, p. 466) suggests that '[t]he word ['then'] should not, however, be interpreted so literally as to mean that a tribunal must therefore disregard the history of the patient's condition or recent fluctuations in his mental state'. Eldergill gives the example of a patient who appears to be 'well' at the time of the hearing, but who had been 'floridly ill' a short time before. This view is supported by the dicta of Donaldson MR in *Perkins* v *Bath District Health Authority* (1989) 4 BMLR 145 at p. 151, that for a tribunal to state that it is satisfied that a patient is not suffering from mental disorder, or to the nature or degree which warrants hospitalisation, 'is not the same thing as saying the tribunal is not satisfied that he is so suffering'. The burden of proof is on the patient, and the task is to prove a negative, and the test is structured so that continued detention is given the benefit of any doubt. In practice, Peay (1989, p. 211) suggests that tribunals, although exercising a civil law jurisdiction, require a patient to prove 'beyond reasonable doubt' that discharge is appropriate. In sum, although it is difficult to generalise, as apparently some tribunals place the burden of proof on the hospital (Hoggett, 1996, p. 193), it is likely that the addition of the word 'then' does very little to improve the patient's chances of discharge, and given the way the dice are loaded against the applicant, it would seem that it is necessary to be very sane indeed to stand even a chance of success.

For patients detained other than under s. 2, and not subject to restrictions, the criteria for mandatory discharge echo those which apply to admission for treatment. The tribunal must discharge the patient if satisfied that he or she is not then suffering from of the four specified forms of mental disorder, or from one of those forms of mental disorder 'of a nature or degree which makes it appropriate for him to be liable to be detained in a hospital for medical treatment' (s. 72(1)(b)(i)); or that detention is not necessary on grounds of the health or safety of the patient or the protection of other persons (s. 72(1)(b)(ii)); or, if the application is made by a NR following the veto by an RMO under s. 25 of an order for discharge made by the NR under s. 23, that the patient would not be likely to act in a manner dangerous to others or himself or herself if released. Again, the word 'then' has been added to the criteria, compared with those in s. 3.

The courts have, until very recently, interpreted these provisions, particularly s. 72(1)(b)(i), in the manner which is least favourable to the patient. In *R v Mental Health Review Tribunal for the South Thames Region, ex parte Smith, The Times,* 9 December 1998 (HC) it was held that the phrase 'nature or degree' in s. 72(1)(b)(i) should be read disjunctively, so that a patient who suffers from a mental disorder of a 'nature' that makes it appropriate that he or she be hospitalised need not be discharged, even if not then suffering from that disorder to a 'degree' that makes hospitalisation appropriate. This decision is in line with, and indeed relied heavily on, academic opinion (Eldergill, 1997, p. 213), and on medical evidence that a patient exhibiting no symptoms of disorder at the time of a tribunal hearing may soon experience acute symptoms if released from hospital prematurely. The court emphasised that there should be some evidence, prior psychiatric history for example, upon which to base such a view, and it is indeed part of the paradox of hospitalisation that the need for it may only be apparent when the individual concerned is not in hospital. But how does a patient prove his or her sanity when evidence of past disorder is admissible? The obvious risk of the decision in *Smith* is that patients who in fact are no longer disordered and in need of hospitalisation will be unable to prove this to the satisfaction of the tribunal. As such, the case is another example of protectionism overriding patients' rights and interests.

The issue in *R v Canons Park Mental Health Review Tribunal, ex parte A* [1994] 2 All ER 659 (CA) was whether the requirement in s. 72(1)(b)(i) that the patient must be discharged if it was not 'appropriate for him to be liable to be detained in a hospital for medical treatment' imported into s. 72 the 'treatability test' that can be found in ss. 3(2)(b), 16(2) or 20(4)(c). A majority of the court decided that it did not. The case involved an application for judicial review made by A, a psychopathically disordered patient who had been refused discharge by an MHRT on the grounds, inter alia, that it did not have to consider whether A was treatable. Kennedy LJ pointed out that the function and position of tribunals differs from that of those concerned with a patient's admission and treatment, as tribunals only have to be satisfied of negatives, i.e., that the patient is not mentally disordered, and so on, whereas on admission, the burden of proof is on those wishing to admit. Section 72, in other words, does not deal with a situation analogous to that covered by s. 3, and Kennedy LJ, consequently, could 'see no reason why the words of s. 72(1)(b)(i) should be read as a form of legal shorthand' referring to the tests in s. 3 (p.683). Instead, s. 72 should be read for what it says, and for what it does not say, and it makes no reference to treatability. Moreover, the criteria relevant to discretionary discharge, contained in s. 72(2) (see 8.5.12) *do* refer to treatability, so there is no purchase to an argument that the absence of treatability as a separate factor in s. 72(1) was an oversight. In the context of s. 72(2) the power to discharge, as discretionary, need not be exercised even if a patient is not treatable, and so to hold that treatability is a factor relevant to mandatory discharge is in effect to turn that discretion into a duty.

There was a powerful dissenting opinion in *Canons Park*. Roch LJ referred to the Percy Commission Report (Royal Commission 1957), which demonstrated that '[t]he policy of the 1983 Act in relation to patients with psychopathic disorders is treatment not containment' (p.675), and to the general principle of statutory interpretation that any ambiguity in a statutory provision should be 'resolved in favour of personal liberty'. He further found that the policy behind the Act was driven by the ECHR decision in *X* v *United Kingdom*, in which the ECHR had held it unlawful to detain a person on grounds of mental disorder if the reasons for initial admission no longer pertained (per Roch LJ at p. 676); and moreover that the policy was reflected in the substance of the Act. Roch LJ's interpretation was that as s. 72(1)(b)(i) used the phrase 'makes it appropriate for him to be liable to be detained' whereas s. 3(2)(a), the comparable subsection, uses the phrase 'makes it appropriate for him to receive medical treatment in hospital', this 'shows that Parliament did not intend to refer simply to the appropriateness test in s. 3(2)(a) ...' (at p. 675). Rather, the addition of the words 'liable to be detained' to the criteria which a tribunal must apply 'clearly refer ... to the treatability test' (ibid.), therefore incorporating that test into the general test of appropriateness.

The decision of the majority in *Canons Park* drew criticism for the reasons given by Roch LJ (Baker and Crichton, 1995; Glover, 1996; Parkin, 1994). In any case it has become clear, as a result of the decision of the House of Lords in the Scots case, *Reid* v *Secretary of State for Scotland* [1999] 1 All ER 481 (HL), that the decision of the majority in *Canons Park* can no longer be regarded as good law. *Reid* concerned the equivalent provision in Scottish law to

s. 72(1)(b)(i), MHA 1983. Although, technically, only of persuasive influence on the law of England and Wales, the appeal in *Reid* was, in the words of Lord Lloyd (at p. 484) 'also in reality an appeal against the decision of the Court of Appeal in the *Canons Park* case'. The House resurrected the policy driven arguments regarding the function of detention and the relevance of the ECHR offered by Roch LJ, holding that a sheriff (who performs the functions of an MHRT for these purposes in Scotland) was bound to order the discharge of an untreatable psychopathic patient. As for the broader policy issue, of whether it is appropriate that dangerously disordered psychopathic persons should be discharged from hospital, this, held Lord Hutton 'is an issue for Parliament to decide and not for judges' (at p. 516). On this, it is worth noting that the decision in *Reid*, although in line with the policy behind the MHA 1983, if not so clearly in line with the policies of the current government. It may be that its effects will be short-lived; and there can be little doubt that *Reid* will provide the government with further impetus for the introduction of 'reviewable deten-tion', although this raises interesting questions concerning how the views expressed in *Reid* as to the relevance of the ECHR and the Human Rights Act 1998 might be negotiated by any new powers (see 6.7).

8.5.1.2 Discretionary discharge

An MHRT should not turn its mind to the possibility of discretionary discharge until it has considered the case for mandatory discharge and rejected it: *R v Mental Health Tribunal for the North Wales Region, ex parte P* (20 May 1990) unreported (DC). There are no powers of discretionary discharge in respect of restricted patients: s. 72(7), *Grant v Mental Health Review Tribunal* (1986) 26 April 1986 (DC). As far as unrestricted patients are concerned, s. 72(1) gives MHRTs a discretionary power to direct the discharge of the patient 'in any case', and s. 72(2) provides that in the exercise of that discretion the tribunal 'shall have regard' to the likelihood of medical treatment alleviating or preventing a deterioration in the patient's condition and, if the patient is suffering from mental illness or severe mental impairment, whether he or she would be able to care for himself or herself, to obtain any care needed, and to be able to guard against serious exploitation. This is not, however, an exclusive list of factors, and an MHRT has a discretion to consider any factor that may be relevant to the exercise of its discretion (per Lord Clyde in *Reid* at p. 504). The discretionary powers are used very rarely, however, and the reason is clear, given that a patient unable to make out his or her case on the basis of the criteria for mandatory discharge is *prima facie* suitable for continued detention.

8.5.2 Discharge of restricted patients

8.5.2.1 Absolute discharge   Section 72(7) disapplies s. 72(1) to restricted patients, except as provided by ss. 73 and 74. Section 73(1) provides that a tribunal *must*, on the application or referral of a patient subject to a restriction, direct the absolute discharge of that patient if satisfied both that at least one of the criteria in s. 72(1)(b) is met *and* 'that it is not appropriate for the patient to remain liable to be recalled to hospital for further treatment': s. 73(1)(b). If an absolute discharge is granted, the hospital order, and with it the restriction order, will cease to have effect: s. 73(3). Absolute discharges are rare. There were only 10 in 1996, down from a high of 21 in 1994 (Home Office, 1997, table 16). The main reason for this is undoubtedly that tribunals, in common with the Home Secretary, take a cautious approach to the interpretation of s. 73(1)(b). Even if the evidence is that an applicant is no longer mentally disordered, or not to a nature or degree which warrants hospitalisation, or that he or she is no longer a danger to other persons, a tribunal anxious that the disorder may only be in remission, or that the risk to others is obscured by the constraints placed on an inmate's behaviour by the fact of hospitalisation, is unlikely to be easily satisfied that it is not appropriate to leave the door open to the possibility of recall. This approach has been approved by the courts on a number of occasions (see 8.5.2.3).

8.5.2.2 Conditional discharge and conditions

If a tribunal concludes that s. 73(1)(b) is not satisfied but that one of the criteria in s. 72(1)(b) is met, it must direct the patient's conditional discharge (s. 73(2)), which can be deferred to allow such arrangements as the tribunal feels are necessary to be made: s. 73(7). In *R v Nottingham MHRT, ex parte Secretary of State for the Home Department, The Times,* 12 October 1988 (HC) it was held that there is no power to adjourn a tribunal hearing under r. 16, 1983 Rules, in the hope that the patient will respond sufficiently well to treatment in the interim that when the tribunal reconvenes an order for discharge can be made. The meeting of the criteria for discharge is intimately related to the practical possibility of attaching conditions to the order. Athough it has been said by Lord Bridge (in *Secretary of State for the Home Department v Oxford Regional MHRT* [1987] 3 All ER 8 at pp.11-12) that a tribunal hearing an application must first decide whether one or both of the criteria for discharge in s. 72(1)(b) are met, and only then turn its mind to the issue of whether discharge should be absolute or conditional, he also held that the first question 'would inevitably be coloured' by the practical possibility of imposing suitable conditions. In practice the answer to the first question is likely to *follow* the answer to the second question, at least in cases where the conditions contemplated by the tribunal, which will be for some form of after care, cannot easily be implemented, not least because it was established in the *Oxford* case that a tribunal, having decided that conditional discharge should be ordered, and having then decided that discharge should be deferred under s. 73(7), is unable to undo either of those decisions. This means that, if arrangements have not been made to the satisfaction of the tribunal, perhaps because of reluctance on the part of the RMO, hospital managers and others to make them, there is no scope for the tribunal to try to force the issue, by replacing its original order with an order for immediate absolute discharge. If there has been a failure to make arrangements, the patient cannot be discharged and the matter can only be reconsidered afresh by a tribunal when the patient's case comes before it again by way of application or reference (s. 73(7), MHA 1983), as happened for example in *R v MHRT, ex parte Booth* [1998] COD 203 (HC). Thus the position of restricted patients on this point is in sharp distinction to that of unrestricted patients, in respect of whom, as was held in *Hempstock* (see 8.5), a tribunal does have powers to reconsider the question of discharge if there has been a failure to act on recommendations that it has made: and this is why the application in *Fox* (see 9.3.2) focused instead on the duty to provide after care under s. 117.

There is no requirement actually to impose conditions (s. 73(4)(b)), but a conditionally discharged patient is subject to recall by the Home Secretary using s. 42(3) (s. 73(4)(a)), and must comply with any conditions which are imposed, either by the MHRT on discharge or at a later date by the Secretary of State, who also has powers to vary any condition, however imposed: s. 73(4)(a),(5). The conditions imposed are the same as may be imposed on conditional discharge under s. 42 (see 8.3.4). Case law has established some limitations to the conditions that may be imposed. In *Secretary of State for the Home Department* v *MHRT for Wales*; *Secretary of State for the Home Department* v *MHRT for Merseyside RHA* [1986] 3 All ER 233 (HC) Mann J held that a condition of discharge that the patient remain in a hospital is 'inconsistent with the duty to discharge' (at p. 238). This is understandable, as to uphold such a condition would undermine the order for discharge, but it also speaks of the lacunae in the powers of tribunals in respect of restricted patients. In the *Merseyside* case at least, the tribunal had concluded that the applicant, who at the time was resident in a special hospital, did not require such a restrictive regime; and the order for discharge was in fact an attempt to transfer the patient to conditions of less security with a view to his eventual release. The High Court vetoed this creative use of the legislation, confirming special hospital applicants to be in an unrealistic 'all or nothing' situation. On the other hand, what is and what is not a hospital can be difficult to detect, and it is clear that residence in a hostel, coupled with compulsory treatment are perfectly proper conditions to be placed on a discharge (per Lord Bridge in the *Oxford* case [1987] 3 All ER 8 at p. 12), but it is *not* clear that, from the point of view of the patient, such would be experienced as 'discharge' in any meaningful sense. Moreover, it has subsequently been decided that a conditionally discharged patient can be detained under s. 3 whilst still liable to recall under part III powers: *Dlodlo* and *ex parte S* (see 6.3.2.2).

8.5.2.3 When a conditional discharge may be ordered Section 73 requires that a mentally disordered patient be discharged if no longer dangerous, and a dangerous person be discharged if no longer mentally disordered. The question whether a person no longer suffering from mental disorder must be absolutely discharged, or could also be conditionally discharged, and hence subject to recall, was considered by the Court of Appeal in *R* v *Merseyside MHRT, ex parte K* [1990] 1 All ER 694. Some months after K had been conditionally discharged by an MHRT on the grounds that he was not then suffering from a mental disorder, he was convicted of assault and sentenced to six years' imprisonment. In prison he applied again to an MHRT, for an absolute discharge under s. 75(2), but the tribunal, although again finding that K was not suffering from a mental disorder, refused to lift the conditions. K sought judicial review, arguing that, as no longer mentally disordered, he was not a patient within s. 145 (defined as 'a person suffering or appearing to be suffering from mental disorder'), and was therefore entitled to an absolute discharge. Butler-Sloss LJ, with whom Kerr LJ concurred, did not answer this difficult point directly, but merely stated that a patient who has been made subject to restrictions 'remains a patient until he is discharged absolutely', and justified this by reference to the policies behind the 1983 Act, of 'protection of the public' and 'the hoped for progression to discharge of the treatable patient' (at p. 699), which, so it was implied, would be upset if a patient was entitled to absolute discharge as soon after detention as he or she was judged no longer to be mentally disordered. Richardson (1993, p. 283) argues that this is a 'strained interpretation' and, had the Court of Appeal taken a more autonomy centred approach, as in treatment cases like *ex parte X* (the Goserelin case, see 7.3.2.1.2), the outcome in *ex parte K* might have been different.

This is an attractive argument but from a different point of view the problem is that, whilst the interpretation of the definition of a 'patient' in *ex parte K* may be problematic (it is worth pointing out that Sir Denys Buckley, the other member of the Court of Appeal, decided the case on the completely different basis that there had been no decision open to judicial review taken by the second tribunal as that tribunal had not 'discharged' K, since he was already discharged), the interpretation of s. 73(2) seems uncontroversial on its face. This is why, presumably, counsel for K felt compelled to look elsewhere, to s. 145(1), in order to raise doubts about the legality of the decision not to discharge K absolutely. If so, then here as elsewhere, the problem is internal to the drafting of the Act, and neither the Court of Appeal's position nor the alternative argued for by Richardson is, as a matter of *legal* interpretation of the provisions of the Act, clearly stronger than the other. It is, however, a cause for concern that persons sentenced by court to a hospital order with restrictions can remain subject to more intrusive control than their peers sentenced to prison, who may be just as dangerous on release, on the grounds that they have been, although are no longer, mentally disordered. It is true that s. 73 reflects both protectionist and beneficent concerns, but all the indicators in the 1983 Act are to the effect that these concerns are limited in focus, to persons who *are* mentally disordered. There is also the argument that the continuance of legal restraints over a person who is not mentally disordered violates Art. 5(1), ECHR, which requires powers of detention to be limited to 'persons of unsound mind'. As discussed above, the Court of Appeal side stepped this question in the later case brought by the same patient to challenge his recall to hospital (*R v Home Secretary, ex parte K* [1990] 3 All ER 562) by holding that the House of Lords ruling in *R v Secretary of State for the Home Department, ex parte Brind* [1990] 1 All ER 649 prevented it from looking to the ECHR unless the UK statute contained ambiguities. There are two points to be made here. First, how to characterise the relation between ss. 73 and 145 as other than ambiguous is not readily apparent. Secondly, this sort of diversionary argument will not be available after the coming into force of the Human Rights Act 1998.

The companion case to *ex parte K* is *R v MHRT, ex parte Cooper* [1990] COD 275 (HC), in which it was held that a patient no longer dangerous (if he ever had been) was not entitled to absolute discharge by virtue solely of that fact, as the tribunal was not satisfied that the patient should not remain liable to recall on therapeutic grounds. The argument of the patient was to the effect that he had been placed under a restriction order at a time (1963) when such orders were made in respect of fairly minor 'nuisance' offences; and if he had been convicted more recently he would have been placed on a hospital order without restrictions, in which case he would have been entitled to discharge without conditions under s. 72(1) when shown not to be dangerous. It was also contended that s. 73(1)(b) should be understood as limited in scope to the need to protect the public. Both arguments were dismissed by Rose J who, relying on the dicta of Butler-Sloss LJ in *ex parte K* that the policy behind the Act is both protectionist and beneficent, saw no reason to limit the scope of the matters to be considered under s. 73(1)(b), and held that a tribunal had no discretion and must order conditional discharge in such a situation. It must be conceded that this is the most straightforward reading of s. 73(1) as a whole and s. 73(1)(b) in particular. However, in *ex parte K*, it was the interests of the general public that had to be balanced against K's interest in being free from liability to recall. Accordingly, *Cooper* is the more paternalistic, and in a sense more problematic, decision. In so far as the issue was considered by the House of Lords in *Reid*, there is nothing in that case which suggests that the decisions in *ex parte K* and *Cooper* were, in the view of their Lordships, wrongly decided.

8.5.2.4   Discharge of restricted patients subject to transfer directions or limitation directions   A different procedure applies, by virtue of s. 74, to patients subject to a transfer direction and a restriction direction or a hospital direction coupled with a limitation direction, even though the effect in hospital is the same as a restriction order (s. 49(2)), since such persons will face the prospect of transfer to prison on discharge from hospital (see 6.7). When such a patient applies or is referred to an MHRT, it must hear the case in the ordinary way, but is under a duty to notify the Secretary of State of the outcome of the hearing, and in particular whether the patient 'would if subject to a restriction order' be entitled to an absolute or conditional discharge (s. 74(1)(a)), and 'entitled' means entitled under the criteria relevant to restriction order patients under s. 73.

If the MHRT decides that the patient should continue to be detained in a hospital, that is what happens. If the patient no longer requires hospitalisation, there are various possibilities. If the transfer was initially made under s. 48 (that is, that the transferee was at the time in prison on remand, or as a 'civil prisoner' or held under immigration laws) the Secretary of State, on notification that the patient is entitled to either version of discharge, 'shall' by warrant direct that the patient be returned to prison (s. 74(4)), usually to face the charges for which the patient had been remanded in custody in the first place, unless the MHRT has used its powers in s. 74(1)(b), which provides that if the patient satisfies the criteria for conditional discharge the MHRT has a discretion to recommend that the patient should continue to be detained in hospital. One reason that a tribunal might conclude that it is appropriate for the patient to remain liable to be recalled to hospital for treatment although not at that time mentally disordered, nor a danger to self or others, is that the illness is in remission, and might reoccur if the patient is returned to a prison environment. If such a recommendation has been made, the Secretary of State need not issue the warrant of remittance to prison: s. 74(4). For s. 48 transferees, then, the only outcome of a successful tribunal application or referral will be either return to prison or continued hospitalisation. In 1996, out of 199 unsentenced or untried prisoners in hospital, 95 returned to prison to await trial or sentence within three months (Home Office, 1997, para. 14), although this will be a slight overestimate as this total includes patients remanded in hospital or given a hospital order without conviction by a court. On the other hand, 74 patients remained in hospital six months after first admission. As might be expected, the vast majority of s. 48 transferees, in both directions, are male.

For patients transferred to hospital under s. 47, or psychopathically disordered patients detained in a hospital by virtue of a hospital direction and a limitation direction under s. 45A (which takes effect as a transfer direction and restriction direction made under ss. 47 and 49: s. 45B(2)(a),(b)), there are more possibilities open. An MHRT must direct the discharge of the patient (with or without conditions), if the Secretary of State agrees, and gives notice to that effect to the tribunal within 90 days of being notified that the grounds for discharge have been made out: s. 74(2). Any discharge will take effect as under s. 73 (s. 74(6)), which means that on absolute discharge the patient ceases to be liable to be detained and the orders authorising detention automatically cease (s. 73(3)), and in the case of conditionally discharged patients the powers to defer the discharge, to impose and vary conditions, and to recall the patient to hospital discussed above (see 8.3.2) also apply. Hence there is a possibility that transferred patients may secure early release from custody via an MHRT, if the Secretary of State consents.

If the Secretary of State does not give such notice, the hospital managers are under a duty to transfer the patient back to prison at the end of the 90-day period: s. 74(3). For both s. 47 and s. 48 transferees, transfer and restriction directions cease to have effect on the return of the patient to prison: s. 74(5). However, this duty, like that of the Secretary of State in respect of s. 48 transferees, need not be exercised by hospital managers if the MHRT has recommended under s. 74(1)(b) that a patient entitled to conditional discharge should nevertheless stay in hospital. An MHRT may feel the need to recommend continued detention in hospital because of the overlap of s. 74 with the powers of the Secretary of State in s. 50, which empowers the Secretary of State, on being notified by the patient's RMO, any other doctor, or an MHRT, that the patient no longer requires treatment in hospital or that there is no effective treatment that can be given, to direct by warrant that the patient be remitted to prison: s. 50(1)(a). A tribunal might wish to counsel against this, for the reasons discussed above.

The Secretary of State is also empowered, by s. 50(1)(b), to 'exercise any power of releasing [the patient] on licence or discharging him under supervision' which would have been available to the Secretary of State had the patient been remitted to prison. These powers comprise, in brief, release on parole or life licence (in the case of prisoners sentenced to life imprisonment): ss. 33, 34, 35, Criminal Justice Act 1991. Home Office policy is that the Home Secretary will refer the case of a patient sentenced to life imprisonment who is deemed ready to leave hospital by an MHRT, and who has 'passed tariff' for the offence in question, to the Parole Board, even if he or she does not agree with the MHRT's decision (see Jones, 1999, p. 233). In addition, the Secretary of State's general power by warrant to discharge a restricted patient from hospital absolutely or conditionally under s. 42(2) applies.

Therefore, when notified that the patient satisfies the criteria for discharge, whether absolute or conditional, the Secretary of State has a choice: to consent to the discharge of the patient into the community by the MHRT, with such conditions as the tribunal sees fit (although of course he or she has powers to vary those conditions); to use his or her own powers of discharge; to remit the patient to prison; to accept the recommendation of the MHRT that the patient should remain in hospital; or, if there has been no recommendation under s. 74(1)(b), to do nothing and effect the transfer to prison by default under s. 74(3). Each case inevitably turns on its own facts. However, it is Home Office policy that, as far as the discharge of life sentence prisoners is concerned, the powers in s. 50(1)(b) are the preferred option over that in s. 42 (see Gunn, 1993, pp.331-3), other than in exceptional cases, which means release on life licence rather than conditional discharge. The key difference between the two is that in the former case liability to recall subsists for the life of the patient, whereas a conditionally discharged patient may apply from between one and two years after conditional discharge for absolute discharge (s. 75(2)), or be absolutely discharged by operation of law if the restriction order ceases to have effect and the patient has not been recalled to hospital: s. 42(5).

The policy was challenged in *R v Secretary of State for the Home Department, ex parte Stroud* (1993) COD 75, which elicited from the Home Office the explanation of this preference on grounds of public policy — that persons sentenced to life imprisonment should not be able to circumvent the sentence imposed by resort to the 1983 Act, and that a clear policy allowed consistency of decision-making — decisions being taken by the Home Secretary on the recommendation of the parole board and in consultation with the Lord Chief Justice and the trial judge, if available. Evidence given on behalf of the Home Office also emphasised that the Home Secretary would consider the use of s. 42 in circumstances when, for example, the sentencing court had wished to make a hospital order but there was no hospital bed available, or if there was evidence, not available to the sentencing court, that the patient had been suffering from a mental disorder at the time the offence was committed (see Gunn, 1993, p. 333). In essence, if the Home Secretary is content that the patient could have been given a hospital order at the time of sentence, s. 42 powers will be used. The High Court in *Stroud* found the policy of the Home Secretary to be unimpeachable and that decision was upheld in the Court of Appeal. Gunn (1993, p. 333) has pointed out that as it is not possible for a court to make a hospital order following a murder conviction, one would presume that the Home Secretary should consider using s. 42 powers in at least some instances involving persons transferred following such a conviction, given the wide range of situations, of varying moral culpability and risk to the public, caught by that offence.

As to the choice between s. 74 and s. 50 powers of discharge, although there is no clear data, it seems that s. 74 is more frequently used in tribunal cases. Of *all* the 165 restricted patients conditionally discharged in 1996, 80 per cent (132) were discharged by an MHRT, with 33 conditionally discharged by the Home Secretary (Home Office, 1997, para. 17 and table 16). There is a discernible general trend whereby MHRTs are discharging more, and the Home Secretary is discharging fewer, patients than previously. For instance, in 1988 55 patients were conditionally discharged by the Home Secretary, and 70 by tribunals. In 1991 the figures were 48 and 101 respectively. In 1995 the Home Secretary conditionally discharged only 24 patients, MHRTs 140 (Home Office, 1997, para. 17 and table 16). It is not clear what story these figures tell; but it is probably a safe bet to venture that they reveal the increasing reluctance of a series of Home Secretaries to take primary responsibility for the release of potentially dangerous individuals into the community (although reconviction rates remain low) and the increasing numbers of restricted patients detained in hospitals over the past decade or so (see 6.5.2). The number of persons returned to prison to resume a sentence (that is, s. 47 transferees) has also increased markedly, although unevenly, over the last decade or so, from 21 in 1986 to 155 in 1996, the highest total being 165 in 1993. Again, this reflects the increased number of prisoners transferred to hospital in recent years. It is not clear whether this is achieved by the use of s. 50 or by the use of the default powers of hospital managers in s. 74(3).

8.6 TRIBUNAL AND DECISIONS

The president of an MHRT may announce its decision immediately after the hearing, but in any case the decision must be communicated in writing within seven days to all parties and, if the patient is subject to restrictions, to the Secretary of State: r. 24(1), 1983 Rules. As with disclosure of documents before a hearing, there is a discretion given to MHRTs to decline to disclose full reasons to the patient, and to impose a duty of confidence on other recipients, such as the AR, if there is thought to be a risk to the health or welfare of the patient or others: r. 24(2). There is an obvious risk that r. 24(2) may be used, in effect, to deprive the patient of his or her right, not merely to know the reasons for the decision, but to challenge that decision. Clearly, this is another reason why the appointment of a lawyer or doctor as AR is advisable.

An MHRT need only reach a majority decision: r. 23(1). Decisions must be recorded in writing, signed by the president of the tribunal, and give the reasons for the decision, and if the decision is based on any of the matters specified in ss. 72(1) or 73(1),(2) the tribunal must state its reasons for being satisfied regarding those matters: r. 23(2). A trilogy of cases in the mid 1980s established that an MHRT must do more than simply state that the statutory grounds are met or not met, as was done in *Bone* v *MHRT* [1985] 3 All ER 330 (DC). Nolan J referred to a line of case law which showed that 'proper, adequate, reasons must be given' (per Megaw J in *Re Poyser and Mills Arbitration* [1963] 1 All ER 612 (HC) at p. 616) which are sufficient to 'enable [the parties to the hearing] to know that the tribunal has made no error of law' (per Donaldson P in *Alexander Machinery (Dudley Ltd)* v *Crabtree* [1974] ICR 120 at 122), holding that merely to rehearse the words of the statute is insufficient. In *R* v *MHRT, ex parte Clatworthy* [1985] 3 All ER 699 (HC), a tribunal decided not to discharge a patient detained under a hospital order on the grounds that the applicant suffered from 'post schizophrenic personality disorder'. Although this was contrary to the opinions given to the tribunal by the patient's RMO and another doctor, the reasons given did not explain why the tribunal had come to a different clinical view. Mann J quashed the MHRT decision as the reasons given were 'a bare traverse' of the statutory criteria which 'do not enable one to see why the contentions of [the two doctors] were not accepted' (at p. 703). In the third of these cases, *R* v *MHRT, ex parte Pickering* [1986] 1 All ER 99 a restriction order patient was not discharged by a tribunal which, by way of giving reasons for that decision, stated that its members were unanimously of the view that the conditions in s. 72(1) were not met; and that it had noted the 'unhappy history' of the applicant, which included a number of convictions for sexual offences and one for manslaughter, associated with the use of alcohol; and that the patient might experience stress if released into the community. Forbes J was 'wholly unable to detect' (at p. 104) from this which element of which ground in s. 72(1)(b) the tribunal had had in mind when refusing the application. Forbes J held that it was 'essential' that the tribunal bear in mind the distinction between the two elements in s. 72(1)(b), that is, the 'diagnostic question' and the 'policy question', and although the decision of a tribunal does not have to be read 'in the air', but need only be comprehensible to those who know what the issues before the tribunal are (at p. 102), it was not so in this case.

Between them, these three decisions have engineered a reasonably precise set of requirements that MHRTs must comply with if their decisions are to survive the scrutiny of the High Court. At least this is the theory. However, it is questionable how legalistic tribunals actually are. Under the 1959 Act regime, it became clear that many MHRT members did not know the law that they were supposed to be applying. In Peay's (1981) research, less than half of the legal members of tribunals questioned knew that they had a power of discretionary discharge. Fennell (1977) found that tribunal members were informed more by their own views of what 'common sense' required of them than by the statutory criteria. Both of these studies took place before the passage of the 1983 Act. However, when Peay (1989) was commissioned by the then DHSS to report on the workings of the tribunal system after the 1983 Act had been implemented, she found that little had changed. According to Peay (1989, p. 212) 'it was not unusual for the decision-making process to be, in essence, back to front; [the members of the tribunal] first determined what outcome they preferred and then selected the evidence to accord with that view'. On occasion the reason for this was to ensure that patients would continue to be supervised on discharge, but more frequently the reasoning was grounded in concerns about public safety. Tribunal members were concerned that the applicant posed a risk to other persons, but there would be no evidence to support that view. In such situations continued detention was authorised 'on the legally acceptable grounds that [the tribunal was] satisfied that the patient remained disordered and in need of medical treatment' (ibid., p. 213). Such creative use of the tests to be applied in ss. 72 and 73 by tribunals will not necessarily lay decisions open to legal challenge, as provided that the reasons given for declining to grant the application sought look reasonable on their face, and given the discretion allowed to tribunals and the way in which the burden of proof lies on the applicant, it will be virtually impossible to go behind them. A recent example is *Smith*, (see 8.5.1.1) in which the court virtually rewrote the tribunal's reasons, for example being prepared to accept that a tribunal's statement, that 'We considered that [the patient] should not be discharged' implied a rejection of the other alternatives open to it. To the extent that Peay's findings continue to hold good, her research gives weight to the thesis of this book that legal criteria mask medical discretion.

Peay's findings on the role of RMOs in tribunal hearings are a further case in point. In theory, the patient's RMO is a witness before the tribunal. In practice, however, 'without some impetus from the RMO neither [the Home Office nor an MHRT is] likely to initiate change' (1989, p. 59). In the case of restricted patients, even where a tribunal recommends the patient's transfer or that leave of absence be given, this is unlikely to be implemented by the Home Secretary without the consent of the RMO; and RMOs, like tribunal members, viewed their role *vis-à-vis* their patients as being determined by clinical rather than legal considerations (1989, p. 61). The most antilegalistic of the RMOs that Peay interviewed in one special hospital simply ignored the law, others were less antagonistic but 'adopted the pragmatic view that it was not possible to make the fine distinctions in human behaviour which the law required' (1989, p. 60); but in either case, legal criteria played at best a marginal role in dictating RMOs' practices, whilst the decisions of MHRTs are frequently dictated by the evidence of RMOs. Of course, this will not always be the case. Sometimes a tribunal will decide against the evidence of an RMO. RMOs have, though, developed strategies to minimise the likelihood of this happening. For instance, one RMO interviewed by Peay explained that if he suspected that an MHRT would make a decision of which he disapproved, he would reduce the patient's medication in the period before the hearing so that the patient would appear before the MHRT in as ill and agitated a state as possible, in order to demonstrate to the tribunal that continued detention was appropriate (1989, p. 70). In summary, although it would be an exaggeration to say that the statutory criteria are irrelevant in practice, it is clear that the criteria in ss. 72 and 73 do not necessarily constitute the sole, or even the most important, of the factors acting on the decision-making processes of MHRTs. Rather, they provide the tools with which decision-makers can justify the outcomes that are reached; and as an attempt to rein in medical discretion with legal criteria it is far from clear that the tribunal procedure has been successful.

Perhaps not surprisingly, tribunals order discharge relatively infrequently. In 1996 there was a total of 7575 hearings, leading to 985 orders for discharge, which is a rate of slightly over 13 per cent (Department of Health, 1997, Appendices 7, 8). Research has shown considerable regional variation, the highest reported figure being 50.3 per cent in Birmingham (Saad and Sashidharan, 1994), compared with 17.1 per cent in Oxford (Wilkinson and

Sharpe, 1993), 18.9 per cent in Bradford (McKenzie and Waddington, 1994) and 9.4 per cent in Middlesborough (Milne and Milne, 1995). This continues to be the case. For example in 1996 there were 804 hearings in the Anglia and Oxford RHA area leading to 65 orders for discharge, whereas in South Thames there were 138 discharges from 826 hearings. In Wales, 349 hearings realised 94 discharges, in the South and West RHA area there were 97 discharges from 634 hearings (Department of Health, 1997, Appendix 7). There are also variations by category of detention and accommodation. One noticeable aspect of the statistics is that non-restricted patients detained in special hospitals have only a slim chance of discharge — in 1996, of 230 applications leading to 164 hearings, there were *no* discharges (1997, Appendix 8) — which reflects the fact that special hospital accommodation is unusual for patients held under part II, and such patients in special hospitals are by definition thought to be the most dangerous of civilly detained patients; and possibly also the fact that the special hospitals house a group of formerly restricted patients who although no longer in need of high security accommodation cannot be found alternative placements and who tend to be heavily institutionalised (see 3.4). This group apart, restricted special hospital patients are much less likely to be discharged than others; only 19 patients were discharged from a special hospital by an MHRT in 1996, out of 562 hearings (1997, Appendix 8). This is to be expected, because as discussed above (8.3.2), discharge is often not a realistic prospect for these patients. Frequently the main purpose of an application is to garner information — through access to medical reports — about their situation that is not forthcoming from RMOs, and to vocalise concerns they may have, rather than to seek discharge. Restricted patients held other than in the special hospitals have a better chance of release. There were 138 orders for discharge from 658 hearings in 1996 (1997, Appendix 7), at a 'success rate' (of 1 in 4.8) greater than that of non-restricted patients detained under s. 2 (of around 1 in 6.75) and other than under s. 2 (of around 1 in 8). Again this is perhaps to be expected, because restricted patients detained other than in special hospitals have most likely been transferred out of a special hospital into less secure accommodation as part of a graduated plan of release. Of course, a tribunal may impose conditions on the discharge of restricted but not other patients, and no doubt this too helps explain these, at first sight counterintuitive, figures.

8.7   CHALLENGING MHRT DECISIONS

8.7.1   Challenges by patients

In 1986 Gunn predicted that the decision of the Court of Appeal in *Hallstrom (No.1)*, that s. 139(2) does not apply to applications for judicial review, 'will permit the resolution of some complex problems of interpretation of the Act' (1986a, p. 292); and it has indeed proved to be the case. Most of the case law that has been discussed in this Chapter and elsewhere has arisen from the High Court's powers of judicial review. Challenges to MHRT decisions are most often based on claims of illegality relating to a tribunal's alleged misreading of the powers given to it by the 1983 Act, but on occasion it will be appropriate instead to argue procedural impropriety, in the form of a breach of the rules of natural justice rather than the terms of the legislation. An example is provided by the decision in *Kelly* (see 8.4.5). In addition, there is the option of an appeal against the decision of an MHRT, which is by way of case stated, under s. 78(8), MHA 1983.

8.7.1.1 Judicial review or appeal by way of case stated under s. 78(8)?

An appeal against the decision of an MHRT on a point of law may be made to the High Court by way of case stated: s. 78(8), RSC Ord 56, rr. 7-12 as reproduced in Civil Procedure Rules (CPR) 1998, sch. 1), and the question arises whether a patient seeking redress is better served by such an appeal or by an application for judicial review. In *Bone* v *Mental Health Review Tribunal* [1985] 3 All ER 330 (HC) the patient, on a s. 78(8) application, was successful in his argument that the tribunal had erred in law in not giving sufficiently clear reasons for its decision not to direct his discharge (see 8.6). Nolan J was invited by counsel for the appellant to say that if the case had come before him by way of an application for judicial review he would have quashed the tribunal's decision, But this Nolan J refused to say, pointing out that if there had been an application for judicial review 'there would have been an opportunity for evidence to be filed as to the facts and issues before the tribunal by all concerned' (at p. 334). He did however advise that 'if any further such case is sought to be brought before the court an application for judicial review should be considered as an alternative to a case stated under s. 78(8) . . . not only because judicial review procedure allows a broader consideration of the issues, but also because it offers a much more comprehensive range of reliefs'. In his lordship's view, all that the High Court could do on upholding an appeal under s. 78(8) was to give any direction that the tribunal could have given (RSC Ord 94, r. 11(6) now reproduced in CPR 1998, sch. 1), and '[n]o such direction could appropriately be made in the circumstances of this case', presumably because the court did not have before it sufficient information upon which any such direction might be based. Gunn (1986b) has taken issue with this view of the powers of the court under s. 78(8), on the basis that the High Court can return a case to the tribunal for amendment (r. 11), which arguably includes the power to ask for further facts as found by the tribunal. This might on occasion serve to provide the High Court with sufficient information to enable it to use its powers under r. 11(6) of Ord. 94 (CPR 1998, sch. 1) to make a decision that the tribunal, had it not erred in law, would have been capable of making, in particular to direct the discharge of the patient, which as Gunn points out (1986b, p. 179) 'seems to provide the court with much greater power than the remedies for judicial review'. Even if, in a technical sense, there is a greater 'range' of remedies on judicial review, discharge by the High Court is the outcome that the most patients wish to see.

In the years after *Bone*, the s. 78(8) route has been the one which is most commonly used (Department of Health, 1993c, Appendix 13). There may not always be a choice, however. Section 78(8) is limited to questions of law, and so challenges based on want of jurisdiction which may not be apparent on the face of information available under s. 78(8) may have to proceed by way of judicial review. In this sense judicial review does allow a broader consideration of the issues, as the High Court may go beyond the facts as found by the tribunal, and admit affidavit evidence from one or more of the parties to the tribunal hearing. Tactics may also be based on the technicalities of application. Gunn (1986b, p. 179) suggests that as a case stated has to be requested of the tribunal within 21 days, and leave for judicial review can be sought up to three months after the events complained of, it may be advisable, when both options are open, to request that the tribunal state a case in the first instance, and if this is not successful then move for leave to apply for judicial review. Not for the first time in this Chapter, it is worth pointing out that under the terms of the Human Rights Act 1998, there is considerable scope for the further development of judicial review as a mechanism by which to challenge the decisions of MHRTs, although much will depend on the attitudes of the judiciary.

8.7.2   Challenges by RMOs

An RMO might not agree with a tribunal decision to discharge a patient. Any party to a tribunal's proceedings can appeal against the decision under s. 78(8), but RMOs have fashioned, and the courts have accepted, other strategies to undermine a tribunal decision. In *R v South Western Hospital Managers and Another, ex parte M* [1994] 1 All ER 161 (HC) a patient, M, had been discharged from detention under s. 2, MHA 1983 on the grounds that she was not then suffering from mental disorder to a nature or degree that justified her detention. Immediately after the hearing, L, a consultant psychiatrist who had examined M earlier the same day, before the hearing, recommended on the basis of that examination that M be compulsorily admitted under s. 3, and, the proper procedures having been followed, she was admitted the following day. She had not left the hospital between being discharged by the tribunal and detained by her RMO.

M applied for leave to apply for judicial review of the decision to readmit her (which was refused) and for a writ of habeas corpus on the grounds, *inter alia* that her readmission immediately after the tribunal's decision was unreasonable in that it frustrated that decision, and this was an abuse of the tribunal's process. Laws J held that M's readmission and continued detention were lawful. The decision to readmit her immediately after her discharge by the tribunal had not been made in bad faith, and the duties bestowed on ASWs to make applications for compulsory detention were not in any way fettered by the existence of a recent tribunal decision. Hence, 'there is no sense in which those concerned with a s. 3 admission are at any stage bound by an earlier tribunal decision' (at p. 173), even if there has been no change in the patient's condition.

Such decisions both highlight the degree to which the 'revolving door' is built into the scheme of the 1983 Act, and demonstrate, here as elsewhere, that the legal controls over medical discretion can prove woefully inadequate. One is left wondering about the point of an MHRT procedure which can be overridden by those charged with deciding who should be admitted under part II, essentially on the grounds that they do not agree with the MHRT's finding of fact. There is a good case to be made that 'new fact' rules, which function in many other common law jurisdictions, should be introduced in the UK.

8.8   ABSENCE WITHOUT LEAVE

Some patients may simply bypass the legal mechanisms by which to challenge detention, and abscond. The MHA 1983 defines 'absent without leave' widely if blandly as 'absent from any hospital or other place and liable to be taken into custody': s. 18(6). A detained patient is deemed to be absent without leave if he or she leaves the hospital at which he or she is detained without having been granted leave; or fails to return to hospital on the expiry of a period of leave or if recalled; or goes absent from a place at which he or she is required to reside as a condition of leave: s. 18(1)(a),(b),(c). These provisions tie in with the widest definition of absconding in the literature, that of Huws and Shubsachs (1993, pp.46-7), namely 'the unauthorised absence of the patient from the hospital, an outside working party, or rehabilitation or compassionate leave from the hospital [including d]eliberate evasion of nursing staff in crowded areas whilst outside the hospital'. It is an offence both to assist or induce a patient who is liable to be detained to abscond and to harbour a patient who is absent without leave or to prevent, hinder or interfere with his or her recapture (s. 128(1), (3)), although a patient commits no criminal offence by absconding: *R v Criminal Injuries Compensation Board, ex p. Lawton* [1972] 3 All ER 582.

The spectre of the 'escaped madman' is a staple of much modern fiction and attracts media attention. Yet the fact is that absconding from the 'deep end' of the hospital system is rare. Huws and Shubsachs (1993) found that in the period 1976-88, during which a total of 4,909 persons were detained in a special hospital, there were only 36 escapes. Only seven of these were from hospital, the majority occurring on outings from the hospital. Even so, Huws and Shubsachs (p. 51) compute that there is only a 1 in 4000 chance that a patient will abscond when on an outing from hospital. A further 30 special hospital patients absconded from RSUs, local hospitals or hostels whilst on leave of absence, at a rate of 1 in 2,800 (p. 52). The majority of absconders — around 75 per cent — are in fact informal patients (Andoh, 1994, p. 135). There is a sense in which the idea of an 'informal absconder' is paradoxical, but in hospital the same recording practices and reactive procedures apply to the unauthorised absences of both detained and informal patients and the main issue is not legal status but whether the absconding is a matter of 'grave concern' or not (Andoh, 1994). It is perhaps to be expected that most absconders would be informal patients, who comprise at least 90 per cent of annual admissions; and the fact that around 25 per cent of absconders are detained patients means that as a proportion of the whole they are markedly more likely to abscond. The research invariably shows that young males, unemployed, admitted under compulsory powers with admission requiring police involvement, with a prior history of hospitalisation, are most likely to abscond (Tomison, 1989; Farid, 1991; Huws and Shubsachs, 1993; Short, 1995), and there is evidence to suggest that Afro-Caribbean patients are more likely to abscond than others (Falkowski et al, 1990).

However, even if the absconder is from the deep end of the hospital system, there is good reason to argue that there will very rarely be cause for 'grave concern'. Offending by patients absent without leave is minimal. Huws and Shubsachs found that between 1976 and 1988 absconders from special hospitals committed a handful of petty theft offences. Two serious offences were committed; a rape, and the shooting of a police officer resulting in a manslaughter conviction. Two serious offences is of course two too many, but it comes nowhere near the public perception of the risk. These offences were committed by patients who had absconded from hospital; patients who absconded whilst on leave committed no serious offences (Huws and Shubsachs, 1993, p. 55). Violence is almost never reported to have been a feature of an escape. In the overwhelming majority of instances, absconders pose no danger to the public. There have long been concerns, on the other hand, that there is a correlation between absconding and risk of suicide (Milner, 1966; Falkowski et al, 1991; Morgan and Priest, 1991; Bannerjee et al, 1995), so that best practice is to respond immediately on discovering an escape.

Most absconders are not hard to find. Homesickness is a common reason for absconding, the patient's view that they do not need to be in hospital is another (Short, 1995, p. 281), and many patients are to be found at home. Most are soon back in the custody of the hospital; a good proportion within hours, and more within 24 hours (89 per cent in Short, 1995, p. 281; 69 per cent in Huws and Shubsachs, 1993, p. 51). A sizeable minority of patients return voluntarily. It is extremely rare that a detained patient absent without leave is not apprehended, although on apprehension a small minority are discharged rather than returned to hospital. Most patients are returned by the police, or by nursing staff, relatives or friends. Very few absconders remain at large for any length of time. Until the passage of the Mental Health (Patients in the Community) Act 1995, a patient, other than one subject to restrictions, who was not taken into custody within 28 days of the date of the absconding ceased automatically to be liable to be detained. Apparently, around 10 per cent of patients detained under a hospital order achieved discharge in this manner (Walker and McCabe, 1973, in Hoggett, 1996, p. 166). However, s. 2(1) of the 1995 Act substituted a new s. 18(4) of the 1983 Act, which now provides that persons detained for treatment, including patients on a s. 37 order, who abscond, may be taken into custody at any time before six months from the first day that he or she was absent without leave, or before the expiry of the period of detention, whichever is the later: ss. 18(4)(a),(b). Thus the maximum period for which a patient may be absent without leave is twelve months, if the authority to detain has been renewed (for at least the second time) shortly before the date of the absconding. A patient who absconds near the end of a period of detention will automatically cause the extension of the period for which he or she is liable to be detained by up to six months. The period of detention (but not the six month period: s. 18(4)) may be extended by one week if the patient is absent without leave on the day or within a week of expiry, and is recaptured or returns voluntarily before the expiry date: s. 21. This is to allow time for arrangements to be made for the renewal of the patient's detention.

None of the above applies to restricted patients, who remain liable to detention regardless of time absent without leave (sch. 1, part II, paras. 2, 4); nor to patients held under the short term part II powers of detention in ss. 2, 4, 5(2) and 5(4), who may not be retaken once the period of detention has expired (s. 18(5)); nor to patients remanded to hospital for medical reports or for treatment, or on conviction made the subject of an interim hospital order, who may be arrested without warrant by a constable, and returned to the court that made the order, who may (although need not) terminate the order and deal with the offender in some other way: ss. 35(10), 36(8), 38(7). There is no time limit on the liability to arrest of absconders in this category.

The 1983 Act provides in s. 18(1) that a detained patient absent without leave may be taken into custody by an ASW, any member of staff of the hospital in question, a police officer, and any person authorised in writing by the hospital managers. If the patient is on leave but with a requirement to reside in another hospital, the staff of that hospital and persons authorised by the managers of that hospital may also retake the patient: s. 18(2). The procedure on absconding depends upon the level of concern raised. Andoh (1994) found that when there is cause for grave concern — usually when a patient is thought to pose a suicide risk or a risk to the safety of other persons, or to be particularly frail, confused or vulnerable — nursing staff would first search the hospital and grounds, and then, if failing to locate the patient, would contact the duty doctor and a decision is taken about whether to book the patient as absent and call the police. Nursing staff would also telephone the home address of the patient and if the patient was there, steps would normally be taken either to compel (if detained) or attempt to persuade (if informal) the patient to return. The patient's home address would also be telephoned in cases causing less than grave concern. It would be possible to use the s. 4 power to compel the return of an informal patient, although the only powers of entry available in the Act are those in s. 135 (see Chapter four), requiring the issue of a warrant. Another option for a police officer is to use s. 17(1)(d), PACE 1984 which gives powers to enter and search premises for a person 'unlawfully at large and whom he is pursuing'. The House of Lords in *D'Souza* v *DPP* [1992] 4 All ER 545 held that a person absent without leave under s. 18 of the 1983 Act is 'unlawfully at large'. As to the reference to pursuit, Lord Lowry held that this limited the availability of this power to situations where there was a chase, and it did not provide a general licence to enter premises. If the requirements of s. 17(1)(d) of the 1984 Act can be made out, reasonable force may be used in their exercise: s. 117, PACE 1984.

Andoh (1994), looking at practices in three hospitals, found that all three always contacted the police when a detained patient had absconded, although if the case was not one of grave concern this would not be done until the patient had broken the hospital's unofficial curfew (typically 11 p. m. or midnight). The police were contacted regarding absconding by informal patients less often, but still perhaps surprisingly frequently, on around 15 per cent of such occasions, although at one hospital, at which there was a relatively small number of absconders, the level was higher, at 55 per cent (Andoh, 1994, p. 135). Police procedure on receipt of a report of absconding shows a high degree of consistency across regions. Cases are categorised as either urgent, requiring full inquiry, or non-urgent, requiring limited inquiry. Cases in the first category involve detained and especially restricted patients, and vulnerable patients. In such cases 'the police would leave no stone unturned in their efforts to find the missing person' (Andoh, 1994, p. 132). For example, forces other than the one initially contacted are brought in if necessary. Otherwise the practice is to go to the home address of the patient, and merely report back to the hospital whether or not the patient was there.

The reason why, until the passage of the Mental Health (Patients in the Community) Act 1995, a patient who remained at large for 28 days ceased to be liable to be detained was that it was assumed that a patient who coped for that period of time outside of hospital did not need to be detained. Although that period has now been extended, the 28 day period retains its significance. Section 21A (which, with s. 21B, was also introduced by the 1995 Act) provides that if a patient is returned or returns voluntarily to hospital within 28 days of absconding, the renewal of authority to detain under s. 20 may be made as if the patient had not absconded, and if the period of liability to detention has been extended by a week through the operation of s. 21, the necessary reports may be made during that period, although the renewal of detention is backdated to the date at which the earlier detention ended. Section 21B, by contrast, lays out a procedure similar to that required for initial admission to be followed in the case of patients being returned or returning to hospital more than 28 days after the date of absconding, and thus maintains something of the philosophy behind the pre-1995, 28 day limit, on liability to recapture. In such a case the patient's liability to detention will automatically terminate one week after his or her return to hospital unless the requirements of the section are complied with: s. 21B(4). These requirements are that the 'appropriate medical officer', which means the RMO for hospital in-patients (ss. 21B(10), 16(5)(b)), must examine the patient within one week of his or her return, to see if the 'relevant conditions' are satisfied: s. 21B(2). These are those in s. 20(4) (s. 21B(10)), which are essentially the same as for admission for treatment under s. 3. If so, the RMO must report to the managers in writing, but before doing so must 'consult' — the decision, though, is solely for the RMO — with one person professionally involved in the patient's treatment and an ASW (who need not be so involved): s. 21B(3). A report, 'duly furnished' to the hospital managers (ss. 21B(2)(b), 10(a)), provides authority for the renewal of the patient's detention in accordance with s. 20(2), that is for six months if it is the first renewal or 12 months for subsequent renewals. As with s. 21A, any renewal made by virtue of s. 21 is backdated: s. 21B(6).

8.9   CONCLUDING COMMENTS

This has been a long chapter, and so our concluding comments will be brief. In terms of the ongoing theme of this book that questions the nature of the relationship between 'medicalism' and 'legalism', it is evident that the material that has been discussed in this Chapter again reveals the limitations in the ability of the law to act as an independent constraint on the exercise of medical discretion. Instead, particularly but not exclusively in the case of restricted patients, medicine and law seem to be able to work effectively 'together' to deliver a policy that subordinates the good of the individual to the safety of the many. But as suggested at 7.5, this should more properly be seen as a colonisation of the legal by the medical. On occasion, as in the M'Naghten rules, that colonisation has gone astray, as the legal fails to move with medical knowledge but rather freezes medical knowledge at a particular point in time. But most of the time it seems to be effective, and law becomes merely procedure, rather than protection. There are of course exceptions. Cases like *Clatworthy*, *Kelly*, *Harry* and *Reid* are examples of courts attempting to place some real legal constraints on the operation of the discharge system. But by and large, the courts have accepted the need to diminish both the importance of substantive rights and due process for the greater public good. These considerations are less to the fore in the case of unrestricted patients (Richardson and Machin, 1999), but even here, in cases like *Smith* and *Canons Park*, this policy preference is very much in evidence.

This much could be argued on the basis of the discussion in the previous Chapter. The particular addition to our understanding of the mental health system that a consideration of the law and practice of discharge from hospital provides is to allow us to see that this notion of colonisation is more complex than first allowed for. It is not just that the legal is colonised by the medical; it is also that the medical is colonised by political and moral discourses. Protectionism, after all, is not a medical concept. In other words, the particular question raised by this Chapter is how the criteria that apply to discharge, at least by tribunal and the Home Secretary, and most probably by RMOs and hospital managers, can be seen as properly medical at all. The paradigm case of this is s. 73(1)(b), which allows for the continuing supervision after discharge, and under the *mental health* legislation, of a person who is then not mentally disordered.

We have seen in this Chapter that the discharge system suffers from shortage of funding, so that at one end of the scale patients may be discharged inappropriately, and at the other discharge may be denied or delayed because of inefficiencies in the system. It is important not to forget that the hospital system provides care and treatment for vulnerable people, and when discharge is governed by factors other than therapeutic ones we should be concerned. It is also appropriate to remember that for most patients prevention of discharge is not an issue. But, important as these considerations are, we should not lose sight of the larger questions raised, about the social function of our mental health system; and we are yet far from a satisfactory answer.

NINE

Care, control and community

9.1 INTRODUCTION

The historical development of the current regime for the care and control of mentally disordered persons in the community has been discussed earlier in this book (see 3.4). The focus in this Chapter, therefore, will be the system as it currently operates. However, it is likely that the current regime will be subject to at least a degree of restructuring in the near future. Two White Papers, published at the end of 1998 (Department of Health, 1998a, 1998b), promised a raft of changes. Some of these are quantitative — there is to be more stock, more resources, better integration of management structures, better quality care, more outreach, more prevention — but others are qualitative. The promise of 'more control' is significant as hitherto the coercive 'end' of the system has been in the form of institutionalisation; and those who adopt a Cohenesque reading of care in the community (see 3.3) will find much ammunition in recent developments. At the same time, however, the White Paper on mental health services (1998a) also promises a new, holistic policy towards mental illness, which recognises for example the housing and civil liberties dimensions of mental health policy; and which has the potential to change not just the 'size' but also the 'shape' of the community care system, by drawing on a more inclusive concept of 'community' than that which came to dominate public policy after 1979.

Even so, both the current situation and the intended reforms can readily be situated within the broader contours that delimit mental health policy generally. The tension between welfarism and managerialism (and the underlying conflict between the politics of left and right which that tension manifests), and that between treatment and control, for example, are absolutely pertinent to an understanding of the law in this area. The White Papers of 1998 do not attempt a paradigm shift, merely a relocation of community care within the already-existing paradigm. As discussed in Chapter 3, this paradigm should be understood as a paradox, in that mental health policy simultaneously constructs mentally disordered persons as being both 'of' the community, needing and deserving of its care; and as 'outsiders' from whom the community is in need of protection. The White Paper on mental health services leaves the reader in no doubt as to how the circle will be squared: '[m]aintaining the highest possible levels of public protection will remain our top priority' (1998a, para. 4.24). For some mentally ill persons currently in the community this may mean that in future in the same circumstances institutionalisation will result. For others, it may mean that life in the community is experienced under conditions of greater supervision and control than is currently the case.

However, as discussed in 3.3.2, the 'failure of community care' which predicated the current round of reforms has been understood not merely as a failure of control. It has also been seen as a failure of coordination and of cooperation between local authority social service departments (SSDs) and health authorities (HAs), caused by inadequate systems, poor management and inadequate resourcing (Department of Health, 1998a, para. 3.2). For the cynically inclined, aware that the last three or four decades are replete with similar sounding government documents, it may be difficult to find much enthusiasm for the latest such document. There can be no doubt that the community care system has a potential demand for resources that is of a magnitude beyond the ability of any government completely to satisfy. Indeed, although the welfare state was introduced on the assumption that better access to services would in the long run decrease overall demand, the opposite has been shown to be true. The consequences of a healthier, longer living population is one of the key social policy questions of our time, as the ongoing debate about pensions and other benefits demonstrates. For the purposes of this chapter, the point is that some of the central controversies in the construction and operation of the current system are unlikely to be resolved quickly or easily, by legislation or by any other means.

On the other hand, however, there is much that can be achieved by policy reorientation and legal reconstruction: there is a widely held view that the current legal framework is a mess and can be improved upon. The key question is how this should be done. This Chapter offers a discussion of current debates around this question through a critical reading of the current law, policy and practice of community care. The discussion will be divided into three main sections, reflecting the argument (see 3.5) that it is misleading to view mental health services as comprising one 'system'. In the present context, there are two systems. The first, discussed at 9.2 to 9.4, is the system of *service provision*. Here the key questions concern the ease with which those in need can access services and the quality of those services. The second, considered at 9.5, is a system of *control* and *supervision*. It is true that in the main, the latter system builds on the former, in that it takes the form of *requiring* compliance with services that are otherwise optional. But the aims of the 'control' based system are significantly different in orientation to those of the 'service' system, and require separate discussion. The third main section of the discussion will return to the proposals contained in the White Papers.

9.2   SERVICES IN THE COMMUNITY FOR MENTALLY DISORDERED PERSONS

9.2.1   Community care plans

Part III of the National Health Service and Community Care Act (NHSCCA) 1990 is the locus of a network of duties and entitlements. However, although attempting to give coherence to the legal framework for the provision of community care services, this is not a consolidating Act. It has not placed all the law relevant to community care under one roof, and can really be seen as no more than a starting point for those who wish to study this area in any detail. Moreover, the Act did nothing to clarify, and in fact complicated, the philosophical or political basis of community care provision. Its consumerist and managerialist principles are very different from the ideology of welfare that underpinned prototypical community care legislation in the post-war period, of which significant elements remain in force. Little attempt has been made as of yet to reconcile these differences (Clements, 1997), and it remains to be seen whether the impending reform of community care will address policy at this deeper level (see further 9.6).

The NHSCCA 1990 places primary responsibility for the effective delivery of community care services on SSDs. Section 46(1) requires every SSD to prepare, publish and keep under review a plan for the provision of community care in its area. This must be done in consultation with HAs, housing authorities, the voluntary sector, and any other persons as the Secretary of State may direct: s. 46(2). There is a significant degree of central government control over service provision at local level. The Secretary of State has powers to inspect premises and evaluate management practices, to make regulations, which must be complied with by SSDs, and to hear complaints and carry out investigations: ss. 48, 49, 50, NHSCCA 1990. The Secretary of State also uses 'approvals' (which are permissive) and, in particular, 'directions' (compliance with which is mandatory) (the latest version of which are to be found in LAC(93)10 published by the Department of Health in March 1993), under powers to be found in ss. 7, 7A Local Authority Social Services Act 1970. Central government also has control of gross local government funding, and can target funds through the use of grant funding for services for the mentally ill under s. 7E of the 1970 Act, and by the Mental Illness Specific Grant, through which £4 million was available in 1998-9 to pump-prime multiagency initiatives: HSC 1998/097 (Department of Health, 1998h). But there is also a significant degree of discretion to be exercised at local level, in terms of which services to provide, to what extent, and to which individuals. This raises issues of entitlement and of inter-agency cooperation. There is a statutory duty on SSDs and HAs to cooperate with each other in the delivery of health and welfare services: s. 22, National Health Service Act (NHSA) 1977. Amongst the most important aims of the NHSCCA 1990 were, first, to bring into being a system of care in the community that was 'much more user driven rather than fitting clients into existing services' (Lord Henley, Under-Secretary of State for the Department of Social Security, *Hansard*, H.L., Vol. 520, col. 645); and, secondly, to 'ensure that a seamless community care service is available which covers both health and social needs' (Baroness Blatch, *Hansard*, H.L., Vol. 518, cols. 1537-38). The extent to which these aspirations have been realised will be discussed at 9.2.3 and 9.2.4 respectively. First, it is necessary to consider what is meant in law by 'community care'.

9.2.2 Community care services

The NHSCCA 1990 does not define 'community care' but 'community care services' are defined by s. 46(3) to comprise those which may be provided under:

- part III, National Assistance Act 1948
- s. 45 Health Services and Public Health Act 1968
- s. 21 and sch 8 National Health Service Act 1977
- s. 117 Mental Health Act 1983

These statutes are concerned with the provision of accommodation services, welfare services, and health services including aftercare to overlapping groups of clients, the main point of overlap being between services for persons with mental illness and for elderly persons. Each of the statutory provisions is supplemented by rules, regulations, and guidance, as well as directions and approvals from the Secretary of State (see fig 9.1).

9.2.2.1 Part III, National Assistance Act 1948 Part III of the National Assistance Act 1948 (NAA) is concerned with the provision of services by SSDs. Sections 21-8 deal with the provision of residential accommodation, s. 29 is concerned with welfare services. Section 21(1)(a) of the 1948 Act, as amended by s. 42(1) of the 1990 Act and LAC 93(10), places a duty on SSDs to make arrangements for the provision of residential accommodation for those ordinarily resident in their area, or having no settled address but being in urgent need (s. 24(1), (2)), who *inter alia* by reason of illness or disability 'are in need of care and attention which is not otherwise available to them'. There is also a power in s. 21(1)(a) to make arrangements for similar provision for persons ordinarily resident in another SSD area. The linkage between the provision of accommodation and the need for care and attention indicates that this provision is not concerned with the provision of accommodation *per se*: s. 21 provides an entitlement to care rather than to housing. An SSD may provide its own accommodation or avail itself of the provision of another SSD, for which it must pay (s. 21(4)), although the SSD in whose area the recipient is ordinarily resident retains the responsibility to provide the accommodation: s. 21(6). Means tested charges are also payable by recipients of accommodation: s. 22. The law has recently been changed to restrict the amount of a capital that may be taken into account: Community Care (Residential Accommodation) Act 1998.

Figure 9.1: The Community Care Legislation

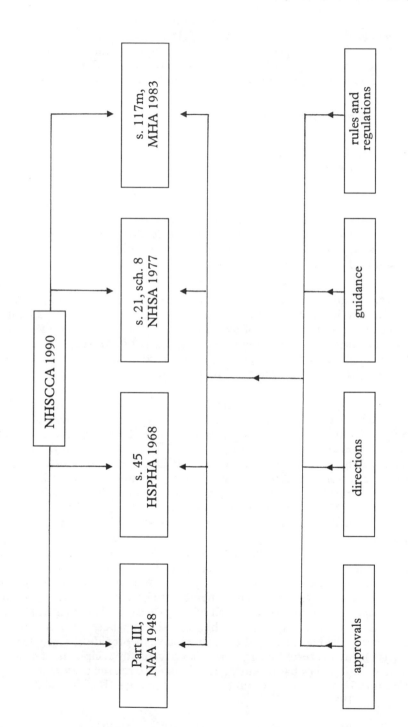

Section 26(1) of the NAA 1948, as amended (most recently) by s. 1(1), Community Care (Residential Accommodation) Act 1992, authorises SSDs to make arrangements for the provision of accommodation with voluntary organisations or 'any other person' — which means privately run residential and other homes — in order to provide board and personal care (s. 26(1A)) or residential accommodation with nursing care (s. 26(1B)), as long as such homes are registered in accordance with the Registered Homes Act 1984, part I or part II, as the case may be. In practice, much residential accommodation is provided by the independent sector (see 3.1.1). The 1984 Act, as amended by the Registered Homes (Amendment) Act 1991, lays down a detailed regime of registration for residential care homes and nursing homes including mental nursing homes, which are defined negatively, as homes which are not 'hospitals' under the terms of the NHSA 1977, (see for example s. 22(3), Registered Homes Act 1984). The 1984 Act gives the Secretary of State a considerable amount of power (mostly delegated to HAs in practice) to make regulations, for example, in the context of mental nursing homes, about the treatments or other 'techniques' that may be used in the homes (s. 21(4)); the qualifications of nursing staff (s. 25(1)(f)); the services which must be supplied (s. 26(a)); entry and inspection of homes (ss. 27(d), 35(1)); the class of patient who may be received into the home in question: s. 29(2) and so on. The Secretary of State may also make regulations concerning applications to run a registered home, and may cancel a registration, and there is a tribunal system (the Registered Homes Tribunal: s. 34(1) and part III) to which appeals against decisions of the Secretary of State lie.

Detailed consideration of the registered homes regime is beyond the scope of this book, but there are two important points that should be made about the regime. First, the courts have decided that there is nothing wrong in principle with SSDs using the mechanism of contracts with independent providers to impose requirements over and above those specified in the statute, provided that such requirements are reasonable: *R* v *Newcastle-upon-Tyne City Council, ex parte Dixon* (1993) 158 Local Government Reports 441 (HC). A contractual term will be found to be unreasonable if compliance with it would threaten the continuing viability of the private homes in question, as that constrains the choice of service users and so frustrates the purpose of the policy behind the Act of 1990: *R* v *Cleveland County Council, ex parte Cleveland Care Homes Association and others* (1993) 158 Local Government Reports 641 (HC). It is perhaps doubtful that the policy of the Act, however, should be seen to be that residential homes should be kept open at any cost. Nevertheless, the judgment in *Cleveland* seems to mean that it is not open to an SSD motivated by a preference for public sector provision to write terms into contracts with independent providers in order to ensure the continued viability of that provision. On the other hand, in *Cumbria Professional Care Limited* v *Cumbria County Council* (1996) 12 *Current Law* 505 (HC) the court was prepared to accept that local circumstances may mean that it is not feasible for an SSD to contract out 85 per cent of the special transitional grant (see 3.3.1) to private providers, but instead to allocate capital resources to its own residential accommodation.

Secondly, although s. 22(3) of the 1984 Act differentiates as a matter of law between registered homes on the one hand and hospitals on the other, other provisions of the 1984 Act operate in the direction of collapsing that distinction. In particular, s. 23(3)(c) requires an application for registration as a mental nursing home to specify whether or not it is proposed that the home should receive patients liable to be detained under the MHA 1983. Obviously, 'residential accommodation' comprises a range of types of accommodation (see 3.3.1), most of which will not receive detained patients. The number of detained patients held in private mental nursing homes has risen considerably over the last decade or so, from 269 admissions in 1986 to 1,005 in 1996-7 (Department of Health, 1998d, table 1), which, although only 4 per cent of the whole still represents a doubling of numbers in real terms. In addition, of course, most hospital in-patients are not detained, and in this much larger group the crossover between 'hospitals' and 'homes' is significantly more substantial. In short, although the 1983 Act draws a rigid distinction between patients who are in hospital and those who are not (although subject to its provisions on leave of absence: see 8.2), in practice, the line between in-patient services and community care can be difficult to draw. This has major implications for the way in which the 'shift' to community care should be understood.

As far as welfare services are concerned, s. 29(1) of the NAA 1948 provides a wide discretion for SSDs, subject to approvals and directions made by the Secretary of State, to make arrangements for promoting the welfare of a wide constituency of 'disabled' clients, which includes *inter alia* those 'who suffer from mental disorder of any description', and s. 29 is used for a wide variety of purposes, including the provision of home help and meals, recreational facilities such as televisions, organised outings and holidays, and services ancillary to these, such as the provision of transport to and from recreational facilities, holidays, and so on.

9.2.2.2 Section 45, Health Services and Public Health Act 1968 This provision empowers SSDs to make arrangements for promoting the welfare of 'old people'. Of course, as has been discussed at various points in this text, there is a considerable number of elderly people with mental health problems and so services for the elderly and services for the mentally disordered will inevitably overlap. However, Department of Health and Social Security Circular 19/71 (Department of Health and Social Security, 1971) makes it clear that s. 45 of the 1968 Act is designed to catch those elderly people who, because not 'disabled' as defined by s. 29 of the 1948 Act, do not qualify for the provision of services under the Chronically Sick and Disabled Persons Act 1970; and this means that this is the least relevant provision for present purposes, as the definition of 'disabled' in s. 29 of the 1948 Act will catch most if not all of those who are mentally disordered within the meaning of the MHA 1983. The range of services available under s. 45 of the 1948 Act is very similar to that available under s. 29 of the 1948 Act.

9.2.2.3 Section 21 and Schedule 8, National Health Service Act 1977 This is the main source of non-residential community care services for

adults suffering from mental disorder. SSDs must make arrangements for the provision of day centres offering facilities for training or occupation, for the provision of an adequate number of approved social workers, and for providing social work support for persons living in their own homes, including the identification, diagnosis, assessment and treatment and after care of mental disorder, and for ensuring that guardianship orders (see 9.5.2) can be made. Schedule 8 also permits the provision of ancillary services, such as domiciliary assistance, to persons living in their own homes.

9.2.2.4 Section 117, Mental Health Act 1983 Section 117(2) of the MHA 1983 places a duty on HAs and SSDs to provide, in cooperation with voluntary agencies, aftercare services to those patients entitled to receive them 'until such time as the [HA and SSD] are satisfied that the person concerned is no longer in need of such services'. Only those released from compulsory detention, under the Act are eligible. Section 117(2A) contained a further duty to provide s. 12 approved doctors and 'supervisors' for the care of persons subject to After Care Under Supervision ('ACUS': see 9.5.3). The nature and profile of 'after care' essentially comprises medical, educational and training services, which may be provided by way of day centres, out-patient provision, or direct to clients in their own homes. Usually such services can be provided without the need for compulsion, but there are powers to force clients to accept services under s. 117 (see 9.5.3).

9.2.2.5 Other sources of care and assistance in the community These, then, are 'community care services' as defined by s. 46(3) of the NHSCCA 1990. There is clearly a considerable degree of overlap between the various provisions. Yet these services by no means fill the field and there are a number of other statutory provisions that in practice are as central to the delivery of community care as those singled out by s. 46(3). These various statutory provisions are linked together and weave in and out of the definition of community care services in s. 46(3). A key example is the provision of welfare services under the Chronically Sick and Disabled Persons Act 1970 (CSDPA), access to which is limited to 'disabled' persons. Section 2(1) of that Act places a duty on SSDs to identify local needs for services, which is broadly similar to the duty in s. 46(1) of the 1990 Act, and lists a range of welfare services which must be supplied to those in need of them. From one point of view, the role of the 1970 Act after the enactment of the 1990 Act is to function as a parallel regime, providing services for 'disabled persons', whilst that set up by the 1990 Act is concerned with providing services to others in need of community care services. Yet things are not that simple, for two reasons.

First, s. 2(1) of the 1970 Act, although listing the welfare services in question, refers to s. 29 of the National Assistance Act, 1948, which gives SSDs a *power* to supply welfare services. The effect of the 1970 Act was to augment that power with a duty. Those to whom the duty under s. 2(1) of the 1970 Act is owed are persons defined as 'disabled' in s. 29 of the 1948 Act, and s. 2(1) of the 1970 Act provides that if it has been assessed as necessary that the SSD make arrangements in order to meet the needs of the person in question, 'it shall be the duty of [the SSD] to make those arrangements in exercise of their functions under ... s. 29 [of the 1948 Act]'. The point is that s. 29 is to be found in part III of the NAA 1948, which *is* on the list of community care services in s. 46(3) of the 1990 Act. Therefore it is arguable that services under the 1970 Act are within the s. 46(3), 1990 Act definition through being linked to part III of the 1948 Act in this way. This view has been rejected by the High Court on a number of occasions. In *R v Gloucestershire County Council ex parte Mahfood and others* (1996) 8 Admin LR 180 at p. 193 McCowan LJ, sitting in the Divisional Court, held that '[w]hat is authorising the local authority to make arrangements under s. 2 is s. 2'; and the same view was reached in the High Court decision in *R v Gloucestershire County Council and another, ex parte Barry* (1995) 30 BMLR 20. *Barry* went to the House of Lords on a different point (see 9.3.1) and there is no particularly strong support to be gleaned from their Lordships' opinions for either of these possible interpretations. However, the view that services which must be provided by virtue of the operation of s. 2(1) of the 1970 Act *are* provided under s. 29 of the 1948 Act was expressed in *R v North Yorkshire County Council, ex parte Hargreaves (No. 2), The Times,* 12 June 1997 (HC), and in *R v Powys County Council, ex parte Hambridge* [1998] 1 FLR 643 (HC). In the latter case Popplewell J held bluntly (at p. 650) that '[w]hen providing welfare services under s. 2 [of the 1970 Act] the local authority are exercising their functions under s. 29 [of the 1948 Act]. They are not providing services under s. 2; they are making arrangements under the 1948 Act for the provision of their services'. On appeal ([1998] 96 LGR 627), the Court of Appeal upheld Popplewell J's decision. The practical importance of this question is that services under the 1948 Act can be charged for under s. 17, Health and Social Services and Social Security Adjudications Act 1983, whereas there are no provisions to permit charges to be levied under the 1970 Act.

Secondly, to confuse matters further still, 'disabled' is defined by s. 29 of the 1948 Act to include *inter alia* people aged 18 or over 'who suffer from mental disorder of any description'. Hence, even if welfare services provided under the 1970 Act are not 'community care services', they may be accessed by persons with mental disorder who would also be *prima facie* entitled to access the same services under the 1990 Act. As might be expected, the complexity of the relationship between the various statutes in this area tends to store up a further set of problems regarding access and entitlement.

9.3   ASSESSING ENTITLEMENT

9.3.1   Entitlement under the NHSCCA 1990

In the scheme of the 1990 Act, access to the services listed in s. 46(3) is dealt with in s. 47. This prescribes a two stage procedure to be used in the assessment of the needs of individuals. When it appears to an SSD that a person may be in need of community care services, it *must*, first, carry out an assessment of his or her needs and secondly the SSD, 'having regard to the results of that assessment, shall then decide whether his needs call for the provision by them of any such services': s. 47(1)(a),(b). It is not open to an SSD to decline to carry out an assessment on the grounds that it does not offer the services required to meet any needs that may be identified: *R v Berkshire CC, ex parte P* [1997] 95 LGR 449 (HC). But it has recently been said that an SSD may refuse to provide a service if it is *impossible* for legal reasons for the SSD to supply it: *R v Swindon BC, ex parte Stoddard* (1998) 2 July, unreported (DC), in which an SSD was unable to provide 'community care' accommodation in a regional secure unit, as such facilities only accept 'sectioned' patients (see further 8.7). In addition, an existent and continuing duty may be terminated if the intended recipient of the services in question refuses to accept them: *R v Kensington and Chelsea London Borough Council, ex parte Kujtim* (1999) *The Times,* 5 August (CA).

At both stages of the assessment process, the way that 'need' is defined is the crucial factor. It is worth pointing out that a 'need' is not a 'right'. As such, although the 1990 Act was purported to herald a new era of user driven services, the statute retains the paternalistic language of the past. An SSD may involve other agencies in the assessment process, yet there is no provision in the statute for input from the client. However, client and carer involvement is a key element of the 'care plan approach' (see 9.4), and so discussion of needs with the client is the norm. But although the client may express preferences, the final decision is with the SSD. On the other hand, the distinction between a 'preference' and a 'need' will not always be clear, and an SSD that draws the distinction inappropriately may be liable to successful challenge by way of judicial review. This is what happened in *R v Avon County Council, ex parte M* [1994] 2 FCR 259 (HC), in which M, a learning disabled client in need of residential accommodation expressed an emphatic preference for a particular care home, but the SSD placed him in another home on grounds of cost. After seeking unsuccessfully to challenge the decision through the SSD's complaints procedure, M sought judicial review, and was successful, on the grounds that his strong preference constituted a psychological need on his part, that required accommodation in the home of his choice in order for it to be satisfied. This seems to hold out a beacon of hope for client involvement, and while this is accurate in a sense, from another perspective it merely emphasises that it is what a client needs rather than what a client wants which is the decisive factor; and if a want is to be satisfied, it must first be redefined as a need. This is antithetical to the concept of empowerment. Indeed, it may be possible to go further and argue that the assessment procedure under the NHSCCA 1990 as constructed by law comes close to systematic disempowerment, and *Avon* expresses the exception that proves the rule; that unless clients present as supplicants, which involves clients recasting themselves in the discursive terms of social work as an essentially paternalist discourse, they will be turned away. Of course, latterday social work no longer espouses this Victorian philosophy, but the law has yet to catch up.

Nevertheless, needs are not abstract entities, and a client's needs must be assessed sensitively. For example, services to be provided to clients in their own homes must take account of the particular circumstances of that homelife. Obviously, attitudes towards, say, the use of residential accommodation will vary from client to client and family to family. Less obviously, perhaps, cultural factors may also often be pertinent. There is some evidence to suggest that mental health services are experienced by actual and potential users from within a particular cultural perspective (Littlewood and Lipsedge, 1982), and the potential of any state system to function as a conduit of racism has been underscored by the events that have unfolded in the wake of the death of Stephen Lawrence. Gender is also a relevant consideration (Thorogood, 1989); and both factors impact on the question of need and how an SSD makes itself aware of needs in its area (Ahmad and Atkin (eds), 1996). For example there are issues surrounding language skills, particularly amongst first generation immigrants from the Indian subcontinent. There is also a reported lack of knowledge of available mental health services, particularly amongst Asian women (Hatfield et al, 1996) which calls for more assertive, but also sensitive, outreach, if needs are to be identified as readily as in other sections of the community. This assumes that (more) intervention is necessarily a good thing, which is in reality an open question. But the point here is that 'need' cannot be assessed outside its broader social context; and in this lies both the potential for empowerment and disempowerment in the assessment process under s. 47.

In the 1990s a dominant and recurring theme has been the relationship between needs and resources: is an individual's 'need' to be assessed without reference to external factors, or is it permissible to take such factors, most importantly available resources, into account? The most significant recent decision is that of the House of Lords in *R* v *Gloucestershire County Council and another, ex parte Barry* [1997] 2 All ER 1, which was not concerned directly with the 1990 Act but rather with the Chronically Sick and Disabled Persons Act 1970. As discussed in 9.2.2.5, the 1970 Act is not listed in s. 46(3) of the 1990 Act, and even if it does come under that section by virtue of its relation to s. 29 of the 1948 Act, it also and simultaneously functions as a parallel regime, concerned with the provision of services to 'disabled' persons. The wording of the provisions of the 1970 Act that deal with access to services is similar but not identical to the wording in s. 47(1) of the 1990 Act, but it is possible nonetheless to apply the implications of the opinions handed down in *Barry* to the question of the interpretation of the 1990 Act.

In *Barry* the situation was that an SSD, pleading lack of resources, intended to withdraw cleaning and laundry services, which it had been supplying to B, a pensioner, under the terms of s. 2(1) of the 1970 Act. This duty is to provide, where 'necessary', a variety of social services to disabled persons who 'need' them. The central thrust of the opinions of a majority of the House of Lords was once a need has been assessed to exist, and it had been decided that it was necessary to meet it (because it was not being met in some other way, for example through the efforts of informal carers) there was a duty to meet it. Lord Clyde said that 'a shortage of resources will not excuse a failure in the performance of the duty' (at p. 16). But that does not mean 'that a consideration of resources may not be relevant to the earlier stage' of deciding whether or not a need recognised by law could be said to exist and whether it was necessary to meet it. In short, in determining whether or not a *legally* recognised need existed, the issue of available resources was a factor that could properly be taken into account. This was because, in Lord Clyde's view, '[t]he words 'necessary' and 'needs' are both relative expressions' and their meaning could only be assessed by reference to other factors, such as other, competing needs, types and extent of disabilities, and so on. Once 'external' factors were acknowledged as relevant, the twin issues of first, cost and, with it, resources inevitably became part of the equation. Lord Nicholls of Birkenhead explained (at p. 12) that:

> Once it is accepted . . . that cost is a relevant factor in assessing a person's needs . . . then, in deciding how much weight is to be attached to cost, some evaluation or assumption has to be made about the impact which the cost will have upon the authority. Cost is of more or less significance depending upon whether the authority currently has more or less money. Thus, depending upon the authority's financial position, so the eligibility criteria . . . may properly be more or less stringent.

As far as its implications for the interpretation of s. 47(1) of the 1990 Act are concerned, the decision of the majority in *Barry* makes clear *both* that the assessment of 'needs' under s. 47(1)(a) *and* the question of whether needs, once identified, must be met under s. 47(1)(b), can properly be answered by the SSD with reference to the availability of resources. Unlike s. 2(1) of the 1970 Act which provides that once needs have been identified which must necessarily be met but which will not otherwise be so 'it shall be the duty of that authority to make those arrangements', s. 47(1)(b) only requires that the SSD make a decision *whether or not* to meet any needs which the assessment has identified, *even if it is 'necessary' that such needs be met* and so an SSD may, subject to the principles of judicial review, plead inadequate resources as sufficient reason for deciding against providing the service in question. In essence the second and third elements of the assessment procedure in the 1970 Act have been telescoped in the 1990 Act. Under the 1970 Act, having, first, decided that there is an unmet need, the SSD must, secondly, decide whether it is necessary to meet that need and, finally, if it is necessary, meet it. Under the 1990 Act by contrast, the issues of whether it is necessary to meet the need and the fact of meeting it have been conflated, with the consequence that the 'third' stage of the process has been 'colonised' by the language of discretion with its subtext of resource awareness.

This means that the 1990 Act allows the possibility that needs will be identified but not met. Lord Clyde explained that under the 1970 Act 'in the strict sense of the word no unmet need will exist' (p.17) because the recognition of needs in the first place is tailored by resource considerations. It may be that there is little difference, from the consumer's point of view, between a need which is legally recognised as such but not met (under the 1990 Act) and a need which is not met because it is not recognised as such through an adjustment of the criteria for assessment to keep needs in line with resources (under the 1970 Act). Nevertheless, Schwehr (1997, pp.664-5) sees this as in part at least a positive development, as 'the notion of unmet need, as widely understood in the field, has finally received attention and recognition by the Lords. Its existence is no longer a matter for shame, concealed by means of mealy-mouthed assessments'. It may well be that the decision in *Barry* will make it easier to challenge decisions to deny services if it does encourage SSDs to explain refusals on grounds of resource limitations rather than by denying the existence of a need. Schwehr suggests that to avoid successful claims for judicial review on grounds of *Wednesbury* unreasonableness, 'authorities will have to set their criteria in their community care plans very much more carefully, and on the basis of much fuller research, consultation and legal advice than is presently the case' (1997, p. 666).

Whilst there is some merit to such points, such an approach really seeks to make a virtue from apparent necessity. The *Wednesbury* test cannot be accused of being overly-protective of the rights of complainants, and to take this approach is to concede that the interpretation of 'need', as it functions in the Acts of 1990 and 1970, adopted by the majority in *Barry* is necessarily the correct one. Ordinarily there is little practical point in disputing a recent and fully reasoned decision of the House of Lords, but in the present state of flux that is community care policy, no point can be assumed to be beyond discussion. And there is a powerful counter argument to the position adopted by the majority of the House, which is to be found in the judgments of the majority in the Court of Appeal and, in particular the dissenting opinion of Lord Lloyd of Berwick in the House of Lords, with which Lord Steyn agreed.

Lord Lloyd accepted that 'need' is a relative concept, but decided that it could nevertheless be defined as 'the lack of what is essential for the ordinary business of living' (at p. 5), which should be 'assessed against the standards of civilised society' (at p. 6). In practice this decision is left to the individual social worker, acting in accordance with standards set at local level by his or her SSD, and although these standards could not be defined precisely, that was no reason to guillotine that judgment through the invocation of questions of resources. His general approach was summed up in his observation that '[e]very child needs a new pair of shoes from time to time. The need is not the less because his parents cannot afford them' (at p. 6). As far as the words of s. 2(1) of the 1970 Act were concerned, 'there is nothing in the language of the section which permits, let alone suggests, that external resources are to be taken into account when assessing the individual's needs' (p.7). Arguably, the same is true of the 1990 Act. If this approach were to be taken — for example if any future statute were positively to exclude any consideration of the availability of resources from the process of assessment of need — it is submitted that both logic and justice would be served. To the extent that Schwehr's argument has force, a true picture of the extent of unmet need is better arrived at by a legal framework which highlights the unavailability of services rather than by denying the existence of needs as a matter of law.

Such an approach also brings into sharp relief the distinction at the stage of meeting identified need that exists between the Acts of 1970 and 1990. Lord Lloyd's opinion rested in part on the relevance of s. 47(2) of the 1990 Act. This provides that if, during the process of carrying out the assessment of needs under s. 47(1)(a), 'it appears to the local authority that [the subject of the assessment] is a disabled person' the SSD 'shall proceed to make such a decision as to the services he requires as is mentioned in section 4 of the Disabled Persons (Services, Consultation and Representation) Act, 1986' (s. 47(2)(a)); and s. 4 of the 1986 Act places a duty on SSDs to assess disabled persons for services under s. 2 of the 1970 Act. Under the terms of s. 4 of the 1986 Act this must be done at the request of the disabled person or their carer, but s. 47(2)(a) of the 1990 Act provides that the SSD must act on its own initiative if the need is identified in the course of an assessment carried out under s. 47(1)(a). In other words, in Lord Lloyd's view, disabled persons are by virtue of s. 47(2) taken out of the discretionary regime of the 1990 Act and relocated into the mandatory regime operating under s. 2 of the 1970 Act. For Lord Lloyd this was a key plank in his reasoning that the duties under the 1970 Act were to be carried out without reference to resources considerations because disabled persons were seen by Parliament 'as a special case' (at p. 8). But if this is correct the more pertinent points for present purposes are, first, why, in principle, disabled persons deserve this privileged status over other community care service users, and secondly, how, in logic, this can be the situation if some service users, in particular, in the context of the present discussion, persons in need of care or assistance by reason of mental disorder, are covered by both Acts. The response of Lord Clyde, for the majority in *Barry*, was to close down on the relevance of s. 47(2) — and so also avoiding these particular difficulties raised at the policy level — by holding that s. 2(1) of the 1970 Act had to be defined not by reference to later legislation but in 'its own terms in the context in which it was enacted' (p.17), and that the rerouting of disabled persons into the 1970 Act regime by s. 47(2) did not imply substantive differences between the regimes but rather speaks merely of 'the desire to recognise the distinct procedural situation relative to the disabled' (p.18). One might be suspicious that this is enough to answer Lord Lloyd's point, particularly, as Schiemann LJ noted in *R v Powys County Council, ex parte Hambridge* [1998] 96 LGR 627 (CA), it is clearly policy that services for the mentally ill are provided free of charge, whilst the policy in regard of services for the disabled is to charge for services. Nevertheless, the labyrinthine nature of this area of community care law makes it impossible to argue authoritatively that Lord Clyde's explanation of the function of s. 47(2) is clearly wrong.

Even so, this does not diminish the point that a service user can demand that his or her identified needs must be met under the 1970 Act but cannot do so under the 1990 Act. Clements (1997, p. 189) has argued, in the context of a discussion of wholesale reform and simplification of community care legislation, that all assessments of entitlement to services should be governed by what is at present s. 47(1) of the 1990 Act, with s. 47(2) of that Act, s. 4 of the 1986 Act and s. 2 of the 1970 Act repealed. This is a proposal of considerable virtue in that it harmonises the assessment process irrespective of the class of user, but its practical effect would be to bring disabled persons 'down' to the level of entitlement currently afforded to other would-be community care service users. This may ultimately be the most realistic proposal, but it is at least arguable that the better option would be to bring other service users 'up' to the level of entitlement currently available under s. 2 of the 1970 Act. One thing is, however, clear. The above analysis of *Barry* reveals that the wording of key statutory provisions is sufficiently loose to bear competing interpretations grounded in competing policy assumptions: here, that which holds that services must, ultimately, be limited by available resources, and, on the other hand, that which holds that resources must be made available to meet such needs as are determined to exist. It is unfortunate that this vital issue is left to the lottery of the court system (in both the Court of Appeal and House of Lords a majority decision was handed down, with four judges deciding the case one way, four the other) and the predilections of unelected judges. Any future statute, whichever policy is decided upon, should make that decision abundantly clear on its face; and if the policy is that services should be needs led rather than resources led, the means to achieve this must also be provided.

Returning to the present situation, however, the above discussion demonstrates that the 1990 Act was always more concerned with the *management* of services, and with the putting in place of a coherent framework of responsibility and accountability for service provision, than with questions of *entitlement*. However, and as if the legal situation were not already complex enough, the 1990 Act did nothing to alter the fact that each of the statutes defined as providing 'community care services' in s. 46(3) of that Act have their own provisions regarding access and entitlement; and increasingly over recent years those seeking access to services have bypassed the 1990 Act altogether and instead sought to argue, with varying degrees of success, that stricter duties are to be found at the 'second level' of the pyramid of community care legislation.

9.3.2 Accessing services at the 'second level'

The nature of the duty imposed under s. 21 of the National Assistance Act 1948 was considered by the Court of Appeal in *R v Sefton Metropolitan Borough Council, ex parte Help the Aged and others* [1997] 4 All ER 532. As discussed above, an SSD has a duty to provide residential accommodation under this section for those who 'by reason of age, infirmity or any other circumstance are in need of care and attention which is not otherwise available to them'. In *Sefton* the defendant SSD had provided an elderly woman, B, with residential accommodation on her leaving hospital. Initially, her available capital was above the £16,000 limit set by s. 22 of the 1948 Act and para. 20 of the National Assistance (Amendment of Resources) Regulations 1992, made by the Secretary of State, which meant that B funded her own placement by way of charges levied by the SSD under s. 22. When B's capital fell to £16,000 the SSD carried out an assessment of her needs and determined that she was in need of residential accommodation. However, as the SSD did not have sufficient funds to provide accommodation for all the elderly people in need in its area, it had developed a policy whereby it would not fund residential accommodation until the resident's capital fell to £1,500. Paragraph 20 of the 1992 Regulations, however, required that charges be reduced for persons with capital below £16,000, and that capital of less than £10,000 be discounted, by an SSD when deciding whether to charge a recipient of residential care for some or all of the cost of that care (see now the Community Care (Residential Accommodation) Act 1998).

The charity, Help the Aged brought an application for judicial review to test the legality of the SSD's policy, and this entailed consideration by the Court of Appeal, *inter alia*, of the nature of the duty owed by an SSD under s. 21 of the 1948 Act. Lord Woolf MR, in the light of *Barry*, felt 'compelled to conclude that there is a limited subjective element in making an assessment of whether the ailments of the person concerned do or do not collectively establish a need for care and attention' (at p. 543). However, in his view, it is 'very much more difficult' for an SSD to plead lack of resources under s. 21 of the 1948 Act than in the context of s. 29 of that Act or s. 2(1) of the 1970 Act. Part of the reason for this was that the nature of the need — for accommodation — is qualitatively different, by definition of greater severity, from a need for other services. In part also, Lord Woolf emphasised that the requirement of s. 2(1) of the 1970 Act — that it must be 'necessary' to provide the services in question — was absent from s. 21 of the 1948 Act, so that under the latter provision there is a duty to meet needs even though it is not 'necessary' that they are met. It is perhaps the case that Lord Woolf's comments would not survive an appeal to the House of Lords. The qualitative distinction between a need for accommodation and a need for other services tends to break down in practice because a failure to provide services in the community increases the likelihood that service users will need residential accommodation. Furthermore, if there is not always a duty, because of limited resources, to meet 'needs' when it has been decided that it is 'necessary' to do so, under the 1970 Act, the implication is, surely, that there should be *greater* scope for the exercise of discretion in the case of needs that are *not* defined as 'necessary' under s. 21 of the 1948 Act and not, as Lord Woolf suggested, *less* scope. Yet this merely points to the problematic nature of the 'policy' on community care provision, as Lord Woolf was surely correct to the extent that there is no reason in principle why it should be have to be 'necessary' that services are provided under s. 2(1) of the 1970 Act, but not under s. 21 of the 1948 Act. Surely there *should* be a duty to provide residential accommodation in cases where it is necessary to do so?

This view clearly informed Lord Woolf's ruling that it was not lawful for an SSD to adopt a system of prioritisation that contradicted the clear policy in s. 22 and the attendant Regulations. Hence, when a resident's capital fell to £16,000 (the specified limit); and following an assessment which revealed a need that, even when resources were taken into account, the SSD concluded that it was under a duty to meet it, then it must do so. It was unlawful to delay meeting a need in such circumstances and 'lack of resources is no excuse' (at p. 543). Nor did the court have much time for the argument that, as an SSD must under the terms of s. 21 of the 1948 Act only provide services 'which are not otherwise available', there was no duty to provide services which were 'otherwise available' by reason of the ability of applicants to fund their own care. This 'totally defeats the intention of s. 22' (ibid.); that under the specified capital limits an SSD must fund care for those under the financial threshold of entitlement regardless of ability to pay. As such, *Sefton* must be counted as at least a partial victory for Help the Aged. The Court of Appeal closed down various 'escape routes' that the SSD had sought to utilise in avoidance of its statutory duty. And although Lord Woolf's reasoning may be somewhat problematic for the reasons discussed above, the decision in this case seems to suggest that there is a greater possibility of ensuring access to residential provision by going directly to s. 21 of the 1948 Act rather than via s. 47 of the NHSCCA 1990, which is effectively to render s. 47(1) of the 1990 Act otiose for these purposes. It is legitimate to wonder, from the point of view of service users, what the function of the passage of the 1990 Act has been other than to complicate the legal situation and to confront would-be applicants with a virtually unintelligible legal maze masquerading as a 'gateway' into securing entitlement. The need for reform is clear.

The effect of *Barry* and *Sefton* is that access to residential accommodation under part III of the 1948 Act is to be assessed differently from access to other welfare services under part III. Access to services under s. 45 of the Health Services and Public Health Act 1968 is if anything more discretionary in nature than access to any other services under any other provisions, as s. 45 provides a power but does not impose a duty on SSDs to provide services for 'the promotion of the welfare of old people'. The main relevance of s. 45 of the 1968 Act for present purposes is that it illustrates yet another permutation of the confused relationship between community care services as defined by s. 46(3) of the 1990 Act and other services, as here the services which are so defined function in effect as a safety net for those falling through the 1970 Act rather than the 1990 Act.

Access to the services to be provided under s. 21, sch. 8, NHSA 1977 is equally problematic. The services to be provided (see 9.2.3) are defined in s. 21 as 'functions exercisable by local social service authorities', whilst para. 2(1) of sch. 8 provides that SSDs 'may, with the Secretary of State's approval, and to such extent as he may direct shall, make arrangements for the purpose of the prevention of illness and for the care of persons suffering from illness and for the after-care of persons who have been so suffering'. Appendix 3 of LAC(93)10 provides that the Secretary of State has approved the making of arrangements under s. 21 in connection with all three of these purposes (LAC(93)10, Appendix 3, para. 3(1), (3)), with the exception of such services for the purpose of prevention of mental disorder, which are the subject of a direction, in para. 3(2). Yet this does not mean that *individual* applicants have a right to access the services in question. The services in question — the provision of training and day centres, a sufficient number of social workers and social work services — are by their nature 'general' provisions; and the reference to 'persons' rather than 'any person' supports the view that this is a 'general duty' not enforceable by individuals and similar, for example, to the general duty that the police have for the detection and investigation of crime (see *R v Commissioner of Police of the Metropolis, ex parte Blackburn* [1968] 1 All ER 763; (No. 2) [1968] 2 All ER 319; (No. 3) [1973] 1 All ER 324 (CA)). This view is further supported by the observation of Lord Clyde in *Barry* (at p. 16) that apart from s. 2(1) of the Chronically Sick and Disabled Persons Act 1970, there was only one other directly enforceable duty to be found in the statutory regime, and that is contained in s. 117, MHA 1983.

Section 117, MHA 1983 imposes a duty on both HAs and SSDs to provides services for mentally disordered persons, but is limited in two ways. First,

s. 117 only authorises the provision of after care, although the term is not itself defined or its components specified. The content of after care has, however, been made clearer by the introduction of 'after care under supervision', which is discussed further at 9.5.3. Secondly, it applies to a limited class of persons, namely only those discharged from hospital following detention under ss. 3, 37 (with or without restrictions) or transfer to hospital under ss. 47 or 48 of the MHA 1983. Section 117 has no application to informal patients or those detained under ss. 2, 4, 5, or 136 if not subsequently transferred to s. 3. Such patients must therefore rely on the general powers in the NHSA 1977, and their attendant problems of enforceability. But for those who do come under the terms of s. 117, it may be that this provision offers a more fruitful avenue for seeking access to services.

That the duties imposed by s. 117 are owed to each individual in receipt of after care was established in *R* v *Ealing District Health Authority, ex parte Fox* [1993] 1 WLR 373; 3 All ER 170 (HC). Otton J pointed out that s. 117(2) provides that 'it shall be the duty' of HAs and SSDs, in consultation with voluntary agencies, to provide after care 'for *any person* to whom this section applies' (emphasis added), holding that the duty is not only a general duty but a specific duty owed to the applicant (1 WLR 373 at p. 385). An order of certiorari was issued to quash the decision of the HA not to provide psychiatric supervision to F, a psychiatric in-patient who had been adjudged suitable for discharge, provided that suitable aftercare was available. However, the same court rather watered down the force of its own judgment by refusing to make an order of mandamus to compel the HA to act, on the grounds that this would be to compel a psychiatrist to treat against his or her clinical judgment (p. 387). It may be that Otton J had in mind the earlier Court of Appeal rulings, *Re J* [1991] 3 All ER 930 and *Re J* [1992] 4 All ER 614, in which it held that no doctor can be compelled to treat against his or her clinical judgment. Otton J did make it clear, however, that an HA, faced initially with staff who refuse to treat or otherwise supervise a patient following discharge 'is under a continuing obligation to make further endeavours to provide arrangements' and it is only when such steps have been taken without success that the HA should admit defeat. *Fox* involved a patient subject to restrictions who was conditionally discharged by an MHRT. But his discharge was to be delayed until necessary arrangements had been made; and it was the refusal of psychiatrists to comply with the tribunal's direction for the continued treatment of the patient in the community which led to the application for judicial review. There was thus the option, which Otton J suggested, of referring the case to the Secretary of State when the 'deadlock' point had been reached (see Chapter eight). This option is unavailable for patients not subject to restrictions, and it is to be hoped that in a similar situation to that which arose in *Fox*, a future court would not be so unwilling to order mandamus. With respect to the view of Otton J, this is not to require psychiatrists or others to act against their best clinical judgments, but rather to require HAs and SSDs to find clinicians willing to treat. To take any other view would be to give rise to the possibility that 'inability to find willing treatment providers' could be used to block discharges that would otherwise be warranted. Yet the approach in *Fox* has recently been adopted by the Court of

Appeal, in *R* v *Mental Health Review Tribunal and others, ex parte Hall* (1999) *The Times*, 5 October (CA). This case involved a patient who had been judged fit for discharge by a tribunal, provided that various conditions, relating to the patient's place of residence and continued supervision after discharge. The arrangements necessary to put these conditions into effect had not been by the relevant HA and SSD, because of various difficulties relating to the patient and the hostility felt towards him by the local community. On an application in the High Court for judicial review, Scott Baker J (reported at [1999] 3 ALL ER 132) attempted to find a mechanism for the enforcement of the s. 117 duty by tribunals. He held, *inter alia*, that the duty under s. 117 extended to the provision, before the hearing, to a tribunal of a care plan for the patient if discharged, and that a tribunal could require the provision of such a plan. The Court of Appeal, however, did not agree: although a tribunal might properly attempt to 'shame' HAs and SSDs into compliance with its orders, it could not require compliance, even if the net effect was that a patient judged suitable for discharge remained in hospital. From the patient's point of view, the decision in *Fox* has been further watered down by the statements made by the Court of Appeal in *Clunis* v *Camden and Islington HA* [1998] 2 WLR 902, in which it was pointed out that complainants should not look to the courts to enforce any duty owed under s. 117 unless having first made a complaint to the Secretary of State to exercise the default powers available in s. 124. These default powers were repealed by s. 66(2) and sch. 10, NHSCCA 1990, although equivalent powers were inserted as s. 7D, Local Authority Social Services Act 1970 by s. 50, NHSCCA 1990. But the important point is that it is unlikely that a complaint would elicit the outcome that the applicant wants, as the Secretary of State is concerned more with the general provision of services than access to them by individuals.

9.3.3   Other avenues of complaint

It is in itself noteworthy that those seeking access to services have used the mechanism of judicial review with such frequency, as this tells the tale of the paucity of other remedies. The House of Lords has effectively closed down the possibility of an action for breach of statutory duty in this area, taking the view that such an action will only be a possibility where there are no avenues of complaint built into the relevant statutory scheme: *Cocks* v *Thanet District Council* [1983] AC 286 and *X* v *Bedfordshire County Council* [1995] 3 All ER 353. Thus, as there are, for example, mechanisms which empower the Secretary of State to issue directions to specific SSDs, it is doubtful that a private law action for breach of statutory duty would lie, and any suggestion that it may do so in the context of services under s. 117, MHA 1983 to be found in the judgment in *Fox* was firmly scotched by the Court of Appeal in *Clunis*. The NHS complaints procedure set up in 1995 and the Patients' Charter are other options, but are unlikely to be effective as a means of securing access to services that have been denied following a community care assessment, since they trade in what Montgomery (1997, p. 61) has termed 'rights in a weak sense', intended to be broad statements of entitlement and expectation, rather than to be enforceable by individuals.

9.4   INTER-AGENCY COOPERATION

In addition to the requirement of collegiate community care planning imposed by s. 46, NHSCCA 1990, and the general duty to work together under s. 22, NHSA 1977, s. 47(3) of the 1990 Act provides that if, during the assessment of needs carried out under s. 47(1), it appears to the SSD that there may be a need for health or housing services, the SSD must notify the relevant HA or local housing authority and 'invite them to assist, to such extent as is reasonable in the circumstances, in the making of the assessment' and the SSD 'shall take into account any services that are likely to be made available by a HA or local housing authority'. The implications of this in the particular context of the provision of independent housing are considered below. But it is first necessary to consider the general position regarding inter-agency cooperation. Policy guidance issued contemporaneously with the NHSCCA 1990 stressed that 'local collaboration is the key to making a reality of community care' (Department of Health, 1990a). The point was repeated in the later document, *Building Bridges: a guide to arrangements for inter-agency working for the care and protection of severely mentally ill people* (Department of Health, 1995a, para. 1.3.6): 'multidisciplinary [community care provision] can only function where all those in the team work effectively together for the good of the patient', not only in formulating and delivering service packages but also in other ways, for example in sharing information and deciding local priorities. The main principles of inter-agency working are listed in *Building Bridges* (para. 1.1.1) as including:

- a commitment to joint working at all levels of the agencies involved, including senior management;
- a focus on service users, including sensitivity to the particular needs of individuals (specifically including people from ethnic minorities);
- an agreed and jointly 'owned' strategy for the care of severely mentally ill people;
- agreed and well understood procedures for accessing services.

In addition, other forms of cooperation, regarding such matters as the effective sharing of information, joint commissioning of services, joint training, and collective and regular review of arrangements are mentioned. With specific regard to mental disorder, the heart of the policy is the Care Programme Approach (CPA), implemented in 1991 by a Department of Health Circular (1990b). While the lead agency for community care services is the SSD, primary responsibility for the CPA lies with HAs, but 'if properly implemented, multi-disciplinary assessment will ensure that the duty to make a community care assessment is fully discharged as part of the CPA, and there should not be a need for separate assessments' (Department of Health, 1995a, para. 1.3.8).

According to the NHS Executive, which in 1994 endorsed the CPA in the form of Guidance (Department of Health, 1994), the main aim 'is to ensure the support of mentally ill persons in the community thereby minimising the possibility of their losing contact with services and maximising the effect of any therapeutic intervention' (para. 9). Paragraph 10 of the Guidance details the main elements of the CPA as:

- *systematic assessment* of health, social care and housing needs, both in the short and long term;
- a written *care plan* agreed by the patient, relevant professionals, and the patient's carers;
- the allocation of a *key worker* to provide a focal point for contact with the recipient of services, monitor service delivery and respond to problems if and when they arise;
- *regular review* of the patient's progress and ongoing needs.

The various limitations in the statutory scheme do not apply to the CPA, which, for example, applies to all patients discharged from hospital and not merely those covered by s. 117, MHA 1983 (Department of Health, 1994, para. 8). In *Building Bridges* it was made clear that 'the CPA can and should be applied to all patients who are accepted by the specialist psychiatric services' (para. 1.3.6). The CPA must be written into contracts with independent and voluntary providers of services. It is the particular task of the 'key worker' (which may be any member of a multidisciplinary team, but will most often be a community psychiatric nurse or psychiatric social worker: see the discussion at Department of Health, 1995a, paras. 3.1.18-3.1.25) to monitor the implementation of the CPA in individual cases. The ideal is a 'tiered approach', in which there is an initial 'needs assessment' which will usually be carried out by the professional (medical or social work) to whom the potential service user has been referred, to be followed by a multi-disciplinary assessment as soon as possible thereafter (para. 3.1.3). However, a full multidisciplinary assessment should be reserved for complex cases. Mindful of the resource implications, *Building Bridges* made clear that the CPA does not mean routine multidisciplinary assessment but rather tailored assessment according to perceived need (para. 3.1.6). Running parallel with the CPA is the broader Department of Health policy of 'care management', which also entails an individualised approach to the treatment of persons within the NHS generally. The CPA is intended to be seen as 'a specialist variant of care management for people with mental health problems' (1995a, para. 3.2.8). Care management may include the appointment of a nominated care manager, or, if the client has complex needs, managers.

There is little doubt that in terms of joint documentation and agreed policies, inter-agency cooperation has improved in the last decade. But it remains the case that the current situation is far from the 'seamless service' that was promised in 1990. In part at least, this may be because the potential for cooperation is delimited by the fact that each agency, and the professions that dominate the various agencies, functions within different paradigms of care. Questions of inter-professional relations were considered in Chapter five. Equally, in the context of community care, a clash of perspective may be a feature of cooperation at ground level between health professionals and social workers. It has been argued that this is the result of differences in professional ideology, overlaid with factors relating to organisational identity, which function as a sort of 'double separation' between SSDs and HAs and their respective staff (Dalley, 1993; Onyett et al, 1994). Divisions are continually recreated by a separation of the level of basic professional education and training. The result is an inevitable politicisation of inter-professional relationships. The professional status of social workers, both in the public mind and in their dealings with psychiatric professionals, especially consultant psychiatrists, remains ambivalent. And it is not just a case of a simple binary split between the professional and organisational cultures of health and social service workers respectively. On the medical 'side' of the divide, psychiatric nurses and psychotherapists are jostling for professional position with psychiatrists (see 7.5). There are two main practical consequences of this. First, that there is a 'grey area' falling between that which is clearly health care and that which is clearly social care, over which responsibility is ill-defined or agreed (Lewis and Glennerster, 1996). Secondly, the assessment process, and the implementation of the CPA, may not always be the consensual experience that the government's guidance might suggest. In this respect, the seemingly innocuous and straightforward advice, that a client's key worker will not always act as care manager, and that for clients with complex needs the functions of care manager may be shared amongst several professionals (1995a, para. 3.2.10), can in fact be seen to carry the risk that service delivery will be experienced by clients as fractured, possibly even as contradictory or incoherent.

There is also evidence to suggest that the introduction of managerialist principles (see 3.3.2) has impacted negatively on the quality of services. This has led to a tendency amongst SSDs and HAs to budget defensively (Wistow, 1994, 1995), a tendency which has accelerated as pressure on resources has increased. The courts have been called upon on a number of occasions in recent years to adjudicate in disputes between various public authorities over responsibility for the provision of a particular service or in the meeting of a particular need. An example is the dispute which spawned *Avon County Council v Hooper and another* [1997] 1 All ER 532 (CA). An SSD had provided services for a severely disabled client, H, from his birth in 1978 until his death in 1991. The services in question were those for which an SSD is entitled to charge under s. 17, Health and Social Services and Social Security Adjudications Act 1983, which now allows charges to be levied by an SSD for the provision of non-residential services: LAC(94)1. At the time, however, SSDs could also charge for residential services under this provision, and it was residential accommodation that had been provided in this case, although no charge had been made by the time of H's death. In 1989 the local HA had paid almost £300,000 to H in settlement of a negligence claim arising out of the circumstances of his birth, and had agreed to indemnify H against claims for care provided prior to the date of that settlement. The SSD, who had funded H's care, sued H's estate and the HA in order to recover a proportion of its cost, amounting to £232,000. The court held that it was reasonable for the SSD to levy such a charge, that charges could be levied retrospectively, and that if a lesser sum is to be payable, the onus is on the chargee to persuade the SSD why that should be the case. But the particular pertinence of this case in the present context is that it shows how far from effective cooperation the actual relationship between an SSD and a HA can be at local level.

In an important recent decision, *R* v *North and East Devon Health Authority ex parte Coughlan* (1999) *The Times*, 20 July (CA), the Court of Appeal has attempted to specify the border between those the responsibilities of HAs and SSDs with greater clarity. The case concerned the care of C, who had been severely disabled and left with a serious neurological condition following a road traffic accident in 1971. Since that time she had been resident in accommodation provided by her HA. The HA now wished to close the facility and transfer C to residential accommodation provided by the SSD. The case involved several issues, but the pertinent one for the present purposes concerned the question of the financing of C's nursing care in the SSD-provided facility. If it was to be provided by the HA as 'nursing care' it had to be provided free of charge (under s. 1(2) National Health Service Act 1977), but if it was to be provided by the SSD then C was liable to charges (under the terms of the legislation discussed above). The Court of Appeal, held that the duty of SSDs to provide accommodation under s. 21, NAA 1948, as it contemplated that those in need of accommodation by reason of age, illness or disability, necessarily implied that some nursing care could properly be provided as part of the 'package of care' for which SSDs are responsible. Such nursing care must be that which is 'provided in connection with the accommodation', as required by s. 21(5), NAA 1948. In C's case, her need for nursing was such that it could not be deemed to be part of any 'social care' package, as her disabilities were such that it would not be reasonable for an SSD to be expected to provide for them. However, this decision does establish that SSDs may provide nursing services and charge recipients for them, and that HAs need not provide those services. This is a neat solution that on the one hand accords with common sense: it seems sensible that those in SSD-provided residential accommodation should have the whole of the package of care that is required provided *as* a package, by one provider. The territory of SSDs, which HAs need not stray into, is now more clearly delineated. But on the other hand, if the need for such 'general' nursing care is that of people living in their own homes, its provision is the responsibility of HAs, as the Court of Appeal acknowledged. It seems odd that whether a client is charged or not depends solely on whether the services are received in residential accommodation of the client's own home; and this also provides a cost-based incentive to prefer the use of residential accommodation over out-patient services in borderline cases. Moreover, the Court of Appeal in *Coughlan* pointed out that where the line is to be drawn between 'social care' and 'nursing care' will sometimes be problematic, depending on 'a careful appraisal of the facts of the individual case'; and although *Coughlan* may have stemmed the stream of legal disputes between HAs and SSDs, it is unlikely that this is the last word to be heard on this issue.

Research carried out by the NHS Executive in conjunction with NHS regional offices and the Social Services Inspectorate in 1997 confirmed that a seamless service is far from being realised in many parts of the country. Only slightly more than half of all SSDs had completed a comprehensive assessment of needs in their areas as required by s. 46, NHSCCA 1990, and HAs had contributed to only two thirds of the assessments of needs that had been carried out under s. 47. The research also found that 'few community teams are integrated' and one reason for this was that SSDs and HAs 'used different systems for recording information about the processes of treatment and care', and more often than not the data accumulated by each was not shared (see Department of Health, 1998a, paras. 3.6 to 3.13). Clearly, the organisational, ideological and financial barriers to better cooperation continue to exert a significant influence. This research also found that in many SSD areas a commitment to client empowerment was noticeably lacking. Only half of all SSDs reported having involved service users in the assessment of local needs required by s. 46 (para. 3.7).

If this is in part an organisational or managerial problem, its solution requires more than organisational reforms. The road, both to client empowerment and inter-organisational efficiency, is also blocked by legal obstacles. Some of these have been discussed above. In the context of housing services, a particular issue is the discretionary language of s. 47(3) of the NHSCCA 1990, under which it is always open for an HA or local housing authority to decline the invitation to assess or meet the needs of an individual who must be assessed by an SSD under s. 47(1). Where does this leave the role and function of local housing authorities in community care provision? The Conservative government's view, expressed in LAC 93(10) (Department of Health, 1993b) was that 'no new category of entitlement to housing is created by 1990 Act'. The need to consider independent housing had been a feature of the debates about the future direction of community care in the 1980s. But by the time of the Griffith Report (1988), upon which the subsequent White Paper and the 1990 Act were largely based, the assumption was that the need was for the provision of services to clients already living in their own homes. Although the much trumpeted intention of the 1990 Act had been to provide 'the right level of intervention and support to enable people to achieve maximum independence and control over their own lives' (Department of Health, 1990a), LAC(93)10 effectively meant that the role of local housing authorities in the realisation of community care practice would be at best marginal. As Cowan (1995a, p. 216) put it, '[t]his message was crystal clear: either own or occupy your own home or be provided with residential care but do not expect us to provide you with your own independent accommodation'. Contrary to the view expressed in social work theory (see 3.3.1), the housing elements of the 1990 Act do not reveal a policy of client empowerment; and the point is that this is above and beyond local policies, practices, or failure of communication. It is true that there have been moves in the direction of greater user choice, the clearest example being the Community Care (Direct Payments) Act 1996 which gives SSDs a power to provide funds directly to certain classes of service user, including mentally ill persons, who may then purchase their own care. However, the service user must first persuade the SSD that he or she is in need of community care services; and there are limitations on the use of direct payments for residential accommodation under s. 21 of the 1948 Act, since an SSD is required under that section to 'make arrangements' and it has been held that the making of direct payments to service users does not comprise such: *R v Secretary of State*

for Health, ex parte LB Hammersmith and Fulham (and others), The Independent,
15 July 1997 (HC), nor does this help the client to access the general public
housing stock.

Moreover, accommodation under ss. 21 or 26 of the 1948 Act is designed as
a last resort provision, to be activated only when care and attention is 'not
otherwise available', a phrase which is for the SSD rather than the client to
define. Although subject to judicial review (see *Sefton,* discussed at 9.3.2), this
can hardly be seen as a measure designed to empower service users. It can be
argued that this situation is far from satisfactory as a matter of policy, all the
more so when this situation is overlaid by the weakly worded responsibility of
local housing authorities to assist in meeting needs identified in a s. 47
assessment. That a local housing authority is not required even to assist at the
stage of assessment of needs, let alone at the stage of actual provision of services
again casts some doubt on the claims that under the 1990 Act service users
would experience a 'seamless service' across local government departments. If
a housing authority declines an invitation to assist, it is perfectly possible that
an SSD will nevertheless go on to decide that there is a need for independent
housing which it, under the terms of the 1948 Act, cannot supply. Even if a
local housing authority does assist at the stage of need assessment, there is no
provision under the 1990 Act to require it to meet any housing needs that are
identified. In sum, this means that the only way for those in need of housing,
other than residential accommodation, to access provision is through private
rental or the general housing legislation. It seems clear that an entitlement to
'ordinary' housing is a prerequisite for a community care policy that has as one
of its intentions to reduce the all-too-frequent triadic equation between mental
illness, homelessness, and avoidable institutionalisation (Abdul-Hamid and
Cooney, 1997). Yet there is no such provision in the current legal regime.

Attempts by service users to enlarge the scope of community care in this
regard by recourse to litigation have met with little success, notwithstanding
that 'a person who is vulnerable as a result of mental illness or handicap' is
defined as being in 'priority need' of local authority or social housing:
s. 189(1)(c), Housing Act 1996, in which case the authority 'shall secure that
accommodation is available for occupation by the applicant' under s. 193(2) of
the same Act. The main blow came in the form of further restrictions on access
to housing, placed on persons in priority need under what is now s. 189(1)(c),
by the decision of the House of Lords in *R v Oldham MBC, ex parte Garlick; R
v Tower Hamlets LBC, ex parte Ferdous Begum* [1993] 2 All ER 65 (HL). The
latter case on this conjoined appeal, which was heard before the passage of the
Act of 1996, although the statutory definition of 'priority need' has not
changed, involved an application for council housing made by F, a learning
disabled woman. This had been rejected by the local housing authority on the
basis, *inter alia,* that F lacked the mental capacity to agree to the application
that had been made in her name (the application was for housing for F and her
family), or to accept an offer of housing if one were made. In the leading
opinion on this point, Lord Griffiths confirmed that no duty arose to provide
accommodation unless the applicant, even if both vulnerable and in priority
need, had sufficient mental capacity to agree to the terms of the tenancy, on the

basis that the housing legislation was concerned with housing provision rather than the provision for the severely disabled, which was instead provided under s. 21, NAA 1948. As Edmunds aptly summarises, 'this significant and regrettable decision denies people with a mental illness or mental handicap who are homeless, access in their own right to the complicated network of provisions on local authority assistance' (1994, p. 358). This does not mean that all persons who are mentally disordered will be unable to access entitlement to housing, but it does mean that those who fail the capacity test (with obscure content) which local housing authorities are licensed to apply after *Garlick* will be excluded. And it is hard to believe that the issue of the resources (in terms of services provided in the home, that would be required to accommodate many such persons in 'conventional' housing) was not within the contemplation of Lord Griffiths in reaching his conclusion on the law (McCabe, 1996); particularly as Lord Slynn dissented, on the basis that there is no reference to a test of capacity on the face of the legislation.

There are further examples of a failure on the part of the courts to embrace and enforce a notion of inter-agency working. For example, in *R* v *Brent LBC, ex parte Mawcan* (1994) 26 HLR 528 (HC) the court refused to find that it was unreasonable of a local housing authority to place community care clients in 'bed and breakfast' accommodation, even though concerns have been expressed that such accommodation is unsuitable for mentally disordered persons, risking 'ghettoisation' of mentally disordered persons, as many people are reluctant to share such accommodation with the mentally ill (Jodelet, 1991). More alarmingly still, in *R* v *Wirral MBC, ex parte B, The Times*, 3 May 1994 (HC), it was held that a local housing authority was under no duty to contact the local SSD when contemplating evicting a person known to be in need of community care services. In *Wirral*, B had been evicted from her council property as a result of her awkward and difficult behaviour. She was then held to be intentionally homeless (under what is now s. 191, Housing Act 1996) even though she was acknowledged by reason of mental illness to be in priority need. Cowan (1995b) has argued that *Wirral* may be wrongly decided because in other cases courts have looked at the background reasons for homelessness when deciding if, in a given case, it can said to be 'intentional'. In *Wirral* Johnson J held that it is for the client rather than the local housing authority to contact the local SSD. This case underlines the point that patient advocacy (see Chapter twelve) is vitally important if client empowerment is to develop as fully in practice as it has in various strands of social work theory, just as it underlines the degree to which the current *legal* framework must accept its share of culpability for the 'failure' of care in the community.

Although the judiciary have hardly improved the situation, it is nevertheless clear that the fundamental problems concern the failure to integrate the community care regime with the housing regime more fully than has been required under s. 47 of the 1990 Act. In an illuminating analysis Cowan (1995a) has argued that although part of the problem can be located in the change in status experienced by both SSDs and local housing authorities by the 1990 Act (in that, as 'purchasers' and 'enablers' respectively, each has been obliged into new, and contradictory roles), and although the abilities of local housing authorities to use their housing stock creatively having been curtailed by the mass sale of council accommodation and central government restrictions on the new building, the key to the problem is in the interrelation of the relevant legislation. One element of this is that under the 1990 Act regime, entitlement is triggered by being 'ordinarily resident' in the SSD area in question. And this remains the case despite the ruling in *R* v *Berkshire CC, ex parte P* [1997] 95 LGR 449 (HC) that there is no such limitation of the right to be assessed under s. 47(1), as in the key 'community care service' of residential accommodation under s. 21 of the 1948 Act the phrase *is* applicable. By contrast, the concept used in the housing legislation is 'local connection', currently contained in s. 199, Housing Act 1996. The two concepts are not coterminous, and whether an applicant has satisfied the requirement is for the SSD or local housing authority respectively. Moreover, s. 198 of the 1996 Act provides that even if an applicant is in priority need, and is not intentionally homeless, a local housing authority may decline to provide accommodation of any sort if of the view that the applicant does not have a local connection with its area but does have a local connection with the area of another local housing authority.

In such circumstances the duty of the first local housing authority in question is only to notify the second one, and the first one need not even offer advice and assistance to the applicant: ss. 197, 198(1), Housing Act 1996. In sum this means that the potential for 'passing the parcel', both as between SSDs and local housing authorities, and between different local housing authorities is built into the statutory scheme. The possibility is exacerbated further by directions made by the Secretary of State in relation to the operation by SSDs of s. 21 of the 1948 Act (by LAC(93)10, Appendix 1), which as detailed above (see 9.2.2.1) require SSDs to provide residential accommodation for persons in urgent need. At 'best', this means that the onus is primarily on SSDs acting under the 1948 Act rather than on local housing authorities acting under the 1996 Act to deal with mentally disordered persons in urgent need of housing, which is to close further the gateway into the general housing stock. At worst 'SSDs might also seek to restrict their definitions of the basis that [the Housing Act 1996] should mop up most cases' (Cowan, 1995a, p. 223), whereas local housing authorities may equally well take the view that the reverse situation should pertain, with SSDs dealing with the bulk of provision. Given the discretionary nature of the community care duties of local housing authorities in s. 47 of the 1990 Act, it is likely that SSDs will be left with the responsibility. In short, if the policy behind decarceration and community care is to deinstitutionalise mental health services, the current regime systematically fails, at the level of statutory provision, to permit the realisation of that aim in policy or practice; and this is because the legal framework exerts a gravitational pull towards the provision of the community care in residential homes. It also tends to make cooperation more rather than less problematic, exacerbating and amplifying already existent tensions. To the extent that there are examples of a 'seamless service' to be found, they exist in spite of rather than because of the statutory regime. Finally, it is worth pointing out that for Cowan, writing in 1995, a chief failing of the housing legislation was that by comparison with the

1990 Act it contained little potential for the empowerment of clients, for example, by including that client in discussion about how best identified needs could be met. Despite the decision in *Avon* (see 9.3.1), it has been made clear by *Barry* that Cowan's assessment of the potential of the 1990 Act in this regard was optimistic. The response of the current government to this situation will be discussed at 9.6.

9.5   CONTROL IN THE COMMUNITY

Community care, and the CPA, are not concerned solely with the provision of 'optional' services. Community care law also embraces a degree of compulsion and control over service recipients, through a variety of statutory and non-statutory mechanisms. This raises the question of whether community care should be seen ultimately in terms of care or of control. Indeed, the question runs through the law that has been discussed above. *Building Bridges*, for example, made it clear that of the target group as a whole, it was the severely mentally ill who were to be the prime focus of service provision, and one would perhaps be forgiven for thinking that this is because there is a perception that clients falling into this category are, by definition, in greater need, not of care, but of control and supervision. Such a view is given support by the fact that services for the mentally ill tend to be provided free of charge regardless of ability to pay, unlike services for disabled persons. There has been a quantitative increase in the number of control-based measures available for use in recent years, but it is more difficult to gauge the extent to which there has been a qualitative shift. Certainly, the public and political will for 'more control' seems to exist, and the main reason for this is the perception that collectively, the mentally ill (particularly schizophrenics) and those with personality disorders constitute a significant risk to public safety. At the heart of this view is an equation between (the failure of) community care and apparently motiveless homicides by mentally disordered persons. Before discussing the available legal powers of control in the community, it is therefore first necessary to consider the extent to which recent developments are based on accurate perceptions of the risk to public safety.

9.5.1   Homicide and community care

The relationship between community care and homicide is one of extreme controversy. The killing of Jonathon Zito by Christopher Clunis on Finsbury Park Tube Station in December 1992, was the first of what has been a prolonged sequence of high profile homicides carried out by persons with known mental health problems. Following this incident, the Department of Health (1994), in the form of the NHS Executive, published guidance on discharge and after care which as well as attempting to lay down standards of best practice also required HAs to initiate independent inquiries following homicides by mentally disordered persons in their areas and to publish the reports generated by the inquiries (para. 34). As discussed at 3.3.2, there have been a considerable number of such reports published. The issue of homicide, particularly committed against strangers in public places, by persons known to the mental health system (although often not in receipt of any care or supervision at the time of the killing) has been the most highly profiled aspect of mental health policy and practice in the media in the 1990s. However, attempting to unravel any precise relationship between homicide and community care is a complex operation.

Homicide rates in England and Wales are low: around 10-12 per million population over the last couple of decades, although homicides over the last few years have been at the high end of the scale, with 635 in 1994, 663 in 1995 and 627 in 1996, a rate over 12 per million, compared with 537 in 1984, 536 in 1985 and 563 in 1986 (Home Office Research and Statistics Directorate, 1996). It can be said that there are, roughly, 100 more homicides a year now than was the case a decade ago. One school of thought, represented for example by Tidmarsh (1995) and Muijen (1996) takes the view that there is no appreciable relationship between community care, mental disorder, and homicide rates. Following a review of the evidence, which shows that '[t]he rate of mentally abnormal homicide appears to be constant world-wide' (1995, p. 2), Tidmarsh argues that '[t]he criminal statistics show no trend over the years which would give ammunition to those who are alarmed about community care' (ibid.). Muijen (1996, p. 151) calculates that somewhere between 3 and 7 per cent of homicides are related to mental disorder. Home Office statistics (Home Office Research and Statistics Directorate, 1996) seem to corroborate this view. They show that in the decade 1986-96 no less than 2 per cent and no higher than 7 per cent of all homicides recorded were committed by persons suspected of being mentally disturbed. The figure was 4 per cent in 1996. The majority (over 50 per cent) of homicides are recorded as being carried out for reasons of quarrel, revenge or loss of temper.

Such conclusions are, however, vigorously disputed by Howlett (1998). Working from the base of the Home Office statistics given above, Howlett points out that they do not show what percentage of homicides carried out following a quarrel or loss of temper or as revenge were committed by mentally disordered persons; and that the statistics for suicide following homicide (usually between 5 and 10 per cent although there were none in 1995 or 1996) may include a number of mentally disordered persons, given the high correlation between suicide and mental illness (1998, pp.77-8, and see 3.2). He goes on to argue that the statistics for the use of s. 2 of the Homicide Act 1957 (the operation of which reduces murder to manslaughter on grounds of diminished responsibility), which show that its use has fallen more or less incrementally over the decade 1986-96, nevertheless indicate that the numbers of mentally disordered persons committing homicide, although relatively small, is at a higher level than that indicated by the 'reasons for homicide' statistics. The other relevant pointer, Howlett argues, is the rising numbers of patients, over 90 per cent diagnosed as suffering from mental illness, who are 'diverted' into hospital from the criminal justice system with restrictions. Of these, the numbers convicted of homicides other than murder have stayed constant (typically 35-45 annually: 48 in 1995, 35 in 1996, Home Office Research and Statistics Directorate, 1997, table 10), but there have been significant increases in the numbers of hospital orders made in respect of those convicted of murder (from 27 in 1986 to 69 in 1996, highest years being 87 in 1995 and 84 in 1993) and other violent offences (116 in 1986, 288 in 1996, highest years being 380 in 1984 and 373 in 1993 (1997, ibid.)).

As Howlett concedes, however, any statistical measure should be treated with caution. For example, the use of s. 2, Homicide Act 1957 cannot be taken to be limited to persons who would be classified under the Mental Health Act 1983 as mentally disordered. And the increase in the numbers transferred from prison to hospital is at least in part a function of increased provision of medium security hospital accommodation over recent years (see 6.6). In addition, the numbers of persons entering hospitals following acts of homicide or violence overestimate the number of individuals actually involved, since these are simply numbers admitted and do not take account of multiple admissions of the same individual (through the exercise of powers of transfer or recall). When such factors are taken into account the number of individuals involved drops substantially (for example, the admission of persons in the 'murder' category drops from 72 to 33 in 1992, 84 to 39 in 1993 and 77 to 35 in 1994, although interestingly, the drop in the 'other homicide' category is much less, from 44 to 33 in 1992, 43 to 38 in 1993 and 46 to 43 in 1994 (Home Office, 1995, p. 14). Howlett concludes that the Home Office statistics 'are insufficiently detailed to ascertain the numbers of mentally ill people who commit homicide' (1998, p. 82), and he turns instead to data produced by the *National Confidential Inquiry into Suicide and Homicide by People with Mental Illness* (Appleby, 1997). A total of 408 homicide convictions were notified to the Inquiry in the year from April 1996. Of these, in 327 instances court files were made available, which showed that in 238 cases a psychiatric report was requested by the court. Of these 238 cases, 17 per cent (39) had 'symptoms of mental illness' at the time of the killing, 43 per cent had a mental disorder of some sort, 25 per cent had previous contact with adult mental health services, and 12 per cent had had contact in the year before the homicide was committed. This gave the Inquiry a figure of 50 homicides (and 1000 suicides) committed by persons who had had contact with mental health services no more than a year before the homicide was committed. However, Taylor and Gunn (1999) found that over the last four decades there has been an annual 3 per cent decline in the contribution of mentally ill persons to criminal homicide statistics.

Whatever the truth of this, it is clear that in relative terms, the numbers of mentally disordered persons involved in homicides, unlike suicides, remain low. But perhaps that is not the point. Appleby's findings do tend to support research suggesting that there is an, albeit complex, link between mental disorder and violence (Bowden, 1996). And included in that 50 or so individuals a year are many of the most highly publicised homicides and other acts of violence by mentally disordered persons in recent years, including those carried out by Micheal Stone, Christopher Clunis, Horrett Campbell, Andrew Robinson, and others. It might be thought that the appropriate policy response to such events would be to improve access to community care services and the framework for the delivery of such services. And the welter of reports that have been made following independent inquiries following homicides and suicides have indeed made many such recommendations. To take one, depressingly typical, recent report, that published by Leicestershire Health Authority following the conviction of a young man for manslaughter by reason of diminished responsibility (Leicestershire Health Authority, 1998), recommendations are made for more explicit national guidance on record keeping, information sharing, changes to training programmes, better monitoring of service delivery, and so on. And although the White Paper on mental health published in December 1998 (Department of Health, 1998a) contains many proposals along these lines, it also incorporates the other strand of policy that has developed through the last decade or so, propelled by public and political concern, towards increased control of mentally disordered persons judged to be a risk to the safety of themselves or others. The government has also revived for further discussion and consultation the concept of a 'community treatment order', which had been discarded in 1995 in favour of more limited powers. But the powers at present, although potentially coercive, have stopped short of requiring compulsory treatment in the community. There are two sets of statutory powers, guardianship and after care under supervision (ACUS). There is also a non-statutory requirement to maintain registers of persons thought to constitute a risk to self or others.

9.5.2 Guardianship

Guardianship is seen as an alternative to compulsory admission to hospital and continuing hospitalisation (Department of Health and Welsh Office, 1999, para. 13.2). It can therefore function as both preventative care and after care. Guardianship is a concept that has long been known to mental health law. The basic idea is that a nominated person or body assumes responsibility for the supervision of a patient's care in the community, and, so the Code of Practice suggests (para. 13.6), acts as 'advocate' in securing necessary services for the person subject to the guardianship order. However, as with admission to hospital under part II, MHA 1983, the making of an order does not require the consent of the patient.

Under the Mental Deficiency Act 1913 'idiots' and 'imbeciles' could be taken into guardianship, the effect of which was to give to the guardian the powers of a father over the person subject to the order. The MHA 1959 extended the scope of guardianship to cover mentally ill persons, but s. 34 of that Act maintained the formula whereby a person appointed as a guardian of a mentally disordered person enjoyed 'all such powers as would be exercisable by him in relation to the patient . . . if he were the father of the patient and the patient were under the age of 14 years'. This would seem to mean that, in so far as this issue was given any thought at the time, a guardian could, amongst other things, consent to medical treatment on behalf of the mentally disordered person.

When the MHA was overhauled in 1983, the opportunity was taken to reword this infantising provision and specify the powers of a guardian with greater clarity and limitation. The White Paper that preceded the reforms of the early 1980s (DHSS, 1981, paras. 43, 44) rejected arguments that guardianship should permit treatment in 'the community' without consent (although these arguments have continued unabated to the present) and opted instead for a more restrictive 'essential powers' approach. Accordingly, the 1983 Act now provides that a guardian has three powers: to require the patient to reside at a specified place; to attend at places and times for the purposes of medical treatment, education, occupation or training; and to require that access to the patient is given to a doctor, ASW, or other person specified by the guardian: s. 8(1), MHA 1983. Whether these 'essential powers' do in fact contain the essentials of guardianship, which according to the Code of Practice 'is to enable patients to receive community care where it cannot be provided without the use of compulsory powers' (para. 13.1), is, at least, debatable. It is accepted law that there is 'no power under the 1983 Act to give treatment to a mentally disordered person who withholds consent [or, presumably, who cannot consent] unless he is detained in hospital': R v *Hallstrom ex parte W (No. 2)* [1986] 2 All ER 306 (HC) per McCullough J at p. 313, see also *T* v *T* [1988] 1 All ER 613 (HC) at p. 617 per Wood J. In addition, the power to require attendance for treatment, and so on, is not supported with any power to take and convey the patient to the place in question, and although a patient absent from the place where he or she has been required to reside by the guardian is deemed to be absent without leave and so can be returned by a social worker or police officer if apprehended before the expiry of the guardianship order or six months from the date first absent, whichever is the later (s. 18(3), (4), MHA 1983), there is no power to detain the patient at the place of residence in question.

If the purpose of guardianship is to give the guardian sufficient powers to ensure and require that patients accept treatment in order to obviate what would otherwise be a need for compulsory detention, then clearly the powers given by s. 8 of the 1983 Act are not sufficient for that purpose. Thus in practice the paradoxical situation is that to be effective these 'compulsory' powers rely on the cooperation, or at least absence of positive resistance, of patients. This is the first reason why guardianship under the 1983 Act failed to live up to the expectations of it. The second reason is concerned with the criteria for the making of a guardianship order. It is open to a criminal court to make a guardianship order rather than a hospital order (s. 37(1), MHA 1983), but this is almost never done. Rather, guardianship orders are usually made under the civil powers contained in part II of the 1983 Act. These largely mirror the requirements of admission for treatment under s. 3. Applications may be made by either an ASW or the patient's NR (s. 11(1)), and must be founded on the written recommendations of two doctors. The requirements and limitations in ss. 11 and 13, discussed in Chapter five in relation to admission to hospital for treatment, also apply here, as does the initial time limitation of six months, and the pattern of renewal, with attendant medical reports (but no consultations) under s. 20(6). Differences are that it must be necessary for the patient's *welfare* (rather than, in s. 3(2)(b), his or her health or safety) that an application be made (s. 7(2)(b)), which is a much broader concept, and there is no treatability test in s. 7. But as with admission under s. 3 the patient must be suffering from one of the four specific forms of mental disorder (s. 7(2)(a)), which incorporates into the criteria for admission into guardianship the requirements of s. 1 of the Act, namely that mentally impaired, severely mentally impaired, and psychopathically disordered persons are only eligible for guardianship if abnormally aggressive or seriously irresponsible conducts results from or is associated with the disorder in question. This is not too much of a problem in practice as far as psychopathy is concerned, as guardianship is rarely if ever used for such patients, but it means that the majority of persons with learning disabilities, for whom guardianship was designed, who are not normally aggressive nor irresponsible, are not eligible for guardianship. This, as Gunn (1986, p. 147) bluntly notes, is 'a mistake', which was poignantly underlined by the case of Beverley Lewis (Fennell, 1989). Nevertheless, in *Re F (a child)* 1999, *Independent*, 12 October (CA), the Court of Appeal has recently confirmed that the criteria for the making of a guardianship order should be construed narrowly, and overruled the High Court, which had found that 'seriously irresponsible' behaviour was exhibited by a person who wished to leave her voluntary residential accommodation and return home against the advice of her carers.

The third reason why guardianship has been used less than was expected before the passage of the 1983 Act is that it usually falls to local authority social services authorities to act as guardian. Section 7(5) of the MHA 1983 provides that an application for guardianship must name the proposed guardian, who can be either a local social services authority or any other person (including the applicant, so that an ASW or NR can both make an application and act as guardian), but SSDs have a power of veto over an application naming any other person as guardian. It is also to the relevant SSD that an application for guardianship must be forwarded, within 14 days of the second medical recommendation: s. 8(2). Once an application for guardianship has been accepted by an SSD, whether or not it will actually act as the patient's guardian, it is required under part III, reg. 13 of the Mental Health (Hospital, Guardianship and Consent to Treatment) Regulations 1983, SI 1983 No. 893 (as amended by SI 1997, No. 807), made by the Secretary of State acting under the powers given in s. 9, to arrange for the patient to be visited by a doctor at least every three months, and by a s. 12 approved doctor at least once every year, in addition to carrying out the functions mentioned in s. 8. If, as rarely happens, a private guardian is appointed, he or she will be under the supervision of the SSD, and must act in accordance with any directions that the SSD gives him or her, as well as appointing a doctor to oversee the patient's medical treatment, and keep the SSD informed of any changes of address of the patient and doctor. An SSD or private guardian will also owe a common law duty of care to the patient. Persons subject to guardianship have much the same rights to apply to an MHRT as do other patients subject to part II of the 1983 Act (s. 66(1)(c)), which will entail a further layer of paperwork for all concerned (the Secretary of State's powers of referral in s. 67 are also applicable here). From the point of view of an SSD, it is easy to see how guardianship can be seen to carry all the burdens of compulsory admission to hospital but few of the benefits. Guardianship should not be used in isolation but only as part of the broader, comprehensive plan of treatment and care for individual patients

(Department of Health and Welsh Office, 1999, paras. 13.1, 13.4); and in the majority of cases it will be hard to demonstrate what the invocation of guardianship will add to the effective operation of such plans.

There has been a noticeable increase in the use of guardianship in recent years, from 41 new cases in 1982-3 to 226 in 1992-3, to 372 in 1995 (MHAC, 1997, para. 8.8), with 564 individuals subject to a guardianship order at the end of that year. This may be because a use has recently been found for guardianship as part of the care plan for persons, mainly female, of pensionable age having dementia or learning difficulties (Gordon, 1998). There are examples of its successful use with younger mentally ill persons, notably Andrew Robinson, who later went on to kill a member of staff whilst he was detained under s. 3. However, as in that case, an order is often allowed to lapse, or is not renewed, and is often a precursor to the provision of residential accommodation (Gordon, 1998). And by comparison with the other powers in part II, its use is still minimal. Not surprisingly, thought has been given to recasting guardianship (Law Commission, 1995), but the Department of Health (1994) decided to hang fire until the impact of the introduction of After Care Under Supervision ('ACUS': see 9.5.3) could be assessed. It is still too early to make that assessment authoritatively, but for reasons to be discussed below, the new after care powers arguably suffer from the same defects as guardianship. And, for reasons that are not absolutely clear, the increase in the use of guardianship seems to have continued despite the introduction of the seemingly more attractive alternative of ACUS in 1996 (MHAC, 1997, para. 8.8). Most probably, this is because the two orders aim at different target populations. ACUS, unlike guardianship, is not used as part of the care plan for elderly mentally infirm, but is aimed, in the main, at young, potentially dangerous, mentally ill (mainly schizophrenic) men.

9.5.3 After care under supervision

New powers to subject an individual, on leaving hospital, to continued care in the community in the form of ACUS were introduced by the Mental Health (Patients in the Community) Act 1995, which came into force on 1 April 1996. These were designed to add some teeth to the duty placed on HAs and SSDs to provide after care under s. 117, MHA 1983. As discussed above (see 9.2.1), SSDs in tandem with other agencies are required to make and review care programmes and to appoint a 'key worker' who is primarily responsible for seeing that the requisite services are provided to patients in the community. Until the 1995 Act, however, the use of these services had been optional. The Royal College of Psychiatrists has been campaigning for a number of years for greater powers of control to be available for patients following discharge, arguing that patients who would be able to cope outside hospital if they could be forced to take necessary medication were being failed by a system that allows the patient total freedom from coercion until sectionable. It is this group of patients — often seen as being caught in the 'revolving door' by the original policy of the 1983 Act — that the 1995 reforms were primarily aimed at. As such, ACUS also had evident attractions for hospital managers who have to manage beds within a system that, as discussed at 3.4, is at breaking point. On the other hand, there was resistance to greater powers of coercion outside of hospital from other quarters (Harrison, 1995), and the presence of the European Convention on Human Rights, which circumscribes measures that impinge on the liberty of the person by a requirement of 'lawful *detention*', also limited the potential of any domestic legislation to introduce compulsion without detention (Crichton, 1994). As a consequence the 1995 Act is essentially a compromise which attempts to mollify both of these views (Parkin, 1996), and, like guardianship, stops short of compulsory treatment in the community.

The main feature of the 1995 Act is to add a degree of compulsion to the use of after care services provided under s. 117, by adding a number of new sections to the MHA 1983 (ss. 25A-25J). As far as the substance of ACUS is concerned, s. 25D gives health and local authorities powers similar to those available under a guardianship order (see 9.5.2) but with the significant additional power of conveyance (s. 25D(4)), using force, if necessary. ACUS is designed for persons aged above 16 who are 'liable to be detained in hospital in pursuance of an application for admission for treatment': s. 25A(1)(a). Thus persons who have been admitted for treatment but given leave under s. 17 are eligible as they continue to be 'liable to be detained', and if this is the case the period of ACUS commences on expiry of the period of leave: s. 25A(9). Also covered are persons detained under the Act at the time that the application for ACUS is made, even if they cease to be so liable by the time they leave hospital. As many patients remain in hospital on the expiry of an authority to detain for treatment, the applicability of ACUS to these patients is not insignificant. Patients detained under s. 37 are also eligible for ACUS: sch. 1, part I, para. 8A, MHA 1983. Conditionally discharged restricted patients are not covered by ACUS (s. 41(3)(aa)) because there is already a separate regime in operation for this group of patients.

Although, unlike guardianship, ACUS is not an alternative to, but in some sense an 'extension', of hospitalisation, ACUS echoes admission for treatment in various ways. A period of ACUS lasts for six months in the first instance (s. 25G(1)), renewable once for a further six months and thereafter annually, and as with renewal of detention in hospital under s. 20, there is an elaborate procedure of examinations, consultations and reports required for the renewal of ACUS (see further below). The criteria for making an order for ACUS are similar to but also distinct from those for compulsory admission into hospital for treatment. The patient must be suffering from one of the four specified forms of mental disorder; there must be a 'substantial risk of serious harm' to the health or safety of the patient or other persons or a risk of the patient being 'seriously exploited' if an application is not made; and it must be that the provision of ACUS is 'likely to help' ensure that the patient receives the services in question: s. 25A(4)(a),(b),(c). The diagnostic elements of these criteria have been discussed in Chapter four, and will not be considered again here. Risk assessment prior to discharge forms a key element in the decision as to whether an application for ACUS should be made (Department of Health, 1994). But it is noteworthy that, compared with the terms of s. 3, the 'dangerousness' and 'vulnerability' criteria here are couched more narrowly: risks must be 'substantial' and harm must be 'serious'. This is comparable with the wording used in s. 41 and it is therefore likely that the discussion of the Court of Appeal in *Birch* (1989, see 6.5) on the interpretation of these terms would also be applicable here. If this is correct, it means that the test for ACUS is harder to satisfy than the test for admission into hospital — which speaks of the reconciliation of opposing interests manifest in the 1995 Act and in particular gives cognisance to the view that the introduction of elements of compulsion into community care programmes is of greater ethico-political significance than the use of compulsion in hospital — and than the test for admission into guardianship under s. 7, as that section uses similar terminology to s. 3. Given the limited use of guardianship, it seems unlikely that an alternative that operates with more restrictive criteria, even if giving a broader range of powers, will be any more successful in meeting its aims than the guardianship regime has been. ACUS, like guardianship, also entitles the person subject to the order to make an application to an MHRT under s. 66 of the 1983 Act, or to have his or her case referred by the Secretary of State under s. 67. This does not entail the medical member of the tribunal being given a right to examine the applicant, as this might amount to treatment without consent, but it is provided by r. 19(2), Mental Health Tribunal Rules 1983 that if a patient refuses to be examined by the medical member of a tribunal, the application will be deemed as having been withdrawn.

There are to date no reported cases of applications being made to an MHRT, and the reason for this is that ACUS has been used only infrequently. For instance, in the South and West Region only 29 persons had been placed on ACUS during the first year in which it was available (Knight, Mumford and Nichol, 1998, see also Mohan, Thompson and Mullee, 1998). The relative restrictiveness of the criteria is one reason for this (Knight, Mumford and Nichol, 1998), but perhaps more significant reasons are the way that the statutory scheme divides up the responsibilities of those charged with its operation; and the limited nature of the powers over a patient on ACUS. As to the first of these issues, it is striking that, unlike the other compulsory powers contained in part II, a supervision application may *only* be made by the patient's RMO rather than an ASW or hospital manager. Before making an application the RMO must consult with the patient; at least one person professionally involved with the patient's treatment in hospital; at least one person who will be professionally involved with the patient in the provision of s. 117 services; and any person whom the RMO thinks will 'play a substantial part in the care of the patient' in a non-professional capacity after release from hospital: s. 25B(2)(a). In addition, the patient's NR should if practicable be consulted about the proposal to make the supervision application: s. 25B(2)(b). Although the patient may request that his or her NR is not consulted, the RMO can override this request if the patient has a propensity for violence towards others *and* the RMO considers consultation is appropriate in the circumstances: s. 25B(3). The RMO must take into account any views expressed (s. 25B(2)(c)), but ultimately the decision to make the application is for the RMO alone. Thus, a patient can be put on ACUS without his or her consent.

In addition to the various consultations that are required, the RMO must also consider which after care services should be provided to the patient and which, if any, conditions should be imposed (discussed below). Each patient will have a supervisor (who will usually be a social worker) and a Community Responsible Medical Officer (CRMO), responsible for the patient's continued treatment and general wellbeing on leaving hospital. Having completed this process and reached the conclusion that putting the patient on ACUS 'is likely to help to secure' that the patient recieves the services in question, the RMO must then complete an application form, confirming the patient's liability to detention; providing the patient's age; confirming that the conditions for ACUS are met; and providing the names of the persons to be the CMRO and supervisor, as well as those of the patient's NR or any other person consulted in a non-professional capacity: s. 25B(5). The supervision application must be accompanied by a written recommendation, in the prescribed form, of a doctor who is to be involved in the patient's after care, or the RMO if that doctor is to be the RMO: s. 25B(6)(a). This recommendation must also confirm that the requirements of s. 25A(4) are met. There must also be an accompanying recommendation from an ASW (although not necessarily one who has had prior contact with the patient), again confirming that the s. 25A(4) requirements are met (s. 25B(6), (8)); and written statements from the intended CRMO and supervisor of their willingness so to act. Details must also be provided of the nature of the s. 117 services and of any conditions to be attached: s. 25B(9). On making an application, the RMO must inform the patient, NR and any other person involved in a non-professional capacity, that the application has been made, and of the names of the intended CMRO and supervisor, as well as any requirements that the RMO wishes to be imposed on the patient.

Section 25B uses language which gives the impression that the *decision* as to the imposition of requirements on a patient on ACUS is one for the RMO, but in fact, the RMO only makes the application, which must be addressed to the relevant Health Authority under s. 117: s. 25A(6). Although the decision to accept the application must be made by the HA in consultation with the relevant SSD (s. 25A(7)), this means that SSDs are not the lead agency here, as is the case with community care provision generally, and with guardianship. It is not clear when an application for ACUS could properly be rejected by the HA, if it is assumed that there is a properly-identified clinical need (see the discussion of *Fox* at 9.3.2). Given that HAs are now only infrequently providers of services, an HA will usually have to purchase the required services from an NHS Trust or private provider, which may well be the same Trust that accommodated the patient during his or her detention in hospital. As Cowan says, this is a 'cumbersome way of doing things' (1995, p. 421), but from the point of view of an RMO this may well be the least worrisome aspect of the scheme. The 1995 Act constitutes a potentially significant new area of non-clinical responsibility for RMOs. Put simply, ACUS if used widely would constitute a substantial increase in the paperwork of RMOs in general psychiatric hospitals (Mohan, Thompson and Mullee, 1998). This in itself may be enough to explain the slow uptake that the 1995 reforms have seen. But in addition, there is widespread agreement that the powers provided by the 1995 Act would lack effective 'bite', even if well resourced.

Section 25D allows HAs and SSDs to impose, on the recommendation of RMOs, requirements as to: place of residence; attendance for treatment, occupation, education or training; and access to the patient by his or her supervisor, any doctor or ASW, or other person authorised by the supervisor. For the purposes of ensuring attendance for treatment, occupation and so on, the supervisor has a power to 'take and convey' the person subject to ACUS (s. 25D(4)) to the place in question. This is an option which is noticeably absent from the powers of a guardian under s. 7, and is what marks off ACUS as a potentially greater imposition on the patient than is guardianship. This power may be delegated by the supervisor, and presumably it was intended that this would be to police officers or psychiatric facility staff. Leaving aside for a moment the ethical issues that the introduction of new powers of compulsion brings with it, there are nevertheless various legal and practical problems with this power. First, as with guardianship, there is *no power to treat without consent*, and so even if a patient is forcibly conveyed to a place for treatment, such treatment cannot be given without consent unless the patient is deemed to lack capacity in which case the common law powers to treat will apply (see Chapters seven, ten and eleven). Secondly, it follows that there is no power to *detain* in s. 25D(4). The word 'detain' is not used in the subsection (as it is, for example, in ss. 6 or 136). To operate as intended, those using this power will have to rely on the patient's compliance and/or ignorance of the strict legal position, and a degree of bluff. As a matter of law a patient who has been taken and conveyed to any such place may simply leave, and attempts to prevent the patient so doing may constitute unlawful imprisonment as comprising a de facto detention. Thirdly, the use of compulsion even to this relatively limited extent may produce negative effects. Speaking in the Parliamentary debates which preceded the 1995 Act, Tessa Jowell MP, who has a good deal of experience in mental health work, expressed concerns that the use of these powers of compulsion 'will damage community care — driving people from services rather than encouraging them to use them, especially if, as will be likely, supervisors try to get the police involved' (*Hansard*, H.C., Vol 264, col.1163, cited in Jones, 1999, p. 137). Fourthly, the power to take and convey must in any case be used only when it is appropriate to do so. Under the ECHR, as interpreted in *X* v *United Kingdom* (1981) 4 EHRR 188, it is lawful to arrest ('take') a person without a medical examination where it would be impracticable to conduct one given the emergency nature of the situation. If the refusal of the patient to attend at the place in question cannot be said to constitute an 'emergency', it is doubtful whether to take and convey that person to a place for treatment would be lawful. If it is training, occupation or education which the patient is refusing to attend, it is unlikely that refusal would *ever* constitute an 'emergency'.

The fact that this type of limitation is not apparent on the face of the Act has led some to argue that as it stands s. 25D(4) falls foul of the ECHR (Parker, 1995, p. 423). From the point of view of a psychiatrist attempting to use ACUS as a device to ensure that a patient continues to take necessary medication following discharge, the power is equally unsatisfactory, and it is easy to see how an RMO might conclude that an ACUS application is not worth the effort, particularly as s. 3 of the 1995 Act extends the maximum period of leave under s. 17 from six months to a year (see 8.2), and a patient on leave of absence *does* remain subject to the powers of compulsory treatment. Eastman (1997) has argued that from a clinical view ACUS is unlikely to improve the quality of community care for patients, and suggests that the explanation for the ineffectual powers in the 1995 Act is that it was propelled more by political than clinical imperatives.

This of course fuels the fires as far as social control theorists are concerned. Yet in many ways ACUS is a weak control mechanism. A patient who refuses or neglects to cooperate may find himself or herself being considered for hospitalisation by the supervisor and CRMO as required by s. 25E(4)(b). Of course, the fact of being on ACUS does not 'protect' a patient from being sectioned if the criteria can be met (in which case ACUS is automatically terminated: s. 25H(5)). By the same token, however, a patient can only be hospitalised for being in breach of ACUS if the criteria for compulsory detention are met; there is no 'sanction for breach' as such. It is not possible to hospitalise simply for breach, as this would circumvent the safeguards for admission in part II of the 1983 Act. And if, as discussed above, there is no power to detain in a place for treatment, nor to treat without consent, then ACUS does take on something of the appearance of a mere facade. But it cannot be disputed that at some level ACUS marks a 'dispersal' of coercive powers, in that it increases the legal powers of supervision over persons not judged to be 'sectionable'. It is this that distinguishes ACUS from the situation when a patient is on leave of absence under s. 17 of the 1983 Act, and makes it fallacious to argue that ACUS does not mark any extension of the mental health system because powers of control, and to require treatment to be undertaken, outside of hospital already exist under that section. And it is not necessary to deny any benevolent intent behind the introduction of ACUS in order to argue that it is also an extension of the state's disciplinary powers: from a Foucaultian perspective, for example, benevolence is a key conduit for the spread of control. This is perhaps how one should interpret the findings of Knight and her colleagues (1998) that in one third of cases in which ACUS was used, an illegal requirement to accept medication *was* stipulated as part of the patient's care plan. Moreover, ACUS does have built in the sort of double bind described by Rosenham (see Chapter two) and endorsed in the context of tribunal applications by the decision of the Court of Appeal in *Perkins* (see 8.5), because an absence of symptoms does not necessarily mean that an order should be discharged, if the view is taken that it is because the patient is on ACUS that he or she appears to be well, there is no logical point at which an order should be discharged.

9.5.4 Supervision registers

ACUS must be seen in conjunction with the use of 'supervision registers'. Department of Health Guidelines published in 1994 (NHS Management

Executive, 1994b) required all HAs to ensure that providers of mental health services were contractually obliged to draw up, maintain and use supervision registers of patients most at risk of harm to self or others, as part of a broader mental health information system by 1 April 1994. The idea of registers is not new: SSDs have maintained 'at risk' registers of children for a number of years, and the register of sex offenders is a recent high profile example of their use. But what is the function of registration in the present context? According to the 1994 Guidance (Department of Health, 1994a), provider units should incorporate the register in the planning of service delivery and the CPA, and the Department of Health Guidelines provide that normal rules of confidentiality apply to the information held on supervision registers. This seems to indicate the information should be anonymous in nature and used quantitatively, but in the '10 point plan' for community care issued in August 1993 by the Secretary of State for health (Department of Health, 1994b), it was made clear that the registers would be used to monitor and support those 'most at risk'. As such, issues of confidentiality are raised, and have been reconciled at local level in ways which have led to an uneven national picture (Cohen, Dolan, and Eastman, 1996).

Concerns about privacy and confidentiality were raised by MIND, which also argued that supervision registers would deter people from seeking help, and would operate in a discriminatory way because of the overrepresentation of black people and women amongst those diagnosed as mentally ill (MIND, 1994). There is also no mechanism to appeal against a decision that an individual be placed on the register. In one small survey, patients did not challenge their inclusion on the register, which suggests that here as elsewhere there is a need for patient advocacy services (Vaughan, 1998). For Foucault, the construction of a detailed knowledge base is axiomatic for the panoptic model of social control, and given the fact that it is by no means clear what such registers add to the provision of care in the community, it is difficult to see what other function they might have. Lowe-Ponsford, Wolfson and Lindesay (1998) report that for a mixture of pragmatic and principled reasons around half of the consultant psychiatrists in one health region felt that the registers should be abolished; and only one quarter of those surveyed felt that they should not. There is much here to confound a simple application of a social control thesis: 'fudged pseudo-coercion' is how Eastman (1997, p. 494) characterises the present situation, and it is difficult to disagree. But perhaps the strongest evidence for control theorists is yet to come, in that the developments in 1995 are not the end of the process, but merely a stepping stone to yet more intrusive measures.

9.6   PROPOSALS FOR REFORM

This brings the discussion around to the question of likely future developments, and the White Paper on the future of mental health services published late in 1998. As mentioned in the introduction to this Chapter, the White Paper proposes a number of changes, and not only to the community care regime which, it is claimed will 'mark a new beginning for mental health' (Department of Health, 1998a, Executive Summary, p. 3). As far as community care is concerned, the White Paper exhibits a sophisticated understanding of the complexity of the problems of the current system (at para. 2.23):

> Effective responses to mental health problems require three elements to be in balance: resources and the systems to make the best use of them, legislative powers, and processes of care. Deficiencies in one area cannot be compensated for by changes in another.

For working age adults there will be a 'national service framework' covering both health and social services; and the whole range of service provision from outreach to high security confinement (1998a, para. 4.3), with increased focus on outreach to prevent avoidable hospitalisation or rehospitalisation. Further community-based accommodation is to be made available and is to be staffed on a 24 hour basis (para. 4.15). The national framework will specify the type of services to be provided in the primary care sector (para. 4.40). The three themes of the White Paper: that mental health services should be 'safe' (from the point of view of the general public); 'sound' (in that access to services based on need should be readily available); and 'supportive' (of clients, their families and carers), is itself set within the broader government policy of 'social inclusionism' (para. 2.4). This requires cognisance to be taken of causes of mental illness, such as environmental stress, poverty and unemployment (paras. 1.13-1.15, 2.3-2.6), and hence the training and employment of persons with mental health problems is part of the government's conception of 'the mental health system'. The importance of the reintegration of SSDs and HAs with local housing authorities is a recurrent theme of the White Paper (see for example paras. 2.6, 4.55); and new technology and procedures are to be introduced to aid in this regard. The first moves towards putting this policy into practice have already been made in the form of a welter of new guidance to services (Department of Health, 1998e; 1998f; 1998g; see also Health Act 1999).

A cursory reading of the White Paper, then, seems to allow a cautious optimism about the prospects for the quality of care in the community over the next few years. But as this Chapter has been at pains to point out, community care is not concerned only with care. In his foreword to the White Paper, the Secretary of State for Health, Frank Dobson, promises to 'ensure that patients who might otherwise be a danger to themselves and others are no longer allowed to refuse to comply with the treatment they need'. Further investigation of the White Paper on this issue, however, tends to perplex rather than elucidate. Given that in 1995 the government stopped short of introducing new powers of compulsory treatment in the community, it might be thought reasonable to suppose that that is what is now intended. However, although the precise details of any new powers are within the remit of the team charged with leading the review of mental health law, the White Paper provides that any new powers will not be in breach of the ECHR, and '[t]he Government does not envisage a situation where treatment is forcibly administered in the individual's own home' (Department of Health, 1998a, para. 4.28). But how is this an extension of powers in comparison with those introduced in the 1995 Act? The answer seems to be the reference to clients' 'own homes', which implies that it *will* be possible in future, not merely to convey a person to a place where treatment is to be given, but also to treat on arrival in that place, and, presumably, to detain for that purpose. It is arguable that even this degree of compulsion would fall foul of the ECHR if the grounds for detention in part II, MHA 1983 are not met.

If one concern is ambiguity and disingenuity regarding the scope of any new coercive powers, the other main point of concern is the lack of discussion in the White Paper of the legal problems and confusion that has been discussed in this Chapter. Although it is made clear that 'the legislative framework, designed when most mental health care was provided in institutions, no longer supports the delivery of care' (1998a, Introduction, p. 1), and that there is a need for 'legislative powers which work with the grain of comprehensive local services' (para. 2.24), the only reference to legal changes in the section of the White Paper headed 'A modern legislative framework' (paras. 4.25- 4.34) are the new powers discussed above; those, relating to capacity which have been the subject of consultation by the Law Commission and the Lord Chancellor (see Chapter ten); and the possibility of a 'reviewable detention' order (see 6.7). There is no acknowledgement by the government of the problems caused by the tangled web of legislation for service delivery (see 9.2 and 9.3); nor any mention of the intention to integrate or consolidate the legal powers and duties of HAs, SSDs and local housing authorities. Yet as the discussion in this Chapter has shown, for the philosophy of social inclusionism to be given any tangible content, without fundamental legal reform all other measures will be of marginal effect.

There are other elements of the current proposals that may lead one to question their likely success. The White Paper has little to say about advocacy. It also puts a faith in new drug treatments and psychotherapeutic interventions that is bound to worry anyone aware of the number of false dawns mental health policy and practice has seen; not to mention the significant cost of the new drug treatments for schizophrenia (see 7.2.1). But even if the new treatments do prove their worth, the lesson from the tragic sequence of homicides and suicides that has shadowed mental health policy over the last decade is that the real problem is not that those who are 'in' the system refuse to take their medication, but that the system fails to maintain contact with persons who are a known risk, sometimes even to themselves. It is worth remembering that Christopher Clunis actually asked for care (Eastman, 1997, p. 493) and that Horrett Campbell passed through both the community care system and the criminal justice system with recognised but unattended problems. From the White Paper, the government's view seems to be that the more fundamental problems are with control rather than with service provision. The suggestion of the present authors is that entirely the reverse is actually the case.

9.7   CONCLUDING COMMENTS

This Chapter has detailed a system in crisis that has 'failed' for a number of complex and interrelated reasons; to do with professional ethos, organisational separation, and legal structure. It is important not to overemphasise this. The White Paper, perhaps for good reason, is a highly political document, one aim of which is to underline the extent to which the failure of community care is a consequence of the policies of the previous administration, and it is important that this dimension be taken on board by its readers. The system is a long way from perfect, but it does work much of the time, particularly for learning disabled clients. In the final analysis it can be suggested that the White Paper's problem is not one of exaggeration but of orientation. Too much emphasis is placed on control and too little on tackling the fundamental *legal* problems and on simplifying procedures for client access and effective inter-agency working. Community care has become a lawyer's playground, and we should not be surprised if others cannot find their way through the legal maze. Moreover, the gravitational pull of residential provision that inheres in the present legal framework functions in practice as a bar to true care 'in' the community and the empowerment of clients. Clements (1997) suggests that the focus of reform should be on philosophical consistency — the current swathe of legislation has substantial elements that reflect the post-war ideals of the Welfare State, which tend to disempower by responding to 'need' and giving over the definition of that concept to professionals, cut across with a number of more empowering provisions (for example the Disabled Persons (Services, Consultation and Representation) Act 1986). The result is that the community care user is incoherently conceptualised by the current regime. The consequences of that incoherence, as this Chapter has shown, are plain to see. It is hard not to suspect that the subtext of policy under the Conservative government was to shift primary responsibility for care in the community from the state to the families and other informal carers of mentally disordered persons (Lewis, 1989). The saving grace of the current White Paper is that it claims to reverse that trend, and to accept on behalf of the community that community care is the responsibility of us all, and of the state, and is not just a problem of individuals and their families. Ultimately, community care law, policy and practice is about the way in which a community sees itself and its aspirations. It is perhaps understandable that this translates easily into a focus on control and public safety. But, *a priori*, this is to fracture 'community', positing the mentally ill as 'other'. It is to be hoped that any new legislation will live up to the claims made for it by the government.

TEN

Mental capacity (I)

10.1 INTRODUCTION

Mental capacity, as distinct from mental illness, has so far been in the background of this book. There have been references to it, in the discussion of *R* v *Bournewood Community and Mental Health NHS Trust, ex parte L* [1998] 3 WLR 107 (HL) in Chapter four and the discussion of the treatment provisions, ss. 57 and 58 of the 1983 Act, in Chapter seven, for example, but the question of how capacity is to be determined, and the effects of a finding of incapacity, have been left unexplored. That is the function of this Chapter.

Capacity determines both the authority of an individual to make a decision, and the legal responsibility for that decision. A patient lacking the capacity to consent to treatment for a specific physical ailment, for example, may be treated for that ailment notwithstanding his or her express objection to the treatment: he or she no longer has control over whether or not treatment will be given, and responsibility for the treatment will lie elsewhere. Precisely what happens when an individual is found incapable of making a decision depends on the decision in question. That will be discussed in some detail below; but the person lacking capacity, the individual most affected, will not normally control the decision. In the usual medical case, for example, the authority to make the decision will pass to the treating physician, who will be under a corresponding responsibility to decide in the patient's 'best interests'.

Capacity is a problematic topic for a book such as this. It cannot be omitted, since it is in part codified within part VII of the MHA 1983, and it so heavily overlaps, or is perceived so heavily to overlap, with the lives of the people with mental health problems; yet at the same time, it also concerns people who are not mentally ill in the conventional sense. Thus a person affected by a severe stroke may lack mental capacity for a variety of decisions (see, for example, *Re S (Hospital Patient: Court's Jurisdiction)* [1995] 3 All ER 290 (CA)). While we would not expect such a person to be within the purview of mental health law as understood in the rest of this book, they are subject to many of the same legal provisions regarding incapacity. In addition, mental disability alone is insufficient to render an individual incapable of making decisions. People with mental health difficulties, like all other adults, are presumed competent until shown to be otherwise: *Re C (Adult: Refusal of Medical Treatment)* [1994] 1 All ER 819 at p. 824. At issue is instead normally the ability to make the specific decision at issue. While characteristics of specific psychiatric conditions may enlighten that investigation, they in no way determine its outcome.

Investigation of the concept of capacity therefore overlays mental illness with a new set of criteria. The issues are substantively broader than much of the discussion in preceding Chapters. Up to now, primary concerns have been confinement, medical treatment, and the mechanics of community care. Incapacity, by comparison, can be raised in a multitude of legal contexts. While particular attention will be given in Chapter eleven to the matters of greatest concern in the MHA, this is an essentially arbitrary restriction. If the concern is capacity, why focus on these subjects rather than capacity to contract, to write a will, to marry, to consent to sexual activity, or to commit a tort or crime, particularly when these issues may also be of relevance to people with mental health problems? In deference to that wider relevance of capacity, and to provide some concrete grounding for the more specific discussion in the next Chapter, an overview of some of the contexts, tests, and results of incapacity are appropriate at this time, both in a specifically mental health context and more broadly. Then, following a discussion of common themes relating to capacity determination, there will be a more detailed discussion of specific contexts in Chapter eleven, namely consent to medical treatment, financial matters, and reforms proposed by the Law Commission to the law of incapacity.

10.2   CONTEXTS, TESTS, AND CONSEQUENCES OF INCAPACITY

The authority of the state as *parens patriae* to assume authority over persons lacking capacity is mediaeval in origin. A series of statutes commencing in the nineteenth century refined the ancient prerogative power until 1959, when the MHA placed both personal and financial guardianship on a purely statutory basis. The jurisdiction in financial matters (although not in personal ones) was for present purposes preserved largely unchanged in part VII of the MHA 1983.

The result is that the financial aspects of incapacity have a long history, a history which has evolved rather than one subject to sudden diversion. While the prerogative authority of the Lord Chancellor gave way to the statutory authority of the Court of Protection, the statutory language of the test for intervention has remained largely unchanged. In 1853, the inquiry was whether the individual was 'of unsound mind, and incapable of managing himself or his affairs, at the time of the inquiry' (s. 47, Regulation of Commissions in Lunacy Act 1853; see also definition of 'lunatic' in s. 2). In the 1983 Act, the court is to intervene where 'after considering medical evidence, [it] is satisfied that a person is incapable, by reason of mental disorder, of managing and administering his property and affairs' (s. 94(2)). If the test is met, the Court of Protection takes control of the estate. Where a hundred years ago, the Lord Chancellor could appoint a person to be committee (pronounced with the emphasis on the first and third syllables) to handle the day-to-day management of the estate, the Master of the Court of Protection can now appoint a receiver to perform an analogous function (s. 99).

Incremental development does not of course mean no development. At one time, the tradition was that those dependent on the incapacitated person would be made guardians of the person, since they had an interest in ensuring the continued good health of the incapacitated person; presumed heirs were instead given the role of committee, as they had an interest in appropriate frugality in the care of the incapacitated individual. That approach disappeared in the nineteenth century, and today family members are frequently appointed as receivers irrespective of their presumed interests in the estate of the individual.

Where the early nineteenth-century procedure required trial of the alleged incapacity by a jury, presided over by three commissioners, the modern statute requires merely that the Master of the Court of Protection be 'satisfied' that the relevant criteria are met (s. 94). Rules 7 and 10 of the Court of Protection Rules 1994 (SI 1994 No. 3046) expressly hold that a hearing is not necessarily required to determine incapacity. That said, the Act and rules do provide a process for a hearing in appropriate cases, albeit without a jury. The provisions relating to notice and representation of the allegedly incompetent person make this a relatively formal process, compared with some of the others which will be noted below. The Court similarly has a staff of visitors, officials able to investigate in support of the Court's work.

The effect of a finding of incapacity in this context has also developed over time. At the beginning of the nineteenth century, it would seem that a finding of lunacy did not necessarily preclude the individual from dealing with their estates, as for example by signing a relevant contract (*M'Adam* v *Walker* (1813) 1 Dow 148 at pp. 177-8). A so-called lucid interval was always acknowledged to be a possibility, and contracts signed in such a condition were binding. That ceased to be the case with *Re Walker* [1905] 1 Ch 160: contracts signed by persons found incapable under the statute were no longer valid (see also *Re Beaney (deceased)* [1978] 2 All ER 595 at p. 600). The result is that the statutory process is in general an extremely blunt instrument: the Court can order either that the individual retain complete control over his or her estate, or forfeit all control. There is no middle ground. Unusually for incapacity law, the finding is global, in so far as it affects all contractual matters relating to the estate. While application to the court may well be prompted by a specific turn of events in the individual's life, the finding of incapacity is based on the individual's situation as a whole, and is not contingent on the specifics of one particular situation. Rule 9 of the Court of Protection Rules 1994 does provide for taking control of small estates for a short period using a simplified process. This allows some flexibility of intervention; yet for the period of the intervention, the entire estate remains in the control of the Court.

The actual substantive matters requiring proof prior to a finding of incapacity under part VII of the MHA 1983 will be discussed, in so far as possible, in Chapter 11.2. Suffice it here to say that there have been changes in substantive matters in the last couple of centuries. Where the original jurisdiction had flowed from the ancient authority over 'idiots' and 'lunatics', nineteenth-century legislation had extended this to anyone of 'unsound mind'. The modern legislation can be seen as returning to a narrower approach, requiring that the individual be suffering from mental disorder, as defined in s. 1 of the Act (s. 93(2)). Consistent with this, a requirement for medical evidence prior to the finding of incapacity was introduced by s. 101, MHA 1959.

Clearly, not all those who may have difficulties caring for their estates are under the control of the Court of Protection. While it is now clear that those under the jurisdiction of that body cannot sign contracts even in a lucid interval, issues may still arise as to the validity of contracts signed by those alleged to be lacking capacity, but not under the control of the Court. The rules here are noticeably different from those of the Court of Protection. Incapacity *per se* does not affect the validity of a contract. The contract can still be enforced by the second party unless that party knew or ought reasonably to have known at the time the contract was signed that the first party lacked capacity: *Imperial Loan Company* v *Stone* [1892] 1 QB 599. In that event, the contract will be voidable rather than void, and in the event of subsequent proceedings under part VII of the MHA 1983 can be confirmed by the court: *Baldwyn* v *Smith* [1900] 1 Ch 588.

In the event that the contract is for 'necessaries', the incompetent person must nonetheless pay the provider a reasonable price for them. The term 'necessaries' in this context is not necessarily to be restricted to the essentials of life, or the least expensive goods or services. The term is defined in the Sale of Goods Act 1979 as 'goods suitable to the condition in life of the ... person concerned and to his actual requirements at the time of sale and delivery', and in so far as it remains appropriate to continue to refer to it, the common law adopts a similar definition (Matthews, 1982). Thus in *In re Bevan* [1912] 1 Ch 196, the incompetent person had made a living letting property. Necessaries in that case included all expenses related to rent audit of the properties and even renovation expenses for one of the rental properties.

Courts are often coy in their definition of what needs to be shown as a matter of substance to find incapacity in contractual and similar matters. In *Manches* v *Trimborn* (1946) 174 LT 344, Scott LJ held (at p. 345):

Therefore, if I were directing a jury, I should tell them that the degree of mental incapacity which the defence would have to establish to their satisfaction, was such a degree of incapacity as would interfere with the capacity of the defendant to understand substantially the nature and effect of the transaction into which she was entering. In some cases, criminal and testamentary, judges have felt able to give juries a good deal more assistance as to what faculties ought to be in question in determining responsibility for the commission of a crime, on the one hand, or for the making of a will, on the other hand; but I doubt if in a case of this kind, I could give the jury any further help than what I have already said.

That said, a few principles may be drawn. Certainly, the individual must be able to understand the nature of the document and the parties.

Some decisions also require the individual to understand the nature of the overall transaction, or the effect of the transaction on their estate more broadly. *Re Beaney (deceased)*, for example, involved a gift by an old lady near the end of her lifetime of her house, her sole significant asset, to one of her children with the effect that at her death, there was little available for her other children. In the circumstances of the case, the court held that it was necessary that Mrs. Beaney understand more than that she was making a gift, that the subject matter of the gift was her house, and that the recipient of the gift was her daughter. It held that she also needed to understand that she was disposing of the bulk of her estate, and the effect that would have upon the claims of the other potential beneficiaries under her will. Similarly, in *Manches* it was held that the individual needed to understand not merely that she was signing a cheque, and that this would involve the transfer of funds in the stated amount from herself to the payee, but also the essentials of the transaction of which the cheque was a part.

Neither incapacity to contract nor being under the authority of part VII of the MHA 1983 preclude an individual from making a will. Once again, capacity in this regard will depend on ability to understand the document in question, but here there is a classic threshold test, defined in *Banks v Goodfellow* (1870) 5 QB 549 at p. 565:

> It is essential to the exercise of such a power that a testator shall understand the nature of the act and its effects; shall understand the extent of the property of which he is disposing; shall be able to comprehend and appreciate the claims to which he ought to give effect.

In the event that the individual fails to meet this standard, the Master of the Court of Protection has authority to draft wills on behalf of the individuals in his or her care: MHA 1983, s. 96(e). If the individual is able to manage his or her existing estate, however, it may be doubted whether the provisions of s. 94(2) apply. If not, no will could be made on behalf of the individual.

The right to marry, interestingly, tends to be available for individuals with a lower level of capacity than the right to make a will. The courts seem content to emphasise that the contract of marriage is an easy one to understand, although it is necessary that the parties understand 'the responsibilities normally attaching to marriage': *In the Estate of Park* [1954] P 89 at p. 127; see also *Durham v Durham* (1885) 10 P 80, *Bennett v Bennett* [1969] 1 WLR 431 at p. 433. In the event that an individual lacks capacity, it would seem that no one may consent to marriage on his or her behalf.

The differential level of capacity between testamentary and matrimonial matters is surprising, since marriage revokes previous wills of the parties: s. 18, Wills Act 1837. The different capacities can in turn lead to ominous results. As with other contracts, marriages of those lacking capacity are voidable, not void, and are not open to challenge following the death of one of the parties. A clandestine marriage of an individual lacking capacity will thus be unchallengeable following the death of the incapacitated party. His or her previous will would be revoked by the supposed marriage, and the new spouse would acquire rights on intestacy (*Re Roberts, decd.* [1978] 1 WLR 653; *In re Davey* [1981] 1 WLR 165). This result seems an invitation for the unscrupulous to prey on wealthy persons of low capacity and poor health.

Personal decisions are considerably more problematic. From 1959, the *parens patriae* power was replaced by the guardianship provisions of the MHA. The 1959 Act had provided the guardian the authority over the incapacitated person possessed by a father over his fourteen-year-old child, a broadly similar authority to the traditional power, but the 1983 Act restricted these powers considerably. Now, the guardian has the power to require an individual to reside at a given place (but not to detain them there), to require that the individual attend at specific times and places for medical treatment (but not to consent to the treatment), and the power to require access to the individual to be given to a medical practitioner, approved social worker, or other person specified in the guardianship order (s. 8). These powers are, of course, restricted to persons with a mental disability as defined by the Act, and about whom an order for guardianship has been made. The authority of the Court of Protection extends only to matters relating to the estate of the individual, not to personal decisions, although admittedly the line between these may often be difficult to draw: *Re W* [1970] 2 All ER 502.

The result was a lacuna in the law: no personal decisions could be made for people incapacitated for reasons outside the mental disability criteria in s. 1 of the 1983 Act, and outside the powers specifically enumerated in s. 8, no personal decisions regarding an incapacitated person could be made at all. Physical treatment by a doctor in such circumstances would, it seemed, have been a battery.

The initial court decisions to deal with this problem involved consent to medical treatment. The facts of *F* v *West Berkshire Health Authority* [1989] 2 All ER 545 (HL) involved the sterilisation of an adult incapacitated by reason of developmental handicap. Surgical intervention without consent is generally a battery, and the question before the court was who could consent on F's behalf. A declaration of the courts was sought in advance of the surgery, to clarify the legal position. By extending the common law doctrine of necessity, the court held that the doctor was permitted to treat an incapacitated adult without consent, so long as the treatment was in the best interest of the patient. Apart from treatments listed in s. 57, MHA 1983, where competent consent of the patient is required and therefore incapacity precludes the provision of the treatment, *F* applies to patients admitted informally to psychiatric facilities. Detained patients are within the scope of s. 58. As their consent is not required in any event during the first three months of confinement, *F* is irrelevant. Its relevance is further limited in the period after three months, since s. 58(3)(b) allows any confined patient to be treated without consent in specific circumstances.

The tests of capacity to consent to treatment will be dealt with at greater length (see 11.1.2). By way of introduction, the most recent test is contained in *Re C (Adult: Refusal of Medical Treatment)* [1994] 1 All ER 819, where

Thorpe J held (at p. 824) that capacity implied that the patient could comprehend and retain treatment information, believe it, and weigh it in the balance to arrive at a choice as to whether or not to consent. This case is significant not merely for the test it establishes, but also because the court was prepared to issue an injunction prohibiting the proposed treatment, in the event that C lost capacity in the future. Where *In re T* [1992] 4 All ER 649 had held that competent patients could refuse treatments in advance, and those treatment refusals ought to be honoured in the event of subsequent incapacity, Butler-Sloss and Staughton LJJ rather unhelpfully held (at pp. 665, 669) that only nominal damages would occur in the event that such treatments were provided to an incapacitated patient, in the patient's best interest. The injunction in *Re C* provided some teeth to the refusal, as treatment in violation of the injunction would constitute contempt of court.

F has since been applied in other contexts related to personal guardianship. Its closest parallel is *R v Bournewood, ex parte L* (see 4.2), where the House of Lords again invoked the doctrine of necessity, per Lords Goff and Steyn. As the question in *F* had been whether a battery would be committed by the doctors performing surgery on an individual unable to consent, so the question in *Bournewood* was whether the tort of false imprisonment would be committed by the facility by restricting the movements of a mentally incapacitated but compliant patient.

Considerably more problematic is the earlier case of *Re S (Hospital Patient: Court's Jurisdiction)* (see 10.1). The case concerned a Norwegian artist, S, who was incapacitated as a result of a stroke. The contest was between his English common law spouse and his Norwegian wife and children as to who would have authority to make personal decisions about him. The immediate question was in which nursing home or private hospital he would live, and whether in Norway or England. At issue before the Court of Appeal was whether there was jurisdiction in the English courts to declare who would make these decisions, the wife or the common law spouse. The court held that there was jurisdiction, and remitted the matter to the High Court for determination on the merits. Note that this is not an analogous situation to *F*, where the doctors would have been understandably curious as to whether they were about to commit a rather serious battery, or *R v Bournewood, ex parte L*, where the local NHS trust actually had custody of L, and therefore might have been seen as wrongfully confining him. S did not involve an application by such a carer, but instead by someone wishing to make decisions about care, a guardianship issue. As noted, there are no rights to personal guardianship outside the MHA 1983, which was agreed to be inapplicable in this case. The question in *S*, therefore, is precisely what right the court thought it was declaring?

The court located the right in contractual doctrine, and specifically the law relating to necessaries (per Bingham MR at p. 303):

> When S suffered his stroke, it is plain that the plaintiff assumed the duty of ensuring that he was properly cared for. Having assumed that duty, she was at risk if she failed to discharge it. ... She did discharge it. She arranged for S to be treated and cared for at the private hospital. If she made that contract

as a principal, no one is prima facie entitled to vary or interfere with performance of it without the consent of either contracting party. If, perhaps more probably, she made the contract as an agent for S, deriving her authority from necessity, then she remains an agent authorised to safeguard the performance of the contract unless and until the best interests of S are shown to require a change in the arrangements.

The difficulty with this is that it turns the matter into one of property and affairs, a matter already covered by part VII of the MHA 1983, when the lacuna in law relates instead to personal guardianship. The Court of Protection takes the view that those with brain damage as a result of accident or illness, into which category S presumably fell, are within its remit (Jones, 1999 p. 328). The Court has authority to do all such things as appear necessary or expedient for the maintenance or other benefit of the patient (s. 95(1)(a)). The rights claimed by the plaintiff in S, in the court's formulation, appear to be no more than a subset of the Court of Protection powers. It certainly creates difficulties in situations where the Court of Protection has been appointed, since it would seem that in that event, the liability for necessaries is extinguished (Matthews, 1982, p. 159). If the S jurisdiction is necessaries-based, it would presumably equally cease to exist with the appointment of the Court of Protection.

The result is at best unfortunate. Are we to understand that those who make contractual decisions relating to necessaries for those lacking capacity, also have authority to make personal decisions? That cannot be right; the distinction between personal and financial decisions is much too entrenched in capacity law. The capacity to determine where one will live is not the same as the capacity to sign the rent cheques; one may have one without the other. And in the event of incapacity, who is to have authority in the event of disagreement between, for example, the nursing home and the family of the incapacitated person? Following R v Bournewood, the home commits no tort by continuing to house the individual; yet such care is a necessary, and if the family is paying, they presumably have authority to make decisions regarding where the individual lives, following Re S. What happens if the care is paid for by the local authority? Presumably, following Re S, the local authority, having assumed contractual responsibility, is now in charge of decisions as to where the incapacitated person will live, excluding family authority and subject only to judicial review. Is it really acceptable that the role of the family in the care of their loved ones will turn on whether it can assume responsibility for payment?

The standards above tend to be based in the individual's understanding of the nature of the decision to be made. There are other ways in which capacity might be conceived. Indeed, the existing law occasionally recognises rather different formulations, depending on the context. Thus while litigation on the point is scarce, it would seem that the standard of capacity for a tort is merely to know the nature and quality of the act in question; there is no requirement that the individual should understand that the act was wrong: Morris v Marsden [1952] 1 All ER 925. It is thus a lower standard than for criminal incapacity in the insanity defence, which may be based either on a lack of knowledge of the nature and quality of the act, or, alternatively, a lack of knowledge that the act was wrong. The reference here is not necessarily to a knowledge of the act's legal ramifications in criminal law, but to a moral standard.

This should be enough to introduce the capacity law landscape. A few overarching principles should be re-enforced. First, there is a legal presumption of capacity: it is in general those claiming incapacity who have the onus of proving it (*Snook* v *Watts* (1848) 11 Beav 105). The exceptions to this rule include that those propounding a will may be required to demonstrate the capacity of the testator, if that has been put in issue by those challenging the will (*Battan Singh* v *Amirchand* [1948] AC 162 (JCPC)). Further, once incapacity of a certain type (such as contractual) is found, the onus will be on the individual alleging a return of capacity so to demonstrate (*Birkin* v *Wing* (1890) 63 LT 80). The presumption of capacity needs to be stressed in part because articulation of tests of capacity, including those in 10.3, tend to be phrased in terms of what is required for capacity to be found. While this does away with a considerable number of negatives and greatly simplifies sentence structures, it is misleading in so far as it suggests that capacity needs to be demonstrated. With the caveats above, it is instead for those who challenge capacity to prove its absence.

Secondly, a finding of incapacity is specific to the decision at issue. A finding that an individual cannot consent to a specific treatment does not preclude the individual from executing contracts or making a valid will or even from consenting to other medical treatments. The sole exception to this is that placement under the Court of Protection removes authority by the individual to sign all contracts, although it does not imply incapacity in testamentary matters or decisions outside the jurisdiction of the Court.

10.3 SOME GENERAL PRINCIPLES

From this, it will be clear that the law of incapacity has a variety of different but related aspects. It first involves a determination of whether the individual will have responsibility and authority over a specific decision in question. This in turn implies both a set of criteria to determine the individual's capacity, and a process by which the individual will be assessed. If the individual is found to be lacking capacity, the law must then determine who if anyone will have authority over and responsibility for the decision in question, and how it will be exercised. Coupled with these are parallel procedural questions of safeguards: how is it to be ensured that the standards of incapacity are being applied appropriately, and how is it to be ensured that the individual charged with making decisions for an incapacitated person is deciding appropriately?

It should be emphasized for the discussion that follows that here, as throughout mental health law, the answers to these must be considered with reference to primary legal sources, and in particular statutes and case law. It will equally be clear, however, that this is an area where the law is very much in the process of development. Not only that; but while the case law which forms the basis of modern thinking is nineteenth-century, the practices and perceptions of incapacity have changed considerably since that time, making application of that law problematic. These changing conceptions mean that a more wide-ranging overview of the problems of incapacity law generally is appropriate, prior to examination of legal approaches in specific contexts; but this pedagogic objective should not detract from the importance of primary legal sources in the relevant contexts.

Up to the late nineteenth century, delusion was pivotal to the finding of incapacity (see Bartlett, 1996). Leonard Shelford (1847), in the leading mid-century legal treatise on lunacy, stated (at p. 42):

> The absence or presence of delusion so understood, forms the true and only test, or criterion, of absent or present insanity. In short, delusion in that sense of it, and insanity, seem to be almost, if not altogether, convertible terms; so that a patient under a delusion, so understood, on any subject or subjects, in any degree, is, for that reason, essentially mad or insane on such subject or subjects in that degree.

If the individual was deluded on a matter relevant to the decision at hand, incapacity followed; otherwise, the courts might be hesitant to intervene, lest the merely eccentric lose their rights.

By the last few decades of the nineteenth century, this point of definition was being lost. *Jenkins* v *Morris* (1880) 14 Ch 674 provides a particularly startling indication of that move. The dispute revolved around the land of Thomas Price who had believed his land to be impregnated with sulphur, and thus of limited value. He sold it to the defendant, Morris, at a price which would have been favourable had the land been polluted with sulphur, but which was in fact well under its real value. The statement of Jessel MR (at p. 683) shows a startling departure from the delusion standard:

> [I]t is suggested that [the trial judge] should have told [the jury] that [Price] was not competent to manage this business unless he was free from delusions as connected with the farm in question, and that he was not free from those delusions because he thought the farm was impregnated with sulphur. I am not prepared to say that he was bound to tell the jury all that under the particular circumstances of this case; for it must be recollected that, although a man may believe a farm to be impregnated with sulphur and not fit for himself to live in, he may still be a shrewd man of business, and may even believe that the other side may not know of the impregnation of the farm with the sulphur, and that in consequence he may get a higher price for it than if it was known that it was so impregnated. He may have been perfectly right in his conclusion upon that subject, and the jury may have thought that it was so. The judge, in fact, says that he was a shrewd man of business.

The delusion went to the heart of the contract concerned; yet the court confirmed capacity. Indeed, the court allowed the possibility of the truth of the delusion, without inquiring into the facts surrounding either the land or the mental state of the vendor — a marked departure from the previous judicial approach. By the close of the twentieth century, language of delusion, which is at the basis of the case law upon which the modern edifice of capacity is built, is rarely used. At times, this seems almost disingenuous. For example, the tendency now, reflected in 10.2, is to stop the classic test of testamentary capacity in *Banks* v *Goodfellow* mid-sentence (on p. 565), ignoring the following:

> but and, with a view to the latter object, [i.e., appreciation of the claims to which the testator ought to give effect] that no disorder of mind shall poison his affections, pervert his sense of right, or prevent the exercise of his natural faculties — that no insane delusion shall influence his will in disposing of his property and bring about a disposal of it which, if the mind had been sound, would not have been made.

While there has been considerable retreat from the hard-line position of Jenkins, the courts have been more circumspect regarding how capacity is now to be assessed. The movement is from a test based on delusion to a test based on intellectual ability, away from the correct perception of facts at the basis of a decision, toward a standard of reasoning capability requisite to reach judgments. Incapacity is now likely to be characterised as a failure to understand or appreciate, a categorisation which would have been quite foreign to the nineteenth-century cases upon which the courts purport to rely. At the same time, there is no obvious acknowledgement in the courts of the changing use of the nineteenth-century language. If the courts have moved from the test of delusion, it is not obvious that they have successfully articulated what they have moved to.

A proper understanding of how the concept of capacity is applied cannot therefore be limited to an assessment of the case law. Not merely are there the usual legal problems that the decisions of the court may or may not be being followed by those in charge of administering the law, it is also that the reported cases themselves are problematic. While referring to the nineteenth-century law, they appear to be applying other standards; but they are relatively silent on what those standards are. A proper assessment would require a systematic analysis of how the decisions are in fact being made.

This is not possible. There is no general mechanism to report those found to be lacking capacity, nor in general to monitor the decisions being made about these people. This makes socio-legal analysis of capacity difficult. It is not known for example what gender or racial mixes in this category are, although a comfortable majority of those under the control of the Court of Protection are women, owing perhaps in part to women's longer average lifespans.

Nonetheless, a number of the same questions arise in assessing the meaning of capacity as arose in the discussion of the meaning of mental illness in Chapter two. Certainly, the test of incapacity, like the test of mental illness, is culturally defined. A particularly clear example of this may be seen in the test of capacity to marry, enunciated in *Durham* v *Durham* (1885) 10 P 80 at p. 82:

> I may say this much in the outset, that it appears to me that the contract of marriage is a very simple one, which does not require a high degree of intelligence to comprehend. It is an engagement between a man and a

woman to live together, and love one another as husband and wife, to the exclusion of all others. This is expanded in the promises of the marriage ceremony by words having reference to the natural relations which spring from that engagement, such as protection on the part of the man, and submission on the part of the woman.

Clearly, the references to protection by the man and submission of the woman would not be understood by all modern bridal couples as part of the bargain. Yet if that attitude is based in a particularly Victorian image of marriage, it is difficult to see what would be substituted at the end of the twentieth century which would be less culturally based. While a modern test might reflect modern culture, the individual would still be judged on whether they had the culturally appropriate understanding.

Further, it is at least open to query how submissive Victorian wives in fact were (and how protective their husbands). Even in the Victorian age, did this represent a realistic view of marriage, a view of marriage which would have reflected the expectation of real nineteenth-century couples? Or was it a moral ideal which many married couples would have viewed with some scepticism? And if the latter, ought people to have been judged according to a standard reflecting a moral ideal rather than a practical reality? A similar difficulty is likely to arise in a modern context. The ideals of marriage remain firm among moralists, but are increasingly challenged in practice. Ought capacity to be judged according to the culture of the moralists?

While particularly clear in the marriage context, these cultural issues extend into all areas of capacity. Thus the testamentary test in *Banks* v *Goodfellow* required that the testator understand, among other things, 'claims to which he ought to give effect'. This tends to refer to close family members; yet it is clearly a mere cultural value that these people are entitled to inherit upon the demise of the testator. Similarly, if jurisdiction of the Court of Protection is based on 'inappropriate' decisions regarding the estate, how is the meaning of 'inappropriate' to be understood outside a cultural context? Even in crime, the knowledge that the act was 'wrong' is to be understood in a moral way, 'according to the ordinary standard adopted by reasonable men': *R* v *Codere* (1916) 12 Cr App R 21 at p. 27.

It seems inappropriate to find individuals incapable owing to the wrong set of cultural values; yet how is a test of capacity to be formulated which is free of cultural bias? This problem circulates at the heart of the academic literature regarding capacity determination.

The law of incapacity creates roles of authority and dependence, discipline and control, power and subordination, themes running through the remainder of this book. In so far as the existing laws relating to incapacity are specific to the decision in question, allowing for capacity in some areas but not others, it is not obvious that the law of incapacity will be analogous to one of Goffman's total institutions (1961/1991). More, like care in the community, it will have some of those characteristics but not others. Thus there will still be issues of learned dependency, particularly significant here as they may affect later capacity. There is also the risk of conflicts in those in charge of decision-making, between the best interests of the person lacking capacity as perceived by that person or by the law, and the personal convenience or view of best interests of the decision-maker.

Similarly, there will be Foucaultean resonances, for the modern view of capacity is linked closely with the concept of rationality. Indeed, it is difficult to find a concept closer to the heart of Foucault's opus than the allocation of rights, of legal personhood, on the basis of a test of rationality. The study of incapacity thus involves the knowledge of the margin of personhood itself. Given the relationship Foucault places on the relationship between knowledge and power, the way in which incapacity is to be understood should be of no small importance to those who take his work seriously.

10.4 TESTS OF CAPACITY

If the case law is at best Delphic on the tests of capacity it uses, medical literature is much more developed as to possible tests of capacity, and the advantages and disadvantages of each. This literature must be approached with some care. It is generally written in the context of consent to medical treatment, and may be difficult to apply to other areas of competency assessment. Nonetheless, it does provide a useful framework for what sorts of option are available to determine capacity.

10.4.1 Status approaches

It would be possible to say that all persons of a certain status were to be deemed incompetent. Laws relying on status tend to be unclear as to whether they are based on a presumption of incapacity in the status group, or a different social policy objective. Thus it is a crime for a man to have sexual intercourse with a woman who is mentally 'defective', and homosexual acts remain criminal for men with severe mental handicaps: see s. 8, Sexual Offences Act 1956, s. 1(3), Sexual Offences Act 1967. It might be asked whether the basis for these prohibitions is that the individuals concerned would be lacking the capacity to consent, or whether it is instead a different social policy against the sexual behaviour in question (see Carson, 1989a, esp. p. 361). Similarly, as discussed in Chapter seven, involuntary patients in psychiatric facilities have no right to refuse most treatment in their first three months following their detention (MHA 1983, ss. 58(1)(b) and 63). Is this based in a belief that such patients would be unable to consent in any event, or that there are other overriding policy considerations which would justify treatment over the objection of a competent patient in these circumstances? The apparent advantage of a status-based test would be its ease of administration, and the certainty which might go along with it. That of course depends on the status chosen. If the status were being involuntarily confined in a psychiatric facility, or indeed being a patient in a psychiatric facility, the line might be relatively clear, but the net thrown too widely, since many people in these groups may be competent in all matters of legal concern. In addition, those lacking capacity to make a decision but not in the status group would remain legally capable.

Selecting a more sensitive status such as 'severe mental handicap' would have similar problems that some people one might expect to remain with authority over decisions might lose that authority, and some who ought perhaps to be relieved of responsibility would keep it. In addition, that sort of standard would lack precise definition, making the apparent ease of administration largely illusory.

A status-based approach would be unlikely to prove acceptable as a test of capacity on any scale, in any event. As noted above, English law has long compartmentalised capacity. Where European jurisdictions may use a concept of judicial personhood to which many legal rights attach together, that has never been the English way. Capacity to contract has always been distinct from capacity to make a will, or to consent to medical treatment, for example.

While this may make for some uncertainty *vis-à-vis* third parties, since a given individual may be competent for some decisions and not others, it does have the advantage of ensuring that the individual retains as much freedom and control over their life as they are capable of exercising. For this reason, the Law Commission rejected any form of a status-based test of capacity (see Law Commission, 1995, p. 32). The rejection of such a test similarly corresponds to the experience of those who work with people with mental health or learning difficulties, that they may well be quite perceptive on some matters, but without capacity on others.

If status is not the appropriate way to go, mechanisms must be articulated to assess the individual choices persons of marginal capacity make, to determine whether the decisions are to be respected. The following discussion presents a variety of alternatives. The overall categorisation relies to a considerable degree upon the classic paper of Roth, Meisel and Lidz (1977).

10.4.2   Evidencing a choice

The ability to evidence a choice is considered a *sine qua non* for capacity. It is unusual as a criterion for incapacity, since the inability to evidence a choice may flow from physical rather than mental factors. Nonetheless, it is difficult to see how the intellectually competent intentions of an individual unable to communicate those intentions can be respected. The concern here, as relating to intellectual capacity, is that all reasonable efforts be made to ascertain any competent wishes. In particular, the distinction must be made between a person who is unable to evidence a choice, and one who acquiesces, who may be able to choose, but for whatever reason does not do so. Query, for example, whether the case presented by Roth et al (1977, p. 280) to illustrate the evidencing of a choice standard is, under that standard, capable or not:

Case 1 A 41-year-old depressed woman was interviewed in the admission unit. She rarely answered yes or no to direct questions. Admission was proposed; she said and did nothing but looked apprehensive. When asked about admission, she did not sign herself into the hospital, protest, or walk away. She was guided to the inpatient ward by her husband and her doctor after being given the opportunity to walk the other way.

The individual was clearly compliant, but notwithstanding Roth's implication, it is not clear that she actually evidenced a choice. Note further that the individual apparently did, rarely, answer yes or no to direct questions. Query whether patient interaction by the person assessing wishes in cases such as these might sometimes yield better indications of what those wishes are.

Acquiescence is an issue which arises particularly in North American systems of health care, where the decision regarding treatment of incapacitated patients belongs not to the doctor, but to a family member. In such systems, a finding that an acquiescing patient is competent to consent saves administrative time, by allowing the treatment to be given without locating and seeking consent of the family member. One can see the logic, if not necessarily the correctness, of this view if the patient is otherwise capable of evidencing a choice and chooses not to do so; but many 'acquiescing' patients do not meet that standard. Their supposed 'acquiescence' may be the result of a physical or mental inability to evidence a choice. It is much less of an issue in England, where the decision in these circumstances would generally fall to the doctor in the event of patient incapacity, resulting in minimal additional administrative hassle.

It is difficult to see that mere acquiescence would be an acceptable standard of capacity in any other legal context. It would be surprising for a court to give effect to a contract or will signed by a merely 'acquiescing' individual, otherwise unable to evidence a choice, for example. It is therefore at best dubious that the standard should apply in a health care context.

While it is difficult to criticise the evidencing of a choice as a necessary condition for capacity, ought it to be a sufficient condition? Such a position is not without its advantages. It would, after all, be inexpensive and easy to administer. Ought any decision which can be articulated by an individual be respected? Buchanan and Brock (1986, pp. 32, 33) provide a rather pointed criticism of the standard:

> This standard respects every expressed choice of a patient, and so is not, in fact, a criterion of *competent* choice at all. It entirely disregards whether defects or mistakes are present in the reasoning process leading to the choice, whether the choice is in accord with the patient's conception of his or her good, and whether the choice would be harmful to the patient. It thus fails to provide any protection for patient well-being, and is insensitive to the way the value of self-determination itself varies with differences in people's capacities to choose in accordance with their conceptions of their own good.

Typical of many modern commentators, Buchanan and Brock equate capacity with the reasoning process to reach a decision, a view which will be reflected in the remainder of the criteria discussed below. Yet why should this be the case? Law and society respect the manifestly irrational decisions of people whose capacity is not called into question. Thus people with cancer may refuse treatment on the manifestly unfounded basis that they do not believe the doctor's diagnosis, and people are permitted to engage in spending sprees or expensive and frivolous hobbies entirely beyond their means. The rationality of some of these decisions is highly dubious, yet they are respected. On what basis should some irrational decisions be respected, and not others? That question will circulate through all the discussions of capacity below. There is an expectation that those of marginal capacity should justify their eccentricities more than those whose capacity is not in doubt; and it is not clear why this should be so (see Carson, 1993, esp. pp. 314-6).

Buchanan and Brock argue that the decision might be at variance with the individual's conception of his or her good. Their point here does not represent paternalism according to the values of an outside source such as a doctor; it is instead that the use of the standard is somehow inconsistent with the *individual's* view of his or her own good. That is a complex statement that warrants unpacking. To begin with, it presupposes a specific vision of self-determination. Margaret Somerville posits various definitions of self-determination and autonomy (Somerville, 1994, pp. 185-8). On one, simple version, self-determination means no more than the ability to register a choice, again rendering a concern about self-determination in the current context circular. Other definitions centre around a more developed notion of the individual as a person, a 'self' in the philosophic sense. Such a higher standard is required in the analysis of Buchanan and Brock, who require as a basis for capacity that the individual have 'a set of values or conception of the good' (p. 25). Various queries flow from this.

To begin with, is it necessarily obvious that the simple version of self-determination is necessarily to be avoided in all cases? The removal of decision-making authority from the individual may have its own costs, both to third parties in the form of assumption of responsibility, and to the individual, in terms of loss of self-respect and the respect of others. Can these costs not sometimes outweigh the benefits? To pick an extreme example, would the simple ability to manifest a choice not be a perfectly acceptable system to decide what sort of sandwich a person will eat for lunch? If it is acknowledged that loss of the decision-making authority *per se* has its costs, should some decisions not merely be left where they are? That suggests that the nature or seriousness of the decision may have a role to play in the standard of capacity applied to it.

A more complex meaning of autonomy raises theoretical difficulties, since it implicitly or explicitly imports a notion of a 'self', with a variety of characteristics. These characteristics will almost certainly be value-laden — as with the discussion of the 'rational' subject above — and much of the discussion of the remaining conceptualisations of capacity will involve defining some of those characteristics. Here, the point is instead to question the appropriateness of relying on that sort of concept. The question becomes not merely whether a concept of the self should be required; but also which self. One view would allow paternalist intervention as a justified displacement of personal autonomy when the latter would 'frustrate the exercise of choices, which are part of the individual's attempts to pursue his own conception of how to live.' (quoted in Fennell, 1990, p. 29). The difficulty here is to ascertain when the 'conception of how to live' is crystallised. As people progress through their lives, including those parts of their lives in which they are to some degree disabled, expectations of what constitutes a good or acceptable level of life may change. Adoption of a more complex standard of self may imply a tendency to privilege the views of the patient when he or she had been of robust capacity, and to marginalise the views of the patient when capacity becomes marginal.

In a testamentary context, there is some support in the case law for this approach, particularly when the will is executed shortly before the death of the testator. Thus *Harwood* v *Baker* (1840) 3 Moore 282, involved a will which left the testator's entire estate to his second wife, disinheriting the remainder of his family. The testator was held to be incompetent to execute the will, on the basis that he had not shown an antipathy to these relatives when his capacity had not been in doubt. (pp. 313-4). Similarly, in *Battan Singh* v *Amirchand* (10.3), a will was disallowed leaving the testator's estate to two friends who had apparently cared for the testator, preferring a will leaving the estate to nephews living on another continent and seen only infrequently, who had been the beneficiaries of an earlier will. While the testator did know the scope of his estate, his prior views as to who should receive the benefit of it held sway.

Certainly, the views of the individual when competent may affect the appropriate decision to be taken when he or she has lost capacity, but it is much less obvious that the fact that a person's views change over the course of time somehow indicates incapacity. If capacity is to be determined with reference to a 'self', it is fair to ask what self that is, the self of robust earlier days, or the self progressing through infirmity. It is not obvious that the answer to that question needs to be the same for all decisions. Should wills be subject to a different test than, for example, treatment to which the patient would have consented in earlier times, but now refuses? The use of mere ability to evidence a choice as the criterion of capacity privileges the existing self to the exclusion of all previous personal characteristics. That is one unambiguous solution to the problem. The versions which follow provide others.

10.4.3   'Reasonable' outcome of choice

Where the previous standard of capacity was based on the mere ability to make a choice, this version assesses capacity on the basis of the outcome of the choice. In theory, it is an objective test: could the reasonable person have reached the decision of the individual in question, in the circumstances in question? This is no more a test of 'capacity' or 'competency' than the previous test, however: reasoning ability does not enter into the equation, nor, at least not expressly, do the reasons for which the choice was made. Here again, the problem of the right to irrational or wrong decisions enters the picture. It is nonsensical to claim that people may do irrational things with their money or refuse life-saving treatment for whatever reason they choose, if when their capacity is called into question, the irrationality of the decision is precisely what will render the individual incapable of making the decision.

Nonetheless, there is a persistent set of claims that this standard is in practice used frequently. Physicians, for example, are alleged often to be content to treat a patient as competent so long as they are accepting treatment, but incompetent if treatment is refused (see, e.g., Law Commission, 1995, para. 3.4; Gunn, 1994, p. 16; Roth et al, 1977, p. 281).

Doctors are by no means the only culprits here, however. While courts do not, at least officially, judge capacity simply on the nature of the decision involved, there is precedent for the application of different standards of capacity, depending on the decision chosen by the allegedly incompetent person. This was the approach in *Evans* v *Knight and Moore* (1822) 1 Add 229 at pp. 237, 238:

> [W]here a mental aberration is proved to have shown itself in the alleged testator, the degree of evidence necessary to substantiate any testamentary act depends greatly on the character of the act itself. If it purports to give effect only to probable intentions, its validity may be established by comparatively slight evidence. But evidence, very different in kind and much weightier in degree, is required to the support of an act which purports to contain dispositions contrary to the testator's probable intentions, or savouring, in any degree, of folly or frenzy.

Here, the will was 'precisely such a disposition as natural affection would dictate' (p. 238), apparently an objective test, and the will was unsurprisingly upheld. More recently, Bernard Dickens has claimed that the common law similarly varies the standard of consent in a medical context, depending on whether treatment is consented to or refused (Dickens, 1994, p. 287). Below, 11.1.2, will re-enforce the view that courts are extremely hesitant to allow a finding of capacity, when the result will be that recommended medical treatment will not be provided.

Certainly, one could see the logic of the standard of capacity varying in proportion to the complexity of the decision; that will indeed be implied in the standards which follow. In so far as 'irrational' decisions have more complex ramifications than socially approved decisions, an assumption which may or may not be true, a higher level of capacity would often be expected of the former decisions. The approach of the courts however would appear to be quite different. The issue is not the complexity of the decision, but the agreeableness of its outcome.

At issue here, then, appears to be a range of social factors, quite independent of the abilities of the individual. The testamentary cases appear to support Victorian ideologies of the family and inheritance of wealth. The medical cases appear to support the desirability of medical treatment. Query whether capacity is an appropriate mechanism to enforce what are effectively social policy goals. Thus if the objective is to re-enforce specific doctrines of the family, it is not obvious why only those of marginal capacity should be subject to the policy, while those clearly possessing capacity enjoy greater freedom to leave their estate to whom they choose. If the objective is to ensure that specific forms of treatment are carried out, it is not obvious why only those of marginal capacity should lose the right to refuse them. In essence, if a specific outcome is worth enforcing, why is it worth enforcing only for those of marginal capacity, rather than through intervention which would affect all in society?

That is not, of course, the same question as the severity of impact of the decision. Ought different standards of capacity apply for decisions which will affect the individual differently? It was posited above for example that the social costs of an incapacity finding may outweigh the benefit of such a finding, so that in some situations the mere ability to evidence a choice may be an appropriate standard of capacity. That is, in its way, a result-oriented test, since the ramifications of a decision either way by an individual of low capacity are viewed as sufficiently small to be outweighed by other social factors. How far should the law go, down this road?

Roth et al (1977, p. 283) propose a system where the test of capacity would vary with the risk-benefit ratio of proposed treatment. Thus treatments of high risk and low benefit would require minimum capacity to refuse, as treatments of high benefit and low risk would require minimum capacity to consent. Consenting to the former, or refusing the latter, would require a higher standard of capacity. The difficulty here is that the risks and benefits are likely to be assessed by the doctor, and may or may not reflect the patient's priorities.

10.4.4 Rational reasons approach

This version of capacity assesses aspects of the reasoning process itself, insisting that the individual reach a decision based on rational reasons. It is thus, to begin with, expected that rational processing of information to reach a rational conclusion will occur: those with, for example, severe affective disorders may be found to lack capacity on that ground alone. The decision may also be found to be irrational if the reasoning process is founded in mental disorder. This approach thus begins to look at the quality of the decision-making process, rather than simply the outcome of the process.

The case law does occasionally expressly reflect the rational reasons test. Certainly, there is a tendency to insist on the ability to manipulate information in a rational way for a finding of capacity to be made. *Jenkins* v *Morris* (10.3) presents a particularly clear example of a rather pure form of the test. Recall that the concern of the court in that case involved the ability of the vendor of the land to reason, based on the apparently incorrect belief that his land was impregnated with sulphur. The focus on the vendor's abilities, the court's view that he might be a 'shrewd man of business', suggests a focus on his abilities. He would fairly clearly not have sold his land in this fashion, however, but for the mistaken belief in the pollution of the land. If this belief were the function of a mental disability, the wrong result would seem to have been achieved by the test.

For this reason, the tendency in recent years has been to attempt to consider irrational reasoning processes based in the mental disorder. The approach has been to examine the reasoning process with reference to the ethical framework of the individual during their life, prior to their capacity being called into question. This is of course only a partial answer to the problem, for it still looks to the process, rather than the information upon which the process is based. The veracity of the information is discussed in other approaches to incapacity, below.

Other problems of this approach will now be obvious. It may well be the case that the individual in question was never of unquestioned capacity, in which case the approach cannot apply. Alternatively, once again, this would expressly privilege a version of the individual's 'self' frozen at a specific point in the past to the prejudice of any legitimate personal progress or change since that time. Consider a decision of an ageing individual, apparently based on religious grounds, when previously the individual had not been a believer. That might well be the product of a mental abnormality; at the same time, many people apparently develop religious beliefs later in life, and it would be inappropriate to deprive those of marginal capacity of that rather common experience. The problem is how it will be determined which of these is the case. Here again, there would appear to be the risk of an objective, result-based test: if the behaviour were that of a reasonable believer, it might be allowed; but then, what constitutes 'reasonableness' of religious belief?

A more fundamental complication going to the heart of the test is that a number of factors used by most people to make decisions are simply not rational in any real sense. Few 'rational' individuals would not be frightened of invasive medical treatment, for example. If that weighs into the decision made by the marginally capable person, is that a point against the decision in this model, notwithstanding that it would equally be a factor in the decision of a person of unquestioned capacity?

10.4.5   Ability to understand

This articulation focuses on the capacity to understand and reason. As such, it bears some similarity to the rational reasons test, but where that test was interested primarily in distinguishing 'true' views from those affected by a mental disorder, this test does not centre on that distinction, but rather directly on the cognitive performance of the individual. As this test focuses on cognitive ability in preference to outcome, it thus acknowledges that the person with capacity may choose to make irrational or unwise decisions. The test is based on the view that an individual who has the relevant reasoning ability should have authority to choose as they see fit.

At least in theory, this may be divorced from the actual information upon which the decision in question is to be made, so long as the level of understanding is such that the individual would have sufficient understanding to make the decision. In practice, since the test is likely to involve a determination of capacity regarding a specific decision, some reference to that context may occur, but not necessarily. The medical profession in particular has developed a variety of apparently objective tests to judge reasoning and understanding ability.

There are a wide variety of these tests, of which the 'mini mental state examination' and the Wechsler scales, particularly the Wechsler Adult Intelligence Scale (WAIS) are the best known. The tests employ a variety of methods. The mini-mental state examination, developed in 1975, is a short test, taking roughly five to ten minutes to administer. It purports to test the individual's spatial and temporal orientation, their attention and calculation abilities, their recall, and their linguistic capacity. In practice, it involves the individual in answering a variety of questions relating to date, time, and place; requires him or her to repeat three objects named by the assessor, count forward by sevens (or spell 'world' backwards), follow simple oral or written commands, write a sentence and copy a design of interlocking pentagons (Folstein et al, 1975). The Hopkins Competency Assessment Test, designed for medical capacity specifically, takes a slightly different approach, where questions were answered relating to essays read aloud to the individual. The essays relate to informed consent to medical treatment, and are written to varying degrees of difficulty (Janofsky et al, 1992). Other tests use vignettes about specific treatment situations, about which the individual is quizzed regarding recall and assessment of relevant information (see, e.g., Marson et al, 1995).

The argument in favour of this sort of test is that it moves away from the judgment of an individual assessor as to the value of the decision in question. The risk of standards based on assessment of relevance of information in the specific situation in which the decision is to be made, is that the person assessing capacity may lack objectivity. Thus doctors recommending treatment presumably want in good faith to give the treatment, believing it to be to the benefit of the patient, and reasons for refusing treatment risk being perceived as lacking capacity. Tests based on ability allow assessment divorced from these professional values. These tests at least purport to be objective.

This very objectivity is equally the difficulty of the tests. The mini-mental state examination, perhaps the most frequently used of this sort of test and strong on objectivity, provides an illustration. The difficulty is that while it may measure cognitive function, it is at best difficult to see how the cognitive function correlates with capacity. As discussed above, capacity is determined with reference to specific decisions, and incapacity in one context does not necessarily imply incapacity in another. The questions on the mini-mental state exam are divorced from all these contexts. Is it really possible that the ability of an individual to make a will, or to consent to medical treatment, or both, is appropriately judged on the basis of their ability to count upwards by sevens, or copy a design of intersecting pentagons? Such tests may be relevant to identify particular cognitive difficulties which may in turn be relevant for some capacity determinations, but it is difficult to see that they can be central to the analysis.

Further, care must be taken in this form of testing to ensure an absence of hidden biases. The mini-mental state exam for example requires the individual both to read and to write a sentence. A person who is illiterate will thus be prejudiced on the test, for reasons entirely divorced from their capacity. Similarly, persons confined for an extended period of time may lose track of the day or month, or indeed even of seasons if they are unable to go outside the institution, where these matters become significant. In this context the test appears particularly problematic, for it would be measuring not cognitive ability, but instead the adverse effects of institutionalisation.

In this context, the approach of reading a paragraph and questioning the individual on the information seems more satisfactory. It, too, can be seen as problematic, however. Do people actually respond to or understand hypothetical situations in the same way that they do their own lives? And further, the vignettes or essays tend to focus on specific factual contexts, generally capacity to consent to treatment. How much assistance will they be outside the area for which they are designed?

The introduction of fact situations also begins to introduce some of the subjective issues that the tests were otherwise to exclude. Consider a Jehovah's Witness patient discussing a hypothetical vignette about a patient to undergo heart surgery. The importance of avoiding a blood transfusion would not be an answer suggested by the vignette in response to a question about the desirability of treatment; but it might well be mentioned by the individual in this case. The vignette approach appears to assume a closed universe of information, and it is not obvious how it would account for information imported by the person being tested.

Even these tests present difficulties in application to specific decisions made by specific individuals. It is not merely that the test will be of limited if any application outside its subject area, it is also that it is unclear how well or badly one must do on a test for a resultant finding of incapacity. Here, the test developed by Marson et al (1995) deserves special note, for that test does attempt to include a variety of thresholds into one instrument. While an interesting approach which may lead the way to testing more sensitive to varying standards, it is nonetheless problematic. Different decisions require different degrees of capacity even within a single subject area: incapacity for one contract or one treatment does not mean incapacity for all. It is difficult to see how statistical scores which are validated according to one set of objective vignettes can take account of capacity when the decision in question may vary considerably from that portrayed in the vignette.

All that would seem to indicate a pressure to assess capacity in the context of the actual decision which occasions the determination of capacity. This does not, at least in theory, mean a departure from a standard of *ability* to understand. This distinction is drawn particularly in the gloss of Stuart-Smith LJ on s. 57(2)(a) of the MHA 1983, where the language reads '"capable of understanding" and not "understands". Thus the question is capacity and not actual understanding.': *R* v *Mental Health Act Commission, ex parte X* (1988) 9 BMLR 77 at p. 85. In cases where, for example, capacity to make a will were contested after the death of the testator, ability to understand might well be determined according to whether the deceased must have been able to understand the required material for the testamentary disposition in question based largely on circumstantial evidence, as there may be no evidence of his or her *actual* understanding of the material. Nonetheless, the move to a focus on the specific situation will often mean that the ability to understand collapses into the actual understanding of the individual.

10.4.6   Actual understanding

This test focuses on the actual understanding of the individual at the time the decision was made, about the actual decision itself. It has a concreteness which ability to understand lacks. Roth et al (1977, p. 282) make this point as follows:

Unlike the ability-to-understand test, in which the patient's comprehension of material of a certain complexity is used as the basis for an assumption of comprehension of other material of equivalent complexity (even if this other material is not actually tested), the actual understanding test makes no such assumption. It tests the very issues central to patient decision-making about treatment.

The move away from the ability to understand in the abstract does, of course, have its difficulties. By placing the assessment back in the context of the specific decision it reintroduces the pressures related to that decision into the capacity assessment. As was the case with the rational reasons approach, the risk is that a failure to decide in a specific way may indicate incapacity: if the decision is unexpected or perceived as inappropriate, the individual *must* have misunderstood.

It further places an onus on the person doing the assessment to ensure that appropriate information has been given to the individual prior to the assessment of capacity being made. This may be relatively unproblematic in some contexts. Doctors are already required to explain treatments to patients prior to performance of the treatment, for example. If the patient understands, they are competent and such an explanation would have been necessary in any event; if not, all that is lost is some of the doctor's time. If the individual is dead, however, as might be the case for a contested will, it may well be difficult to determine whether a lack of knowledge flowed from a lack of understanding, the test for capacity here, or a failure by those surrounding the individual to make information about the estate available to the testator.

Under this standard, the individual clearly needs to understand the information relevant to making the actual decision in question. Do they need to believe it? The nineteenth-century tradition was very much in the affirmative: decisions based on delusions were at the core of incapacity (Bartlett, 1996). Particularly if the temptation to use the fact of an 'inappropriate' decision as indicating a lack of understanding is resisted, the standard of actual understanding may still be met if the decision is made under a delusion. The way understanding has been defined in the previous sections, after all, is based largely on abstract information, and the ability to manipulate it. Even in the test of actual understanding, the question is whether an individual is actually aware of relevant material and able to manipulate it. There is no obvious requirement that the individual *believe* the information in question. That is the problem addressed by the next test, appreciation.

10.4.7 Appreciation of information

Appreciation of information is the test adopted by the Law Commission in its 1995 proposals on mental capacity, to be discussed (see 11.3.1). Under this test, individuals will lack capacity if they are 'unable to make a decision based on the information relevant to the decision, including information about the reasonably foreseeable consequences of deciding one way or another or failing to make the decision.' (Law Commission, 1995, p. 39). This suggests not merely a minimum level of ability to understand information, but also that the individual must use that information, including information about the probable consequences of a decision one way or the other, as the basis of their decision. While the Law Commission is clear that an individual is not to be found lacking capacity on the basis of imprudence (Law Commission, 1995, p. 40), it does seem that the apparently imprudent decision must be based on objectively relevant grounds.

Gunn suggests that this is probably not the standard currently reflected in English law (1994, p. 18). In so far as this comment is restricted to the law as it relates to consent to treatment, he is probably correct; but outside that area, it would seem that something closely akin to this relatively high standard of capacity has indeed been required, at least occasionally, in English law. Thus for testamentary capacity, *Banks* v *Goodfellow* required that the testator understand 'the nature of the act *and its effects*', and also 'to comprehend and appreciate the claims to which he ought to give effect': (1870) 5 QB 565, emphasis added. The failure to realise that signing a will would, for example, disinherit a child, and perhaps to understand the relative needs of children for a share in the estate, would thus render the will invalid. This was certainly the result in *Re Beaney (deceased)* (10.2) where it was held that capacity to make a gift of the sole major asset of the donor, as the donor approached the end of her life, required not merely that she was making a gift, and that the recipient of that gift was one daughter, but also that the gift would effectively deny the donor's other children a share in her estate. In *In the Estate of Spier (decd)* [1947] WN 46, a man was held not to have the capacity to marry, since while he certainly knew that he was going through a ceremony of marriage, he 'was lacking in a proper capacity to take care of his own person and property, and that the very nature of the disease was such as to act towards incapacitating him from deciding whether his own health justified him in taking this very important step'. In this formulation, although not some of the others regarding capacity to marry discussed above (10.2, 10.3), the expectation that capacity to marry would involve understanding the property ramifications and consideration of one's health suggests a much more sophisticated standard of capacity than mere understanding information; it suggests a standard more analogous to appreciation.

The standard raises various sets of problems. One will now be familiar: the expectation that a decision will be based on specific criteria, requiring acknowledgement of specific future results of the decision, risks privileging one set of criteria over others. For example, the individual must not be competent, because they are failing to give adequate concern to the fact that they might die without the treatment, or, more controversially, that a foetus might be terminated unless the potential mother is treated. Such cases will be considered below, in the context of consent to medical treatment (see 11.1.2, 11.1.3); but the problem is not necessarily confined to medical issues. The testamentary standard, for example, would seem to make it relatively difficult for a person of marginal capacity to disinherit someone. It is perhaps possible to minimise this risk by interpreting the test to allow the individual to weight criteria as they wish, so long as they acknowledge the possible result. Nonetheless there is a real potential that the criteria be used for ends not relevant to capacity itself. Another familiar problem concerns how one is to determine how much the lack of appreciation is the result of an inability to appreciate, a skill which the medical tests discussed above do not measure, and how much a problem of information not being provided, or not provided in an accessible form?

An additional problem is simply whether this sets the standard of capacity too high. What level of specificity is expected for the understanding of future ramifications of deciding in various ways? The reality is that people of robust capacity may make decisions quickly, or for reasons which ignore longer-term effects. Does a standard which requires appreciation of these factors require decisions of marginally capable people which are of higher standard than those of unquestioned capacity? The higher the standard, the more people will fall outside it. The standard of appreciation is sufficiently high that it does not tend to occur in the medical literature; is it therefore a standard too high for at least some legal contexts?

It will be clear from the smattering of cases that have been cited that the law does not adopt a single, coherent approach to capacity. The case law cites nineteenth-century precedent selectively, and the result is a mixture of standards and tests. The Law Commission's proposals relating to incapacity, if enacted, will go some way to sorting out this hotchpotch. Michael Gunn comments (1994, p. 13):

If for no other reason than introducing certainty and clarity, the proposals of the Law Commission will be welcomed. If legislation follows, all involved in decision-making and medical treatment will have a clearer idea of what the parameters are for assessing whether an individual is capable of making a particular decision.

It is difficult to disagree with that sentiment, favouring coherence and certainty. The Commission's proposals themselves will be discussed in 11.3.

10.5   HOW SHOULD DECISIONS BE MADE FOR THOSE LACKING CAPACITY?

Once it has been determined that an individual lacks capacity to make a specific decision or set of decisions by the appropriate process, the issue arises as to how, if at all, those decisions should be able to be made regarding the individual. That implies both the selection both of a decision-maker and a set of criteria or principles upon which to base the decision. These are, at least in theory, quite separate processes. A doctor might be selected as the decision maker, for example, but be required to make the decision on non-medical criteria, such as what the patient would have chosen prior to losing capacity.

It would be possible, of course, to devise a system where no one made the decision. As discussed in 10.2, this was the situation introduced for personal decisions by the 1983 MHA, but currently in retreat after cases such as *F* and *Re S*. While it is fashionable to disparage such a system, it may well be the case that no action is the best action. If an individual is on the evidence reasonably likely to regain capacity with reasonable promptness, it may well be that the best course of action is to leave things unchanged, so that the individual can make their own decisions when capacity is regained. Often, however, this will not be an appropriate response. Failure to act might result in an individual remaining incapacitated, when their condition might be improved. It might result in a pointless diminution of their assets, or a life of poverty because assets are not realised. It may also leave the individual unprotected, and subject to exploitation by those who would wish to take advantage.

If intervention is appropriate, there are a variety of approaches to the substantive criteria for decision-making.

10.5.1   The place of the incapacitated person

Conceptually, capacity is a gatekeeper concept, a mechanism by which individuals either retain or lose authority over and responsibility for decisions that affect their lives. If the individual loses that authority and responsibility through incapacity, the question arises as to what status, if any, they continue to hold in the criteria of decision-making. As Buchanan and Brock point out (1986, pp. 50, 51), the tradition in legal, ethical and biomedical literature has tended to place their interests at the centre of the decision-making process:

> The dominant tendency, both in recent legal doctrine and in the bioethics literature, has been to view the rights of incompetent individuals as an extension of the rights of competent individuals, through arrangements by which these rights are exercised for the incompetent by others. Although many bioethicists are sharply critical of attempts to apply this approach to those incompetent individuals who were never competent, it is generally agreed that the appropriate starting point for a theory of decision-making for incompetents is in the rights of competent individuals.

This appears initially counterintuitive. If the finding of incapacity is a process by which the individual is taken out of the decision-making process, why should the criteria of decision-making be perceived in terms of the rights that individual would have possessed if competent? Obviously, they remain human people whose views, even if lacking capacity ought to be considered; and clearly that is particularly important when the decision in the area of incapacity will affect options in areas where the individual continues capable. Yet is this sufficient to exclude all other criteria? The reality is that the individual has lost personal autonomy, and no surrogate decision-making structure will reintroduce that personal control over their life. If the individual control which is the value at the heart of autonomy is irretrievable, why should the rights of a competent individual serve as the model for decision-making? What is wrong with allowing factors unrelated to the individual, such as social interests or the interests of carers, into the decision-making equation?

Historically, relations between trustee and beneficiary and between guardian and ward, the relations created under the old *parens patriae* system, were fiduciary in nature. Students familiar with the law of equity will recognize the maxims and principles which will apply to these relationships. It is expected that those in fiduciary positions will act to safeguard the interests of those under their care, and they must avoid even potential conflicts of interest. This will of course be problematic if carers, be they family or professionals, are the decision-makers, since it is difficult to see that they will not be personally affected by decisions made regarding the incapacitated person. While the fiduciary relationship would require the trustee or guardian to act solely for the benefit of the vulnerable person, that is of course quite a different matter from making the decisions which the vulnerable person would have made. That the law of equity never required; indeed, the trustee or guardian was, and is, expected to exercise independent judgment.

If the principle is that the interests of the incapacitated person hold sway to the exclusion of the interests of professionals, family, carers, the state and society at large, the question still remains as to how the incapacitated person is to be embodied in the decision-making. There have traditionally been three ways, which will be examined in turn: advance directives, substituted judgment and best interests.

10.5.2 Advance directives

Advance directives allow an individual to make decisions while competent, which will be binding in any subsequent period of incapacity. Historically, they had no formal recognition in England. A move towards this form of advance planning was made by the Enduring Powers of Attorney Act 1985, which allowed donors of powers of attorney in a specific form to determine who would manage their estate in the event of subsequent incapacity (see Chapter eleven). They did not, however, allow advance determination of how decisions would be made in the personal realm, where property or affairs were not at issue. The first step in that direction was taken by Thorpe J in *Re C* [1994] 1 All ER 819 (HC) regarding medical treatment (discussed at 10.2). Such advance refusals of treatment are without formality requirements: they do not need to be in writing, signed or witnessed. All that appears to be required is clear evidence of a decision by a patient that the treatment in question should not be performed in the event that the patient lacks capacity to consent at the time.

These remain the only contexts in which advanced decisions have been formally recognised in English law, although the Law Commission has advocated their extension into the broader realm of personal decision-making (see Law Commission, 1995, part VII). Other jurisdictions already have these broader provisions in place: see, for example, the Ontario Substitute Decisions Act 1992, SO 1992, c. 30, which effectively allows an individual to create binding preferences for virtually all decisions related to personal care, consent to treatment, or estate management.

If the model of decision-making for those lacking capacity is deemed to be an extension of the rights of the individual when competent, the advance directive has a considerable theoretical attraction. How better to introduce the wishes of the incapacitated individual into the process, than by his or her own proclaimed wishes prior to incapacity?

While certainly appealing in this regard, the matter is not so straightforward as would first appear. The individual may have made a variety of directives at different times. Is it only the most recent that is to be taken into account for purposes of the decision? Alternatively, how well informed was the individual about the consequences of their statement? Did they realise, for example, that the refusal of a certain treatment might cause death, or the failure to sell certain shares might result in insufficient funds to pay nursing home costs? Did they realise the legal effect of the statement, that it would indeed bind a subsequent decision? How are changes of circumstance to be accounted for? Thus an individual refusing treatment for a physical condition in advance might or might not have refused a treatment for the condition discovered after the directive had been made. Should the directive still preclude such treatment? The appeal of the advance directive is that the individual would decide now, if competent, in the manner they proscribed earlier. That is not necessarily true. As people's capacities change, their expectations of life may change with them; and what was unthinkable previously becomes acceptable or even desirable.

Some of these matters may be appropriately addressed through the provision of formal safeguards. It is difficult to see for example that an individual with capacity attending at a lawyer's office to sign an official looking document purporting to restrict future choices in the event of incapacity will have any doubt as to what they are doing. That does not address all the problems, however; and it must be remembered that increasing formality restricts the use of the process, through both social and economic rationing. The risk of a formal system is that it will be available only to those with money and in the know about the process.

10.5.3   Substitute judgment

The substitute judgment model of decision-making requires that decisions be made as they would have been by the incapacitated person, but for the incapacity. In *In re D (J) (Court of Protection)* [1982] 1 Ch 237 at pp. 243, 244, Sir Robert Megarry V-C establishes five principles for making decisions in this way, in the context of the authority of the court to make a will for a person lacking capacity:

(1)   It is to be assumed that the patient is having a brief lucid interval at the time when the will is made.

(2)   During the lucid interval the patient has a full knowledge of the past, and a full realisation that as soon as the will is executed he or she will relapse into the actual mental state that previously existed, with the prognosis as it actually is.

(3)   It is the actual patient who has to be considered and not a hypothetical patient. One is not concerned with the patient on the Clapham omnibus.

(4)   During the hypothetical lucid interval, the patient is to be envisaged as being advised by competent solicitors.

(5)   In all normal cases, the patient is to be envisaged as taking a broad brush to the claims on his bounty, rather than an accountant's pen.

While some of these apply most directly to the specific context of a testamentary disposition, a slightly more detailed account of them will provide insight into the precise nature, and the strengths and weaknesses of the substitute judgment approach.

The essence of the substitute judgment approach is in the first three principles. The objective is for the decision-maker to stand in the shoes of an incompetent person experiencing a hypothetical, temporary return to capacity, albeit a capacity tempered by the knowledge that immediately the decision is made, they will return to their incapacitated state. The decision is thus to be grounded in the character the incapacitated individual would have if competent, but the specific situation the individual actually finds themself in. While conceptually clear, this may involve complications in practice. People are not consistent, and here, as with the advance directive model, inconsistencies are difficult to absorb into the system.

According to the third principle, the decision-maker is to take into account the idiosyncrasies of the incapacitated individual: the approach is one of substituting judgment. Thus the decision-maker should take into account the religious or political views, and antipathies or affection for specific persons or causes of the individual affected by the decision. To this end, reference is to be made to the individual as they were prior to losing capacity (p. 244). A formal advance directive or a clearly stated view when competent therefore will normally be of considerable evidential value in determining the decision to be taken. Nonetheless, the court in *D(J)* does leave itself with some leeway (p. 244):

> No doubt allowance may be made for the passage of years since the patient was last of full capacity, for sometimes strong feelings mellow into indifference, and even family feuds evaporate.

This may perhaps be merely an acknowledgement that people change over time, and that people lacking capacity may do so as well as anyone else. Earlier in this Chapter, the danger was noted of assessing capacity on the basis of an earlier time when the subject was of undisputed capacity. Similarly, it was noted that advance directives are problematic when circumstances change, as for example when new treatments become available for a condition where the directive would refuse all treatment. In so far as the court here is addressing this sort of problem, the statement seems unobjectionable, and indeed conceptually necessary to distinguish the substitute decision model from the less flexible advance directive.

It is questionable however whether the statement is instead a mechanism to allow other non-subjective factors to enter into the determination of the decision-maker. It continues as follows (at p. 244):

> Furthermore, I do not think that the court should give effect to antipathies or affections of the patients which are beyond reason. But subject to all due allowances, I think that the court must seek to make the will which the actual patient, acting reasonably, would have made if notionally restored to full mental capacity, memory and foresight.

The reference to antipathies which are 'beyond reason', and to the individual 'acting reasonably' suggest a move from the pure subjective standard. In so far as the antipathies are the result of mental disorder, the reservation is uncontroversial; indeed, the purpose of substitute decision-making rules is to ensure that such delusional notions are not part of the decision-making process. If instead it refers to antipathies of the individual when competent, as seems likely given the context, it is a notable departure from the subjective standard. On a subjective basis, the incapacitated person should after all be allowed to continue their irrational dislike of some of their family. The comment seems to be opening the way for factors, such as a respect for family values, to be introduced to paper over the cracks of old family disputes.

Perhaps in this context it is appropriate to remember that substitute decision-making involves the law awarding authority to another. Arguably, there are some things in which the law ought not to allow itself to be involved, or there are assumptions law ought to make, whether true or not. This can be seen in the fourth principle, the assumption that the individual would have the benefit of competent professional advice. The reality is that many people do not get such advice, if indeed they receive advice at all, and do not discover the deficiency until it is too late. Assume the individual's previous will had been badly drafted. If one looks to the individual and their specific situation to the exclusion of all else, there is no reason to assume they would have had better luck with the lawyer, when they sought to draft a new will. Yet the courts, reasonably, have rejected this approach, since it would not meet social expectations of the court's function. The court cannot be seen to make decisions on the basis of bad advice, even if that is the advice the client would probably have received. Similarly, it would be difficult to defend the Court of Protection taking investment decisions for a client by selecting random stocks from the daily newspaper, even if this was how the client invested. At some point, fetishising a substitute decision model in its purest form becomes counter-productive and unhelpful to the client.

The final principle identified in $D(\mathcal{J})$, that the incapacitated person is deemed to take 'a broad brush to the claims on his bounty, rather than an accountant's pen' (p. 244) applies most directly to the specific situation of that case, the writing of a will by the court. The point is that a legacy is not to be decided on the basis of a minute arithmetical calculation of previous gifts and specific kindnesses to the testator. It would seem to have little application outside the specific context of that case.

A problem with the substitute decision model becomes immediately obvious: what if the individual never had capacity for the decision in question? How is the decision-maker to infer what the views of the incapacitated person would be, if he or she has never had capacity? The tendency would appear to be to lapse into other social values to justify a decision. In the testamentary context, some of these are contained in the test of capacity itself. Recall that capacity to draft a will required among other things an ability to 'comprehend and appreciate the claims to which he ought to give effect' (*Banks* v *Goodfellow* (1870) 5 QB 549 at p. 565). *Smee* v *Smee* (1879) 5 P 84 elaborated upon this, indicating that the testator ought to be able 'rationally to consider the claims of all those who are related to him, and who, according to the ordinary feelings of mankind, are supposed to have some claim to his consideration when dealing with his property as it is to be disposed of after his death.' (p. 92). At issue was 'not merely the amount and nature of his [the testator's] property but, the interest of those who by personal relationship or otherwise had claims upon him' (p. 92).

There seems to be something of an expectation that the person who had never been competent would behave in a way something akin to the social norms identified above. In *Re C* [1991] 3 All ER 866, for example, the individual in question was aged seventy-five and had been institutionalized for sixty-five years owing to a severe developmental disability. At the time of the application to draft a statutory will, Hoffman J held that she had 'little memory, understanding or capacity to communicate,' (at p. 867) and that she had always been incapable of making a testamentary disposition (at p. 868). At issue was whether the statutory will might include a considerable bequest to the institution in which C lived, and where she appeared to have been happy for a considerable time.

Hoffman J acknowledged that there was no way of knowing what C's preferences would have been, as she had never been competent: 'In all relevant respects, the record of her individual preferences and personality are a blank on which nothing has been written. Accordingly, there is no material on which to construct a subjective assessment of what the patient would have wanted to do.' (p. 870). In these circumstances, 'the court must assume that she would have been a normal decent person, acting in accordance with contemporary standards of morality' (p. 870). Here, C's decision would be swayed by two factors: that she had been in the care of the community, through the National Health Service and voluntary organisations, for much of her life; and that she had inherited her wealth. The court therefore held that she would have bequeathed her estate to the mental health charity associated with her institution and to her family on this basis. At the time of the hearing, the estate was valued at £1.5 million. The court ordered an immediate gift of £400,000 to the family and £100,000 to the charity. A will was then to be drawn giving a special legacy of £10,000 to B, a volunteer with the charity who had been particularly kind to C, taking her on outings and visiting her regularly, which 'will I hope be accepted as symbolic of the debt which people like Miss C and their families owe to voluntary workers who ameliorate their lives' (p. 872). A special bequest of £15,000 was to be made to a first cousin twice removed who had Down's Syndrome, since 'Miss C would wish to recognise her community of misfortune with this child by a special provision' (p. 872). The residue of the estate would be divided equally between the family and the charity.

It is as difficult to fault this result as it is disarmingly easy to do so. It is fair to ask why the facility should benefit, albeit indirectly through its charitable arm. The point of the National Health Service is that a reasonable quality of service ought to be available to people such as C as a matter of right. We do not expect individuals to leave bequests to their general practitioners, even if they have received long and good service from them; indeed, the law presumes against the validity of such gifts and bequests in such situations are void for undue influence: see *Rhodes* v *Bate* (1866) 1 Ch App 252; *Mitchell* v *Homfray* (1881) 8 QBD 587; *Dent* v *Bennett* (1839) 4 My & Cr 268. Why would we expect C to leave a bequest to the facility, which is in some ways in an analogous position? At the same time, the family's moral claim is doubtful. C's mother died in 1918, and it was not clear whether her father had maintained any contact prior to his death in 1953. Hoffman J held that 'few if any other members of her fairly extensive family appear to have been aware of her existence' (p. 867). It is not entirely obvious why C would wish to leave funds to such people. The court found that it was because she had inherited her money; yet it is not obvious that this is sufficient to justify a share to the relatives. The recognition of 'community of misfortune' with the child with Down's Syndrome seems at best speculative, and while it is certainly easy to sympathise with the gift to B, the reasons appear to flow directly from Hoffman J's view of social obligation, rather than C's substituted judgment.

On the other hand, without the will, the family would inherit the entire estate on intestacy. This seems an equally inappropriate result, given the limited relationship between the parties.

If competent, C would presumably have made a will; and thus on a substituted judgment approach the court was right to do so in her stead; yet in order to do so, the decision-maker must create a fictional construction of the character of the incapacitated person, a construction which is entirely fictional in the case of a person who has never had capacity, and at least partly fictional in any event, if supposed circumstances following incapacity are to be taken into account, as in *Re D(J)*. The values of autonomy implied in the model, the respect provided to the individuality of the person and the right for decisions to be made in a fashion consistent with their views when competent, are laudable; but in the end, the reality cannot be expected to match the ideal.

10.5.4   Best interests

The best interests approach is perhaps the most frequently applied of the mechanisms to determine decision outcome in English incapacity law. It is certainly the test of general application in matters of consent to medical treatment (*F*). Further, in so far as the 'best interests' of the individual may be equated with 'benefit' to the individual, it is one part of the approach contained in the MHA 1983 for decisions related to the property and affairs of incapacitated persons (s. 95(1)).

For such a significant portion of incapacity law, remarkably little guidance is provided as to what the approach actually entails. *F* says nothing. A certain amount may perhaps be surmised. If the substituted judgment approach can be characterised in legal terms as a set of subjective criteria, the best interests approach, reasonably, should be objective. At issue ought to be how the reasonable individual would decide in the position of the incapacitated person in question, rather than how the actual incapacitated person would have decided.

There is judicial support for this view, in the words of Ungoed-Thomas J, that the decision-maker should act 'as a properly advised decent sane person in the patient's position would act.': *In re TB* [1967] Ch 247 at p. 253. This does not restrict the best interests test to a specific set of professional criteria. If the 'sane person' in the position of the patient would consider a wide variety of factors, that same variety would fall to be considered under the best interests test. This is confirmed in *Re MB (Medical Treatment)* [1997] 2 FLR 426, a case involving surgical intervention, where Butler-Sloss LJ held that 'Best interests are not limited to best medical interests' (p. 439). A similar view can be seen in *In re W(EEM)* [1971] 1 Ch 123 at p. 125, where the court was charged with deciding whether commencement of divorce proceedings would be to the 'benefit' of the incapacitated person:

> The first question which arose on these sections was the scope of the word 'benefit'. It seems clear to me that it is not restricted to material benefit, but that it is of wide significance comprehending whatever would be beneficial in any respect, material or otherwise.

In that case, the court considered the following relevant to determining whether the divorce proceedings would be to the benefit of W: the sanctity of marriage, in so far as that would be relevant to the reasonable person in W's position; the religious views of W; public policy in so far as it would have affected W's views; the effects on W's children; and pending legal changes to divorce legislation; as well as financial considerations for W.

The focus on how W would approach matters suggests a blurring of the distinction between the substitute judgment and best interest approaches. Indeed, the court in *W* goes so far as to cite *In re CL* [1969] 1 Ch 587 for the proposition that 'it is for the benefit of the patient that the court should do what it is satisfied that he would have done even though it be not for his financial or material benefit.' (*W* pp. 135-6, citing *CL* p. 597). This may in part be a reflection of the specifics of the statutory provisions further defining the court's role, although not specifically relevant to the issue in question, which allowed the court to act 'for making provision for other persons or purposes for whom or which the patient might be expected to provide if he were not mentally disordered', perhaps but not necessarily a substitute judgment test. It may also reflect a view that the individual would be the best judge of their best interests, given the breadth of factors which may be taken into account in assessing best interests.

If that is the case, it suggests that the distinction between substitute judgment and best interests approaches is not merely that of subjective versus objective view. Where characteristics of the subject are known, the test would become a substitute judgment; as less reliable or recent information were available, the application of an objective standard, the reasonable individual in the position of the one in question, would become increasingly significant. As noted above, a similar process must of necessity happen in the substitute judgment approach: if the individual never had capacity, a decision must be made according to a mythical personality constructed for the incapacitated person. The two tests start to look remarkably similar.

The best interests approach is however open to other interpretations. In some formulations, external factors could be used to override the competent wishes previously expressed of the incapacitated person. The Law Commission proposals on mental incapacity, for example, would codify that ascertaining the best interests of an individual lacking capacity would include consideration among other factors of his or her present (and therefore incompetent) wishes, and the need to permit and encourage the individual to be involved as fully as possible in any decision made for them (Law Commission, 1995, pp. 45-6). That seems laudable. Perhaps more troubling, counsel in *W(EEM)* argued that both the sanctity of marriage and social policy supporting marriage militated against allowing the divorce to proceed (p. 132). In the actual case, the court rejected that contention, except in so far as it might have affected W's views, but it does raise the issue of what policy factors ought to be insisted upon, if any, in the determination of best interests.

The result of these outside factors could be decisions being made about the individual, or treatment performed on the individual, to which they may be known to have objected when capable. This seems, intuitively, to be a violation of the individual's autonomy. There is rationally (or not) a sense that the incapacitated individual is somehow a vestige of the capable one, and the failure to acknowledge the continuity of the person by respecting prior wishes or relying on the decision that he or she would have made appears at best to marginalise, if not violate, that person.

It is these tensions which render problematic the failure of the courts to articulate the best interests test in greater detail. If it were simply an extension of the substitute judgment approach to take account of individuals whose personal characteristics when competent cannot be known, a detailed set of criteria would be difficult to create, as each decision would be so heavily reliant on its facts; but if this is the approach, the courts should say so. If, on the other hand, other factors are to be taken into consideration, the courts should be clear as to what those factors are.

10.6   WHO SHOULD MAKE DECISIONS FOR THOSE LACKING CAPACITY?

If the authority to make decisions on behalf of another is to be granted, there are various possible bodies which might exercise it. The selection of such a decision-maker involves a variety of concerns. The authority to make decisions on another's behalf may involve the delegation of considerable power. The decision-maker must be trusted to make the decisions of appropriate standard, according to the appropriate criteria. The incapacitated person may be in a vulnerable position *vis-à-vis* the decision-maker, physically, emotionally, or financially. The decision-maker must be an individual who will not abuse that position of vulnerability. At the same time, there is a social and practical interest that decisions be made expeditiously and efficiently.

Traditionally, this decision-making has been the role of the court, or has at least been overseen by the court. Thus prior to the MHA 1959, authority over personal decisions rested with High Court judges, through their *parens patriae* jurisdiction. Courts remain involved, albeit in an advisory capacity, after *F* for some forms of particularly intrusive medical treatments such as sterilisation.

The difficulty with courts assuming this role more broadly is similar to the difficulty of courts making incapacity determinations. They tend to be expensive, impersonal, often slow, and bureaucratic, and these difficulties compound themselves when moving from the temporally specific determination of incapacity, to the long-term supervision of the care of persons lacking capacity. They are also likely to have no direct knowledge of the individual: whatever approach of decision-making is adopted, the court will need to be instructed by evidence. This will be problematic if a quick decision is required, and is likely to be expensive in any event. That said, courts do tend to be strong on due process safeguards, which at their best provide some protection to the person lacking capacity against abuse.

Alternatively, the decisions might be allocated to an administrative body. This is currently the situation, for example, for estate management by the Court of Protection, which is less a real court than an administrative office. Such professionalisation of the caring functions has the advantage that those in charge of decisions are themselves sufficiently talented to make good decisions, or at least decisions meeting a professional standard. Administrative bodies again risk the perception that decision-making is too far removed from the individual, performed by bureaucrats. If all the work is done by professionals, it can also be expensive. For both these reasons, courts and administrative bodies have tended to find individuals who are closer to the individual to make the day-to-day decisions. These have variously been called committees, guardians, tutors, receivers and managers, depending on the system in question, but generally keep some sort of overarching control to ensure appropriate exercise of the decision-making power by the individual.

Other systems appoint individuals to make the decisions, without the intervention of a court or administrative body. Frequently, a family member will be designated by statute to make decisions on behalf of an incapacitated individual (see, for example, Ontario's Consent to Treatment Act, S.O. 1992, c. 31, s. 17(1)). *F* offered a different approach, where the doctor proposing treatment would make the decision. While often bringing the decision much closer to the individual, and rendering decisions considerably less bureaucratic, less expensive and more flexible, both have their problems.

The professional is likely to be recommending a certain course of conduct because of a belief that it is the right course of conduct. There are professional values at stake, and quite possibly a bona fide desire that a specific decision be made in a specific way. For doctors and lawyers alike, involvement of a competent client in the decision-making allows those values to be tested by the individual most affected, according to values outside those of the professional. At issue is a reality check on the professional vision, an acknowledgement that the decision of the client or patient is not merely based on a professional standard of quality of outcome. Whether the decision-making criterion is substitute judgment or best interests, it is nonetheless to be based on how the outcome would best suit the life of the incapacitated individual as a whole, not merely according to a specific professional code. Professionals are generally not trained to take account of this wider array of factors. The advantage of involving the family or other lay person in the decisions involving an incapacitated individual is that this reference to the individual circumstances of the incapacitated person, outside the professional gaze, is maintained.

At the same time, there is no guarantee that the family member will be intellectually or emotionally able to interrogate the decision of the professional, or otherwise to manage the affairs of the incapacitated person. The family member may be well-meaning, but not qualitatively good at decision-making, on whatever standard of quality is selected. Equally problematic is that they, like the professionals, may well be affected by the outcome of the decision, and it is doubtful that either family or professional can keep their own interest separate from those of the incapacitated person. Sending mother to a private nursing home may mean the decision-maker's inheritance will be spent on nursing home fees, and the decision-maker may feel, wrongly in law but perhaps consistent with some social views, that they have some sort of quasi-proprietorial claim over the inheritance. Can he or she really be relied upon to keep this factor outside consideration when deciding accommodation for mother?

Equally problematic is the availability of information upon which to base decisions, and how it is to be safeguarded. It seems indisputable that the individual with authority to make a decision on behalf of another must have access to the information upon which to base the decision. In most if not all cases, this will mean a considerable amount of personal information must be made available. The current law is generally silent about availability of such information. Doctors will have the relevant medical information in their files already, removing that access problem in the event that they make the treatment decision. They will not, or at least not necessarily, have the non-medical information which seems to be relevant for decision-making under any of the models above. Other professionals are likely to be in a similar situation for decisions in their fields. On the other hand, there is nothing in the current law which gives family members access to doctors' or other professionals' files in the event of the client's incapacity. It must be the case that access can be given to those with decision-making authority; but release of the information has its problems too.

The first difficulty concerns the privacy of the incapacitated person. This is in part a matter of personal dignity: it is not obvious that the individual concerned would have wished family members for example to know aspects of their private life. Consider *Re S*, the case of the Norwegian artist whose care was the subject of dispute between his current common law spouse and his estranged wife. The wife eventually received custody of S's person and estate, a set of duties which might well have included support for the common law spouse. The personal and financial relations between S and the common law spouse might well be something he would have wished to keep private from his wife; yet she may well need to be given access to the information to fulfil her duties over the estate. This situation is particularly problematic, since it also affects the privacy rights of the common law spouse, who might also have wished the details of her relationship with S to have been kept private from the wife. The result, disclosure to the wife, may therefore be a less than ideal solution.

Involvement of lay people as decision-makers also carries with it the complication that it may be difficult to control the information after it is disclosed to them. The relations between decision-maker and incapacitated person are almost certainly fiduciary in nature. A duty of confidentiality is a classic fiduciary duty, and such a duty would presumably attach to the information. As a matter of practice, however, can the family member be relied upon not to disclose the information to others? Enforcement would have to be by way of court application — an expensive process, and one often requiring an additional guardian figure to take the action on behalf of the person lacking capacity. Even if successful, the result would be fine or imprisonment, and it is doubtful that these would be appropriate for what may well have been an indiscretion by the family member. At the same time, lack of confidentiality can be problematic, as it may alert the less scrupulous in society to a vulnerable individual.

All of this suggests that decisions might be better made by professionals, be they doctors, lawyers, court staff or professional trustees. These people tend to be overseen by their relevant professional bodies, and are likely better to understand their duty of confidentiality. The first difficulty here of course is that these people also generally would expect payment, and that must come either from the public purse or from the incapacitated person. They are also unlikely to have the personal knowledge of the incapacitated person for high calibre decisions to be made without considerable investigation, and the corresponding time commitment. The professionals concerned are not necessarily trained in such investigation, and such investigations would be unlikely to be seen by them as an efficient use of time.

From all this, it should be clear that the selection of determinations of capacity, decision-making criteria, and the selection of a surrogate decision-maker are all value-laden concepts. In the next Chapter, these concepts will be considered in the contexts of capacity law as it relates to consent to treatment, and estate management. Finally, there will be an overview of the proposals by the Law Commission for reform of the law of incapacity.

ELEVEN

Mental capacity (II): specific contexts

11.1 CAPACITY AND CONSENT TO TREATMENT

11.1.1 Overview and structure of the law

The substantive law relating to medical treatment of those in the psychiatric system is detailed elsewhere in this book. Nonetheless, at this time, an overview of this law as it relates to capacity is appropriate, to place the remainder of this section in context.

All persons over the age of 16 are presumed competent to consent to medical treatment. This applies not merely to the public at large, but also, specifically, to those in psychiatric facilities (whether formally or involuntarily admitted): *Re C (Adult: Refusal of Medical Treatment)* [1994] 1 All ER 819; *St. George's NHS Trust* v *S* [1998] 3 All ER 673 at 693. *A fortiori*, the presumption must also exist for those with psychiatric difficulties living in the community.

If the presumption of capacity is not rebutted, treatment may not be given to an adult unless the patient consents: *Re T (Adult: Refusal of Medical Treatment)* [1992] 3 WLR 782; *Re MB (An Adult: Medical Treatment)* [1997] 2 FLR 426; *St. George's NHS Trust* v *S*, above. Such patients are entitled to refuse treatment even if, in the words of Lord Donaldson MR, 'the reasons for the refusal were rational or irrational, unknown or nonexistent.' (*Re T*, p. 799). 'Adult' for these purposes means an individual over the age of eighteen years. Individuals between the ages of sixteen and eighteen years may be treated notwithstanding their active objection through the consent of a custodial parent, or by leave of the court: *Re R (A Minor) (Wardship: Medical Treatment)* [1991] 4 All ER 177, esp at p. 185; *Re W (A Minor) (Medical Treatment)* [1992] 3 WLR 758.

The major exception to the rule that competent adults may be treated only with their consent concerns treatment provided under ss. 63 and 58, MHA 1983. These and related sections were discussed in detail in Chapter seven: they are restricted to treatment of mental disorders of people legally detained in psychiatric facilities. The common law applies to informal patients, and to detained patients other than for treatment for mental disorder.

For all patients, neither psychosurgery nor the surgical implantation of hormones to reduce the male sex drive may be performed on a patient lacking the capacity to consent to these treatments (s. 57, MHA 1983; see Chapter seven above). Beyond this, if a patient lacks capacity to consent to a specific treatment, the general rule is that treatment can be provided to the patient without consent, if it is in the view of the treating physician in the patient's best interest: F v *West Berkshire HA* [1989] 2 All ER 545. This general rule applies both to informal patients in psychiatric facilities and to patients living in the community. It also applies to treatment other than treatment for mental illness of patients confined in psychiatric facilities.

At the same time as the courts have been affirming the propriety of physicians treating incapacitated patients without independent consent, as in the F case, courts have equally been affirming the rights of competent patients to make their own treatment decisions. In *Re C*, this was held to extend to the right of a competent patient to express treatment wishes which would be binding in the event of subsequent incapacity (p. 825). While that case dealt with physical treatment, there is no reason that its basic principle should not extend into the sphere of treatment for mental disorder, at least for treatment occurring outside ss. 63 and 58, MHA 1983. It therefore stands as an exception to the principle in F: if a patient in a period of competence indicates a wish that a psychiatric treatment not be performed or drug not administered during a period of subsequent incapacity, that wish supersedes the general authority to treat under F (see also Code of Practice (Department of Health and Welsh Office, 1999) para. 15.12).

The theoretical problems of prior decisions regarding treatment were noted in Chapter ten. There are also practical problems. There are no formal requirements as a threshold for these advance directives to take effect. They are not required to be in writing, nor is it clear what information the patient must have been given prior to expressing the wish. Certainly, there is case law that the failure of the minor to be aware of the specific results of refusing treatment may lead to his or her refusal of treatment not being honoured: *Re L (Medical Treatment)* [1998] FLR 810 at p. 813. The factors in that case involved a particularly unpleasant mode of death which L would suffer, not disclosed to her because of her youth. If similar detailed knowledge of potential consequences were found to be a prerequisite for adult advance refusals of treatment, their validity would be very difficult to determine.

Should knowledge of consequences be required for a valid advance refusal of treatment by an adult? L was, after all, a minor, and therefore subject to the broad supervisory jurisdiction which the court reserves for children. If one of the points of adulthood is an assumed maturity, should the courts not find that adults refusing treatment in advance and on inadequate information do so at their peril? This seems a coherent argument, as yet untried. It does run up against an apparent predisposition of the court to find ways of allowing treatment to occur, consistent with medical views of the patient's best interests.

Among the geriatric population, and in psychiatric contexts, competency may fluctuate considerably in a brief period of time, in some cases within hours. Unless the doctor was present when the wish was made, it may be therefore virtually impossible for him or her to know whether the patient had mental capacity at the time the wish was expressed. Once again, the validity of advance directives may be difficult to determine.

Re C does make it clear that the court has jurisdiction to determine the validity of such a directive. This nonetheless seems an insufficient substitute for clearer regulation. Court applications are cumbersome and expensive. Further, while perhaps more detached from the immediacies of the situation, it is difficult to see how a court is in a better position than the doctor to determine the validity of an advance directive.

While an advance directive would restrict the application of *F*, it would not preclude treatment being provided under ss. 63 or 58 of the MHA 1983. An advance refusal of treatment can have no greater effect than the current refusal of a competent patient, and such competent patients can of course be treated under those sections in any event, albeit upon the fulfilment of the relevant due process safeguards if the treatment is provided under s. 58.

11.1.2   Determination of capacity

When viewed in summary, there appears to be an essential split not merely in the consequences of a finding of incapacity, but also perhaps in the meaning of capacity itself, between the common law and the Mental Health Act 1983. The apparent splintering of legal coherence might be expected merely to be aggravated by the variety of sources in which treatment capacity is discussed: the statute, the Code of Practice, cases under the statute, and cases under the common law. Further, capacity tends to be litigated in specific contexts, such as the refusal of treatment on religious grounds or by pregnant women, or treatment regarding minors, where particularly emotive factual situations arguably further threaten the coherence of the concept (see 11.3). While it would be misleading to ignore these differences and pressures, at least some of the existing case law suggests that capacity is a more coherent concept than would first appear.

The leading case involving an adult psychiatric patient is *Re C (Adult: Refusal of Medical Treatment)* (see 11.1.1). C had long been a psychiatric patient at Broadmoor Hospital. He developed a gangrenous leg, and risked death unless it were amputated promptly. He nonetheless refused to consent to the amputation. While involving a detained psychiatric patient, the case involved physical treatment, and is therefore to be understood as an application of the common law rules rather than the statute. Nonetheless, Thorpe J held that the issue was whether C's capacity had been so reduced that he did not sufficiently understand 'the nature, purpose and effects' of the proposed treatment (p. 824). This language mirrors precisely the words of ss. 57(2)(a) and 58(3)(a) of the MHA 1983, suggesting consistency between the two legal regimes.

Thorpe J divided the decision-making process into three stages: first, comprehending and retaining treatment information; second, believing the information; and third, weighing the information in the balance to arrive at a choice. (p. 824). It would therefore seem, to use the language of Chapter ten, that the test at common law involves actual understanding and appreciation of the consequences of giving or withholding consent.

At first blush, this would appear to contradict the precise wording of the MHA 1983 sections, which would require merely that the patient be 'capable' of understanding the relevant information, not that it necessarily be actually understood, nor that the patient's ability reach the apparently higher standard of appreciation. There is some authority to support this view: see *R* v *Mental Health Act Commission, ex parte X* (1988) 8 BMLR 77 at p. 85. More recently, the authorities seem not to draw this reading of the Act, instead following Thorpe J's tripartite analysis in *C*: see *Tameside and Glossop Acute Services Trust* v *CH* [1996] 1 FLR 762; *B* v *Croydon District Health Authority* (1994) 22 BMLR 13. At the same time, *C* continues to be cited in a common law context, re-enforcing the consistency of tests between the statutory and common law contexts: *Re MB (medical treatment)* [1997] 2 FLR 426; *A Metropolitan Borough Council* v *DB* [1997] 1 FLR 767.

The 1999 Code of Practice (Department of Health and Welsh Office, 1999) adopts Thorpe J's tripartite test in its discussion of capacity. Following the Act, it phrases each term in terms of ability to understand, rather than actual understanding; but it then undercuts that distinction by citing *C* and *MB* without further comment.

Some of the cosy congruence between these legal sources may perhaps be called into question when the specifics are examined, for where Thorpe J on one hand seems to establish the tripartite test of understanding, reasoning and appreciation, he is equally prepared to allow considerable latitude in a patient's view of their circumstances. Specifically, while it is clear that the patient must take medical opinion seriously in Thorpe J's view, the patient is not required to view the internalist medical world uncritically. *B* v *Croydon* concerned a woman with a personality disorder which manifested itself in part in her refusing to eat. On the question of insight and appreciation of her situation, the court (at p. 20) specifically acknowledges that medical opinion is open to critical appraisal and question by the competent patient:

> The overall impression that I firmly derived from her evidence was of a tortured human being with a frustratingly incomplete comprehension of her condition, but struggling to understand more, not rejecting professional help and in overall control of her life. I did not share Dr. Eastman's interpretation of her reaction to medical advice in times of crisis as possibly amounting to disbelief. I conclude that she was only expressing the tendency which most people have when undergoing medical treatment to self-assess and then to puzzle over the divergence between self-assessment and medical assessment. . . . Nothing in what she said, or in her manner of saying it, suggested that she was imprisoned in an isolation which was impervious to reason, divorced from reality, or incapable of adjustment after reflection.

This decision on capacity was expressly doubted by the Court of Appeal in brief reasons and *obiter*, based on a different finding of facts from the evidence. His Lordship must nonetheless surely be right that such questioning does not bespeak incapacity; if anything, such an ability to analyse and interrogate information indicates quite the reverse. Nonetheless, can the 'self-assessing' patient with 'a frustratingly incomplete comprehension of her condition' really be said to 'understand what will be the consequences of not receiving the proposed treatment', as contained in the Code of Practice? The Code's language seems to reflect instead the internalist, medicalised view of doctors, with which the patient must simply concur.

The *C* case and some of the subsequent litigation acknowledges that capacity is not simply a question to be left to the attending physician. The risk, of course, is that the attending physician will conflate the decision for or against treatment with the capacity of the patient (see 7.3 and 10.4.3). The inevitability of that conflict has resulted in the questioning of the appropriateness of the treating physician assessing capacity. Thorpe J is clearest on this point, in *Croydon* (at p. 23):

> I also reject the defendant's submission that the assessment of capacity is primarily a medical matter for the medical practitioner with clinical responsibility. Obviously, that assessment will suffice where capacity, or the lack of it, is manifest. But in cases where a decision as to capacity is very finely balanced, I accept the opinion of Dr. Eastman and Dr. Trowell that the clinician should seek at least an assessment from an authoritative medical expert, if not a ruling from the court. The clinician's judgment is too liable to be affected by emotions engendered by the manipulative patient, as well as pressures that inevitably arise from the instinct and the responsibility to preserve life.

This on its face is difficult to reconcile with the advice in the Code of Practice that 'the assessment of a patient's capacity to make a decision about his own medical treatment is a matter for clinical judgment, guided by current professional practice and subject to legal requirements' (para. 15.9). The effect of the difference as yet remains untested. The issue is not merely one of when the patient's choice will be respected, but also of when the physician will be liable for treating without consent an objecting patient, incorrectly believed to lack capacity. The reference to clinical judgment in the Code of Practice suggests an internalist medical standard, where a decision consistent with a responsible body of medical opinion might suffice to preclude the doctor from liability, in the style of *Bolam* v *Friern Hospital Management Committee* [1957] 2 All ER 118. The more guarded view of the court in *B* by comparison instead suggests a duty to enquire further, to ensure a more authoritative determination.

The case law has not, as of yet, reached a satisfactory articulation of precisely what needs to be understood in order for a patient to have capacity. The ambiguity surrounds whether capacity refers to a defence to an action for battery, or whether it is instead to be measured according to the information a competent patient must be given prior to consenting, as a matter of negligence law. In the former case, a defence based on consent will be upheld if the patient knew 'in broad terms of the nature of the procedure which is intended': *Chatterton* v *Gerson* [1981] QB 432, at p. 443. This may be considerably less than the information a doctor is required by the law of negligence to provide to the patient: *Sidaway* v *Board of Governors of the Bethlem Royal Hospital* [1985] AC 871. While the latter adopts a test based in reasonable professional practice, a more detailed explanation of risks and benefits of the proposed treatment is likely to be required than under (*Chatterton*: see Gunn, 1994, pp. 10-12). The distinction makes it possible that an individual will have the required capacity to understand the information which would found a defence to battery, but insufficient ability to understand the more complex treatment information which must be provided under *Sidaway*. Does the person have the capacity to consent to the treatment?

To view the problem as related to battery would have the virtue of consistency within the common law. That was the focus of the *F* v *West Berkshire* case (see 11.1.1), upon which so much of the current law relating to treatment of those lacking capacity is based. It does not appear to be the standard adopted by either the Code of Practice or the *C* case, each of which insists on understanding of the risks, benefits and consequences of the proposed treatment. In the context of the Code, this makes sense, as it reflects the language of the Act. There is nothing in the law of trespass, however, which would demand such a standard, although the approach in *C* does have the virtue of relative consistency with the MHA 1983 standard. It may seem counterintuitive to honour the decisions of an individual who is, *ex hypothesi*, unable to understand the information a responsible doctor would provide to serve as the basis of treatment. It seems equally dubious however to hold that a patient who understands the nature of the procedure in broad terms as required by the law of battery and does not consent to the intervention is nonetheless precluded from redress, even if they were unable to understand some of the finer points of information required by *Sidaway*.

Remaining to be litigated is the question of what requires disclosure, and whether a failure to disclose relevant facts can result in an adult being rendered incapable. *Re L (Medical Treatment)* (see 11.1.1) was a case of such non-disclosure regarding a fourteen-year-old girl. L had suffered serious burns, and risked a particularly gruesome death unless she received treatment which involved a blood transfusion, which she refused on religious grounds. She had not however been told the details of the death she faced, an omission the court viewed as appropriate given her age, background, and condition. That failure to disclose was material to a finding that L lacked capacity to consent since, in the words of the judge, 'it is quite clear in this case that she has not been able to be given all the details which it would be right and appropriate to have in mind when making such a decision' (p. 813).

Can a similar argument be made for adults of marginal capacity? The courts have steadfastly allowed a so-called therapeutic exception to the duty to disclose the risks of operations (*Sidaway*). A similar approach is reflected in the Code of Practice, which sets disclosure of information prior to obtaining consent as the norm, but further allows that 'there may be a compelling reason, in the patient's interest, for not disclosing certain information' (para. 15.16). If information is not given to a patient pursuant to this exception, does that in turn render the patient incapable of making the decision?

The answer must be in the negative. In all the tests discussed in Chapter ten except that of reasonable outcome, and also in the existing case and statute law, the test of capacity concerns the abilities intrinsic to the patient. The ability is not affected by a failure to disclose information. While the case law also speaks of the actual appreciation of the patient, that again refers to the ability of the patient rather than disclosure of information, as in the words of Butler-Sloss LJ in *Re MB (Medical Treatment)* (at p. 437):

> the patient is unable to use the information and weigh it in the balance as part of the process of arriving at the decision. If, as Thorpe J observed in *Re C*, a compulsive disorder or phobia from which the patient suffers stifles belief in the information presented to her, then the decision may not be a true one.

This is of course a very different situation from that where the patient is denied the relevant information. If denial of information were of itself sufficient to deprive an individual of capacity, even those of robust and otherwise unquestioned abilities would lose the right to consent to treatment in cases of therapeutic priviledge. *L* must instead be understood in the context of child law, where even a competent refusal of treatment may be overriden. The result in *L* should be understood as flowing from that protectionism.

This situation raises the broader question of the role of the physician in obtaining a competent consent. As Thorpe J recognised in the *Croydon* case, the treating physician may well have a professional concern that treatment be given, in an efficient manner. This can be understood variously in terms of a humanitarian concern to ensure that the health of patients improves to an optimal level, a desire to foster both peace on the ward and the shortest admissions possible, and practical concern that their job be free of unnecessary diversions or administrative hassles. It does mean that the treating doctor may well not be neutral as to how treatment progresses, and therefore how capacity is assessed.

That is relevant not merely for the test and standard of capacity which is adopted, but also for the practices by which those standards are administered. The ability and lucidity of an individual patient may vary considerably in a short space of time, or even according to the time of day. Ought the doctor to arrange the capacity assessment and consent to treatment at a time when the patient might reasonably be expected to be at optimal capacity? The way in which information is conveyed to a patient may also affect how it is understood. For example, it would seem that patients understand information better if disclosed to them part by part, rather than as an uninterrupted whole (Grisso and Applebaum, 1995b, p. 173) Is the doctor required to adopt this approach, even though it may take longer?

The law has not addressed these issues, apart perhaps from the comments of Thorpe J in *Croydon* suggesting that the treating physician ought not be the arbiter of capacity at all, except in clear cases. The Code of Practice would seem to have a preference for treatment based on capable consent (see, e.g., para. 15.7, 15.14-17, 16.4, 16.16-17), but it, too, does not address these questions directly. The medical profession itself has addressed the questions, however, in a joint report with the Law Society. The view therein is that the doctor is under a duty to maximise capacity (British Medical Association and the Law Society, 1995, para. 12.7). This encourages doctors, for example, to delay a decision if the patient's capacity is likely to improve; to conduct assessments at a time and place conducive to capacity; to beware of symptoms such as difficulties in communication which merely appear to affect capacity; and to re-explain and if necessary write down information for the patient's consideration. Such approaches are no doubt desirable to buttress patient autonomy and dignity; it remains to be seen the degree to which they will be found to be legal requirements of capacity assessment.

11.1.3   Capacity in context

The case law presents a seeming paradox. In theory, capacity is a prerequisite for consent, and thus in general a *sine qua non* for the provision of treatment. In practice, however, the issue arises when the patient is refusing a treatment proposed by the doctor. This is because if a patient were apparently consenting, the treatment could generally be provided even if the patient was incompetent on the basis of F. The risk is that this product of legal procedure begins to be understood as forming part of the substance of the law, and that the substantive question becomes not whether the patient was competent to consent, but instead whether the patient was competent to refuse to consent. It is difficult to see how this view can be justified in law. The rule remains that interference with the body of a patient constitutes a battery unless a defence can be shown. Consent of a competent patient is a defence. There is no presumption that a patient consents: this must be an act of the patient. It makes no sense to question a patient's capacity to refuse to do something which they have not done, and which there is no presumption they have done.

The presumption of capacity for those with mental health difficulties is not a legal fiction: it reflects the actual abilities of a majority of psychiatric patients. The MacArthur Treatment Competence Study set out to measure capacity of newly admitted in-patients in psychiatric facilities in three American cities (Applebaum and Grisso, 1995; Grisso et al, 1995a; Grisso and Applebaum, 1995b). Patients with schizophrenia were tested, along with those with major depression. There were two control groups. The first was drawn from the population living in the communities served by the facilities, but without psychiatric histories. This allowed control based on socio-economic factors. A second control was drawn from a population hospitalised for a purely medical problem, ischemic heart disease (angina), to allow a control based on the possible effect of hospitalisation upon capacity. A variety of measures were used to assess whether the patients could understand treatment disclosures, whether patients could perceive, acknowledge and understand their disorder, and whether they were able to think rationally about proposed treatments. Readers will recognise these as pivotal concepts in the assessment of capacity, discussed in Chapter ten.

The findings of the MacArthur study (Grisso and Applebaum, 1995b) make very interesting reading. The study did find that patients with mental illness scored less favourably as a group on the tests of understanding, appreciation and reasoning than the physically ill and community controls. This was due largely to relatively poor performance by some schizophrenic patients, a group tending to manifest more severe symptoms. They were at pains to point out (at p. 169) that this result could not however be applied indiscriminately to individual people with schizophrenia:

> Even so, on any given measure of decisional abilities, the majority of patients with schizophrenia did not perform more poorly than other patients and non-patients. The poorer mean performance of the schizophrenia group for any particular measure was due to a minority within that group.

In concrete terms, roughly a quarter of the schizophrenic group showed impaired performance on each of the particular tests, understanding information, appreciation and reasoning. Roughly half the group of schizophrenic patients showed impairment on at least one of these tests. For the depressed patients, impairment on the individual tests ranged from about 5 to 12 per cent, and just under a quarter showed impairment in at least one of the three areas. About 12 per cent of those hospitalised for angina showed such impairment in at least one area, and 4 per cent of the community control.

While the MacArthur study is refreshing in its statistical rigour, it is not without its problems, as its authors acknowledge. Of those approached to participate in the study, 15 to 20 per cent, depending on the site, declined. Between 1 and 20 per cent of psychiatric admissions, again depending on the site, were not approached to participate due to the intervention of their doctors (Grisso and Applebaum, 1995b, p. 151). The authors cite the latter group as perhaps resulting in underestimation of impairment, since clinicians' requests were 'often' based on judgments that the patient was too acutely disturbed to participate, suggesting they would be likely to fall in the impaired range on the tests (pp. 152 and 169-70). Sadly, there is no indication of the reasons that the former, larger, group did not participate, and so no indication how they would have altered the statistical profile.

Notwithstanding their best attempts, the patient samples are not entirely evenly matched. This shows up most significantly in the angina control group. Roughly 20 per cent of the angina group were from a relatively high socio-economic class, compared with 1 per cent of the schizophrenics and 4 per cent of the patients with major depression. Fully 80 per cent of the schizophrenics, and 64 per cent of the depressives, were from the lowest socio-economic classes, compared with 51 per cent of the angina patients. These criteria were based on education and level of employment (p. 151n). While the study was administered orally, therefore removing literacy as a factor, it is difficult to see that articulateness could have been removed, and the authors acknowledged that results for the understanding of treatment information tests were correlated positively with socio-economic status (p. 161). On that basis, it is unsurprising that the psychiatric patients scored lower on these tests than the angina patients. This argument, it must be said, is not persuasive when comparing the psychiatric sample with the community groups, where considerably better pairing was achieved.

Perhaps more problematic, it is not obvious that the study escaped the medical internalism which can so easily monopolise capacity determination.

This is perhaps clearest on the tests of appreciation (perceptions of disorder), a section which evaluated both whether the patient acknowledged their disorder, and whether they acknowledged the potential of treatment. This test was not administered to the community groups, sensibly enough since they had been screened to ensure that they had no disorder. It is the second of these tests which is interesting for current purposes. About 13 per cent of the schizophrenic patients, and 14 per cent of the depressive individuals, failed to acknowledge the potential value of treatment. For angina patients, this number was zero. The authors elaborate (at p. 164) on the reasons for denial among the psychiatric patients:

> The most frequent reasons given by schizophrenia patients for devaluing treatment, especially medication, involved beliefs that it was intended to harm them in some way. In contrast, the most frequent reason given by depression patients for devaluing treatment was the belief that they were 'too sick' for anything to help them.

The account fails to acknowledge a distinctive quality of the psychiatric sample groups: they were much more likely to have been veterans of the psychiatric system. The breakdown of statistics does not indicate how many of the angina patients were on their first admission and thus their first major encounter with treatment, but almost three-quarters had been admitted no more than twice before. By comparison, 84 per cent of the schizophrenic patients and 45 per cent of the depressives had been admitted to a psychiatric facility at least three times previously. The statistics offer no insight into the experiences of the patients in these prior admissions. To what degree can the comments of the schizophrenics be read as at least partly coloured by adverse effects of medication in past admissions? If the confinement was not a happy one, and an appropriate sense of trust not established between patient and doctor, could this in part explain the belief that the medication was not merely harmful, but intended to harm? Admittedly, three-quarters of the individuals in this class were diagnosed with schizophrenia of a paranoid type, but that cannot be understood as a full explanation, as about half of those giving full acknowledgement to the treatment shared that diagnosis.

As for the people with severe depression, is it not possible that they are right? If previous treatments had failed to provide a lasting solution for them, is a belief that they are 'too sick' to be helped necessarily an indicator of incapacity? Is it possible that, instead of the depressives lacking capacity for not acknowledging the potential of treatment, the angina patients were unduly optimistic about treatment? It has been speculated that mild depression might indeed improve rationality to make treatment decisions (Taylor, 1989), since persons in full health tend to undervalue risks of treatment and overvalue benefits, relative to a hypothetical 'rational' person. There is some empirical study to support this view (Costello, 1983). In the MacArthur study, the patients instead were diagnosed with major depression; nonetheless, it is fair to ask whether a pattern of repeat confinements and no lasting medical solution might lead a competent patient to believe that more medication was not the answer.

The design of the MacArthur study must also be remembered. The patients were tested promptly upon admission, generally before any psychiatric medication would have time to take effect (Grisso and Applebaum, 1995b, p. 152). Assuming that the beneficial effects of these drugs would outweigh increased impairment caused by adverse effects, it would be reasonable to expect these people to score better on the three tests as time passed, suggesting that the levels of impairment in entire patient psychiatric populations may be lower than the study would suggest. Equally, the fact of admission would generally suggest a particularly acute point in the patient's psychiatric symptoms. As the study finds a correlation between severe symptoms and impairment, it may well be the case that impairment of those with psychiatric problems in the community is also less frequent than the rate contained in the study.

Finally, as the authors make clear (at p. 170), the study measured impairment, not incapacity:

> [D]eterminations of incompetence require a judgment that the *degree* of deficits in the abilities relevant in a particular case is sufficiently great to warrant a declaration of incompetence, with consequent invalidation of the person's choice. There is no numerical criterion that can represent this judgment across cases, because the degree of deficits in ability that logically will be required may be expected to vary in relation to the specific disorder, proposed treatments, probable consequences, and other contextual factors that vary from one case to another . . . (emphasis in original)

Some patients may have been impaired relative to the control groups in ways which one might expect to be relevant to capacity to make treatment decisions; but the study does not purport to claim that they were impaired enough that they would lack capacity to make a specific treatment decision. That determination would depend on the specific information needed to be understood in the context of the specific treatment in question.

The study does demonstrate that the discussion of the variety of tests of incapacity in Chapter ten is not a mere academic exercise. If ability to understand proposed treatment were alone the test of capacity, 72 per cent of the schizophrenic sample and 95 per cent of the severely depressed sample would presumably be of unquestioned capacity, as they showed no impairment in this area. If the test of capacity were instead understanding, reasoning and appreciation jointly, a different picture results. Roughly half of the schizophrenic sample and 24 per cent of the severely depressed sample showed impairment on at least one of these tests, making their capacity appropriately the subject of particular scrutiny.

For this reason, inconsistencies in the determination of capacity are unfortunate, and notwithstanding the fairly uniform adoption of the standard in *C*, the case law shows considerable variation in application. This may in part be because capacity determination has tended to be litigated in unusual and specific fact situations. The capacity of pregnant women refusing treatment has been particularly prominent in recent case law: see *St. George's Healthcare NHS*

Trust v *S* (11.1.1); *Norfolk and Norwich Healthcare (NHS) Trust* v *W* [1996] 2 FLR 613; *Re MB* (11.1.1); *Re T* (11.1.1); *Tameside* (11.1.2); *A Metropolitan Borough Council* v *DB* [1997] 1 FLR 767; *Re S (Adult: Refusal of Medical Treatment)* [1992] 4 All ER 671. The refusal to consent to a blood transfusion owing to religious beliefs is another common theme: *Re S (Adult: Refusal of Medical Treatment)*; *Re L* (11.1.1); *Re S (A Minor) (Consent to Medical Treatment)* [1994] 2 FLR 1065; *Re T*. None of these cases purport to distinguish their facts from the more general common law. In a few of the pregnancy cases, the pregnant woman had been admitted to a psychiatric facility, so the capacity and treatment provisions of the MHA 1983 were discussed expressly. These cases are nonetheless very specific fact situations, with particular pressures. Treatment was eventually authorised in every one except *St. George's NHS Trust*, which was an appeal of a treatment authorisation by the court after the treatment had been performed. It remains to be argued and considered how far they may be extended to cases involving impairment of understanding rather than religous belief, when the viability of a foetus is not at issue.

The selection of cases involving the capacity of minors must also be approached with some care. Often, the litigation will be in the context of particularly controversial fact situations. The leading case, *Gillick* v *West Norfolk and Wisbech AHA* [1985] 3 All ER 402, for example, concerns whether children with capacity but under the age of sixteen years may receive birth control treatment. *L*, and *S* involved religous objections to blood transfusions, and *DB* was a pregnancy case. Perhaps more significant, minors are subject to a different legal regime. While consent by a minor with capacity will render medical treatment legal, a treatment refusal by a competent minor can still be overridden by the minor's parent or the courts. This reflects a policy decision in society that minors are to be particularly protected by the state, and decisions made about them to be subject to special scrutiny, to ensure that the decisions are in the minor's best interests. It is not a policy which has general legal foundation for adults.

The test in *C* has the advantage of avoiding these difficulties: this was a case about an adult psychiatric patient, whose situation was uncomplicated by pregnancy or religious views. As discussed in 11.1.2, the case requires all three of the comprehension measures of the MacArthur survey or, to place it in the language of Chapter ten, establishes a test where information must be appreciated.

While this test tends to be adopted on its face in the more recent cases above, its application tends to vary markedly from that of Thorpe J. In *Re C* itself, there was no doubt that C had impaired decision-making ability, but this did not result in a finding of incapacity. C's evidence in court was described by the court as follows (at pp. 822–3):

> He expressed the grandiose delusions of an international career in medicine during the course of which he had never lost a patient. He affirmed his complete faith in God and, subject to one reservation, in the Bible. He expressed complete confidence in his ability to survive his present trials aided

by God, the good doctors and the good nurses. Although he recognised that he would die, death would not be caused by his foot. As he made clear in re-examination, that was his belief, although he could not say that that would not happen. Throughout he expressed his rooted objection to amputation. He did not ascribe the condition of his foot to persecution by authority. As in his interview with Dr. Gall, he accepted the possibility of death as a consequence of his retaining his limb.

While this was his evidence in court, his doctor at Broadmoor testified that C did also have a 'persecutory delusion that whatever treatment is offered is calculated to destroy his body.' (p. 823). Thorpe J also summarized his view of C's behaviour in court (at p. 823):

C himself throughout the hours that he spent in the proceedings seemed ordinarily engaged and concerned. His answers to questions seemed measured and generally sensible. He was not always easy to understand and the grandiose delusions were manifest, but there was no sign of inappropriate emotional expression. His rejection of amputation seemed to result from sincerely held conviction. He had a dignity of manner that I respect.

Pivotal to the court's finding that C had requisite capacity to consent was the legal finding that causation between delusion and decision must be demonstrated for a finding of incapacity, another theme discussed in Chapter ten, above. His Lordship must be right on the law here, but it is applied in a spirit very generous to C. The persecutory delusion cited by his Broadmoor doctor does not seem to figure in his analysis, reliance instead being placed on C's testimony in court. Similarly, C's grandiose delusion that he had previously had an international medical career, his belief notwithstanding medical advice that he would survive his injury, and his belief again in direct contradiction to the medical evidence that he would not die from his injured foot, were held insufficient to warrant a finding that he lacked capacity. The court drew the following conclusion (at p. 824):

Although his general capacity is impaired by schizophrenia, it has not been established that he does not sufficiently understand the nature, purpose and effects of the treatment he refuses. Indeed, I am satisfied that he has understood and retained the relevant treatment information, that in his own way he believes it, and that in the same fashion he has arrived at a clear choice.

How are we to understand this finding, and in particular the phrase 'in his own way he believes it'? While he sets the most stringent criteria for the test of capacity, Thorpe J appears to require a considerable weight of evidence to displace the presumption of capacity. To use the MacArthur language, while he holds that inadequate ability in any one of the tests of understanding of information, appreciation and reasoning will be sufficient to render an individual incapable, he equally seems to find that a very significant impairment is necessary to deprive the individual of capacity — a much more significant impairment than that used by the MacArthur authors for their statistics.

C can be juxtaposed in this context with *Tameside and Glossop Acute Services Trust* v *CH* (11.1.2). CH was already pregnant when she was detained in a psychiatric ward, and throughout the litigation it was clear that she wanted her child to be born alive and healthy. She also had a history of schizophrenia, dating back some fifteen years. It was discovered in her thirty-first week of pregnancy that her foetus was suffering from intra-uterine growth retardation. By her thirty-seventh week of pregnancy, the medical evidence was that the situation was becoming serious: either the baby would need to be born through induction or Caesarean section, or it would not be born alive. CH had agreed to induction to occur several days hence, but her doctor was concerned that she would change her mind. He therefore approached the court for a declaration that a Caesarean section could be performed, should it be necessary.

The issues in the case are various. The question of whether the Caesarean section could constitute treatment for mental disorder within the meaning of s. 63 of the MHA 1983 were noted in Chapter seven: it could. Here, the issue is whether CH had capacity to consent. Strictly speaking of course, it did not matter, as the treatment could be imposed upon her over her competent objection anyway, due to the court's view of the first issue. Nonetheless, the findings of the court on the capacity point are striking.

While represented by a guardian *ad litem*, CH was not called in the case, notwithstanding that the matter was not yet an emergency, and as a result all evidence is seen through the filter of the Trust's submission and an affidavit from the Official Solicitor's agent. While it is dangerous to speculate what evidence CH might have provided if called, the case report does cry out that there is another side to the story.

The court purports to follow the test in *C*, but adopts a markedly different approach to the evidence. First, it is difficult to characterise CH's fundamental position as incorrect, irrelevant, or irrational. This basic position was summed up by her doctor as follows (at p. 765):

In her deluded way she is doing the best to protect the baby. Her understanding is that the baby is premature and that if it is delivered small it will not survive. I cannot get through to her that if we leave it where it is it will die.

She was correct in her belief that the child, if induced, would be born prematurely. The second statement must be viewed with some scepticism. On the facts, it was not obvious that CH rejected the medical advice she was given: she had, after all, consented to the induction of the delivery; the application was occasioned by a concern of the doctor that she would change her mind. The possibility of a Caesarean section had been raised with her, but she had declined on the basis that 'it was unnecessary at the moment — she wanted to hang on because she wanted a week of antibiotics' (p. 766). The statement from the Official Solicitor's agent, who interviewed her, indicated that the antibiotics had indeed assisted the development of the foetus. In that interview, she reiterated that she would consent to a Caesarean section or induction of labour should it become necessary. One is left to wonder where the evidence of incapacity in this position was.

The second part of the statement might suggest that there had been a failure of trust between CH and her medical advisors, a failure the doctors appear to acknowledge in the case. Again, it is not difficult to see why this might be the case. CH had a history of pathological reactions to the major tranquillisers which would have been the drug of choice during her current psychiatric treatment. The reactions had been sufficiently severe that the foetus would be put at risk if she experienced them while pregnant, and as a result she was on less intrusive medication. Such problematic treatment in the past might be unlikely to engender a relationship of trust between CH and the treatment staff on a subsequent admission. It would seem that she believed some of the drugs she was receiving for her psychiatric disorder were harming her foetus (p. 766). Whether or not she was right, would not any expectant mother be sceptical? There was evidence from her doctor that CH 'is unable to accept [the medical staff's] advice and perceives it as malicious and harmful to her child.' (p. 766). Once again, must this be evidence of incapacity? CH was in a controlled situation where, effectively, she could not select her own doctors. Is it really a mark of incapacity to be sceptical of doctors the patient did not select and cannot change?

The court's finding regarding her capacity is nothing if not pithy, perhaps in part because CH's guardian *ad litem* conceded her incapacity (at p. 771):

> As to the first of the questions posed by Mr. Francis, the evidence is overwhelming that the defendant lacks the capacity to consent to, or to refuse medical treatment in relation to the management of her pregnancy. Mr. Francis accepts this on her behalf. I agree with Dr. M's evidence that she fails all three of the tests laid down in *Re C*. In particular, she is suffering from the delusion that the doctors wish to harm her baby and is incapable of understanding the advice which she is given.

Yet is the standard in *Re C* really applied here? Thorpe J seemed to insist merely on a minimal level of capacity. Can it really be said that CH did not meet that standard? The court in *Tameside* makes no reference to the degree of impairment necessary to found an incapacity finding, but its approach seems to set a much higher threshold than that envisaged by Thorpe J.

How are these differing approaches to be understood? The temptation is to view *Tameside* as the anomaly, as it involves the complicating factor of the viability of the foetus. *C*, too, involved an unusual situation in its way, however. As Broadmoor did not have a resident surgeon who would perform the amputation, C was admitted on a temporary basis to a general hospital. The doctor at that hospital took the view that C was competent, and that his refusal of the amputation should be respected; it was the view of Broadmoor that the operation should go ahead, either now or in the event that it was medically necessary at a future time when C lacked capacity, which created the need for the court decision. The *C* case can therefore be understood not so much as a conflict between C and the doctor wishing to treat him, but as between C and Broadmoor, with the surgeon in charge of the amputation supporting C's position.

Viewed in this light, the *C* case can be seen as part of a line of cases about whether the courts ought to encourage treatments about which the treating doctors have reservations. The courts have traditionally been extremely hesitant to do this: see, e.g., *Re J* [1992] 4 All ER 614 at pp. 623, 625, 626. Usually, there will be no such medical dispute between the patient's treatment team, and the medical view of best interests will be clear. Where that is the case, it is rare if ever that the courts have not found a way for the treatment to occur. On this view, *Tameside* is the more typical case.

Indeed, one can occasionally see the courts adopting a lower threshold of capacity, when necessary to allow treatment. *R v Mental Health Act Commission, ex parte X* (1988) 9 BMLR 77 was a case involving a treatment arguably under s. 57 of the MHA 1983. Section 57 treatments cannot be given to patients lacking capacity, so for the treatment to proceed, a finding that X was capable was of more than academic interest. In that case, where both X and his medical advisors favoured the treatment, the court was content that competency would be shown on the basis of adequate capacity to understand, whether or not there was actual understanding or actual appreciation. This is certainly a correct literal reading of s. 57(2)(a) of the statute, which refers expressly to a patient '*capable* of understanding the nature, purpose and likely effects of the treatment in question' (emphasis added), but it nonetheless stands in rather stark contrast to the approach in the later cases of *C* and *Tameside*.

It would be harsh to view the law of capacity as simply a mechanism by which courts allow treatment to occur, but it would be equally unwise to accept uncritically the claim of Jones and Keywood that 'the courts have been emphatic in rejecting the rationality or reasonableness of the outcome as a measure of incompetence' (1996, p. 112) That is certainly the courts' claim; but it is less obviously a description of the courts' practice.

11.1.4 Best interests

If the patient is found to lack capacity to consent to a certain treatment, they lose control over that treatment. If it is treatment under s. 57 of the MHA 1983, it cannot be given at all. If it is treatment under s. 58 of the Act, it may be provided if a second medical practitioner attests that the patient lacks capacity, and that the treatment should be given 'having regard to the likelihood of its alleviating or preventing a deterioration of his [the patient's] condition' (s. 58(3)(b)). Otherwise, the treatment may be given if it is in the 'best interests' of the patient.

Best interests, like capacity, has tended to be litigated in unusual, emotive and specific fact situations. A number of the pregnancy cases cited above move from a discussion of incapacity to a discussion of best interests. Other cases, including *F* v *West Berkshire*, involve sterilisation of developmentally handicapped women. Occasionally, there are also cases involving the termination of life-support systems for individuals in a persistent vegetative state or similar situation: see, e.g., *Airedale NHS Trust* v *Bland* [1993] AC 789. Because of the unusual situations in which the cases tend to be decided, here once again general principles can be derived only with caution.

In the *F* case itself, best interests was left startlingly undefined. The most complete substantive definition is that of Lord Brandon (at p. 551):

> The operation or other treatment will be in their best interests if, but only if, it is carried out in order either to save their lives or to ensure improvement or prevent deterioration in their physical or mental health.

While this may appear less a legal test than a paraphrase, it is relevant for a couple of reasons. First, the similarity of wording with the MHA 1983 section suggests a similarity of approach between the statute and the common law. Secondly, the approach does suggest that best interests in this context refers to medical best interests. This in turn is reflected in the unanimous view of the Law Lords that the doctor would not be liable, if he or she understood best interests in a fashion consistent with a responsible body of opinion among their professional colleagues. In the view of Lord Goff, it would be 'good practice' to consult relatives and others involved in the care of the patient (p. 567). In cases of doubt, and in any event for particularly intrusive treatments such as sterilisation, the court would be available to offer a view (pp. 552, 562, 569; see further 11.5). Nonetheless, in the general case, the responsibility to act lay with the doctor.

This substantive medical focus may be more apparent than real in the common law. Even *F* itself was not, strictly, about a medically necessary procedure (p. 549). While it was clear that pregnancy would be 'disastrous' to F from a psychiatric point of view (p. 550), pregnancy is not the same as sterilisation, and the sterilisation was not necessary except as, on the facts, the only means to avoid pregnancy. In subsequent cases, it would appear that this nontherapeutic character of *F* is not an irrelevant issue. Where the judges in *F* indicated that court approval ought to be sought prior to a sterilisation operation (p. 562), it has been held that there is a distinction between cases where the hysterectomy is 'required for genuine therapeutic purposes and where the operation is designed to achieve sterilisation.'. For the former, distinguishing *F*, advance court approval was held not merely not to be required; it was inappropriate (*Re E (A Minor) (Medical Treatment)* [1991] 2 FLR 585 at p. 587). In this context, the *F* case ceases to be about medical best interests, and is instead about a broad range of social factors related to the sterilisation of the developmentally handicapped. Nonetheless, the decision is left with the doctors.

More recent cases have clarified that the criteria of best interests are not simply medical. The gloss given to the *F* case by Lord Keith in *Bland* (at p. 858) makes this clear:

> The ground of the decision [in *F*] was that sterilisation would be in the patient's best interests because her life would be fuller and more agreeable if she were sterilised than if she were not.

Yet in the move away from a purely medical approach, it is not entirely obvious what is to be considered in determining the patient's best interests. Lord Keith's remarks make it perhaps possible to see *F* as a case of selecting the least restrictive alternative, for it would presumably have been possible to separate F from her romantic partner, or indeed to segregate her on an all-women ward, a course the court does not consider. In *Bland*, Lord Goff held that the first consideration was the wishes of the patient, and in the event of incapacity, regard would be had to the wishes of the patient expressed during an earlier period of capacity (p. 864). This approach can be seen reflected in the *C* case, with the court's willingness to issue an injunction restraining the removal of the gangrenous leg during a subsequent period of incapacity.

This approach may be reflected in *Re MB (Medical Treatment)* (11.1.1). This case involved treatment of a woman in labour, found by the court to lack capacity. While the court held that the best interests of the foetus could not be determinative of whether or not to treat, the best interests of the woman could be understood with reference to her desire for her child to be born alive. The case was an unusual one. The woman was generally of robust capacity, but had a phobia of needles, resulting in her panicking and withdrawing her consent just before the performance of a Caesarean section operation. This panic was held to remove her capacity to consent at that moment. Butler-Sloss LJ (at p. 439) held that B's wishes were relevant in determining her best interests:

Best interests are not limited to best medical interests.

It is clear on the evidence that the mother and the father wanted this child to be born alive and Miss MB was in favour of the operation, subject only to her needle phobia. It must be in the best interests of a woman carrying a full-term child whom she wants to be born alive and healthy that such a result should if possible be achieved.

This suggests a quite broad interpretation of patient wishes, for the wishes here refer not to the treatment itself, but to the result of the treatment, a healthy baby, a result also no doubt emotionally easy for the court to support. It remains to be seen whether the court will adopt such a robust approach to patient wishes on harder facts.

In *Bland*, Lord Goff makes it clear that the invasiveness of the treatment, and both the potential benefits and risks are appropriate for consideration of best interests, as is the indignity the patient will suffer during the treatment (p. 869). His Lordship views this as an extension of the principle of self-determination, quoting with approval the following extract from *Superintendent of Belchertown State School* v *Saikewicz* 370 NE 2d 417 (1977) (p. 428; quoted in *Bland* at p. 865):

To presume that the incompetent person must always be subjected to what many rational and intelligent persons may decline is to downgrade the status of the incompetent person by placing a lesser value on his intrinsic worth and vitality.

Bland is, again, a case on unusual facts, the termination of treatment needed by a young man in a persistent vegetative state to remain alive. From that case, it is clear that there is no simple duty to provide treatment if that treatment has no reasonable likelihood of success. It again is not clear how far the courts will extend the principle of autonomy in other contexts. As discussed in Chapter seven, psychiatric drugs may have severe adverse effects, rendering the patient nauseous, affecting their physical movement, or damaging their nervous system. In disputes over psychiatric and related treatment, it remains to be seen how the courts will address issues of best interests.

It is startlingly unclear the degree to which interests other than those of the patient may be considered in the determination of best interests. Certainly, family and carers are to be consulted as a matter of good practice by the doctor, but it is equally clear in *F* that the decision as to best interests rests with the doctor (p. 567). While Lord Goff in *Bland* reiterates that view (pp. 871), he also refers (at p. 869) to the effects of the treatment on family members:

> It is reasonable also that account should be taken of the invasiveness of the treatment and of the indignity to which, as the present case shows, a person has to be subjected if his life is prolonged by artificial means, which must cause considerable distress to his family — a distress which reflects not only on their own feelings but their perception of the situation of their relative who is being kept alive.

A similar view is taken by the court in *Re S (Medical Treatment: Adult Sterilisation)* [1998] 1 FLR 944 (at p. 946-7):

> The question is what is best for S? As to the wishes of her parents, their opinions as to the nature and extent of the risk of pregnancy and their reaction to an adverse decision by the court — these are matters to be taken into account. However, the opinion of the parents as to the outcome of the central balancing exercise is certainly not determinative of the matter; that is one for the court alone.

The counterveiling authority is found in the argument of Lord Mustill, again in the *Bland* case (at p. 896), where both the pain caused to the family and the expense or other unpleasantness caused to the state as a whole, are held to be matters inappropriate for the court's consideration:

> Threaded through the technical arguments addressed to the House were the strands of a much wider position, that it is in the best interests of the community at large that Anthony Bland's life should now end. The doctors have done all they can. Nothing will be gained by going on and much will be lost. The distress of the family will get steadily worse. The strain on the devotion of a medical staff charged with the care of a patient whose condition will never improve, who may live for years and who does not even recognise that he is being cared for, will continue to mount. The large resources of skill, labour and money now being devoted to Anthony Bland might in the opinion

of many be more fruitfully employed in improving the condition of other patients, who if treated may have useful, healthy and enjoyable lives for years to come.

This argument was never squarely put, although hinted at from time to time. In social terms it has great force, and it will have to be faced in the end. But this is not a task which the courts can possibly undertake. A social cost-benefit analysis of this kind, which would have to embrace 'mercy-killing' to which exactly the same considerations apply, must be for Parliament alone, and the outcome of it is at present quite impossible to foresee. Until the nettle is grasped, we must struggle on with the existing law, imperfect as it is.

Lord Mustill's view is certainly the more consistent with the themes of self-determination which Lord Goff espouses elsewhere in *Bland*, and he is right to point to the difficulty of moving beyond the individual patient to allow other social factors to enter the equation. The difficulties are at least twofold. First is the difficulty of ascertaining what would constitute best interests, when the interests of a wide variety of people and of the state as a whole might be theoretically relevant. Second is the risk of creeping extension of this approach: when do matters of convenience to carers (professional or family) and the state become matters of legitimate interest and concern in the determination of overall best interests?

This issue is of course of considerable importance in a mental health framework. In a climate of increased concern by the state of controlling patients living in the community, and at a time when both community care and institutional budgets are increasingly stretched, resulting in increasingly overstretched staff, the use of drugs risks blurring the line as to best interests of the patient, or best interests of others. While an increasingly important area of concern, it is not obvious that the courts will have an occasion to address it, since there is at this time no requirement except in unusual circumstances that courts oversee treatment provided in the best interests of incompetent patients.

11.1.5 The process, extent and effect of court applications

In general, the decision as to whether or not to treat lies in the authority of the treating medical officer. The case law does establish a number of exceptions to this general rule, however: court applications ought to be made when the treatment in question is one of therapeutic sterilisation (*F*, pp. 552, 562; see also *Practice Note* at [1996] 2 FLR 111), termination of life for an individual in a persistent vegetative state (*Bland* pp. 859, 874, 875–6), in cases where the capacity of the patient is in doubt (*St. George's NHS Trust*, p. 703) and treatment over the objections of a woman in labour (*MB*, p. 445). There is further no provision in the MHA 1983, for review by court or tribunal of treatment decisions made under ss. 58 or 63: court applications are instead limited to treatment of incapable people under the common law.

Cases such as *Bland* and *F* have encouraged doctors more broadly to apply to court in cases where they are unsure how to proceed. This has on occasion happened. Thus in *Re H (Mental Patient: Diagnosis)* [1993] 1 FLR 28, the court ruled on an application as to whether relatively intrusive diagnostic procedures could be performed on an incapacitated patient on the authority of *F* (they could). At the same time, the courts have sometimes actively discouraged such applications. Sometimes, this seems justifiable. In *Re JT* [1998] 1 FLR 48, for example, an application was made by a doctor to withhold dialysis treatment in a case where the competent patient had refused treatment. The doctor agreed with the withholding, since the treatment could not be given effectively without the patient's cooperation. The court's reluctance to be involved seems justifiable here: it is not obvious that anyone's interests are served by court applications, when competent patient and doctor agree on a course of action, or where a competent patient refuses treatment entirely (*St. George's NHS Trust*, p. 703).

In other cases, the reluctance of the courts is not so obviously warranted. Thus in *Re SG (Adult Mental Patient: Abortion)* [1991] 2 FLR 329, it was held that court approval would not be required prior to the performance of an abortion on an adult, incapacitated woman, on the basis that regulation by the Abortion Act 1967 provided adequate safeguards. This is not entirely obvious. The court application should ensure that attention is directed to the best interests of the incapacitated patient. The regulation of the Abortion Act 1967 is not directed to this end, but rather to whether specific social standards are met such that an otherwise illegal act may be performed. The two roles seem quite distinct. Similarly, in *Re E (A Minor) (Medical Treatment)* [1991] 2 FLR 585, the court held that a hysterectomy performed on an incapacitated seventeen-year-old girl which was medically necessary for reasons not related to birth control did not require prior court approval. The court's position is that approval should not be required for treatment which is properly therapeutic. While that has its attractions, it is problematic. Treatments do not necessarily divide neatly into the therapeutic and the nontherapeutic. A hysterectomy remains a profoundly intrusive process, which will result in the patient's sterilisation. If the court application is in part to ascertain the patient's best interests in the context of a treatment with an important, lasting and certain adverse effect, it is not obvious that the motivation for the procedure ought to determine the desirability of a court declaration.

The clearest indication of the nature of the court proceedings may be found in *St. George's NHS Trust*. That was a case where virtually everything seemed to go wrong in law. The patient, thirty-six weeks pregnant, was diagnosed with eclampsia. When she refused treatment, an approved social worker was called, and she was admitted to a psychiatric facility, illegally as it turned out. An *ex parte* approach was made to a judge for authorisation to perform a Caesarean section. The information provided to the judge was in part incorrect; she was told for example that S had been in labour for twenty-four hours when in fact labour had not yet commenced. Information was incomplete on other material points. The court was not told, for example, that the evidence was that S had capacity to consent, but was nonetheless refusing treatment. S had earlier contacted lawyers about her situation, but they were not informed of the court application. In this context, the court laid down a set of substantive and procedural guidelines for the conduct of cases of alleged incapacity, which both provide a clearer structure for the applications, and also clarify what the court declaration actually does.

Consistent with *F*, the procedure is intended to provide protection for doctors against subsequent adverse criticism or claims. There are limitations to the degree to which this can occur through the declaration process, however. The court in *St. George's* quotes *Imperial Tobacco Ltd* v *A-G* [1980] 1 All ER 875 to the effect that a declaration cannot shield the parties against a subsequent criminal prosecution, although 'authoritative guidance ... would in practice inhibit prosecution' [*St. George's*, p. 700, quoting Lord Goff in *Bland*]. Further, the declaration will bind only those persons who are parties to the process. Here, since S was not herself present or represented at the hearing, it had no effect on her, and she remained free to bring a civil action against the doctors and hospital. In the event that the patient lacked capacity to instruct solicitors, a different standard of course from treatment capacity, the Official Solicitor should be contacted to act as guardian *ad litem*; and even if the patient was competent and represented, the Official Solicitor might be involved as *amicus curiae* (p. 704; see also *MB*, p. 445). The hearing could only result in a final order; an 'interim declaration' was 'a contradiction in terms' (p. 700). The hearing would instead proceed on full and complete evidence (p. 704):

> It is axiomatic that the judge must be provided with accurate and all the relevant information. This should include the reasons for the proposed treatment, the risks involved in the proposed treatment, and in not proceeding with it, whether any alternative treatment exists, and the reason, if ascertainable, why the patient is refusing the proposed treatment. The judge will need sufficient information to reach an informed conclusion about the patient's capacity, and, where it arises, the issue of best interest.

The circumstances of the *St. George's* case are striking and unfortunate, and the strictures established by the court are convincing in that context. Appropriately, they establish procedural standards to protect patients from violations of their rights, and foundations for the information required for a decision as to whether treatment should proceed. It remains to be seen whether that court's firmness of approach will be continued in other less dubious fact situations.

At the same time, the structures contained in *St. George's* highlight the difficulties of the declaration procedure in the context of treatment of incapable people. The declaratory procedure is advisory only. The point here is not merely that it does not in theory preclude criminal charges, since in practice it would be a rare case where such charges proceeded. It is also that it is theoretically difficult to see how the court can impress the importance of court applications prior to treatment in cases such as sterilisation or termination of life support, since such applications merely proclaim the existing rights between the parties: they are not formal legal prerequisites. It may well be that the social view is that these treatments are sufficiently intrusive that they ought to require court approval; but that is not what the declaration process does.

It further becomes difficult or impossible to invoke the declaration procedure on short notice. Consider the situation of women in labour, for example, a situation where doctors are told they 'ought' to apply to court prior to treating a woman without consent (*MB*, p. 445). Even if they have the capacity to instruct solicitors, it is an inappropriate time to ask them to do so; yet if the patient is not present, the fundamental issue of whether the doctor can be assured that a tort will not be committed if treatment proceeds will not be resolved. If the patient lacks capacity, the Official Solicitor will be called in, but in some cases may not provide an appropriate substitute. The gathering of the relevant evidence can take time, particularly since best interests extend beyond a medical frame of reference. If time is not available, of necessity the Official Solicitor may not fully be prepared. In what way in such a situation is his presence a safeguard to the rights of the patient, or an assurance of the integrity of the process or the outcome?

These are, in part, inevitable outcomes of legal process. They are, nonetheless, real problems with the declaratory approach, suggesting that the current situation is not ideal and that a coherent and considered approach such as that proposed by the Law Commission may well be preferable to the organically grown response of the courts.

11.2   THE COURT OF PROTECTION AND THE PROPERTY AND AFFAIRS OF PEOPLE LACKING CAPACITY

As discussed in Chapter ten, the *parens patriae* jurisdiction of the Crown over the property and affairs of people lacking capacity has evolved by statute into the Court of Protection, currently constituted by part VII of the Mental Health Act 1983. It is staffed by nominated superior court judges, in practice those appointed to the Chancery Division, along with a Master, a Deputy Master, and a variety of other officers.

The court has jurisdiction over the estates of roughly 30,000 individuals at any given time. As noted in Chapter ten, these individuals will as a result of the court's involvement lose authority to contract, and to deal with their own affairs. Atypically for incapacity law, this loss of control is not determined by the ability to make the individual decision in question: the capacity to deal with one's property and affairs is an all-or-nothing matter.

Notwithstanding its statutory construction, the Court remains something of an anomaly. Despite its title, it is not exactly a court, in the sense that it does not have routine sittings. In spite of its roots and the fact that its nominated judges are all drawn from the superior courts, it is not juridically part of the Supreme Court: Supreme Court Act 1981, s. 1(1). It therefore has no inherent jurisdiction, but is instead constituted entirely through the relevant provisions of the MHA 1983. The Civil Procedure Rules 1998 do not apply directly to the Court of Protection, although some of those rules which concern costs are incorporated by the Court of Protection (Amendment) Rules 1999, SI 1999 No. 2504, r. 8. In addition, as guidance was sought from the former court rules in the silence of the Court of Protection Rules, so similar guidance is likely to be sought from the Civil Procedure Rules 1998.

The author of the current edition of *Heywood and Massey, Court of Protection Practice*, the Bible of Court of Protection practice, describes it instead as 'merely the title of an office' (p. 8). This may be equally misleading for the student, however, since the Court does make judicial decisions according to established processes, and its decisions are appealable to the Court of Appeal. Nonetheless the processes are markedly different from those that traditional common lawyers would recognise. Applications to the court are normally in writing, and are decided without the formality of a hearing. In the event of dispute, the court does not normally hear evidence directly, but instead sends its agents, the Lord Chancellor's Visitors, to assess the situation and provide a report. This process derives from the older practices of the court, when exercising *parens patriae* jurisdiction. The court may hold a hearing on the basis of that evidence, but this will generally be to entertain argument based on the evidence, not to hear new evidence.

11.2.1 Jurisdiction of the court

The court's jurisdiction extends only to 'property and affairs' of those lacking capacity (s. 94(2)). In *Re W* [1970] 2 All ER 502 at p. 510, the phrase was read expansively:

'Affairs', prima facie, has a wider and more general meaning than 'property.' The coupling of the two words in the section emphasises a difference of meaning; and the substance of the section indicates that the only object of referring to the patient's incapacity as extending to affairs as well as property is to give the Court of Protection jurisdiction for the protection and management of the patient's 'affairs' as well as 'property'.

The court goes on to hold that the court has 'exclusive jurisdiction over all the property and all the affairs of the patient in all their aspects; but not to the management or care of the patient's person.' (p. 511). As we have seen, this distinction between personal and property and affairs is significant since there is no statutory system to deal with personal decisions of an incapacitated person.

The court in *W* provides a relatively broad reading of property and affairs, and a correspondingly narrow reading of decisions relating to the person. The facts in *W* must also, of course, be taken into account. The issue was whether litigation, and in particular a divorce proceeding, was within the range of the phrase 'property and affairs'. The couple had been estranged for some time, and the husband was living with a different partner whom he wished to marry. Financially, it would have been in W's interest to bring the petition prior to anticipated divorce reforms. In so far as W's views could be ascertained, she favoured the divorce, and the court was prepared to hold that such a divorce would be in her best interests. The conduct of legal proceedings, into which divorce proceedings must unquestionably fall, was in the list of specifically enumerated powers granted to the Court of Protection by the MHA 1983. It is in this context that the court was prepared to move outside a narrow reading of property and affairs (pp. 510–1):

The conduct of legal proceedings, and in particular of divorce, may involve far more than the management, protection or administration of property, which may indeed form an insignificant aspect of the proceedings. Nor does it seem to me conceivable that the court, in considering legal proceedings, should consider that merely as an aspect of administering the patient's property; otherwise other aspects of such proceedings of no property significance would not receive their proper consideration. Nor, I would emphasise, particularly in view of references in the correspondence before me to the 'financial affairs' of the patient being in the hands of the Court of Protection, in contrast with the personal care of the patient being in the hands of the mental after-care home, is the court's protection of the patient's affairs limited to her financial affairs. There is no such limitation to 'affairs' in the Act.

In the context of litigation, a matter specifically reserved to the court, these comments must be correct. The question is how far they can be generalised to the court's role as a whole. The matter will be particularly relevant in two contexts: significant decisions relating to the individual's personal affairs, which are not covered by a narrow reading of the phrase 'management or care of the patient's person', and decisions with financial ramifications which are clearly relevant to the individual's personal care. Decisions regarding the care and upbringing of the individual's children might serve as a paradigm example of the former; and the payment of nursing home fees or fees for private medical treatment of the latter.

The MHA 1983 may provide some guidance. The general principles to be exercised by the court are contained in s. 95. These are not particularly helpful in determining the scope of the phrase 'property and affairs', since the section itself uses the phrase without further definition. Section 96 provides a list of specific powers of the court. While subject to the generality of s. 95, it may nonetheless provide an illustrative list of the types of powers envisaged for the court, and thus the sorts of decisions the individual might be expected to lack capacity in making. The list in s. 96 concerns the control, disposition or acquisition of property, the making of a will, the carrying on of the individual's business, the dissolution of a partnership of which the individual is a member, the conduct of legal proceedings, the carrying out of contracts, and the payment of debts. In so far as this is an illustrative list, and with the possible exception of the conduct of litigation, the list appears to be focused on the business, financial and property affairs of the individual.

If this is taken as illustrative, the affairs of the patient might be read in a somewhat more narrow sense than *Re W* might at first glance be thought to suggest. Purely personal decisions, such as those involving the raising of children, would generally fall outside the jurisdiction of the court, even though they do not obviously involve the 'management or care of the patient's person'.

Issues such as nursing home fees raise different complexities. The court currently takes the view that these are within their jurisdiction, notwithstanding their overlapping relevance to the management or care of the individual. This view must surely be correct, as these fees will often be the primary expense to the individual's maintenance. This would appear to be precisely analogous to the overlap between personal and 'property and affairs' envisaged by the court in *W*. It is not an entirely satisfactory situation. If the individual is competent to decide where they will live, but lacking capacity in their property and affairs, for example, how is the court to proceed? Its first priority is to make decisions 'as appear necessary or expedient' for the maintenance and benefit of the patient, but it also has authority to consider the interests of creditors and others such as family members (s. 95). The exercise of these criteria might result in the individual's choice of accommodation, a decision which they are competent to make, being overridden, a significant intrusion into the personal capacity of the individual. It would be tempting to define the court's role in terms merely of overall budget for accommodation, subject to direction by those with personal decision-making authority as to how that money is to be spent; yet this is fairly clearly not what the statute directs, and raises the difficulty that if the individual lacks capacity, there will usually, in law, be no one to provide that direction.

The court's jurisdiction arises, of course, only if the individual is demonstrated to be 'incapable, by reason of mental disorder' of managing their property and affairs (s. 94(2)). A mental disorder, as defined by s. 1 of the Act, must therefore be shown, although there is no need to specify one of the four specific types of disorders described in that section. There is further no need that that individual be otherwise in the mental health system, let alone in hospital. While the term 'patient' is specifically applied in the MHA 1983 to refer to those under the jurisdiction of the court, (s. 94(2)) and will for consistency be applied in the following discussion, it is nonetheless therefore somewhat misleading.

No guidance is provided by the 1983 Act or supporting rules as to how incapacity is determined, although the powers of the court over 'property and affairs', discussed above, may provide some guidance as to the sorts of decisions the patient should lack the capacity to make, in order for the jurisdiction to be invoked. While medical evidence is expressly required, it need not be from a psychiatric specialist. The notes accompanying the form (Notes accompanying Certificate of Incapacity, Form CP3) to be completed by the doctor may provide some indication of the proof of incapacity expected by the court:

> 5. ... What is required is not merely a diagnosis (although this may be included) but a simple statement giving clear evidence of incapacity which an intelligent lay person could understand, e.g., reference to defect of short-term memory, of spatial and temporal orientation or of reasoning ability, or to reckless spending (sometimes periodic as in mania) without regard for the future, or evidence of vulnerability or exploitation.

> 6. In many cases of senile dementia, severe brain damage, acute or chronic psychiatric disorder and severe mental impairment the assessment of incapacity should present little difficulty. Cases of functional and personality disorders may give more problems and assessment may depend on the individual doctor's interpretation of mental disorder. The Court tends towards the view that these conditions render a person liable to its jurisdiction where there appears to be a real danger that they will lead to dissipation of considerable capital assets.

While there is little law on the point, it would seem axiomatic that the mental disorder must cause the incapacity to manage property or affairs: eccentric spending does not necessarily bespeak incapacity in people with mental disabilities, as it does not do so in the general population.

11.2.2 Process issues

Applications for the initial appointment of receivers, the standard first application regarding people thought to lack capacity, are likely to be dealt with by the Master. Appeal of that decision, if necessary, lies to a nominated judge, thence to the Court of Appeal.

The failure of the statute further to define the test of incapacity may in part be compensated for through the provision of process safeguards. The patient and, generally, some relatives of the patient must be served with notice of the application: Court of Protection Rules 1994, rr. 21, 27. The relatives must generally be all those at least as close in kinship to the patient as the applicant. While the court has authority to dispense with service, it tends to be hesitant to do so: *Re B (Court of Protection)* [1987] 2 FLR 155. These protections may appear at least partially illusory, since legal aid is not available for proceedings before the court. Nonetheless, it is to be remembered that the court has its own investigative unit, the Lord Chancellor's Visitors. While the court is not required to investigate all objections, it has the power to do so, and thus even a letter from the patient may be sufficient to induce some procedural safeguards.

Anyone may launch a first application for the appointment of a receiver, although it is generally instigated by a close relative of the patient. It is usually made through solicitors, although in some cases, the Public Trust Office will assist lay people to complete the relevant forms. The application consists of a general application form for the appointment of a receiver, accompanied by statements containing the medical evidence of incapacity, an enumerated list of the patient's family, property and personal circumstances, a copy of the patient's will if available, and the required fee.

The proposed receiver may be, but need not necessarily be the applicant. Professional receivers such as solicitors, accountants, or bank managers may be allowed in some cases, but will generally be permitted to be paid from the patient's estate for their services, and may thus be undesirable. Currently, roughly 19,000 receivers (68 per cent) are relatives or friends of the patient, and 4000 (14 per cent) are professionals such as solicitors, bank managers. The public trustee is receiver in about 2,600 cases (10 per cent); and agents of local authorities fulfil the role in about 2,400 cases (9 per cent). (Jones, 1999, p. 336). The receiver will be required to post security prior to appointment, generally by purchasing a fidelity guarantee bond with an insurance company. The premium for this bond, as the other court fees, is generally payable from the patient's estate upon appointment of the receiver. The receiver will generally be required to render accounts annually, although there is a simplified process for small estates, where the receiver is the spouse of and shares a house with the patient. The receiver's powers will be enumerated in the order of appointment, and can be as wide as those possessed by the court in appropriate circumstances. Often, but not necessarily, investments will be held by the court rather than by the receiver.

Unless there is an objection by the patient or other relative to the application, it will be dealt with on the basis of the application, without the formality of an oral hearing. The appointment will remain in effect until either the death of the patient, or until revoked by the court: s. 99, MHA 1983. There is no routine review of these orders, to see whether the patient continues to lack capacity.

The jurisdiction of the court upon the grant of an order was noted above. It here remains merely to emphasise that while the court's first responsiblity is to the requirements of the patient, it also has authority to do such things as may be 'necessary or expedient' for maintenance or benefit of the patient's family, or 'for making provision for other persons or purposes for whom or which the patient might be expected to provide if he were not mentally disordered' (s. 95(1)(c)). The interests of creditors must also be taken into account (s. 95(2)). Section 95(2) further makes it clear that the court can, in appropriate circumstances, make these provisions notwithstanding that they are not legally enforceable. The interests of the patient are to be understood as 'true' interests, not merely financial ones, and, as discussed in Chapter ten, a substitute judgment test is to apply.

While this is the most usual procedure to invoke the jurisdiction of the court, it is not the only one. Urgent applications allow for court intervention when the court merely 'has reason to believe' that a person may be incapable of managing and administering their property and affairs, and the court believes immediate provision to be necessary: s. 98. Medical evidence is not a prerequisite.

The court's jurisdiction may also be invoked using the so-called short process, described in r. 9 of the Court of Protection Rules 1994. This is designed for small estates, generally those under £5,000, when court intervention is required for a specific and defined purpose. An example would be where the patient has become entitled to funds, as for example as beneficiary of a will, and short, one-off intervention is required to deal with the money. It is not appropriate when on-going supervision will be required, or for particularly major transactions such as the sale of real estate. The order can be designed to effect that end, without further intrusion into the patient's affairs. Applications require medical evidence of incapacity, and an explanation of the facts justifying the use of the application.

The general result of the court's involvement, however, is the appointment of a receiver. This is an extraordinarily blunt intervention: the patient loses control over all their estate, until such time as the receivership is terminated either by court order, or the death of the patient. It might be noted that there is no obligation on anyone to apply to the Court of Protection for intervention; in the event that the person lacking capacity, or of marginal capacity, is able to continue without the intervention, this is in no way contrary to law. Sympathetic carers may be well-advised to consider other, less drastic strategies. In so far as the patient forgetting to pay routine household expenses such as rent and utilities is the root of potential problems, for example, these can be moved to payment by direct debit. For social security benefits, reg. 33 of the Social Security (Claims and Payments) Regulations 1987 allows the Secretary of

State to appoint an 'appointee' to act on behalf of a claimant when the claimant is himself or herself 'unable to act'. This allows the appointee to exercise rights and duties of the claimant under social security legislation, receive the claimant's benefits, and spend that money in the interests of the claimant and his or her dependants. Again, this may be of assistance in limiting the broad intervention into the life of many clients which the involvement of the Court of Protection would entail.

Finally, the enduring powers of attorney may provide a mechanism by which the broad intervention of the Court of Protection may not be necessary. These are discussed in 11.2.4.

11.2.3 Wills

The authority of the Court of Protection to draft wills on behalf of an incapacitated patient is contained in ss. 96(1)(e), (4), and 97, MHA 1983. The content of the will is to be determined using a substituted judgment test, with some variations (*In re D (J)* [1982] 1 Ch 237). The test of capacity grows from *Banks* v *Goodfellow* (1870) 5 QB 549. Both of these were discussed at length in Chapter ten and will not be repeated here. Instead, this section will limit itself to the procedural specifics of the Court of Protection in these matters.

The Court of Protection drafts in the order of 90 to 140 wills per year. Applications may be made by the patient's receiver; an applicant for the appointment of a receiver, if the application has not yet been determined; a person who, under any known will of the patient or under the patient's intestacy may become entitled to property of the patient; a person for whom the patient might be expected to provide if not mentally disordered; an attorney acting under an enduring power of attorney; or any other person by leave of the court: Court of Protection Rules 1994, r. 20. A formal hearing will be held, at which the patient will be represented, generally by the Official Solicitor. Notice of the hearing should normally be given to those who may be materially and adversely affected by the application. These will include beneficiaries of a previous will and those who would take on intestacy, as well as any party for whom the patient 'might be expected to make some substantial provision if of sound mind, regard being paid to the size of the estate . . . and the size of the provision which might have been expected to be made for that party' (*Re B (Court of Protection)* (11.2.2), p. 160). In the event of urgency, there is jurisdiction to proceed without complete notification (*Re Davey* [1981] 1 WLR 165).

The evidence required for the application is detailed in *Heywood and Massey*, and includes details of the patient's family, current assets, estimated annual income and expenses, a statement of anticipated future needs, a statement as to the patient's current health, the resources of the proposed beneficiaries and the tax implications of the proposed allocation, and a copy of the patient's current will (*Heywood and Massey*, pp. 195-6). The jurisdiction of the court may only be invoked upon specific proof of the patient's testamentary incapacity (s. 96(4)), a matter narrower than the general incapacity warranting Court of Protection involvement in the estate of the patient. Such proof must therefore be provided as part of the application.

The principles guiding the drafting of the will remain those in s. 95 of the MHA 1983, as they are for the other interventions of the Court of Protection. As illustrated in Chapter ten, family members are often beneficiaries, although in unusual circumstances, even a spouse may be disinherited (see *Re Davey*). Charities may be beneficiaries, if the evidence discloses that such a bequest would probably have been made by the patient, if of sound mind (*Re C (A Patient)* [1991] 3 All ER 866).

Once the will is signed by the court staff on behalf of the patient, it takes effect as if it were the will of the patient. It has been doubted whether at that time, a nominated judge has jurisdiction to consider the appropriateness of the will (Re *Davey*, pp. 171-2).

11.2.4 Enduring powers of attorney

Enduring powers of attorney provide the most effective mechanism for persons to plan for their own incapacity. Like regular powers of attorney, they are mandates signed by a donor, allowing the person named in the power, the attorney, to act on the donor's behalf in those matters listed in the power. Once again, these powers may confer authority only over matters relating to the property and affairs of the donor: powers of attorney for personal decisions have no basis in law and are at this time unenforceable.

While based on an old form, enduring powers of attorney are nonetheless creatures of statute. At common law, the incapacity of a donor revoked any power of attorney: *Drew v Nunn* (1879) 4 QB 661. This remained the case until the Enduring Powers of Attorney Act 1985, which allowed powers executed in a specific form to remain valid, notwithstanding incapacity. A caveat is appropriate here: the rules contained in the Act are not overly onerous, but they are quite precise; and reference ought to be made to the Act for specifics.

The general scheme is that anyone with requisite capacity may, along with the proposed attorney, execute a continuing power. At the time of execution, the attorney must be either an individual aged eighteen years or older, or a trust corporation. After execution, the attorney may only disclaim the power (indicate an unwillingness to act) if notice is given to the donor. Unlike regular powers of attorney, which operate entirely in the private law of agency and without state intervention, enduring powers must be registered when the individual is or is becoming incapable. The Court of Protection then acquires some supervisory powers over the attorney, to ensure that the power is being carried out consistently with the donor's expressed wishes: see s. 8, Enduring Powers of Attorney Act (EPAA) 1985. After registration, the power may not be modified by the donor, and may only be revoked by order of the court. In addition, the attorney cannot cease to act without notice to the court: s. 7(1). EPAA 1985.

To be valid, the enduring power of attorney must include statements that the donor has read or had read to him or her prescribed information as to the effect of creating a power, that the donor intends the power to continue in spite of subsequent mental incapacity, and that the attorney understands the duty of registration imposed by the Act. Both the attorney and the donor must sign the form, and those signatures must be witnessed. In the event that the donor or attorney is unable to sign the form, whether through illiteracy or through physical disability, an individual may sign instead at the individual's direction, but this signature must be witnessed by two people.

The enduring power of attorney can be tailored to the wishes of the donor to a considerable degree. That said, there are a few presumptive clauses, which will apply unless the contrary is stipulated. Thus for example it is presumed that the attorney may provide for himself or herself and third parties as the donor might be expected to have provided, consistent with the needs of those individuals, and do whatever the donor might have done to meet those needs. Specifically, it is assumed that the attorney may make gifts such as those of a seasonal nature to these individuals, and donate to charity as the donor might have been expected to donate, provided these gifts are reasonable in the context of the size of the donor's estate: ss. 3(4),(5), EPAA 1985.

A variety of due process safeguards are contained in the Act. The first is that the donor is expected to read the information on the form, which explains the nature of the power, including its continuation notwithstanding subsequent incapacity. Secondly, registration provides some protection against the premature use of the power. Registration must occur when the attorney believes the donor is or is becoming incapacitated. While there is no formal requirement for medical evidence of incapacity as a matter of routine, the registration provisions require not merely that the donor, but at least three relatives of the donor be notified when the power is to be registered. The rule is somewhat complex. Schedule I to the Act establishes class of relatives, with the donor's spouse at the head of the list, followed by children, parents, siblings, and so forth. At least three relatives must be notified, with those higher in the list preferred to those lower. If at least one person in the class is notified, all must be notified. All these individuals have the right to object to the registration of the power, on the basis that the power is invalid or no longer subsists; that the application is premature since the donor is not yet becoming incapable; that the creation of the power was induced by fraud or undue pressure; or that with regard to all circumstances and in particular the attorney's relationship to the donor, the attorney is unsuitable (s. 6(5)). In the event of objection, a hearing is held by the Master of the Court of Protection, who may affirm the registration, order the power to be given up for cancellation, or, in the event that the application is premature, refuse the registration but leave the power intact to be registered in the future (s. 6(6)). Appeal of this decision lies to a nominated judge of the court. Once registered, however, a separate motion is required to cancel the power. There is no routine review to ensure that the individual remains incapable.

Finally, if the instrument is registered, the court does attain some supervisory jurisdiction over the attorney. Specifically, the court can give directions with respect to the management or disposal by the attorney of the property and affairs of the donor, require the rendering of accounts by the attorney, and give directions regarding remuneration of the attorney: s. 8(2). In the extreme, the appointment of a receiver through the regular Court of Protection route will give the court jurisdiction to cancel the registration of the power of attorney (s. 8(4)).

The powers of the court were considered in the case of *In re R (Enduring Power of Attorney)* [1990] 1 Ch 647. That case involved the alleged promise of a life interest in property and continuing support for a paid companion, formerly housekeeper, employed by R for some twenty years. It was alleged that in detrimental reliance upon these promises, the companion remained with R, accepting wages well below the market value of her labour. R executed a power of attorney containing an express prohibition of gifts to friends or relatives. When R was admitted to a nursing home, the attorney terminated the employment of the companion, and commenced proceedings to evict her from the flat where she and R had lived. The companion applied to the court to enforce the promise of continued support, relying on the general authority of the court to give directions with respect to the management or disposal by the attorney of the property and affairs of the donor (s. 8(2)(b)(i), EPAA 1985).

The court declined to order the attorney to honour the promises. The court held that the powers of the court in s. 8(2)(b) concerned merely administrative matters; they could certainly not be used to override the clause of the power, expressly permitted by the Act, precluding gifts to friends or relatives. The court's approach should instead be one of non-intervention (p. 652):

> The purpose and effect of the Enduring Powers of Attorney Act 1985 is to enable somebody to give a power of attorney, which will endure despite a supervening incapacity, to a person of his choice, and to empower that person to deal with his property in the way that he thinks fit.

In part this is irreproachable. It is difficult to see that it would be an appropriate exercise of the court's powers to circumvent a clause in the power, expressly authorised by the Act. In this context, the case stands as a warning of the need to ensure proper advice prior to execution, since mistakes (if indeed this was a mistake) cannot necessarily be rectified later.

The broader principle, that the court ought to adopt a non-interventionist approach generally, may be more controversial. It is certainly an arguable view, but it does not flow inevitably from the text of s. 8. The powers contained in that section may be used to assist or to control the attorney. Thus the rendering of accounts is one way in which attorneys are shown to be doing their job appropriately, and the clause concerning remuneration of attorneys specifically allows for the repayment of excessive fees. The power of the court in s. 8(2)(a) to determine the meaning or effect of the instrument is similarly ambiguous: it may be seen to assist or to confine the attorney's discretion, depending on the circumstance. Further, the power in s. 8(2)(c) to require the attorney to furnish information or documents may be an important tool in controlling an attorney. To label these powers as concerning 'administrative matters' (p. 651) solves nothing; presumably the manner in which moneys are spent could equally be characterised as an 'administrative matter', coming with the 'management or disposal of property' in s. 8(2)(b)(i).

The court's view of the clause risks reducing it to mere surplusage. If the approach is one of non-intervention, what import could the clause have? Certainly, the court may have jurisdiction to entertain an application from an attorney as to whether a specific decision is within the authority conferred by the power; but if the question is merely one of the extent of the power, it would more appropriately be considered under s. 8(2)(a), which allows the court to determine the meaning or effect of the power. If s. 8(2)(b)(i) is to have a different effect, it must be to instruct the attorney to behave in a specific way. This is consistent with its plain wording. And if that is the case, it is not obvious why any potentially interested persons ought not in theory be able to avail themselves of the provision.

Whether the court has the power to intervene, of course, is a different question from whether the court ought to exercise such a power. The issue here is how one is to view the enduring power of attorney. The court in *R* emphasised its private law roots, and certainly it may well be the case that donors execute such powers in the expectation that it will leave the management of their affairs in the private sphere of the family. It is similarly arguable that those who wish their affairs administered by a particular person following incapacity should have that wish respected, and the court should not usurp that role. Further, an expansive reading of the court's power to intervene does reduce the distinctions between the enduring power of attorney process and receivership under the Court of Protection: if the attorney is not to have independent power, how are they in practice to be different from a receiver appointed under part VII of the Mental Health Act 1983? If a non-interventionist approach is adopted, as it is in *R*, it does emphasise the importance of the donor selecting an attorney who can be trusted to administer the estate as the donor would wish, since they will have a broad discretion, broadly free of court intervention.

Arguments may also be advanced for a more expansive view of the court's intervention. The protection of those lacking capacity has been understood as an appropriate role of the state for close to a millennium. It can be difficult to know how successful or appropriate an attorney will be in their role, until they have actually taken it up. Are we really to leave an unfortunate and incapacitated donor in the largely unmonitored control of the attorney? Are the other safeguards on enduring powers really so strong that we can rest assured that such powers cannot be used by the unscrupulous for self-advantage? If an attorney is sufficiently inept at his or her role, they may be removed on the ground of unsuitability and a receiver appointed, but this is an extreme outcome. Is there not space for some role of the court in supporting an attorney of mixed abilities in the exercise of their functions rather than removing them entirely, thereby more closely approximating the relations envisaged by the donor? And how, if not through the use of the court's directory powers, is this to be accomplished? The *R* case leaves a stark choice in the case of this sort of difficulty: remove the attorney and appoint a receiver, or live with the less-than-ideal administration. Is it at least arguable that a less severe use of s. 8, EPAA 1985 allows for a kinder middle ground, more in keeping with what the donor must presumably have wanted?

In order to execute an enduring power, the donor must of course have the mental capacity to do so. The Act makes no requirement of medical evidence to this effect, although it is of course prudent for such evidence to be collected at the time the power is signed, in cases of doubt. The meaning of incapacity in this context has been litigated in the case of *Re K, Re F* [1988] 1 All ER 358. In these cases, the donor was agreed to be incapable of managing their property and affairs at the time the power was signed, but understood the nature and effect of the power. The court upheld the powers, establishing the following test of capacity (at p. 363):

> What degree of understanding is involved? Plainly one cannot expect that the donor should have been able to pass an examination on the provisions of the 1985 Act. At the other extreme, I do not think that it would be sufficient if he realised only that it gave cousin William power to look after his property. Counsel as amicus curiae [for the Official Solicitor] helpfully summarised the matters which the donor should have understood in order that he can be said to have understood the nature and effect of the power: first, if such be the terms of the power, that the attorney will be able to assume complete control over the donor's affairs; second, if such be the terms of the power, that the attorney will in general be able to do anything with the donor's property which the donor could have done; third, that the authority will continue if the donor should be or become mentally incapable; fourth, that if he should be or become mentally incapable, the power will be irrevocable without the confirmation of the court.

There is certainly an appeal to this approach. Intuitively, there does seem to be a difference between understanding what an enduring power of attorney does, and understanding the full range of one's property and affairs and what needs to be done to maintain them. A donor may not understand the full range of their property, but still be perfectly aware that they want their child, for example, to manage the property in the event of their incapacity.

While the result of the court may be defensible and desirable, reaching the result is not nearly so easy, for as noted above, incapacity revoked a power of attorney at common law: *Drew* v *Nunn*. The reason for this would seem to be that the essence of the power is to allow the attorney to act for the donor. When the donor ceases to have a contracting mind, he or she cannot perform the acts the power purports to grant to the attorney. Therefore, the attorney can no longer perform them either, and the power is revoked (*Drew* v *Nunn*, p. 666). The argument in *K* was that the donor could not create a power which the law would have revoked. The court circumvents this argument by suggesting that the revocation in this context is metaphoric, since no actual act was performed by the donor to revoke it, and that a more accurate phrasing was that 'at least for some purposes the power ceased to have effect *as if* he had revoked it' (pp. 361, 364):

> The rule is therefore concerned with whether the power can be validly exercised rather than with its essential validity. Of course, for most purposes it will make no difference whether one says that the power has ceased to be exercisable or has become invalid. But the fact that the power cannot be validly exercised does not commit one to the proposition that it is for all purposes invalid.

This approach raises the issue of what the status of the power is in such circumstances at common law. Is it a valid power, but held in abeyance? Would the restoration of the donor to full capacity resurrect the authority of the attorney, since the power itself was valid but not exercisable? There is no suggestion of this in *Drew* v *Nunn*, where the donor did recover capacity. In that case, the court seemed to think that revoked meant revoked.

Even if this theoretical distinction is accepted, it is still not entirely adequate to reach the result in *K*, for at the time the powers in that case were signed, the donors did not have the legal ability to deal with their property. On the theory of *Drew* v *Nunn*, how could they purport to pass on to the agent powers which they did not have at the time the powers were signed? The court addressed this problem in the following terms (p. 362):

> In one sense Miss K did possess the powers to manage her property because she owned it. She could not exercise those powers on a regular basis because she lacked the mental capacity. But there is no logical reason why, though unable to exercise her powers, she could not confer them on someone else by an appropriate juristic act.

Surely this is sophistry. The force of the *Drew* judgment is that an attorney cannot do things which the donor cannot do. If that is the case, the distinction drawn by the court is specious: it would be contrary to *Drew* that the agent be able to exercise powers that the donor could not. It might, theoretically, be possible for the donor to grant the agent the powers of an incapacitated person over property, but it is difficult to see that such powers would be much use. Such an approach follows the old rule that a person lacking capacity to manage their affairs could not appoint an agent. This rule is contained in cases such as *Stead* v *Thornton* 3 B & Ad 357n and *Tarbuck* v *Bispham* 2 M & W 2 at p. 8, cases cited in argument to the court in *Drew* (p. 664), but apparently not to the court in *K*. Whatever the merits of the result in K, the reasoning is problematic.

In many ways, the enduring power of attorney is potentially an astonishingly flexible tool for those contemplating the possibility of incapacity. It may refer to all, or only to part of the donor's affairs. It may give instructions or set restrictions as to how those affairs are to be handled, although as seen in *Re R*, appropriate care should be taken in setting such restrictions. It may take effect immediately, as a regular power of attorney would, or may contain a clause that it is not to be effective until it is registered. While the power must not authorise an attorney to appoint a successor attorney, joint attorneys may be appointed by the power, allowing some mechanism to allow continuation of the power even after the death of one of the attorneys.

At the same time, there are complications in the use of the instrument. While in general it may be attractive to some clients because the involvement of the Court of Protection is minimised, the involvement of the Court cannot be excluded entirely. Unlike the provisions of part VII of the Mental Health Act 1983, where the Court of Protection becomes involved only in case of need, registration of the enduring power of attorney is mandatory, with the consequent supervision of the court that registration implies. In addition, as with any other power of attorney, the existence of the power does not of itself restrict the donor from acting on his or her own behalf. In some ways, this is a real advantage: the donor may retain control over those decisions for which they continue to have capacity. On the other hand, if capacity is lost, anyone contracting with the donor in good faith not knowing of the incapacity will be able to rely on the contract, suggesting that fairly intense supervision of the incapacitated person may be necessary to ensure that inappropriate contracts are not entered into. This is of course unnecessary with the appointment of a receiver under the Court of Protection procedures in the Mental Health Act 1983, for in that process, the patient loses the ability to contract: *In Re Marshall* [1920] 1 Ch 284.

11.3   THE LAW COMMISSION AND PROPOSALS FOR REFORM

The *F* case prompted an extended and detailed appraisal of the law relating to capacity by the Law Commission. Following four consultation documents, the Commission issued its final report in 1995 (Law Commission, 1995). The Commission's work and proposals received broadly, although not universally, favourable responses (Carson, 1993; Gunn, 1994; Fennell, 1994; Freeman, 1994; Parkin, 1995; Fennell, 1995; Bartlett, 1997). Nonetheless, the proposals were put out for further consultation with the publication of a green paper by the Lord Chancellor's Department in 1997 (Lord Chancellor's Department, 1997). The fate of the proposals thus remains unclear, although some indication of proposed government policy is expected in late 1999. While there is overwhelming consensus that the current state of affairs is in need of reform, the government has not formally indicated how closely the amendments will resemble the Law Commission's proposals, or indeed whether it is prepared to proceed with reform at all.

In essence, the Law Commission's proposals envisage three mechanisms at the core of the legal response to incapacity. The first can be seen as an extension of the *F* approach outside the medical sphere. Under a proposed general authority to act, any person would be empowered to make decisions in the best interests of a person lacking capacity. Secondly, two mechanisms would be available for the control by a competent person of decisions made during subsequent incapacity. First, an advanced directive precluding medical treatment of the sort used in the *C* case would be placed on statutory footing. Secondly, enduring powers of attorney (renamed continuing powers of attorney) would be continued, but expanded so that powers over personal as well as estate-related decisions may be included. Finally, a new court jurisdiction corresponding very broadly to the old *parens patriae* power would be introduced, incorporating both personal decision-making and the current Court of Protection, as well as serving to oversee the remainder of the system. All of these mechanisms would operate within statutory definitions of incapacity and best interests.

Several issues are completely excluded from the proposed authority to act: consent to marriage; consent to sexual relations; consent to a divorce petition based on two years of separation; agreement to an adoption order; voting in public elections; and the discharge of parental responsibilities other than those relating to the child's property. While the proposals go a long way into recovering jurisdiction to intervene in the personal decisions of individuals lacking capacity, there thus remain some things which are deemed to be sufficiently personal that decisions are better not made than made by an outside party.

11.3.1 The definition of incapacity

The gateway to the proposed reforms is the definition of incapacity. Much of this reflects themes discussed previously. Thus there is a presumption of capacity (Law Commission, 1995, para. 3.2), and the distinction between adults and children is maintained, with those under sixteen years of age outside the scope of the proposed reforms and instead continuing to be subject to the more general provisions of child law (para. 2.52).

Those unable to communicate a decision will be considered incapacitated, although this would take effect only if 'all practicable steps' have been taken to effect communication (Law Commission, 1995, draft Bill, cl. 2(1)(b), (5)). Otherwise the powers proposed by the Bill would take effect only if an individual were 'unable by reason of mental disability to make a decision for himself on the matter in question' (draft Bill, cl. 2(1)(a)). The Law Commission understands that this would impose a diagnostic threshold (para. 3.8). It is not obvious that this is the case, however, for 'mental disability' is not defined in diagnostic terms, but rather as 'a disability or disorder of the mind or brain, whether permanent or temporary, which results in an impairment or disturbance of mental functioning' (draft Bill, cl. 2(2)). Medical involvement or testimony is further not expressly required by the draft Bill prior to its provisions being acted upon. The Commission may thus have intended a diagnostic threshold, but it is not clear that this is reflected in the drafting of the Bill.

The desirability of such a threshold was the subject of some debate in the development of the Law Commission's proposals. David Carson in particular argued against such a threshold, arguing that it was inconsistent with the remainder of the proposed definitional structure, and risked in practical application pre-empting the more relevant, capacity-based aspects of capacity determination. Doctors are used to diagnostic criteria and in so far as they can be expected in practice to be powerful in capacity determination, the risk is that they would focus on their expertise, and marginalise the more important questions of the individual's ability to make decisions. Carson further pointed to the risk that those lacking capacity, but failing to meet a diagnostic threshold, would be left without the support of the Act, rhetorically asking 'Must everyone be open to exploitation and confusion unless we are prepared, and able, to claim the stigma of mental disorder?' (Carson, 1993, p. 313).

The Commission's response to Carson is not entirely convincing, since it claims in part that the diagnostic process 'would in no sense prejudice or stigmatise those who are in need of help with decision-making' (Law Commission, 1995, para. 3.8). Diagnosis of mental difficulties in some circumstances is clearly perceived by some people as profoundly stigmatising, suggesting that the Commission's claim is not obvious.

The other branch of the Commission's response is that the diagnostic threshold would 'provide a significant protection' (para. 3.8). The concern here would appear to be that the other branches of the test, relating to decision-making ability, may not be clear enough on their own to prevent the inappropriate use of the Bill's powers. The Bill specifically provides that a person will not be considered to lack capacity 'merely because he makes a decision which would not be made by a person of ordinary prudence' (draft Bill, cl. 2(4)). If one is to look beyond the result of the decision to the ability of the decision-maker, it is fair to ask which irrational or imprudent decisions will appropriately invoke the powers of the state. The requirement of a causal nexus between disability and decision provides some framework to consider this. Less obvious is that this needs to be a diagnostic conception of disability.

The draft Bill does further define the phrase 'unable to make a decision', in the following terms (in cl. 2(2)):

(a)   he is unable to understand or retain the information relevant to the decision, including information about the reasonably foreseeable consequences of deciding one way or another or of failing to make the decision; or
(b)   he is unable to make a decision based on that information.

No further guidance is provided on how the phrase 'information relevant to the decision' is to be understood, although the threshold is held to be understanding the information 'in broad terms and in simple language' (cl. 2(4)). This may perhaps suggest that, consistent with the C case, a relatively low level of understanding may suffice to attain capacity (see Gunn, 1994, p. 24). The draft Bill is further silent as to any duty to determine capacity at a time or in conditions where one might expect it to be optimal. While the ethos of the Law Commission reforms would suggest the desirability of reliance on decisions of the competent individual, the desirability of organising assessment to obtain such decisions does not appear to be reflected in concrete terms in the drafting of the statute.

Like the test in the current MHA 1983 and Code of Practice, this is a functional test, based ostensibly on the ability to understand, rather than actual understanding or actual appreciation. We have seen, however, the expansion of the test under that statute to include actual understanding and appreciation, and Gunn may well be right in querying whether the phrasing proposed by the Law Commission may be read in the same way (Gunn, 1994, p. 24). Clause 2(2)(b) similarly raises questions of interpretation. Will any decision based on the information suffice, or will some form of normative or other criteria be read into the sub-clause, validating some decisions and not others?

11.3.2   The definition of best interests

All decisions under the proposed powers would be taken in light of the individual's best interests. Clause 3(2) of the draft Bill would require that regard be had to the following in determining a person's best interests:

(a)   so far as ascertainable, his past and present wishes and feelings and
the factors he would consider if he were able to do so;

(b)   the need to permit and encourage that person to participate, or to
improve his ability to participate, as fully as possible in anything done for and
any decision affecting him;

(c)   if it is practicable and appropriate to consult them, the views as to
that person's wishes and feelings and as to what would be in his interests of—

(i)   any person named by him as someone to be consulted on those
matters;

(ii)   anyone (whether his spouse, a relative, friend or other person)
engaged in caring for him or interested in his welfare;

(iii)   the donee of any continuing power of attorney granted by him;

(iv)   any manager appointed for him by the court;

(d)   whether the purpose for which any action or decision is required can
be as effectively achieved in a manner less restrictive of his freedom of action.

No guidance is given as to how these factors ought to be weighed relative to one
another. Further, the list is not phrased restrictively, so that other factors
relevant to the individual's best interests may be considered.

The section is peculiar in its phrasing. It refers to both substance (the current
wishes of the individual, for example), and process (who needs to be consulted)
without distinction. It rolls together various models of decision-making, from
advance directive (the past wishes of the individual), perhaps to substitute
judgment (in the people who are to be consulted), to a presumption of minimal
intrusion. The failure to provide guidance as to how the factors and
information gleaned are to be weighted provides scope for considerable
flexibility to arrive at appropriate results in individual cases; but it also leaves a
lack of clarity as to what test is actually to be adopted. The risk, of course, is
that such a lack of clarity will allow the decision-maker to adopt such test as
they please. This difficulty is reinforced by cl. 3(3) of the draft Bill, which
allows sufficient compliance with the best interest standard if the decision-
maker 'reasonably believes that what he does or decides is in the best interests
of the person concerned.'. While this may relieve lay decision-makers of the
need for skills of statutory interpretation, it also risks removing much of the
directive authority of cl. 3(2).

The flexibility does have its advantages too, however, as may be seen in the
first subclause quoted above. As we have seen, and as the Commission
proposals would not change, capacity is a gatekeeping concept, determining
whether the individual retains authority over a given decision. As such, it is a
stark concept: for a given decision, either the individual keeps all authority for
the decision, or loses it all. The first paragraph quoted here goes a considerable
distance to soften that stark dichotomy, as the current wishes and feelings of the
incapacitated individual are to be taken into account in reaching a decision
about best interests. Clearly, if capacity is to be retained as a gatekeeping
concept, these wishes cannot be controlling of the decision, since that would
return authority over the decision to the individual who lacks capacity. At best,
they can be merely one factor in a larger selection, to be balanced by the

decision-maker in determining best interests. This is possible only in a flexible system, such as that proposed by the Commission.

The express inclusion of a right for the views of carers to be considered may provide a safeguard to the incapacitated person, but it also reflects a broadly sympathetic attitude of the Commission to carers in general. Here again, both advantages and disadvantages result. On the one hand, carers will often be the people most directly aware of the individual's needs and current and former wishes and feelings. On the other, as discussed above, the carer also has needs and feelings, and these may well be bound up with the decision relating to the incapacitated person, and may influence the carer's view of the best interests of the person. Again, the risks of a rigid system become apparent. If the views of carers as to best interests are to be taken into account, it is perhaps desirable that they should not necessarily be determinative.

11.3.3   The general authority to act

The general authority to act is created by cl. 4(1) of the proposed Bill:

> 4(1)   Subject to the provisions of this Chapter, it shall be lawful to do anything for the personal welfare or health care of a person who is, or is reasonably believed to be, without capacity in relation to the matter in question ('the person concerned') if it is in all circumstances reasonable for it to be done by the person who does it.

The remaining sub-clauses of cl. 4 allow the person making such a decision either to be reimbursed for the costs of these decisions, or to use funds or credit of the incapacitated person to pay for these decisions.

There are some restrictions on the proposed general authority. The powers of the section would not be able to overrule the authority of a court-appointed manager or donee of a continuing power of attorney (cl. 6); nor to authorise treatments within the scope of an advanced refusal of treatment (cl. 9); nor, by implication, to terminate artificial nutrition of those who are unconscious and lacking activity in the cerebral cortex (cl. 10). It would in general apply neither to non-therapeutic sterilisation treatments, nor to treatments involving the donation of non-regenerative tissue or bone marrow, and a power would be given to the Secretary of State to expand this list (cl. 7). The general authority could not be used to authorise acts to which the incapacitated person objected, nor to confine or detain the person (cl. 5). Second medical opinions as to best interests would further be required for treatments under s. 58 of the MHA 1983, the administration of medicine for mental disorder for more than three months, abortions, and therapeutic sterilisation operations, again with a power of the Secretary of State to expand this list (cl. 8).

It is with the general authority that the Commission is at its boldest and most innovative. Effectively, what they propose is the expansion of the decision-making structure in F, where doctors make necessary decisions on behalf of patients following appropriate consultation and consideration of best interests, to most personal decisions regarding incapacitated individuals. The proposal has considerable strengths. It is nearly infinitely flexible, allowing the individual to retain control over those decisions where they remain competent but allowing other decisions to be made with the minimum of administrative hassle. It reflects what is actually happening, in the sense that the move to increased community living is inevitably resulting in more decisions being taken by carers ranging from live-in family to well-meaning neighbours and friends on a relatively *ad hoc* basis. The legal status of these decisions is now at best complicated; the proposed Bill would place them on a firm legal footing.

While these advantages are significant, the proposed general authority to act has not been without its critics. Bartlett (1997) notes that there is no expectation that all decisions under the general authority will be taken by the same individual, leading to a potential lack of coordination between decision-makers, who may not even know of each other's existence. Similarly, it is not clear how a potential decision-maker under this power would know of the court orders or continuing power of attorney which would deprive them of authority. Particularly if the person exercising the power is not closely related to the individual, it is not clear how they would know enough about the financial situation of the individual to know whether some of the more significant interventions anticipated by the Law Commission under this power, such as replacing a roof, would be within the budget of the individual. There is no restriction on the decision-maker himself or herself receiving payment for goods or services rendered to the incapacitated individual, suggesting the risk of conflicts of interest. And here, as with many of the Law Commission's proposals, Bartlett argues that there are insufficient mechanisms of policing proposed, to ensure that the powers granted are being exercised effectively and appropriately.

Is Bartlett unduly alarmist? He is also the primary author of this Chapter, and thus obviously does not think so. To put the other side, however, the problems will be minimised if the procedural aspects of the best interests test, requiring communication between carers, work effectively and if those carers feel it appropriate to share necessary information. Yet it is appropriate to remember here that law operates as part of a broader social structure. Will persons with knowledge of the finances or life expectancy of an individual necessarily feel it appropriate to share that information with someone else, perhaps outside the family, who thinks (perhaps quite rightly) that a new roof is necessary? The proposal does not handle disagreement or lack of trust between carers particularly effectively. The best interest provisions appear to be directory only, and the views of other carers do not bind the decision-maker as to their view of the best interests of the incapacitated person. For doctors operating under *F*, there are professional disciplinary structures and employment hierarchies which can be brought into play to challenge decisions in a relatively informal and inexpensive way. Such mechanisms do not exist outside professional bodies. The only obvious control on these decisions is a court application, an expensive process for which legal aid may not be available.

The proposal is promising in cases where reasonable people make good decisions in good faith. The problems arise outside this protected realm. How frequently will people make bad decisions, albeit in good faith, relying on the general authority? How frequently will bad people take advantage? Will the stereotypical double glazing salesman for example really use the general authority to sell new windows to vulnerable old ladies of marginal capacity? Even if the draft Bill is enacted, we will not know the answer to these questions, for the general authority operates entirely in the private realm: we will not know on any systematic basis what decisions are being made, and therefore will have no way to judge the relative merits and demerits of its impact. The problem is deeper than such a statistical survey in any event. Even if, as will almost certainly be the case, the considerable bulk of decisions are good ones, is this sufficient? If the state is to grant powers to third parties over its most vulnerable citizens, is there not a corresponding political duty to ensure that these powers are exercised appropriately? Or, to put the reverse philosophical view, do we really trust the state to second-guess personal decisions made about vulnerable people by their friends, neighbours, and family — the people who know the vulnerable person best?

11.3.4   Advance directives and continuing powers of attorney

The Law Commission proposes that advance directives for medical treatment be placed on a statutory footing. Unlike the remainder of the proposed Act, which would apply to those aged sixteen and over, cl. 9 of the draft Bill would restrict advance directives to those who have reached eighteen years of age. If in writing, an advanced directive would be presumed to be validly made; but the draft Bill stops short of insisting that all such directives be in written form. Further, 'basic care', defined as care required to maintain bodily cleanliness or to alleviate severe pain, or the provision of direct oral nutrition and hydration, could not be refused by an advance directive (cl. 9(7), (8)). The presumption would be that the advanced refusal will not take effect if the failure to treat would endanger the life of the individual, or the life of the foetus if the individual is pregnant (cl. 9(3)). This is a rebuttable presumption, however, so that if the proposals are enacted, the presumption will not apply in the face of clear language indicating a contrary intent.

By comparison, continuing powers of attorney would have to be in writing, and in a prescribed form. Here again, both donor and donee must have attained eighteen years of age. The major departure from the existing law here is that the power would be able to cover personal decision-making, as well as property and financial decisions. While this could include medical consent, it could not preclude the provision of basic care as defined above. In addition, there are some alterations to the registration processes; for example only the donor, and not family members, would be required to be notified of the intent of the donee to register the power. As in the existing Enduring Powers of Attorney Act 1985, the court under the draft Bill would be given considerable power over attorneys. It remains to be seen whether the same restrictive reading of these provisions would be applied, as was the case in *Re R* (11.2.4).

As we have seen, the general rule about powers of attorney is that they create a power in the attorney, but do not of themselves remove the power from the donor. If the donor remains capable of making a specific decision, it may be made either by the attorney, or by the donor. Regarding health care, this dual authority would be restricted by the draft Bill. Notwithstanding registration of the power, the attorney could only consent to treatment if the donor were incapable of so doing. Whether or not the donor had capacity, the attorney could not informally admit the donor to a psychiatric facility over the donor's objection.

11.3.5   The new court jurisdiction

The Law Commission proposes a new court be created called the Court of Protection. Unlike the existing body of that name, which as we have seen functions more as an administrative office than as a court, this would be a superior court of record, staffed by judges. Its jurisdiction would subsume that of the current Court of Protection, but would also be expanded to include personal welfare decisions and health care matters. While perceived primarily as an option of last resort, when the other mechanisms proposed by the Bill have proven insufficient or unworkable, it would have authority over the administration of the whole incapacity system. Like the existing Court of Protection, it would have the authority to appoint managers, although such appointments would be limited to five years subject to renewal, and the appointments would be required to be as limited as possible in scope and duration. The power of the managers could of course reflect the court's increased jurisdiction into personal and health care decision-making.

Consistent with the view of the court as a place where unforeseen problems can be sorted out, the court is given very broad powers. While the court would be bound by an advance refusal of treatment, (cl. 26(2)(b)(ii)) it would not expressly be bound by the provisions of a continuing power of attorney. It would have express authority to make declarations relating to the capacity of an individual, and to determine the validity of advance refusals and continuing power of attorney (cl. 23); and to make orders or give directions as to decisions regarding a person without capacity, including all matters relating to personal welfare, health care, or property and affairs of the incapacitated person (cl. 24). The scope of these decisions would expressly include matters of where the person would live, contact with third parties, rights to obtain information on behalf of the individual, and the obtaining of benefits and services for the individual (cl. 25). Consent to medical treatment could be given or refused (except for basic care, as defined above, which could not be refused); doctors could be changed; and health records obtained. The powers relating to the property of the incapacitated person remain largely unchanged from the existing Mental Health Act powers, and in particular, the power to write a will on behalf of an incapacitated person remains.

Special provisions are proposed regarding admission to psychiatric facilities. Effectively, the court would be able to order the admission to psychiatric facilities if and only if the criteria for civil confinement were met, and the court were convinced of the appropriateness of the admission. Such an order would require two medical certificates in support, including at least one from a medical practitioner approved pursuant to s. 12 of the MHA 1983 (cl. 26(2),

(4)). The order of the court would take the place of the initial order and certificates of doctor and approved social worker under ss. 2 or 3 of the Mental Health Act 1983, but the individual would after admission be treated as if admitted under one of those sections, except that the nearest relative would not be permitted to apply for the patient's release under s. 66 of the MHA 1983.

The checks on these powers are, presumably, the standard due process safeguards which accompany full-scale court processes. While the experience of the last number of years makes it difficult to argue against a court process, the criticism of court decisions relating to people arguably lacking capacity over the same period suggests that vigilance will be required to ensure an appropriate standard of decision-making. This may in part be assisted by the appointment of a specialised bench, who may be expected to become increasingly expert in issues related to incapacity.

11.3.6 Conclusion

The revisions proposed by the Law Commission effectively respond to the lacuna in law left following the 1983 alterations to the Mental Health Act. The proposals have much to recommend them, and implementation of them, or something very much like them, is to be hoped for.

Considerable care was taken in an attempt to make the proposed processes dovetail with the existing Mental Health Act. Thus particular restrictions are imposed to ensure that people lacking capacity cannot be admitted against their will to psychiatric facilities, under the guise of informal admission. Treatments under s. 58 of the Mental Health Act 1983, which cannot be provided to patients lacking capacity, are similarly precluded by the proposed incapacity reforms. That said, it should be noted that the definition of mental disability was specifically designed not to match the definition of mental disorder in s. 1 of the Mental Health Act 1983, on the basis that the diagnostic criterion ought to be broader than a psychiatric criterion. It remains to be seen whether or not this will cause some confusion among practitioners.

While the reforms are wide-ranging in their sphere, it is equally appropriate to recognise what the proposals do not cover. Notwithstanding their comprehensiveness, they are in no way a complete code of incapacity law: the enforceability of contracts, the validity of marriages, the insanity defence, and other similar aspects of the law relating to incapacity will remain intact. While the laws relating to assignment of social security benefits to third parties would be modified by the proposals, they would continue to operate outside the incapacity statute, in their own social security framework. In this context, it is more appropriate to think of the proposals as affecting the law of guardianship, rather than the law of capacity *per se*. Even here, and assuming the proposals become law, it is not clear that the existing law will be able to be simply set aside. Minors, for example, will still be subject to the intricacies of existing child law, although from the age of sixteen, they will begin to be subject to the new rules as well. Similarly, if a diagnostic threshold is found to exist for the invocation of the new rules, then in so far as there is a group which lacks capacity but does not meet the diagnostic threshold, it is a nice question whether the common law as developed in cases such as *F* will continue to apply. To be fair, doctors can be adept at finding a medical label for a situation when required, suggesting cases of this sort would be expected to be rare indeed.

The fate of the proposals remains unclear. The current situation is broadly believed to be seriously flawed, a cobbled-together set of responses, *ad hoc* in form. The hesitancy of the previous government in enacting the reforms is said to concern alleged ethical difficulties relating to medical research on people lacking capacity, and euthanasia (Wilson, 1996, p. 228). This seems perverse. The proposals regarding medical research would ensure for the first time appropriate safeguards for incapacitated participants in research; and as we have seen, the proposals have nothing obvious to do with euthanasia at all. It would be a shame if these collateral diversions scupper the other, broadly desirable aspects of the reforms. It is to be hoped that the Commission's proposals, or something like them, will be introduced at some time in the near future. Time will tell.

TWELVE

Legal responses and advocacy for clients

12.1   INTRODUCTION

In conclusion, I may say that this seems to me one of the very cases which Parliament had in mind when they said that such an action as this should not be brought without the leave of the court. It is an unfortunate feature of mental illness that those afflicted by it do not realise the need for their being under the care and control of others. They resent it, much as a small child or a dumb animal resents being given medicine for its own good, and they are apt to turn round and claw and scratch the hand that gives it.

Richardson v *London County Council*
[1957] 1 WLR 751 at pp. 760–1, per Denning LJ

The quotation is shocking to readers at the end of the twentieth century. After thirty years of the politics of disability and patients' rights, Lord Denning's words may sound like reflections of a bygone era; but are they?

As we have seen in the preceding Chapters, there is no shortage of legal rules and standards contained in the MHA 1983, community care legislation and common law. These rules are of course relevant only if there are mechanisms in place to ensure that they are followed. The question underlying this Chapter is whether the law provides adequate mechanisms for those brought under the mental health system to ensure that they are dealt with consistently with the substantive and procedural rules provided by the law, and whether sufficient recompense is available in the event that the standards are not complied with.

In addition, as we have seen, involvement in the psychiatric system can impact fundamentally on the lives of individuals. The extreme example is institutionalisation, which affects all aspects of the individuals' lives: how they spend their time, what they eat, when and where they sleep, what treatment they receive, who they are permitted to have contact with, and so forth. Care in the community is less overtly controlling, but may nonetheless structure the lives of clients in particular ways. Much of this lies outside the scope of the legal or statutory standards, but nonetheless has a considerable impact on the individual's life. Lawyers who work with disadvantaged clients will recognise this sort of situation, where the client is concerned about a complex set of problems, where the legal and extralegal mix together in a tangled mass. This Chapter will also ask whether there is a role for law or for lawyers in addressing client dissatisfaction with these less expressly legal issues.

The legal forms of redress are primarily judicial review, civil or criminal actions, and the various complaints processes associated with NHS trusts. These will be examined in turn below. In the event that a lawyer, paralegal or other authorised person is to act on behalf of the client, involvement in any of these systems raises pragmatic issues of advocacy. Some of these will be examined at the end of the Chapter.

12.2 MENTAL HEALTH REVIEW TRIBUNALS AND JUDICIAL REVIEW

These remedies have been discussed at many points in this text (see, primarily, 5.5, 8.4–8.7). The objective here is not to repeat that substantive discussion, but instead to summarise what these remedies can do in a mental health context.

12.2.1 Mental health review tribunals

Although mental health review tribunals (MHRTs) have substantial powers, their jurisdiction is purely statutory. There is no jurisdiction to consider matters beyond those listed in ss. 66 and 70, MHA 1983. The tribunal system's governing legislation is not geared to require a patients' rights approach. Thus a tribunal is required to release a detained patient only if the patient demonstrates that the confinement criteria are not met. The onus is on the patient to show an error, rather than on the doctor or hospital manager to justify the decision in question. That said, MHRTs do have a discretion to release patients, even if the confinement criteria are met. While this does not require a patients' rights approach, it gives advocates scope for argument that the patient should be released, notwithstanding the terms of the statute.

The discretion given to MHRTs rarely results in an unqualified release, but an MHRT can recommend the grant of a leave of absence to an unrestricted patient, or the transfer of the patient to another hospital or into guardianship, or into after care under supervision: ss. 72(3), 72(3A), and can further consider the case in the event that these recommendations are not complied with. Again, this allows some flexibility of outcome, which may work for or against the patient. Yet as seen in Chapter eight, the indications are that the tribunals are extraordinarily sympathetic to the doctors' positions. Moreover, many issues important to patients are not within the remit of MHRTs. Tribunals have no direct role in determination of appropriateness of treatment, for example, or inappropriate living conditions in the facility. While in theory these are matters that could be considered under a tribunal's general discretion to release an individual from confinement, this would be an extraordinarily tangential way to approach disagreements regarding treatment or conditions.

The Mental Health Review Tribunal Rules do contain some basic due process provisions, such as right to notice (r. 20), the right to representation (r. 10), and the duty on MHRTs to give reasons for their decisions: r. 23 (see 8.4.3, 8.6). Several of these rules are, at best, problematic. Rule 11 requires the medical member of the tribunal to be both witness and judge. The exceptions and limitations in r. 12, relating to the disclosure of documents to the patient and/or his authorised representative, may considerably restrict the ability of advocates to determine the truth of factual allegations contained in any document disclosed with the r. 12(3) limitation (that the information must not be disclosed to the client: see 8.4.3), since an advocate may be unable to verify the accuracy of statements without disclosing the information in question to his or her client. Similarly, it would seem very difficult to ask other persons who might be able to confirm or deny the information about its veracity, since it is difficult in practice to see how this could be accomplished without disclosing the content of the document.

Rule 12(3) can therefore drive a wedge between advocate and client. The difficulty was recognised in the Ontario case of *Re Egglestone and Mousseau and Advisory Review Board* (1983) 42 OR (2d) 268 (at p. 276):

I would expect that faced with the order made here counsel should obtain the consent of his client to accept the documentary review on this limited basis, otherwise he may not feel at liberty to receive the information at all.

Such instructions in advance cannot be perceived as a solution, however. Either the client refuses the disclosure on this basis, in which case neither advocate nor client will know the information and it is difficult to see how the case can properly be argued; or the client consents, and the advocate will know information which will inform decision-making which the client will not know, furthering the marginalisation and disempowerment of the client. In this latter scenario, the result may be little short of Kafka: the client will be asked for instructions on the conduct of the case, without being able to be told why the instructions are being asked for.

12.2.2 Judicial review

As has been seen at various points throughout this book, both judicial review and habeas corpus are potentially powerful mechanisms by which to challenge decisions made by those who implement mental health services, both in hospital and in the community. But as has also been seen, both are of limited effect, and if the decision of the Court of Appeal in *Barker* (see 5.5.4) is anything to go by, it seems that the availability of habeas corpus will become increasingly limited in the future. Despite our misgivings about such a development, judicial review is of potentially broad scope, extending to any statutory power of decision. There have been some notable victories using judicial review by those seeking access to community services, although overall it can be said that the courts have more often than not failed to take a stance that is likely to empower clients or give their advocates much scope to challenge decisions (see 9.3). As far as in-patients are concerned, both the decisions of

MHRTs and of individual doctors, social workers and others made pursuant to MHA 1983 are subject to review. Thus in *Hallstrom* (see 8.2), the detention of a patient under s. 3 was successfully challenged on the basis that one of the medical reports did not represent the true view of the doctor: see also Gunn (1986a, p. 292). The amenability of individual certifications or opinions by doctors to judicial review makes this, in theory at least, a particularly useful tool for the enforcement of the statute, but for reasons not immediately obvious, it does not appear to have been used to challenge the sometimes somewhat perfunctory second opinions pursuant to s. 58 of the 1983 Act, for example. Indeed, there seems to be no reason why treatment decisions made pursuant to s. 63 during the first three months of a patient's detention should not be amenable to judicial review. Hence there is reason to think that the potential of judicial review from the point of view of patients and their advocates is to date far from being fully exploited, and the passage of the Human Rights Act 1998 gives further scope for arguments in judicial review proceedings based on the terms of the European Convention of Human Rights.

Several limitations of judicial review must be noted, however. To begin with, remedies are discretionary: a prima facie case by an applicant will not necessarily result in relief (see 5.5). Secondly, the courts are content to accord specialist tribunals such as the MHRTs considerable latitude both in their findings of fact and, to a lesser degree, in their interpretation of their constitutive legislation. Similarly, if the decisions regarding treatment under s. 63 are judicially reviewable, it is difficult to imagine the court establishing a threshold beyond 'reasonableness' to satisfy judicial scrutiny, although this might still leave some room for argument in cases of medication beyond recommended maximum dosages, for example. Finally, judicial review will only be available when there is a statutory power of decision: decisions occurring outside the statute will not be within its scope.

The review tribunal process, habeas corpus, and judicial review all have their place in assuring that the standards contained in the various legislation are applied. They do little to affect decisions made regarding patients or situations not directly subject to legislation, however. They have virtually no application, for example, to informal hospital in-patients. Further, while they may ensure that decisions are corrected after they are made, they are unlikely to provide recompense in damages for the results of such decisions, nor do they hold individuals directly responsible. That is the function of civil and criminal law, and it is to those areas that this Chapter now turns. There are, as we have seen, numerous statutes applicable to the care and treatment of mentally disordered persons. The following discussion will focus on the relevant provision of the MHA 1983, but the points made here also provide a flavour of the issues relevant to statutory provisions regarding civil and criminal liability more generally.

12.3   CONTROLLING THE STARTING GATE: S. 139

Section 139, MHA 1983 provides:

139   (1)   No person shall be liable, whether on the ground of want of jurisdiction or on any other ground, to any civil or criminal proceedings to

which he would have been liable apart from this section in respect of any act purporting to be done in pursuance of this Act or any regulations or rules made under this Act, or in, or in pursuance of anything done in, the discharge of functions conferred by any other enactment on the authority having jurisdiction under Part VII of this Act, unless the act was done in bad faith or without reasonable care.

(2)   No civil proceedings shall be brought against any person in any court in respect of any such act without the leave of the High Court; and no criminal proceedings shall be brought against any person in any court in respect of any such act except by or with the consent of the Director of Public Prosecutions.

These subsections do not apply to actions against the Secretary of State, health authorities or NHS trusts (s. 139(4), as amended by the National Health Service and Community Care Act 1990, s. 66(1), sch. 9, para. 24(7)), nor to offences for which leave of the Director of Public Prosecutions is already required as condition precedent to prosecution: s. 139(3). Nonetheless, s. 139 does limit recourse by patients against those who control them. For this reason, the scope and effects of the section should be analysed with some care.

12.3.1   Scope

Section 139 expressly applies to both criminal and civil matters, and to actions taken relating to the management of the property and affairs of the patient under part VII of the statute. Regarding the part VII protection, the section would seem broad enough to cover both persons involved in applications to invoke the jurisdiction of the Court of Protection, and receivers and others putting the orders of that body into effect. It does not apply to judicial review: *Hallstrom*, see 8.2. The logic here is that notwithstanding that judicial review applications are heard in the civil court structure, they do not determine 'liability' for decisions, but rather correctness of decisions ([1985] 3 All ER 775 at pp. 783, 784).

The provisions extend, not merely to acts actually done pursuant to the statute but also to acts purporting to be done pursuant to the statute. The leading case here is *Poutney* v *Griffiths* [1976] AC 314 (HL). As will be recalled from 7.4.2.1, the case concerned the use of restraint by a nurse in ushering a patient back to his ward at the end of a visit from his family. The patient alleged that he had been assaulted by the nurse, and the nurse, although claiming that he had only lightly brushed against the patient, was duly convicted. The House of Lords held that the conviction could not stand as the events occurred in pursuance of the statute, and therefore there could be no proceedings without leave having first been obtained. The court noted that the detention of an individual in hospital necessarily involved the exercise of control and discipline, as a necessary corollary to the administration of treatment (see 7.3.2.1.1). This would perhaps be uncontroversial if the nurse's version of the facts were accepted; but it is at best doubtful that they were so accepted by the triers of fact at first instance. It is far less obvious that an unprovoked punch, as was the case in the patient's version of events, is appropriately considered part of the exercise of control and discipline. That said, could it be seen to be an act '*purporting* to be done' in pursuance of the legislation? The view of the House of Lords is extraordinarily expansive on the scope of s. 139(1), particularly when combined with the expansive readings of 'medical treatment' which have flowed from s. 145.

The current view is that s. 139 refers only to detained patients, not to those admitted informally: *R* v *Runighian* [1977] Crim LR 361. This authority is merely the Crown Court level, suggesting some hesitation is appropriate before uncritical reliance is placed upon it. The summary of the case in the *Criminal Law Review* is brief, but it suggests that the decision was reached on the basis that s. 5 of the 1959 Act, now s. 131 of the 1983 Act, did not mandate the admission of informal patients; it merely indicated that the statute did not preclude such admissions. Informal admissions were instead by private arrangement. Such a reading would of course not apply to situations where the statute specifically governs informal patients, such as the treatment safeguards contained in s. 57. More generally, the reading is not obviously consistent with *R* v *Kirklees MBC ex parte C* [1992] FLR 117, discussed in Chapter four, where the court appears to see s. 131 and private arrangements as creating separate admission routes, with the bulk of informal patients admitted pursuant to s. 131. Nevertheless, as the possibility of admission pursuant to s. 131 was not disputed in that case, the argument may still be open.

Also problematic will be the issue of when an individual living in the community falls outside the scope of the Act, so as to render s. 139 inoperative. Clearly, the creation of a plan for after care pursuant to s. 117 of a person formerly detained under the Act and about to be released will be within the scope of the section. Will the performance of the after care, as distinct from the formation of the plan for after care, also fall within the scope of the section? The preferable view would be not, in so far as the individual has been released from the facility and is a regular individual in the community, separate from the facility. In reality, such a clean split is unlikely to occur. If the individual is not simply released, but subjected to after care under supervision under s. 25A, then the implementation of the care plan under s. 25D would appear to be caught by s. 139. If the discharged individual is not subjected to a s. 25A order, he or she is still likely to remain an out-patient. Should out-patients be covered by the section? It would seem not. They have no status under the Act, and it is therefore difficult to see that they can be treated pursuant to it. If an out-patient is actually a detained patient on leave of absence pursuant to s. 17, however, a much closer nexus to the Act is present, and the applicability of s. 139 is considerably more likely.

Prosecutions of offences under the MHA 1983, which already may be only instituted by or with the consent of the Director of Public Prosecutions are not subject to the section: s. 139(3). This currently applies only to offences under s. 127, concerning ill treatment or wilful neglect of patients.

The section covers not merely events in purported compliance with the legislation, but also with 'any regulations or rules' made under the statute. This extension will be particularly important for matters flowing from review tribunal proceedings and applications before the Court of Protection, both of which are regulated to a considerable degree by statutory instruments. It is a nice question whether purported reliance on the Code of Practice brings a defendant within the protection of the section. Often, the question will be merely academic, since acts performed within the guidance of the Code will be sufficiently related to some authority in the statute that a plea of *purported* pursuance of the statute will be successful. In the event that informal patients are deemed to be admitted and treated outside the statute, however, there may still be an issue as to whether their admission, treatment and management as advised in the Code of Practice renders the section applicable. Alternatively, it is perhaps arguable that the applicability of many of the provisions of the Code to informal patients suggests that these patients are treated pursuant to the statute, rather than as a result of the private arrangements by which they were admitted.

Section 139 refers specifically to 'acts' performed in purported pursuance of the statute. It is another nice question as to whether acts include omissions in this context. Jaconelli and Jaconelli (1998, p. 153) argue that it does not. If that is correct, it would be the case that failure to treat would be outside the scope of the section, but maltreatment would be within it, for example. While this seems counterintuitive, the section is quite clear in its reference to 'any act purporting to be done'; it is not obvious that this wording can conveniently include omissions.

The section will, of course, be relevant to patients and former patients who wish to pursue remedies against those administering the legislation. The wording does not limit the category of plaintiff to whom it applies, however. Thus the section will also apply to a plaintiff suing for example on the basis that an individual acted negligently in allowing a detained patient to escape, when that escape results in an assault on the plaintiff: see *In re Shoesmith* [1938] 2 KB 637.

12.3.2   Leave to commence an action

The immediate effect for a plaintiff or complainant whose action falls within s. 139 is that leave must be sought to commence the action. In the case of a criminal matter, consent must be sought from (or the prosecution instituted by) the Director of Public Prosecutions. For a civil action, it is the leave of the High Court that is required. The requirement for leave to be granted is that the plaintiff demonstrate that the act complained of was done in bad faith, or without reasonable care: s. 139(1).

The section might loosely be understood as creating standards relating both to the defendant's conduct and to the appropriateness of the plaintiff's case. On the one hand, there is a sense that people charged with the administration of the MHA 1983 should not be held liable because they genuinely and in good faith make a mistake in their duties. This approach is manifest, for example, in *Richardson* v *London County Council* [1957] 1 WLR 751 (at p. 760):

Parliament has wisely provided that he [the plaintiff] is not to be allowed to bring an action of this kind unless there is substantial ground for believing them [the officers who confined the plaintiff] to have been guilty of want of good faith or want of reasonable care. . . . [A]lthough these public authorities may have misconstrued the Act and although they may have done things which there was no jurisdiction to do, nevertheless, so long as they acted in good faith and in a reasonable manner, they are to be protected from having actions brought against them.

While the need for 'substantial' grounds must be read in the context of subsequent statutory reform and case law, the remainder of the comment continues to reflect one judicial approach to the section. In general, wrongful confinement is a tort of strict liability; an action will succeed whenever a detention is unlawful. Section 139 may therefore be understood as precluding otherwise winnable cases. As Jaconelli and Jaconelli point out, this alteration will be particularly significant in torts of strict liability, such as breach of statutory duty, false imprisonment, and battery (1998, p. 154). It will be less likely to be significant when the action is in negligence, since a want of due care forms a part of the action in these cases in any event. Even in these cases, as Hoggett (1996, p. 250) points out, there are residual disadvantages. The plaintiff must approach receive leave from a High Court judge, even if the claim is in the jurisdiction of the county courts; and at that hearing, they have the burden to show that the case should continue.

The section also looks to the plaintiff, on a longstanding assumption that those with histories of mental health difficulties will be more likely than the general public to sue unreasonably and with unwinnable cases. It was to these claims that Lord Denning referred in the quotation with which this Chapter commenced. In this context, the section can be seen to overlap considerably with the restrictions already available to the courts relating to claims having no real prospect of success: see Civil Procedure Rules, r. 24.2. Indeed as Hoggett suggests, given the existence of these rules, it is not obvious that this aspect of the section is necessary or desirable (1996, p. 250):

> Only a minority of patients, even of those compulsorily detained, are suffering from disorders which make it at all likely that they will harass other people with groundless accusations. Rather more of them are suffering from disorders which make it likely that they will not complain at all, even if they have every reason to do so. . . . There is no evidence that the floodgates would open if section 139 were entirely repealed. There is more evidence, from a series of reports and investigations, that mental patients are in a particularly powerless position which merits, if anything, extra safeguards rather than the removal of those available to everyone else.

The recent trend seems at least at first blush to be to restrict the application of s. 139, and thus to provide the plaintiff with increased access to the courts. This is in part the result of changes to the wording of s. 139(2) in the 1983 legislation. Where the 1959 Act had required a potential plaintiff to demonstrate a 'substantial ground' for the contention that the potential defendant had acted in bad faith or without reasonable care, that requirement was removed from the 1983 legislation. The leading case is *Winch v Jones* [1985] 3 All ER 97 (CA). Lord Donaldson MR identified the problems the section is intended to address in the following fashion (pp. 100, 101):

> To be more specific, there are two fundamental difficulties. First, mental patients are liable, through no fault of their own, to have a distorted recollection of facts which can, on occasion, become pure fantasy. Second, the diagnosis and treatment of mental illness is not an exact science and severely divergent views are sometimes possible without any lack of reasonable care on the part of the doctor. The intention of Parliament, as it seems to me, was quite clearly that no one should be prevented from making a valid claim that they have suffered by reason of negligence in the exercise of powers conferred by the Mental Health Acts and that no one should be harassed by an invalid claim.

Thus both the aspects of the section discussed above were noted. His Lordship then addressed the standard by which the court should decide whether leave ought to be granted (p. 102):

> As I see it, the section is intended to strike a balance between the legitimate interests of the applicant to be allowed, at his own risk as to costs, to seek the adjudication of the courts on any claim which is not frivolous, vexatious or an abuse of the process and the equally legitimate interests of the respondent to such an application not to be subjected to the undoubted exceptional risk of being harassed by baseless claims by those who have been treated under the Mental Health Acts. In striking such a balance, the issue is not whether the applicant has established a prima facie case or even whether there is a serious issue to be tried, although that comes close to it. The issue is whether, on the materials immediately available to the court, which, of course, can include material furnished by the proposed defendant, the applicant's complaint appears to be such that it deserves the fuller investigation which will be possible if the intended applicant is allowed to proceed.

While the onus therefore remains on the plaintiff, it is necessary to meet only a relatively low threshold in order for leave to be granted. This is consistent with the procedures for the hearing of the application. Affidavit evidence from both parties may be considered (*Carter v Metropolitan Police Commissioner* [1975] 1 WLR 507), but it is not to be turned into a trial on the affidavit evidence, and Parker LJ in *Winch v Jones* holds that cross-examination on that evidence ought never to be permitted (p. 103). Affidavits might show that 'some allegation made by an intending plaintiff is totally refuted by incontrovertible evidence', but he was unwilling to go much further in interrogating the merits of the case. For Parker LJ the appropriate standard was whether there was a 'reasonable suspicion that the authority had done something wrong' (at p. 103).

The approach in *Winch* is intended to keep the leave application from turning into a full scale trial. While that end is laudable, it does raise possible difficulties. For example, if the relatively low threshold and summary investigation process required by *Winch* is relied upon, can the standards contained in s. 139(1) be relied upon as the case progresses and more facts become available? For the vexatious plaintiff, this is likely to be an academic problem, for the granting of leave under s. 139(2) does not preclude an application to strike the proceedings as frivolous or vexatious at a later point in the process: *X v A, B and C and the MHAC* (1991) 9 BMLR 91. If instead the facts show that there was no want of reasonable care, a negligence action can be dismissed either at trial or on summary judgment.

If instead the action is for wrongful confinement, for example, the question arises as to whether s. 139(1) actually alters the nature of the tort, or merely provides a procedural safeguard at the beginning of the process. In the event that leave is granted, does the eventual trial include the bad faith or want of due care provisions as a part of the substance of the tort that the plaintiff must demonstrate? Or once leave is granted, does the tort revert back to its usual rules, where any illegal confinement can yield damages? The law is not clear on this point. The cases in which s. 139 have been cited have been leave cases, not final trials, and the section is generally understood to be about leave to bring an action, not the nature of the law once the action is brought. This is consistent with the precise wording of s. 139(1), which refers to whether the defendant ought to be liable 'to proceedings'. In that event, the issues of bad faith or want of reasonable care must be considered at the leave application, if they are to be considered at all; and a relatively low threshold of consideration for leave to be granted does work to the continuing advantage of the plaintiff.

12.3.3   Section 139 and vicarious liability

The issue of the precise, technical effect of the section is relevant also because it may affect the liability of the defendants' employers. In general, employers are liable for the torts of employees acting within the scope of their employment, through the doctrine of vicarious liability. This is of course a separate matter from direct liability of employer in situations where a tort performed by an employee is not involved, such as a failure by an NHS trust to maintain a building adequately, or to provide adequate staffing for a facility. In such situations of direct liability, only the employer will be liable. In situations of vicarious liability, liability will be joint: both employer and employee will be liable, as would be the case when leave is given pursuant to s. 139 and a plaintiff is successful in their suit. In most cases, the employer of the doctors and nurses charged with the administration of the MHA 1983 will be a health authority or NHS trust, parties specifically excluded from the protection of s. 139. The question therefore arises as to whether the employers can remain vicariously liable, notwithstanding that leave is not granted under s. 139 to sue the doctor or nurse individually.

The arguments turn on whether vicarious liability is a 'master tort' or a 'servant tort'. If the former, vicarious liability of the employer is based on a theory that the employee acts on express or implied instructions of the employer, and therefore the tort of the employee is equally the tort of the employer. If the latter, the liability is based solely on the tort of the employee, and the liability of the employer is some form of indemnity flowing from the employment relationship.

The standard view in English tort law texts is that vicarious liability is a servant tort (Jones, 1998, p. 376; Stanton, 1994, p. 128; Rogers, 1994, pp. 593–4, 620–2). These accounts tend to rely to a considerable degree on *Imperial Chemical Industries Ltd* v *Shatwell* [1965] AC 656 (HL). In that case, it has to be said, the view was stated by all five Law Lords that unless the servant could be held liable in damages, the employer could not be. That said, the facts in that case were rather unusual, and there are still occasional judicial pronouncements to the contrary: see, e.g., *Twine* v *Bean's Express Ltd* [1946] 1 All ER 202; *Norton* v *Canadian Pacific Steamships* [1961] 1 WLR 1057 at p. 1063. The possibility that vicarious liability remains a master tort was specifically left open by Henry J in *Furber* v *Kratter* (1988) unreported (HC), a case involving inappropriate solitary seclusion in a psychiatric facility, allegedly without nursing care and without clothing, reading or writing material, where leave was sought pursuant to s. 139. If, following the opening left in *Furber*, vicarious liability is perceived as a master tort, the employer might well remain liable, notwithstanding the unavailability of an action against the employee because of s. 139.

This line of argument is complicated by the fact that in some parts of the MHA 1983 duties are vested directly in employees such as approved social workers or medical officers. Specific statutory duties are not generally delegable. It becomes problematic to adopt a theory of implied instructions from employer to employee, when the employee and not the employer is charged with the duties alleged to be violated.

Even if vicarious liability is a servant tort, that does not necessarily end the matter. If, as was argued to be a possibility above, s. 139 does not alter the substantive law but instead merely removes an action for damages against some people, the tort arguably continues to exist. Just because (in the absence of bad faith or a want of reasonable care) an individual doctor cannot be sued for wrongful confinement, the argument would go, it does not necessarily follow that the tort has ceased to exist, but merely that one of the parties cannot be sued for it: see Jaconelli and Jaconelli (1998, p159). The issues here would seem to be first, the degree to which s. 139 does in fact affect substantive law; and second, whether the employer can be called upon to indemnify damages for which the employee has not been found liable.

Can this arrangement of split liability reflect the legislative intent of the section? While such an intent may seem improbable Jaconelli and Jaconelli point to the fact that the subsection removing health authorities and the Secretary of State from the scope of the provision was drafted as the case of *Ashingdane* v *UK* neared the European Court of Human Rights, challenging the authority of the predecessor of s. 139. While both the Commission recommendation, reported at (1984) 6 EHRR 69 and the eventual court decision, (1985) 7 EHRR 528, upheld the predecessor of s. 139, it was more reluctant to do so for the health authority and government than it was for individual members of staff. Jaconelli and Jaconelli argue that the exclusion of health authorities and the Secretary of State from the scope of the section is to be read in that context. If this is correct, the continued liability of the Secretary of State and health authorities (along, now, with NHS trusts) can be seen as consistent with legislative intent.

12.4   CRIMINAL PROSECUTIONS

Subject to the provisions of s. 139, the regular criminal law continues to apply to those contained in the mental health system. In addition, however, the MHA 1983 provides its own, additional offences in part IX of the Act.

Section 126 provides penalties of up to two years' imprisonment and an unlimited fine for persons who without lawful authority or excuse possess documents relating to the administration of the Act which they know or believe to be false. While the documents to which the section applies are specified in s. 126(3), the class is quite broad, including applications under part II, medical or other recommendations or reports under the Act, and 'any other document required or authorised to be made for any of the purposes of this Act.'. The actual deception by the person creating the document remains under the broader criminal law; this section makes it an offence knowingly to possess such documents.

Section 128 makes it an offence to induce or knowingly assist detained persons to absent themselves without leave. The provision extends not merely to those detained under part II of the Act, but also to persons detained in a place of safety under s. 137, and also to those subject to guardianship under s. 7. Similarly, the harbouring of individuals absent without leave, or assisting them to prevent their recapture, is made an offence. Section 129 essentially makes it an offence to interfere with inquiries and inspections authorised by the Act. The interferences prohibited are listed specifically in the section: refusing to allow the inspection of premises; refusing to allow access to or visiting, interviewing, or examination of persons; refusing to produce records and documents; and refusing to withdraw when an interview is permitted under the Act to be held in private.

Section 127 creates a number of offences related to the ill-treatment or wilful neglect of patients. Managers, officers and staff of hospitals and mental nursing homes can be held liable for ill-treating or wilfully neglecting persons receiving treatment as in-patients of those facilities. These individuals can similarly be held liable regarding ill-treatment or wilful neglect on the premises of out-patients on receiving treatment at the hospital or mental nursing home: s. 127(1). The offences in s. 127(1) are restricted to the staff of the facilities in question. Not so the remaining offences provided in the section. Section 127(2) is broader still:

It shall be an offence for any individual to ill-treat or wilfully to neglect a mentally disordered patient who is for the time being subject to his guardianship under this Act or otherwise in his custody or care (whether by virtue of any legal or moral obligation or otherwise).

This applies to any individual who cares for another who is mentally disordered, be it through guardianship or otherwise. Thus in *R v Newington* (1990) Cr App R 247 (CA), the statute was applied to the owner of a residential home for the elderly. There was no doubt that the section could apply to her, although the mental disorder of the individuals allegedly ill-treated had to be demonstrated (p. 254).

While s. 127(2) will be of particular relevance for those living in the community and in facilities other than those identified in s. 127(1), it is also presumably broad enough to encompass many of the situations contained in s. 127(1). The elements of the offences are nonetheless somewhat different. Section 127(2) requires proof of the mental disorder of the individual, and of a specific relation between the accused and the individual — guardian, custodian or carer. Section 127(1) requires a patient/staff relationship in a hospital or mental nursing home, and, it would seem from the wording of the subsection, that the individual is 'receiving treatment for mental disorder'. The current trends in case law would seem to be according a markedly broad interpretation to the phrase 'treatment for mental disorder', suggesting that it may not be a high hurdle for a prosecutor to leap; nonetheless, in the event of ill-treatment of an individual not actually receiving such treatment, s. 127(2) might be considered, in the event that the complainant is mentally disordered and in the care of the potential accused.

Section 127(2A) inserted by the Mental Health (Patients in the Community) Act 1995, s. 2(1), sch. 1, para. 18, is broader still:

It shall be an offence for any individual to ill-treat or wilfully to neglect a mentally disordered patient who is for the time being subject to after care under supervision.

Here, no express relationship is implied between the potential defendant and the patient. Indeed, it is not even expressly required that the defendant know that the individual is mentally disordered and subject to after care under supervision, although proof of those facts would undoubtedly be required to make out the offence. Curiously, this provides people subject to after care under supervision to wider protection than those subject to guardianship under s. 7. While ill-treatment or wilful neglect of either by a carer would found a remedy, additional protection to those subject to guardianship is within the remit of s. 127(2), which prohibits ill-treatment or wilful neglect only by their guardians. The lives of those subject to each form of control in the community may be quite similar; it is not obvious why the punitive sanctions against those abusing them ought to be different.

Common to all the s. 127 offences is the phrase 'ill-treat or wilfully to neglect'. The leading case on the meaning of this phrase is *Newington*. In that case, the Court of Appeal held that ill treatment should be pleaded separately from wilful neglect, as the latter would require consideration of a particular state of mind, where the former would not (p. 252). The nature of the state of mind was not particularly articulated, as *Newington* was a case of ill-treatment. The court summed up the elements of this aspect of the offence in the following terms (at p. 254):

In our judgment the judge should have told the jury that for there to be a conviction of ill-treatment contrary to the Act of 1983 the Crown would have to prove (1) deliberate conduct by the appellant which could properly be described as ill-treatment irrespective of whether this ill-treatment damaged or threatened to damage the health of the victim and (2) a guilty mind involving either an appreciation by the appellant at the time that she was inexcusably ill-treating a patient or that she was reckless as to whether she was inexcusably acting in that way.

The court held that a case may be made out notwithstanding no actual injury or unnecessary suffering or injury to health was caused (p. 253). This suggests a relatively wide scope to 'ill-treatment'. Michael Gunn (1990, p. 361) has suggested that it could well be wide enough to include inadequate feeding or heating, the use of harsh words or bullying. Violence does not necessarily constitute ill treatment if it was used, for example 'for the reasonable control of a patient' (*Newington*, at p. 253). From the earlier case of *R* v *Holmes* [1979] Crim LR 52, it is clear that the offence can be made out from a single assault; a course of conduct is not necessary.

Proceedings under s. 127 must be instituted by, or with leave of, the Director of Public Prosecutions (DPP): s. 127(4). The effect of this provision is to take s. 127 offences outside the scope of s. 139. Thus s. 127 prosecutions may be commenced without proof of bad faith or want of due care.

Local social service authorities are given specific authority to 'institute proceedings' for all the offences in part IX by s. 130, although this is 'without prejudice to any provision of this Part of this Act requiring the consent of the Director of Public Prosecutions for the institution of such proceedings.'. The effect of this caveat is ambiguous. To begin with what is clear, local social service authorities have standing to prosecute the offences under the Act. They must also seek consent of the DPP to institute a prosecution under s. 127, the only section in part IX where such consent is expressly required. The ambiguity arises in the interface between ss. 130 and 139. Does the authority to 'institute proceedings' mean an authority to institute such proceedings without the leave of the DPP otherwise required by s. 139(2)? The specific maintenance of the role of the DPP 'under this Part' could be taken to imply a modification of that officer's role under s. 139, which is contained in a different part of the Act. On this reading, s. 139 would not apply. At the same time, s. 139(3) specifically exempts from its remit part IX offences which the DPP must already institute or consent to the institution of. This implicitly brings the remaining part IX offences under the scope of s. 139(2), and there is nothing which would remove the local social services authority from that subsection. It is not clear which of these readings the courts would adopt.

In some cases, the issue will be academic. It is difficult to see how leave would be required under s. 139 for an action against an individual who assists another to escape, for example, even given the broadest interpretation of acts 'purporting to be done in pursuance of this Act'. In other cases, the matter will be effectively a procedural nicety. It is difficult to see how an individual who knowingly makes false statements on an admission application can be said to be acting other than in bad faith, suggesting the grant of leave under s. 139 would be a formality. Cases may well be more complicated, however. The obstruction offences contained in s. 129 provide an example. Arguably, these may involve imperfect compliance with the Act, and a misguided view of the law by the potential defendant. Prima facie, s. 139 might provide a defence, if prosecutions by the local social services authority are in fact covered by that section. The relationship between ss. 130 and 139 is thus not entirely of academic interest.

A variety of offences outside the current MHA refer specifically to people with mental disabilities. Thus s. 128, MHA 1959 remains in force to prohibit extramarital sexual relations between male staff members of hospitals and mental nursing homes with persons receiving treatment in those facilities, for men to have extramarital sexual relations with the women subject to their guardianship, and for male carers generally to have such sexual relations with mentally disordered women in their care or custody. More generally, the Sexual Offences Act 1956 prohibits men from engaging in sexual intercourse with and procuring for sexual intercourse women who are 'defective': ss. 7, 9.

It is appropriate to close this section by returning to its first point: the broader criminal law also applies to people contained in the mental health system. Thus assaults of patients by staff is not merely an offence under s. 127; it may also give rise to a charge of common assault: see, e.g., *Newington*. A manifest lack of care such as results in the death of a person with mental disorder, unable to care for himself or herself, may result in a conviction for manslaughter in the event that an individual undertakes to provide care to that individual and fails adequately to do so: *R v Stone, R v Dobinson* [1977] 1 All ER 341. Advocates should be aware of such wider possibilities of the criminal law.

12.5   CIVIL ACTIONS FOR DAMAGES

Subject again to the provisions of s. 139, the general laws of contract and tort apply to people in the mental health system as much as anywhere else. Contract will be of limited assistance when dealing with NHS trusts and health authorities, for no contract exists between these bodies and their patients: *Pfizer v Ministry of Health* [1965] 1 All ER 152. The same logic would apply to community care facilities, unless the client pays directly for the care received.

Tort provides a more encouraging line of authorities. Any exhaustive analysis of the torts that might assist people in the mental health system is of course beyond the scope of this book: it could well be a text on its own. That said, advocates should think creatively, and not leap instantly to an action in negligence. Assault or battery may be an effective mechanism to seek redress for inappropriately aggressive behaviour directed at the client by hospital or community care staff. Occupier's liability applies as much in psychiatric facilities as it does elsewhere, providing redress for injury flowing from a person's entry into premises, whether on a short-term or long-term basis. Wrongful confinement may be used to challenge detentions, and has the advantage that once the confinement is shown, it is for defendant to justify their actions. Rather than discuss the variety of torts in a summary fashion, the discussion which follows will instead examine a few more specific difficulties raised in recent mental health litigation. Those issues have tended to arise in the context of negligence law.

To begin with a basic principle, it is uncontroversial that there is a duty of care between health care professionals such as doctors and nurses, and their patients. The duty arises when the doctor/patient relationship is crystallised, or when the patient is accepted as a patient in a hospital (McHale and Fox with Murphy, 1997, p. 149). This duty is therefore broad enough to include care both inside and outside psychiatric facilities. This gives the patient the right to expect the standard of care which the 'reasonable doctor' occupying the position of the potential defendant would have provided: general practitioners are subject to the standard of the reasonable general practitioner; psychiatric specialists are subject to the standard of the reasonable psychiatric specialist, and so forth.

In theory, this ought to provide many people in the mental health system with civil redress for medical misadventure or other errors by these professionals. For example, patients given megadoses of cocktails of psychiatric medication (see 7.3.3) might think they can sue in the event that they suffer adverse effects. Until recently, it would be difficult to see that such an action would succeed. The test of whether the standard of care was breached was whether a responsible body of medical opinion would have behaved as the defendant did: *Bolam* v *Friern HMC* [1957] 2 All ER 118. As megadosing is not uncommon in psychiatric facilities, this test would be difficult to surmount. Recently, however, a caveat has been introduced on the Bolam test, by *Bolitho* v *City and Hackney HA* [1997] 3 WLR 1151, where the House of Lords acknowledged, per Lord Browne-Wilkinson at p. 1159, that the professional views must stand up to objective scrutiny:

> The court has to be satisfied that the exponents of the body of opinion relied upon can demonstrate that such opinion has a logical basis. In particular, in cases involving, as they so often do, the weighing of risks against benefits, the judge before accepting a body of opinion as being responsible, reasonable or respectable, will need to be satisfied that, in forming their views, the experts have directed their minds to the question of comparative risks and benefits and have reached a defensible conclusion on the matter.

The intrusiveness of this revised standard on medical authority is limited. The views of doctors will clearly continue to have considerable sway in court. In megadosing, however, doctors are failing to be governed by the maximum dosages of drugs recommended by the manufacturers of those drugs, maxima presumably based on scientific testing and experimentation. In such extreme situations, *Bolitho* might be invoked to challenge the appropriateness of the doctor's decision. Except in such rather unusual situations, however, a fairly uniform medical view that the doctor's actions were inappropriate would be necessary to found a negligence action; and such uniform views opposing a course of action by a doctor are uncommon.

Megadosing might also be addressed through a negligence action based on insufficient information provision. Informal patients, of course, have the same treatment rights as any other member of the community. That means they must consent to any treatment they are given, assuming they have the capacity to do so (see Chapters ten and eleven). Similarly, some confined patients are treated on their consent pursuant to s. 58. Treatment on the patient's consent in these contexts must meet the usual common law standard, as established by *Sidaway* v *Governors of Bethlem Royal Hospital* [1985] AC 871. This means that they must be informed of the major risks and benefits of treatment. The precise scope of this in a megadosing context has yet to be litigated, but it seems at the very least arguable that it would be necessary to disclose that the dosage is in excess of the manufacturer's recommended maximum. Information provision can be a double-edged sword, however, since if the information is provided, including possible adverse effects from the megadose, a court might find that the patient had voluntarily assumed the risk of resulting adverse effects, and no action would therefore lie: *volenti non fit injuria*. It is questionable whether this is an appropriate result. If consenting to the medication is understood by the patient as the only hope for release from the facility, is the consent to the risk 'voluntary' in the sense that ought to invoke the defence?

The legal relationship between doctor and patient becomes more complex when the doctor is exercising a statutory function under the 1983 Act. Liability for signing a medical certificate as part of a process for involuntary admission will serve as an example. Recently, it has been expressly held that the duty of care of doctors signing such certificates is still an open question: *X (minors)* v *Bedfordshire County Council* [1995] 3 All ER 353 at p. 384; *Clunis* v *Camden and Islington Health Authority* [1998] 2 WLR 902 at p. 914. This was somewhat surprising, as the broadly held belief up until that time had been that a duty of care did exist, as evidenced by a considerable trail of litigation: e.g., *Winch* v *Jones* (see 12.3.2; leave granted to sue doctor for negligence in confinement); *O'Neill* v *Morrison* (CA, unreported, 1994) (similar situation, leave refused but no implied doubt as to duty of care); *Buxton* v *Jayne* [1960] 1 WLR 783 (leave granted to bring action against duly authorised officer of local authority — analogous in the 1959 Act to the social worker in the 1983 Act — for lack of care in confining plaintiff).

Both *X* and *Clunis* rely for this proposition on the case of *Everett* v *Griffiths* [1921] 1 AC 631 (HL), where notwithstanding the tentative views of Viscounts Haldane and Cave that such a duty did exist, the fact that no negligence was found in the completion of the medical certificate in question allowed the matter to be left open. A majority of the House of Lords continued to leave the matter open in *Harnett* v *Fisher* [1927] AC 573, although Lord Atkinson offers the opinion that the doctor signing such a certificate 'is simply engaged as a medical man by a patient to give an opinion as to the patient's state of health, as he would be to diagnose the state of health of any patient who in his daily practice called upon him to prescribe for him.' (p. 596). This suggests that in his Lordship's view, the standard duty of care applied to the duties of a doctor in signing such certificates. The content of these cases may be inconclusive, but reliance upon these cases is not convincing in any event. The statutory regime under consideration was that contained in the Lunacy Act 1890 where the medical certificate was but one piece of evidence necessary to apply for an order for confinement. The order itself was signed by, and was subject to the discretion of, a justice of the peace. The removal of this extra layer of bureaucracy is significant. Now, the requisite medical certificates and the application pursuant to ss. 2 or 3 are sufficient for confinement. The certificates therefore have a legal effect that they did not have previously, suggesting a new analysis is necessary.

The obvious starting place for such an analysis is *X* v *Bedfordshire*. In that case, one of the issues was whether the social workers and psychiatrists interviewing children as part of the determination as to whether the children ought to be placed in care gave rise to an action in damages, in the event that it was performed negligently. Lord Browne-Wilkinson, speaking for a unanimous House of Lords, held that it did not, on the basis that such a duty would not be 'just and reasonable' within the meaning of *Caparo Industries plc* v *Dickman* [1990] 2 AC 605. His Lordship reasoned that a complex and interdisciplinary statutory system had been established, in which liability of individuals could not easily be disentangled. Second, child protection proceedings were inherently delicate, involving a complex balancing exercise, and the court should hesitate before criticising the balancing of conflicting priorities by the authorities. Third, liability in damages might induce local authorities to be more cautious and defensive in their approach. Fourth, he held that the fraught relations that often existed between parents of the children concerned and social workers would breed hopeless, vexatious and costly litigation. He further held that the statutory remedies, although not providing for compensation, did allow for scrutiny of decisions. Finally, he held that the doctors were retained to advise the local authorities, not the plaintiffs, and hence that no patient/doctor relationship was in fact established (pp. 380–4).

A number of these arguments simply do not apply to the doctor or social worker involved in a confinement under the MHA 1983. Certainly, the statutory regime is complex, but the roles of the various professionals is kept distinct. Any negligence or impropriety of these individuals would be clearly definable by reference to the statute. Issues of the delicacy of the proceedings and the risk of vexatious litigation are already dealt with through s. 139, discussed at 12.3. Two others can be dismissed relatively briefly. Certainly, the availability of a civil remedy might induce those in charge to 'adopt a more cautious and defensive approach to their duties' (p. 381); but is caution necessarily a bad thing, particularly when considerable violations of civil rights will result from the actions? It should further be recalled that the existence of a duty of care is but one element required for success in a negligence action. A breach of the duty is also necessary, and success on this head will require proof of a want of reasonable care, a criterion already allowing room for error in the event of difficult circumstances. The negligence action is to provide a mechanism to call decision-makers to account, to explain themselves. This is further relevant to the issue of statutory remedies, for as discussed above, the review tribunals provided by the statute do not determine the validity of the initial detention, but only the appropriateness of continued detention. The statute does not provide a mechanism for the initial detention to be considered;

unlike the child welfare situation, that is left to the broader law of judicial review.

This leaves the most interesting of the grounds for decision in X, the question of who is the client of the doctor or social worker. In X, Lord Browne-Wilkinson addressed the matter as follows (at p. 383):

> The social workers and the psychiatrists were retained by the local authority to advise the local authority, not the plaintiffs. The subject matter of the advice and activities of the professionals is the child. Moreover, the tendering of any advice will in many cases involve interviewing and, in the case of doctors, examining the child. But the fact that the carrying out of the retainer involves contact with and a relationship with the child cannot alter the extent of the duty owed by the professionals under the retainer from the local authority. The Court of Appeal drew a correct analogy with the doctor instructed by an insurance company to examine an applicant for life insurance. The doctor does not, by examining the applicant, come under any general duty of medical care to the applicant. He is under a duty not to damage the applicant in the course of the examination: but beyond that his duties are owed to the insurance company and not to the applicant.

The role of the certifying doctors and social worker is by no means as clear cut. Certainly, some doctors or social workers will be brought in for purposes of the certification only, and will have no other professional relationship with the individual. This suggests a relatively close parallel to the doctors and social workers in X. Frequently, however, at least one of the certifying doctors will be the patient's general practitioner. In the event that the certificate will involve a readmission, the other doctor may well be the individual's psychiatrist, who may continue to serve in that role following the individual's admission to hospital. In both these cases, the medical professionals signing the certificates are in an ongoing professional relationship with a patient. Can it really be said that the signing of the certificates is severable from the remainder of that relationship, so that it, unlike the programme of treatment of which the admission must form an integral part, is not contained within the doctor-patient relationship?

A finding that the actions of doctors related to medical certification was not within the patient/doctor duty of care would lead to anomaly. Consider a case where a doctor informed a patient that if he or she did not consent to informal admission, the doctor would institute civil confinement. If the patient relied on the doctor and went into hospital as an informal patient, the situation would be analogous to a patient entering hospital for a physical ailment on doctor's advice, and the duty of care would be beyond question. If instead the patient called the bluff of the doctor and the doctor signed the certificate, the duty of care would not exist. The duty would be a function of whether the patient agreed to follow the doctor's advice voluntarily — a most unusual result.

The move towards increasing care in the community similarly raises difficulties relating to the scope of the duty of care and the doctor/patient relationship. The leading case is *Clunis*. In that case, the plaintiff was released from Guy's Hospital in south London. As he wished to live in north London, after care was arranged by Guy's with a north London hospital, and a Dr Sargeant, a psychiatrist at that hospital agreed to serve as responsible medical officer under the after-care plan. Notwithstanding appointments established for him on 9 October and 13 November 1992, the plaintiff, Clunis failed to attend at the hospital. Dr Sargeant contacted Clunis's last general practitioner, who indicated that Clunis had been removed from his list due to aggressive and threatening behaviour. Dr Sargeant then contacted Guy's Hospital, and social services to arrange a mental health assessment visit. This was to take place on 30 November, but Clunis was not at home at the relevant time, and the assessment therefore did not take place. Dr Sargeant made an appointment to see Clunis on 10 December, which again he did not attend. On 17 December, social services notified Dr Sargeant of a phone call from the police, indicating that Clunis was 'waving screwdrivers and knives and talking about devils'. Later that day, Clunis killed a bystander in an unprovoked attack, by stabbing him with a knife. At trial, a plea of diminished responsibility was accepted, based on a diagnosis of schizoaffective disorder.

Clunis commenced a suit against Dr Sargent, alleging negligence in her follow up of his care plan. The case is therefore interesting because it lies at the intersection of several issues. First, there is the issue of the duty of care owed by doctors to persons in care in the community in general, and on after-care under s. 117 in particular. Secondly, there is the issue that the negligence alleged was one of omission: the doctor should have intervened more to ensure that appropriate care was given, notwithstanding the inevitable conclusion that Clunis did not, at the time, want the treatment. Finally, there was the issue of whether the action was barred on policy grounds, because it stemmed from Clunis's own criminal act in killing the bystander: *ex turpi causa non oritur actio*. The defendants applied to have the claim struck out as disclosing no cause of action. This was unsuccessful, but their appeal succeeded and the case was dismissed on the basis of the first and third of these issues. In neither case is the reasoning of the court entirely satisfactory.

On the issue of *ex turpi causa*, the court held (at p. 911) that the claim arose out of the commission of a criminal offence:

> In the present case we consider the defendant has made out its plea that the plaintiff's claim is essentially based on his illegal act of manslaughter; he must be taken to have known what he was doing and that it was wrong, notwithstanding that the degree of his culpability was reduced by reason of mental disorder. The court ought not to allow itself to be made an instrument to enforce obligations alleged to arise out of the plaintiff's own criminal act and we would therefore allow the appeal on this ground.

The difficulty with the court's reasoning is that the court conflated the entire action for damages to an action for damages flowing from the death of the bystander. No doubt in monetary terms this was where most of the damages lay; but the failure to provide appropriate medical care would appear to have had adverse effects not directly related to the homicide. Certainly, it would appear that by the morning in question, Clunis was psychotic. The unpleasant experience of having those psychotic delusions before the attack would presumably constitute actionable damage, if the duty of care and breach were successfully shown.

Of greater relevance for current discussion is the fact that the Court of Appeal failed to find a duty of care between Dr Sargeant and Clunis. Perhaps unsurprisingly given the lack of express statutory language, the court held that s. 117, the duty to provide after-care services to a formerly detained patient, created a public law duty, rather than a private law action in damages. More problematically, it held (at p. 913–14) that the provision of after-care services under the statute was inconsistent with a coexisting common law duty of care:

> Bearing in mind the ambit of the obligations under s. 117 of the Act and that they affect a wide spectrum of health and social services, including voluntary services, we do not think that Parliament intended so widespread a liability as that asserted by Mr Irwin [counsel for Clunis]. The question of whether a common law duty exists in parallel with the authority's statutory obligations is profoundly influenced by the surrounding statutory framework. . . . So, too, in this case, the statutory framework must be a major consideration in deciding whether it is fair and reasonable for the local health authority to be held responsible for errors and omissions of the kind alleged. The duties of care are, it seems to us, different in nature from those owed by a doctor to a patient whom he is treating and for whose lack of care in the course of such treatment the local health authority may be liable.

Certainly, a variety of professional individuals and voluntary agencies may be involved in the patient's after-care. It is not obvious that this should negate a duty of care, however, for the after-care received by a formerly detained patient under s. 117 may well in all outward appearances be similar to the care in the community received by any other patient, only for the latter, the care will be outside the terms of the statute. Precisely analogous arguments to those rehearsed by the court above will apply. Therefore, either the court is saying that there is no duty of care between psychiatrists or health authorities and their patients living in the community — a truly startling statement — or it must be asked why the provision of essentially similar services by statutory obligation under s. 117 rather than merely by good practice should *remove* the duty of care.

Perhaps the escape route for the court could have been that Clunis terminated one therapeutic relationship with Guy's upon his release from that facility, and since he never attended an appointment with Dr Sargeant, never commenced a new one. As a result, at the time of the homicide, there was no duty of care in effect: Clunis had slipped through the cracks between therapeutic relationships. Even that is problematic. In general, the duty of care between hospital and patient arises when there is an express or implied undertaking that the patient will be treated: *Cassidy* v *Ministry of Health* [1951] 1 All ER 574. Such an express undertaking would appear to have existed in this case, and was manifest by Dr Sargeant's continuing, albeit unsuccessful, attempts to establish a therapeutic relationship with Clunis. It is perhaps arguable that the relationship, and hence the duty, did not exist in this case, as it had been repudiated by Clunis's refusal to attend the treatments. In any event, this is not how the court approached the issue.

A broader question arises as to the strategic benefits from a patient's rights perspective of litigation complaining of a doctor's failure to intervene in the life of a patient, either by failing to confine the individual under ss. 2 or 3, or to launch guardianship proceedings under s. 7. Certainly, there is a legal coherence to such actions. If a duty of care exists between doctor and patient, then the patient has a right to expect the doctor to exercise a certain standard of care. Since the doctor's role appropriately includes diagnosis of mental illness and consequent responsibilities under the Act, it seems tautological that the patient ought to be able to insist that these roles are fulfilled to the appropriate standard of care. The failure to do so, as was alleged in the *Clunis* case, can be tragic; more often it is more mundane, but nonetheless may detract from the longer term quality of life of the patient, and may therefore be actionable. All that is asked, the argument runs, is the exercise of a reasonable professional standard of care. At the same time, such litigation must encourage doctors to err on the side of intervention. As we saw in Chapter four, the dangerousness of the mentally ill is significantly over-predicted, and institutionalisation has its disadvantages as well as its benefits. Is it really the case that doctors should be encouraged to intervene more?

12.6 COMPLAINT PROCESSES

For much of what clients will want, litigation is not the appropriate model. Not merely is it expensive, it frequently will not provide a remedy to the client's actual problem. There may not be a lot of point to suing because a client is unhappy with the medication they are receiving, or unable for religious or cultural reasons to eat the food served in a hospital, although these may be significant problems for the client. It is not obvious that civil actions would succeed for such problems; and even if they did, they would provide a remedy in damages, not preferable medication or different food. For many such day-to-day difficulties, a direct approach to the doctor or hospital manager may provide the best chance of a resolution to the problem. The presence of an advocate may give the client's concerns increased credence by such authority figures, which may trigger a solution. In other instances, the advocate's negotiation skills may allow otherwise unforeseen solutions to be reached.

Even if the matter is one for which other legal avenues appear appropriate, informal dispute resolution mechanisms should be considered. Thus tribunals tend to be sympathetic to the RMO's views of the appropriateness of detention, for example. It may well be the case that some sort of negotiated plan with the RMO directed towards release of the client may bring results more effectively than a review tribunal hearing.

Particularly for issues of day-to-day living outside the scope of tribunals, internal complaint processes within the hospital or community care facility might be considered. A variety of such mechanisms exist. NHS trusts are now required to operate complaints processes, headed by a complaints manager. This is a separate structure from the trust's disciplinary system, although the structure of most complaint systems seems to assume that the complaint will be about an individual, rather than an inappropriate policy. Increasingly, these processes will have advocacy programmes running in parallel in the trust, to assist complainants. At their best, these advocacy services will be staffed by people whose knowledge of the workings of the trust will be considerably better than an external advocate, and who may therefore be particularly effective at having the complainant's matter resolved.

In the event that the client is not content with the result of a complaint through one of these internal processes, the complaint may then be forwarded to the MHAC. The Commission has a fairly broad authority under the Act to visit people detained pursuant to the Act in hospitals and mental nursing homes; and to investigate complaints of detainees under the Act if the complaint has not been adequately dealt with through an internal process: s. 120(1), MHA 1983. The Commission has powers of investigation — a distinct advantage in ensuring that the substance of a complaint is considered — but its jurisdiction extends only to confined patients, not to those informally admitted, nor to out-patients or persons on after care with supervision, although the Commission does have jurisdiction to investigate complaints relating to events which occurred during a period of detention even if that detention has now ceased.

Complaints may also be lodged with the Health Services Commissioner for England, a position established through the Health Service Commissioner Act 1993. The Commissioner's jurisdiction extends to individuals providing health services, and also health authorities and NHS trusts. Until 1996, complaints relating to clinical judgment were outside his remit; that was changed by s. 6 of the Health Service Commissioner (Amendment) Act 1996. The Commissioner has powers of investigation, suggesting that this may be an inexpensive way for a client's concern to be investigated.

There can thus be seen to be a potential overlap between the jurisdictions of the Mental Health Act Commission and the Health Services Commissioner. The bodies have informally agreed that matters relating to the circumstances or consequences of detention of psychiatric patients will be dealt with by the former body; otherwise, it will fall to the latter.

Finally, many professionals working in the mental health sector are subject to internal professional disciplinary processes. For example, doctors, nurses and health visitors are all subject to such professional regulation. In the event that the concern is with the professionalism of such an individual, a complaint to the relevant professional body, be it the General Medical Council or the United Kingdom Central Council for Nursing, Midwifery and Health Visiting, might be considered.

12.7   ADVOCACY

The right of people with mental health difficulties to representation is established in a variety of sources. The Mental Health Review Tribunal Rules

1983 establish a right of a party to representation before those tribunals. The representative may be virtually anyone authorised by the party. Legal aid is available for these proceedings (see 8.4.3).

For litigation before the courts, the usual rules regarding representation apply. The apparent openness of the courts is however subject to the individual's right to participate in litigation. The rule is that a 'patient' may sue or be sued only through a 'litigation friend': CPR r. 21.2. These take effect if the individual is 'a person who, by reason of mental disorder within the meaning of the Mental Health Act 1983, is incapable of managing and administering his own affairs': CPR r. 21.1. While this is identical to the test under s. 94(2), MHA 1983 for the invocation of the jurisdiction of the Court of Protection, the procedural standards are not the same. Where the Court of Protection must decide on the basis of medical evidence, there is no such express requirement in the court rules: CPR r. 21.6(4). The provisions may be invoked for specific litigation if the Court of Protection remains uninvolved with the individual's affairs: *In re S(FG) (Mental Health Patient)* [1973] 1 WLR 178. This avenue may be appropriate in situations where, apart from litigation, there would be no need to invoke the jurisdiction of the Court.

In the event that the individual is under the jurisdiction of the Court of Protection, however, the Court assumes jurisdiction over 'the conduct of legal proceedings in the name of the patient or on his behalf': s. 96(1)(i), MHA 1983. It would seem that this is an authority not generally granted by the Court to receivers as a matter of routine, and therefore receivers must apply to the Court for authorisation to represent that individual's interests in litigation.

It is a nice question the degree to which the authority of the Court of Protection extends to legal proceedings before MHRTs. Such proceedings are clearly not within the rules of the courts, but are they 'legal proceedings' within the meaning of s. 96(1)(i)? If the client is not eligible for legal aid, it is difficult to see that the Court of Protection can be uninvolved, since the payment of a solicitor's fees may result in considerable expense to a patient's estate, particularly if the case is complex or goes to judicial review. At least on the question of expense, it is difficult to see that the Court can be uninvolved, since management of the patient's assets is central to its role. That jurisdiction can be understood to flow from the authority to contract on behalf of the patient, however, as much as from the authority over litigation. What would be the case if the individual were eligible for legal aid, or able to convince a solicitor to act for free, or indeed decided to represent himself or herself before the review tribunal? Here the matter is much more debatable. As costs cannot be awarded for proceedings before the review tribunals, there would be no direct financial exposure of the estate: unless covered by s. 96(1)(i), the proceedings look very much like matters related to the personal care of the individual, and thus not obviously within the core jurisdiction of the court. In such circumstances where there is no financial exposure, it is inappropriate that the Court of Protection should be involved. The purpose of the tribunal processes is to accord the individual the right to challenge their confinement; it would be inappropriate if that individual right were lost, because of a different incapacity, to manage their property and affairs.

Advocates should be aware that the authority of the client to conduct proceedings is not merely an issue upon the commencement of proceedings. The authority of a solicitor to act ceases upon a client subsequently becoming a person under disability, and proceedings occurring after that time would seem to be a nullity. In civil actions, the solicitor may become personally liable for costs thrown away by other parties, in the event that the case proceeds after the client becomes a person under disability and without the appointment of a next friend: *Yonge* v *Toynbee* [1910] 1 KB 215.

The effect of the appointment of a litigation friend, or the conduct of the litigation by the Court of Protection, is that the patient, while remaining technically the party in the matter, ceases to be involved in the conduct of the litigation. That role is taken by the next friend. Next friends can be anyone the court sees fit to appoint, although the Official Solicitor often assumes this role. The litigation is of course to be conducted for the benefit of the patient, there is an inevitable loss of control of the litigation by the patient himself or herself. In the event that the loss of capacity is likely to be temporary, it may be worth considering delay of the proceedings until it is regained. In this context, it should be noted that limitation periods do not run against people in their incapacity: s. 28, Limitations Act 1980.

As to the mechanics of representing individuals within the mental health system, Eldergill (1997, chapter 16) provides a valuable 'how to' guide, complete with not merely discussion of general principles, but also checklists, a *pro forma* case summary, and advice on the minutiae of conducting interviews. Quite appropriately, he emphasises the essential similarity between representation in this context with any other form of client advocacy (1997, p. 884):

> In terms of professional conduct, the principles are the same as for any client attending the office: to serve the client without compromising the solicitor's integrity or his overriding duty to the court and the judicial process. . . . To summarise, the usual principles governing the solicitor-client relationship apply and few problems will arise provided the solicitor is courteous and avoids being patronising.

While this is and must be the overarching principle, as Eldergill acknowledges, representation of this sort of client has its own quirks. Additional patience and empathy may be required to gain the client's trust, to help the client to formulate their wishes and instructions. Particular care may be necessary to explain the situation the client is in. While information about detention and treatment rights is required to be given to clients by s. 132, MHA 1983, the client may or may not remember the information. In a study of detentions under the Scots Mental Health Act, for example, Goldbeck et al (1997, p. 577) found that less than a third of detained patients recalled receiving this information. While 87 per cent understood that they were detained, only 30 per cent could correctly identify the legal order which was the basis of the detention. This is not necessarily an indictment of those providing the information. Section 132 requires that the information be given 'as soon as practicable after the commencement of the patient's detention', and thus at a time when the client may well be facing new and frightening surroundings, and a barrage of other information. It is perhaps unsurprising that they do not remember it. Nonetheless, the advocate may have to explain the legal situation, starting at the basics.

As in all relationships with clients, the solicitor should not jump to conclusions about what the client wants. The client may well want to be released from the facility; but alternatively or additionally, the client may want a different treatment regime which, if provided, might make continuation in the facility considerably more palatable or even agreeable. Assuming the client has the capacity to instruct, it is inappropriate that advocates 'second-guess' the client's wishes or instructions due to concerns about whether the instructions are in the client's clinical or social best interests. Virtually all other professionals in the mental health system are professionally obliged to act in the client's best interests: that role is already taken, many times over. In the same way that a solicitor would not second-guess the instructions of other clients, the instructions of these clients should be respected, consistent of course with the solicitor's duty to the court and judicial process. The fact that the client's views should not be second-guessed does not of course mean that the advocate should encourage the client to have a closed mind about other results. An advocate may be able to negotiate a partial solution to a problem, and here as in any other solicitor/client relationship, a partial victory may be preferable to the client than the risk of an all or nothing hearing.

All of this is based on the assumption that the client is able to give competent instructions. What is the role of the advocate if the client does not have this ability? Romano (1997, pp. 750–9) identifies four logically possible responses of the advocate in this situation: follow the client's wishes as if the client is competent; have a guardian appointed; have the advocate act as *de facto* guardian; and withdraw. None of these is ideal; but some are perhaps more problematic than others. In court proceedings, the directions are fairly clear: withdraw until a litigation friend is appointed. The hard line of the court rules does not directly apply to tribunal applications, however, and it seems counterintuitive to remove to a third party the rather specific right to challenge a confinement, for example, which is provided to the patient under the Act. For this reason it is also dubious whether the advocate should act as guardian: it is still not the client making the decisions. In addition, as Romano points out (1997, p. 755), the role of advocate is different and conflicting from that of guardian:

> While the advocate has an obligation to consult with the client regarding what the advocate should do on his behalf, the guardian's role is to determine the best interests of the client and act accordingly. This shift in responsibility from taking instructions to giving them can result in the advocate disregarding many important ethical rules which should ordinarily govern the advocate-client dynamic.

Arguably, the advocate is in a particularly poor position to fulfil the role of guardian in any event. He or she is unlikely to have known the client prior to the commencement of the professional relationship, and therefore unlikely to be aware of the values of the client when capable. There is real danger here that the advocate will move in directions of which the client may not approve, if they regain capacity.

Continuing based on the client's wishes is also a profoundly problematic option, even in a review tribunal setting where the rules of court do not apply. The difficulty is that continuation with a hearing may have an adverse result. The client has a right to only one hearing per certificate, and if the client is detained under s. 3, it will be six months or a year before the right to another tribunal hearing arises. It is conceivable that a negligence action might lie against a solicitor for the loss of the right to a hearing in this period, in the event that the solicitor proceeded on instructions of an incapable client to a hearing early in the certificate.

That leaves withdrawal, which would seem to be the only appropriate course of action. It, too, is problematic, particularly if the advocate sees what appears to be a winning argument. It also does not preclude the client from proceeding to the tribunal and representing themself. It seems counterintuitive to deny representation to which the client has a prima facie right under the rules of the tribunal, for a hearing that is going to go forward in any event. Withdrawal finally suggests that the client must pass two hurdles to obtain relief from the tribunal: they must not merely convince the tribunal of the justice of their case; but also convince their advocate of their ability to instruct. Care must therefore be taken not to set the standard of capacity to instruct so high as to preclude meritorious cases from reaching the appropriate forum. Yet if the advocate really cannot get proper instructions, it is not obvious what else can be done.

Above all, clients should be treated professionally, with respect, dignity, and emotional commitment. We are now at the end of this book — the time for the reader to look back and to consider where we have been. The legal issues described in this book involve fundamental rights and liberties, and the needs of some of society's most vulnerable people. Conceptually, mental health law contains implied premises as to what it is to be a citizen, what the role of the state is with reference to the vulnerable and the bizarre in society, and what the relative roles of law and medicine are in the regulation and control of deviance. It is a field where what is usually assumed becomes problematic. It has been suggested that the law may have unforeseen effects — some beneficial, some not. Above all, it has been argued that this is an area of considerable legal and social complexity. It is not a realm of simple answers. It is instead a field of considerable difficulty, but a field offering corresponding intellectual rewards. Mediocre advocacy will not suffice. Clients deserve — and need — better. That is the final challenge of this book, to the advocates and potential advocates who read it.

Bibliography

Abdul-Hamid, W. and Cooney, C. (1997) 'Homelessness, Mental Illness and the Law', *Medicine Science and Law*, vol. 37(4), p. 341-4.

Adams, R. (1998) *The Abuses of Punishment*, London: Macmillan.

Adshead, G. (1998) 'Psychiatric staff as attachment figures: understanding management problems in psychiatric services in the light of attachment theory', *British Journal of Psychiatry*, vol. 172, p. 64.

Ahmad, W.I.U. and Atkin, K. (1996) *'Race' and Community Care*, Buckingham: Open University Press.

Akinkunmi, A. and Murray, K. (1997) 'Inadequacies in the Mental Health Act, 1983 in relation to Mentally Disordered Remand Prisoners', *Medicine Science and Law*, vol. 37(1), p. 53.

Allderidge, P. (1985) 'Bedlam: fact or fantasy?', in W.F. Bynum, R. Porter, and M. Shepherd, (eds), *The Anatomy of Madness*, vol. 2, London: Tavistock.

Andoh, B. (1994) 'Hospital and Police Procedures when a Patient Absconds from a Mental Hospital', *Medicine Science and Law*, vol. 34(2), p. 130.

Andoh, B. (1995) 'Jurisprudential Aspects of the "Right" to Retake Absconders from Mental Hospitals in England and Wales', *Medicine Science and Law*, vol. 35(3), p. 225.

Anon. (1996) 'Why We Run for Cover' in Read J. and Reynolds J. (eds), *Speaking Our Minds: An Anthology*, Basingstoke: Macmillan.

Appelbaum, P. and Grisso T. (1995) 'The MacArthur Treatment Competence Study I. Mental Illness and Competence to Consent to Treatment', *Law and Human Behavior*, vol. 19(2), p. 105.

Appelbaum, P.S. (1985) 'Standards for Civil Commitment: A Critical Review of the Literature', *International Journal of Law and Psychiatry*, vol. 7, p. 133.

Appleby, L. (1997) *The National Confidential Inquiry into Suicide and Homicide by People with Mental Illness: Progress Report*, London: Department of Health.

Arber, S., Gilberty, G. N. and Evandrou, M. (1988) 'Gender, household composition and receipt of domiciliary services by elderly disabled people' *Journal of Social Policy*, vol. 17, p. 153.

Ashworth, A. (1996) 'Sentencing Mentally Disordered Offenders', *Criminal Law Review*, p. 457.

Atkinson, P. (1995) *Medical Talk and Medical Work*, London: Sage.

Audit Commission. (1986) *Making a Reality of Community Care*, London: HMSO.

Bailey J. and MacCulloch, M. (1992) 'Patterns of reconviction in patients discharged directly to the community from a Special Hospital: implications for after-care' *Journal of Forensic Psychiatry*, vol. 3(3), p. 445.

Baker, E. (1992) 'Dangerousness. The neglected gaoler: disorder and risk under the Mental Health Act 1983' *Journal of Forensic Psychiatry*, vol. 3(1), p. 31.

Baker, E. (1994) 'Human Rights, M'Naghten and the 1991 Act', *Criminal Law Review*, p. 84.

Baker, E. and Crichton J. (1995) '*Ex Parte A*: psychopathy, treatability and the law' *Journal of Forensic Psychiatry*, vol. 6(1), p. 101.

Bannerjee, S. et al. (1995) *Deaths of Detained Patients: A Review of Reports to the Mental Health Act Commission*, London: Mental Health Foundation.

Barham, P. (1992) *Closing the Asylum: The Mental Patient in Modern Society*, London: Penguin.

Barnes, M. and Maple, N. (1992) *Women and Mental Health: Challenging the Stereotypes*, Birmingham: British Academy of Social Workers and Ventura Press.

Barnes, M., Bowl, R. and Fisher, M. (1990) *Sectioned: Social Services and the Mental Health Act 1983*, London: Routledge.

Bartlett, P. (1996) 'Sense and Nonsense: Sensation, Delusion and the Limitation of Sanity in Nineteenth-Century Law', in L. Bently and L. Flynn (eds), *Law and the Senses*, London: Pluto.

Bartlett, P. (1997) 'The Consequences of Incapacity', *Web Journal of Current Legal Issues*, vol. 4.

Bartlett, P. (1999) *The Poor Law of Lunacy: The Administration of Pauper Lunatics in Mid-Nineteenth-Century England*, London: University of Leicester Press/Cassell.

Bartlett, P. (1999a) 'The Asylum, the Workhouse and the Voice of the Insane Poor in Nineteenth-Century England', *International Journal of Law and Psychiatry*, vol. 21(3), p. 1.

Bartlett, P. and Wright, D. (eds) (1999) *Outside the Walls of the Asylum: The History of Care in the Community 1750–2000*, London: Athlone.

Bartlett, P. and Wright, D. (1999a) 'Community care and its antecedents' in P. Bartlett and D. Wright (eds), *Outside the Walls of the Asylum*, London: Athlone.

Baxter, R. (1991) 'The mentally disordered offender in hospital: the role of the Home Office' in K. Herbst and J. Gunn (eds), *The Mentally Disordered Offender*, London: Butterworth-Heinemann.

Bean, P. (1980) *Compulsory Admissions to Mental Hospitals*, Chichester: John Wiley.

Bean, P. (1986) *Mental Disorder and Legal Control*, Cambridge: Cambridge University Press.

Bean, P. and Mounser, P. (1993) *Discharged from Mental Hospitals*, London: Macmillan.

Bean, P. and Nemetz, T. (n.d) *Out of Depth and Out of Sight*, London: Mencap.

Bean, P., Bingley, W., Bynoe, I. et al. (1991) *Out of Harm's Way*, London: MIND.

Bebbington P.E., Feeney, S.T., Flannigan, C.B., Glover, G.R., Lewis, S.W. and Wing J.K. (1994) 'Inner London Collaborative Audit of Admissions in Two Health Districts: II. Ethnicity and the Use of the Mental Health Act', *British Journal of Psychiatry*, vol. 165, p. 734.

Beebe, M., Ellis, D. and Evans, R. (1973) 'Research Report on Statutory Work under the Mental Health Act 1959: Experience in the London Borough of Camden', *The Human Context*, vol. 5, p. 377.

Bentall, R.P., Jackson H.F. and Pilgrim D. (1988) 'Abandoning the concept of "schizophrenia": some implications of validity arguments for psychological research into psychotic phenomena', *British Journal of Clinical Psychology*, vol. 27, p. 303.

Bentall, R.P., Jackson H.F. and Pilgrim D. (1988a) 'The concept of schizophrenia is dead: long live the concept of schizophrenia', *British Journal of Clinical Psychology*, vol. 27, p. 329.

Berger, P. and Luckmann, T. (1967) *The Social Construction of Reality*, London: Penguin.

Berthoud, R. and Nazroo J. (1997) 'The mental health of ethnic minorities', *New Community*, vol. 23(3), p. 309.

Birchwood, M., McGorry, P. and Jackson, H. (1997) 'Early intervention in schizophrenia', *British Journal of Psychiatry*, vol. 170, p. 2.

Bird, A. (1998) *Philosophy of Science*, London: UCL Press.

Birmingham, L., Mason, D. and Grubin, D. (1996) 'Prevalence of Mental Disorder in Remand Prisoners: Consecutive case study', *British Medical Journal*, vol. 313, p. 1521.

Black Health Workers and Patients Group (1983) 'Psychiatry and the Corporate State', *Race and Class*, vol. 25, p. 49.

Bluglass, R. (1987) 'The Mental Health Act 1983 in practice', *Medico-Legal Journal*, vol. 55(3), p. 151.

Blumenthal, S. and Wessely, S. (1992) 'National Survey of Current Arrangements for Diversion from Custody in England and Wales', *British Medical Journal*, vol. 305, p. 1322.

Blumenthal, S. and Wessely, S. (1994) *The patterns of delay in Mental Health Review Tribunals*, London: HMSO.

Boast, N. and Chesterman, P. (1995) 'Black People and Secure Psychiatric Facilities', *British Journal of Criminology*, vol. 31(2), p. 218.

Bordo, S. (1988) 'Anorexia nervosa: Psychopathology as the Crystallisation of Culture', in I. Diamond and L. Quinby (eds), *Feminism and Foucault: Reflections on Resistance*, Boston: Northeastern University Press.

Bordo, S. (1993) *Unbearable Weight: Feminism, Western Culture and the Body*, Berkeley: University of California Press.

Bott, E. (1976) 'Hospital and society', *British Journal of Medical Psychology*, vol. 49, p. 97.

Bowden, P. (1996) Violence and Mental Disorder', in N. Walker (ed), *Dangerous People*, London: Blackstone Press.

Boyle, M. (1990) *Schizophrenia: A scientific delusion?*, London: Routledge.

Boyle, M. (1994) 'Schizophrenia and the art of the soluble', *The Psychologist*, vol. 7, p. 399.

Brabbins, C. J., and Travers, R. F. (1994) 'Mental Disorder among Defendants in Liverpool Magistrates' Court', *Medicine Science and Law*, vol. 31 (4), p. 279.

Bradford, B., McCann, S. and Mersky, H. (1986) 'A survey of involuntary patients' attitudes toward their commitment', *Psychiatric Journal of the University of Ottawa*, vol. 11, p. 162.

Bridgeman J. and Millns, S. (eds) (1998) *Feminist Perspectives on Law: Law's Engagement with the Female Body*, London: Sweet and Maxwell.

British Medical Association and Association of Police Surgeons. (1994) *Health Care of Detainees in Police Stations*, London: BMA.

British Medical Association and the Law Society. (1995) *Assessment of Mental Capacity: Guidance for Doctors and Lawyers*, London: BMA.

Brook, R. (1573) *La Grande Abridgement*, 2 vols. , n.p.

Brooke, D., Taylor, C., Gunn J. and Madden, D. (1996) 'Point Prevalence of Mental Disorder in Unconvicted Male Prisoners in England and Wales', *British Medical Journal*, vol. 313, p. 1524.

Brown, D., Ellis, T. and Larcombe, K. (1993) *Changing the Code: Police Detention Under the Revised PACE Codes of Practice*, London: HMSO.

Brown, H. and Smith, H. (1992) (eds) *Normalisation: A Reader for the Nineties*, London: Routledge.

Brown, N. (1991) 'Section 5(2) audit', *Psychiatric Bulletin*, vol. 15, p. 706.

Buchanan, A. and Brock, D. (1986) 'Deciding for Others', *The Milbank Quarterly*, vol. 64 (Suppl. 2), p. 17.

Busfield J. (1986) *Managing Madness: Changing Ideas and Practice*, London: Unwin Hyman.

Busfield J. (1996) 'Professionals, the state and the development of mental health policy' in T. Heller, et al (eds), *Mental Health Matters: A Reader*, London: Macmillan.

Butler, R. and Rosenthal, G. (1985) *Behaviour and Rehabilitation*, Bristol: Wright.

Butler, T. (1993) *Changing Mental Health Services: The politics and the policy*, London: Chapman and Hall.

Bynum, W. (1981) 'Rationales for Therapy in British Psychiatry, 1780-1835' in A. Scull, (ed), *Madhouses, Mad-Doctors and Madmen*, London: The Athlone Press.

Campbell, D. (1996) 'Cash-hit courts 'are not using' mental tests', *Guardian*, July 11 1996, p. 1.

Caplan, P. (1995) *They Say You're Crazy: How the World's Most Powerful Psychiatrists Decide Who's Normal*, Reading, Mass.: Addison-Wesley.

Cardinal, M. (1996) 'The Words To Say It', in S. Dunn, B. Morrison and M. Roberts (eds) *Mind Readings: Writers' Journeys through Mental States*, London: Minerva.

Carson, D. (1989a) 'The Sexuality of People with Learning Difficulties', *Journal of Social Welfare and Family Law*, p. 355.

Carson, D. (1989b) 'Prosecuting People with Mental Handicap', *Criminal Law Review*, p. 87.

Carson, D. (1993) 'Disabling Progress: The Law Commission's Proposals on Mentally Incapacitated Adults' Decision-making', *Journal of Social Welfare and Family Law*, p. 304.

Castel, R. (1985) 'Moral Treatment: Mental Therapy and Social Control in the Nineteenth Century', in S. Cohen and A. Scull (eds), *Social Control and the State*, Oxford: Basil Blackwell.

Cavadino, M. (1989) *Mental Health Law in Context: Doctor's Orders?*, Aldershot: Dartmouth.

Cavadino, M. (1991) 'Mental illness and neo-Polonianism', *Journal of Forensic Psychiatry*, vol. 2, p. 295.

Cavadino, M. and Dignan J. (1997, 2nd edition) *The Penal System: An Introduction*, London: Sage.

Central Council for Education and Training in Social Work. (1993) *Requirements and Guidance for the Training of Social Workers to be considered for Approval in England and Wales under the Mental Health Act 1983*, CCETSW Paper No.19.27, London: CCETSW.

Cheadle J. and Ditchfield J. (1982) *Sentenced Mentally Ill Offenders*, London: Home Office Research and Planning Unit.

Cheung, P., Schweitzer, I., Tuckwell, V. and Crowley, K. (1997) 'A Prospective Study of Assaults on Staff by Psychiatric In-patients', *Medicine Science and Law*, vol. 37(1), p. 46.

Chrichton, J. (1995) 'Psychiatric In-Patient Violence: issues of English law and discipline within hospitals, *Medicine, Science and the Law*, vol. 35(1), p. 53.

Clarkson, C. and Keating, H. (1990, 2nd edition) *Criminal Law: Text with Materials*, London: Sweet and Maxwell.

Clarkson, P (1994) 'The nature and range of psychotherapy' in P. Clarkson and M. Pokorny, (eds), *The Handbook of Psychotherapy*, London: Routledge.

Clarkson, P and Pokorny, M. (eds) (1994) *The Handbook of Psychotherapy*, London: Routledge.

Clements, L. (1997) 'Community Care — Towards a Workable Statute', *Liverpool Law Review*, vol. 19(2), p. 181.

Cocozza J. and Steadman, H. (1978) 'Predictions in Psychiatry: an example of misplaced confidence in experts', *Social Problems*, vol. 25(3), p. 265.

Cohen, A., Dolan, B. and Eastman, N. (1996) 'Research on the supervision registers: inconsistencies in local research ethics committees responses' *Journal of Forensic Psychiatry*, vol. 7(2), p. 413.

Cohen, R. and Hart J. (1995, 2nd ed) *Student Psychiatry Today: A comprehensive textbook*, Oxford: Butterworth-Heinmann.

Cohen, S. (1985) *Visions of Social Control*, Cambridge: Polity.

Coid J. (1988) 'Mentally Abnormal Offenders on Remand I: Rejected or Accepted by the NHS?', *British Medical Journal*, vol. 296, p. 1779.

Committee on Mentally Abnormal Offenders (the 'Butler Committee'). (1975) *Report of the Committee on Mentally Abnormal Offenders*, Cmnd. 6244, London: HMSO.

Comyn J. (1822, 5th ed) *Digest of the Laws of England*, 8 vols. , Anthony Hammond (ed), London: Strahan.

Cooke, D. (1991) 'Treatment as an alternative to prosecution: offenders diverted for treatment', *British Journal of Psychiatry*, vol 158, p. 785.

Cope, R. (1989) 'The compulsory detention of Afro-Caribbeans under the Mental Health Act', *New Community*, vol. 15(3), p. 343.

Cope, R. (1993) 'A survey of forensic psychiatrists' views on psychopathic disorder' *Journal of Forensic Psychiatry*, vol. 4, p. 215.

Cornell, D. (1992) *The Philosophy of the Limit*, London: Routledge.

Costello, E. (1983) 'Information processing for decision-making in depressed women: A study of subjective expected utilities', *Journal of Affective Disorders*, vol. 5, p. 239.

Cowan, D. (1995a) 'Accommodating Community Care' *Journal of Law and Society*, vol. 22(2), p. 212.

Cowan, D. (1995b) 'Community Care and Homelessness', *Modern Law Review*, vol. 58(2), p. 256.

Cowen, H. (1999) *Community Care, Ideology and Social Policy*, Hemel Hempstead: Prentice Hall.

Crawford, D. (1984) 'Problems with Assessment of Dangerousness in England and Wales', *Medicine and Law*, vol. 3, p. 141.

Crepaz-Keay, D. (1996) 'A sense of perspective: the media and the Boyd Inquiry', in G. Philo (ed), *Media and Mental Distress*, London: Longman.

Crichton J. (1994) 'Supervised Discharge', *Medicine Science and Law*, vol. 34(4), p. 319.

Crow, T., MacMillan, J., Johnson, A. and Johnstone, E. (1986) 'The Northwick Park study of first episodes of schizophrenia II: a controlled trial of prophylactic neuroleptic treatment', *British Journal of Psychiatry*, vol. 148, p. 120.

Cumming, E. and Cumming, J. (1957) *Closed Ranks: An Experiment in Mental Health Education*, Cambridge, Mass: Harvard University Press.

Dalley, G. (1993) 'Professional ideology or organisational tribalism?' in J. Walmsley, J. Reynolds, P. Shakespeare, and R. Wollfe (eds), *Health, Welfare and Practice: Reflecting on Roles and Relationships*, London: Sage.

Dally, P. and Connolly J. (1981) *Physical Methods of Treatment in Psychiatry*, Edinburgh: Churchill Livingstone.

Davis, S. (1991) 'Violence by psychiatric inpatients: a review', *Hospital and Community Psychiatry*, vol. 42, p. 585.

Deahl, M, and Turner, T. (1997) 'General psychiatry in no-man's land', *British Journal of Psychiatry*, vol. 171, p. 6.

Dean, C. and Webster, L. (1991) 'The Mental Health Act 1983: characteristics of detained patients' *Journal of Forensic Psychiatry*, vol. 2(2), p. 185.

Dell, S. (1980) 'Transfer of Special Hospital patients into National Health Service hospitals' in J. Gunn, and D. Farrington (eds), *Abnormal Offenders, Delinquency and the Criminal Justice System*, Chichester: John Wiley.

Dell, S. (1982) 'Diminished Responsibility Reconsidered', *Criminal Law Review*, p. 809.

Dell, S., Grounds, A., James, K., and Robertson, G. (1991) *Mentally Disordered Remand Prisoners: Report to the Home Office*, unpublished.

Dell, S. and Robertson, G. (1988) *Sentenced to Hospital*, Oxford: Oxford University Press.

Department of Health and Home Office. (1992) *Review of Health and Social Services for Mentally Disordered Offenders and others requiring similar services, final summary report*, Cm 2088.

Department of Health and Home Office. (1996) *Mentally Disordered Offenders: Sentencing and Discharge Arrangements*, Discussion paper, London: Department of Health and Home Office.

Department of Health and Social Security. (1971) *Welfare of the elderly: implementation of section 45 of the Health Services and Public Health Act 1968*, DHSS Circular 19/71, London: DHSS.

Department of Health and Social Security. (1981) *Reform of Mental Health Legislation*, Cmnd.8405, London: HMSO.

Department of Health and Social Security. (1984) Circular No. DDL (84) 4, *Mental Health Act Commission: Guidance For Responsible Medical Officers — Consent to Treatment*.

Department of Health and Social Security. (1971) *Better Services for the Mentally Handicapped*, London: HMSO.

Department of Health and Social Security. (1975) *Better Services for the Mentally Ill*, London: HMSO.

Department of Health and Welsh Office. (1993) *Mental Health Act 1983 Code of Practice*, London: HMSO.

Department of Health and Welsh Office. (1998) *Mental Health Act 1983: Memorandum on Parts I to VI, VIII and X*, London: The Stationery Office.

Department of Health and Welsh Office. (1999, 3rd edition) *Mental Health Act 1983 Code of Practice*, London: The Stationery Office.

Department of Health. (1986) *Mental Health Act — Approved Social Workers*, Circular No. LAC (86)15, London: Department of Health.

Department of Health. (1989) *Discharge of Patients from Hospital*, HC(89)5, London: Department of Health.

Department of Health. (1989a) *Caring for People*, London: Department of Health.

Department of Health. (1989b) *Working for Patients*, London: Department of Health.

Department of Health. (1990a) *Community care in the next decade and beyond*, London: HMSO.

Department of Health. (1990b) *The Care Programme Approach for people with a mental illness referred to specialist psychiatric services*, HC(90)23/LASSL(90)11.

Department of Health. (1992) *Mental Health Review Tribunals for England and Wales Annual Report 1991*, London: Department of Health.

Department of Health (1993a) *Community Care Plans (Consultation) Directions 1993*, LAC(93)4, London: Department of Health.

Department of Health (1993b) *Approvals and Directions for Arrangements from 1 April 1993 Made Under schedule 8 to the National Health Service Act 1977 and sections 21 and 29 of the National Assistance Act 1948*, LAC(93)10, London: National Health Service Executive, Department of Health.

Department of Health (1993c) *Mental Health Review Tribunals for England and Wales Annual Report 1992* London: Department of Health.

Department of Health. (1994a) *Guidance on the Discharge of Mentally Disordered People and their Continuing Care in the Community*, HSG(94)27.

Department of Health (1994b) *Introduction of supervision registers for mentally ill people from 1 April 1994*, HSG(94)5, London: National Health Service Executive, Department of Health.

Department of Health. (1995a) *Building Bridges: a guide to arrangements for inter-agency working for the care and protection of severely mentally ill people*, London: Department of Health.

Department of Health. (1995b) *Mental Health Act 1983: Memorandum on Parts I to VI, VIII and X*, London: HMSO.

Department of Health. (1995c) *Mentally Disordered Offenders* produced for LAG and Doughty Street Chambers Conference.

Department of Health. (1995d) 'In-Patients Formally Detained under the Mental Health Act 1983 and Other Legislation, England: 1987-88 to 1992-93', *Department of Health Statistical Bulletin 1994/9*, London: Department of Health.

Department of Health. (1996a) *The Spectrum of Care*, London: Department of Health.

Department of Health. (1996b) *The Use of 'Trial Leave' under section 17 of the Mental Health Act 1983 to Transfer Patients between Hospitals*, HSG (96)28, London: Department of Health.

Department of Health. (1997) *Mental Health Review Tribunals for England and Wales Annual Report 1996*, London: Department of Health.

Department of Health. (1998a) *Modernising Mental Health Services: Safe, Sound and Supportive*, London: The Stationery Office.

Department of Health, (1998b) *Modernising Social Services: Promoting independence, improving projection, raising standards*, Cm 4169, London: The Stationery Office.

Department of Health. (1998c) *Community Care Statistics 1998*, London: Department of Health.

Department of Health. (1998d) *In-patients formally detained in hospitals under the Mental Health Act 1983 and other legislation, England: 1987-88 to 1997-98*, London: Department of Health.

Department of Health. (1998e) *A First Class Service: Quality in the new NHS*, London: The Stationery Office.

Department of Health. (1998f) *National Service Frameworks*, HSG(98) 074, LASSL (98)6, London: Department of Health.

Department of Health. (1998g) *Partnership in Action: new opportunities for joint working between health and social services*, London: Department of Health.

Department of Health (1998h) *Specific grant to local authorities in 1998/9 for the development of integrated social care services for adults with a mental illness*, HSC 1998/097, London: National Health Service Executive, Department of Health.

Department of Health. (1999) *Report of the Committee of Inquiry into the Personality Disorder Unit, Ashworth Special Hospital* (the 'Fallon Report'), Cm 4194-II, London: The Stationery Office.

Dershowitz, A. (1970) 'The Law of Dangerousness: Some Fictions about Predictions', *Journal of Legal Education*, vol. 23, p. 24.

Deutsch, A. (1973) *The Shame of the States*, New York: Arno.

Dickens, B. (1994) 'Medical consent legislation in Ontario', *Medical Law Review*, vol. 2, p. 283.

Digby, A. (1985) 'Moral Treatment at the Retreat, 1796-1846', in W. Bynum, R. Porter, and M. Shepherd (eds), *The Anatomy of Madness Volume II Institutions and Society*, London: Tavistock.

Digby, A. (1985a) *Madness, Morality and Medicine: A Study of the York Retreat, 1796-1914*, Cambridge: Cambridge University Press.

Dolan, M., Coorey, P. and Kulupana, S. (1993) 'An audit of recalls to a Special Hospital' *Journal of Forensic Psychiatry*, vol. 4(2), pp. 249-60.

Dolan, M. and Shetty, G. (1995) 'Transfer Delays in a Special Hospital Population', *Medicine Science and Law*, vol. 35(3), p. 237.

Duff, R. (1986) *Trials and Punishment*, Cambridge: Cambridge University Press.

Dunn, S., Morrison, B. and Roberts, M. (eds), (1996) *Mind Readings: Writers' Journeys Through Mental States*. London: Minerva.

Eagles J. (1991) 'The Relationship between Schizophrenia and Immigration: Are There Alternatives to Psychosocial Hypotheses?', *British Journal of Psychiatry*, vol. 159, p. 783.

Eastman, N. (1996) 'Hybrid orders: an analysis of their likely effects on sentencing practice and on forensic psychiatric practice and services' *Journal of Forensic Psychiatry*, vol. 7(3), p. 481.

Eastman, N. (1997) 'The Mental Health (Patients in the Community) Act 1995: A Clinical Analysis', *British Journal of Psychiatry*, vol. 170, p. 492.

Eastman, N. and Peay, J. (1998) 'Sentencing Psychopaths: Is the 'Hospital and Limitation Direction' an Ill-Considered Hybrid?', *Criminal Law Review*, p. 93.

Eckermann, L. (1997) 'Foucault, embodiment and gendered subjectives: The case of voluntary self-starvation', in A. Peterson and R. Bunton (eds), *Foucault Health and Medicine*, London: Routledge.

Edelsohn, G. and Hiday, V. (1990) 'Civil commitment: A range of patient attitudes', *Bulletin of the American Academy of Psychiatry and Law*, vol. 18, p. 65.

Edmunds, R. (1994) 'Locking the mentally ill out of the homelessness legislation' *Journal of Forensic Psychiatry*, vol. 5(2), p. 355-369.

Egglestone, F. (1990) 'The Home Office: The advisory board on restricted patients' in R. Bluglass and P. Bowden (eds), *Principles and Practice of Forensic Psychiatry*, Edinburgh: Churchill Livingstone.

Eisner, H. (1989) 'Returning the not-guilty by reason of insanity to the community: A new scale to determine readiness', *Bulletin of the American Academy of Psychiatry and the Law*, vol. 17(4), p. 401.

Eldergill, A. (1997) *Mental Health Review Tribunals Law and Practice*, London: Sweet and Maxwell.

Eldergill, A. (1999) 'Casenote on *Barker* v *Barking and Brentwood Community NHS Trust and others*', *Journal of Mental Health Law*, vol. 1(1), p. 68.

Emmins, C. (1986) 'Unfitness to Plead: Some Thoughts Prompted by Glenn Pearson's Case', *Criminal Law Review*, p. 604.

Evans J. and Tomison, A. (1997) 'Assessment of the Perceived Need for a Psychiatric Service to a Magistrates' Court', *Medicine Science and Law*, vol. 37(2), p. 161.

Exworthy, T. and Parrott J. (1997) 'Comparative evaluation of a diversion from custody scheme' *Journal of Forensic Psychiatry*, vol. 8(2), p. 406.

Fahy, T. (1989) 'The police as a Referral Agency for Psychiatric Emergencies', *Medicine Science and the Law*, vol. 29(4), p. 315.

Falkowski J., Watts, V., Falkowski, W. and Dean, T. (1990) 'Patients Leaving Hospital without Knowledge or Permission of Staff — Absconding', *British Journal of Psychiatry*, vol. 156, p. 488.

Fanthorpe, U. A. (1996) 'Walking in Darkness' in S. Dunn, B. Morrison and M. Roberts (eds), *Mind Readings: Writers' Journeys through Mental States*, London: Minerva.

Farid, B. (1991) 'Absconders from a District General Hospital', *Psychiatric Bulletin*, vol. 15, p. 736.

Farrell, E. (1997) *The Complete Guide to Mental Health*, London: Vermilion.

Fennell, P. (1977) 'The Mental Health Review Tribunal: A Question of Imbalance', *British Journal of Law and Society*, vol. 2, p. 186.

Fennell, P. (1986) 'Law and Psychiatry: The Legal Constitution of the Psychiatric System' *Journal of Law and Society*, vol. 13(1), p. 35.

Fennell, P. (1988) 'Sexual Suppressants and the Mental Health Act', *Criminal Law Review*, p. 660.

Fennell, P. (1989) 'The Beverley Lewis Case — was the law to blame?', *New Law Journal*, vol. 139, p. 559.

Fennell, P. (1990) 'Inscribing Paternalism in the Law: Consent to Treatment and Mental Disorder' *Journal of Law and Society*, vol. 17(1), p. 29.

Fennell, P. (1991a) 'Diversion of Mentally Disordered Offenders from Custody', *Criminal Law Review*, p. 333.

Fennell, P. (1991b) 'Double Detention under the Mental Health Act 1983 — A Case of Extra-Parliamentary Legislation' *Journal of Social Welfare and Family Law*, p. 194.

Fennell, P. (1992) 'The Criminal Procedure (Insanity and Unfitness to Plead) Act 1991', *Modern Law Review*, vol. 55(4), p. 547.

Fennell, P. (1994) 'Statutory Authority to Treat, Relatives and Treatment Proxies', *Medical Law Review*, vol. 2, p. 30.

Fennell, P. (1994a) 'Mentally Disordered Suspects in the Criminal Justice System' *Journal of Law and Society*, p. 57.

Fennell, P. (1995) 'The Law Commission Proposals on Mental Incapacity', *Family Law*, p. 420.

Fennell, P. (1996) *Treatment Without Consent: Law, Psychiatry and the Treatment of Mentally Disordered People since 1845*, London: Routledge.

Fenton, W., Blyler, C., Wyatt R. and McGlashan T. (1997) 'Prevalence of spontaneous dyskinesia in schizophrenic and non-schizophrenic patients', *British Journal of Psychiatry*, vol. 171, p. 265.

Finch J. (1984) 'Community care: developing non-sexist alternatives', *Critical Social Policy*, vol. 9, p. 6.

Firestone, S. (1971/1979) 'Freudianism: The Misguided Feminism', in *The Dialectic of Sex: the case for a feminist revolution*, London: Jonathan Cape/The Women's Press.

Flannigan, C., Glover, G., Feeney, S., Wing J., Bebbington, P. and Lewis, S. (1994) 'Inner London Collaborative Audit of Admissions in Two Health Districts: I. Introduction, Methods and Preliminary Findings', *British Journal of Psychiatry*, vol. 165, p. 734.

Flannigan C., Glover, G., Wing J., Lewis, S., Bebbington, P. and Feeney, S. (1994) 'Inner London Collaborative Audit of Admissions in Two Health Districts: III. Reasons for Acute Admission to Psychiatric Wards', *British Journal of Psychiatry*, vol. 165, p. 750.

Folstein, M., Folstein, S. and McHugh, P. (1975) '"Mini-Mental State": A Practical Method for Grading the Cognitive State of patients for the Clinician' *Journal of Psychiatric Research*, vol 12, p. 189.

Forsythe, B., Melling, J. and Adair, R. (1999) 'Politics on Lunacy: Central state regulation and the Devon Pauper Lunatic Asylum, 1845–1914' in J. Melling and B. Forsythe (eds), *Insanity, Institutions and Society, 1800–1914: A social history of madness in comparative perspective*, London: Routledge.

Foucault, M. (1965) *Madness and Civilization: A History of Insanity in the Age of Reason*, Trans (1973) R. Howard, New York: Random House.

Foucault, M. (1977) *Discipline and Punish: The Birth of the Prison*, London: Allen Lane.

Foucault, M. (1980) 'Lecture Two, 14 January 1976' in C. Gordon (ed), *Power/Knowledge*, Brighton: Harrvester Press.

Foucault, M. (1986) *The Foucault Reader*, Rabinow, P. ed, London: Penguin.

Foucault, M. (1988) 'The dangerous individual', in L. Kritzman (ed), *Michel Foucault: Politics, Philosophy, Culture: Interviews and Other Writings*, London: Routledge.

Fraser, K. and Hepple J. (1992) 'Prescribing in a Special Hospital' *Journal of Forensic Psychiatry*, vol. 3(2), p. 311.

Freedman, A., Kaplan, H. and Sadock, B. (1975) *Comprehensive Textbook of Psychiatry*, 2 vols. , Baltimore: Williams and Wilkins.

Freeman, M. (1994) 'Deciding for the Intellectually Impaired', *Medical Law Review*, vol. 2, p. 77.

Frith, C. (1994) Letter to *The Psychologist*, vol. 7, p. 490.

Gallon, I. (1999) 'Issues around Control and Restraint Training currently used in UK Hospitals', http://www.imhl.com/candr.htm

Ganesvaran, T. and Shah, A. (1997) 'Psychiatric In-patient Suicide Rates: a 21-year study', *Medicine Science and Law*, vol. 37(3), p. 202-9.

Garfinkel, H. and Bittner, E. (1967/1984) '"Good" organizational reasons for "bad" clinical records', in H. Garfinkel, *Studies in Ethnomethodology*, Cambridge: Polity.

Garrett, T. (1994) 'Sexual contact between psychotherapists and their patients', in P. Clarkson and M. Pokorny (eds), *The Handbook of Psychotherapy*, London: Routledge.

Gelder, M., Gath, D., Mayou, R. and Cowen, P. (1996, 3rd ed) *Oxford Textbook on Psychiatry*, Oxford: Oxford University Press.

Gilboy J. and Schmidt J. (1971) "Voluntary' hospitalization of the mentally ill', *Northwestern Law Review*, vol. 66, p. 429.

Glasgow Media Group. (1996) *Media and Mental Distress*, G. Philo (ed), London: Longman.

Glover, N. (1996) '"Treatability": its scope and application' *Journal of Forensic Psychiatry*, vol. 7(2), p. 353.

Goffman, E. (1961/1991) *Asylums: Essays on the Social Situation of Mental Patients and other Inmates*, London: Penguin.

Goldbeck, R., Mackenzie, D. and Bennie, P. (1997) 'Detained patients' knowledge of their legal status and rights' *Journal of Forensic Psychiatry*, vol. 8, p. 573.

Goldberg, D., Benjamin, S. and Creed F. (1994, 2nd ed.) *Psychiatry in Medical Practice*, London: Routledge.

Gondolf, E., Mulvey, E. and Lidz, C. (1991) 'Psychiatric Admission of Family Violent Versus Nonfamily Violent Patients', *International Journal of Law and Psychiatry*, vol. 14(2), p. 245-54.

Gordon, C. (1998) 'Guardianship in Oxfordshire: hits and misses', *Psychiatric Bulletin*, vol. 22, p. 233.

Gostin, L. (1975) *A Human Condition*, vol. 1, London: MIND.

Gostin, L. (1977) *A Human Condition*, vol. 2, London: MIND.

Gostin, L (1982) 'Human Rights, Judicial Review and the Mentally Disordered Offender', *Criminal Law Review*, p. 792.

Gostin, L. (1983) 'The ideology of entitlement: the application of contemporary legal approaches to psychiatry', in P. Bean (ed), *Mental Illness: Changes and Trends*, Chichester: John Wiley.

Gostin, L. (1986a) *Institutions Observed*, London: King's Fund.

Gostin, L. (1986b) *Mental Health Services, Law and Practice*, London: MIND.

Gostin, L. and Fennell, P. (1992) *Mental Health: Tribunal Procedure*, London: Longman.

Government Statistical Service (1998) *Health and Personal Social Service Statistics England 1998*, London: The Stationary Office.

Green, B. and Baglioni Jr, A. (1997) 'Judging Suitability for Release of Patients from a Maximum Security Hospital by Hospital and Community Staff', *International Journal of Law and Psychiatry*, vol. 20(3), p. 323.

Greenhalgh, N., Wylie, K., Rix, K. and Tamlyn, D. (1996) 'Pilot Mental Health Assessment and Diversion Scheme for an English Metropolitan Petty Sessional Division', *Medicine Science and Law*, vol. 36(1), p. 52.

Griffiths, R. (1988) *Community Care: Agenda for Action*, London: HMSO.

Grisso, T., Appelbaum, P., Mulvey, E. and Fletcher, K. (1995a) 'The MacArthur Treatment Competence Study. II. Measures of Abilities Related to Competence to Consent to Treatment,' *Law and Human Behavior*, vol. 19(2), p. 127.

Grisso, T. and Appelbaum, P. (1995b) 'The MacArthur Treatment Competence Study. III. Abilities of Patients to Consent to Psychiatric and Medical Treatments', *Law and Human Behavior*, vol. 19(2), p. 149.

Grounds, A. (1990) 'Transfers of Sentenced Prisoners to Hospital', *Criminal Law Review*, p. 544.

Grounds, A. (1991) 'The Transfer of Sentenced Prisoners to Hospital 1960-1983: A Study of One Special Hospital', *British Journal of Criminology*, vol. 31(1), p. 54.

Grubin, D. (1991) 'Unfit to Plead in England and Wales 1976-1988: A Survey', *British Journal of Psychiatry*, vol. 158, p. 540.

Grubin, D. (1993) 'What Constitutes Unfitness to Plead?', *Criminal Law Review*, p. 748.

Gudjonsson, G. (1992) *The Psychology of Interrogations, Confessions and Testimony*, Chichester: Wiley.

Gudjonsson, G. (1995) '"Fitness for interview" during police detention: a conceptual framework for forensic assessment', *Journal of Forensic Psychiatry*, vol. 6(1), p. 185.

Gudjonsson, G., Clare, I., Rutter, S. and Pearse J. (1993) *Persons at Risk During Interviews in Police Custody: The Identification of Vulnerabilities*, RCCJ research study no.12.

Gunn J. and Joseph, P. (1993) 'Remands to hospital for psychiatrists' reports: a study of psychiatrists' attitudes to section 35 of the Mental Health Act 1983', *Psychiatric Bulletin*, vol. 17, p. 197.

Gunn J., Maden, A. and Swinton, M. (1991) 'Treatment needs of prisoners with psychiatric disorders', *British Medical Journal*, vol. 313, p. 338.

Gunn, M. (1986) 'Mental Health Act Guardianship: Where Now?', *Journal of Social Welfare Law*, p. 144-52.

Gunn, M. (1986a) 'Judicial Review of Hospital Admissions and Treatment in the Community under the Mental Health Act 1983', *Journal of Social Welfare Law*, p. 290.

Gunn, M. (1986b) 'Casenote on *Bone* v *Mental Health Review Tribunal*', *Journal of Social Welfare Law*, p. 177.

Gunn, M. (1986c) 'Case note on *R* v *Mental Health Review Tribunal, ex parte Clatworthy*', *Journal of Social Welfare Law*, p. 249.

Gunn, M. (1990) 'Casenote on *R* v *Newington*', *Journal of Forensic Psychiatry*, vol. 1, p. 360.

Gunn, M. (1993) 'Patients subject to restriction direction and release', *Journal of Forensic Psychiatry*, vol. 4(2), p. 330.

Gunn, M. (1994) 'The Meaning of Incapacity', *Medical Law Review*, vol. 2, p. 8.

Hall, A., Puri, B., Stewart, T. and Grahame, P. (1995) 'Doctors' Holding powers in Practice: Section 5(2) of the Mental Health Act 1983', *Medicine Science and Law*, vol. 35(3), p. 231-6.

Halleck, S. (1979) 'The Future of Psychiatric Criminology', in C Jeffrey (ed), *Biology and Crime*, Beverley Hills, California: Sage.

Hamilton J. (1990) 'Special Hospitals and the State Hospital' in R. Blugrass and P. Bowden (eds), *Principles and Practice of Forensic Psychiatry*, London: Churchill Livingstone.

Hardie, T., Bhui, K., Brown, P., Watson, J. and Parrott, J. (1998) 'Unmet Needs of Remand Prisoners', *Medicine Science and Law*, vol. 38(3), p. 233.

Hargreaves, D. (1997) 'The transfer of severely mentally ill prisoners from HMP Wakefield: a descriptive study', *Journal of Forensic Psychiatry*, vol. 8(1) p. 62.

Harrison, G., Ineichen, B., Smith, J. and Morgan, H. (1984) 'Psychiatric Hospital Admissions in Bristol: II. Social and Clinical Aspects of Compulsory Admission', *British Journal of Psychiatry*, vol. 145, p. 605.

Harrison, K. (1995) 'Growing opposition to "uncontroversial" bill', *Openmind*, April/May, p. 5.

Hart, H. (1961/1994) *The Concept of Law*, Oxford: Clarendon Press.

Hart, L. (1995) *Phone At Nine Just To Say You're Alive*, London: Pan.

Hart, L. (1996) 'Stay Calm and Charm Them', in J. Read and J. Reynolds (eds) *Speaking Our Minds: An Anthology*, London: Macmillan.

Hatfield, B., Huxley, P. and Mohamad, H. (1997) 'Social Factors and Compulsory Detention of Psychiatric Patients in the UK: The Role of the Approved Social Worker in the 1983 Mental Health Act', *International Journal of Law and Psychiatry*, vol. 20(3), p. 389-97.

Hatfield, B., Mohamad, H., Rahim, Z. and Tanweer, H. (1996) 'Mental Health and the Asian Communities: A Local Survey', *British Journal of Social Work*, vol. 26, p. 315.

Haycock J. (1993) 'Comparative Suicide Rates in Different Types of Involuntary Confinement', *Medicine Science and Law*, vol. 33(2), p. 128.

Health Education Authority. (1997) *Making Headlines: mental health and the national press*, London: Health Education Authority.

Heywood and Massey. See Whitehorn.

Hiday, V. (1992) 'Coercion in Civil Commitment: Process, Preferences and Outcomes', *International Journal of Law and Psychiatry*', vol. 15, p. 359.

Hirst, D. and Michael, P. (1999) 'Family, community and the lunatic in mid-nineteenth-century North Wales' in P. Bartlett and D. Wright (eds), *Outside the Walls of the Asylum*, London: Athlone.

Hodgson J. (1997) 'Vulnerable Suspects and the Appropriate Adult', *Criminal Law Review* p. 785.

Hogarty G. and Ulrich, R. (1972) 'The Discharge Readiness Inventory', *Archives of General Psychiatry*, vol. 23, p. 419.

Hoge, S., Appelbaum, P. and Greer, A. (1989) 'An Empirical Comparison of the Stone and Dangerousness Criteria for Civil Commitment', *American Journal of Psychiatry*, vol. 146, p. 170.

Hoggett, B. (1996, 4th ed) *Mental Health Law*, London: Sweet and Maxwell.

Hogman, G. (1996) *Is cost a factor? A survey by the National Schizophrenia Fellowship of the experiences and views of psychiatrists on new drugs for the treatment of schizophrenia*, London: National Schizophrenia Fellowship.

Holdaway, S. (1983) *Inside the British Police*, Oxford: Basil Blackwell.

Holden, A. (1974) *The St. Albans Poisoner*, London: Hodder and Stoughton.

Home Office. (1973) *Report on the Review of Procedures for the Discharge and Supervision of Psychiatric Patients subject to Special Restrictions* (The 'Aarvold Committee'), Cmnd 5191.

Home Office. (1980) *Report of the Review of Rampton Hospital*, Cmnd 8073, London: HMSO.

Home Office. (1990) *Provision for Mentally Disordered Offenders*, Circular 66/1990, London: HMSO.

Home Office. (1991) HO Circular No. 93/91.

Home Office. (1992) *Report of the Committee of Inquiry into Complaints about Ashworth Hospital.* 2 vols. Cmnd 2028, London: HMSO.

Home Office. (1996) *Protecting the Public*, Cm. 3190, London: The Stationery Office.

Home Office. (n.d) *Restricted Patients Detained in Special Hospitals: Information for the Special Hospitals Service Authority*, London: Home Office.

Home Office and Department of Health. (1992) *Review of Health and Social Services for Mentally Disordered Offenders and Others Requiring Similar Services*, Cmnd 2088, London: HMSO.

Home Office and Department of Health (1999) *Managing Dangerous People with Severe Personality Disorders: Proposals for Policy Development*, London: Home Office and Department of Health.

Home Office, Mental Health Unit. (1997) *Crime Sentences Act*, Home Office Circular 52/1997.

Home Office Research and Statistics Directorate. (1996) *Criminal Statistics: England and Wales 1996 Statistics Relating to Crime and Criminal Proceedings for the Year 1995*, London: HMSO.

Home Office Research and Statistics Directorate. (1997) *Statistics of mentally disordered offenders in England and Wales 1996*, London: Home Office Research and Statistics Directorate.

Home Office Research and Statistics Directorate. (1998a) *Statistics of mentally disordered offenders in England and Wales 1997*, London: Home Office Research and Statistics Directorate.

Home Office Research and Statistics Directorate. (1998b) *The Prison Population in 1997: A Statistical Review*, London: Home Office Research and Statistics Directorate.

Horne J. (1999) 'The Advisory Board on Restricted Patients and Tribunal Recommendations', *Journal of Mental Health Law*, vol. 1(1), p. 62-7.

Houston, R. (1999) '"Not simple boarding": care of the mentally incapacitated in Scotland during the long eighteenth century' in P. Bartlett and D. Wright (eds), *Outside the Walls of the Asylum*, London: Athlone.

Howlett, M. (1998) *Medication, Non-Compliance and Mentally Disordered Offenders*, London: The Zito Trust.

Hoyer, G. (1986) 'Compulsorily Admitted Patients' Ability to Make Use of their Legal Rights', *International Journal of Law and Psychiatry*, vol. 8, p. 413.

Huckle, P. (1996) 'A Survey of Sentenced Prisoners Transferred to Hospital for Urgent Psychiatric Treatment over a Three-Year Period for One Region', *Medicine Science and Law*, vol. 36(4), p. 37.

Hughes, D. (1991) 'The Reorganisation of the National Health Service: The Rhetoric and Reality of the Internal Market', *Modern Law Review*, vol 54, p. 88.

Hume, C. and Pullen, I. (1994, 2nd ed) *Rehabilitation for Mental Health Problems: an introductory handbook*, Edinburgh: Churchill Livingstone.

Huws, R. and Shubsachs, A. (1993) 'A study of absconding by Special Hospital patients: 1976 to 1988', *Journal of Forensic Psychiatry*, vol. 4(1), p. 45.

Huws, R., Longson, D., Reiss, D. and Larkin, E. (1997) 'Prison transfers to Special Hospitals since the introduction of the Mental Health Act 1983', *Journal of Forensic Psychiatry*, vol. 8(1), p. 74.

Huxley, P. *Social Work Practice in Mental Health*, Aldershot: Gower, 1985.

Ineichen, B., Harrison, G. and Morgan H. (1984) 'Psychiatric Hospital Admissions in Bristol: I. Geographic and Ethnic Factors', *British Journal of Psychiatry*, vol. 145, p. 600.

Jacob J. (1976) 'The Mental Patient's Right to his Psychosis', *Modern Law Review*, vol. 17, p. 17.

Jaconelli J. and Jaconelli, A. (1998) 'Tort liability under the Mental Health Act 1983', *Journal of Social Welfare and Family Law*, vol. 20, p. 151.

James, D. and Hamilton, L. (1991) 'The Clerkenwell Scheme: Assessing Efficacy and Cost of a Psychiatric Liaison Service to a Magistrates' Court', *British Medical Journal*, vol. 303, p. 282.

James, D., Cripps J. and Gray, N. (1998) 'What demands do those admitted from the criminal justice system make on psychiatric beds?', *Journal of Forensic Psychiatry*, vol. 9(1), p. 74.

James, D., Cripps J., Gilluley P. and Harlow P. (1997) 'A court-focused model of forensic psychiatry provision to central London: abolishing remands to prison?', *Journal of Forensic Psychiatry*, vol. 8(2), p. 309.

Jameson, R. (1996) 'Schizophrenia from the inside', in J. Read and J. Reynolds (eds), *Speaking Our Minds: An Anthology*, London: Macmillan.

Jamison, K. (1993) *Touched with Fire: Manic-Depressive Illness and the Artistic Temperament*, New York: Simon and Schuster.

Jamison, K. (1996) *An Unquiet Mind: A Memoir of Moods and Madness*, London: Picador.

Janofsky J., McCarthy, R. and Folstein, M. (1992) 'The Hopkins Competency Assessment Test: A Brief Method for Evaluating Patients' Capacity to Give Informed Consent', *Hospital and Community Psychiatry*, vol. 43:2, p. 132.

Jefferson, T. (1988) 'Race, Crime and Policing: Empirical, Theoretical and Methodological Issues', *International Journal of the Sociology of Law*, vol. 16, p. 521.

Jefferys, M. and Blom-Cooper, L. (1975) 'Foreword' to Gostin, L. (1975) *A Human Condition*, vol. 1, London: MIND.

Jodelet, D. (1991) *Madness and Social Representations*, Hemel Hempstead: Harvester Wheatsheaf.

Johnson, C., Smith J., Crowe, C. and Donovan, M. (1993) 'Suicide amongst Forensic Psychiatric Patients', *Medicine Science and Law*, vol. 33(2), p. 137.

Johnson, D. (1990) 'Organising a Depot Clinic', *Practical Reviews in Psychiatry*, vol. 2(10), p. 1.

Johnstone, G. (1996) *Medical Concepts and Penal Policy*, London: Cavendish.

Jones, K. (1972) *A History of the Mental Health Services*, London: Routledge & Kegan Paul.

Jones, M. (1998, 6th ed) *Textbook on Torts*, London: Blackstone.

Jones, R. (1999, 6th ed) *Mental Health Act Manual*, London: Sweet and Maxwell.

Jones, M. and Keywood, K. (1996) 'Assessing the Patient's Competence to consent to Medical Treatment', *Medical Law International,* vol. 2, p. 107.

Joyce J., Morris, M. and Palia, S. (1991) 'Section 5(2) audit', *Psychiatric Bulletin,* vol. 15, p. 224.

Justice. (1994) *Unreliable Evidence? Confessions and the safety of convictions,* London: Justice.

Kaltiala-Heino R., Laippala, P. and Salokangas, R. (1997) 'Impact of Coercion on Treatment Outcome', *International Journal of Law and Psychiatry,* vol. 20(3), p. 311.

Kendell, R. (1991) 'Relationship Between the *DSM-IV* and the *ICD-10*' *Journal of Abnormal Psychology,* vol. 100, p. 297.

Kesey, K. (1977) *One Flew Over the Cuckoo's Nest,* Harmondsworth: Penguin.

King, M. (1991) 'Child Welfare Within Law: The Emergence of a Hybrid Discourse', *Journal of Law and Society,* vol. 18(3), p. 303.

Kjellin, L. and Westrin, C-G. (1998) 'Involuntary Admissions and Coercive Measures in Psychiatric Care', *International Journal of Law and Psychiatry,* vol. 21(1), p. 31-42.

Knight, A., Mumford, D. and Nichol, B. (1998) 'Supervised discharge order: the first years in the South and West Region', *Psychiatric Bulletin,* vol. 22, p. 418.

Lacey, R. (1996, 2nd ed) *The Complete Guide to Psychiatric Drugs,* London: Vermilion.

Laing J. (1995) 'The Mentally Disordered Suspect at the Police Station', *Criminal Law Review,* p. 371.

Laing J. (1996) 'The Proposed Hybrid Order for Mentally Disordered Offenders — A Step in the Right Direction?', *Liverpool Law Review,* vol. 18(2), p. 127.

Laing J. (1997) 'The likely impact of mandatory and minimum sentences on the disposal of mentally disordered offenders', *Journal of Forensic Psychiatry,* vol. 8(3), p. 504.

Larkin, E. and Close, A. (1996) 'Performing well? Referrals to Rampton Hospital in 1993', *Journal of Forensic Psychiatry,* vol. 7(1), p. 177.

Law Commission. (1995) *Mental Incapacity,* Law. Com., No. 231, London: HMSO.

Lawson W., Hepler, N., Holliday, J. and Cuffel, B. (1994) 'Race as a Factor in Inpatient and Outpatient Admissions and Diagnosis', *Hospital and Community Psychiatry,* vol. 45, p. 72.

Leff J. (1993) 'Comment on crazy talk: Thought disorder or psychiatric arrogance by Thomas Szasz', *British Journal of Medical Psychology,* vol. 66, p. 77.

Legemaate J. (1988) 'Legal Aspects of Voluntary Psychiatric Hospitalization', *International Journal of Law and Psychiatry,* vol. 11, p. 259.

Leicestershire Health Authority. (1998). *Report of the Independent Inquiry into the Treatment and Care of Sanjay Kumar Patel,* Leicester: Leicestershire Health Authority.

Lewis, B. (1996) 'Therapy room', in J. Read, and J. Reynolds (eds), *Speaking Our Minds: An Anthology,* London: Macmillan.

Lewis, G., Croft-Jeffreys, C., David, A. (1990) 'Are British Psychiatrists Racist?', *British Journal of Psychiatry*, vol. 157, p. 410.

Lewis J. (1989) "It all really starts in the family" Community Care in the 1990s', *Journal of Law and Society*, vol. 16, p. 83.

Lewis J. and Glennerster, H. (1996) *Implementing The New Community Care*, Buckingham: Open University Press.

Lindsay, W. (1996) 'By Definition', in J. Read and J. Reynolds (eds), *Speaking Our Minds: An Anthology*, London: Macmillan.

Littlechild, B. (1995) 'Reassessing the Role of the "Appropriate Adult"', *Criminal Law Review*, p. 540.

Littlewood, R. (1992) 'Psychiatric Diagnosis and Racial Bias: Empirical and Interactive Approaches', *Social Science and Medicine*, vol. 34, p. 141.

Littlewood, R. and Lipsedge, R. (1982) *Aliens and Alienists*, Harmondsworth: Penguin.

Long, C. and Midgely, M. (1992) 'On the closeness of the concepts of the criminal and the mentally ill in the nineteenth century: yesterday's opinion reflected today', *Journal of Forensic Psychiatry*, vol. 3(1), p. 63.

Lord Chancellor's Department. (1997) *Who Decides? Making Decisions on Behalf of Mentally Incapacitated Adults*, Cm 3803, London: The Stationery Office.

Loring and Powell, (1988) 'Gender, Race and DSM-III', *Journal of Health and Social Behaviour*, vol. 29, p. 1.

Lowe-Ponsford, F., Wolfson, P. and Lindesay J. (1998) 'Consultant psychiatrists' views on the supervision register', *Psychiatric Bulletin*, vol. 22, p. 409.

Lupton, D. (1997) 'Foucault and the medicalisation critique', in A. Peterson and R. Bunton (eds), *Foucault, Health and Medicine*, London: Routledge.

Mackay, R. (1990) 'Fact and Fiction about the Insanity Defence', *Criminal Law Review*, p. 247.

Mackay, R. (1995) *Mental Condition Defences in the Criminal Law*, Oxford: Clarendon.

Mackay, R. and Kearns, G. (1994) 'The Continued Underuse of Unfitness to Plead and the Insanity Defence', *Criminal Law Review*, p. 576.

Mackay, R. and Kearns, G. (1997) 'The Trial of the Facts and Unfitness to Plead', *Criminal Law Review*, p. 644.

MacLeod, S. (1996) 'The Art of Starvation', in S. Dunn, B. Morrison and M. Roberts (eds), *Mind Readings: Writers' Journeys through Mental States*, London: Minerva.

Manor, O. (1994) 'Group psychotherapy', in P. Clarkson and M. Pokorny (eds), *The Handbook of Psychotherapy*, London: Routledge.

Marson, D., Ingram, K., Cody, H. and Harrell, L. (1995) 'Assessing the Competency of Patients With Alzheimer's Disease under Different Legal Standards', *Archives of Neurology*, vol. 52, p. 949.

Mason, T. (1992) 'Seclusion: definitional interpretations', *Journal of Forensic Psychiatry*, vol. 3(2), 261-9.

Mason, T. (1993) 'Seclusion: an international comparison', *Medicine Science and Law*, vol. 34(1), p. 54.

Mathiesen, T. (1983) 'The Future of Control Systems — the case of Norway' in D. Garland, and P. Young (eds), *The Power to Punish: Contemporary Penality and Social Analysis*, London: Heinemann.

Matthews, P. (1982) 'Contracts for Necessaries and Mental Incapacity', *Northern Ireland Legal Quarterly*, vol. 33(2), p. 149.

Mays J. (1995) *In the Jaws of the Black Dogs: A Memoir of Depression*, Toronto: Penguin.

McCabe, D. (1996) 'No place like home', *Community Care*, 22 August, p. 27.

McConville, M. and Hodgson J. (1993) *Custodial Legal Advice and the Right to Silence*, RCCJ research report no.16, London: HMSO.

McGue, M., Gottesman, I. and Rao, D. (1985) 'Resolving genetic models for the transmission of schizophrenia', *Genetic Epidemiology*, vol. 2, p. 99.

McHale J. and Fox, M. with Murphy, J. (1997) *Health care law: text and materials*, London: Sweet and Maxwell.

McKenzie, I., Morgan, R. and Reiner, R. (1990) 'Helping the police with their enquiries', *Criminal Law Review*, p. 22.

McKenzie, I. and Waddington, D. (1994) 'Mental Health Review Tribunals in Bradford', *Psychiatric Bulletin*, vol. 18, p. 55.

Mental Health Act Commission. (1985) *First Biennial Report 1983-1985*, London: HMSO.

Mental Health Act Commission. (1987) *Second Biennial Report 1985-1987*, London: HMSO.

Mental Health Act Commission. (1989) *Third Biennial Report 1987-1989*, London: HMSO.

Mental Health Act Commission. (1991) *Fourth Biennial Report 1989-1991*, London: HMSO.

Mental Health Act Commission. (1993) *Fifth Biennial Report 1991-1993*, London: HMSO.

Mental Health Act Commission. (1995) *Sixth Biennial Report 1993-1995*, London: HMSO.

Mental Health Act Commission. (1997) *Seventh Biennial Report 1995-1997*, London: HMSO.

Midelfort, E. (1980) 'Madness and Civilisation in Early Modern Europe: A Reappraisal of Michel Foucault', in Malament, B. (ed), *After the Reformation: Essays in honor of J.H. Hexter*, Manchester: Manchester University Press.

Milne, E. and Milne, S. (1995) 'Mental Health Review Tribunals. Why the delay?', *Journal of Forensic Psychiatry*, vol. 6(1), p. 93.

Milne, S., Barron, P., Fraser, K. and Whitfield, E. (1995) 'Sex Differences in Patients Admitted to a Regional Secure Unit'), *Medicine Science and Law*, vol. 35(1), p. 57.

Milner, G. (1966) 'The Absconder', *Comprehensive Psychiatry*, vol. 7, p. 147.

MIND. (1994) *MIND's response to the Department of Health's Guidance on Supervision Registers and on Hospital Discharge*, London: National Association for Mental Health.

Ministry of Health (1963) *Health and Welfare: the Development of Community Care*, London: HMSO.

Mohan, D., Thompson, C. and Mullee, M. (1998) 'Preliminary evaluation of supervised discharge in the South and West Region', *Psychiatric Bulletin*, vol. 22, p. 421.

Mokhtar, A. and Hogbin, P. (1993) 'Police may underuse section 136', *Medicine Science and Law*, vol. 33(3), p. 188.

Monahan, J. (1981) *Predicting Violent Behavior*, Beverly Hills: Sage.

Monahan, J. (1984) 'The Prediction of Violent Behavior: Toward a Second Generation of Theory and Policy', *American Journal of Psychiatry*, vol. 141(1), p. 10.

Monahan J. (1988) 'Risk Assessment of Violence Among the Mentally Disordered: Generating Useful Knowledge', *International Journal of Law and Psychiatry*, vol. 11, p. 249.

Monahan J., Hoge, S., Lidz, C., Roth, L., Bennett, N., Gardner, W. and Mulvey, E. (1995) 'Coercion and commitment: understanding involuntary mental hospital admission', *International Journal of Law and Psychiatry*, vol. 18(3), p. 249.

Monahan J., Ruggiero, M. and Friedlander, H. (1982) 'Stone-Roth Model of civil commitment and the California dangerousness standard', *Archives of General Psychiatry*, vol. 39, p. 1267.

Monahan, J. and Steadman, H. (eds) (1994) *Violence and mental disorder: developments in risk assessment*, Chicago: Univeristy of Chicago Press.

Montandon, C. and Harding, T. (1984) 'The Reliability of Dangerousness Assessments: A Decision Making Exercise', *British Journal of Psychiatry*, vol. 144, p. 149.

Montgomery J. (1997) *Health Care Law*, Oxford: OUP.

Moodley, P. and Thornicroft, G. (1988) 'Ethnic Group and Compulsory Detention', *Medicine Science and Law*, vol. 28(4), p. 324-8.

Morgan, H. and Priest, P. (1991) 'Suicide and Other Unexpected Deaths among Psychiatric In-patients: the Bristol Confidential Inquiry', *British Journal of Psychiatry*, vol. 158, p. 368.

Morris J. (1993) *Independent Lives: Community care and disabled people*, London: Macmillan.

Morrison, W. (1997) *Jurisprudence: from the Greeks to Postmodernism*, London: Cavendish.

Muijen, M. (1996) 'Scare in the community: Britain in moral panic' in T. Heller, J. Reynolds, R. Gomm, R. Muston and S. Pattison, (eds), *Mental Health Matters: A Reader*, Basingstoke and London: Macmillan.

Murphy, E. (1991) *After the Asylums: Community care for people with mental illness*, London: Faber.

NHS Health Advisory Service/DHSS Social Services Inspectorate. (1988) *Report on the Services Provided by Broadmoor Hospital*, HAS/SSI(88) SH 1, London: DHSS.

NHS Management Executive. (1994a) *Introduction of Supervision Registers for Mentally Ill People from 1 April 1994*, London: Department of Health, HSG(94)5.

NHS Management Executive. (1994b) *Guidance on the Discharge of Mentally Disordered People and their Continuing Care in the Community*, HSG(94)27, London: Department of Health.

Nicholson, R., Ekenstam, C. and Norwood, S. (1996) 'Coercion and the Outcome of Psychiatric Hospitalisation', *International Journal of Law and Psychiatry*, vol. 19:2, p. 201.

Norfolk, G. (1997) 'Fitness to be interviewed' — a proposed definition and scheme of examination', *Medicine Science and Law*, vol. 37(3), p. 228.

Norris, C., Fielding, N., Kemp, C. and Fielding J. (1992) 'Black and blue: an analysis of the influence of race on being stopped by the police', *British Journal of Sociology*, vol. 43(2), p. 207.

Onyett, S., Heppleston, T. and Bushnell, D. (1994) 'A national survey of community mental health team structure and process', *Journal of Mental Health*, vol 3, p. 175.

Openmind. (1995) 'Older women and ECT', *Openmind*, vol. 74, p. 10.

Orbach, S. (1993) *Hunger Strike: The Anorectic's Struggle as a Metaphor for our Age*, Harmondsworth: Penguin.

Palmer, C. (1996) 'Still Vulnerable After All These Years', *Criminal Law Review*, p. 633.

Parkin, A. (1994) 'Case note on *R v Canons Park Mental Health Review Tribunal, ex parte A'*, *Journal of Social Welfare and Family Law*, p. 331.

Parkin, A. (1995) 'Where now on Mental Incapacity?', *Web Journal of Current Legal Issues*, vol. 2.

Parkin, A. (1996) 'Caring for Patients in the Community', *Modern Law Review*, vol. 59(3), p. 414.

Peay J. (1981) 'Mental Health Review Tribunals: Just or Efficacious Safeguards?', *Law and Human Behaviour*, vol. 5, p. 161.

Peay J. (1988) 'Offenders Suffering from Psychopathic Disorder: The Rise and Demise of a Consultation Document', *British Journal of Criminology*, vol. 28, p. 67.

Peay J. (1989) *Tribunals on Trial: A Study of Decision-Making under the Mental Health Act 1983*, Oxford: Clarendon.

Peay J. (1997) 'Mentally Disordered Offenders', in M. Maguire, R. Morgan and R. Reiner (eds), *The Oxford Handbook of Criminology*, Oxford: Oxford University Press.

Perkins, R. (1996) 'Choosing ECT', in J. Read and J. Reynolds (eds), *Speaking Our Minds: An Anthology*, London: Macmillan.

Perring, C. (1992) 'The experience and perspectives of patients and care staff of the transition from hospital to community-based care', in S. Ramon, (ed), *Psychiatric Hospital Closure: Myths and Realities*, London: Chapman and Hall.

Perrucci, R. (1974) *Circle of Madness: On being insane and institutionalized in America*, Prentice-Hall: New Jersey.

Pilgrim, D. (1995) Letter to *The Psychologist*, vol. 8, p. 9.

Pilgrim, D. and Rogers A. (1993) *A Sociology of Mental Health and Illness*, Buckingham: Open University Press.

Pokorny, M. (1994) 'Structure of the United Kingdom Council for Psychotherapy and list of its member organisations' in P. Clarkson and M. Pokorny (eds), *The Handbook of Psychotherapy*, London: Routledge.

Porter, R. (1987a) *Mind-Forg'd Manacles: A history of madness in England from the Restoration to the Regency*, London: Athlone Press.

Porter, R. (1987b) *A Social History of Madness: Stories of the Insane*, London: Nicholson and Weidenfeld.

Pourgourides, C., Prasher, V. and Oyebode, F. (1992) 'Use of section 5(2) in clinical practice', *Psychiatric Bulletin*, vol. 16, p. 14.

Price, D. (1994) 'Civil commitment of the mentally ill: compelling arguments for reform', *Medical Law Review*, vol. 2, p. 321.

Prins, H. (1995) 'What Price the Concept of Psychopathic Disorder?', *Medicine Science and Law*, vol. 35, p. 307.

Prior, L. (1993) *The Social Organisation of Mental Illness*, London: Sage.

Prior, L. (1996) 'The appeal to madness in Ireland' in Tomlinson, D and Carrier, J (eds) *Asylum in the Community*, London: Routledge.

Prior, P. (1992) 'The Approved Social Worker — Reflections on Origins', *British Journal of Social Work*, vol. 22, p. 105.

Prochaska, F. (1988) *The Voluntary Impulse: Philanthropy in Modern Britain*, London: Faber and Faber.

Rabin, C. and Zelner, D. (1992) 'The Role of Assertiveness in Clarifying Roles and Strengthening Job Satisfaction of Social Workers in Multidisciplinary Mental Health Settings', *British Journal of Social Work* vol. 22, p. 17.

Ramon, S. (1992) 'The Context of Hospital Closure in the Western World, or why now?' in S. Ramon (ed) *Psychiatric Hospital Closure: Myths and Realities*, London: Chapman and Hall.

Rassaby, E. and Rogers, A. (1987) 'Psychiatric Referrals from the police', *Bulletin of the Royal College of Psychiatrists*, vol. 11, p. 78.

Read, J. and Reynolds, J. (eds). (1996) *Speaking Our Minds: An Anthology*, London: Macmillan.

Reed J. (1994) *Report of the Department of Health and Home Office Working Group on Psychopathic Disorder*, London: Department of Health and Home Office.

Reed J. (1996) 'Psychopathology: A Clinical and Legal Dilemma', *British Journal of Psychiatry*, vol. 168, p. 4.

Richardson, G. (1993) *Law, Process and Custody: Prisoners and Patients*, London: Weidenfeld and Nicolson.

Richardson, G. and Machin, D. (1999) 'A clash of values? Mental Health Review Tribunals and Judicial Review', *Journal of Mental Health Law*, vol. 1(1), p. 3.

Roberts, J. and Pines, M. (eds) (1991) *The Practice of Group Analysis*, London: Routledge.

Robertson, G. (1989) 'The Restricted Hospital Order', *Psychiatric Bulletin*, vol. 13, p, 4.

Robertson, G., Pearson, R. and Gibb, R. (1996) 'Police interviewing and the use of appropriate adults', *Journal of Forensic Psychiatry*, vol. 7(2), p. 297.

Rogers, A. (1990) 'Policing Mental Disorder: Controversies, Myths and Realities', *Social Policy and Administration*, vol. 24, p. 226.

Rogers, A. (1993) 'Coercion and "voluntary" admission: An examination of psychiatric patient views', *Behavioral Sciences and the Law*, vol. 11, p. 259.

Rogers, A. and Faulkner, A. (1987) *A Place of Safety: MIND's Research into police referrals to the pscyhiatric services*, London: MIND.

Rogers, A., Pilgrim, D. and Lacey, R. (1993) *Experiencing Psychiatry: Users' Views of Services*, London: Macmillan.

Rogers, A. and Pilgrim, D. (1996) *Mental Health Policy in Britain: A Critical Introduction*, London: Macmillan.

Rogers, W. (1994, 14th ed) *Winfield and Jolowicz on Tort*, London: Sweet and Maxwell.

Romano, D. (1997) 'The Legal Advocate and the Questionably Competent Client in the Context of a Poverty Law Clinic', *Osgoode Hall Law Journal*, vol. 35, p. 737.

Romilly, C., Parrott J. and Carney, P. (1997) 'Limited duration restriction orders: what are they for?', *Journal of Forensic Psychiatry*, vol. 8(3), p. 562.

Rose, N. (1985) 'Unreasonable Rights: Mental Illness and the Limits of the Law', *Journal of Law and Society*, vol. 12(2), p. 199.

Rose, N. (1986) 'Law, psychiatry and rights' in Miller, P., and Rose, N., (eds) *The power of psychiatry*, Cambridge: Polity Press.

Rosenhan, D.L. (1973) 'On Being Sane in Insane Places', *Science*, vol. 179, p. 250.

Rossau, C. and Mortensen, P. (1997) 'Risk factors or suicide in patients with schizophrenia: nested case-study analysis', *British Journal of Psychiatry*, vol. 171, p. 355-69.

Roth, L. (1979). 'A commitment law for patients, doctors and lawyers', *American Journal of Psychiatry*, vol. 136, p. 1121.

Roth, L., Meisel, A. and Lidz, C. (1977) 'Tests of Competency to Consent to Treatment', *American Journal of Psychiatry*, vol. 134:3, p. 279.

Roth, M. (1990) 'Psychopathic (sociopathic) personality', in R. Blugrass and P. Bowden (eds) *Principles and Practice in Forensic Psychiatry*, London: Churchill Livingstone.

Rowlands, R., Inch, H., Rodger, W. and Soliman, A. (1996) 'Diverted to where? What happens to the diverted mentally disordered offender', *Journal of Forensic Psychiatry*, vol. 7(2), p. 284.

Royal College of Psychiatrists. (1993) *Consensus Report on the Use of High Dosage Antipsychotic Medicine*, Council Report CR.26, London: Royal College of Psychiatrists.

Royal College of Psychiatrists (1998) *Management of Imminent Violence*, London: Royal College of Psychiatrists.

Royal Commission on Criminal Justice. (1993) *Report of the Royal Commission on Criminal Justice*, Cm 2263, London: HMSO.

Royal Commission on Criminal Procedure. (1981) *Report of the Royal Commission on Criminal Procedure*, Cmnd 8092, London: HMSO.

Royal Commission on the Law relating to Mental Illness and Mental Deficiency 1954-1957, (Chair, Lord Percy of Newcastle) (The Percy Commission) (1957), *Report*, Cmnd 169, London: HMSO.

Ruschena, D., Mullen, P., Burgess, P., Cordner, S., Barry-Walsh J., Drummer, O., Palmer, S., Browne, C. and Wallace, C. (1998) 'Sudden death in psychiatric patients', *British Journal of Psychiatry*, vol. 172, p. 331.

Russell, D. (1995) *Women, Madness and Medicine*, Cambridge: Polity.

Saad, K. and Sashidharan, S. (1994) 'Mental Health Review Tribunals', *Psychiatric Bulletin*, vol. 16, p. 470.

Sackett, K. (1996) 'Discharges from Section 3 of the Mental Health Act 1983; changes in practice', *Health Trends*, vol. 28, p. 66.

Sammut, R. (1993) 'Disagreements between psychiatrists and social workers over compulsory admissions under the 1983 Mental Health Act', *Psychiatric Bulletin*, vol. 17, p. 462.

Sandland, R. (1994) 'The common law and the "informal" minor patient', *Journal of Forensic Psychiatry*, vol. 5:3, p. 569.

Schwehr, B. (1997) 'The relevance of resources to the assessment of need and the provision of services for the disabled', *Journal of Forensic Psychiatry*, vol. 8(3), p. 662.

Scull, A. (1977) *Decarceration: Community Treatment and the Deviant — A Radical View*, Englewood Cliffs, NY: Prentice Hall.

Scull, A. (1979) *Museums of Madness*, Harmondsworth: Penguin.

Scull, A. (1993) *The Most Solitary of Afflictions: Madness and Society in Britain, 1700-1900*, New Haven: Yale University Press.

Scull, A. (1996) 'Mental Patients and The Community: A Critical Note', *International Journal of Law and Psychiatry*, vol. 9, p. 383.

Sedgwick, P. (1982) *Psychopolitics*, London: Pluto Press.

Shah, A. (1993) 'An increase in violent behaviour among psychiatric in-patients: real or apparent?', *Medicine, Science and the Law*, vol. 33, p. 227.

Shelford, L. (1847, 2nd ed) *Practical Treatise of the Law concerning Lunatics, Idiots, and Persons of Unsound Mind*, London: Sweet.

Short J. (1995) 'Characteristics of absconders from acute admission wards', *Journal of Forensic Psychiatry*, vol. 6(2), p. 277.

Shubsachs, A., Huws, R., Close, A., Larkin, E. and Falvey, J. (1995) 'Male Afro-Caribbean Patients Admitted to Rampton Hospital Between 1977 and 1986', *Medicine Science and Law*, vol. 35(4), p. 336.

Silverstone, T. and Turner, P. (1995, 5th ed) *Drug Treatment in Psychiatry*, London: Routledge.

Smith, A. and Humphreys, M. (1997) 'Physical Restraint of Patients in a Psychiatric Hospital', *Medicine, Science and the Law*, vol. 37(2), p. 145.

Smith, D. (1990) 'K is Mentally Ill: The Anatomy of a Factual Account', in *Texts, Facts, and Femininity: Exploring the Relations of Ruling*, London: Routledge.

Smith J., Donovan, M. and Gordon, H. (1991) 'Patients in Broadmoor Hospital from the South Western Region: an audit of transfer procedures', *Psychiatric Bulletin*, vol. 15, p. 81.

Smith, R. (1981) *Trial by Medicine: Insanity and Responsibility in Victorian Trials*, Edinburgh: Edinburgh University Press.

Solomka, B. (1996) 'The role of psychiatric evidence in passing "longer than normal" sentences', *Journal of Forensic Psychiatry*, vol. 7(2), p. 239.

Somerville, M. (1994) 'Labels versus Contents: Variance between Philosophy, Psychiatry and Law in Concepts Governing Decision-Making', *McGill Law Journal*, vol. 39, p. 179.

Soothill K., et al. (1981) 'Compulsory admissions to mental hospitals in six countries', *International Journal of Law and Psychiatry*, vol. 4, p. 327.

Soothill, K., Kupitksa, P., Badiani, D. and Macmillan F. (1990a) 'Compulsory Admission to Mental Hospitals: A Replication Study', *International Journal of Law and Psychiatry*, vol. 13, p. 179.

Soothill K., Kupitksa, P. and Macmillan, F. (1990b) 'Compulsory Hospital Admissions: dangerous decisions?', *Medicine, Science and Law*, vol. 30(1), p. 17.

Spence, S. and McPhillips, M. (1995) 'Personality Disorder and Police Section 136 in Westminster: a retrospective analysis of 65 cases over six months', *Medicine, Science and Law*, vol. 35(1), p. 48.

Spitzer, R. (1976) 'More on Pseudoscience in Science and the Case for Psychiatric Diagnosis', *Archives of General Psychiatry*, vol. 33, p. 459.

Stanton, K. (1994) *The Modern Law of Tort*, London: Sweet and Maxwell.

Stein, G. (1993) 'Drug treatment of personality disorders' in P. Tyre and G. Stein (eds), *Personality Disorder Reviewed*, London: Gaskell Books.

Stone, H. (1992) 'Depot neuroleptics: involuntary castration?', *Journal of Forensic Psychiatry*, vol. 3(1), p. 7.

Street, R. (1998) *The restricted hospital order: from court to the community*, Home Office Research Study 186, London: Home Office Research and Statistics Directorate.

Sturdy, H. and Parry-Jones, W. (1999) 'Boarding-out insane patients: the significance of the Scottish system 1857-1913', in P. Bartlett and D. Wright (eds), *Outside the Walls of the Asylum*, London: Athlone.

Styron, W. (1990) *Darkness Visible*, London: Cape.

Styron, W. (1996) 'Darkness Visible', in S. Dunn, B. Morrison and M. Roberts (eds), *Mind Readings: Writers' Journeys through Mental States*, London: Minerva.

Suzuki, A. (1991) 'Lunacy in seventeenth- and eighteenth-century England: analysis of Quarter Sessions records Part I', *History of Psychiatry*, vol. 2, p. 437.

Suzuki, A. (1992) 'Lunacy in seventeenth- and eighteenth-century England: analysis of Quarter Sessions records part II', *History of Psychiatry*, vol. 3, p. 29.

Suzuki, A. (1995) 'The Politics and ideology of non-restraint: the case of the Hanwell Asylum', *Medical History*, vol. 39, p. 1.

Szasz, T. (1970) *Ideology and Insanity: Essays on the Psychiatric Dehumanisation of Man*, Garden City: Doubleday.

Taylor, J. and Gunn J. (1984) 'Violence and Psychosis: 1 — Risk of Violence among psychotic men', *British Medical Journal*, vol. 288, p. 1945.

Taylor, L. (1996) 'ECT is Barbaric', in J. Read and J. Reynolds (eds), *Speaking Our Minds: An Anthology*, London: Macmillan.

Taylor, P. and Gunn J. (1999) 'Homicides by people with mental illness: myth and reality', *British Journal of Psychiatry*, vol. 174, p. 9.

Taylor, S. (1989) *Positive Illusions: Creative self-deception and the healthy mind*, New York, Basic Books.

Tennent, G., Tennent, D., Prins, H. and Bedford, A. (1993) 'Is Psychopathic Disorder a Treatable Condition?', *Medicine Science and Law*, vol. 33, p. 63.

Thackrey, M. and Bobbitt, R. (1990) 'Patient aggression against clinical and non-clinical staff in a VA medical center', *Hospital and Community Psychiatry*, vol. 41, p. 195.

Thomas, C., Stone, K., Osborn, M., Thomas, P. and Fisher, M. (1993) 'Psychiatric Morbidity and Compulsory Admission Among UK-Born Europeans, Afro-Caribbeans and Asians in Central Manchester', *British Journal of Psychiatry*, vol. 163, p. 91.

Thomas, P. (1997) *The Dialectics of Schizophrenia*, London: Free Association Books.

Thomas, T. (1986) *The Police and Social Workers Community Care Practice Handbooks*, London: Gower.

Thomson, M. (1996) 'Family, Community and State: the Micro Politics of Mental Deficiency', in A. Digby and D. Wright (eds), *From Idiocy to Mental Deficiency*, London: Routledge.

Thomson, M. (1998) 'Community Care and the Control of Mental Defectives in Inter-War Britain', in P. Horden and D. Smith (eds), *The Locus of Care*, London: Routledge.

Thorogood, N. (1989) 'Afro-Caribbean women's experience of the health service', *New Community*, vol. 15(3), p. 319.

Tidmarsh, D. (1978) *Broadmoor Ins and Outs*, unpublished paper presented to the Forensic Section of Royal College of Psychiatrists, Broadmoor Hospital, 23 May 1978.

Tidmarsh, D. (1995) 'Homicide and Community Care', *Journal of Forensic Psychiatry*, vol 6(1), p. 1.

Toews J., el-Guebaly, N. and Leckie, A. (1984) 'Patients' attitudes at the time of their commitment', *Canadian Journal of Psychiatry*, vol. 26, p. 251.

Tomison, A. (1989) 'Characteristics of Psychiatric Hospital Absconders', *British Journal of Psychiatry*, vol. 154, p. 368.

Unsworth, C. (1987) *The Politics of Mental Health Legislation*, Oxford: Oxford University Press.

Vaughan, P. (1998) 'Supervision registers in practice', *Psychiatric Bulletin*, vol. 22, p. 412.

Walker, N. (1996) 'Hybrid orders', *Journal of Forensic Psychiatry*, vol 7(3), p. 469.

Walker, N. and McCabe, S. (1973) *Crime and Insanity in England Vol. One: The Historical Perspective*, Edinburgh: Edinburgh University Press.

Wallcraft, J. (1996) 'Some models of asylum and help in times of crisis', in D. Tomlinson and J. Carrier (eds) *Asylum in the Community*, London: Routledge.

Walmsley J., Atkinson, D. and Rolph, S. (1999) 'Community care and mental deficiency 1913 to 1945', in P. Bartlett and D. Wright (eds), *Outside the Walls of the Asylum: History of Care in the Community 1750-2000*, London: Athlone.

Webb, A. and Hobdell, M. (1980). 'Co-ordination and team work in the health and personal social services', in S. Lonsdale, A. Webb and T. Briggs (eds), *Teamwork in the Personal Social Services*, London: Croom Helm.

West, D. 'Sexual Molesters', in N. Walker (ed), *Dangerous People*, London: Blackstone, 1996.

Whelan, R. (1999) *Involuntary Action: How Voluntary is the 'Voluntary' Sector?*, London: Institute of Economic Affairs.

White, S. (1992) 'The Criminal Procedure (Insanity and Unfitness to Plead) Act', *Criminal Law Review*, p. 4.

Whitehorn, N. (1991) *Heywood and Massey, Court of Protection Practice*, London, Sweet and Maxwell.

Widdett, C. and Thomson, M. (1997) 'Justifying Treatment and Other Stories', *Feminist Legal Studies*, vol. 5, p. 84.

Wilkinson, P. and Sharpe, M. (1993) 'What Happens to Patients Discharged by Mental Health Review Tribunals?', *Psychiatric Bulletin*, vol. 17, p. 337.

Wilson, P. (1996) 'The Law Commission's report on mental incapacity: medically vulnerable adults or politically vulnerable law?', *Medical Law Review*, vol. 4, p. 227.

Wing J. (1988) 'Abandoning what?', *British Journal of Clinical Psychology*, vol. 27, p. 325.

Winick, B. (1994) 'The Right to Refuse Mental Health Treatment: A Therapeutic Jurisprudence Analysis', *International Journal of Law and Psychiatry*, vol. 17(1), p. 99.

Wistow, G. (1994) 'Community care futures: inter-agency relationships — stability or continuing change', in M. Titterton (ed), *Caring for People in the Community*, London: Jessica Kingsley.

Wistow, G. (1995) 'Coming apart at the seams', *Health Service Journal*, vol. 2, p. 24.

Wolberg, L. (1954) *The Technique of Psychotherapy*, New York: Grune and Stratton.

Wood J. (1999) 'Foreword' in Department of Health, (1997) *Mental Health Review Tribunals for England and Wales Annual Report 1996*, London: Department of Health.

Wright, D. (1997) 'Getting out of the Asylum: Understanding Confinement of the Insane in the Nineteenth Century', *Social History of Medicine*, vol. 10, p. 137.

Zedner, L. (1991) *Women, Crime and Custody in Victorian England*, Oxford: Oxford University Press.

Index